Index to Baptisms, Burials and Confirmations

Second German Evangelical Lutheran Church

Baltimore City Maryland

1835-1867

Gary B. Ruppert, M.D.

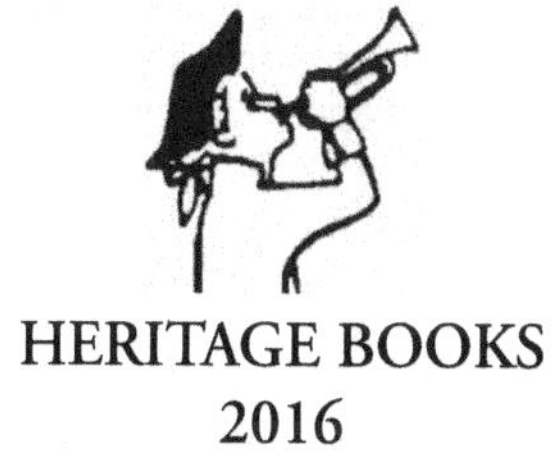

HERITAGE BOOKS
2016

HERITAGE BOOKS
AN IMPRINT OF HERITAGE BOOKS, INC.

Books, CDs, and more—Worldwide

For our listing of thousands of titles see our website at www.HeritageBooks.com

Published 2016 by
HERITAGE BOOKS, INC.
Publishing Division
5810 Ruatan Street
Berwyn Heights, Md. 20740

Heritage Books by the author:

Index to Baptisms, Burials and Confirmations, Second German Evangelical Lutheran Church, Baltimore City, Maryland, 1835–1867

Obstetrical Casebooks of Dr. Ferdinand E. Chatard: An Alternative Genealogical Resource for Baltimore City [Maryland], 1829–1883

The German Correspondent, *Baltimore, Maryland; Translation and Transcription of Marriages, Deaths and Selected Articles of Genealogical Interest: Volume I, Death Notices & Obituaries, 1879–1883*
Volume II, Marriages & Selected Articles of Genealogical Interest, 1879–1883

Trinity German Lutheran Church Records, 1853–1877: Baltimore, Maryland

Cover illustration: The illustration of the church on the cover is taken from a pamphlet (*Jubelfeir der Baltimore Gemeinden, 1836-1911*) celebrating the seventy-fifth anniversary of St. Paul's Lutheran Church, Missouri Synod. This pamphlet is part of the Works Progress Administration Historical Church Records Survey, Record Group S1512-2481, housed at the Maryland State Archives in Annapolis, Maryland.

International Standard Book Numbers
Paperbound: 978-0-7884-3370-2
Clothbound: 978-0-7884-6323-5

Second German Evangelical Lutheran Church
Baltimore City
1835-1867

During the eighteenth-century, Baltimore was not yet a hub of German immigration in Maryland; however the foundations of the German-language houses of worship were already established in both the Protestant and Catholic communities. By 1850, the beginning of a tidal wave of new German-speaking immigrants was flooding the city. The second half of the nineteenth-century witnessed an unprecedented flourishing of ethnic communities and their churches. Second German Evangelical Lutheran, established in 1835 was one of the earliest German-speaking congregations.

The first protestant German-language congregations in Baltimore City included (1) Zion Lutheran established 1755 (2) First German Reformed, 1750 or 1757 (3) Second German Reformed in 1771 (4) Trinity German Lutheran in 1833 and (5) Second German Lutheran in 1835. Excepting Trinity, which began independently as Fell's Point Lutheran, all of these congregations share common roots.

For a short time in the 18th century, Zion Lutheran (rarely identified as First Lutheran in very early records) and First German Reformed shared the same building. This short-lived arrangement ended when both communities had grown sufficiently to sustain their own building, cemetery and pastor.

By 1771, Second German Reformed Church, was created as a filial congregation of First Reformed, establishing a presence further west of the centrally located mother church. Not many years later Philipp Otterbein became pastor at Second Reformed. And it was not many years thereafter that Otterbein established his own denomination, the first American denomination, United Brethren in Christ. The Second Reformed congregation followed Otterbein changing both name and denomination of the church while maintaining its mother tongue.[i]

Meanwhile, by 1834, the Zion Lutheran congregation had been through a very difficult period experiencing turmoil within the congregation, absence of ministers and general decline in attendance. Johann Philipp Haesbert (Häsbert, Haysbert. Haesbaert) was called to Zion Lutheran as pastor.

Unfortunately, the Reverend Haesbert did not bring peace to this community.

Haesbert believed that the council and previous ministers at Zion had strayed from the orthodox teachings of the Lutheran Church. Depending on which version of history you accept, it was at this point that Haesbert either left voluntarily or was dismissed by the council. Either version attests to the fact that he took a large number of Zion's congregants, perhaps as many as 150 souls and on 1 November 1835, established *Der Zweite Deutsche Evangelische Gemeinde in Baltimore*, otherwise known as Second German Evangelical Lutheran Church of the Unaltered Augsberg Confession.

The new congregation was successful. By 1844 however, Haesbert resigned, relocating to New Orleans and then Brazil where he was a prominent Lutheran missionary.

For a few months thereafter, the elderly 81-year old retired pastor from Zion Lutheran, Daniel Kurtz voluntarily chose to lead the Second German Lutheran congregation demonstrating what surely must have been considerable Christian charity toward members of his former flock.

In 1845, Pastor Friederich Conrad Dietrich Wyneken was installed. According to the congregation history, "Pastor Wyneken found that the practices of the church were not strictly Lutheran." Apparently some members of the congregation were of the Reformed persuasion. These members were asked to leave Second German Lutheran and joined the First German Reformed Church. Actually, the "official" history of Second German church states that the dismissed congregants *formed* First Reformed Church. Of course, First German Reformed congregation had existed since the 18th century.

Pastor Wynecken began referring to his congregation as St. Paul's Lutheran Church, however church registers still reflect the name of Second German Lutheran. Wynecken worked to expand the congregation and especially its German-language schools.

By 1849, Pastor Wynecken left Baltimore and became affiliated with the newly established Lutheran Church, Missouri Synod. As a matter of fact, he became the second president of this young church body. Second German, or St. Paul's Lutheran has remained affiliated with the Missouri Synod from 1848 to the present. At one time it was one of the largest and most active congregations of this synod.

The next minister of this congregation was the Reverend Ernst Gerhard Wilhelm Keyl, who served from 1850 until the church closed two decades later. During his pastorate, the congregation established a cemetery in Druid Hill Park in 1857.[ii]

In 1856, some of the congregation wanted an English-language religious service. This led to the founding of St. Peter's Evangelical Lutheran which disbanded in 1865 but reorganized in 1875 as the mother church of the Lutheran Church, Ohio Synod in Baltimore. St. Peter's Lutheran, disbanded in the 1990s when it was last located on Loch Raven Boulevard.

By the end of the Civil War, circumstances were changing in central Baltimore City. The following is the official church recognition of the situation:

> By the end of 1864 the area surrounding the church was being crowded by business and many members of the church had moved to outlying districts of the city. The building was greatly in need of repair but in light of these circumstances, it seemed inadvisable to spend much money in renovation.

By 1865, a decision had been made to sell the church buildings, however the congregation did not entirely disappear. In a somewhat unique series of events, the members, finances, church fittings and school buildings of Second German Lutheran were divided between three newly established congregations which were or would soon become affiliated with the Missouri Synod.

1. St. Paul's Lutheran, officially established in 1866 at Fremont and Saratoga Streets retained the name of the mother church. When first constructed it was said to be of "good Lutheran architecture" and had the tallest steeple in town, 190 feet. At the final service of Second German Lutheran, held on 15 December 1867, the entire congregation of some 1000 souls marched from the old location at Holliday and Lexington to the new building. It was a snowy day and Pastor Keyl, being of advanced years was taken by horse drawn sleigh to the new church where he installed the new pastor, Reverend W. G. Hugo Hanser. St. Paul's Lutheran Church later relocated to Catonsville, Maryland where it remains an active Missouri Synod congregation.[iii]

2. Immanuel Lutheran Church was established in 1864 in part by members of Second German Lutheran's congregation in East Baltimore. It had begun as one of the outreach schools of Second German Additionally, members of other Lutheran congregations in Baltimore, namely Trinity and St. Matthews formed the nucleus of this new congregation. In 1874 a church cemetery was established.[iv] Immanuel Lutheran subsequently relocated to Loch Raven Boulevard and Belvedere Avenue where it remains an active Missouri Synod congregation.

3. Thirdly, Martini Lutheran Church was established in 1867 in South Baltimore again originally an outreach of the German-language schools established by Second German Lutheran. Martini, first located at the corner of Sharp and Henrietta Streets, moved in 1976 a block east to the corner of Hanover and Henrietta Streets. The move was made at

the request of the city because of a planned highway that never actually materialized. Martini Lutheran remains an active Missouri Synod congregation.

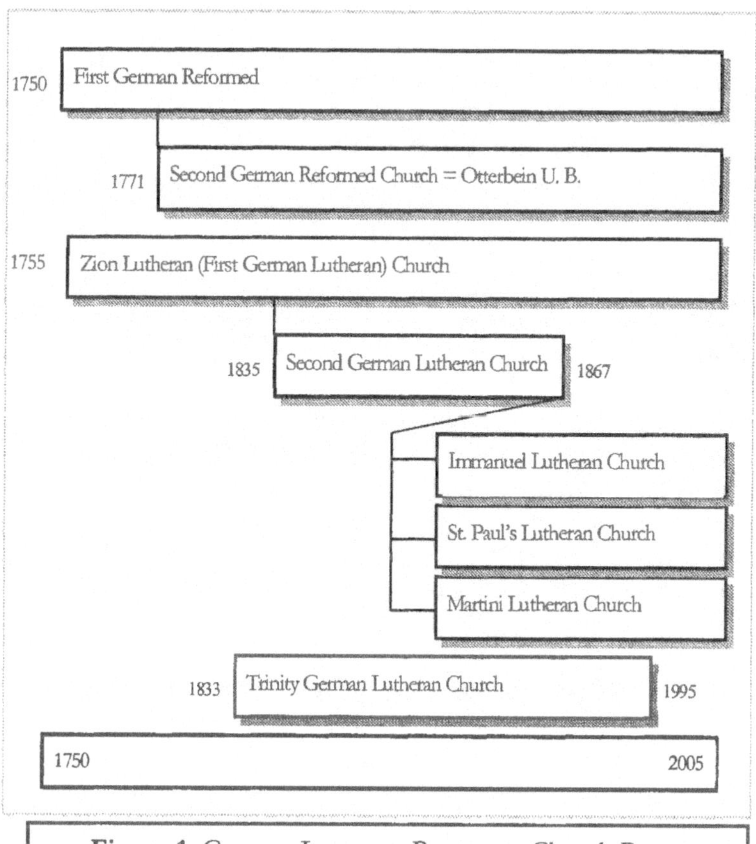

Figure 1. German-Language Protestant Church Roots

Records of Second German Lutheran Church

The burial register and a list of congregants from the original Second German Lutheran Congregation in Baltimore have been archived at the Concordia Historical Institute in St. Louis, Missouri. This facility serves as the Archives and History Department for the Lutheran Church, Missouri Synod. These records have been microfilmed by the Concordia Historical Institute where they are available as films number 595, 596 and 597. Additionally, microfilms were created by the Genealogical Society of Utah and are available at the Family History Library in Salt Lake City, Utah and through the affiliated Family History Centers. The microfilm number is 1,479,675-10.

The baptismal register of the original Second German Lutheran Church has been housed at Martini Lutheran Church in South Baltimore, one of the three filial congregations of Second German. This register as well as church minutes, various financial records, cemetery interments, a few confirmations and other official documents from the congregation have been at Martini for nearly 140 years, basically inaccessible to the genealogist.

With the consent of the church council and church pastor, Rev. Elliott M. Robertson and the patience of the church secretary, Ms. Krantz, I was able to review the baptismal register and again with consent from Martini, these records were microfilmed by The Genealogical Society of Utah for the Family History Library. Additionally, the church registers of Martini Lutheran and the former South Baltimore congregation of The Lutheran Church of the Messiah (which merged with Martini) were also microfilmed. These records are now available through the Family History Centers on microfilm 2,312,943.[v]

The whereabouts of the original marriage register from Second German Lutheran is unfortunately not known at this time.

Transcription of Records

The surviving baptismal and burial registers of Second German Lutheran Church are intact from its founding in late 1835 until closure in late 1867. The entries are entirely in German, some of it extremely dense German script (Suetterlin). Spelling was not exactly a strong point of any of the scribes, presumably the ministers. Names and words within the same entry may be spelled in a variety of ways.

Fortunately, most of the pastors provided a great deal of information concerning the people about whom these entries were made. Rarely, do we find just a name, but rather full names, dates, places of events, often parents' names including birth names for females and witnesses. Occasionally, marginal notes provide interesting tid-bits of information.

Burial Register: begins in 1837 with the burial of Magdalena Arins Klein who died 24 October 1837, was buried the next day and had been born on 24 October 1811. These earliest burial records, which correspond with the pastorate of Rev. Haesbert are generally very brief providing birth and death dates and not much more. In 1845, presumably with the arrival of Pastor Wyneken, considerably more information is provided such as parents' names, place of birth (including a specific village, *Kreis* and kingdom) and often an age in years, months and days. In the late 1840s, the handwriting changes most likely to that of Pastor Keyl, however the same level of detail in the entries continues.

The last funeral entry is that of Karl Schwab who died on the 19 of November 1867 and was buried on the following day. He was the youngest son of Christian Schwab from Gersbach being only five days of age at his death.

The total number of burials entered from 1837 to 1867 is 1,046 with roughly 2500 names.

Baptismal Register: begins in 1837 as follows: "*Im Namen Gottes des Vaters und des Sohnes und der Heiligen Geistes wurde in der Zweiten Deutschen Lutherischen Kirche getauft durch Pastor Joh. P. C. Haesbaert ...*" The first entry is for Margaretha Elisabeth, born 16 December 1836 to Heinrich Schliessler and Christina Elisabetha nee Kummer.

The pattern of entries is identical to that described under Burials, namely minimal detail for entries by Pastor Haesbert and considerable detail for those by Pastors Wyneken and Keyl.

The last baptism was recorded on Christmas Day 1867 for Johann Hermann born on 9 December to Christian Ecksturm from Useborn in Hessen and his wife Katharina born Weber from Volkortshain in Hessen. The witnesses were Heinrich Ecksturm and Mrs. Margaretha Wirth.

Total baptisms from 1837 until 1867 were 3,042 with more than 12,000 names.

Scattered among the baptisms are Confirmation entries. Unfortunately, there is an incomplete record of confirmations.

The total number of confirmations is 822.

How to Use This Index

I have transcribed the German entries as closely as possible to the original within the limits of legibility and my understanding of the text. Obviously, neither is perfect, so please follow the age-old *caveat* for all works of this type - ***check the original records!***

Information included in this index is not complete. Because of space limitations and formatting, some witnesses and other data have been omitted. There were often three or more witnesses to a baptism which sometimes included places of birth of the witnesses or other notations. There is just not enough room to include such detail in this index.

The major body of this work is divided into an alphabetical listing for subjects of Baptisms, Burials and Confirmations followed by indices to names of other persons mentioned in the baptismal, confirmation and burial entries. Finally, a Place Name Index includes a listing of all geographic names extracted from the baptismal and burial registers.I have not provided a chronological transcription but have arranged the three sections by Surname.
The section on Baptisms is sorted by (1) surname and (2) child's given name. Each baptism includes the following columns of information: Surname, Child's Given Name, Birth Date, Baptismal Date, Father's Given Name, Father's Place of Birth, Mother's Surname and Given Name, Mother's Birthplace, Witness I Surname and Given Name, Witness II Surname and Given Name and Comments.

The pastors included illegitimate births often with a notation to this effect. In this situation, seldom is a father's name provided. In the transcription, the father is entered by the notation [--?--] which sorts at the beginning of the list before entries starting with the letter 'A'.

The section on Burials is arranged in a similar manner with ranking by (1) Surname (2) Given Name and (3) Date of Death. Because Survivor information is provided, it is relatively easy to see how the deceased fit into a given family.

Each burial includes the following columns of information: Given Name of Decedent, Date of Death, Date of Burial, Birth Date or age, Birthplace, Survivor and Comments. Note that under Birthplace, when the entry is followed by [f], this refers to the birthplace of the father, not of the deceased. If the entry is followed by [m], the birthplace is that of the mother.

Confirmation data are rather scant, generally including just the confirmand's name and a date. This section of the transcription is ranked by (1) Surname and (2) Given Name and (3) Date. The data are printed two columns to a page, to be read from left top to left bottom and then right top to right bottom.

The Index at the back of the book provides an entry for all names excluding the subject of the event, since the subjects are contained in the primary alphabetical listing in the body of this work. Entries in the index therefore consist of witnesses, parents, survivors, etc. Since there are so many geographic place names extracted from this church register, a Place Name Index is also included.

Therefore to make the best use of this transcription, follow this order of search:

1. Check the surname of interest in the main body of the book in the sections for Baptism, Burial and Confirmation. This will provide an index to persons baptized, buried and confirmed.
2. Check the index in the back of the book to see if there are individuals of the surname you are searching who were witnesses, spouses, survivors, parents, etc included in the Baptismal, Confirmation and Burial entries.

3. Finally, you can check the Place Name Index to find all individuals in Second German Lutheran Church who were from any given locality in Europe.

Bibliography

Friends of Allen County. Immanuel Lutheran Cemetery, Baltimore, Maryland. Online at http://wwwfriendsofallencounty.org/search immlutheran.php. Downloaded 15 August 2005.

Immanuel Lutheran Church and School [Baltimore, Maryland]. Online at http://www.immanuellutheran.org/index/htm. Downloaded 15 August 2005.

Martini Lutheran Church [Baltimore, Maryland]. Online at http://martinilutheran.org/. Downloaded 15 August 2005.

Scarborough, Katherine (14 December 1947). St. Pauls downtown moved 80 years ago. *The Baltimore Sunday Sun*.

Scharf, J. Thomas, *History of Baltimore City and County from the earliest period to the present day: including biographical sketches of their representative men.* Philadelphia, Pennsylvania: Louis H. Everts, 1881.

Shepherd, Henry Elliot, editor. *History of Baltimore, Maryland from its founding as a town to the current year 1729-1898*. n.p.: S. B. Nelson Publisher, 1898.

St. Paul Lutheran Church & School Catonsville, Maryland. Online at: http://www.stpaul-lcms-md.org/church/church.shtml. Downloaded 15 August 2005.

St. Paul's Lutheran Church, Missouri Synod. *Jubelfeir der Baltimore Gemeinden, 1836-1911.* Second German

Evangelical Lutheran Church, 1835-1864, Saratoga and Holliday Streets. Works Progress Administration Historical Church Records Survey. Record Group S1512-2481, Maryland State Archives, Annapolis

Wentz, Rev. Prof. Abdel Ross, *History of the Evangelical Lutheran Synod of Maryland of the United Lutheran Church in America, 1820-1920.* Harrisburg, Pennsylvania: Evangelical Press, 1920.

Wentz, Rev. Prof. Abdel Ross, *A Basic History of Lutheranism in America.* Revised edition. Philadelphia, Pennsylvania: Fortress Press, 1964.

Wust, Klaus G., *Zion in Baltimore 1755-1955, the Bicentennial History of the Earliest German-American Church in Baltimore, Maryland.* Baltimore, Maryland: Zion Church of the City of Baltimore, 1955.

Wyneken, Matthew. Wynecken Genealogy. 2003. University of Freiburg, Germany. Online at: http://top10.physik.uni-freiburg.de/~mpw/Wynekens/. Downloaded 15 August 2005.

Zimmerman Elaine O. and Kenneth Zimmerman. *Records of St. Pauls Cemetery, 1855-1946.* Westminster, Maryland: Willow Bend Books, 1992.

Zion Church of the City of Baltimore, The Virtual Tour, History of Zion. Online at http://www.zionbaltimore.org/vthistory.htm. Downloaded 15 August 2005.

[i] Second German Reformed Church became Otterbein United Brethren which through a variety of mergers is now Otterbein United Methodist Church. Though it has changed names and even denominations, the congregation still worships in the original church building located on Conway Street at Sharp.

[ii] Over the years, three church cemeteries have been established. The first, established 1838, was located on Madison Avenue near North Avenue and was closed with all graves moved to a new cemetery in 1857 where the congregation purchased four acres in 1854 in what is now Druid Hill Park. Although the cemetery in Druid Hill still exists, the church opened a third burial ground in Violetville about 1880. Many interred in Druid Hill were removed to Violetville, but not all. There are several sources of information on interments. See Zimmerman's published book as well as the on-line sites noted in the Bibliography. Original records from Druid Hill are maintained at Martini Lutheran (and have been microfilmed). Records relating to Violetville are maintained by St.Paul's Lutheran Church, Catonsville.

[iii] See website http://www.stpaul-lcms-md.org/church/church.shtml

[iv] See http://friendsofallencounty.org/search_immlutheran.php

[v] Items 1-5 on this microfilm are the registers of Martini Lutheran Church. Item 6 is the baptismal register of Second German Lutheran. Item 7 is the original constitution and a list of members of Second German Lutheran through 1853. Item 8 contains a list of interments for St. Paul's Cemetery beginning in 1844 through 1946. Item 9 is a copy of the registers of The Lutheran Church of the Messiah roughly 1911 through 1956. Lastly, item 10 is a register of minutes of the Missouri Synod in Baltimore.

Surname Father; Child's Given Name; Birth Date; Baptismal Date; Father's Given Name; Father's Place of Birth; Mother's Surname and Given Name; Mother's Place of Birth; Witness 1 Surname and Given Name; Witness 2 Surname and Given Name; Witness 3 Surname and Given Name; Comments

[--?--]; Anna Martha; 22-Jun-50; 10-Aug-50; [--?--]; —; Christ, Maria; Elgenroth, Hessen; Treibert, Martha Steube; —; —; born at sea, illegitimate

[--?--]; Catharina Elisabeth; 5-Dec-54; 4-Mar-55; [--?--]; —; Schmidt, Maria; Aklosthausen, Baden; Hufnagel, Catharina; Einwachter, Elisabeth; —; mother fled with Joh. Georg Hoffmann

[--?--]; Catharina Louise; 17-Aug-52; 29-Aug-52; [--?--]; —; Hankel, Elisabeth; Obernost, Kurhessen; Mansdorfer, Catharine Louise; —; —; illegitimate

[--?--]; Elias; 6-Oct-36; 15-Jan-37; [--?--]; —; Dietz, Elisab. Marg.; —; —; —; —; illegtimate

[--?--]; Heinrich August; 25-Sep-48; 7-Jan-49; [--?--]; —; Dreyer, Maria; Liebenau, Hannover; Heidmuller, Heinrich; Jungstus, Auguste; —; illegitimate

[--?--]; Henriette Julie; 3-Aug-37; 28-Aug-37; [--?--]; —; Otto, Magdalena; —; —; —; —; illegitimate

[--?--]; Hermann Friedrich; 10-May-51; 7-Sep-51; [--?--]; —; Fraske, Friedrike; Siecke, Hannover; Aichele, Jakob; —; —; illegitimate

[--?--]; Jacob Heinrich; 28-Nov-38; 4-Dec-38; [--?--]; —; Bahlmanns, Katharina; —; —; —; —; illegitimate

[--?--]; Johann Adam; 17-Feb-46; 8-Mar-46; [--?--]; —; Jung, Clara; Ferth, Konigruaiern [?]; Jakob, Johann Adam; —; —; illegitimate

[--?--]; Johann Joseph; —; 13-Jun-48; [--?--]; —; —; —; —; —; —; —

[--?--]; Katharine; 8-Jan-39; 17-Mar-30; [--?--]; —; Grössen, Maria; —; —; —; —; illegitimate

[--?--]; Luise Marg.; 13-Sep-38; 18-Sep-38; [--?--]; —; Fischbeck, Luise; —; —; —; —; illegtimate

[--?--]; Maria Friedericke; 5-Mar-56; 6-Apr-56; [--?--]; —; Heyse, Irsina Christiana; Liebenau, Hannover; Klinkmeier, Maria Friederike; Heyse, Maria; —; —

Surname Father; Child's Given Name; Birth Date; Baptismal Date; Father's Given Name; Father's Place of Birth; Mother's Surname and Given Name; Mother's Place of Birth; Witness 1 Surname and Given Name; Witness 2 Surname and Given Name; Witness 3 Surname and Given Name; Comments

[--?--]; Marie Elisabeth; 31-Jan-51; 1-Feb-51; [--?--]; —; Gingnagel, Sophie; Krumstadt, Hessen; Gingnagel, Widow; Schumacher, Elisabeth; —; illegitimate

Achenbach; Johann Heinr.; 12-Jan-39; 16-Feb-39; Johann; —; [--?--], Emeline; —; —; —; —; —

Ackler; Dorothea; 11-May-43; 28-Jul-44; Jacob Bernh.; —; Teufel, Maria; —; —; —; —; —

Ackler; Georg; 11-Dec-41; 28-Jul-44; Jacob Bernh.; —; Teufel, Maria; —; —; —; —; —

Ackler; Jacob; 18-Mar-38; 28-Jul-44; Jacob Bernh.; —; Teufel, Maria; —; —; —; —; —

Ackler; Maria Elisabeth; 21-Dec-39; 28-Jul-44; Jacob Bernh.; —; Teufel, Maria; —; —; —; —; —

Aichele; Anna Sarah; 28-Feb-66; 15-Apr-66; Johann; Baltimore; Erdmann, Martha Taeilin; Baltimore; Muhly, Georg; Bauer, Sarah; Erdmann, Amande; —

Aichele; Caroline; 13-Feb-46; 16-Mar-46; Jakob; Furstenhoff, Backnang, Wurttemberg; Frank, Rosine; Aschbach, Backnang, Wurttemberg; Frank, Christian; —; —; —

Aichele; Jacob; 6-Oct-44; 13-Nov-44; Jacob; —; Arant, Regine; —; —; —; —; —

Aichele; Jakob Gottlieb; 21-Jun-64; 14-Jul-64; Johann; Baltimore; Erdmann, Cacilie; Baltimore; Muhly, Hermann; Bauer, Elisabeth; —; —

Aichele; Johannes; 11-Aug-42; 25-Sep-42; Jacob; —; Frank, Regina; —; —; —; —; —

Aichele; Karoline Magd.; 22-May-41; 2-Jun-41; Jacob; —; Frank, Regine; —; —; —; —; —

Aichele; Sophie; 20-Jun-47; 14-Jul-47; Jakob; Furstenhoff, Backnang, Wurttemberg; Frank, Regine; Gross Aschbach, Backnang, Wurttemberg; Frank, Jakob; —; —; wit is grandfather

Albach; Louise Caroline; 5-Sep-44; 23-Mar-45; Johann; Niedrohm, Hessen; Mohr, Catharina; Niedrohm, Hessen; Sehrt, Heinrich; Sehrt, Elise; Messinger, Caroline; —

Surname Father; Child's Given Name; Birth Date; Baptismal Date; Father's Given Name; Father's Place of Birth; Mother's Surname and Given Name; Mother's Place of Birth; Witness 1 Surname and Given Name; Witness 2 Surname and Given Name; Witness 3 Surname and Given Name; Comments

Albach; Maria Elisabeth; 21-Dec-36; 10-Feb-37; Georg; —; Herrschaft, Anna; —; —; —; —; —

Albert; Alexander; 14-Jun-42; 17-Jul-42; Johann; —; Mohr, Anna Kathr.; —; —; —; —; —

Albrecht; Anna Katharina; 13-Nov-63; 13-Nov-63; Karl Julius; Sengerhausen, Preussen; Osten, Barbara; Exinct [?], Baiern; Briel, Anna Katharine; —; —; —

Albrecht; infant daughter; 7-Sep-57; —; Karl Eul.; Sangerhausen, Preussen; Osten, Barbara; —; —; —; —; stillborn

Albrecht; Julie Barbara; 26-Mar-59; 26-Mar-59; Karl Julius; Sangerhausen, Preussen; Oster, Barbara; —; parents, ; —; —; in house

Aldinger; Carl Wilhelm Heinrich; 10-May-45; 1-Jun-45; David; Fellbach, Kanstadt, Wurttemberg; [--?--], Regina; Nill bei Kirchheim, Wurttemberg; Weber, Heinrich; Pitz, Hrnch.; —; —

Alfken [--?--]; Adeline Marie; 28-Dec-47; 24-May-47; Heinrich Dietrich; Varel, Oldenburg; Mahlers, Catharine; Bremen; Stessen, Adeline; Schragen, Marie; —; —

Allniger; Catharina; 31-Dec-49; 10-Feb-50; Jakob; Laufen, Bessingheim, Wurttemberg; Wissinger, Maria; Bulzbach, Duspach, Baiern; Horn, Catharina; —; —; —

Almang; Johannes; 23-May-41; 21-Jun-41; Philip; —; Geissert, Christine; —; —; —; —; —

Altekruse; Friedrich Wilh.; 11-Feb-41; 9-Mar-41; Heinrich R.; —; Gert von do Mark!, Sophie; —; —; —; —; —

Altekruse; Heinrich Rudolph; 8-Aug-39; 15-Sep-39; Heinrich; —; Hert von der Mark!, Sophie; —; —; —; —; —

Altrieth; Elisabeth Kathr.; 6-Mar-44; 21-Apr-44; Christian; —; Kätes, Christine; —; —; —; —; —

Altrith; Wilhelm; 28-Feb-48; 9-Apr-48; Christian; Jaxthausen, Wurttemberg; Kothe, Christine; Diegenthal bei Hall, Wurttemberg; Hissel, Wilhelm; —; —; —

Altritt; Marianne; 28-Mar-46; 17-May-46; Christian; Jaxthausen, Nekarsulm; Kote, Christine; Tipelnthal, Wurttemberg; Kote, Marianne; —; —; —

Surname Father; Child's Given Name; Birth Date; Baptismal Date; Father's Given Name; Father's Place of Birth; Mother's Surname and Given Name; Mother's Place of Birth; Witness 1 Surname and Given Name; Witness 2 Surname and Given Name; Witness 3 Surname and Given Name; Comments

Am Rain [Amrhein]; Wilhelm; 16-Jun-45; 12-Nov-45; Heinrich; Wahle bei Alsfeld, Hessen; Schneider, Anna Elisabeth; Bernsburg bei Alsfeld; —; —; —; born Long Green, Baltimore Co.

Am Rhein; Anna Maria; 20-Aug-37; 24-Dec-37; Johann; —; Wahl, Elisab.; —; —; —; —; —

Am Rhein; Heinrich; 26-Sep-40; 26-Dec-40; Johann; —; Wahl, Elisab.; —; —; —; —; —

Am Rhein; Karoline; 19-Sep-36; 22-Sep-38; Johann; —; Braun, Susanne; —; —; —; —; —

Amrein; Johannes; 18-Aug-44; 27-Mar-45; Johann; Wahlen, Hessen; Braunroth, Susanne; Bernsburg, Hessen; Nau, Johannes; —; —; —

Amrhein; Eleonora; 10-Oct-43; 29-Nov-43; Johann; —; Wahl, Elisab.; —; —; —; —; —

Amrhein; Ludwig; 23-Aug-46; 25-Oct-46; Johann; Wahlen, Alsfeld, Hessen; Wahl, Elisabeth; Philadelphia; —; —; —; —

Amthor; Johann Andreas; 29-Apr-62; 29-Jun-62; Dr. Johann Michael Robert; Gotha; Aschmann, Johanne Friederike Dorothea; —; Schimpf, Johann Heinrich Gottfried; —; —; —

Andre; Johann; 15-Sep-49; 11-Nov-49; Christoph; Ilmeneu, Sachsen Weimar; Malesch, Johanne; Neustadt an derHeudt, Sachsen Coburg; Rother, Johann; —; —; —

Angelmeyer; Georg; 16-Aug-43; 10-Dec-43; Mathaus; —; Lugensland, Katharine; —; —; —; —; —

Angelmeyer; Luise; 16-Jan-48; 18-Jul-48; Mathias; Siedelbach, Maulbronn, Wurttemberg; Luginsland, Catharine; Ubdingen, Vairingen, Wurttemberg; Luginsland, Luise; —; —; —

Angelmeyer; Maria Elisabetha; 11-Mar-50; 21-Apr-50; Matthias; Grundelbach, Maulbronn, Wurttemberg; Lugisland, Katharina; Ubdingen, Wurttemberg; —; —; —; —

Angelmeyer; Matthaus; 21-Sep-45; 4-Jan-46; Matthaus; Gundelbach, Maulbronn, Wurttemberg; Luginsland, Catharine; Ubteigen, Wurttemberg; Geigle, Joh.; —; —; —

Angromann; Margaretha; 19-Nov-42; 11-Dec-42; [--?--]; —; Hacker, Susanne; —; —; —; —; —

Surname Father; Child's Given Name; Birth Date; Baptismal Date; Father's Given Name; Father's Place of Birth; Mother's Surname and Given Name; Mother's Place of Birth; Witness 1 Surname and Given Name; Witness 2 Surname and Given Name; Witness 3 Surname and Given Name; Comments

Anschütz; Ludwig Philip; 28-May-42; 14-Jun-42; Philip; —; Emmrich, Wilhelmine; —; —; —; —; —

Anschütz; Wilhelm; 21-Dec-37; 14-Feb-38; Philip; —; Emmart, Wlhelmine; —; —; —; —; —

Antrop; Hermann Rudolph; 27-Oct-38; 4-Nov-38; Hermann; —; Barlmeyer, Kathr.; —; —; —; —; —

Apel; Johann; 7-May-48; 4-May-48; Caspar; Hain, Weismain, Baiern; Hopf, Margarethe; Harb, Lustenfels, Baiern; Kohler, Johann; —; —; —

Apel; Johann; 18-Dec-46; 28-Dec-46; Caspar; Hain, Weismain, Baiern; Hopf, Margarethe; Horp a. M., Lichtenfels, Baiern; Senft, Johann Wilhelm; —; —; child died

Apodofsky; Johann; 9-Apr-40; 31-May-40; Georg; —; Heil, Marg.; —; —; —; —; —

Apothofsky; Heinrich; 19-Jun-36; 29-Jul-38; Georg; —; Heil, Marg.; —; —; —; —; —

Arel; Georg Friedrich; 5-Apr-51; 21-Apr-51; Johann; Ried, Sachsen Meiningen; Roner, Christine; —; Rittger, Georg; —; —; —

Arend; Gottfried August Wilh.; 6-Jan-40; 26-Jan-40; Gottfried; —; Sprank, Charlotte; —; —; —; —; —

Arnd; Heinrich Gottfr.; 5-Mar-43; 27-Mar-43; Gottfr.; —; Sprank, Charlotte; —; —; —; —; —

Arndt; Johann; 27-Jan-47; 1-Feb-47; Jakob; Hempfershausen, Sachsen Meiningen; Betzenberger, Catharine; Dernbach, Sachsen Weimar; Tripp, Johann; Tripp, Barbara; —; child died

Arnold; August Eduard; 9-Jan-51; 21-Feb-51; Richard Hugo; Lommetzsch, Sachsen; Borgelt, Maria Amilie; —; Borgelt, Hermann Heinrich; —; —; —

Arnold; August Heinrich; 22-Oct-57; 8-Nov-57; Georg; Heidelberg, Baden; Gansmuller, Magdalena; —; Dietz, Heinr.; Arnold, Kunigunde; —; —

Arnold; Auguste Emilie; 16-Apr-58; 25-Apr-58; Richard Hugo; Lommatesch, Sachsen; Bargelt, Maria Amalie; —; Hoffmann, Anna Maria Amalia; —; —; —

Surname Father; Child's Given Name; Birth Date; Baptismal Date; Father's Given Name; Father's Place of Birth; Mother's Surname and Given Name; Mother's Place of Birth; Witness 1 Surname and Given Name; Witness 2 Surname and Given Name; Witness 3 Surname and Given Name; Comments

Arnold; Eberhard Johann Georg; 2-Jul-55; 3-Feb-56; Georg; Leunheim, Baden; Gansmuller, Madgalena; —; Ortmann, Eberhard Heinr.; Sunop [?], Joh.; Begerlein, Joh.; —

Arnold; Heinrich Friedrich R.; 31-Jan-64; 6-Mar-64; Richard Hugo; Lomatzsch, Sachsen; Borchalte, Anna Maria; —; Schaumburg, Joh. Heinr.; Thiemeyer, Frdch.; —; —

Arnold; Johann Heinrich; 11-Jun-55; 24-Jun-55; Richard Hugo; Loommatxch, Sachsen; Bargelt, Anna Maria Amalia; —; Bargelt, Heinrich; Bargelt, Anna Maria Louise; —; —

Arnold; Katharine Marie Susanne; 9-Dec-60; 23-Dec-60; Georg; Heidelberg, Baden; Gansmuller, Magdalena; —; Arras, Katharine; Waldschmidt, Marie; Bremer, Susanne; —

Arnold; Louis Oscar; 12-Oct-66; 23-Dec-66; Richard Hugo; Lammotzsch, Sachsen; Bargelt, Anna Emilie; Engter, Hannover; Schomberg, Wilhelm; Thiemeyer, Elisabeth; —; —

Arnold; Louise Julianne; 1-May-60; 19-Aug-60; Hugo Richard; Lommetzsch, Sachsen; Bargelt, Anna Emilie; —; Vorderwusten, Heinrich; Thiemeyer, Julianne; —; —

Arnold; Lousie Sophie; 6-Jul-52; 22-Jul-52; Hugo Richard; Lommatsch, Sachsen; Borgelt, Anna Maria Amalia; —; Borgelt, Maria Wilhelmine; Borgelt, Louise; —; —

Arnold; Richard Wilhelm; 6-Dec-53; 18-Dec-53; Richard Hugo; Lommatzsch, Sachsen; Borgelt, Anna Amalia; —; Borgelt, Wilhelm; —; —; —

Arnold; Theodor Adolph; 22-Dec-1861; 26-Jan-62; Hugo; Lommatzsch, Sachsen; Borgelt, Anna Marie; —; Weidemeier, Adam; Wiebking, Heinrich; —; —

Arnolds; infant daughter; 15-Jan-57; —; Richard Hugo; Lomatsch; Borgelt, Anna Maria Amalie; —; —; —; —; stillborn

Auerheim; Eva Elisabeth; 26-Jun-49; 22-Jul-49; Johann; Wahlen, Alsfeld, Hessen; Wahl, Elisabeth; Philadelphia, PA; Lehr, Eva; —; —; —

Auermann; Caroline Wilhelmine; 19-Dec-45; 14-Jun-46; Jakob; Naumberg a.d., Preussen; Hoffmann, Wilhelmine; Naumberg a.d., Preussen; Hellwig, Carline; —; —; —

Surname Father; Child's Given Name; Birth Date; Baptismal Date; Father's Given Name; Father's Place of Birth; Mother's Surname and Given Name; Mother's Place of Birth; Witness 1 Surname and Given Name; Witness 2 Surname and Given Name; Witness 3 Surname and Given Name; Comments

Bach; Anna Eleonora Wilhelmine; 10-Nov-61; 17-Nov-61; Adam; Eckartsbrunn, Hessen; Stein, Katharine; —; Blonch [?]; anna Margarethe, Weddiger; Theodor; —

Bach; Anna Elisabeth Katharine; 19-Feb-56; 2-Mar-56; Adam; Eckartsborn, Hessen; Stein, Katharine; —; Riedel, Anna Elisabeth; Riedel, Konrad; Schneider, Katharine;

Bach; George Heinrich; 22-Feb-66; 4-Mar-66; Adam; Eckhartsborn, Hessen; Stein, Elisabeth Katharin; Oberohm, Hessen; Winter, Wilhelmine; Stein, Heinrich; Lange, Bernhard; —

Bach; Johann Jacob; 21-Jul-42; 16-Aug-42; Joseph; —; Grünwald, Juliane; —; —; —; —; —

Bach; Karl Heinrich Theodor; 23-May-57; 1-Jun-57; Adam; Eckartsborn, Hessen; Stein, Elisabeth Katharina; —; Schafer, Heinrich; Weddiger, Theodor; —; —

Bach; Maria Magdalena Henrietta; 9-Aug-59; 21-Aug-59; Adam; Eckartsborn, Hessen; Stein, Katharine; —; Spielmann, Maria Margaretha; Ecksturm, Elis. Maria; Beck, Henrietta; —

Bach; Rosine Friederike; 18-Nov-53; 11-Dec-53; Adam; Eckartsbrun, Hessen; Stein, Kathainre; —; Walthers, Rosina Friederike; Walthers, Aug.; —; —

Bach; Susanne Emilie; 6-Mar-64; 20-Mar-64; Adam; Eckertsbrunn, Hessen; Stein, Katharine; Oberohm, Hessen; Stein, Kaspar; Winter, Wilhelmine; Weddiger, Auguste; —

Bachmann; Anna Margaretha; 10-Oct-55; 21-Oct-55; Heinrich Wilh.; Holzthallebon; Meier, Anna Margar.; —; Radecka, Margaretha; Meier, Anna Adelheid; —; posthumous baptism

Bachmann; Anna Maria; 19-Jul-49; 19-Aug-49; Heinrich Wilhelm; Holzthalnben, Sondershausen, Preussen; Meier, Anna Margaretha; Leste, Sieke, Hannover; Meier, Adelheid Maria; Bachmann, Maria; —; —

Bachmann; Georg Karl; 16-Nov-40; 4-Jul-41; Wilhelm; —; Heyse, Henriette; —; —; —; —; —

Bachmann; Heinrich Wilhelm; 21-Dec-50; 26-Jan-51; Franz Joh.; Schillingsfurst, Baiern; Suss, Marie Dorothea; —; Erbe, Heinrich Wilhelm; —; —; —

Surname Father; Child's Given Name; Birth Date; Baptismal Date; Father's Given Name; Father's Place of Birth; Mother's Surname and Given Name; Mother's Place of Birth; Witness 1 Surname and Given Name; Witness 2 Surname and Given Name; Witness 3 Surname and Given Name; Comments

Bade; Maria Margaretha; 29-Jan-52; 22-Feb-52; Wilh. Heinr.; Schlitthausen, Hannover; Meinicke, Margarehte; —; Engel, Margarethe; Bade, Sophie Dingler; —; —

Bade; Wilhelm Ludw.; 5-Sep-40; 11-Oct-40; Wilhelm; —; Meinecke, Marg.; —; —; —; —; —

Bader; Johann Hermann; 1-Jul-65; 16-Jul-65; Johann Veit; Baltimore; Redinger, Kathrine Regine; Baltimore; Muhly, Hermann; Brauer, Joh. Wilh.; Brenner, Susanne Katharine; —

Bader; Johann Veit; 18-Jul-42; 31-Jul-42; Heinrich; —; Werther, Agathe; —; —; —; —; —

Bader; Karl Heinrich; 13-Mar-67; 24-Mar-67; Johann Veit; Baltimore; Reddinger, Katharine Regina; Baltimore; Meier, Karl; Whittler, Heinrich; —; —

Bahr; Johann Friedrich; 20-May-48; 4-Jun-48; Mathaus; Frankenberg, Pegnitz, Baiern; Hossmann, Margarethe; Machs, Bodenstein, Baiern; Viertel, Johann Friedrich; —; —; —

Baier; Elisabeth Kunigunde; 14-Dec-48; 14-Jan-49; Georg; Oberhochstadt, Neustadt a.d. Reuss, Baiern; Kestler, Margarethe; Markuhlfeld, Neustadt a.d. Reuss, Baiern; Kestler, Kunigunde; —; —; —

Baier; Georg Wilhelm; 13-Jan-52; 18-Feb-52; Joh.; Oberheckstadt, Baiern; Schmidt, Anna Kunigunde; —; Baier, Georg; —; —; —

Baier; Susanne Margarethe; 28-Sep-51; 26-Oct-51; Georg; Oberheckstadt, Baiern; Lissler, Anna Margaretha; —; Kohler, Susanne Margarethe; Baier, Katharina; —; wit #1 in Markuhlfeldt, Baiern

Baiswanger; Elisabethe; 4-Mar-41; 23-Mar-41; Jacob; —; Engelken, Christine; —; —; —; —; —

Baiswanger; Johann Jacob; 13-Jan-40; 26-Jan-40; Jacob; —; Engelken, Christine; —; —; —; —; —

Baiswanger; Karoline Christiane; 13-Oct-44; 24-Nov-44; Jacob; —; Engelken, Christine; —; —; —; —; —

Baiswänger; Rebecca Maria; 16-Jan-38; 4-Feb-38; Jacob; —; Engelken, Christine; —; —; —; —; —

Surname Father; Child's Given Name; Birth Date; Baptismal Date; Father's Given Name; Father's Place of Birth; Mother's Surname and Given Name; Mother's Place of Birth; Witness 1 Surname and Given Name; Witness 2 Surname and Given Name; Witness 3 Surname and Given Name; Comments

Balla; Elisabeth Florentine; 23-Jul-41; 6-Feb-42; Johann R.; —; Dinkelmann, Salome; —; —; —; —; —

Balla; Karl Theodor; 4-Oct-38; 28-Oct-38; Johann R.; —; Diekelmann, Salome; —; —; —; —; —

Ballau; Karl Eduard; 25-Feb-37; 30-Jun-39; August; —; Dehof, Karoline; —; —; —; —; —

Baltz; Eva Katharina; 19-Sep-43; 12-Nov-43; Philip; —; Weber, Elisab.; —; —; —; —; —

Baltz; Wilhelm; 26-Jan-42; 6-Mar-42; Philip; —; Weber, Elisab.; —; —; —; —; —

Balz; Elise Kathr.; 8-Nov-40; 15-Dec-40; Philip; —; Weber, Elisab.; —; —; —; —; —

Balz; Philipine; 21-Aug-39; 9-Sep-39; Philip; —; Weber, Elisab.; —; —; —; —; —

Bambach; Elise; 28-Dec-50; 29-May-51; Aug.; Biedekopf, Hessen; Pfeister, Elise; —; father, ; —; —; —

Barbiens; Maria Susanne; 17-Nov-51; 21-Mar-52; Joseph; —; Vogelmann, Wilhelmine; —; Vogelmann, Carl Wilh.; —; —; —

Bargen; Anna; 9-Dec-65; 31-Dec-65; Eberhard; Allendorf a. d. Lumda, Hessen; Fuchs, Marie; Frankenberg, Kurhessen; Schlerf, Anna Katharina; Fuchs, Katharine; Fuchs, Eleonora; —

Bartel; Henriette Caroline; 28-Aug-49; 30-Sep-49; Heinr. Ludw.; Benderode, Münden, Hannover; Farber, Margaretha Friederike; Oberstäaben, Baiern; Farber, Joh. Heinrich; Farber, Caroline; —; —

Barth; Elisabeth; 5-Mar-38; 16-Apr-38; Christian; —; Kraft, Maria; —; —; —; —; —

Barthold; Rosine Margarethe; 18-Jun-52; 14-Jul-52; Christian; Schleitz, Reuss; Keller, Margarethe; —; Keller, Margarethe; —; —; —

Bartram; Anna Sophia Elisabeth; 19-Mar-67; 31-Mar-67; Karl Friedrich; Burem, Preussen; Balz, Anna Elisabeth; Baltimore; Stamm, Rev. Alexander; Scherrer, Sophia Elisabeth; Balz, Maria; —

Surname Father; Child's Given Name; Birth Date; Baptismal Date; Father's Given Name; Father's Place of Birth; Mother's Surname and Given Name; Mother's Place of Birth; Witness 1 Surname and Given Name; Witness 2 Surname and Given Name; Witness 3 Surname and Given Name; Comments

Batjer; Elise Luise; 9-Sep-46; 24-Jan-47; Heinrich; Bremen; Briegel, Luise Dorothea; Feldbach, Wurttemberg; —; —; —; —

Battjer; Carl Heinrich; 24-Mar-49; 10-Jun-49; Heinrich; Habenhausen bei bremen; Bringel, Luise; Feldbach, Canstadt, Wurttemberg; Briegel, Carl; Briegel, Mrs.; —; —

Bauer; Christine Marg.; 1-Jul-41; 25-Jul-41; Gottfr.; —; Plessing, Marg.; —; —; —; —; —

Bauer; Elisabeth Barbara; 6-Jun-45; 15-Jun-45; Georg; Doerzbac, Kinzelsau, Wurttemberg; Bless, Margaretha; Hesselwart, Wurttemberg; Nicklas, Georg; Bless, Barbara; —; wit#2 is grandmother

Bauer; Emilie Elisabeth; 15-Jun-54; 25-Jun-54; Georg; Torzbach, Wurttemberg; Blessing, Margaretha; —; Blessing, Barbara; Picklas, Elis.; —; —

Bauer; Engelbert Carl Friedrich; 18-Jun-50; 18-Aug-50; Johann; Roizheim, Wurttemberg; Eisemann, Rosine; —; Meister, Engelbert; Meister, Dorothea; Scheibe, Carl; 2 child, 1 son

Bauer; Franz Wilhelm; 9-Jun-65; 18-Jun-65; Georg Ludwig; Tharzbach, Wurttemberg; Blasing, Margaretha; Baltimore; Hampe, Franz; Trager, Heinrich; —; —

Bauer; Georg Friedr.; 18-Jul-43; 25-Jun-43; Georg; —; Plessing, Marg.; —; —; —; —; —

Bauer; Heinrich Ludwig; 16-Dec-60; 23-Dec-60; Georg Ludwig; Diezbach, Wurttemberg; Blasing, Margarethe; —; Trager, Heinrich; Bauer, Ludwig Georg; —; —

Bauer; Johann Benjamin; 30-Aug-50; 8-Sep-50; Goerg; Terzbach, Wurttemberg; Blessing, Margaretha; —; Niklas, Georg; Blessing, Margaretha; —; 5 child, 2 son

Bauer; Johann Heinrich; 24-Jun-45; 16-Jul-45; Friederich; Schanbach, Canstadt, Wurttemberg; Saemann, Cath.; Isingen, Sulz, Wurttemberg; Kurle, Gottfried; Saemann, Christine; —; —

Bauer; Johannes; 21-Oct-51; 25-Nov-51; Johannes; Mergenseitz, Hessen; Lyess, Margarethe; —; Lentz, Johannes; —; —; —

Surname Father; Child's Given Name; Birth Date; Baptismal Date; Father's Given Name; Father's Place of Birth; Mother's Surname and Given Name; Mother's Place of Birth; Witness 1 Surname and Given Name; Witness 2 Surname and Given Name; Witness 3 Surname and Given Name; Comments

Bauer; Katharina Maria; 8-May-50; 23-Jun-50; Johannes; Merkenfritz, Birting, Darmstadt; Hess, Margaretha; Bleichenbach, Nidda, Darmstadt; Lenz, Maria; —; —; —

Bauer; Louise Julianna; 8-Aug-57; 16-Aug-57; Georg Ludwig; Tortzbach, Wurttemberg; Blasing, Margaretha; —; Blasing, Barbara; Albrecht, Jul.; —; —

Bauer; Margarethe Elisabeth; 16-Feb-47; 6-Apr-47; Georg; Niederstatten, Wurttemberg; Weingart, Margareth; Greuth, Hochstadt, Preussen; Senft, Marg. Elis.; —; —; —

Bauer; Marianne Maria; 9-Oct-43; 27-Oct-43; Michael; —; Haun, Elisab.; —; —; —; —; —

Bauer; Sarah; 14-Jan-48; 23-Jan-48; George; Dorzbach, Kinzelsau, Wurttemberg; Blessing, Margarethe; Hesselbach, Wurttemberg; Blessing, Barbara; Niklas, Elisabeth; —; —

Bauer; Wilhelmine Henriette; 26-Oct-62; 2-Nov-62; Georg Ludwig; Tortzbach, Wurttemberg; Blosing, Margarethe; —; Trager, Emilie; Hampe, Frau; —; —

Bauerle; Elisabeth Margareth; 4-Mar-49; 26-May-49; Johann Michael; Hersichau, Kirchheim a. d. Deck, Wurttemberg; Hammann, Maria Catharine; Herrsichau, Kirchheim a.d. Deck, Wurttemberg; Hermann, Anna Barbara; —; —; —

Baum; Johann; 8-Sep-45; 16-Nov-45; Johann; Kleinmunster, Hosfert, Baiern; Schwingler, Anna Barbara; Neustadt a.d. Reuss; Wolfram, Johann; —; —; —

Baumann; Dorothea Elisabetha; 3-Apr-67; 5-May-67; Georg; Blumenthal, Hannover; Wiebking, Maria Sophie; Liebenau, Hannover; Wiebking, Dorothea; Thiemeier, Elisabeth; —; —

Baumann; Eberhard Jacob; 23-Sep-37; 29-Oct-37; Arnold; —; Schepp, Maria; —; —; —; —; —

Baumann; Johann Heinrich; 28-Aug-48; 24-Sep-48; Johann Thomas; Staben, Neilau, Baiern; Horn, Henriette; Staben, Neilau, Baiern; Burger, Johann Heinrich; —; —; child died

Baumann; Maria Elisabeth; 18-Aug-44; 6-Apr-45; Arnold Rudolph; —; Schöp, Maria; —; —; —; —; —

Surname Father; Child's Given Name; Birth Date; Baptismal Date; Father's Given Name; Father's Place of Birth; Mother's Surname and Given Name; Mother's Place of Birth; Witness 1 Surname and Given Name; Witness 2 Surname and Given Name; Witness 3 Surname and Given Name; Comments

Baumann; Maria Friderika; 19-Apr-50; 19-May-50; Johann; Steben, Bayern; Horn, Heinrike; Steben, Bayern; Horn, Heinrike Maria; Baumann, Friederike M.; —; —

Baumgart; Anna Christine Pauline; 16-Mar-48; 19-Mar-48; Paul Israel; Oberlauringen, Hofheim, Baiern; Albach, Catharine Elisabeth; Baltimore; Albach, Anna Christine; —; —; wit is grandmother

Baumgärtel; Margaretha Elisabeth; 30-Aug-39; 10-Sep-39; Andreas; —; Ludwig, Kathr.; —; —; —; —; —

Baurichter; Margaretha Amalie Christiane; 4-Nov-38; 25-Nov-38; Christian; —; Tözters, Elise; —; —; —; —; —

Bayer; Barbara; 16-Mar-36; 7-May-37; Jacob; —; Koch, Barbara; —; —; —; —; —

Bayer; Johann Georg; 30-Mar-50; 5-May-50; Johann Conrad; Olerhochstadt, Bayern; Schmidt, Anna Katharina; Milnersbach, Bamberg, Bayern; Stierhof, Johann Georg; —; —; wit from Hierfeld

Beck; Anna Elisabeth; 19-Feb-46; 1-Jun-46; Ernst; Wixhausen, Hessen; Koch, Anna Magdalene; Oberrodt, Frankfurt a.M.; Horn, Anna Elisabeth; —; —; —

Beck; Anna Maria; 19-Jul-40; 13-Sep-40; Johann; —; Sebold, Dorothea; —; —; —; —; —

Beck; Catharine Friederike; 11-Aug-49; 19-Aug-49; Georg Friedrich; Waldtham, Kreilsheim, Wurttemberg; Hemmdorf, Sybilla Friederike; Feuchtwangen, Baiern; Kohnlein, Johann Jakob; Horn, Johann Michael; Horn, Catharine; —

Beck; Ferdinand Ludwig; 18-Mar-49; 8-Apr-49; Ernst; Wixhausen bei Darmstadt, Hessen; Koch, Anna Margaretha; Oberrod bei Frankfurth a.M, Hessen; Brauns, Ferdinand Ludwig; —; —; —

Beck; Georg; 1-Sep-38; 16-Sep-38; Jacob; —; Wissmann, Maria; —; —; —; —; —

Beck; Johann Kasper; 24-Jun-41; 2-Aug-41; Joh. E. W. P.; —; Koch, Magd.; —; —; —; —; —

Beck; Margaretha; 6-Sep-40; 20-Sep-40; Jacob; —; Wismann, Maria; —; —; —; —; —

Surname Father; Child's Given Name; Birth Date; Baptismal Date; Father's Given Name; Father's Place of Birth; Mother's Surname and Given Name; Mother's Place of Birth; Witness 1 Surname and Given Name; Witness 2 Surname and Given Name; Witness 3 Surname and Given Name; Comments

Beck; Maria; 6-May-38; 16-Sep-38; Georg; —; Koch, Marg.; —; —; —; —; —

Beck; Maria Magd. Henr.; 25-Jul-44; 3-Nov-44; Ernst; —; Koch, Magd.; —; —; —; —; —

Beckel; Anna Philippine; 29-Jul-51; 24-Aug-51; Heinrich; Lisberg, Hessen; Karmroth, Martha; —; Karmroth, Anna; Beckel, Eleonore; —; —

Beckel; Karoline Sophie; 4-May-61; 19-May-61; Heinrich; Lisberg, Hessen; Kamroth, Martha; —; Spielmann, Sophie; Brauer, Karoline; —; —

Beckemeyer; Maria; 22-May-41; 25-Jul-41; Wilhelm; —; Sonez, Barb.; —; —; —; —; —

Becker; Carl; 6-Sep-45; 26-Feb-47; Louis; Nidda, Hessen; Karmroth, Elisabeth; Oberdella bei Muhlhausen, Preussen; Roth, Carl; —; —; —

Becker; Carl August; 10-Mar-48; 2-Apr-48; August; Marburg, Kurhessen; Schumacher, Elisabeth; Marburg, Kurhessen; Schuhmacher, Karoline; —; —; —

Becker; Conrad Wilh.; 30-Oct-42; 14-Nov-42; August; —; Schumacher, Elisab.; —; —; —; —; —

Becker; Emilie; 25-Dec-36; 31-Jan-37; Joh.G.; —; Braun, Philipine; —; —; —; —; —

Becker; Friedrich Wilhelm; 21-Jun-67; 15-Jul-67; Konrad Heinrich; Marburg, Kurhessen; Bauer, Elisabeth; Volkartshain, Hessen; Nagel, Friedrich; —; —; —

Becker; Johann Lorenz; 25-Dec-47; 6-Apr-47; Gottlieb Friedr.; Rudersberg, Weltheim, Wurttemberg; Koch, Luise; Kloster, Baiern; Bopp, Lorenz; Bopp, Catharine; —; —

Becker; Johann Michael; 7-May-50; 26-May-50; August; Marburg, Kurhessen; Schuhmacher, Elisabeth; Marburg, Kurhessen; Jacob, Johann Michael; —; —; wit from Schweinsberg, Kurhessen

Becker; Johannes Wilhelm; 16-Feb-49; 2-Jul-49; Gottlieb Friedrich; Rudesberg, Walsheim, Wurttemberg; Koch, Luise; Kloster Loirum, Hannover; Senft, Joh. Wilh.; Ziegler, Eva; —; —

Surname Father; Child's Given Name; Birth Date; Baptismal Date; Father's Given Name; Father's Place of Birth; Mother's Surname and Given Name; Mother's Place of Birth; Witness 1 Surname and Given Name; Witness 2 Surname and Given Name; Witness 3 Surname and Given Name; Comments

Becker; Maria; 24-Dec-52; 2-Jan-53; Conrad; Marburg, Kurhessen; Muller, Elisabeth; —; Reinhard, Maria; —; —; —

Becker; Maria Elisabeth; 27-Mar-46; 20-Apr-46; August; Marburg, Kurhessen; Schumacher, Elisabeth; Marburg, Kurhessen; Becker, Maria; —; —; wit is grandmother

Becker; Wilhelm Conrad Dietrich; 10-Jul-64; 24-Jul-64; Christoph Wilhelm; Battenberg, Hessen; Kattenkamp, Juliane; Baltimore; Kattenkamp, Dietrich; Schulz, Conrad; —; —

Beckmeyer; Heinrich Ludwig; 17-Aug-43; 3-Dec-43; Wilh.; —; Bartes, Charlotte; —; —; —; —; —

Bedheimer; Georg Jakob; 20-Oct-44; 29-Jun-45; Christian; Coburg; Neubrand, Christiana; Unterderdingen, Wurttemberg; Bentz, Andreas; —; —; —

Begerlein; Elisabeth Louise Johanna; 23-Jan-56; 27-Jan-56; Joh. Michael; Bayreuth, Baiern; Mietzel, Justine; —; Leutner, Louise; Schorrer, Joh.; Schorrer, Elisabeth; —

Beisswanger; Jakob Ludwig; 6-Jul-50; 22-Jul-50; Jakob Peter; Bizfeld, Wurttemberg; Engelkind, Christine; —; Mix, Jakob; Hellwig, Ludwig; —; 7 child, 3 son

Beiswanger; Anna Clara; 3-Sep-47; 19-Sep-47; Jakob; Bizfeld, Weinsbach, Wurttemberg; Engelking, Christine; Quetzen bei Windheim, Preussen; Nix, Jakob; Nix, Anna Clara; —; —

Beitzel; Wilhelmine; 17-Feb-45; 27-Apr-45; Carl; —; Winther, Elisabeth; Berleberg, Witgrenstein, Arensberg, Preussen; Borsch, Wilhelmine; —; —; wit from Marburg

Bender; Barbara; 11-Oct-39; 1-Dec-39; Wilhelm; —; Emon, Barbara; —; —; —; —; illegitimate

Bender; Johannes Eduard; 30-Jun-66; 15-Jul-66; Heinrich; Marburg, Kurhessen; Rein, Katharine; Allendorf a. d. L., Hessen; Muth, Joh.; Mess, Johann; —; —

Bender; Karl Ludwig Eberhard; 18-Sep-64; 9-Oct-64; Heinrich; Marburg, Kurhessen; Rein, Maria; Allendorf a. d. L., Hessen; Rein, Christine; Wiesner, Eberhard; —; —

Bender; Katharine; 5-Nov-41; 21-Nov-41; Johann Chr.; —; Hecker, Maria; —; —; —; —; —

Surname Father; Child's Given Name; Birth Date; Baptismal Date; Father's Given Name; Father's Place of Birth; Mother's Surname and Given Name; Mother's Place of Birth; Witness 1 Surname and Given Name; Witness 2 Surname and Given Name; Witness 3 Surname and Given Name; Comments

Benker; Margaretha Julianne; 10-Feb-46; 22-Feb-46; Johann; Eutin, Holstein; Tönjes, Margaretha; Neuenwalde, Hannover; —; —; —; twin child died

Benker; Wilhelmine Elisabeth; 10-Feb-46; 22-Feb-46; Johann; Eutin, Holstein; Tönjes, Margaretha; Neuenwalde, Hannover; —; —; —; twin

Bepler; Anna Maria; 11-Sep-48; 11-Oct-48; Heinrich; Helpershain, Grunberg, Hessen; Reuwer, Catharine; Vorden, Melgarten, Hannover; Reuwer, Dorothea; —; —; —

Berchtold; Ferdinande Caroline; 13-Jul-49; 2-Oct-49; Christoph; Waldmilsbach, Musbach, Baden; Muller, Margaretha; Diepholz, Hannover; Schreiner, Ferdinande; Braun, Helene; —; —

Berg; Heinrich; 24-Jul-39; 13-Oct-39; Johann; —; Bornmann, Elisab.; —; —; —; —; —

Berg; Katharine; 30-Jun-41; 15-Jul-41; Johann; —; Bormann, Elisab.; —; —; —; —; —

Berg; Lorenz; 28-Jan-38; 4-Feb-38; Johann; —; Bornau, Elise; —; —; —; —; —

Bergen; Christiane Wilhelmine Karoline; 12-Mar-63; 29-Mar-63; Eberhard; Allendorf a. d. Lumda, Hessen; Fuchs, Marie; —; Leutner, Anna Katharine; Fuchs, Christiane; Reinhard, Wilhelmine; —

Bergen; Emil Christoph Melchior; 16-Mar-69; 27-Mar-59; Eberhard; Allendorf a.d.L., Hessen; Kuhl, Maria; —; Schlerf, Melchior; Leutner, Christoph; Schlerf, Emilia; —

Bergen; Heinrich Christian; 22-Apr-61; 28-Apr-61; Eberhard; Allensdorf a.d. Lumda, Hessen; Fuchs, Marie; —; Fuchs, Heinrich; Fuchs, Eleonore; Reinhard, Christoph; —

Berlau; Elisabeth; 10-Apr-54; 10-Apr-54; Johannes; Rheinroth, Hessen; Flauaus, Anna Catharina; —; Flauaus, Elisabeth; —; —; twin

Berlau; infant daughter; 10-Apr-54; —; Johannes; Rheinroth, Hessen; Flauaus, Anna Catharina; —; —; —; —; twin stillborn

Bernhard; Elisabeth; 26-May-47; 17-Jun-47; Andreas; —; Fath, Elisabeth; —; —; —; —; child died

Surname Father; Child's Given Name; Birth Date; Baptismal Date; Father's Given Name; Father's Place of Birth; Mother's Surname and Given Name; Mother's Place of Birth; Witness 1 Surname and Given Name; Witness 2 Surname and Given Name; Witness 3 Surname and Given Name; Comments

Bernhard; Magdalena Elisabeth; 19-Nov-45; 1-Feb-46; Andreas; Unnterlautern, Sachsen Coburg; Fath, Elisabeth; Klein Umstadt, Hessen; Oster, Magdalena; —; —; —

Bernhard; Maria Elisabeth; 29-Aug-48; 24-Sep-48; Andreas; Coburg; Fath, Elisabeth; Kleinumstadt, Hessen; Schafer, Maria Elisabeth; —; —; —

Bernhard; Wihelm Heinrich; 16-Jan-42; 30-Jan-42; Andr.; —; Fath, Elisab.; —; —; —; —; —

Bertelkamp; Maria Magd. Karol.; 19-Feb-37; 5-Mar-37; Herm. Heinr.; —; Rietborck, Mariane; —; —; —; —; —

Bertram; Heinrich Johann Phillip; 6-Nov-59; 13-Nov-59; Wilhelm; Burren, Preussen; Hellwigs, Friederike Karoline; —; Habermehl, School teacher; Schlerf, Phillip; Bruns, Joh.; —

Bertram; Johann Adam; 19-Oct-65; 5-Nov-65; Wilhelm; Buren, Preussen; Sellwege, Friedrike Karoline; Lubbecke, Preussen; Ruppel, Johann; Hinkel, Adam; —; —

Bertram; Johann Heinrich; 28-Jul-58; 8-Aug-58; Wilhelm; Buren, Preussen; Helbig, Friedrike; —; Ruppel, Joh.; Thiemeyer, Joh.; Broning, Johann; —

Bertram; Karl Johann Paul; 19-Apr-63; 10-May-63; Karl; Buren, Preussen; Balz, Elisabeth; —; Balz, Elisabeth; Schorrer, Paul; Schimpf, Johann Gottfried; —

Bertram; Karl Wilhelm; 30-Jan-53; 6-Feb-53; Wilhelm; Buren, Paderborn, Preussen; Gollmann, Anna Margaretha; —; Bertram, Karl; —; —; —

Bertram; Maria Agens; 4-May-55; 13-May-55; Wilhelm; Buren, Preussen; Helbig, Friedericka; —; Salzner, Agnes; Kaufmann, Maria; —; —

Bertram; Sophie Auguste Elisabeth; 30-Dec-63; 17-Jan-64; Wilhelm; Buren, Preussen; Fellwig, Friedrike Karoline; Lubecke, Preussen; Schimpf, Auguste; Ruppel, Elisabeth; —; —

Bertram; Therese Henrietta Maria; 13-May-57; 24-May-57; Wilhelm; Buren, Preussen; Hellwig, Friedericka Karolina; —; Bertram, Therese; Habermehl, Heinr.; Spielmann, Maria; —

Surname Father; Child's Given Name; Birth Date; Baptismal Date; Father's Given Name; Father's Place of Birth; Mother's Surname and Given Name; Mother's Place of Birth; Witness 1 Surname and Given Name; Witness 2 Surname and Given Name; Witness 3 Surname and Given Name; Comments

Bertram; Wilhelm Karl Gottfried; 13-Nov-61; 24-Nov-61; Wilhelm; Buren, Preussen; Fellwig, Friederike; —; Schorrer, Paul; Bertram, Karl; Schimpf, Gottried; —

Bertsch; Georg Jakob; 16-Apr-51; 1-Jun-51; Jakob; Grona, Wurttemberg; Weber, Dorothea; —; Bruning, Heinr.; Bruning, Mrs.; —; —

Betz; Johann Ludwig; 6-Feb-40; 1-Mar-40; Johann; —; Fritz, Maria; —; —; —; —; —

Betz; Maria Dorothea; 31-Oct-38; 18-Nov-38; Johann; —; Fritz, Anna M.; —; —; —; —; twin

Betz; Sabine Kathr.; 31-Oct-38; 18-Nov-38; Johann; —; Fritz, Anna M.; —; —; —; —; twin

Bick [?]; Johann Georg; 21-Sep-41; 31-Oct-41; Georg; —; Ritz, Elisab.; —; —; —; —; —

Biehler; Gerog Ernst; 1-Mar-52; 12-Apr-52; Granz; Klosten Maulbron, Wurttemberg; Bauer, Charlotte; Harrisburg, PA.; Willner, Georg; Willner, Margaretha; —; witness from Washington

Bier; Johann; 25-Feb-37; 26-Mar-37; Kaspar; —; Buckardt, Maria; —; —; —; —; —

Biewend; Charles Friedrich James; 29-Jun-47; 5-Aug-47; Rev. Adolph Friedrich Theodor; Rothehutbe bei Elbingerode, Hannover; Martin, Sophie; Colombier, Neufchatel, Schweiz; Estcourt, James; Werlisch, Friedrich; Marsch, Caroline; born in Georgtown, DC

Biewend; Sophia Albertine Mathilde; 23-Jul-49; 30-Aug-49; Adolph Friedrich Theodor; Rothehutte bei Elbingerode, Hannover; Martin, Sophia; Colombier, Canton Neufchatel, Schweiz; Koch, Hermann; Koch, Mathilde Biewend; Martin, Albertine; —

Billmann; Barbara; 23-Dec-47; 25-Dec-47; Johann Mathias; Egersdorf, Mark Gelbbach, Baiern; Streger, Margarethe; Biegarten, Herzogaurach, Baiern; Zehn, Barbara; —; —; —

Billmann; Elisabeth Katharine; 9-Feb-56; 24-Feb-56; Johann; Elgersdorf, Baiern; Zeh, Margarethe; —; Schmidt, Georg; Schmidt, Katharine; —; —

Surname Father; Child's Given Name; Birth Date; Baptismal Date; Father's Given Name; Father's Place of Birth; Mother's Surname and Given Name; Mother's Place of Birth; Witness 1 Surname and Given Name; Witness 2 Surname and Given Name; Witness 3 Surname and Given Name; Comments

Billmann; Georg; 26-Nov-46; 2-Dec-46; Johann; Egersdorf, Neustadt a.d. Reuss, Baiern; Riegler, Marg.; Bingarten, Herzogaurach, Baiern; Beck, Johann; —; —; child died

Billmann; Georg Heinrich Johann; 19-Sep-66; 7-Oct-66; Georg; Bingarten, Baiern; Demme, Emilie; —; Billmann, Johann; Billmann, Fr. Margaretha; —; —

Billmann; Johann; 13-Jul-51; 20-Jul-51; Joh.; Elgersdorf, Baiern; Picker, Margaretha; —; Beck, Joh.; Spielmann, Joh.; —; —

Billmann; Katharina; 13-Oct-53; 23-Oct-53; Johann; Elgersdorf, Baiern; Beikardt, Margaretha; —; Schmidt, Georg; —; —; —

Billmann; Margaretha Sabina; 27-Jun-63; 9-Jul-63; Georg; Bingarten, Baiern; Damm, Emilie; Grendelsburg, Hessen Kassel; Billmann, Margarethe; Horr, Maria; —; —

Binder; Johann Heinr.; 29-Mar-44; 28-Apr-44; Johann Chr.; —; Hecker, Maria; —; —; —; —; —

Binder; Luise; 28-Mar-47; 25-Jul-47; Johann Christian; Marbach, Wurttemberg; Hecker, Maria; Gemund bei Marburg, Kurhessen; Hecker Catharine, ; —; —; wit is aunt

Bindermann; Adam; 30-Apr-40; 3-May-40; Johann M.; —; Vogel, Elisab.; —; —; —; —; —

Binting; Wilhelm; 4-Apr-46; 3-May-46; Georg; Nieder Gemunde, Alsfeld, Hessen; Steinhard, Elisabeth; Nieder Gemunde, Alsfeld, Hessen; Pfeifer, Wilhelm; —; —; —

Binzer; Heinrich; 20-Jan-40; 16-Feb-40; Heinrich; —; Gunz, Helene; —; —; —; —; —

Birksler; Louise; 29-Oct-50; 10-Nov-50; Andreas; Ruppertsweiler, Baiern; Busch, Eva; —; Stephan, Heinrich; —; —; 2 child, 2 dau

Bisser; Elisabeth; 5-Jan-43; 29-Jan-43; Jacob; —; Heldmann, Christine; —; —; —; —; —

Blaich; Karl Robert Andreas; 15-Mar-61; 24-Mar-61; Johann Friedrich; Stammheim, Wurttemberg; Wagner, Margarethe; —; Lange, Robert; Bach, Katharine; Winter, Andreas; school teacher

Blase; Luise Wilhelmine; 9-Jan-40; 24-May-40; Heinrich; —; Jahrmann, Christine Wilh.; —; —; —; —; —

Surname Father; Child's Given Name; Birth Date; Baptismal Date; Father's Given Name; Father's Place of Birth; Mother's Surname and Given Name; Mother's Place of Birth; Witness 1 Surname and Given Name; Witness 2 Surname and Given Name; Witness 3 Surname and Given Name; Comments

Blatter; Jacob; 28-Dec-36; 17-Aug-37; Georg; —; Hedderich, Maria; —; —; —; —; —

Blei; Henriette Auguste; 28-Aug-38; 15-Sep-39; Friedrich; —; Oberlien, Auguste; —; —; —; —; —

Bleihschmidt; Anna Maria; 25-Feb-46; 17-Mar-46; Johann Peter; Vorschenkreud, Somenberg, Sachsen Meiningen; Ruppert, Johanne Marg.; Neubrunn, Sachsen Meiningen; [--?--], Anna Maria; —; —; —

Blessing; Marie Emnilie; 8-Feb-52; 31-May-52; Daniel; Hesselvort, Wurttemberg; Egelston, Marie; —; Bauer, Geoerg; Bauer, Margaretha Blessing; —; —

Blocher; Anna Eva; 2-May-41; 16-May-41; Johann; —; Gross, Kathr.; —; —; —; —; —

Blöcher; Franz; 5-Aug-42; 18-Aug-42; Johann; —; Gross, Kathr.; —; —; —; —; —

Blohs; Catharine; 22-Aug-45; 19-Oct-45; Lorenz; Farbau, Rehau, Baiern; Kiesel, Elisabeth; Munchberg, Baiern; Becher, Catharine; —; —; —

Blons; Anna Katharine Wilhelmine; 10-Feb-63; 22-Feb-63; Johann Friedrich; —; Werner, Anna Margaretha; Bobenhausen, Hessen; Bach, Katharine; Feiertag, Benjamin; Winter, Wilhelmine; school teacher

Blum; Johann Georg; 2-Nov-41; 21-Nov-41; Valent; —; Schmidt, Kathr.; —; —; —; —; —

Blum; Johann Herrmann; 8-Jun-39; 16-Jun-39; Valentin; —; Schmidt, Katharine; —; —; —; —; —

Blum; Katharine; 10-Dec-42; 23-Dec-42; Valentin; —; Schmidt, Kathr.; —; —; —; —; —

Blum; Luise; 16-Apr-41; 6-Oct-41; Friedrich; —; Schenk, Elisab.; —; —; —; —; —

Blum; Maria; 17-May-39; 6-Oct-41; Friedrich; —; Schenk, Elisab.; —; —; —; —; —

Blume; Johann; 3-Aug-47; 15-Dec-47; Johann; Tedinghausen, Braunschweig; Cordes, Sophie; Rethem, Hannover; Rudinger, Eduard; Homann, Johann; —; —

Surname Father; Child's Given Name; Birth Date; Baptismal Date; Father's Given Name; Father's Place of Birth; Mother's Surname and Given Name; Mother's Place of Birth; Witness 1 Surname and Given Name; Witness 2 Surname and Given Name; Witness 3 Surname and Given Name; Comments

Blumlein; Wilhelm; 15-Apr-51; 1-Jan-52; Andreas; Emskirchen, Baiern; Schudern, Catharine; —; Aichner, Jakob; Blumlein, Wilh.; —; —

Bockel; Heinrich Wilhelm; 2-Apr-64; 17-Apr-64; Johann Heinrich; Lisberg, Hessen; Karmroth, Martha; —; Spilmann, Karl; Schaumlussel, Wilh.; —; —

Bode; Anna Catharina; 19-Nov-47; 15-Dec-50; Adam; Schleddehausen, Osnabruck; Degler, Sophie; —; Bode, Catharina; Degler, Anna; —; 2 child, 2 dau

Bode; Anna Maria Friederike; 14-Mar-45; 27-Apr-45; Wilhelm; Schledehausen bei Kerlgock [?]; Meineke, Margaretha; Buckenbruck, Hannover; Buschmann, Friederich; Bode, Anna; —; —

Bode; Helene Elisab.; 5-Sep-42; 6-Oct-42; Wilhelm; —; Meineke, Marg.; —; —; —; —; —

Bode; Maria Elisabeth; 1-Dec-47; 15-Dec-50; Hermann Heinrich; Schleddehausen, Osnabruck; Honnicke, Catharina; —; Drewing, Maria; Drewing, Elisabeth; Bade, Adam; wit 3 father's brother

Bode; Maria Helene; 30-Nov-38; 6-Jan-39; Wilhelm; —; Meineke, Maria Marg.; —; —; —; —; —

Bode; Sophie Christine; 6-Sep-49; 26-Sep-49; Wilhelm; Schledehausen bei Osnabruck; Meineke, Margarethe; Quakenbruck, Hannover; Bode, Sophie; Eberle, Christian Daniel; —; —

Boesser; Johann; 3-May-47; 23-May-47; Jakob; Allendorf, Hessen; Heldmann, Christine; Marburg; Weye, Johann; —; —; —

Bohde; Sophia Maria; 15-Aug-48; 3-Sep-48; Adam; Sledehusen, Osnabruck, Hannover; Tegeler, Sophia Margaretha; Sudburg, Ehrenburg, Hannover; Bohde, Maria Margaretha; —; —; —

Bohde; Wilhelm Heinrich; 26-Jul-47; 29-Aug-47; Wilhelm; Schledehesen, Osnabruck; Meineke, Cath. Margarethe; Quakenbruck; Meineke, Joh. Heinrich; —; —; —

Bohme; Maria Catharine; 28-Oct-47; 13-Jan-48; Heinrich; Zeitz, Sachsen, Preussen; Petzold, Therese; Drösig, Sachsen, Preussen; Baur, Maria Cath.; —; —; —

Surname Father; Child's Given Name; Birth Date; Baptismal Date; Father's Given Name; Father's Place of Birth; Mother's Surname and Given Name; Mother's Place of Birth; Witness 1 Surname and Given Name; Witness 2 Surname and Given Name; Witness 3 Surname and Given Name; Comments

Bokelmann; Friedrich Wilhelm; 18-Apr-46; 14-Jun-46; Johann Heinrich; Assen, Diepholz, Hannover; Schröder, Sophie; Drebber, Diepholz, Hannover; Bokelmann, Conrad Heinr.; Hohnemann, Heinrich; Bunk, Margarethe Christine; —

Bokelmann; Hermann Heinrich; 28-Aug-48; 28-Aug-48; Johann Heinrich; Aschen, Diepholz, Hannover; Schroder, Sophie; Jakobi Drebber, Hannover; —; —; —; child died

Böker; Fritz Theodor; 9-Apr-42; 5-May-42; Karl H.; —; Harper, Sahra Anna; —; —; —; —; —

Böker; Johann Aug.; 10-Aug-39; 9-Sep-39; Kar V.; —; Harger, Sahra Anna; —; —; —; —; —

Bolde; Anna Maria; 19-Mar-53; 10-Apr-53; Kluas Heinrich; Ottersberg, Hannover; Threw, Anna; —; Warnecke, Anna; —; —; —

Bomhoff; Margarethe Magdalene; 9-Apr-48; 30-Apr-48; Heinrich Wilhelm; Barnstorf, Diepholz, Hannover; Muller, Maria Magdalena; Diepholz; Muller, Anna Margarethe; —; —; —

Boppler; Andreas; 28-Jul-50; 17-Aug-50; Heinrich; Helbischhain, Hessen; Reiber, Catharina; —; Papst, Andreas; —; —; 4 child, 3 son

Boppler; Anna Catharina; 23-Aug-54; 27-Aug-54; Heinr.; Helpersheim, Hessen; Reiber, Catharina; —; Leutner, Anna Catharina; —; —; —

Boppler; Anna Susanna Barbara; 15-Mar-57; 22-Mar-57; Heinr.; Holbershain, Hessen; Reuwer, Katharina; —; Einwachter, Anna Elisabeth; Habermehl, Susanna; —; —

Boppler; Elisabeth; 4-Jul-52; 8-Jul-52; Heinrich; Helbershain, Hessen; Reuber, Catharine; —; Reuber, Elisabeth; —; —; —

Boppler; Georg Wilhelm; 14-Jan-61; 27-Jan-61; Heinrich; Heigershain, Hessen; Reuber, Engel Katharine; —; Lammer, Wilhelm; Schwarz, Elisabeth; —; —

Boppler; Henriette Karoline Louise; 1-Mar-63; 15-Mar-63; Heinrich; Helgershain, Hessen; Reuber, Katharine; —; Lettmade, Henriette Louise Wilhelmine; Einwachter, Alexander; Thiemeyer, Linna Maria; —

Surname Father; Child's Given Name; Birth Date; Baptismal Date; Father's Given Name; Father's Place of Birth; Mother's Surname and Given Name; Mother's Place of Birth; Witness 1 Surname and Given Name; Witness 2 Surname and Given Name; Witness 3 Surname and Given Name; Comments

Boppler; Magdalena Maria Elisabeth; 20-Oct-58; 31-Oct-58; Heinrich; Gelpershausen, Hessen; Reuwer, Katharina; —; Schwarz, Daniel; Papst, Maria; Will, Elisabeth; —

Bormer; Agathe; 18-Nov-50; 28-Nov-50; Andreas; Preussen; Werder, Catharina; —; Bader, Agatha Werder; —; —; 3 child, 2 dau

Bornmann; Christine; 17-Feb-40; 9-Feb-40; Heinrich; —; Schwelm, Magdalene; —; —; —; —; —

Boss; Luise; 16-Jun-45; 10-Aug-45; Ludwig; —; Habicht, Margaretha; Lauterbach, Hessen; —; —; —; —

Bothe; Heinrich Julius; 9-Mar-66; 18-Mar-66; Gerhard Friedrich Julius; Engter, Hannover; Muhly, Louise; Baltimore; Muhly, Eberhard; Bothe, Ludwig; Labahn, Heinr.; —

Bothe; Katharine Karoline Louise; 15-May-64; 5-Jun-64; Gerhard Friedrich Julius; Engter, Hannover; Muhly, Louise; Baltimore; Labahn, Karoline; Bender, Katharine; Lange, Karl; School teacher

Bothe; Lous Julius; 9-Jan-63; 15-Feb-63; Hermann Heinrich; Engter, Hannover; Beranberg, Louise; Allendorf a.d. Werra, Kurhessen; Bothe, Julius; Thiemeyer, Louis; Labahn, Elise Karoline; —

Bothmann; George Washington; 22-Jun-46; 29-Aug-46; [--?--]; —; Buts, Maria; Schledehausen, Osnabruck, Hannover; —; —; —; illegitimate

Bötjer; Anna Kathr. Gesina; 19-Apr-42; 29-May-42; Heinrich; —; Brügel, Luise Dor.; —; —; —; —; —

Bötjer; Johann Georg; 8-Dec-43; 31-Mar-44; Heinrich; —; Brügel, Luise; —; —; —; —; —

Botsch; Anna Margaretha; 20-Nov-44; 25-Nov-44; Johann Adam; —; Geschwind, Anna B.; —; —; —; —; —

Botsch; Joh. Michael Ludwig; 10-Oct-50; 10-Mar-51; Joh. Adam; Schwartzberg, Wurttemberg; [--?--], ; —; Horn, Marie Catharine; —; —; child died

Botsch; Johann; 27-Sep-46; 25-Oct-46; Johann Adam; Schrotsberg, Gerbronn, Wurttemberg; Geschwind, Anna Barbara;

Schrotsberg, Gebronn, Wurttemberg; Suttelmeyer, Johann; —; —; child died

Boxtorfer; Heinrich; 3-Feb-47; 7-Feb-47; Gottlieb; Weidnitz, Obernfranken, Baiern; Munch, Barbara; Atzendorf, Obernfranken, Baiern; Dietrich, Heinrich; Ehefrau; —; —

Boys; Georgine Anna; 3-Nov-47; 13-Jan-48; George; —; Vogelmann, Friederike; Bredsfeld, Wurttemberg; Frank, Catharine Vogelmann; —; —; illegitimate

Braasch; Johann Karl; 23-May-43; 4-Jun-43; Johann; —; Bencken, Wilhlmine; —; —; —; —; —

Brackmann; Katharine Karoline Louise; 1-Nov-66; 2-Dec-66; Albert Friedrich; Besgerode, Braunschweig; Kramer, Friedricke Wilhelmine Emilie; Gottingen; Briel, Fr. Kaspar; Lettmade, Louise; Weckesser, Karoline; —

Bracks; Julius Niklaus; 11-Sep-64; 14-Oct-64; Gottlieb; Meiningen; Reinhard, Katharine; Herrnbreitungen, Kurhessen; During, Julius; Ruppel, Jr., Niklaus; —; —

Brandau; Maria; 4-Jul-40; 9-Jul-40; [--?--]; —; [--?--], Marg.; —; —; —; —; —

Brauer; Anna Karoline Elise; 20-Mar-58; 28-Mar-58; Johann Konrad; Lisberg, Hessen; Schnabel, Maria; —; Schaumloffel, Karoline; Ecksturm, Elise; —; —

Brauer; Eleonore Lisette Wilhelmine; 21-Mar-65; 2-Apr-65; Johann Konrad; Lisberg, Hessen; Schnabel, Marie; Allendorf a. d. L., Hessen; Herrlich, Lisette; Reinhard, Wilhelmine; —; —

Brauer; Karl Heinrich; 17-Dec-66; 30-Jan-66; Heinrich Karl Joh. August Christoph; Lisberg, Hessen; Hederich, Elise; Raustadt, Hessen; Spilmann, Karl; Schaumlusel, Karoline; Hederich, Heinrich; —

Brauer; Karoline; 11-Jan-61; 20-Jan-61; Konrad; Lisberg, Hessen; Schnabel, Maria; —; Brauer, Eleonora; Brauning, Katharine; —; —

Brauer; Konrad; 9-Sep-53; 14-Sep-53; Johannes; Armsfeld, Waldeck; Schmidt, Marie; —; Brauer, Konrad; —; —; —

Surname Father; Child's Given Name; Birth Date; Baptismal Date; Father's Given Name; Father's Place of Birth; Mother's Surname and Given Name; Mother's Place of Birth; Witness 1 Surname and Given Name; Witness 2 Surname and Given Name; Witness 3 Surname and Given Name; Comments

Brauer; Sophie Karoline Marie; 20-Dec-64; 1-Jan-65; Heinrich Karl August; Lisberg, Hessen; Hederich, Elise; Raustadt, Sachsen; Klenke, Sophia; Spilmann, Joh.; Karl, Karoline; —

Braun; August Johann Georg; 22-Feb-57; 7-Feb-57; Wilhelm; Frankfurt a. M.; Brauerlein, Louise Julia; Forchtenberg, Wurttemberg; Billmann, Joh.; Schmidt, Georg; —; probably illegitimate

Braut; Katharine Christine Philipine; 27-Mar-39; 7-Jun-39; Heinrich; —; Matterer, Maria; —; —; —; —; —

Breil; Johann Wilhelm; 15-Feb-47; 1-Mar-47; Jakob; Statten, Hohenzolern, Hechingen; Brandt, Maria Cath.; Badbergen, Bersenbruck, Hannover; Brandt, Johannes; Lassig, Joh. Christoph; —; wit #1 is grandfather

Bremer; Johann Ludwig; 7-Dec-57; 13-Dec-57; Andreas; Waldgermer, Hessen; Worter, Katharine; —; Waldschmidt, Ludwig; Konig, Christine; Bader, Joh.; —

Brendel; Johann Heinrich; 16-Dec-47; 30-Jan-48; Johann Georg; Untereichenbach, Herzogaurach, Baiern; Muller, Dorothea; Osterholz, Sieke, Hannover; Muller, Joh. Heinr.; —; —; wit is grandfather

Brendel; Johann Matthaeus; 31-Mar-1850; 21-Apr-50; Johann; Unterreichenbach, Bayern; Muller, Rebekka Dorothea; Hannover; Brendel, Matthaus; Muller, Johann Heinrich; —; —

Brendel; Katharine Margarethe; 8-Aug-51; 24-Aug-51; Johann Georg; Unterreiherbach, Baiern; Muller, Rebecca Dorothea; —; Strove, Katharina Marie; Hoffmann, Katharina; —; —

Brenner; Elisabeth; 4-Dec-45; 14-Feb-47; Johann Georg; Waldgermes, Giessen, Hessen; Arzt, Dorothea; Altkrug, Baiern; Waldschmidt, Ludwig; Brenner, Christine; —; wit #2 is grandmother

Briegel; Johann Georg; 21-Aug-48; 24-Sep-48; Johann Jakob; Feldbach, Canstadt, Wurttemberg; Burk, Margaretha; Schmieden, Canstadt, Wurttemberg; Horst, Johann Georg; —; —; —

Briegel; Philipine Karoline; 6-Jun-38; 1-Jul-38; Jacob; —; Birkle, Marg.; —; —; —; —; —

Surname Father; Child's Given Name; Birth Date; Baptismal Date; Father's Given Name; Father's Place of Birth; Mother's Surname and Given Name; Mother's Place of Birth; Witness 1 Surname and Given Name; Witness 2 Surname and Given Name; Witness 3 Surname and Given Name; Comments

Briegel; Samuel Andreas; 9-Dec-45; 15-Mar-46; Johann Jakob; Felbach, Canstadt, Wurttemberg; Burk, Margaretha; Shmieden; Horst, Georg; Horst, Mrs.; —; child died

Briehl; Johann Heinrich; 9-Aug-49; 9-Sep-49; Johann; Wolmer, Marburg; Urban, Catharine; Schlichten, Kurhessen; Weckesser, Johann; Weckesser, Anna Catharine; —; —

Briehl; Johannes; 29-Aug-48; 29-Aug-48; Johann; Wollmar, Wetter, Kurhessen; Urbach, Catharine; Schlichten, Kurhessen; —; —; —; child died

Briel; Amalie Christine Friedrike; 6-Sep-63; 20-Sep-63; Johann; Wollmer, Kurhessen; Urbach, Marie; —; Henkel, Christine; Kowalik, Friedrich; Henkel, Christine; twin

Briel; Ernst Wilhelm Heinrich; 6-Sep-63; 20-Sep-63; Johann; Wollmer, Kurhessen; Urbach, Marie; —; Rudolph, Ernst; Lettmade, Henriette Louise Wilhelmine; Briel, Heinr.; twin

Briel; Georg Martin; 20-Jan-47; 28-Feb-47; Johann; Wollmer bei Marburg, Kurhessen; Urbach, Cath.; Hannaus, Schlichter; Brabandt, Georg; —; —; —

Briel; Maria Christine; 12-Aug-58; 12-Aug-58; Johann; Wollmer, Kurhessen; Urbach, Katharine; —; Spielmann, Maria; —; —; emergency baptism

Briel; Regine Lisette Karoline; 6-Mar-61; 17-Mar-61; Johann; Wollmer, Kurhessen; Urbach, Katharine; —; Aichele, Regine; Happel, Heinrich; Frank, Lisette; —

Briel; Wilhelm; 16-Oct-65; 23-Oct-65; Johann; Wollmar, Kurhessen; Urbach, Anna Katharine; Schlichten, Kurhessen; —; —; —; emergency baptism

Briel; Wilhelm Emil Gerhard; 1-Oct-67; 13-Oct-67; Johann; Wollmar, Kurhessen; Oppachaus, Katharine; Schlichte, Kurhessen; Sommer, Rev. Michael Wilhelm; Brinckmann, Emilia; Schaumlustel, Wilhelm; —

Brocks [Brooks]; Maria Katharine; 26-May-55; 1-Sep-64; Gottlieb; Meiningen; Reinhard, Katharine; Herrnbreitungen, Kurhessen; Winter, Wilhelmine; Bach, Katharine; —; —

Surname Father; Child's Given Name; Birth Date; Baptismal Date; Father's Given Name; Father's Place of Birth; Mother's Surname and Given Name; Mother's Place of Birth; Witness 1 Surname and Given Name; Witness 2 Surname and Given Name; Witness 3 Surname and Given Name; Comments

Brocks [Brooks]; Moritz Ludwig; 05-Oct-1850; 1-Sep-64; Gottlieb; Meiningen; Reinhard, Katharine; Herrnbreitungen, Kurhessen; Diering, Heinr. Ludiwg; Winter, Johann; —; —

Brodt; Christine; 6-Oct-43; 4-Nov-43; Johann; —; Frank, Susanne; —; —; —; —; —

Bronhard; Johann Ludwig; 23-Feb-43; 12-Mar-43; Andr.; —; Fath, Elisab.; —; —; —; —; —

Broning; Friederika Maria; 25-May-59; 5-Jun-59; Heinrich; Langenbergheim, Hessen; Brust, Katharina; —; Spielmann, Maria; Bertram, Friederika; —; —

Broning; Karolina; 26-Dec-56; 11-Jan-57; Heinr.; Langenberg, Hessen; Brust, Katharina; —; Schaumloffel, Karolina; Brauer, Karolina; —; —

Brosenne; Margarethe Frances; 5-Oct-39; 18-Nov-39; Friedrich; —; Fuchs, Luise; —; —; —; —; —

Brosius; Jacob Friedrich; 23-Jan-43; 5-Feb-43; Jacob; —; Schmidt, Luise; —; —; —; —; —

Brosius; Johanne; 17-Apr-40; 20-Apr-40; Jacob; —; Schmidt, Luise; —; —; —; —; —

Brosius; Katharine; 13-Mar-41; 21-Mar-41; Jacob; —; Schmidt, Luise; —; —; —; —; —

Brucks; Georg; 16-Jan-1853; 03-Dec-1866; Gottlieb; Meiningen; Reinhard, Katharine; Herrenbreitungen, Kurhessen; Garbadi, Heinr. Wilhelm; Bartram, Elisabeth; —; —

Brucks; Katharine Wilhelmine Karoline; 31-Jul-62; 3-Mar-63; Gottlieb; Meiningen, Sachsen; Reinhard, Katharine Karoline; Herrenbreitinger, Hessen; Winter, Wilhelmine; Bach, Katharine; —; —

Brugel; Wilhelm Jakob; 1-Feb-50; 17-Mar-50; Joseph Friedrich; Wurttemberg; Fross, Caroline; —; Brugel, Johann Jakob; Christ, Wilhelmine; —; —

Brügel; Anna Elisab.; 13-Sep-39; 20-Oct-39; Jacob; —; Burkler, Marg.; —; —; —; —; —

Brügel; Maria Rebecca; 18-Sep-45; 22-Oct-43; Joh. Jac.; —; Beiklin, Anna M.; —; —; —; —; —

Surname Father; Child's Given Name; Birth Date; Baptismal Date; Father's Given Name; Father's Place of Birth; Mother's Surname and Given Name; Mother's Place of Birth; Witness 1 Surname and Given Name; Witness 2 Surname and Given Name; Witness 3 Surname and Given Name; Comments

Bruggemann; Gerhard Eduard; 12-Jan-47; 31-Jan-47; Friedrich; Dassel, Hannover; Bischoff, Charlotte; Lubbeke, Preussen; Edeler, Gerhard; —; —; —

Bruggemann; Ludwig Theodor; 27-Jul-52; 15-Aug-52; Friedrich; Dossel, Hannover; Buscher, Charlotte; —; Bruggemann, Friedrich; —; —; father is witness

Brüggemann; Karl Aug.; 16-Sep-42; 2-Oct-42; Friedrich; —; Buscher, Charlotte; —; —; —; —; —

Bruhl; Anna Katharine Auguste; 29-Aug-56; 7-Sep-56; Johann; Wollmar, Kurhessen; Urbach, Katharine; —; Riedel, Anna; Kaltenkamp, Dietr.; Weddigen, Auguste; —

Bruhl; Elisabeth; 29-Feb-52; 14-Mar-52; Joh.; Wollmar, Kurhessen; Urbach, Catharine; —; Bruhl, Elisabeth; Bruhl, Wilhelm; —; —

Bruhl; Friedrich Immanuel Conrad; 7-Jul-54; 23-Jul-54; Johann; Wollmar, Kurhessen; Urbach, Catharina; —; Flemming, Immanuel; Waltjen, Catharina; Schultz, Conrad; —

Bruning; Heinrich Wilhelm; 6-Dec-47; 13-Dec-47; Heinrich Hermann; Dickel; Dannettel, Maretha Sophia; Deka, Diepholz, Hannover; Dannettel, Karl Heinr.; Timmermann, Heinr. Ludw.; —; —

Bruning; Ludwig Wilhelm; 26-Aug-45; 5-Sep-45; Herrmann Heinrich; Jakobi Drebber; Dannettel, Maria Sophia; Maria Drebber, Hannover; —; —; —; —

Bruning; Margaretha Wilhelmine; 3-Jun-37; 23-Jul-37; Hermann; —; Dannettel, Marg.; —; —; —; —; —

Bruning; Maria Johanna; 5-Aug-50; 12-Aug-50; Hermann Heinrich; Amt Diepolts, Hannover; Danettel, Margaretha Sophie; —; Brockmeier, Maria Christine Friedricke; Meier, Heinrich Dietrich; —; 7 child, 4 dau

Brüning; Henriette Karoline; 30-Mar-43; 30-Jun-43; Herm. Heinr.; —; Dannettel, Maria S.; —; —; —; —; —

Brüning; Maria Wilhelmine; 3-Mar-40; 13-Apr-40; Hermann; —; Dannettel, Sophie; —; —; —; —; —

Brunner; Margaretha; 5-Jun-40; 16-Aug-40; Johann L.; —; Hewit, Mary; —; —; —; —; —

Surname Father; Child's Given Name; Birth Date; Baptismal Date; Father's Given Name; Father's Place of Birth; Mother's Surname and Given Name; Mother's Place of Birth; Witness 1 Surname and Given Name; Witness 2 Surname and Given Name; Witness 3 Surname and Given Name; Comments

Bruns; Anna Margaretha Katharine; 27-Jun-60; 1-Jul-60; Johann; Dellinghausen, Braunschweig; Radecke, Rebecca; —; Radecke, Sr., Hermann Heinrich; Louise, Margarethe; Radecke, Katharine; —

Bruns; Johann Dietrich; 8-Jul-52; 11-Jul-52; Johann; Thellinghausen, Branschweig; Bierfischer, Margaretha Dorothea; —; Radecke, Dietrich Eberhard; —; —; —

Bruns; Johann Friedrich Wilhelm; 29-Aug-57; 6-Sep-57; Joh.; Dechinghausen, Braunschweig; Radecke, Maria Rebecca; —; Radecke, Joh. Frdch.; Radecka, Wilhelmina Friedericka; Thiemeyer, Johann; —

Bruns; Karl Hermann Heinrich; 20-Jul-65; 30-Jul-65; Johannes; Dellinghausen, Brunschweig; Radecke, Rebekka Maria; Susstedt, Hannover; Louis, Karl Friedrich; Radecke, Hermann Friedrich; Osenderf, Georg Heinrich; —

Bruns; Margaretha Adelheid; 24-Jan-54; 29-Jan-54; Joh.; Dellinghausen, Braunschweig; Bierfischer, Dorothea Margaretha; —; Dunker, Adelheid; —; —; —

Bruns; Maria Anna; 25-May-55; 28-May-55; Johann; Dellinghausen, Braunschweig; Bierfischer, Maria Dorothea; —; Thiemeyer, Maria; Kunker, Maria Elisabeth; —; child died

Bruns; Rebecca Marie; 15-Dec-62; 25-Dec-62; Johann; Thetinghausen, Braunschweig; Radecke, Rebecca Marie; —; Radecke, Margarethe Rebecca; Heyse, Marie; —; —

Buchler; Katharine Elise; 1-Mar-37; 19-Mar-37; Nickolas; —; Horn, Regine; —; —; —; —; —

Bucking; daughter; 25-May-62; —; Franz; Marburg, Kurhessen; Damann, Elisabeth; —; —; —; —; stillborn

Buhler; Heinrich Wilhelm; 2-Apr-48; 25-May-48; Franz; Maulbronn, Wurttemberg; Bauer, Charlotte Maria; Harrisburg, PA; Morris, Dr. Johann; —; —; —

Bühler; Anna Margaretha; 8-Feb-50; 17-Feb-50; Franz; Maulbronn, Wurttemberg; Bauer, Charlotte Maria; Harrisburg, PA; Tschagkonz, Juliane; —; —; —

Bühler; Charlotte Maria; 24-Mar-39; 18-Jun-39; Franz; —; Bauer, Charlotte; —; —; —; —; —

Surname Father; Child's Given Name; Birth Date; Baptismal Date; Father's Given Name; Father's Place of Birth; Mother's Surname and Given Name; Mother's Place of Birth; Witness 1 Surname and Given Name; Witness 2 Surname and Given Name; Witness 3 Surname and Given Name; Comments

Bühler; Maria Elisabeth; 7-Nov-45; 7-Dec-45; Franz; Maulbronn, Wurttemberg; Bauer, Charlotte Maria; Harrisburg, PA; Conrad, G. J.; —; —; —

Bühler; Marianne; 27-Feb-41; 3-May-41; Franz; —; Bauer, Charlotte; —; —; —; —; —

Bunemann; Marianne Elisab.; 23-Apr-39; 4-Jul-39; Johann G.; —; Meibinger, Elisab.; —; —; —; —; —

Burgdorf; Minna Emilie; 4-Sep-53; 16-Oct-53; Karl; Pfortingsleben, Sachsen Gothe; Kaiser, Anna Martha; —; Burgdorf, Emilie; —; —; —

Burger; Anna Catharine; 21-Dec-46; 3-Jan-47; Johann; Lauffen, Bern; Schmidt, Catharine; Mariasreuth bei Feireuth, Baierh; Schmidt, Johann; —; —; —

Burger; Johann Heinrich; 27-Jun-49; 13-Jul-49; Christian; Oberstaben, Neila, Baiern; Rank, Caroline; Oberstaben, Neila, Baiern; Burger, Johann Heinrich; —; —; —

Burmann; Anna Katharine Wilhelmine; 31-Mar-60; 15-Apr-60; Heinrich Christoph Wilhelm; Potzwenden, Hannover; Lenz, Susanne Margaretha; —; Lenz, Katharine; Heyse, Wilhelm; Lenz, Anna Adelheid; —

Burmann; Anna Margarethe; 7-Apr-52; 18-Apr-52; Ernst Heinr.; Amt Grunenberg, Hannover; Schnitker, Elise; —; Thiemeyer, Margaretha Charlotte; Theimeyer, Frdch.; —; —

Burmann; Anna Maria Caroline; 30-May-54; 11-Jun-54; Ernst Heinr.; Bur, Hannover; Schnittker, Linna Maria Elise; —; Thiemeyer, Anna Maria; —; —; —

Burmann; Ernst Heinrich Wilhelm; 18-Jan-64; 31-Jan-64; Ernst Heinrich; Bur, Hannover; Schnitker, Elisabeth; —; Sieck, Heinr. Adolph Clomer; Schulz, Henriette; Schrader, Friedrich Wilhelm; —

Burmann; Friedrich Wilhelm; 8-Mar-51; 26-Mar-51; Joh. Frdch.; Bur, Hannover; Heidmann, Catharine Charlotte; —; Burmann, Ernst Heinrich; —; —; —

Burmann; Helena Charlotte; 28-Jul-50; 25-Aug-50; Ernst Heinrich; Gronberg, Hannover; Schnidtker, Elise; —; Schnidtke, Louise; —; —; 2 child, 2 dau

Surname Father; Child's Given Name; Birth Date; Baptismal Date; Father's Given Name; Father's Place of Birth; Mother's Surname and Given Name; Mother's Place of Birth; Witness 1 Surname and Given Name; Witness 2 Surname and Given Name; Witness 3 Surname and Given Name; Comments

Burmann; Henrietta Elise Amalie; 26-Jun-59; 3-Jul-59; Ernst Heinrich; Bur, Hannover; Schnitker, Elisabeth Maria; —; Lettmade, Henriette Louise Wilhelmine; Kattenkamp, Dietrich; Wiebking, Anna Maria Amalie; —

Burmann; Johann Friedrich Wilhelm; 1-Sep-61; 8-Sep-61; Ernst Heinrich; Puer, Hannover; Schnitker, Maria Elisabeth; —; Langschmidt, Wilhelm; Lettmade, Friedrich; —; —

Burmann; Johann Heinrich; 19-Dec-61; 29-Dec-61; Wilhelm; Potzwenden, Hannover; Lenz, Susanne; —; Lenz, Wittern; Lenz, Heinrich; —; —

Burmann; Johann Heinrich Wilhelm; 17-Sep-56; 28-Sep-56; Ernst Heinr.; Bompte, Hannover; Schnitker, Maria Elise; —; Schnitker, Joh. Frdch.; Lettemade, Wilhelm; —; —

Burmann; stillborn child; 16-Jun-67; —; Ernst Heinrich; Bur, Hannover; Schnittker, Maria Elisabetha; Bomste, Hannover; —; —; —; —

Burmann; Wilhelmine Luise; 4-Mar-49; 25-Mar-49; Ernst Heinrich; Bur, Gronenberg; Snitzer, Marie Elise; Bohmde, Witlage, Hannover; Snitzer, Wilhelmine Luise; —; —; —

Burus; Maria Elisabeth; 13-May-53; 29-May-53; Georg; —; Eitel, Elisabeth; —; Otto, Maria; —; —; —

Buscher; Charlotte Lisette; 14-Feb-49; 4-Mar-49; August; Lubbeke, Minden, Preussen; Hoffmann, Elisabeth; Dauernheim, Nidda, Hessen; Bruggemann, Charlotte; Schuldhaus, Lisette; —; —

Büscher; Georg; 19-Jun-43; 16-Aug-43; Friedr.; —; Lipp, Pauline; —; —; —; —; —

Busta [?]; Christine Wilhelmine; 5-Aug-37; 17-Sep-37; Johann; —; Schmidt, Regina; —; —; —; —; —

Butschke; Wilhelm; 7-Feb-41; 14-Feb-41; Johann; —; Raber, Marg.; —; —; —; —; —

Büttner; Friedrich Wilhelm; 22-Dec-44; 26-Dec-46; Rudolph; Ostheim, Sachsen, Weimar; Keller, Catharine; Ostheim, Sachsen Weimar; Gast, Leonhard; —; —; —

Butz; August; 11-Apr-51; 17-Jun-51; Andreas; Malmerz, Sachsen Meiningen; Metzler, Christiane; —; Waltjen, Aug.; —; —; —

Surname Father; Child's Given Name; Birth Date; Baptismal Date; Father's Given Name; Father's Place of Birth; Mother's Surname and Given Name; Mother's Place of Birth; Witness 1 Surname and Given Name; Witness 2 Surname and Given Name; Witness 3 Surname and Given Name; Comments

Butz; Catharine; 26-Feb-47; 18-Apr-47; Andreas; Maimertz, Sachsen Meiningen; Metzler, Christiane; Judenberg, Sachsen Meiningen; Metzler, Cath.; —; —; —

Capeller; Maria Luise Henr.; 21-Dec-42; 1-Jan-43; Georg Casp.; —; Diemann, Marg. E.; —; —; —; —; —

Carl; Johanna; 21-Jan-55; 4-Feb-55; Carl; Bellmuth, Hessen; Brauer, Maria; —; Schafer, Heinrich; Brauer, Heinr.; Mohring, Joh.; —

Carle; Anna Maria Catharine; 2-Apr-48; 16-Apr-48; Johann Christian; Jaxthausen, Wurttemberg; Heinzmann, Catharine; Jagsthausen, Wurttemberg; Wust, Johann; Hauer, Catharine; Carle, Barbara; —

Carle; Catharina Margaretha; 10-Mar-50; 15-Mar-50; Conrad; Gross Herzogth, Hessen; Pfeil, Catharina Margartha; —; Siegel, Cath. Margaretha Pfeil; —; —; —

Carle; Johann Heinrich; 27-Feb-46; 22-Mar-46; Christian Heinrich; Siedringen, Ehringen, Wurttemberg; Snukel, Eva; Obermoor, Baiern; [--?--], Georg; —; —; —

Casten; Maria Caroline; 30-Jan-48; 13-Feb-48; Carl; Eikhorst, Minden, Preussen; Rosener, Maria Luise; Eikhorst, Minden, Preussen; Wilson, Erline; —; —; —

Christ; Philip; 7-Dec-38; 16-Dec-38; Philip; —; Hummerich, Charlotte; —; —; —; —; —

Christ; Wilhelm; 23-May-37; 4-Jun-37; Philip; —; Hummerich, Charlotte; —; —; —; —; —

Colubus; Heinrich; 12-Oct-52; 13-Oct-52; Heinrich; Preussen; , ; —; Lentz, Widow; —; —; child died

Crome; Johann Friedr.; 20-Jan-38; 3-Jul-38; Johann; —; Muller, Karoline; —; —; —; —; —

Crumar; Karl Friedr.; 4-Apr-42; 15-Oct-42; Nathan; —; Meyer, Friedricke; —; —; —; —; —

Crumar; Nathan John; 14-Jul-1811; 15-Oct-42; John; —; [--?--], Margath.; —; —; —; —; —

Curd; Ernst Wilhelm; 19-Dec-49; 27-Jan-50; Heinrich; Hedemuhlen bei Münden, Hannover; Volmers, Maria Louise Charlotte;

Hedemuhlen bei Münden, Hannover; Schmidt, Georg Wilhelm; Wilhelm, Friedrich; —; —

Curt; Georg Friedrich; 24-Dec-52; 20-Feb-53; Georg Friedr. Heinr.; Hedminden, Hannover; Volmers, Maria Louise Charlotte; —; Treude, Joh. Heinr. Gottlieb; —; —; —

Curtain; Anna Emilie; 11-Jun-41; 7-Nov-41; Henry; —; Ebert, Sahra; —; —; —; —; —

Curtain; Emma Ebert; 19-Jun-49; 15-Aug-49; Henry; Baltimore Co., MD; Ebert, Salome; Brumath bei Strezsburg, Elsass; Ebert, Margareth; —; —; —

Curtain; Gottfried Heinrich; 2-Jan-40; 2-Mar-40; James; —; Ebert, Kathr.; —; —; —; —

Curtain; Maria Catharina; 6-Oct-46; 11-Dec-46; Henry; Baltimore Co.; Ebert, Salome; Brumath, Elsass bei Strassberg; —; —; —

Curtain; Sahra Elisab.; 6-Feb-43; 22-Mar-43; Henry; —; Ebert, Sahra; —; —; —; —

Curtan; Jakob Thomas; 3-Jan-45; 29-May-45; Henry; Baltimore; Ebberts, Salome; Brumath, Elsass; —; —; —

Danettel; Maria Margaretha; 9-Feb-52; 19-Mar-54; Joh. Heinr.; Deka, Hannover; Stoll, Elisabeth; —; Danettel, Kurt Heinr.; Waltjen, Friederike; —

Danettel; Wilhelm Heinrich; 16-Jan-52; 29-Feb-52; Heinr. Ludwig; Theka, Hannover; Brackerung, Friedericke; —; Bruning, Jr., Hermann Heinr.; Bruning, Sophie; —

Dankmeier; Heinrich Theodor; 10-Jun-62; 25-Jun-62; Johann Friedrich; Rabba, Hannover; Brockmeier, Wilhelmine; —; Karstens, Heinrich; Lenz, Heinrich; —

Dankmeier; Johann Friedrich; 16-Jun-60; 1-Jul-60; Johann Friedrich; Rabber, Hanner; Brockmeier, Wilhelmine; —; Bruns, Johann; Kunker, Johann Heinrich; —

Dankmeier; Marie Wilhelmine Katharine; 31-Jul-64; 21-Aug-64; Friedrich; Robber, Hannover; Brockmeier, Wilhelmine; Helle, Preussen; Bruns, Marie Rebecca; Karstens, Marie; Kunker, Katharine

Dankmeier; Sophia Karoline Wilhelmine; 29-Jan-67; 17-Feb-67; Johann Friedrich; Robber, Hannover; Brockmeier, Fredricke

Wilhelmine; Halle, Preussen; Sieck, Heinrich Adolph; Schultheiss, Sophia; Sieck, Karoline

Dannettel; Anna Elisabeth; 30-May-49; 24-Sep-49; Heinrich Ludwig; Deke, Diepholz, Hannover; Meinhardt, Isabelle; Baltimore; —; —; —

Dannettel; Baltimore; 20-Jun-46; 14-Jan-47; Heinrich Ludwig; Drebber, Diepholz, Hannover; Georg Friedrich, Reinhardt; Isabella; —; —; —

Dannettel; Johann Heinrich; 26-Mar-49; 14-May-49; Johann Heinrich; Dekau, Diepholz, Hannover; Stoll, Elisabeth; Lankaster, Penna.; Dannettel, Cord Heinrich; Dannettell, Maria Margarethe; —

Dannettel; Sophie Emilie; 2-Mar-47; 5-May-47; Heinrich; Drelber, Hannover; Stoll, Elisabeth; Lancaster, PA; Bruning, Sophie; —; —

Dantz; Maria; 9-Sep-64; 25-Sep-64; Heinrich; Wege, Waldeck; Minna, Dun; Dantzig b. Berlin; Boppler, Maria; Hampe, Wilh.; —

Däsch; Carl Wilhelm; 28-Dec-44; 16-Mar-45; Peter; Schaafheim, Hessen; Kull, Justine; Wurttemberg; Ruff, Samuel Fr.; —; —

Daub; Christine Susanne; 4-Mar-37; 15-Apr-37; Christoph; —; [--?--], Magdalene; —; —; —; —; —

David; Johann Heinrich; 22-Aug-42; 4-Sep-42; Georg; —; Damm, Philipine; —; —; —; —; —

Deckert; Johann Ernst; 18-Jan-66; 11-Feb-66; August; Winkel, Sachsen Weimar; Sieck, Eleonore Marie; Husede, Hannover; Sieck, Johann; Sieck, Heinr. Adolph; Ebeler, Ernst; —

Deckert; Karoline Louise; 3-Jun-67; 16-Jun-67; August; Winkel, Sachsen Weimar; Sieck, Maria Elenora; Ennsede; Mohring, Karoline; Sieck, Louise; Sieck, Heinrich; —

Dehsing; Maria Adelheid; 31-Jul-47; 15-Aug-47; Johann; Quackenbruck, Hannover; Imwolde, Catharine; Quackenbruck, Hannover; Imwolde, Catharine; —; —; —

Deichmann; Reinhard; 3-Jan-41; 23-Mar-41; Heinrich; —; Sippel, Sophie; —; —; —; —; —

Surname Father; Child's Given Name; Birth Date; Baptismal Date; Father's Given Name; Father's Place of Birth; Mother's Surname and Given Name; Mother's Place of Birth; Witness 1 Surname and Given Name; Witness 2 Surname and Given Name; Witness 3 Surname and Given Name; Comments

Dellbrügge; Katharine Maria; 11-Nov-37; 1-Dec-37; Jacob; —; Stille, Maria; —; —; —; —; —

Dengel; Jacob; 20-Sep-37; 21-Oct-37; Heinrich; —; Weller, Dorothea; —; —; —; —; —

Dengel; Sophie; 13-Feb-39; 22-Feb-39; Heinrich; —; Weller, Dorothea; —; —; —; —; —

Derflein; Christian; 2-May-45; 25-May-45; Jakob; Aufenau, Baiern; Steiernagel, Catharina; Zerbach, Hessen; Fischer, Caspar; Fischer, Christine; —; —

Desing; Johann Gerhard; 23-Apr-50; 19-May-50; Johann; Quackenswurt, Hannover; Beismanns, Helena Maria; Badburgen, Hannover; von der Heide, Johann Gerhard; —; —; wit from Badbergen

Dickel; Elisabeth; 23-Jun-58; 11-Jul-58; Konrad; Romeroth, Hessen; Karel, Maria Dorothea; —; Ruppel, Elisabeth; Wolf, Anna Elisabeth; —; —

Dickel; Karoline; 31-Mar-42; 7-Jan-44; Johann; —; Supfling, Kathr.; —; —; —; —; —

Dickel; Kaspar Ludwig; 12-Aug-44; 17-Nov-44; Johann; —; Zöpslin, Kathr.; —; —; —; —; —

Dickel; Valentin Friedrich Christian; 3-May-66; 13-May-66; Konrad; Rameroth, Hessen; Krotell, Maria Dorothea; Strebendorf, Hessen; Wolf, Valentin; Hollebein, Friedrich; Meier, Christian; —

Dickhauf; Maria; 2-Nov-37; 25-Dec-37; Adam; —; Ramp, Elisab.; —; —; —; —; —

Dickhaut; Georg; 15-Oct-39; 15-Dec-39; Adam; —; Ramze, Elisab.; —; —; —; —; —

Diering; Emma Louise Emilie; 11-Nov-64; 20-Nov-64; Heinrich Ludwig; Baltimore; Rauch, Christine; Kitzschebach, S. Koburg; Steger, Emilie; Langer, Louise; Ruppel, Johann; —

Diering; Marie Katharina; 14-Dec-62; 18-Jul-63; Heinrich Ludwig; Baltimore; Rausch, Christine; Kitschebach, Sachsen, Coburg; Diering, Marie Katharine; Harmes, Thomas; —; —

Dieter; Ferdinand Heinrich; 12-Jun-39; 8-Jul-39; Anastasius; —; Fetter, Ursula; —; —; —; —; —

Surname Father; Child's Given Name; Birth Date; Baptismal Date; Father's Given Name; Father's Place of Birth; Mother's Surname and Given Name; Mother's Place of Birth; Witness 1 Surname and Given Name; Witness 2 Surname and Given Name; Witness 3 Surname and Given Name; Comments

Dieterle; Caroline Elisabeth; 20-Mar-46; 7-Jun-46; Christoph; Ensing, Veisingen, Wurttemberg; Hildebrandt, Maria; Bleichenbach, Hessen; Josenhans, Carl Christoph; Josenhans, Mrs.; —; —

Dieterle; Christiane; —; 3-Mar-44; Christoph; —; Hildebrand, Maria; —; —; —; —; 30 Feb 44

Dieterle; Christoph Friedr.; 4-Sep-37; 1-Oct-37; Christoph; —; Hildebrand, Maria; —; —; —; —; —

Dieterle; Emma; 12-Sep-67; 29-Sep-67; Christoph Friedrich; Baltimore; Waltjen, Anna Maria; Baltimore; Stegner, Amalie; Waltjen, Friedrich; —; —

Dieterle; Georg Christoph; 17-Jun-60; 24-Jun-60; Christoph Friedrich; Baltimore; Waltjen, Anna Maria; —; Hecke, Gerog; Ober, Sophie; —; —

Dieterle; Georg Heinrich; 24-Nov-41; 12-Dec-41; Christopf; —; Hildebrand, Maria; —; —; —; —; —

Dieterle; Gustav; 7-Nov-65; 26-Nov-65; Christoph Friedrich; Baltimore; Waltgen, Anna Maria; Baltimore; Stegner, Gustav; Waltjen, Anna Marie; —; —

Dieterle; Karl Eduard; 22-Jun-62; 6-Jul-62; Christoph Frieddrich; Baltimore; Waltjen, Anna Marie; —; Spielmann, Karl; Spielmann, Marie; Lange, Auguste Wilhelmine; —

Dieterle; Maria Kathr.; 10-Aug-39; 22-Sep-39; Christoph; —; Hildebrand, Maria; —; —; —; —; —

Dieterle; Robert Friedrich; 9-Apr-64; 24-Apr-64; Christoph Friedrich; Baltimore; Waltjen, Anna Marie; Baltimore; Lange, Robert; Waltjen, Louise; —; —

Dieterle; Wilhelm Heinrich; 26-Jul-58; 1-Aug-58; Christoph Friedrich; Baltimore; Waltjen, Maria; —; Waltjen, Friedrich; Waltjen, Heinrich; —; —

Dietrich; Elisabeth; 2-Apr-44; 28-Apr-44; Bernhard; —; Schneider, Friedricke; —; —; —; —; —

Dietrich; Elisabeth; 14-Jun-49; 14-Jun-49; Leonhard; Marburg, Kurhessen; Schneider, Friedrike; Bermesins, Rheinbaiern; —; —; —; child died

Surname Father; Child's Given Name; Birth Date; Baptismal Date; Father's Given Name; Father's Place of Birth; Mother's Surname and Given Name; Mother's Place of Birth; Witness 1 Surname and Given Name; Witness 2 Surname and Given Name; Witness 3 Surname and Given Name; Comments

Dietrich; Elisabeth Friedericke; 10-Jun-55; 17-Jun-55; Leonhard; Marburg, Kurhessen; Schneider, Friederike; —; Frank, Elisabeth Friederike; —; —; —

Dietrich; Friederike Henriette; 7-Jan-47; 17-Jan-47; Leonhard; Marburg, Kurhessen; Schneider, Friederike; Bermesins, Rheinbaiern; Dietrich, Friederike; Dietrich, Henriette; —; wit #1 is grandmother

Dietrich; Gottlieb; 13-Mar-47; 21-Mar-47; Heinrich; Reuth, Turnau, Baiern; Schmidt, Eva; Neudorf, etc; Buxtorfer, Gottlieb; Buxtorfer, Mrs.; —; —

Dietrich; Heinrich Karl; 11-Aug-60; 26-Aug-60; Leonhard; Marburg, Kurhessen; Schneider, Friederike; —; Wortmann, Karl; Schneider, Heinr.; Frank, Lisette Friederike; —

Dietrich; Johann Georg; 5-Aug-52; 15-Aug-52; Leonhard; Marburg, Kurhessen; Schneider, Friederike; —; Frank, Georg; —; —; —

Dietrich; Julia; 12-Jul-50; 29-Jul-50; Leonhard; Marburg, Kurhessen; Schneider, Friederike; —; Maurer, Julia; —; —; 5 child, 4 dau

Dietrich; Karolina; 20-Oct-57; 1-Nov-57; Leonhardt; Marburg, Kurhessen; Schneider, Friedericka; —; Frank, Lisette Friedericka; —; —; —

Dietsch; Friederich Ferdinand; 4-Feb-45; 8-Jun-45; Friederich; Fistenbergsgreuth, Höchstadt, Baiern; D'Emerix, Philippine; Freuderichsthal, Baden; —; —; —; —

Dietz; Amalia Sophie; 27-Feb-54; 12-Mar-54; Heinr. Ludwig; Westerburg, Hessen Nassau; Waldschmidt, Catharina; —; Waldschmidt, Jakob; Hollebein, Sophie; —; —

Dietz; Anna Maria; 31-Oct-51; 16-Oct-51; Heinr. Ludwig; Westerberg, Hessen Nassau; Waldschmidt, Catharine; —; Waldschmidt, Maria; —; —; —

Dietz; Christian Karl; 7-Nov-58; 14-Nov-58; Georg Andreas; Jagsthausen, Wurttemberg; Gutmann, Barbara; —; Frank, Karoline Elislabeth; Ermold, Georg Michael; Dietz, Johanna; —

Surname Father; Child's Given Name; Birth Date; Baptismal Date; Father's Given Name; Father's Place of Birth; Mother's Surname and Given Name; Mother's Place of Birth; Witness 1 Surname and Given Name; Witness 2 Surname and Given Name; Witness 3 Surname and Given Name; Comments

Dietz; Georg Heinrich; 24-Aug-61; 6-Oct-61; Georg Tobias; Jacthausen, Wurttemberg; Lechner, Johanne; —; Dietz, Georg Andreas; Wiedemann, Joh.; —; —

Dietz; Georg Tobias; 15-Jan-57; 25-Jan-57; Georg Tobias; Jagsthausen, Wuerttemberg; Lechner, Johanna; —; Wiedemann, Joh.; Dietz, Barbara; —; —

Dietz; Johann Georg; 17-Feb-56; 24-Feb-56; Goerg Andreas; Jagsthausen, Wurttemberg; Gutmann, Barbara; —; Frank, Georg; Dietz, Johann; —; —

Dietz; Johann Gottfried; 13-Feb-59; 20-Mar-59; Georg Tobias; Jagthausen, Wurttemberg; Lehner, Johanna; —; Wiedemann, Joh.; Dietz, Andreas; —; —

Dietz; Johann Konrad; 14-Mar-51; 13-Jul-51; Joh.; Brun, Waldeck; Danz, Wilhelmine; —; Dietz, Joh.; —; —; —

Dietz; Johanna Barbara; 11-Jan-55; 25-Jan-55; Georg Tobias; Jagsthausen, Wurttemberg; Lehner, Johanna; —; Dietz, Maria Barbara; Dietz, Sophia; —; child died

Dietz; Johannes; 5-Aug-39; 1-Nov-40; Johannes; —; Horst, Kathr.; —; —; —; —; —

Dietz; Maria Catharine; 13-Jul-52; 25-Jul-52; Reinhard; Ermenrode, Hessen; Graf, Catharine; —; Ermold, Catharine; Grimm, Catharine; —; —

Dietz; Wilhelm Heinrich; 17-Sep-65; 8-Oct-65; Georg Andreas; Jagsthausen, Wurttemberg; Gutmann, Barbara; Jagsthausen, Wurttemberg; Dietz, Georg Tobias; Frank, Joh. Georg; —; —

Dietz; Wilhelm Ludwig; 5-Jan-57; 18-Jan-57; Heinr. Ludwig; Westerburg, Hessen Nassau; Waldschmidt, Katharina; —; Bach, Elisasbeth Katharina; Waldschmidt, Ludwig; —; —

Dihm; Elisabeth; 31-Jul-40; 7-Aug-40; Philip; —; Weigand, Anna M.; —; —; —; —; —

Dihm; Eva; 22-Oct-42; 4-Dec-42; Philip; —; Stauf, Eva; —; —; —; —; —

Dihm; Georg Ludwig; 7-Nov-37; 19-Nov-37; Philip; —; Weiand, Maria; —; —; —; —; —

Dihm; Luise; 20-Oct-37; 5-Nov-37; Christoph; —; Kares, Kathr.; —; —; —; —; —

Surname Father; Child's Given Name; Birth Date; Baptismal Date; Father's Given Name; Father's Place of Birth; Mother's Surname and Given Name; Mother's Place of Birth; Witness 1 Surname and Given Name; Witness 2 Surname and Given Name; Witness 3 Surname and Given Name; Comments

Dill; Johann Georg; 9-May-47; 12-Jul-47; Michael; Egersdorf bei Beireuth, Baiern; Haker, Eva; Obernsees bei Baiereuth; Obitz, Johann Georg; —; —; —

Dingfelder; Maria Magdalena; 12-Oct-49; 19-Dec-49; Andreas; Herhardshofen bei Neustadt a.d.A., Baiern; Gross, Barbara; Nürnberg; Sommers, Maria; —; —; —

Dirrenberger; Johann Georg; 6-Jun-40; 5-Aug-40; Georg; —; Grimm, Magdal.; —; —; —; —; —

Dirrenberger; Philip Georg; 13-Oct-41; 24-Aug-42; Christian; —; Rihm, Salome; —; —; —; —; —

Dirrnberger; Sophie Magd.; 15-Apr-43; 7-Jun-43; Georg; —; Grimm, Sophia M.; —; —; —; —; —

Dittus; Johann Friedr.; 5-Jan-43; 27-Jun-43; Johann Fr.; —; Gettier, Julianne; —; —; —; —; —

Dittus; Wilhelm Peter; 9-May-44; 14-Jun-44; Johann Fr.; —; Gettier, Juliane; —; —; —; —; —

Ditus; Elisabeth Kathr. Maria; 1-Jul-39; 4-Aug-39; Johann Friedr.; —; Gettier, Juliana; —; —; —; —; —

Doberer; Carl Heinrich; 20-Feb-46; 1-Jul-46; Johann; Lehrenberg, Waiblingen; Ackermann, Anna Maria; Lehrenberg,Waiblingen; —; —; —; —

Doberer; Johann Christian; 9-Mar-48; 12-Jun-48; Johann; Lehnenberg, Waiblingen, Wurttemberg; Ackermann, Maria; Lehnenberg, Waiblingen, Wurttemberg; Wildermuth, Adam; Wildermuth, Elisabeth; —; —

Doberer; Johann Christian; 1-Sep-41; 16-Dec-41; Johann; —; Ackermann, Anna M.; —; —; —; —; —

Doberer; Johann Georg; 8-Oct-43; 17-Jan-44; Johann; —; Ackermann, Anna M.; —; —; —; —; —

Doberer; Ludwig Friedrich; 8-Nov-51; 27-Jul-52; Johannes; Lehnenberg, Wurttemberg; Ackermann, Anna Maria; —; Wildemuth, Adam; Wildemuth, Elisabeth; —; —

Doberer; Luise Dorothea; 16-Sep-39; 16-Oct-39; Johann; —; Ackermann, Anna Maria; —; —; —; —; —

Doberer; Margaretha Kathr.; 11-Sep-37; 11-Oct-37; Johann; —; Ackermann, Maria; —; —; —; —; —

Surname Father; Child's Given Name; Birth Date; Baptismal Date; Father's Given Name; Father's Place of Birth; Mother's Surname and Given Name; Mother's Place of Birth; Witness 1 Surname and Given Name; Witness 2 Surname and Given Name; Witness 3 Surname and Given Name; Comments

Dolch; Margaretha; 9-Sep-47; 26-Sep-47; Conrad; Trefurth, Preussen; Freitag, Maria; Trefurth, Preussen; Kustner, Margarethe; —; —; child died

Dolch; Margarethe; 27-Oct-48; 5-Nov-48; Johann Conrad; Trefurth, Preussen; Freitag, Maria; Trefurth, Preussen; Kistner, Johann Conrad; —; —; emergency baptism

Doler; Johann Georg; 23-Nov-52; 2-Jan-53; Georg; Baireuth, Baiern; Kermann, Christine; —; Krauss, Joh. Georg; —; —; —

Dölfel; Alexander; 10-Oct-39; 8-Dec-39; Friedrich; —; Mathil, Elisab.; —; —; —; —; —

Dölfel; Carl; 14-Feb-46; 16-Feb-46; Friedrich; Disbeck bei Neustadt a.d. Reuss, Baiern; Mathail, Elisabeth; Thalsweiler, Bermesins, Baiern; Dollinger, Kunigunde; —; —; —

Dölfel; Karoline; 15-Jan-44; 3-Mar-44; Friedr.; —; Mathil, Elisab.; —; —; —; —; —

Dölfel; Maria; 21-Mar-38; 29-Apr-38; Johann; —; Mathil, Elisab.; —; —; —; —; —

Dölsel; Peter; 21-Nov-41; 6-Dec-41; Friedrich; —; Mathil, Elisab.; —; —; —; —; —

Donges; stillborn child; 4-Jun-67; —; Heinrich; Blauhenbach, Hessen; Dietrich, Henriette; Baltimore; —; —; —; —

Döring; Friedrich August; 16-Jan-48; 13-Feb-48; Valentin; Frischborn, Lauterbach, Hessen; Grevermann, Dorothea; Neundorf, Stolzenau, Hannover; Walding, Fried. Aug.; —; —; —

Dorsch; Anna Luise; 24-Jan-49; 25-Feb-49; Heinrich Friedrich; Mitterhude bei Bremen, Hannover; Scharlmann, Margarethe Luise; Rissen, Diepholz, Hannover; Lährs, Marianne; Wortmann, Anna Helene; —; —

Dorsch; Carl Herrmann; 12-Nov-46; 20-Dec-46; Heinrich Friedrich; Ritterhude bei Bremen, Hannover; Scharlmann, Marg. Luise; Russen, Diepholz, Hannover; Wortmann, Carl Fried.; Lohr, Claus; —; —

Draband; Georg Wilhelm; 2-Dec-44; 19-Jan-45; Georg; —; [--?--], Elisabetha; —; Urbach, Fr. Wm.; Urbach, Erolina Johanna; —; —

Surname Father; Child's Given Name; Birth Date; Baptismal Date; Father's Given Name; Father's Place of Birth; Mother's Surname and Given Name; Mother's Place of Birth; Witness 1 Surname and Given Name; Witness 2 Surname and Given Name; Witness 3 Surname and Given Name; Comments

Drechsel; Carl Heinrich; 12-May-46; 5-Jul-46; Johann; Creussen, Pegnitz, Baiern; Leutner, Kunigunde; Creussen, Pegnitz, Baiern; Dreschel, Carl Heinrich; —; —; wit is uncle

Drechsel; Georg Friedr.; 22-Jan-41; 21-Feb-41; Johann; —; Lautner, Kunigunde; —; —; —; —; —

Dunker; Hermann Heinrich Andreas; 7-Jun-55; 10-Jun-55; Joh. Kasten Heinr.; Mattfeld, Hannover; Meier, Caroline; —; Waltjen, Heinr.; Dunker, Adelheid; Purner, Joh. Andreas; —

Dunker; Johann Heinrich Christian; 17-Jun-57; 21-Jun-57; Kasten Heinr.; Mattfelde, Hannover; Meier, Karolina; —; Meier, Christian; Vordewosten, Joh.; Vordewosten, Mrs.; —

Dunker; Johann Karl Wilhelm; 20-Jun-66; 1-Jul-66; Joh. Kasten Heinr.; Martfeld, Hannover; Meier, Karoline; Liebenau, Hannover; Meier, Johann Christian; Prufer, Louise; Siemers, Wilhelm; —

Dunker; Kasten Friedrich Gottfried; 26-May-59; 29-May-59; Johann Kasten Heinr.; Mattfelde, Hannover; Meier, Karolina; —; Schimpf, Gottfried; Kowalik, Friedrich; Meier, Minna; —

Dunker; Maria Margareth Elisabeth; 24-May-63; 31-May-63; Kasten; Mattfeld, Hannover; Meier, Karoline; Liebenau, Hannover; Vorderwesten, Margarethe; Vornhofe, Frdch. Theodor; Mess, Elisabeth; —

Ebeling; Sophi Elise; 23-Oct-46; 27-Dec-46; Wilhelm; Obernkirchen, Kurhessen; Zetzenert, Dorothea; Minden, Preussen; Ebeling, Sophie; —; —; wit is grandmother

Eberhard; Sophie Karl.; 29-Oct-39; 4-Nov-39; Friedrich; —; Reiz, Sophia; —; —; —; —; —

Eberle; Caroline Wilhelmine; 11-Dec-46; 10-Jan-47; Friedrich; Kohlenberg, Niddinger, Wurttemberg; Imhardt, Wilhelmine; Mohringen bei Stuttgart, Wurttemberg; Fehler, Joseph; S..euth [?]; —; —

Eberle; Conrad; 28-Sep-39; 27-Oct-39; Friedrich; —; Einhard, Wilhelmine; —; —; —; —

Eberle; Friedrich; 15-Aug-44; 22-Sep-44; Friedrich; —; Emhart, Wilhelmine; —; —; —; —

Surname Father; Child's Given Name; Birth Date; Baptismal Date; Father's Given Name; Father's Place of Birth; Mother's Surname and Given Name; Mother's Place of Birth; Witness 1 Surname and Given Name; Witness 2 Surname and Given Name; Witness 3 Surname and Given Name; Comments

Eberle; Johann Jac. Friedr.; 20-Oct-41; 21-Nov-41; Friedr.; —; Emhard, Wilhelmine; —; —; —; —

Eberle; Wilhelm; 17-Dec-48; 28-Jan-49; Friederich; Kohlberg, Niddingen, Wurttemberg; Imhard, Wilhelmine; Mehringen, Stuttgart, Wurttemberg; Reith, Catharine; —; —

Eberleh; Louis Wilhelm Friedrich; 17-Mar-47; 5-Apr-47; Daniel; Quakenbruck, Hannover; Bohde, Anna; Schelenburg, Osnabruck, Hannover; Eberleh, Ludwig; Bode, Wilhelm; Eberleh, Friederike

Eck; Pauline Friedrieke; 14-Jun-37; 19-Jun-37; Paulus; —; Albrecht, Maria; —; —; —; —

Eckard; Georg; 21-Feb-41; 7-Mar-41; Johann; —; Schmidt, Emeline; —; —; —; —

Eckard; Margarethe Maria; 29-Dec-45; 11-Jan-46; Ernst; Hermsdorf, Sachsen Altenburg; Stuver, Barbara; Ditzmansberg, Baiern; Benker, Heinrich; Benker, Margaretha; —

Eckardt; Friedrich Andreas; 28-Aug-1861; 13-Oct-61; Johann; Nidda, Sachsen; Kilian, Henriette; —; Kowalik, Friedrich; Winter, Andreas; —

Eckardt; Johann August Andreas; 18-Jul-59; 7-Aug-59; Johann; Nidda, Hessen; Kilian, Henrietta; —; Winter, Andreas; Winter, Wilhelmine; Waltjen, August

Eckart; Christine; 22-Feb-52; 3-Mar-52; Ernst; Altenburg; Stiebinger, Barbara; —; Eckart, Christine Friedrike; —; —

Eckart; Elisabeth Barbara; 14-Nov-47; 25-Dec-47; Ernst; Hermsdorf, Sachsen, Altenburg; Stievering, Barbara; Betsmansberg bei Culmbach, Baiern; Webersperger, Elise Barbara; —; —

Eckart; Elisabeth Wilhelmine; 28-Apr-64; 3-Jul-64; Johann; Nidda, Hessen; Kilian, Henriette; Selbitz, Baiern; Eckart, Wilhelmine; —; —

Eckart; Hoia, Hannover; 20-Mar-65; 21-May-65; Konrad Johann; Grunberg,; Hessen, Gunther; Sophie; Wiedner, Ernstine Krantrike; Eckart, Wilhelmine; —

Surname Father; Child's Given Name; Birth Date; Baptismal Date; Father's Given Name; Father's Place of Birth; Mother's Surname and Given Name; Mother's Place of Birth; Witness 1 Surname and Given Name; Witness 2 Surname and Given Name; Witness 3 Surname and Given Name; Comments

Eckart; Johann Christian Heinrich; 31-May-63; 14-Jun-63; Johann Konrad; Grunberg, Hessen; Gunther, Maria Sophie; Hoia, Hannover; Knochele, Christian; Kaufmann, Heinrich; Hampe, Franz

Eckart; Matthaus; 23-Jun-42; 3-Jul-42; Johann; —; Schmidt, Anna M.; —; —; —; —

Eckhardt; Alexander Heinrich Wilhelm; 1-May-67; 30-Jun-67; Konrad; Grünbert, Hessen; Günther, Sophia; Hoga, Hannover; Stamm, Pastor Alexander; Schafer, Joh. Heinrich; —

Eckhardt; Friedericke; 17-Mar-49; 1-Apr-49; Ernst; Hermisdorf, Altenburg; Stiewinger, Barbara; Pittsmansberg bei Kulmbach, Baiern; Eckhardt, Friederike; —; —

Ecksturm; Anna Louise Maria; 3-Sep-56; 14-Sep-56; Heinrich; Useborn, Hessen; Brauer, Elise; —; Harmes, Katharine; Brauer, Konrad; Karl, Elisabeth Maria

Ecksturm; Elise; 25-Nov-54; 30-Nov-54; Heinrich; Useborn, Hessen; Brauer, Elise; —; Winter, Friederike Wilhelmine; Schaumloffel, Caroline Wilhelmine; —

Ecksturm; Elise Catharine Mathilde; 14-Sep-63; 27-Sep-63; Heinrich; Aseborn, Hessen; Brauer, Elise; Lisberg, Hessen; Wendel, Elise; Ecksturm, Katharine; Klingelhofer, Wilh.

Ecksturm; Heinrich Adam Wilhelm; 8-Jul-61; 21-Jul-61; Heinrich; Useborn, Hessen; Brauer, Elisabeth; —; Brauer, Sr., Heinrich; Bach, Adam; Schaumloffel, Wilhelm

Ecksturm; Johann Heinrich Andreas; 17-Sep-60; 30-Sep-60; Christian; Useborn, Hessen; Weber, Katharine; —; Winter, Andreas; Mieth, Margarethe; Ecksturm, Heinrich

Ecksturm; Johann Hermann; 11-Aug-62; 31-Aug-62; Christian; Useborn, Hessen; Weber, Katharine; Volkertshain; Thiemeyer, Johann Heinrich; Waltjen, Hermann Heinrich; Ecksturm, Elisabeth

Ecksturm; Johann Hermann; 11-Aug-62; 31-Aug-62; Christian; Useborn, Hessen; Weber, Catharine; Volkortshain, Hessen; Ecksturm, Heinrich; Wirth, Margaretha; —

Surname Father; Child's Given Name; Birth Date; Baptismal Date; Father's Given Name; Father's Place of Birth; Mother's Surname and Given Name; Mother's Place of Birth; Witness 1 Surname and Given Name; Witness 2 Surname and Given Name; Witness 3 Surname and Given Name; Comments

Ecksturm; Katharina Wilhelmina; 7-Mar-59; 20-Mar-59; Heinrich; Useborn, Hessen; Brauer, Elise; —; Broning, Katharina; Ecksturm, Christian; Regener, Katharine

Ecksturm; Melchior; 11-Jul-64; 14-Jul-64; Christian; Useborn, Hessen; Weber, Katharine; Volkortheim, Hessen; Schlerf, Melchior; —; —

Edeler; Auguste Ernestine Rudolphine; 20-Sep-47; 17-Oct-47; Johann Christoph Gerhard; Lubbeke, Preussen; Snitzer, Christine Margaretha Elisabeth; Lubbeke, Preussen; Buscher, Auguste Ernestine; —; —

Edeler; Carl Heinrich; 16-Sep-45; 8-Feb-46; Gerhard; Lubbeke, Minden, Preussen; Snitzer, Elise; Lubbeke, Minden, Preussen; Landmann, Heinrich; —; —

Edeler; Christine Elise; 11-Dec-46; 17-Jan-47; Joh. Heinrich Wilhelm; Lubbeke, Preussen; Buscher, Auguste Ernstine Adolphine; Lubbeke, Preussen; —; —; —

Edelmann; Karl Heinrich; 25-Aug-67; 15-Sep-67; Johannes; Wingershausen, Hessen; Kratz, Karoline; Freienser ?, Hessen; Edelmann, Karl; Kratz, Elisabeth; —

Eger; Anna Kathr.; 29-Jan-40; 16-Feb-40; Heinrich; —; Butzner, Kathr.; —; —; —; —

Eger; Hartmann; 18-Feb-42; 20-Mar-42; Heinrich; —; Bützner, Kathr.; —; —; —; —; —

Eger; Tobias; 26-Aug-44; 14-Sep-44; Tobias; —; Joseph, Barka; —; —; —; —; —

Eger; Wilhelm Tell; 7-Jul-44; 8-Sep-44; Heinrich; —; Putzner, Kathr.; —; —; —; —; —

Egger; Elisabeth; 14-Nov-45; 4-Jan-46; Tobias; Jusbach, Kirchheim, Kurhessen; Joseph, Walburga; Dern, Badenschen; —; —; —; —

Eggers; Heinrich Friedr. Wilh.; 28-Jan-38; 11-Feb-38; Karl; —; [--?--], Maria; —; —; —; —; —

Ehlwein; Gustav Adolph; 10-Feb-38; 9-Apr-38; Friedrich; —; Schmidt, Cumalie; —; —; —; —; —

Surname Father; Child's Given Name; Birth Date; Baptismal Date; Father's Given Name; Father's Place of Birth; Mother's Surname and Given Name; Mother's Place of Birth; Witness 1 Surname and Given Name; Witness 2 Surname and Given Name; Witness 3 Surname and Given Name; Comments

Ehrhard; Jakob; 19-Mar-48; 26-Mar-48; Georg; Hermausfeld, Sachsen Meiningen; Kohn, Margareth; Zweickershausen, Sachsen Meiningen; Bach, Jakob; —; —; child died

Ehrhardt; Henriette; 19-Sep-47; 12-Dec-47; Johann Heinrich; Ebelem, Schwarzburg, Sonderhausen; Stedefeld, Caroline; Arnsstadt, Schwarzburg Sondershausen; Gabeler, Henriette; Rusperg, Ros; Reinhardt, J. G.; —

Ehrmann; Critius; 4-Sep-40; 1-Oct-40; Mathaus; —; Weller, Rosine; —; —; —; —; —

Eigenbrod; Adam Heinrich Ludwig; 8-Dec-45; 25-Dec-45; Christian; Königshagen, Waldeck; Batz, Maria; Bergheim, Waldeck; Jäger, Ludwig; Kramer, Henriette; —; —

Eigenbrodt; Maria Auguste; 30-Sep-49; 25-Dec-49; Christian; Königshagen, Waldeck; Batz, Maria; Lergheim, Waldeck; Lohrmann, Maria Elisabeth; Dill, Auguste; —; —

Einnrauch; Anna Margarethe; 06-Jan-1860; 8-Jan-62; Weil. Georg; Bleichenbach, Hessen; Friedrich, Margarethe; —; Friedrich, Anna; Friedrich, Susanne Margarethe; —; —

Einwachter; Anna Elisabetha; 30-May-50; 2-Jun-50; Adam; Niederohm, Hessen; Momberger, Maria Elisabeth; Merlau; Momberger, Georg; —; —; —

Einwachter; Friedrich Ferdinand; 30-Aug-51; 14-Sep-51; Alexander; Niederohm, Hessen; Lyeger [?], Catharine; —; Brande, Friedrich Ferdinand; —; —; —

Einwachter; Georg Alexander; 16-Jul-53; 31-Jul-53; Joh. Adam; Niederohm, Hessen; Momberger, Elisabeth; —; Einwachter, Alexander; Momberger, Georg; —; —

Einwachter; Johann Adam; 10-Apr-47; 29-Apr-47; Alexander; Niederohm, Grunberg, Hessen; Hoyer, Catharine; Langensteinbach, Dorlach, Baden; Einwacther, Adam; Musch, Johann; —; —

Einwachter; Johann Adam Wilhelm; 18-Jan-61; 27-Jan-61; Joh. Adam Wilhelm; Niederohm, Hessen; Momberger, Maria Elisabeth; —; Wildermuth, Adam; Immrich, Elisabeth; —; at house

Surname Father; Child's Given Name; Birth Date; Baptismal Date; Father's Given Name; Father's Place of Birth; Mother's Surname and Given Name; Mother's Place of Birth; Witness 1 Surname and Given Name; Witness 2 Surname and Given Name; Witness 3 Surname and Given Name; Comments

Einwachter; Johannes; 25-Jun-63; 9-Jul-63; Adam; Niederohm, Hessen; Momberger, Elisabeth; Kirschgarten, Hessen; Einwachter, Jr., Alexander; Walther, Jr., Heinr.; —; —

Einwachter; Katharina Marg.; 24-Jul-39; 4-Aug-39; Alexander; —; Hager, Kathr.; —; —; —; —; —

Einwachter; Maria; 6-Feb-45; 16-Mar-45; Alexander; —; Hager, Catharina; Hessen; Lohrmann, Maria; —; —; —

Einwachter; Maria Elisabeth Katharina; 12-Aug-57; 23-Aug-57; Adam; Niederohm, Hessen; Momberger, Elisabeth; —; Ermold, Katharina; Einwachter, Elisabeth; —; —

Einwachter; Maria Katharina Elisabeth; 17-Jan-59; 30-Jan-59; Adam Wilhelm; Niederohm, Hessen; Momberger, Elisabeth; —; Wildermuth, Elisabeth; Einwachter, Katharina; Momberger, Maria; —

Einwachter; Maria Katharine; 7-Jun-49; 17-Jun-49; Alexander; Stiederohen, Grunberg, Hessen; Hoger, Catharine; Landensteinbach, Durlach, Baden; Momberger, Elisabeth; —; —; —

Einwächter; Anna Maria; 22-Nov-37; 3-Dec-37; Alex.; —; Heger, Kathr.; —; —; —; —; —

Einwächter; Georg Alexander; 19-Nov-42; 18-Dec-42; Alexander; —; Heger, Kathar.; —; —; —; —; —

Einwalde; Gottfried Samuel; 7-May-58; 16-May-58; Johann Hermann Heinrich; Quackenbruck, Hannover; Weltner, Katharina; —; Schimpf, Gottfried; Kleppsch, Heinrich; —; twin

Einwalde; Katharine Christiane; 7-May-58; 16-May-58; Johann Hermann; Quackenbruck, Hannover; Weltner, Katharina; —; Siegel, Katharine; Repp, Catharine; Schmidt, Christian; twin

Eisenach; Johannes; 10-Mar-55; 8-Apr-55; Johannes; Hofgarten, Hessen; Krotell, Maria; —; Berlau, Johannes; —; —; —

Eiser; Christoph Daniel; 20-Oct-40; 1-Nov-40; Johann A.; —; Minnich, Marg.; —; —; —; —; —

Eitel; Catharine Elisabeth; 24-Feb-48; 27-Mar-48; Jakob; Biesheim, Baiern; Horst, Maria Christine; Zell, Alsfeld, Hessen; Reinhardt, Catharine Elisab. Horst; —; —; —

Surname Father; Child's Given Name; Birth Date; Baptismal Date; Father's Given Name; Father's Place of Birth; Mother's Surname and Given Name; Mother's Place of Birth; Witness 1 Surname and Given Name; Witness 2 Surname and Given Name; Witness 3 Surname and Given Name; Comments

Emerich; Johann August Wilhelm; 1-Apr-64; 1-May-64; Johann; Bleichenbach, Hessen; Bickel, Charlotte; Spangenberg, Hessen; Lenz, Joh.; Krell, Joh.; Lenz, Katharine; —

Emmerich; Heinrich Christian Rudolph; 18-Apr-52; 15-Apr-55; Johann; Bleichenbach, Hessen; Bickel, Charlotte; —; Repp, Conrad; Schmidt, Christian; —; —

Emmerich; Johann Georg; 12-Jul-49; 16-Jul-49; Johann; Bleichenbach, Nidda, Hessen; Lipp, Sophia; Liedheim, Nidda, Hessen; Kircher, Johann; Lipp, Joh.; —; —

Emmerich; Katharine Elisabeth Margaretha; 10-Dec-60; 30-Dec-60; Johann; Reichenbach, Hessen; Pickel, Charlotte; —; Repp, Katharine; Krell, Elisabeth; Friedrich, Margarethe; —

Emmert; Elisabeth; 23-Jul-39; 8-Sep-39; Andreas; —; Grünwald, Amalie; —; —; —; —; —

Emmrich; Elisabeth; 13-Mar-42; 6-May-42; Peter; —; Hallenberger, Elisab.; —; —; —; —; —

Emrich; Heinrich; 25-Feb-45; 30-Mar-45; Conrad; Lissberg, Hessen; Werner, Anna Maria; Zeilbach, Hessen; Sehrt, Heinrich; Pabst, Adam; —; —

Emrich; Johann; 4-Sep-43; 1-Oct-43; Konrad; —; Werner, Anna M.; —; —; —; —; —

Enders; Johann; 30-Aug-48; 17-Sep-48; Joseph; —; Lundin, Sophia; Waltendorf, Sachsen Meiningen; Fritz, Johannes; Fritz, Magdalena; —; —

Endler; Philipp Adolfus; 22-Nov-60; —; Friedrich; Krezten, Baiern; Salzner, Agnes; —; —; —; —; emergency baptism

Engel; Christina Rosina; 6-Mar-50; 28-Apr-50; Gottlieb; Durrn, Pfortzheim, Baden; Demer, Margareth; Billertshausen, hessen; Horst, Ludwig; —; —; —

Engel; Christine Luise; 1-Mar-48; 16-Apr-48; Gottlieb; Durrn, Pforzheim, Baden; Diemer, Margarethe; Aillertshausen, Groschtheim, Hessen; Horst, Maria; —; —; —

Engel; Gottlieb; 23-Jun-40; 26-Jul-40; Gottlieb; —; Thiemer, Marg.; —; —; —; —; —

Engel; Maria Marg.; 8-Dec-42; 16-Apr-43; Gottlieb; —; Diemann, Marg.; —; —; —; —; —

Surname Father; Child's Given Name; Birth Date; Baptismal Date; Father's Given Name; Father's Place of Birth; Mother's Surname and Given Name; Mother's Place of Birth; Witness 1 Surname and Given Name; Witness 2 Surname and Given Name; Witness 3 Surname and Given Name; Comments

Engelhardt; Elisabeth Anna; 17-Jan-50; 30-May-52; Eduard; Erfurt, Preussen; Schneider, Anna; —; Kleppisch, Carl Frdch.; Kramer, Helene Elisabeth; —; —

Engelhardt; Johann; 4-May-52; 30-May-52; Eduard; Erfurt, Preussen; Schneider, Anna; —; Saar, Joh.; —; —; —

Engelhaupt; infant son; —; —; Frdch. Wilh.; Belzig, Preussen; —; —; —; —; —; stillborn

Engelhaupt; Johanna Maria Louise; 24-Jun-58; 17-Jul-58; Friedrich Wilhelm; Belzig, Preussen; Schreiner, Anna Maria; —; Zink, Eva Rosina; Mohring, Louise; Bruns, Johann; —

Engelhaupt; Sarah Maria; 6-Nov-61; 17-Nov-61; Friedrich Wilhelm; Belzig, Preussen; Schreiner, Anna Maria; —; Spielmann, Maria Elisabeth; Schreiner, Sarah; —; —

Engelhausen; Ernistine Emilie; 13-Aug-47; 25-Sep-47; Heinrich; Grindau, Bissendorf, Hannover; Bauersfeld, Anna Elisabeth; Wundersleben bei Erfurt, Preussen; Bauersfeld, Ernestine; —; —; —

England; Maria; 11-Sep-36; 6-May-38; Adam; —; Ungemach, Karoline; —; —; —; —; —

Erbe; Franz Johann; 26-Mar-52; 11-Apr-52; Heinrich; Sterckoltshausen, Kurhessen; Suss, Catharine; —; Horn, Johannes; Pechmann, Franz Joh.; —; Pechman from Philadelphia

Erbe; Heinrich Georg; 21-Dec-49; 25-Dec-49; Heinrich; Starkelshausen, Rothenburg a.d.F., Kurhessen; Sus, Catharine; Schrotsberg, Herbram, Wurttemberg; Schlein, Heinrich; Sus, Michael; —; —

Erdelmann; Karoline Louise; 3-Dec-64; 16-Apr-65; Karl; Wingershausen, Hessen; Kratz, Katharine; Freuensner, Hessen; Kratz, Karoline; Einwachster, Jr., Alex.; Erdelmann, Louise; —

Erdmann; Susanne Rebecka; 2-Apr-48; 22-May-48; Mathaus; Baltimore Co., MD; Hauser, Luise; Baltimore Co., MD; Erdmann, Susanne; —; —; —

Erhart; Johanne Henriette Caroline; 12-Aug-44; 20-Apr-45; Joh. Heinrich; Ebleben; Sedefeld, Caroline; Anstadt, Schwarzburg

Sondershausen; Gerber, Heinrich; Bertholdt, Johanne Maria Christiane; England, Caroline; —

Ermold; Christiana Catharina; 7-Dec-50; 22-Dec-50; Georg Michael; Jagsthausen, Wurttemberg; Bender, Catharine; —; Wiedemann, Christiana; Wiedemann, Gottfried; Graf, Catharina; 1 child

Ermold; Gottfried; 3-Apr-53; 5-Apr-53; Georg; Jagsthausen, Wurtemberg; Bender, Katharina; —; Wiedemann, Gottried; Einwachter, Adam; —; —

Ermold; Katharina Christiana Elisabeth; 7-Dec-56; 7-Dec-56; Georg; Jagsthausen, Wurttemberg; Bender, Katharina; —; Wiedemann, Christiane; Volgerlmann, Wilhelm; Einwacther, Elisabeth; —

Ernst; August; 1-Oct-46; 16-Mar-47; Christopher; Staben, Langweiler, Baiern; Herwig, Sophia; Staben, Langweiler, Baiern; Walther, August; —; —; —

Ernst; Catharine Margarethe; 4-Jul-49; 22-Jul-49; Georg Christoph Martin; Steben, Neila, Baiern; Herbich, Sophia Dorothea Johanne; Steben, Neila, Baiern; Siegel, Margaretha Catharine; Bluhm, Catharine; —; —

Esch; Wilhelm; 9-Dec-46; 27-Jan-47; Gerhard Heinrich; Schaln, Ippenbuhren, Hannover; Kleinschmidt, Elisabeth; Schaln, Ippenbuhren, Hannover; Dopke, Marie; —; —; illegitimate

Escherich; Johann Andreas; 11-May-50; 2-Jun-50; Georg; Malishausen, Schwarzburg, Sondershausen; Metzler, Elisabetha; Judsbach, Sachsen Meinungen; —; —; —; —

Escherich; Pauline Sophia; 16-Nov-47; 21-Nov-47; Georg; Marrelshausen, Neupreussen; Metzler, Elisabeth; Judenbach, Sachsen Meiningen; Metzler, Pauline Sophia; —; —; —

Etchington; Johann Thomas; 19-Jan-42; 13-May-42; Abraham; —; Fitzgerald, Cathr.; —; —; —; —

Evers; Katharine Salome; 28-Jul-38; 18-Sep-38; Johann; —; Pfeffer, Salome; —; —; —; —

Ewers; Carl Dietrich; 8-Jul-45; 24-Aug-45; Johann; Brake, Oldenburg; [--?--], Wilhelmine; Stolzenau, Hannover; Bluhm, Carl; —; —

Surname Father; Child's Given Name; Birth Date; Baptismal Date; Father's Given Name; Father's Place of Birth; Mother's Surname and Given Name; Mother's Place of Birth; Witness 1 Surname and Given Name; Witness 2 Surname and Given Name; Witness 3 Surname and Given Name; Comments

Ewighausen; Eva Katharine Charlotte; 08-Jun-1860; 03-Jul-1861; Ludwig; Siewershausen, Hannover; Bohnhagen, Charlotte; —; Schmidt, Katharina Elisabeth; Weissbrod, Eva Barbara; Stetter, Anna Marie

Fahrenau; Therese Rosine; 17-Feb-46; 15-Mar-46; Heinrich; Dielmgen, Lubbeke, Preussen; Uebehauen, Cath.; Diedersdorf, Schwarzburg, Rudolstadt; Junken, Therese Rosine; Höker, Heinrich; —

Faitz; Elisabeth; 26-Jun-39; 28-Jun-39; Heinrich; —; Groh, Gertraut; —; —; —; —

Farnbacher; Ursula; 15-Mar-50; 7-Apr-50; Georg; Barbach, Mustadt a.A., Bayern; Ameyer, Dorothea; Nienburg, Hannover; Ameyer, Ursula; —; —

Fasler; Catharine; 14-Sep-46; 27-Sep-46; Heinrich; Zeuserswehr, Maulbronn; Mauth, Catharine; Elbronn, Wurttemberg; Fischer, Conrad; Fischer, Mrs.; —

Fassberg; Augustine Dorothea Juliane; 19-Mar-61; 21-Jun-61; Friedrich; Schwecke; Lauer, Sophie; Bruchstal, Baden; Waldhauer, Dorothe; Seitz, Juliane; —

Fassler; Johann Wilh.; 3-Jan-41; 1-Sep-41; Heinrich; —; Maude, Kathr.; —; —; —; —

Fassler; Karoline; 11-Apr-38; 6-May-38; Christian; —; Siebeler, Christine; —; —; —; —

Fassler; Katharina; 8-Aug-44; 13-Oct-44; Heinrich; —; Mauthe, Kathr.; —; —; —; —

Fassler; Philip Gottlieb; 24-Jul-42; 14-Aug-42; Heinrich; —; Makthen [?], Kathr.; —; —; —; —

Fath; Anna Maria; 13-Jun-49; 8-Jul-49; Heinrich; Kleinaustadt, Diburg, Hessen; Oste, Maria Magdalene; Bermesins, Rheinbaiern; Fehndrich, Anna Maria; —; —

Fath; Maria Magdalene; 23-Apr-47; 13-May-47; Heinrich; Klein Umstadt, Diburg, Hessen; Oster, Maria Magd.; Schopp, Wallfischbach, Rheinbaiern; —; —; —

Faust; Catharine Elisabeth; 3-Sep-43; 9-Mar-46; Samuel; Lancaster, PA; Dorsch, Christiane Margaretha; Lancaster, PA; Fick, Catharine; —; —

Surname Father; Child's Given Name; Birth Date; Baptismal Date; Father's Given Name; Father's Place of Birth; Mother's Surname and Given Name; Mother's Place of Birth; Witness 1 Surname and Given Name; Witness 2 Surname and Given Name; Witness 3 Surname and Given Name; Comments

Faust; Georg Wilhelm; 5-Jul-45; 9-Mar-46; Samuel; —; Dorsch, Christiane Margarethe; Lancaster, PA; Fick, Georg Adam; —; —; —

Fauth; Johann Philip; 18-May-37; 28-May-37; Friedrich; —; Schramm, Kathr.; —; —; —; —; —

Fedder; Georg; 2-Jan-38; 3-Oct-38; Benjamin; —; Bollinger, Christine; —; —; —; —; —

Feger; Friedrich Wilhelm; 16-Dec-50; 16-Feb-51; Joseph; Solzau, Wurttemberg; Ernhardt, Friedericke; —; List, Mrs. Jakob; Eberle, Friedrich; —; —

Feger; Joseph Friedrich; 13-Sep-41; 10-Jul-42; Joseph; —; Emhard, Friedrieke; —; —; —; —; —

Feger; Josephine; 25-Dec-48; 28-Jan-49; Joseph; Saulgau, Wurttemberg; Imhard, Friederike; Mehringen, Stuttgart, Wurttemberg; Reith, Catharine; —; —; —

Feger; Katharine Wilh.; 22-Feb-44; 19-May-44; Joseph; —; Emhard, Friedricke; —; —; —; —; —

Feger; Luise Sophie; 19-Aug-46; 11-Oct-46; Joseph; Saulgau, Wurttemberg; Imhardt, Friederike; Mehringen, Stutgart, Wurttemberg; Reuth, Catharine; —; —; —

Feger; Wilhelm; 24-Mar-41; 10-Jul-42; Joseph; —; Emhard, Friedrieke; —; —; —; —; —

Fehringer; Maria Elise Lisette; 6-Aug-37; 20-Aug-37; Friedr.; —; Meyer, Kathr.; —; —; —; —; —

Feiertag; Gustav Heinrich Johannes; 22-Sep-65; 1-Oct-65; Samuel Benjamin; Schullehner, Baden; Beutner, Sophie; Heroldsberg, Baiern; Stegner, Gustav; Beutner, Barbara; Feiertag, Rev. Joh.; —

Feiertag; Marie Louise Friedericke; 3-Oct-62; 12-Oct-62; Samuel Benjamin; Berlin; Beutner, Sophie; —; Spielmann, Marie Elisabeth; Beutner, Louise; Birkner, Friedrich; school teacher

Felchner; Dorothea; 9-Jan-47; 31-Jan-47; Christian; Nurnberg; Gindern, Dorothea; Diepholz, Hannover; Ohlers, Dorothea; —; —; —

Surname Father; Child's Given Name; Birth Date; Baptismal Date; Father's Given Name; Father's Place of Birth; Mother's Surname and Given Name; Mother's Place of Birth; Witness 1 Surname and Given Name; Witness 2 Surname and Given Name; Witness 3 Surname and Given Name; Comments

Felder; Friedrich Wilhelm; 14-Sep-63; 27-Sep-63; Georg; Gerbenroth, Hessen; Kummel, Elisabeth; Wiesick, Hessen; Leutner, Friedrich; Muller, Wilhelmine; —; —

Fellner; Friedrich August; 4-Dec-43; 14-Apr-44; Karl H.; —; Lenzer, Juliane M.; —; —; —; —; —

Fertsch; Friedrich; 18-Jun-38; 22-Jul-38; Christoph; —; Koch, Kathr.; —; —; —; —; —

Fessel; Christian Friedrich; 15-Sep-43; 22-Oct-43; Heinrich; —; Bach, Marg.; —; —; —; —; —

Fessel; Christian Heinrich; 8-Jun-38; 30-Sep-38; Heinr.; —; Bach, Marg.; —; —; —; —; —

Fessel; Jacob; 25-Sep-40; 22-Oct-43; Heinrich; —; Bach, Marg.; —; —; —; —; —

Fetting; Anna Sophie; 3-Dec-43; 29-May-44; Johann; —; Meyer, Sophie; —; —; —; —; —

Fetting; Johann Heinrich; 24-Apr-46; 24-May-46; Johann Friedrich; Schwedt, Ukermark, Preussen; Meyner, Sophia; Bossum, Diepholz, Hannover; Riemenschneider, Gottlieb; Waltjen, Mrs.; —; born 11 PM

Fetting; Wilhelm Gerhard; 23-Dec-50; 5-Jan-51; Johann Friedrich; Schwed, Preussen; Meier, Sophie; —; Duhle, Wilhelm Friedrich; —; —; —

Fichtmeyer; Johann; 6-Apr-37; 13-Aug-37; Jacob Friedr.; —; Mussgen, Rosine; —; —; —; —; —

Fick; Jacob; 9-Jan-43; 29-Jan-43; Georg A.; —; Huth, Barbara; —; —; —; —; —

Fick; Karoline; 9-Sep-41; 15-Sep-41; Georg Adam; —; Richberger, Barb.; —; —; —; —; —

Fiese [?]; Katherine Gertrud; 24-Sep-66; 7-Oct-66; Christian; Wreren, Fursten. Waldeck; Kochaut, Anna Philippine; Bauernschwand, Hessen; Lapp, Ludwig; Lapp, Katharine; Zwick, Gertrud; —

Filbert; Sophia Elisabeth; 2-Apr-47; 9-May-47; Georg; Eschau, Baiern; Medinger, Dorothea; Dem Remsthal, Wurttemberg; Medinger, Sophia; —; —; child died

Surname Father; Child's Given Name; Birth Date; Baptismal Date; Father's Given Name; Father's Place of Birth; Mother's Surname and Given Name; Mother's Place of Birth; Witness 1 Surname and Given Name; Witness 2 Surname and Given Name; Witness 3 Surname and Given Name; Comments

Finkbein; Magdalaena; 3-May-37; 4-May-37; Georg; —; Taub, Magdal.; —; —; —; —; —

Fischer; Caroline Dorothea; 9-Jul-46; 26-Jul-46; Ernst; Sikingen, Baden; Schröder, Adelheid Gesche; Wachendorf, Sieke, Hannover; Stille, Dorothea; Wortmann, Caroline; —; —

Fischer; Conrad; 17-Mar-52; 30-May-52; Georg; Hitzkirchen, Hessen; Geiss, Elisabeth; —; Nagler, Conrad; —; —; —

Fischer; Johann; 25-Oct-37; 5-Nov-37; Martin; —; Hartmann, Anna Kathr.; —; —; —; —; —

Fischer; Katharine Elisabeth; 22-Oct-44; 8-Dec-44; Ernst; —; Schröder, Helena; —; —; —; —; —

Fischer; Margaretha; 2-Feb-40; 3-Mar-40; Georg; —; [--?--], Hanna; —; —; —; —; —

Fitzberger; Anna Elisabeth; 30-Dec-46; 26-Dec-47; Heinrich; Lidingen, Hessen; Schickner, Catharine; Ochsenburg, Rappenheim, Wurttemberg; Meyer, Philipp; Meyer, Elisabeth; —; —

Fitzberger; Rosine; 23-Jun-44; 25-Dec-44; Heinrich; —; Schickner, Katharine; —; —; —; —; —

Flauaus; Elisabeth; 14-Oct-58; 31-Oct-58; Heinrich; Hergersdorf, Hessen; Schneider, Maria; —; Flauaus, Elisabeth; —; —; —

Flauaus; Johann Friedrich Wilhelm; 16-Sep-61; 29-Sep-61; Heinrich; Hergersdorf, Hessen; Schneider, Anna Maria; —; Schneider, Heinrich Friedrich; Klinkmeier, Wilhelm; —; —

Flauaus; Wilhelm Gottlieb Heinrich; 2-Mar-64; 4-Mar-64; Emil Heinrich; Ergersdorf, Hessen; Schneider, Anna Maria; Engter, Hannover; Heyse, Wilhelm; Schulz, Louise; —; —

Fleischmann; Georg Michael Cranford; 14-Mar-63; 29-Mar-63; Georg; Markt Dietenhofen, Baiern; Friedrich, Margarethe Susanne; Baiersdorf, Baiern; Friedrich, Michael; Friedrich, Cranford; Rossel, Maria Barbara; —

Fleischmann; Johanna Louise Barbara; 31-Jul-67; 11-Aug-67; Georg Friedrich; Markt, Dictehofen, Baiern; Friedrich, Susanna Margaretha; Baiernsdorf, Baiern; Fleischmann, Georg; Harmes, Louise; Zink, Barbara; —

Surname Father; Child's Given Name; Birth Date; Baptismal Date; Father's Given Name; Father's Place of Birth; Mother's Surname and Given Name; Mother's Place of Birth; Witness 1 Surname and Given Name; Witness 2 Surname and Given Name; Witness 3 Surname and Given Name; Comments

Fleischmann; Marie Margarethe Johanne; 18-Mar-65; 2-Apr-65; Georg; Markt Dietenhofen, Baiern; Friedrich, Margaretha; Baiersdorf, Baiern; Fleischmann, Marie; Friedrich, Marg.; Zink, Joh.; —

Fluhardt; Rosina; 1-Mar-58; 20-Jun-58; Andreas; —; , ; —; Repp, Conrad; —; —; Foster father

Fordtmann; Maria Anna; 13-Nov-47; 4-May-48; Adolph; Engde beiOsnabruck; Fischer, Anna Maria; Herde, Berhnbruck, Hannover; Lange, Maria Adelheid; —; —; illegitimate

Forster; Philipp; 25-Oct-50; 1-Dec-50; Leonhard; Markerlbach, Baiern; Vogel, Marie; —; Kress, Philipp; —; —; 5 child, 2 son

Fortmann; Georg; 28-Mar-52; 22-May-52; Adam; Engter, Hannover; Ricken, Marie; —; Fortmann, Marie; —; —; mother is witness

Frank; Carl Johann; 16-Nov-47; 26-Dec-47; Johann Georg; Adolshausen, Mergertsheim, Wurttemberg; Wortmann, Elisabeth; Diepholz, Hannover; Wortmann, Carl August; Dorr, Johann; —; —

Frank; Caroline Elisabetha; 13-Jun-45; 13-Jul-45; Georg; Adolshausen, Wurttemberg; Wortmann, Lisette; Diepholz, Hannover; Wortmann, Caroline; —; —; —

Frank; Friederike Elisabeth; 23-Jun-54; 16-Jul-54; Georg; Adolshausen, Wurttemberg; Wortmann, Lisette Friederike; —; Dietrich, Friederike; Wortmann, Caroline; —; —

Frank; Jakob; 16-Feb-51; 23-Feb-51; Christian Ludwig; Grossaschbach, Wurttemberg; Getner, Margarethe; —; Aichele, Jakob; —; —; child died

Frank; Johann; 22-Mar-38; 29-Apr-38; Jacob; —; Kienzle, Regine Kath.; —; —; —; —; —

Frank; Johann August Leonhard; 23-Mar-59; 3-Apr-59; Johann Georg; Adolshausen, Wurttemberg; Wortmann, Lisette; —; Dietrich, Joh. Leonhard; Mieth, Joh.; Wortmann, Karl; —

Frank; Johann Georg Heinrich; 6-Mar-57; 15-Mar-57; Georg; Adolphshausen, Wurttemberg; Wortmann, Lisetta; —; Treide, Joh. Heinr.; Mieth, Joh.; Willner, Georg; —

Surname Father; Child's Given Name; Birth Date; Baptismal Date; Father's Given Name; Father's Place of Birth; Mother's Surname and Given Name; Mother's Place of Birth; Witness 1 Surname and Given Name; Witness 2 Surname and Given Name; Witness 3 Surname and Given Name; Comments

Frank; Johann Jakob; 5-Feb-55; 25-Feb-55; Jakob; Grossaschbach, Wurttemberg; Schmidt, Louise; —; Aichele, Jakob; —; —; —

Frank; Katharine Lisette Friedrike; 29-Mar-62; 6-Apr-62; Johann Georg; Adelshausen, Wurttemberg; Wortmann, Friedrike Lisette; —; Briel, Katharine; Dietz, Andreas; Dietrich, Friederike; twin

Frank; Klara Henriette Emilie; 15-May-64; 29-May-64; Johann Georg; Adolshausen, Wurttemberg; Wortmann, Lisette; Diepholz, Hannover; Wildermuth, Joh.; Mieth, Karoline; Wortmann, Eleonore; —

Frank; Louise Johanne Regine; 29-Mar-62; 6-Apr-62; Johann Georg; Adelshausen, Wurttemberg; Wortmann, Friedrike Lisette; —; Treide, Louise; Mieth, Johann; Aichele, Regine; twin

Frank; Margarethe Emilie Barbara; 14-Aug-66; 2-Sep-66; Johann Georg; Adolshausen, Wurttemberg; Wortmann, Lisette Friedrike; Diepholz, Hannover; Dietz, Barbara; Wildermuth, Johann; Mieth, Marg.; —

Franke; Marie Wilhelmine; 11-Apr-50; 12-May-50; Georg; Adolshausen, Wurttemberg; Wortmann, Lisette; Diepholz, Hannover; Egelstein, Maria; Gunther, Wilhelmine; —; —

Frech; Peter August; 10-Oct-45; 28-Dec-45; August; Ludwigsberg, Wurttemberg; Hotmann, Caroline; Buschaus, Wurttemberg; Keil, Peter; Keil, Mrs.; —; —

Fredrich; Carl; 9-Oct-46; 30-May-47; Rudolph; Laufenburg, Aargau, Schweitz; Fischer, Sophia; Linsburg, Wolpe, Hannover; Schmidt, Moritz; Schmidt, Mrs.; —; —

Fredrich; Rudolph; 28-Dec-45; 30-May-47; Rudolph; Laufenburg, Aargau, Schweitz; Fischer, Sophia; Linsburg, Wolpe, Hannover; Schmidt, Moritz; Schmidt, Mrs.; —; —

Frei; Maria Sophia Caroline; 5-Mar-56; 2-Jul-54; Heinr.; Holstein; Kortulla, Anna; —; Schaumloffel, Mrs.; —; —; —

Freimann; Heinrich; 21-Sep-55; 27-Sep-55; Georg; —; Klein, Christiane; —; Schwab, Heinr.; —; —; —

Freudenberg; Eva; 30-Apr-43; 30-Jun-43; Martin; —; Ruhl, Maria; —; —; —; —; —

Surname Father; Child's Given Name; Birth Date; Baptismal Date; Father's Given Name; Father's Place of Birth; Mother's Surname and Given Name; Mother's Place of Birth; Witness 1 Surname and Given Name; Witness 2 Surname and Given Name; Witness 3 Surname and Given Name; Comments

Freudenberg; Johannes; 15-Oct-41; 26-Dec-41; Martin; —; Kuhl, Maria; —; —; —; —; —

Freudenberger; Jakob; 8-Feb-49; 24-Feb-49; Martin; Eschau bei Aschaffenburg, Baiern; Ruhl, Maria; Steinberg bei Giessen; Arndt, Jakob; —; —; —

Fricke; Kardelie; 21-Dec-42; 8-May-43; Heinrich; —; Bauerbach, Rosine; —; —; —; —; —

Fricke [?]; Anna Catharine; 27-Feb-48; 9-Apr-48; Friederich; Diepholz, Hannover; Winkelmann, Margarethe; Kirchspiel, Essen, Oldenburg; Klare, Anna Catharine; —; —; twin

Fricke [?]; Margaretha Wilhelmine; 27-Feb-48; 9-Apr-48; Friederich; Diepholz, Hannover; Winkelmann, Margarethe; Kirchspiel, Essen, Oldenburg; Bobert, Wilhelmine; —; —; twin

Friedrich; Barbara Margarehta Dorothea; 1-Mar-60; 11-Mar-60; Johann Michael; Baiersdorf, Baiern; Weninger, Anna; —; Friedrich, Margarethe; Zink, Barbara; Reuter, Dorothea; —

Friedrich; Barbara Margarethe; 24-Nov-61; 8-Dec-61; Leonhard; Baiersdorf, Baiern; Weiss, Margaretha; —; Weiss, Barbara; Friedrich, Margarethe; —; —

Friedrich; Carl Heinrich; 18-Jan-46; 22-Feb-46; Peter; Remheld, Sachsen; Rothing, Margaretha; Coburg; —; —; —; —

Friedrich; Elis; 10-Jun-50; 14-Jul-50; Peter; Reiningen, Sachsen Meiningen; Hein, Anna Maria; —; Schneider, Elisa; —; —; 4 child, 3 dau. Died

Friedrich; Johann Georg; 30-Oct-57; 17-Oct-57; Michael; Baiersdorf, Baiern; Weninger, Anna; —; Heck, Joh.; Meier, Georg; —; —

Friedrich; Johann Georg Leonhard; 10-Oct-62; 26-Oct-62; Johann Michael; Baiersdorf, Baiern; Weninger, Linna; —; Zink, Johann; Fleischmann, Susanne Margarethe; Friedrich, Leonhard; —

Friedrich; Louise; 9-May-52; 16-May-52; Michael; Baiersdorf, Baiern; Weniger, Anna; —; Harmes, Louise; —; —; —

Friedrich; Luise; 20-Jan-39; 22-Feb-39; Ludwig; —; Helmuth, Christiane; —; —; —; —; illegitimate

Surname Father; Child's Given Name; Birth Date; Baptismal Date; Father's Given Name; Father's Place of Birth; Mother's Surname and Given Name; Mother's Place of Birth; Witness 1 Surname and Given Name; Witness 2 Surname and Given Name; Witness 3 Surname and Given Name; Comments

Friedrich; Margarethe; 7-Sep-52; 17-Oct-52; Heinrich; Fellberg, Kurhessen; Schabel, Christiane; —; Salzner, Anna Barbara; —; —; —

Friedrich; Maria Catharine; 31-May-55; 10-Jun-55; Micahel; Baiersdorf, Baiern; Weineger, Anna; —; Momberger, Georg; —; —; —

Friedrich; Philippine; 5-Feb-48; 7-Apr-48; Peter; Rehmhild, Sachsen Meiningen; Reding, Margarethe; Coburg; —; —; —; —

Friedrich; Susanna Margarethe; 15-Sep-59; 25-Sep-59; Leonhard; Baiersdorf, Baiern; Weiss, Margarethe; —; Friedrich, Anna; Friedrich, Susanna Margaretha; —; —

Friedrich; Wilhelm Michael Georg; 24-Oct-63; 8-Nov-63; Leonhard; Baiersdorf, Baiern; Theiss, Margaretha; Beigheim, Baiern; Friedrich, Michael; Klingelhofen, Wilh.; Fleischmann, Susanne Margarethe; —

Frisch; Anna Margaretha Elisabeth; 28-Nov-44; 16-Mar-45; Johann Wolfgang; Thurnau, Oberfranken; Dreide, Sophia; Schweinsberg, Kurhessen; Frisch, Conrad; —; —; wit is father's brother

Frisch; Johann Wolfgang; 22-Sep-51; 16-Oct-51; Konrad; Burnau; [--?--], Christine; —; Frisch, Wolfgang; —; —; —

Frisch; Marie Elisabeth; 25-Dec-51; 29-Feb-52; Joh. Wolfgang; Thurnau, Baiern; Treude, Wilhelmine; —; Treude, Anna Catharine Louise; —; —; —

Frische; Catharine Elisabeth; 10-Feb-48; 26-Mar-48; Johann Wolfgang; Turnau, Culmbach, Baiern; Hess, Sophia; Carlshafen, Hessen Cassel; Frische, Anton; —; —; —

Frische; Gerhard Louis Wilhelm; 26-Mar-67; 7-Apr-67; Andreas; Bremen, Hannover; Keyl, Anna Dorothea; Perry Co., Missouri; Vogel, Wilhelm; Lettenack, Louise; Keyl, Pastor Ernst Gerhard W.; —

Frische; Heinrich; 14-Aug-47; 28-Nov-47; Conrad; Turnau, Baiern; von Buhren, Christine; Petershagen, Preussen; von Buhren, Heinrich; —; —; —

Surname Father; Child's Given Name; Birth Date; Baptismal Date; Father's Given Name; Father's Place of Birth; Mother's Surname and Given Name; Mother's Place of Birth; Witness 1 Surname and Given Name; Witness 2 Surname and Given Name; Witness 3 Surname and Given Name; Comments

Fritsch; Philipp; 20-Nov-45; 11-Jan-46; Johann; Thurnau, Baiern; Treiter, Maria; Karlshafen, Kurhessen; Kraft, Philipp; —; —; —

Fritz; Catharine; 21-Dec-49; 13-Jan-50; Johannes; Eberbach, Kinzelsau, Wurttemberg; Vogel, Magdalena; Aufdenthal, Grafenberg, Baiern; Eybert, Johann; Eybert, Catharine; —; —

Fritz; infant son; 11-May-56; —; Joh.; Ebersbach, Wurttemberg; Vogel, Magdalena; —; —; —; —; still born

Fritz; Johan Thomas Adam; 31-Jul-55; 5-Aug-55; Michael; Eberbach, Wurttemberg; Ostheim, Eleonore; —; Kraus, Rosina; Harmes, Thomas; Bach, Adam; —

Fritz; Johann; 4-Aug-51; 24-Aug-51; Joh.; Eberbach, Wurttemberg; Vogel, Magdalena; —; Albert, Joh.; Fritz, Mich.; —; —

Fritz; Michael; 30-Dec-53; 22-Jan-54; Joh.; Eberbach, Wurttemberg; Vogel, Magdalena; —; Fritz, Michael; Kruger, Joh. Philipp; —; —

Fritze; Anna Maria Barbara; 3-Aug-57; 16-Aug-57; Johann; Eberbach, Wurttemberg; Vogel, Magdalena; —; Brauer, Maria Katharina; Kruger, Barbara; Fritze, Michael; —

Fritze; Barbara Maria; 3-Dec-66; 30-Dec-66; Johann; Eberbach, Wurtemberg; Vogel, Magdalena; Afterthal, Wurtemberg; Harmes, Barbara; Schneider, Maria; —; —

Fritze; infant daughter; 29-Mar-54; —; Michael; Eberbach, Wurttemberg; Osthaim, Eleonore; —; —; —; —; stillborn

Fritze; Johann Leonhard; 21-Jun-58; 27-Jun-58; Michael; Eberbach, Wurttemberg; Ostheim, Eleonore; —; Hoffmann, Leonhard; Harmes, Louise; Alt, Johann; —

Fritze; Johann Ludwig Thomas; 9-Mar-61; 24-Mar-61; Johann; Eberbach, Wurttemberg; Vogel, Magdlaena; —; Hoffmann, Bernhard; Harmes, Louise; —; —

Fritze; Magdalena; 2-Dec-52; 12-Dec-52; Georg Michael; Eberbach, Wurttemberg; Ostheim, Eleonore; —; Fritze, Magdalena Vogel; —; —; —

Fritze; Thomas Heinrich; 12-Aug-60; 19-Aug-60; Georg Michael; Ebersbach, Wurttemberg; Ostheim, Eleonora; —; Hoffmann, Katharine; Harmes, Thomas; —; —

Surname Father; Child's Given Name; Birth Date; Baptismal Date; Father's Given Name; Father's Place of Birth; Mother's Surname and Given Name; Mother's Place of Birth; Witness 1 Surname and Given Name; Witness 2 Surname and Given Name; Witness 3 Surname and Given Name; Comments

Fritzschler; Wilhelmine; 23-Nov-37; 29-Jan-38; Wilh.; —; Braun, Helmine; —; —; —; —; —

Fuchs; Eberhard Gottlieb Johannes; 10-May-65; 28-May-65; Heinrich; Frankenberg, Kurhessen; Spiess, Katharine; Frankenberg, Kurhessen; Bergen, Eberhard; Kuhnert, Gottlieb; Lemmermann, Johannes; —

Fuchs; Eleonora Marie Christiane; 30-Dec-63; 24-Jan-64; Heinrich; Frankenberg, Kurhessen; Spiess, Katharine; Frankenberg, Kurhessen; Fuchs, Eleonora; Taubert, Marie; —; —

Fuller; Johann Georg; 8-Sep-41; 28-Oct-41; Leonh.; —; Peter, Elisab.; —; —; —; —; —

Funk; Anna Karolina; 15-Mar-59; 8-May-59; Rudolph; Wetter, Kurhessen; Dominick, Charlotte; —; Beck, Anna Magdalena; Waltjen, Maria Magdalena; —; —

Funk; Karl Georg; 5-Aug-61; 25-Aug-61; Karl Georg; Wetter, Kurhessen; Dominick, Charlotte; —; Beck, Ernst; Horn, Valentin; Vogel, Emil; —

Funk; Rudolph; 2-Apr-57; 26-Apr-57; Rudolph; Wetter, Kurhessen; Dominick, Charlotta Friedericka; —; Rudolph, Ernst Benjamin; Schulz, Konrad; —; —

Furst; Rosine Magdalene; 23-Aug-48; 3-Sep-48; Johann Leonhard; Gunzendorf, Markelbach, Baiern; Vogel, Anna Maria; Eckenberg, Markelbach, Baiern; Hecker, Heinrich; Hecker, Rosina; —; —

Gacker; Margaretha Katharine; 10-Sep-42; 15-Jan-43; Christian; —; Detlendaler, Maria; —; —; —; —; —

Gahm; Catharine; 6-Feb-52; 22-Feb-52; Leonhard; Tristshausen, Wurttemberg; Koster, Marie; —; Kruger, Catharine; —; —; child died

Gahm; Friedrich Wilhelm; 20-Dec-64; 15-Jan-65; Georg; Tristhausen, Wurttemberg; Keyster, Marie; Krell, Preussen; Tormolen, Frdch. Wilh.; Tormolen, Fr. Marie Christine Karoline; —; —

Gahm; Friedrich Wilhelm; 23-Oct-60; 11-Nov-60; Georg; Tristshausen, Wurttemberg; Lester, Marie; —; Becker, Wilhelm; —; —

Surname Father; Child's Given Name; Birth Date; Baptismal Date; Father's Given Name; Father's Place of Birth; Mother's Surname and Given Name; Mother's Place of Birth; Witness 1 Surname and Given Name; Witness 2 Surname and Given Name; Witness 3 Surname and Given Name; Comments

Gahm; Johann; 2-Sep-58; 5-Sep-58; Leonhard; Triftshausen, Wurttemberg; Kunkel, Maria; —; Kruger, Johann; —; —

Gahm; Katharine Barbara; 8-Jun-56; 15-Jun-56; Georg; Tristshausen, Wurttemberg; Kuster, Marie; —; Kruger, Katharine Barbara; Kruger, Barbara; —

Gahm; Katharine Barbara; 30-Jul-62; 17-Aug-62; Georg; Triftshausen, Wuerttemberg; [--?--], Marie; —; Kruger, Barbara; Kruger, Katharine; —

Gahm; Maria Philippine; 20-May-67; 2-Jun-67; Georg; Tristenhausen,Wurttemberg; Keyster, Maria; Krell, Preussen; Thiemeier, Hermann Friedrich; Ober, Sophia; —

Gahm; Wilhelm; 6-Feb-53; 20-Feb-53; Georg Bernhard; Greilsheim, Wurttemberg; Koster, Maria; —; Becker, Wilhelm; —; —

Gail; Emilie Whilemine Karoline; 28-Jul-66; 12-Aug-66; Emil Adolph Ludwig; Giessen, Sachsen; Fent, Christine; Schotten, Hessen; Lettmade, Wilhelm; Schroder, Karoline Louise; —

Gail; Heinrich August Wilhelm; 12-Feb-64; 21-Feb-64; Emil Adolph Ludwig; Giessen; Fenk, Christine; Schotten, Hessen; Schroder, Frdch. Wilh.; Langschmidte, Frdch. Wilh.; Lettmade, Auguste Louise

Gantenbein; Heinrich; 3-Jan-40; 16-Jan-40; Johann; —; König, Jacobine; —; —; —; —

Gantinbein; Jacob; 10-Dec-38; 16-Dec-38; Johann Mich.; —; König, Jacobine; —; —; —; —

Gantinbein; Sophie Kathr.; 9-Apr-37; 7-Sep-37; Johann; —; König, Jacobine; —; —; —; —

Gantner; Anna Elisabeth; 14-Jan-45; 24-Mar-45; Johann; lauffen, Rothweil, Wurttemberg; Loos, Elisabeth Cath.; Bernsburg, Hessen; Kramer, Heinrich; —; —

Gantner; Johann Conrad; 31-Dec-42; 29-Jan-43; Johann; —; Loos, Elisab. K.; —; —; —; —

Gantner; Maria Elisab.; 2-Jan-41; 14-Mar-41; Johann; —; Loos, Elisab.; —; —; —; —

Gardner; Rosine; 25-Oct-40; 23-Aug-41; Wilhelm; —; Knöller, Justine; —; —; —; —

Surname Father; Child's Given Name; Birth Date; Baptismal Date; Father's Given Name; Father's Place of Birth; Mother's Surname and Given Name; Mother's Place of Birth; Witness 1 Surname and Given Name; Witness 2 Surname and Given Name; Witness 3 Surname and Given Name; Comments

Gauss; Christine; 30-Aug-48; 3-Sep-48; Emanuel Friedrich; Hildrichshausen, Herrenberg, Wurttemberg; Kuhn, Elisabeth; Bobenhausen, Hessen; Braier, Christine; —; —

Gayer; Christian Friedrich; 7-May-43; 4-Jun-43; Christian Fr. Tit.; —; Gayer, Christine M.; —; —; —; —; —

Geibeck; Margaretha; 22-Sep-50; 13-Oct-50; Daniel; Allstadt b Anspach, Baiern; Hirschmann, Maria Catharine; —; Paulick, Margaretha; —; —; 3 child, 2 dau

Geiger; Barbara; 30-Mar-38; 8-Jul-38; Heinrich; —; Rauch, Barbara; —; —; —; —; —

Geiger; Johann Georg; 10-Jul-39; 27-Oct-39; Jacob; —; Blickensdörfer, Friedricke; —; —; —; —; —

Geiger; Karoline Elisab.; 22-May-37; 18-Jun-37; Jacob; —; Blickensdörfer, Friedrieke; —; —; —; —; —

Geiger; Kunigunde Katharine; 27-Jul-51; 3-Aug-51; Joh.; Rauschenberg, Kurhessen; Weber, Catharine; —; Kraft, Kunigunde; —; —; —

Geiger; Margaretha Elisabeth; 13-Sep-49; 23-Sep-49; Johann; Rauschenberg, Kurhessen; Weber, Catharine; Gemunden, Kurhessen; Olny, Elisabeth; Weber, Margaretha; —; —

Geigle; Caroline; 16-Nov-46; 17-Jan-47; Johann Conrad; Luhringen, Herrenberg, Wurttemberg; Luginsland, Caroline; Ebdingen, Feingen, Wurttemberg; Angelmeyer, Mathaus; —; —; —

Geigle; Elisabeth; 23-Feb-52; 16-May-52; Joh. Conrad; Nufringen, Wurttemberg; Luckensland, Caroline; —; Muller, Elisabeth; —; —; —

Geigle; Jakob Friedrich; 3-Jun-48; 16-Jul-48; Johann Conrad; Nufringen, Herrenberg, Wurttemberg; Luginsland, Caroline; Ubdingen,Vairingen, Wurttemberg; Knapp, Johann; —; —; —

Geigle; Johann Heinr.; 29-Jan-43; 7-May-43; Johann Conrad; —; Luginsland, Karoline; —; —; —; —; —

Geigle; Katharina; 9-May-50; 23-Jun-50; Johann Conrad; Nusringer, Wurttemberg; Luginsland, Caroline; Ubdingen, Wurttenberg; Luginsland, Catharina; —; —; —

Surname Father; Child's Given Name; Birth Date; Baptismal Date; Father's Given Name; Father's Place of Birth; Mother's Surname and Given Name; Mother's Place of Birth; Witness 1 Surname and Given Name; Witness 2 Surname and Given Name; Witness 3 Surname and Given Name; Comments

Geigle; Maria Catharina; 1-Nov-44; 16-Mar-45; Johann Conrad; Uffringen, Wurttemberg; Luginsland, Caroline; Ebdingen, Wurttemberg; Angelmeyer, Mathais; —; —; —

Geiglein; Friederich Christoph; 2-Feb-46; 2-Mar-46; Andreas; Turnau, Baiern; Diethorn, Gertrud; Bamberg, Baiern; Volmers, Friedrich; Haker, Chrstoph; —; —

Geischel; Wilhelm; 5-May-49; 26-May-49; Johann Adam; Obermelzungen, Melzungen, Kurhessen; Zicklam, Catharine; Beischforth, Melzungen, Kurhessen; Lindemann, Christoph Wilhelm; —; —; —

Gelrinus; Johann Heinrich Gottlieb; 19-Feb-55; 28-May-55; Gottfried; Heppach, Baiern; Haas, Dorothea; —; Treide, Joh. Heinr. Gottlieb; —; —; —

Gemp; Johann Wilh.; 16-Jan-41; 24-Nov-41; Jacob; —; Bühler, Maria; —; —; —; —; —

Gemp; Juliane; 19-Oct-42; 30-Oct-42; Georg Fr.; —; Armbruster, Marg. Barb.; —; —; —; —; —

Gent; Amalia Charlotte; 23-Dec-47; 6-Feb-48; Johann; Armersbach, Backnang, Wurttemberg; Ahlers, Chrisinte Catharine; Gross Ashbach, Backnang, Wurttemberg; Ahlers, Joh. Georg; Ahlers, Christine; —; wits are grandparents

Gent; Anna Maria; 9-Aug-37; 13-Aug-37; Johann; —; Ahlers, Christine; —; —; —; —; —

Gent; Heinrich; 3-Feb-37; 12-Feb-37; Joh.; —; Stanger, Friedrieke; —; —; —; —; illegitimate

Gent; Luise; 1-Jan-43; 5-Feb-43; Johann; —; Ahler, Christine K.; —; —; —; —; —

Gent; Rosine Kathr.; 8-Nov-38; 2-Dec-38; Johannes; —; Ahlers, Christine K.; —; —; —; —; —

Genz; Georg Fr.; 13-Apr-39; 28-Apr-39; Georg Fr.; —; Armbrust, Marg.; —; —; —; —; —

George; Caroline Elisabeth; 18-Dec-49; 6-Jan-50; Conrad; Solz, Rothenburg, Kurhessen; Hessler, Catharine; Grumbach, Ascaffenburg, Baiern; Heidmuller, Caroline; Becker, Elisabeth; —; —

Surname Father; Child's Given Name; Birth Date; Baptismal Date; Father's Given Name; Father's Place of Birth; Mother's Surname and Given Name; Mother's Place of Birth; Witness 1 Surname and Given Name; Witness 2 Surname and Given Name; Witness 3 Surname and Given Name; Comments

George; Johann Philipp; 20-May-51; 1-Jun-51; Konrad; Solz, Kurhessen; Heller, Catharine; —; Kruger, Joh. Philipp; —; —; —

Gerber; Maria Kathr.; 16-Dec-37; 1-Jan-38; Christian; —; Klein, Luise; —; —; —; —; —

Gerboth; Emil; 2-Apr-38; 16-Apr-38; Johann Chr.; —; Rödel, Sophie; —; —; —; —; —

Gerlach; Maria Chatinre; 6-Jun-49; 11-Jul-49; Peter; Dittelsheim bei Hanau, Hessen; Schüssel, Margareth; Dittelsheim bei Hanau, Hessen; Bauer, Maria Catharina; —; —; child died

Germuth; Emma Katharina; 23-May-57; 31-May-57; Andreas; Eschau, Baiern; Weckesser, Anna Elisabeth; —; Weckesser, Katharina; —; —; —

Germuth; Eva Sophia; 5-Aug-55; 19-Aug-55; Andreas; Eschau, Baiern; Weckesser, Anna Elisabeth; —; Weckesser, Eva; —; —; —

Germuth; Johann Heinrich Ferdinand; 6-Jun-59; 26-Jun-59; Andreas; Eschbach, Baiern; Weckesser, Elisabeth; —; Weckesser, Joh.; Habermehl, Schoo teacher; —; —

Gerthe; Heinrich; 4-Sep-52; 12-Sep-52; Johannes; Geissmar, Kurhessen; Hille, Louise; —; Boppler, Heinrich; —; —; father died 21 Jul 52

Gerwig; Georg; 2-May-42; 3-Jul-42; Jacob Fr.; —; Lehmann, Christine Kathr.; —; —; —; —; —

Gerwig; Karoline; 18-Jan-39; 17-Feb-39; Jacob; —; Lehmann, Christine; —; —; —; —; —

Gesell; Katharine Margaretha; 26-Aug-37; 17-Sep-37; Wilhelm; —; Neibert, Marg.; —; —; —; —; —

Gettier; Georg Franz; 30-Mar-43; 23-Oct-43; Georg; —; Kraft, Marg.; —; —; —; —; —

Gettier; Margaretha Ellen; 5-Sep-38; 6-Jan-39; Georg; —; Kraft, Marg.; —; —; —; —; —

Gettier; Sahra Anna Mathilde; 19-Apr-40; 7-Sep-40; Heinrich; —; Kraft, Susanne; —; —; —; —; —

Gettier; Susanne; 23-Feb-37; 10-Apr-37; Heinrich; —; Kraft, Susanna; —; —; —; —; —

Surname Father; Child's Given Name; Birth Date; Baptismal Date; Father's Given Name; Father's Place of Birth; Mother's Surname and Given Name; Mother's Place of Birth; Witness 1 Surname and Given Name; Witness 2 Surname and Given Name; Witness 3 Surname and Given Name; Comments

Gettier; Wilhelm Heinr.; 17-Jan-43; 23-Oct-43; Heinrich; —; Kraft, Susanne; —; —; —; —; —

Gippert; Friedrich Georg; 30-Jun-37; 2-Jul-37; Friedr.; —; Bey, Christine; —; —; —; —; —

Glassner; Johann Georg; 29-Aug-50; 14-Oct-50; Ernst Friedrich; Dreuchslingen, Baiern; Wegemann, Catharina Barbara; —; Steinert, Georg; Huber, Wilhelmine Glassner; —; 4 child, 2 son

Gluck; Elisabetha Dorothea; 17-May-50; 2-Jun-50; Karl Friedrich; Gondelsheim, Bretten, Baden; Schön, Veronika; Oberöbisheim, Bruchheit, Baden; Morlock, Elisabeth; —; —; wit from Gondelsheim

Gobel; Catharine; 16-Aug-52; 26-Sep-52; Martin; Fuldau, Hessen; Kettenring, Catharine; —; Schneider, Catharine; —; —; —

Goebel; Katharina Francisca; 17-Mar-50; 1-Apr-50; Martin; Felda, Grunberg, Hessen; Kettenring, Katharina; Sommerset Co., PA; Göbel, Katharina; —; —; wit is father's sister

Goetz; Catharina Elisabeth; 18-Nov-45; 14-Dec-45; Christian; Bernthal, Elsass; Oestreich, Maria Magdalene; Doldesheim, Hessen; Ostreich, Adam; Vetter, Gottlieb; —; wit#1 is grandfather

Goetz; Margaretha Christine; 15-Dec-45; 2-Feb-46; Adam; Schenglengsfeld, Kurhessen; Rehbein, Christine; Schenglengsfeld, Kurhessen; Rehbein, Catharine Orr; —; —; child or mother died [?]

Goller; Johann; 18-Oct-46; 25-Oct-46; Johann Friedrich; Munchberg bei Hoff, Baiern; Kiesling, Anna Magdalene; Marktlauthen, Kirch, Baiern; Kiesling, Johann; —; —; —

Gompf; Maria; 24-Jun-51; 20-Jul-51; Peter; Niederofleiden, Hessen; Schott, Anna Catharine; —; Schott, Catharina; —; —; —

Gorn; Johann Peter; 20-Apr-53; 8-May-53; Joh. Michael; Grossbernweiler, Wurttemberg; Renner, Maria Katharine; —; Brisswanger, Jakob; Kruger, Philipp; —; —

Goss; Rebecca Anna; 27-Jan-39; 16-Aug-43; Robert; —; Towers, Nancy; —; —; —; —; —

Surname Father; Child's Given Name; Birth Date; Baptismal Date; Father's Given Name; Father's Place of Birth; Mother's Surname and Given Name; Mother's Place of Birth; Witness 1 Surname and Given Name; Witness 2 Surname and Given Name; Witness 3 Surname and Given Name; Comments

Goss; William Robert; 7-May-37; 16-Aug-43; Robert; —; Towers, Nancy; —; —; —; —; —

Götz; Margaretha Christine; 1-Jul-43; 16-Aug-43; Christian; —; Oestreicher, Maria; —; —; —; —; —

Götz; Maria Anna; 8-Apr-48; 14-May-48; Christian; Bernthal, Elsass; Oesterich, Maria Magdalene; Doljersheim bei Mainz; Carle, Mathaus; Carle, Barbara; —; —

Götze; Caroline Josephine; 18-Dec-45; 12-Apr-46; Carsten; Köln, Bederkes, Hannover; Clark, Marianne; Eastern Shore, MD; von Holten, Johann Peter; von Holten, Anna Cath.; —; —

Götze; Hermann Heinr.; 7-Apr-44; 16-Jun-44; Karsten; —; Klark, Marianne; —; —; —; —; —

Gräb; Ludwig; —; 20-Feb-48; Johann; Meiches, Grunberg, Hessen; Binderwald, Margaretha; Meinhes, Grunberg; Gräb, Georg; —; —; wit is grandfather

Graner; Catharine Margarethe; 22-Nov-47; 6-Jan-48; George Friedrich; Wilferdingen bei Carlsruhn, Baden; Seidler, Caroline; Hinter Weidenthal bei Bermesins, Rheinbaiern; Seigel, Margaretha; Kettenring, Peter; Kettenring, Cath.; —

Graulich; Catharina Louise; 9-Dec-54; 25-Dec-54; Conrad; Bleichenbach, Hessen; Papst, Christiane; —; Papst, Catharina; —; —; —

Grein; Heinrich; 27-Jan-40; 9-Feb-40; Paul; —; Ries, Elisab.; —; —; —; —; —

Grenzenbach; Katharine Emma; 28-Sep-43; 3-Mar-44; Heinr.; —; Schmidt, Elisab.; —; —; —; —; —

Gries; Anna Martha; 20-Mar-37; 26-Mar-37; Bernh.; —; Frave, Anna Kath.; —; —; —; —; —

Gries; Christine Elisab; 1-Apr-41; 16-May-41; Tobias; —; Brehringer, Christine; —; —; —; —; -- Apr 1841

Grieser; Marianne; 7-Oct-38; 9-Apr-39; Sylvester; —; Wolf, Anna; —; —; —; —; —

Grieser; Sophie Maria; 23-Mar-44; 22-Aug-44; Sylvester; —; Wolf, Anna B.; —; —; —; —; —

Surname Father; Child's Given Name; Birth Date; Baptismal Date; Father's Given Name; Father's Place of Birth; Mother's Surname and Given Name; Mother's Place of Birth; Witness 1 Surname and Given Name; Witness 2 Surname and Given Name; Witness 3 Surname and Given Name; Comments

Gross; Johann Emanuel; 14-Jan-49; 24-Jan-49; Jakob Wilhelm; Baltimore; Hender, Friederike; Eselshalterhoff bei Schönbach, Wurttemberg; Bringel, Caroline Gross; —; —; child died

Gross; Julie; 10-Jan-35; 7-Sep-39; Jacob; —; Burger, Kathr.; —; —; —; —; —

Gross; Maria; 1-Oct-33; 7-Sep-39; Jacob; —; Burger, Kathr.; —; —; —; —; —

Grösser; Hermann Friedr.; 22-Dec-36; 25-May-38; Sylvester; —; Wolf, Anna B.; —; —; —; —; —

Guehl; Carl; 9-Oct-41; 30-Apr-42; Conrad; —; Portz, Anna M.; —; —; —; —; —

Gunther; Johann Heinrich; 7-Jul-41; 15-Aug-41; Heinrich; —; Feiler, Marg.; —; —; —; —; illegitimate

Gunther; Sophie Kathr.; 21-Jan-38; 25-Mar-38; Heinrich; —; Meyer, Maria; —; —; —; —; —

Guntrum; Elisabeth; 22-May-38; 1-Jul-38; Christian; —; Dittmar, Anna; —; —; —; —; —

Gutenmuth; Margaretha Elisabeth; 8-Oct-45; 9-Nov-45; Nicolaus; Thalherta, Bruckenau, Baiern; Maul, Barbara; Thalherta, Bruckenau, Baiern; Grick, Margaretha; —; —; —

Hacker; Johann Andreas; 5-Aug-45; 31-Aug-45; Johann Christopfer; Thurnau, Oberfranken; Windenheimer, Cathar.; Oberringelheim, Hessen; Hacker, [--?--]; —; —; wit is father's brother

Hacker; Johann Christian; 4-May-41; 19-May-41; Christian; —; Dettendaler, Maria; —; —; —; —; —

Hacker; Karl Ludwig; 21-Nov-41; 26-Dec-41; Johann Andr.; —; Werner, Eva Rosine; —; —; —; —; —

Hagemuth; Caroline Elisabeth; 3-Jan-46; 8-Mar-46; Georg Heinrich; Birmesins, Rheinbaiern; Keim, Elisabeth; Birmesins, Rheinbaiern; Wild, Caroline; Muhly, Eberhard; —; —

Hagen; Sophie Henriette Caroline; 24-Aug-50; 15-Sep-50; Johann; Neile bei Baiereuth, Baiern; Weisleder, Rebecca; —; Farber, Henriette Caroline; —; —; 1 child

Surname Father; Child's Given Name; Birth Date; Baptismal Date; Father's Given Name; Father's Place of Birth; Mother's Surname and Given Name; Mother's Place of Birth; Witness 1 Surname and Given Name; Witness 2 Surname and Given Name; Witness 3 Surname and Given Name; Comments

Hagey; Samuel; 9-Nov-48; 12-Aug-49; John; Baltimore, MD; Muller, Eva; Frickenhofen, Gailsdorf, Wurttemberg; Schafer, Philipp; —; —; —

Hahn; Elisabeth; 23-Oct-42; 13-Aug-43; Johann; —; Muller, Anna; —; —; —; —; —

Hahn; Heinrich; 22-Sep-43; 25-Nov-43; Nikolas; —; Schmidt, Elisab.; —; —; —; —; —

Hahn; Hermann; 14-Dec-40; 11-Apr-41; Johann; —; Muller, Elisab.; —; —; —; —; —

Hahn; Jacob; 18-Sep-41; 31-Oct-41; Nikolas; —; Schmidt, Elisab.; —; —; —; —; —

Hahn; Margaretha Barb.; 16-Mar-44; 31-Mar-44; Johann; —; Ladebach, Dorothea; —; —; —; —; —

Hainlein; Jakob; 30-Nov-48; 25-Dec-48; Johann; —; [--?--], Kunigunde; —; Geben, Johann; —; —; Rev Biewend

Hammann; Peter; 6-Aug-45; 12-Aug-45; Johannes; —; Bauerle, Anna Barbara; Kirchheim an der Drost, Wurttemberg; Sauerwein, Peter; —; —; child died, father died 17 jul

Hammel; Eduard; 5-Oct-40; 24-Jan-41; Valentin; —; Schmidt, Elisab.; —; —; —; —; —

Hammel; Margaretha; 27-Jun-38; 2-Jun-39; Valentin; —; Schneider, Elisab.; —; —; —; —; —

Hammel; Margaretha; 17-Jul-43; 19-May-44; Valentin; —; Schneider, Elisab.; —; —; —; —; —

Hammelsdorfer; Christian; 17-Mar-44; 8-Apr-44; Kaspar; —; Dörfner, Anna K.; —; —; —; —; —

Hammer; Georg Heinrich; 10-Feb-65; 5-Mar-65; Wilhelm; Radtheim, Hessen; Reuwer, Dorothea; Vohrden, Hannover; Schwartz, Daniel; Boppler, Heinrich; —; —

Hammer; Johann Anton; 3-Dec-42; 3-Jan-43; David; —; Tim, Rosine; —; —; —; —; —

Hammer; Karoline Elisabeth; 13-Mar-45; 10-Apr-45; Johann David; Wahlheim, Wurttemberg; Tim, Rosine; Amsterdam; Seitz, Gottlieb; Tim, Elisabeth; —; —

Hammer; Sophie Henriette; 17-Jun-38; 2-Aug-38; David; —; Tim, Rosine; —; —; —; —; —

Surname Father; Child's Given Name; Birth Date; Baptismal Date; Father's Given Name; Father's Place of Birth; Mother's Surname and Given Name; Mother's Place of Birth; Witness 1 Surname and Given Name; Witness 2 Surname and Given Name; Witness 3 Surname and Given Name; Comments

Hampe; Franz Wilhelm; 11-Aug-45; 31-Aug-45; Franz; Norten, Hanover; Gobrecht, Wilhelmine; Göttingen; [--?--], Wilhelm; —; —; —

Hampe; Nikolas Friedr. Adolph; 1-Dec-37; 28-Apr-39; Friedr. Ad.; —; Fennarre, Christine; —; —; —; —; —

Hampe; Wilhelm Franz; 8-Jul-66; 22-Jul-66; Franz Wilhelm; Baltimore; Gorsuch, Clara Virginia; Baltimore; Hampe, Franz; Trager, Heinr.; —; —

Handgrätinger; Friedrich Wilh.; 14-Jul-39; 19-Aug-39; Mathias; —; Keppler, Kathr.; —; —; —; —; —

Happel; Peter Johann; 4-Apr-41; 29-May-41; Peter; —; Stuhlmann, Christine; —; —; —; —; —

Harmes; Anna Barbara Rosina; 29-Jun-55; 8-Jul-55; Thomas; Baiersdorf, Baiern; Helm, Louise; —; Fritz, Michael; Kraus, Rosina; Rose, Barbara; —

Harmes; Anna Katharina Magdalena; 4-Jan-66; 14-Jan-66; Thomas; Beirsdorf, Baiern; Helen, Louise; Beirsdorf, Baiern; Fritze, Michael; Fritze, Magdalena; Schneider, Katharine; —

Harmes; Anna Margaretha Adelheid; 10-Jan-67; 17-Feb-67; Joh. Heinrich; Hildesheim, Hannover; Lindemann, Anna; Ottersberg, Hannover; Eggers, Adelheid; Lindemann, Margeretha; —; —

Harmes; Friederike Katharine Elise; 8-May-63; 17-May-63; Thomas; Baiersdorf, Baiern; Helmz, Louise; —; Ecksturm, Elise; Schneider, Heinr.; Reitzel, Friederike; —

Harmes; Friedrich Gerhard; 6-Dec-60; 6-Dec-60; Thomas; Baiersdorf, Baiern; Helm, Louise; —; —; —; —; emergency baptism by midwife

Harmes; Johann; 13-Oct-52; 17-Oct-52; Thomas; Baiersdorf, Baiern; Helm, Louise; —; Heck, Johann; —; —; —

Harmes; Karl Johann Gottfried; 27-Jun-60; 8-Jul-60; Paul; Heroldsberg, Baiern; Bertram, Sophie Elisabeth; —; Scherrer, Sr., Joh.; Raumusser, Joh. Gottfried; —; —

Harmse; Johann Heinrich Gustav; 25-Sep-65; 22-Oct-65; Johann Heinrich; Hildesheim, Hannover; Lindemann, Anna;

Ottenberg, Hannover; Lindemann, Ludolph Gustav; Radecke, Kath.; —; —

Harries; Meta Marg.; 1-Jan-38; 16-Apr-38; Johann H.; —; Eschenforst, Sophie M.; —; —; —; —; —

Harris; Charlotte Karoline; 21-Jun-40; 28-Sep-40; Johann H.; —; Eschenhapt, Sophie Dor.; —; —; —; —; —

Hartlein; Johann Peter; 7-Feb-46; 12-Apr-46; Johann; Kaferbach, Anspach; Horn, Maria Margaretha; Ohrenbach, Rotenburg a.d. Tauber, Baiern; Hartlein, Jaohnn Peter; —; —; —

Hartmann; Charlotte Magdalene; 19-Mar-40; 20-Apr-40; Christian G.; —; Knobloch, Kathr.; —; —; —; —; —

Hartmann; Georg; 11-Oct-43; 17-Jan-44; Johann; —; Ott, Marg.; —; —; —; —; —

Hartmann; Heinrich Christian; 19-Jul-41; 22-Aug-41; Christian G.; —; Knobloch, Kathr.; —; —; —; —; —

Hartmann; Johann Phil. Friedr.; 11-Jul-37; 23-Jul-37; Johann; —; Orth, Marg.; —; —; —; —; —

Hartmann; Johann Philip; 2-Nov-40; 17-Nov-40; Johannes; —; Orth, Maria; —; —; —; —; —

Hartmann; Maria Margarethe; 15-Nov-46; 3-Feb-47; Johann; Engelsdorf bei Darmstadt; Orth, Margarethe; Hohenhailach, Wurttemberg; Hartmann, Margarethe; —; —; wit is grandmother

Hascher; Elisabeth; 13-Mar-49; 8-Apr-49; Philipp; Niedergeilsbach, Hessen; Siebhahn, Marie; Festenberg, Kreutz, Hachstadt, Baiern; Dries, Elisabeth; —; —; —

Haslob; Anna Mathilde Elisabeth; 20-Sep-65; 8-Oct-65; Johann; Blumenthal, Hannover; Heyse, Marie; Liebenau, Hannover; Hucksohlen, Mathilde; Ober, Elisabeth; Heyse, Anna; —

Hassbach; Marie Margarethe; 15-Jan-51; 9-Feb-51; Joh. Adam; Gross Bechle, Preussen; Schuhmann, Elise; —; Lange, Margarethe; Waldschmidt, Mrs.; —; —

Hauber; Franciska; 23-Oct-47; 14-Nov-47; Philipp; Schriesheim, Baden; Kuhl, Anna Margaretha; Meidehausen bei Wetzlar, Preussen; Sohl, Catharina; —; —; child died

Surname Father; Child's Given Name; Birth Date; Baptismal Date; Father's Given Name; Father's Place of Birth; Mother's Surname and Given Name; Mother's Place of Birth; Witness 1 Surname and Given Name; Witness 2 Surname and Given Name; Witness 3 Surname and Given Name; Comments

Hauch; Catharina; 29-Dec-44; 2-Feb-45; Christoph; —; [--?--], Rosina; —; Walters, Johannes; —; —; —

Hauer; Marie Elisabeth; 26-Jul-48; 1-Aug-48; Christoph Friedrich; Seichardshausen, Sleckarsulm, Wurttemberg; Herold, Marie Catharine; Adelsheim, Baden; Wust, Johann Gottfried; Heim, Elisabeth; —; —

Hauf; Christoph Friedrich; 12-Dec-47; 31-Jan-48; Christoph Friedrich; —; Velte, Rosine; Aschenbach, Calw, Wurttemberg; Velte, Johannes; —; —; child died

Hauf; Georg Friedrich; 5-Jun-49; 15-Jun-49; Christoph Friedrich; Apenbach, Culw, Wurttemberg; Felde, Rosine; Apenbach, Culw, Wurttemberg; Felde, Jakob Friedrich; —; —; —

Hauss; Maria; 30-Jul-47; 7-Aug-47; Friedrich Emanuel; Hildritzhausen, Herrenberg, Wurttemberg; Kuhl, Elisabeth; Babenhausen, Hessen; —; —; —; child died

Häussler; Hermann Ludwig; 22-Mar-50; 7-Apr-50; Johann; Kleinmunster, Hassfort, Bayern; Sachse, Margaretha; Melsungen, Kurhessen; Zulauf, Ludwig; —; —; wit from Hessen

Haynel; Eduard Adolph; 1-May-44; 9-May-45; Dr. Ferdinand Adolph; Doebra, Sachsen; Baesmer, Maria Amalia; Danzig; Haynel, Carl Friedrich; Baesmer, Rev. Carl Friedrich; Baesmer, Luise; wit#2 is grandfather

Haznel; Emilie Luise; 4-Dec-43; 2-Feb-43; Dr. Adolph Fred.; —; Bansamer [?], Maria Amalie; —; —; —; —; —

Heck; Carl James; 6-Apr-49; 29-Apr-49; Conrad Christian; Obernkirchen; Dorn, Sophie Leonore Amalia; Sinteln, Kurhessen; Dorn, Georg Ludwig; —; —; —

Heck; Caroline Eleonore Rebecka; 9-Jul-46; 16-Aug-46; Friederich; Obernkirchen bei Minden, Kurhessen; Dorn, Sophia Eleonore Amalie; Rinteln, Kurhessen; Heck, Sophia; Dorn, Christine; —; wit #1 is grandmother

Heck; Catharine; 14-Feb-48; 2-Apr-48; Andreas; Eglofstein, Grafenberg, Baiern; Keilholz, Barbara; Bieberbach, Bodenstein, Baiern; Kuhn, Catharine; —; —; child died

Surname Father; Child's Given Name; Birth Date; Baptismal Date; Father's Given Name; Father's Place of Birth; Mother's Surname and Given Name; Mother's Place of Birth; Witness 1 Surname and Given Name; Witness 2 Surname and Given Name; Witness 3 Surname and Given Name; Comments

Heck; Christina Sophia; 25-Jun-59; 3-Jul-59; Georg Karl; Oberkirchen, Kurhessen; Waltjen, Julianna; —; Ober, Sophia; Dieterle, Christoph Friedrich; —; —

Heck; Friedrich Heinrich Andreas; 26-Jan-55; 4-Feb-55; Georg; Neuenkirchen, Kurhessen; Waltjen, Julianne Christine Elisabeth; —; Waltjen, Friedrich; Waltjen, Heinr.; Waltjen, Andreas; —

Heck; infant daughter; 17-Sep-50; —; Wilhelm; Oberkirchen, Kurhessen; , ; —; —; —; —; stillborn

Heck; Johann Georg; 9-Jan-52; 25-Jan-52; Wilhelm; Obernkirchen, Kurhessen; Winter, Wilhelmine; —; Heck, Georg; —; —; —

Heck; Johannes; 25-Dec-46; 10-Jan-47; Andreas; Egloffstein, Grafenberg, Baiern; Keilholz, Barbara; Bieberbach, Bodenstein, Baiern; Hoffmann, Johann; —; —; —

Heck; Juliane; 2-Jun-66; 15-Jul-66; Georg Karl; Oberkirchen, Kurhessen; Waltjen, Juliane Christiane; Baltimore; Dieterle, Christoph; Waltjen, Katharine; —; —

Heck; Karl Heinrich; 10-Dec-62; 28-Dec-62; Georg Karl Louis; Obernkirchen, Kurhessen; Waltjen, Juliane Christine; —; Wittler, Karl; Schafer, Heinr.; —; —

Heck; Sophie Louise; 9-Jun-65; 2-Jul-65; Georg Karl; Oberkirchen, Kurhessen; Waltjen, Julianne; Baltimore; Waltjen, Sophie; Schulz, Louise; —; —

Heck; Stephan; 9-Aug-49; 2-Sep-49; Andreas; Eglofstein, Baiern; Keilholz, Barbara; Eglofstein, Baiern; Schmidt, Stephan; —; —; —

Heck; Stephanus Heinrich Wilhelm; 2-Jul-60; 8-Jul-60; Georg Karl Louis; Obernkirchen, Kurhessen; Waltjen, Julianne; —; Waltjen, Sr., Frdch. Hermann Wilh.; Waltjen, Andreas; Waltjen, Heinrich; —

Hecker; Catharine Mariaum Luise; 22-Feb-48; 23-May-48; Friedr. David; Buxtelhude, Hannover; Grosskopf, Luise; Neckarels bei Manheim, Baden; Fischer, Mariane; Reiz, Catharine; —; —

Hegener; Maria; 7-Feb-47; 10-Feb-47; Johann Christian; Goldmuhl, Berneck, Baiern; Kisbert, Catharine; Wunsiedel, Baiern; Hegener, Maria; —; —; —

Surname Father; Child's Given Name; Birth Date; Baptismal Date; Father's Given Name; Father's Place of Birth; Mother's Surname and Given Name; Mother's Place of Birth; Witness 1 Surname and Given Name; Witness 2 Surname and Given Name; Witness 3 Surname and Given Name; Comments

Heidmuller; Friedrich Wilhelm Ferdinand; 27-Feb-56; 9-Mar-56; Wilhelm; Liebenau, Hannover; Salge, Charlotte; —; Wittlerhle, Friedrich; —; —; —

Heim; Anna Kunigunde; 17-May-49; 25-Jun-49; Johann; Hitzelsdorf, Ebermanstadt, Baiern; Graf, Johanne; Litzelsdorf, Ebermanstadt, Baiern; Graf, Anna Kunigunde; —; —; —

Heim; Margaretha; 26-Jul-51; 3-Aug-51; Joh.; Hezzelsdorf, Baiern; Graf, Johanne; —; Graf, Margaretha; —; —; —

Heimer; Adam; 12-Mar-44; 8-Apr-44; Georg; —; Rein, Kathr.; —; —; —; —; —

Heimrodt; Georg Adolph; 27-Aug-48; 28-May-49; August Adolph; Neuendorf, Kurhessen; Engels, Caroline; Preussisch, Minden; —; —; —; —

Heinemann; Heinrich Wilhelm Dietrich; 26-Sep-67; 6-Oct-67; Justus Heinrich; Balhorn, Kurhessen; Bohne, Maria Sophia Lucia; Neustadt, Hannover; Kettenkamp, Dietrich Christian; Nobbe, Friedrich Wilhelm; Bohne, Heinrich; —

Heinemann; Sophie Hardine; 14-Jul-38; 13-Aug-38; Nikolaus; —; Kühn, Kathr.; —; —; —; —; —

Heiner; Katharine; 23-Dec-41; 21-Jan-42; Georg; —; Kreiner, Kathr.; —; —; —; —; —

Heinlein; Catharine; 4-Jun-52; 11-Jul-52; Joh.; Oflerdahl, Baiern; Hoffmann, Kunigunde; —; Grupp, Catharina; —; —; —

Heinlein; Katharine; 27-Apr-43; 7-May-43; Michael; —; Leppit, Kathr.; —; —; —; —; —

Heinlein; Margaretha; 26-Jul-50; 25-Aug-50; Johann; Landzer, Baiern; Hoffmann, Kunigunde; —; Heinlein, Meurer; Margaretha Heinlein; —; 4 child, 2 dau

Heinlein; Maria Katharina; 4-Aug-56; 31-Aug-56; Joh.; Melkendorf, Baiern; Geisel, Margaretha; —; Heinlein, Katharine; —; —; —

Heinrich; Anina Mathilde; 10-Apr-65; 3-Aug-65; Christoph; Bremen; Behn, Anna Louise Theodora; Bremen; Behn, Heinrich; Behn, Louise; —; —

Heinrich; Elisabeth; 16-Jan-39; 8-Sep-39; Jacob; —; Hettich, Kathr.; —; —; —; —; —

Surname Father; Child's Given Name; Birth Date; Baptismal Date; Father's Given Name; Father's Place of Birth; Mother's Surname and Given Name; Mother's Place of Birth; Witness 1 Surname and Given Name; Witness 2 Surname and Given Name; Witness 3 Surname and Given Name; Comments

Heins; Johann Heinrich; 15-Sep-48; 22-Sep-48; Heinrich; Schornsheim, Hessen; Weber, Elisabeth; Bernsburg, Hessen; Marschal, Ludwig Wilhelm; Weber, Johann; —; child died

Heinz; Heinrich Emanuel; 22-Dec-49; 27-Jan-50; Heinrich; Schornsheim, Alzey, Hessen; Weber, Elisabeth; Bernsburg, Hessen; Weber, Wilhelm; —; —; —

Heinz; Johann Friedrich; 28-Jul-42; 25-Sep-42; Johann Friedr.; —; Tim, Sophie; —; —; —; —; —

Heinz; Rosine; 24-Aug-44; 7-Oct-44; Friedrich; —; Tim, Sophie; —; —; —; —; —

Heinzmann; Maria Catharine; 13-May-48; 28-May-48; Heinrich; Jaxthausen, Wurttemberg; Schmidt, Maria; —; Wust, Johann; Kraft, Catharine; Carle, Cath.; —

Heise; Georg Friedrich Wilhelm; 1-Aug-66; 12-Aug-66; Heinrich; Liebenau, Hannover; Ernst, Marie Katherine; Staben, Baiern; Hollebein, Georg Friedrich; Suchting, Friedrich Wilhelm; Heise, Mrs. Beda; —

Heise; Heinrich August Wilhelm; 7-Jun-58; 20-Jun-58; Wilhelm; Liebenau, Hannover; Lenz, Maria; —; Lenz, Heinr.; Klinkmeier, August; Repp, Heinr.; —

Heiser; Caroline Christine; 8-Apr-47; 6-Aug-47; Heinrich; Kinsdorf, Hessen; Schlee, Dorothea Friederike; Kasteldorf, Baiern; Stroh, Catharine Christine; —; —; —

Heitmuller; Sophie Henriette Elisabeth; 2-Oct-52; 17-Oct-52; Wilhelm; Biebenau, Hannover; Salge, Charlotte; —; Wittler, Anna Sophie; —; —; —

Helbig; Friederike Sophie; 21-Jun-52; 27-Jun-52; Louis; Lubbeke, Preussen; Thunes, Louise; —; Helbig, Friederike Sophie; —; —; —

Hellwig; Catharine Caroline; 2-Jan-51; 26-Jan-51; August; Lubbecke, Preussen; Grune, Clara; —; Hellwig, Friedericke Caroline; Hossner, Catharine; —; —

Hellwig; Heinrich Conrad Wilhelm; 24-Nov-44; 19-Jan-45; Ludwig; —; [--?--], Louise; —; Thurner, Wilhelm; Hellwig, Heinrich; —; —

Surname Father; Child's Given Name; Birth Date; Baptismal Date; Father's Given Name; Father's Place of Birth; Mother's Surname and Given Name; Mother's Place of Birth; Witness 1 Surname and Given Name; Witness 2 Surname and Given Name; Witness 3 Surname and Given Name; Comments

Hellwig; Henrich Dietrich; 2-May-48; 14-May-48; August; Lubbeke, Preussen; Gruner, Clara; Lobenstein, Reuss; Hellwig, Dietrich; —; —; child died

Hellwig; Louise Sophie; 26-Nov-50; 8-Dec-50; Ludwig; Lubbecke, Preussen; Tauer, Louise; —; Hellwig, Louise Sophie Sudmeier; Sohns, Henriette Louise; Waltjen, Rosine Friedrike; 6 child, 3 dau

Hellwig; Rosine Maria; 6-Jan-45; 9-Feb-46; August; Lubbeke, Minden, Preussen; Gruner, Clara; Lobenstein; Maissel, Rosine Maria; —; —; —

Heltz; Albertine Kathr.; 30-May-40; 5-Jul-40; Wingold; —; Aner, Christine M.; —; —; —; —; —

Helwig; Anna Sophie; 6-Jan-40; 23-Feb-40; Heinrich Ludwig; —; Thiene, Luise M.; —; —; —; —; —

Helwig; August Heinr.; 10-Oct-42; 4-Dec-42; Ludwig H.; —; Thime, Luise; —; —; —; —; —

Helwig; Florentine Henriette Wilhelmine; 18-Jan-49; 28-Jan-49; Heinrich Ludwig; Lubbeke, Minden, Preussen; Theuw [?], Luise; Osnabruck; Melching, Wilhelmine; Sohns, Henriette Wilhelmine; —; child died

Helwig; Ludwig Wilhelm; 11-Mar-47; 21-Mar-47; Heinr. Ludwig; Lubbeke, Minden, Preussen; Thuner, Luise; Osnabruck; Thuner, Wilh.; —; —; —

Henkel; Caroline; 7-Mar-47; 5-Apr-47; Johann; Semchach bei Hanau; Rehberger, Catharine; Krainfeld, Nidda, Hessen; Rehberger, Caroline; —; —; —

Henkel; Georg Wilhelm; 15-Feb-55; 25-Feb-55; Adam; Mossenheim b. Frankfurt a. M.; Schafer, Christine; —; Becker, Wilhelm; —; —; —

Henkel; Heinrich Ferdinand; 1-Feb-58; 21-Feb-58; Adam; Massenheim, Kurhessen; Schafer, Christine; —; Becker, Wilhelm; —; —; —

Henkel; Johann Georg; 17-Jan-42; 30-Jan-42; Johann P.; —; Aschbach, Anna M.; —; —; —; —; —

Henkel; Maria Elisab.; 7-May-40; 17-May-40; Jacob; —; Muller, Kathr.; —; —; —; —; —

Surname Father; Child's Given Name; Birth Date; Baptismal Date; Father's Given Name; Father's Place of Birth; Mother's Surname and Given Name; Mother's Place of Birth; Witness 1 Surname and Given Name; Witness 2 Surname and Given Name; Witness 3 Surname and Given Name; Comments

Henkel; Peter; 3-Dec-44; 19-Jan-45; Peter; Schaffelbach, Kurhessen; Oehler, Anna Maria; Apsbach, Wurttemberg; Hind [?], Johannes; Hind [?], Mrs.; —; —

Henning; Wilhelm; 4-Dec-41; 1-Jan-42; Johann; —; Melcher, Marg.; —; —; —; —; —

Henry; Adeline Elisabeth; 20-Sep-35; 11-Aug-39; Johann Georg; —; Dieterle, Sybille; —; —; —; —; —

Henry; Karoline Isabelle; 18-Nov-39; 11-Aug-39; Johann Georg; —; Dieterle, Sybille; —; —; —; —; birth year wrong

Hentze; Caroline Marie Auguste; 22-Oct-45; 24-Mar-46; Adolph; Mengershausen bei Göttingen, Hannover; Schnell, Caroline; Blankenhain, Sachsen Weimar; Preiss, Michael; Hentze, Marie; —; —

Henze; Georg Heinrich; 29-Jan-48; 26-Mar-48; Adolph; Mengershausen bei Gottingen; Rohden, Caroline; Blankenheim, Sachsen, Meiningen; Muller, Heinrich; —; —; —

Henze; Maria Elisab.; 11-Jun-44; 25-Aug-44; August; —; Andermann, Maria; —; —; —; —; —

Herbig; Heinrich Carl; 21-Oct-54; 29-Oct-54; Heinrich; Oberstehmen, Baiern; Burger, Margaretha; —; Burger, Heinr.; Burger, Caroline; —; —

Herbig; Johann; 15-May-53; 22-May-53; Heinrich; Gonsbach, Kurhessen; Happel, Philippine; —; Schmick, Johann; —; —

Herbig; Karoline Henriette; 8-Mar-53; 20-Mar-53; Joh. Heinrich; Obersteben, Baiern; Burger, Margaretha; —; Burger, Heinrich; Burger, Karoline; —

Herbner; Elisabeth; 4-Apr-40; 19-Apr-40; Justus; —; Vogel, Kathr.; —; —; —; —

Hermansdörfer; Margarethe; 14-Dec-41; 19-Dec-41; Kaspar; —; Dörfler, Kathr.; —; —; —; —

Hertlein; Wilhelm; 10-May-50; 23-Jun-50; Johann; Elpnersdorf, Ausbach, Bayern; Horn, Maria Margaretha; Ohrenbach, Rothenburg a.d. T, Bayern; Hertlein, Peter; —; —

Surname Father; Child's Given Name; Birth Date; Baptismal Date; Father's Given Name; Father's Place of Birth; Mother's Surname and Given Name; Mother's Place of Birth; Witness 1 Surname and Given Name; Witness 2 Surname and Given Name; Witness 3 Surname and Given Name; Comments

Herzog; Louis Adam; 16-May-49; 20-Jan-50; Christian; Hanar, Hessen; Diemers, Marie; Hanar, Hessen; Wildermuth, Adam; —; —

Hess; Christian Friedrich; 23-Jun-49; 15-Jul-49; Friedrich; Jurste bei Osterode, Hannover; Gluck, Franziska Caroline Luise; Ebersdorf, Reusischen Voigtland; Schafer, Christian Jakob; —; —

Heugrad; Sophie; 3-Feb-37; 4-Jun-37; Wilhelm; —; Henrich, Elisab.; —; —; —; —

Heyde; Eduard; 17-Feb-38; 1-Jul-38; Anton; —; Biedengratt, Marg.; —; —; —; —

Heyde; Emilie; 3-Apr-36; 1-Jul-38; Anton; —; Biedengratt, Marg.; —; —; —; —

Heyde; Georg Anton; 15-Oct-40; 15-Dec-40; Georg A.; —; Windekop, Anna M.; —; —; —; —

Heyer; Margaretha Luise; 29-Mar-37; 23-Apr-37; Georg Ludw.; —; Lormann, Marg.; —; —; —; —

Heyse; Friedericke Katharina Susanne; 1-Jun-56; 8-Jun-56; Wilhelm; Liebenau, Hannover; Lenz, Marie; —; Klinkmeier, Friedericke; Repp, Katharine; Lenz, Susanne

Heyse; Gottlieb Ludwig; 20-Oct-65; 5-Nov-65; Heinrich Dietrich Wilhelm; Liebenau, Hannover; Lenz, Marie; Bleichenbach, Hessen; Schulz, Gottlieb; Thiemeyer, Louis; Lenz, Katharine

Heyse; Johannes Ludwig Dietrich; 1-Aug-63; 23-Aug-63; Heinrich Dietrich Wilhelm; Liebenau, Hannover; Lenz, Marie; Bleusenbach, Hessen; Lenz, Johannes; Haslob, Johann; Bruns, Johann

Heyse; Karl Heinrich Wilhelm; 27-Mar-61; 7-Apr-61; Wilhelm; Liebenau, Hannover; Lenz, Marie; —; Klinkmeier, Heinrich Wilhelm; Burmann, Wilhelm; Prufer, Karl

Heyser; Elisabeth Friedr.; 16-Feb-38; 20-Jun-38; Heinrich; —; Wahl, Elisab.; —; —; —; —; —

Heyser; Fraces Therese; 16-Dec-42; 14-Jul-43; Heinrich; —; Schlen, Dorothea; —; —; —; —; —

Heyser; Johann Heinrich; 15-Jan-41; 14-Jul-43; Heinrich; —; Schlen, Dorothea; —; —; —; —; —

Surname Father; Child's Given Name; Birth Date; Baptismal Date; Father's Given Name; Father's Place of Birth; Mother's Surname and Given Name; Mother's Place of Birth; Witness 1 Surname and Given Name; Witness 2 Surname and Given Name; Witness 3 Surname and Given Name; Comments

Heyser; Luise Anna; 23-Feb-39; 7-Apr-39; Heinrich; —; Schlee, Dorothea; —; —; —; —; —

Hickmann; Friedrich Wilh.; 23-Jul-41; 15-Aug-41; Georg; —; Haftmeyer, Kathr.; —; —; —; —; —

Hickmann; Georg Samuel; 16-Jan-40; 26-Jan-40; Georg; —; Hartmeyer, Kathr.; —; —; —; —; —

Hickmann; Jacob Eduard; 15-Aug-43; 24-Sep-43; Georg; —; [--?--], Kathr.; —; —; —; —; —

Hilbert; Heinrich; 9-Mar-52; 11-Apr-52; Georg; Eschau, Baiern; Fellbusch, Marie; —; Fellbusch, Heinr.; —; —; —

Hilbert; Johannes; 9-Mar-52; 11-Apr-52; Georg; Eschau, Baiern; Fellbusch, Marie; —; Bauer, Widow Elisabeth; —; —; twin

Hildebrand; Heinrich Justus; 16-May-40; 2-Jan-42; Christoph; —; Ritz, Rosine K.; —; —; —; —; —

Hildebrand; Katharine Rosine; 13-Sep-41; 2-Jan-42; Christoph; —; Ritz, Rosine K.; —; —; —; —; —

Hildebrand; Lisette Leonore Georgiane; 24-Mar-43; 30-Jul-43; Christian; —; Snedt, Leonore; —; —; —; —; —

Hildebrand; Ludwig Eduard; 13-Mar-43; 25-May-43; Christoph; —; Ritz, Karoline; —; —; —; —; —

Hildebrand; Wilhelm Ludw.; 16-Feb-38; 22-Sep-39; Christoph; —; Retze, Karoline; —; —; —; —; —

Hildebrandt; Maria Luise; 4-Jul-45; 20-Jul-45; Heinrich Wilh.; Osnabruck, Hannover; Palgemeyer, Cath. Regina Julie; Osnabruck, Hannover; Hildebrandt, Maria Elisabeth; Palgemeyer, M. Elis.; —; wits are grandmothers

Hilgartner; Ludwig Heinrich; 26-Sep-67; 6-Oct-67; Johannes; Landerf, Hessen; Einwachter, Anna Elisabeth; Baltimore; Schafer, Heinrich; Hilgartner, Heinrich; Einwachter, Maria Katharine; —

Hilgemann; Katharine Sophie; 4-Jun-41; 27-Jun-41; Wilhelm; —; Henschner, Elisab.; —; —; —; —; —

Hilgemann; Maria Karoline; 7-Nov-44; 15-Dec-44; Wilhelm; —; Hentsch, Elisab.; —; —; —; —; —

Surname Father; Child's Given Name; Birth Date; Baptismal Date; Father's Given Name; Father's Place of Birth; Mother's Surname and Given Name; Mother's Place of Birth; Witness 1 Surname and Given Name; Witness 2 Surname and Given Name; Witness 3 Surname and Given Name; Comments

Hillen; Caroline; 4-Mar-49; 11-Jun-49; Carl; Baltimore County; Frank, Magdalena; Gross Aschbach, Backnang, Wurttemberg; Aichele, Jakob; Regner, Mrs.; —; —

Hillgartner; Anna Katharine Margaretha; 3-Oct-64; 16-Oct-64; Johann; Londorf, Hessen; Einwachter, Anna Elisabeth; Baltimore; Siegel, Katharine; Schafer, Katharine; —; —

Hillgartner; Johann Heinrich; 30-Oct-63; 31-Oct-63; Johannes; Londorf, Hessen; Einwachter, Anna Elisabeth; Oberohm, Hessen; Frank, Georg; Dietz, Tobias; —; emergency baptism

Hillgartner; Katharine Elisabeth; 8-Jul-61; 14-Jul-61; Johannes; Londorf, Hessen; Einwachter, Anna Elisabeth; —; Einwachter, Alexander; Einwachter, Katharine; —; —

Hillgartner; un-named son; 31-Jul-66; —; Joh.; Londorf, Hessen; Einwachter, Elisabeth; —; —; —; —; died without baptism

Hink; Anna Catharina; 11-Aug-46; 23-Aug-46; Heinrich; Reigstadt, Baierspesa, Hannover; Brummer, Gesche Margaretha; Reigstadt, Baierkesa, Hannover; Schmidt, Christine; —; —; wit is aunt

Hinkel; Johann Adam; 7-Jul-56; 20-Jul-56; Adam; Mossenheim, Kurhessen; Schafer, Christina; —; Schafer, Martha; —; —; —

Hinkel; Karoline Emilie Katharine; 18-Aug-64; 28-Aug-64; Adam; Mosenheim, Kurhessen; Schafer, Christine; Baltimore; Mieth, Karoline; Briel, Helen Katharine; —; —

Hintener; Johann Andreas; 5-Sep-64; 8-Sep-64; Andreas; Hessen; Kruger, Margaretha Barbara; Kuhnhardt, Wurttemberg; Kruger, Joh. Philipp; Kruger, Katharine; —; —

Hirsch; Elisabeth; 7-Aug-45; 11-Dec-45; Daniel; Walldorf, Sachsen, Meiningen; Wagner, Barbara; Soltz, S. M.; Hirsch, Elisabeth; —; —; —

Hirsch; Johann Heinrich Ludwig Daniel; 1-Sep-46; 13-Sep-46; Daniel; Braunau, Waldeck; Wagner, Elisabeth; Braunau, Waldeck; Lohrmann, G. H.; Raabe, Luise; —; —

Hittmeyer; Adolph Chrisian Gerhard; 25-Feb-48; 19-Mar-48; Adolph Christ.; Dorrerden, Hannover; Schulte, Maria Clara; Horinghausen bei Osnabruck, Hannover; Schulte, Gerhard; —; —; wit is grandfather

Surname Father; Child's Given Name; Birth Date; Baptismal Date; Father's Given Name; Father's Place of Birth; Mother's Surname and Given Name; Mother's Place of Birth; Witness 1 Surname and Given Name; Witness 2 Surname and Given Name; Witness 3 Surname and Given Name; Comments

Hoffmann; August Konrad; 2-Apr-57; 12-Apr-57; Aug.; Bierdekopf, Hessen; Hoffmann, Magdalena; —; Magin, Anna Katharina; Schulz, Konrad; —; —

Hoffmann; Friederich; 16-Feb-50; 17-Feb-50; Valentin; Mauweiler, Elsass; Eitel, Salome; Lemberg bei Bernesins, Rheinbaiern; Dill, Friedrich; Eitel, Elisabeth; —; —

Hoffmann; Friedrich; 20-May-51; 8-Jun-51; Valentin; Nouweiler, Elsass; Eitel, Salome; —; Till, Frdch.; Till, Mrs.; —; —

Hoffmann; Heinrich Johann Christian; 10-Jan-60; 12-Feb-60; August; Biedkopf, Hessen; Klein, Magdalena; —; Grun, Heinrich; Trapp, Johann; Hoffmann, Christian; by Rev. Gratzel

Hoffmann; Henrietta Louise Wilhelmina; 8-Apr-58; 25-Apr-58; Valentin; Nerxweider, Elsass; Eitel, Salome; —; Muller, Wilhelmina; Muhly, Christian; Jackel, Henrietta; —

Hoffmann; Karl; 15-Sep-53; 9-Oct-53; August; Biedekopf, Hessen; Klein, Magdalena; —; Muller, Karl; Schwab, Katharine; —; —

Hoffmann; Katharine Louise Karoline; 22-Oct-60; 4-Nov-60; Valentin; Elsass; Eitel, Salome; —; Jackel, Katharine; Lange, Johann; Muhly, Louise; —

Hoffmann; Maria Elisabeth; 14-Mar-46; 13-Apr-46; Wilhelm; —; Eitel, Salome; —; Eitel, Maria Elisabeth; Kamp, Bernhard; —; —

Hoffmann; Maria Katharina; 11-Sep-58; 27-Oct-58; August Heinrich; biedekopf, Hessen; Klein, Magdalena; —; Magin, Anna Katharina; —; —; —

Hoffmann; Maria Kunigunde; 12-Jul-45; 14-Mar-46; Conrad; Reinhardshofen, Neustadt, Baiern; Kreuzer, Margarethe; Landerstadt, Höchstadt, Baiern; Friewold, Mar. Kunig.; —; —; —

Hoffmann; Marie Elise; 14-May-51; 1-Jun-51; Joh.; Volkershausen, Baiern; Bachmann, Henriette; —; Sieck, Marie; —; —; —

Hoffmann; Wilhelmina; 4-Jul-55; 2-Sep-55; August; Biedekopf, Hessen; Klein, Magdalena; —; Muller, Wilhelmine; Schwab, Heinrich; —; —

Hofmann; Christine; 8-Jun-65; 8-Jun-65; Valentin; Elsass; Eitel, Salome; Lemberg, Rheinbaiern; —; —; —; emergency baptism

Surname Father; Child's Given Name; Birth Date; Baptismal Date; Father's Given Name; Father's Place of Birth; Mother's Surname and Given Name; Mother's Place of Birth; Witness 1 Surname and Given Name; Witness 2 Surname and Given Name; Witness 3 Surname and Given Name; Comments

Hofmann; Elisabeth; 3-Oct-47; 24-Oct-47; Caspar; Stetten vor der Hohn, Ostheim, Sachsen Weimar; Peter, Elisabeth; UnterAlba, Dermbach, Sachsen Weimar; Arnold, Elisabeth; —; —; —

Hofmann; Friedrich Wilhelm; 18-Jun-61; 29-Sep-61; August; Biedkopf, Hessen; Klein, Magdalene; —; Bierau, Friedrich; Feige, Marie Christiane; Schmidt, Katharine; —

Hofmann; Friedrich Wilhelm; 18-Jun-61; 29-Sep-61; —; —; , ; —; —; —; —; —

Hofmann; Georg; 8-Jun-65; 8-Jun-65; Valentin; Elsass; Eitel, Salome; Lemberg, Rheinbaiern; —; —; —; emergency baptism

Hofmann; Georg Gottfried; 18-Mar-63; 12-May-63; Johann August; Biedenkopf, Hessen; Klein, Magdalena; Lemberg, Baiern; Muhly, Georg; Muller, Katharine; —; —

Hofmann; Heinrich; 8-Jun-65; 8-Jun-65; Valentin; Elsass; Eitel, Salome; Lemberg, Rheinbaiern; —; —; —; emergency baptism

Hofmann; Louise Henriette; 22-Feb-63; 29-Mar-63; Valentin; Elsass; Eitel, Salome; —; Bothe, Julius; Dietrich, Henriette; Muhly, Louise; —

Hofmann; Ludwig Christian; 17-Feb-65; 19-Mar-65; August; Birckkopf, Hessen; Klein, Magdelena; Lemberg; Schwab, Christian; Bollander, Louise; —; —

Hofmeister; Heinrich; 1-Jul-41; 22-Aug-41; Heinrich; —; Heldmann, Elisab.; —; —; —; —; —

Höhnemann; Johann Georg; 8-Feb-44; 10-Mar-44; Heinrich; —; Witzen, Maria; —; —; —; —; —

Holdgrefe; Anna Katharine Elisabeth; 29-Oct-64; 13-Nov-64; Louis; Engter, Hannover; Vollers, Katharine; Bewertstadt, Hannover; Holdgrefe, Anna; Will, Elisab.; Boppler, Kathar.; —

Holdgrefe; Friedrich Wilhelm; 2-Jun-66; 8-Jul-66; Friedrich Wilhelm; Engter, Hannover; Schneider, Anna; Engter, Hannover; Thiemeyer, Friedrich; Klinkmeyer, Wilhelm; —; —

Holdgreve; Heinrich Ferdinand; 26-Sep-67; 20-Oct-67; Louis; Engter, Hannover; Vollers, Katharine; Bekerstedt, Hannover; Vollers, Ferdinand; Thiemeier, Henriette; —; —

Surname Father; Child's Given Name; Birth Date; Baptismal Date; Father's Given Name; Father's Place of Birth; Mother's Surname and Given Name; Mother's Place of Birth; Witness 1 Surname and Given Name; Witness 2 Surname and Given Name; Witness 3 Surname and Given Name; Comments

Holdtgrafe; Katharine Marie; 10-Dec-62; 10-Dec-62; Wilhelm; Engter, Hannover; Schneider, Anna Maria; —; Holdtgrafe, Katharine; Klinkmeier, Marie; —; —

Hollebein; Conrad; 18-Jun-55; 1-Jul-55; Georg Friedrich; Axselbrunn, Hessen; Herbig, Sophie; —; Schultz, Conrad; —; —; —

Hollebein; Georg Friedrich Bernhard; 9-Feb-61; 17-Feb-61; Friedrich; Asselbrunn, Hessen; Herbig, Sophie; —; Zink, Georg Friedrich; Dietrich, Bernhard; —; —

Hollebein; Georg Ludwig; 15-Mar-53; 27-Mar-53; Friedrich; Osselbrunen, Hessen; Herbig, Sophie Ernst; —; Koch, Georg Ludwig; —; —; —

Hollebein; Henrietta Rebecca; 19-Apr-58; 2-May-58; Friedrich; Asselbrunn, Hessen; Ferbig, Sophia; —; Bruns, Rebecca; Schulz, Henrietta; —; —

Hollebien; Konrad Franz; 22-Aug-62; 7-Sep-62; Friedrich; Assolbrunn, Hessen; Herbeg, Sophie; —; Schultz, Konrad; Hampe, Franz; —; —

Hölscher; Johann Heinr.; 7-Aug-37; 11-Sep-37; Heinrich; —; Wenner, Maria; —; —; —; —; —

Holtgrave; Friedrich Wilhelm; 3-Aug-62; 17-Aug-62; Hermann Friedrich Louis; Engter, Hannover; Vollers, Anna Katharine; —; Klinkmeier, Wilhelm; Thiemeyer, Friedrich; —; —

Holtgrave; Johann Friedrich Louis; 8-Aug-61; 20-Aug-61; Louis; Engter, Hannover; Vollers, Katharine; —; Thiemeyer, Friedrich; Thiemeyer, Heinrich; —

Holthaus; Johann Gerhard; 9-Jul-41; 25-Jul-41; Franz Th. L.; —; Nöhlenkamps, Maria E.; —; —; —; —

Holthaus; Johann Wilh.; 27-Oct-37; 5-Nov-37; Franz Ludw.; —; Muhlenkamp, Maria; —; —; —; —

Holthus; Theodor Wilhelm; 8-Sep-45; 10-Oct-45; Franz Theodor Ludwig; Atter bei Osnabruck; Wohlenkamp, Engel; Fenne bei Osnabruck; Kolkmenzer, Joh. Wilh.; —; —

Holzhaus; Johann Heinr. Kaspar; 3-Sep-43; 27-Sep-43; Franz Theod.; —; Möllenkamp, Maria; —; —; —; —

Surname Father; Child's Given Name; Birth Date; Baptismal Date; Father's Given Name; Father's Place of Birth; Mother's Surname and Given Name; Mother's Place of Birth; Witness 1 Surname and Given Name; Witness 2 Surname and Given Name; Witness 3 Surname and Given Name; Comments

Homann; Johannes; 20-Jun-45; 5-Oct-45; Caspar; Staten, Sachsen Weimar; Peter, Elisabeth; Unterallbuck Dainbach, S. Weimar; Machwerth, Adam; —; —

Hopner; Theodor Benjamin; 1-Mar-52; 2-Apr-52; Benjamin; Bramberg, Posen; Guntrum, Margarethe; —; Purnes, Jilindr. [?]; Hickmann, Georg; —

Hoppel; Margarethe; 14-Feb-41; 18-Apr-41; Karl; —; Röhling, Gertrurde; —; —; —; —

Horklein; Johann Peter; 5-Nov-48; 26-Nov-48; Johann; Kaferbach bei Anspach; Horn, Margarethe; Ohrenbach bei Rothenburg a d. Tauber, Baiern; Horklein, Johann Peter; —; —

Hormes; Georg Michael; 1-Jun-57; 7-Jun-57; Thomas; Baiersdorf, Baiern; Helm, Louise; —; Meier, Georg; Fritz, Anna; Friedrich, Michael

Horn; Anna Elisab.; 5-Jul-37; 17-Sep-37; Johann Valentin; —; Koch, Philipine; —; —; —; —

Horn; Clara Virginia; 20-Aug-44; 7-Oct-44; Benjamin; —; Reppert, Regina; —; —; —; —

Horn; Emma Sophia Amalia; 29-Oct-52; 2-Dec-52; Joh. Valentin; Erbach, Hessen; Koch, Maria Philippine Eulalia; —; Keyl, Sophia Amalia; —; —

Horn; Ernst Jakob Bernhard; 14-Jan-47; 24-May-47; Johann Valentin; Erbach, Odenwald, Hessen; Koch, Philippine Maria; Oberad bei Frankfurth a.M.; Beck, Ernst; Beck, Bernhard Jakob; —

Horn; Friedrich Leonhard; 10-Feb-48; 19-Mar-48; Johann Michael; Gross Bernweil, Herbronn, Wurttemberg; Renner, Catharine; Rodamsen, Herbronn, Wurttemberg; Beck, Friedrich; Rappold, Leonhard; —

Horn; Friedrich Wilhelm; 25-Nov-50; 12-Jan-51; Joh. Valentin; Erbach, Hessen; Koch, Philippine Eulalia; —; Beck, Friedrich Wilhelm; —; —

Horn; Jakob; 19-Nov-49; 2-Dec-49; Johann Michael; Grossbernweiler; Renner, Maria Catharine; Roth am See, Hernbronn, Wurttemberg; Altinger, Jakob; Beck, Georg Fr.; Rappold, Leonhard

Surname Father; Child's Given Name; Birth Date; Baptismal Date; Father's Given Name; Father's Place of Birth; Mother's Surname and Given Name; Mother's Place of Birth; Witness 1 Surname and Given Name; Witness 2 Surname and Given Name; Witness 3 Surname and Given Name; Comments

Horn; Johann Friedr. Valentin; 5-Feb-43; 5-Jun-43; Johann V.; —; Koch, Maria; —; —; —; —

Horn; Karoline Emilie; 18-Nov-36; 9-Jul-37; Benjamin; —; Reppert, Regina; —; —; —; —

Horn; Katharine Susanne; 26-Apr-41; 2-Aug-41; Johann V.; —; Koch, Philipine; —; —; —; —

Horn; Maria; 12-Nov-48; 22-Apr-49; Friedrich; Bobengrun, Neila, Baiern; Spörl, Caroline Christine; Fichten, Neila, Baiern; Spörl, Anna Maria Dorette; —; —

Horn; Maria Christine; 23-Oct-44; 3-Nov-44; Johann Wl.; —; Renner, Maria; —; —; —; —

Horn; Marie Elisabeth; 2-Mar-51; 29-Jun-51; Frdch; Bobengrun, Baiern; Sporrer, Caroline Christiane; —; Sporrer, Joh. Christian; —; —

Horn; Marie Friedricke Catharine; 1-Jan-51; 26-Jan-51; Joh. Michael; Oberweiler, Wurttemberg; Reuwer, Maria Catharina; —; Bollinger, Mrs.; Beck, Friedrich; Kruger, Mrs. Philipp

Horn; Philipine Eulalia; 13-Jul-39; 22-Sep-39; Johann Val.; —; Koch, Philipine E.; —; —; —; —

Horn; Rosamunde Albertine; 13-Dec-48; 4-Feb-49; Johann Valentin; Erbach, Odenwald, Hessen; Koch, Philippine Maria; Oberad bei Frankfurth a M.; Happe, Rosamunde Albertine; —; —

Horn; Wilhelm Caspar; 19-Nov-44; 12-May-45; Joh. Valentin; Erbach, Odenwald, Hessen; Koch, Philippine Maria; Obern bei Frankfurth a M.; Becker, Ernst Wilhelm; Koch, Joh. Caspar; —

Hornung; Georg David; 12-Feb-44; 28-Feb-44; Georg D.; —; Daum, Philipine; —; —; —; —

Horst; Anna Catharine; 31-Oct-52; 14-Nov-52; Conrad; Bobenhausen, Hessen; Kladenbach, Catharine; —; Theisser, Maria; —; —

Horst; Catharine; 21-Sep-49; 28-Oct-49; Leonhard; Kindersbuhl, Lauf; Grask, Kunigunde; Lutzelsdorf, Ebermanstadt, Baiern; Griesacker, Catharine; —; —

Horst; Heinrich Martin; 16-Jan-49; 4-Feb-49; Conrad; Boboenhausen bei Grunberg, Hessen; Schuster, Catharine;

Glatenbach, Biedenkopf, Hessen; Horst, Martin; Schneider, Heinr.; —

Horst; Johann Martin; 30-Jul-54; 12-Aug-54; Conrad; Bobenhausen, Hessen; Schuster, Catharina; —; Otterbein, Johann; —; —

Horst; Johanne; 23-May-48; 13-Aug-48; Leonhard; Gundersbach, Lauf, Baiern; Graff, Kunigunde; Litzelsdorf, Ehrenstadt, Baiern; Heim, Johanne; —; —

Horst; Marie Elisabeth; 10-Apr-51; 4-May-51; Konrad; Pobenhausen, Hessen; Kladenbach, Catharina; —; Hagel, Marie; —; —

Horstmann; Heinrich Rudolph; 26-Apr-54; 7-May-54; Georg Heinrich; Holte, Osnabruck; Thiemeyer, Anna Maria; —; Thiemeyer, Joh. Heinr.; —; —

Horstmann; Maria Elisa; 14-Sep-55; 23-Sep-55; Jorgen Heinrich; Holte, Hannover; Thiemeyer, Anna Maragertha; —; Thiemeyer, Maria Charlotte; —; —

Horstmeyer; Johann Wilhe.; 28-Nov-37; 29-Dec-37; Eberhard W.; —; Uttmeyer, Kathr.; —; —; —; —

Hossmann; Amalie; 21-Feb-48; 2-Apr-48; Valentin; Nawarn, Elsass; Eitel, Susanne; Bermesins, Rheinbaiern; Hoffmeister, Amalie; —; —

Hotze; Elisabeth; 10-Nov-46; 13-Feb-47; Johann Rudolph Albrecht; Bern; Jakob, Maria; Wilsbach, Klarenbach, Hessen; —; —; —

Hotze; Luise; 15-Dec-48; 3-Jul-49; Johann Rudoph Alberth; Leugerswyl, Caton Bern, Schweitz; Jakobs, Maria; Wilsbach, Gladenbach, Hessen; Ammenhauser, Luise; —; —

Huber; Johan Georg; 26-May-49; 17-Jun-49; Friedrich; Treuchtlingen, Heidenheim, Baiern; Admansbacher, Sophie; Treuchtlingen, Heidenheim, Baiern; Walther, Johann; Walther, Margaretha; —

Hubner; Anna Maria; 5-Dec-48; 14-Dec-48; Johann; Hohlmusle bei Beirnuth, Baiern; Ziegler, Barbara; Oldenburg; Schaumann, Anna Maria; —; —

Hubner; Elisabeth; 4-Dec-45; 21-Nov-47; Heinrich Daniel; Schlechtenweg, Lauterbach, Hessen; Muller, Anna Catharine; Stockhausen, Lauterbach, Hessen; Paul, Elisabeth; —; —

Surname Father; Child's Given Name; Birth Date; Baptismal Date; Father's Given Name; Father's Place of Birth; Mother's Surname and Given Name; Mother's Place of Birth; Witness 1 Surname and Given Name; Witness 2 Surname and Given Name; Witness 3 Surname and Given Name; Comments

Hubner; Johann Gottfried; 13-Jul-47; 10-Aug-47; Johann Martin Math.; Culmbach, Baiern; Diethorn, Caroline; Bamberg, Baiern; Schneider, Gottfried; —; —

Hubner; Sophia Wilhelmine; 5-Nov-47; 21-Nov-47; Heinrich Daniel; —; [--?--], Catharine; —; Rinkel, Sophia Cath.; —; —

Hübschmann; Johannes; 21-Oct-45; 9-Nov-45; Johann; Egloffstein, Baiern; Bolster, Margaretha; Egloffstein, Baiern; Heim, Johann; —; —

Huck; Elise; 13-Jun-47; 8-Aug-47; Jakob; Diedorf, Eisenach, Sachsen Weimar; Engelhardt, Catharine; Diedorf, Eisenach, Sachsen Weimar; Arndt, Jakob; Arndt, Mrs.; Arndt, Elise

Hucksall; Ernst Wilhelm Engelhard; 24-Dec-66; 20-Jan-67; Ernst; Rethem, Hannover; Haslob, Mathilde; Blumenthal, Hannover; Heise, Maria; Klinkmeier, Wilhelm; —

Hucksoll; Maria Johanne Adelheid; 14-Sep-64; 9-Oct-64; Ernst Christian Friedrich; Retheim, Hannover; Haslop, Mathilde; Blumenthal, Hannover; Thiemeyer, Marie; Haslob, Joh.; Haslob, Adelheid; —

Hufnagel; Carl; 13-Aug-54; 27-Aug-54; Peter Carl Ludwig; Gnadenthal, Wurttemberg; Altvater, Catharina; —; Altvater, Frdch.; Hoffmann, Georg; —; —

Huhn; Maria Elisabeth; 15-Jun-38; 18-Nov-38; Johann; —; Söllers, Elisab.; —; —; —; —; —

Huhn; Philipine Elise; 27-Jan-37; 26-Mar-37; Johann; —; Zeller, Elisab.; —; —; —; —; —

Hummer; Abraham; 15-Oct-36; 9-Jul-40; Cornelius; —; Stöhr, Maria; —; —; —; —; —

Hummer; Maria Elisabeth; 11-Mar-40; 9-Jul-40; Cornelius; —; Stöhr, Maria; —; —; —; —; —

Hundermark; Karoline; 21-Mar-42; 15-May-42; Conrad; —; Walter, Karoline; —; —; —; —; —

Hundt; Katharine Susanne; 6-Feb-40; 28-Feb-40; Shaden; —; Stanger, Kathr.; —; —; —; —; illegitimate

Hüsing; John Dietrich; 21-Jan-49; 27-Mar-49; Johann Dietrich; Hamburg; Desige, Mary; New York; Walther, Rosine; —; —; —

Surname Father; Child's Given Name; Birth Date; Baptismal Date; Father's Given Name; Father's Place of Birth; Mother's Surname and Given Name; Mother's Place of Birth; Witness 1 Surname and Given Name; Witness 2 Surname and Given Name; Witness 3 Surname and Given Name; Comments

Huss; Benjamin Franklin; 4-Feb-46; 21-Nov-47; Alexander; Harford County; Schmal, Sarah; Little York; —; —; —; —

Huss; Cassandra Elisabeth; 25-Aug-47; 21-Nov-47; Alexander; —; [--?--], Sarah; —; —; —; —; —

Hüter; Maria Kathr.; 11-Oct-38; 18-Nov-38; Ludwig; —; Fuchs, Elisab.; —; —; —; —; —

Iggleston; Karl Eduard; 16-Jul-61; 23-Aug-61; Edward C.; —; Waltjen, Christiane; Baltimore; Heck, Georg Karl; Jeck, Juliane; —; illegitimate

Ihle; Georg David; 20-Jul-41; 16-Jan-42; Philip Jac.; —; Conrad, Christine; —; —; —; —; —

Imwalde; Caroline Wilhelmine; 29-Jun-55; 1-Jul-55; Johann; Quzckenbruck, Hannover; Weldner, Catharine; —; Luck, Caroline; —; —; —

Imwalde; Heinrich Samuel; 4-Jul-51; 10-Jul-51; Joh. Heinr.; Quackenbruck, Hannover; Weltner, Catharine; —; Imwalde, Heinr.; —; —; wit is grandfather

Imwalde; Johann Heinrich; 18-Nov-57; 6-Dec-57; Hermann Heinrich; Quackenbruck, Hannover; Wilken, Anna; —; Imwalde, Joh.; Imwalde, Mrs. Joh.; —; —

Imwalde; Karl Friedrich; 24-May-53; 30-May-53; Johann; Quackenbruck, Hannover; Weldner, Katharine; —; Kleppisch, Karl Frdch.; —; —; —

Imwolde; Friedrich Franz; 19-Jul-62; 27-Jul-62; Johann Heinrich Bernhard; Quackenbruck, Hannover; Weldner, Catharine; —; Thiemeyer, Friedrich; Hampe, Franz; —; —

Imwolde; Johann Anton; 29-Oct-47; 7-Nov-47; Johann; Quackenbruck, Hannover; Waltner, Catharine; Heimarshausen, Kurhessen; Imwolde, Anton Bernhard; Imwolde, Maria; —; —

Imwolde; Johann Heinrich; 10-Apr-46; 29-May-46; Johann; Quackenbruck, Hannover; Waltner, Cath.; Heimarshausen, Kurhessen; Dietrich, Johann Heinrich; —; —; —

Imwolde; Maria Adele; 18-Jul-49; 5-Aug-49; Johann; Quakenbruck, Hannover; Weldner, Catharine; Heimarshausen, Kurhessen; Imwolde, Adelheid; Imwolde, Maria Elisabeth; —; —

Surname Father; Child's Given Name; Birth Date; Baptismal Date; Father's Given Name; Father's Place of Birth; Mother's Surname and Given Name; Mother's Place of Birth; Witness 1 Surname and Given Name; Witness 2 Surname and Given Name; Witness 3 Surname and Given Name; Comments

Intrau; Adam; 24-Oct-48; 6-Jul-50; Johann Friedrich; Stotternhaim bei Erfurt; Heugen, Katharina; Oberfladungen, Rhonzeberg; Felbinger, Adam; —; —; wit from Kuthenbach

Isermann; Johann Silas; 21-Oct-42; 6-Mar-43; Jacob; —; Gilka, Susanne; —; —; —; —; —

Isermann; Margaretha; 2-Feb-39; 24-Mar-39; Jacob; —; Gilke, Susanne; —; —; —; —; —

Ittner; Anna Maria Barb.; 21-Nov-42; 25-Dec-42; Andr.; —; Wimmer, Maria B.; —; —; —; —; —

Jackel; Carl; 3-Mar-55; 15-Apr-55; Heinrich; Lisberg, Hessen; Uhl, Elisabeth; —; Carl, Carl; —; —; —

Jackel; Elisabeth Kunigunde Henriette; 4-Oct-60; 28-Oct-60; Friederich; Nidda, Hessen; Rausch, Barbara; —; Jackel, Elisabeth; Dlein, Kunigunde; Jackel, Henriette; —

Jackel; Friedrich Adam; 26-Apr-64; 8-May-64; Friedrich; Nidda, Hessen; Rausch, Barbara; Blankenfels, Baiern; Klein, Adam; Jackel, Katharine; —; —

Jackel; Wilhelm Karl; 12-Sep-66; 23-Sep-66; Friedrich; Nidda, Hessen; Rausch, Barbara; Blankenfeld, Baiern; Jackel, Katharine; Stetter, Wilhelm; —; —

Jäckel; Heinrich Wilh. Georg; 25-May-43; 11-Feb-44; Georg; —; Buschmann, Sophie; —; —; —; —; —

Jager; Katharina; 26-Jun-53; 17-Jul-53; Anton; Oberohm, Hessen; Muhlenkamp, Katharina; —; Schneider, Katharina; Schneider, Heinr.; —; —

Jakob; Charlotte Johanne; 1-Sep-46; 9-Sep-46; Lorenz; Weissendorf, Baiern; Frische, Ursula Margarethe; Weissendorf, Baiern; Wunder, Charlotte; —; —; child died

Jakob; Elisabeth Catharina; 5-Apr-45; 18-May-45; Michael; Schweinsberg, Kkurhessen; Frisch, Catharina; Hammermuhl, Kolnbach, Baiern; Frisch, Elisa; —; —; child died

Jakob; Johann; 12-Jun-67; 19-Jun-67; Johann; Blumenthal, Hannover; Heise, Maria; Liebenau, Hannover; Jakob, Johann; Jakob, Johann Heinrich; Baumann, Gerhard; —

Surname Father; Child's Given Name; Birth Date; Baptismal Date; Father's Given Name; Father's Place of Birth; Mother's Surname and Given Name; Mother's Place of Birth; Witness 1 Surname and Given Name; Witness 2 Surname and Given Name; Witness 3 Surname and Given Name; Comments

Jakob; Johann Georg; 5-Jul-50; 15-Jul-50; Joh. Michael; Scheinsberg, Hessen Cassel; Frisch, Elisa; —; Jakob, Joh. Georg; —; —; 2 child, 1 son

Jakob; Lorenz; 3-Apr-46; 8-Apr-46; Johann; Weissendorf, Nurnberg; Wunder, Charlotte; Rauschenberg beiNeustadt a.d. Reuss, Baiern; Jakob, Lorenz; —; —; child died

Jakob; Wilhelm Heinrich Ernst; 15-Dec-63; 10-Jan-64; Johann; Blumenthal, Hannover; Heyse, Marie; Liebenau, Hannover; Heyse, Wilhelmn,; Klinkmeier, Wilh.; Hucksohl, Ernst; —

Jakobs; Christine; 18-Oct-47; 28-Nov-47; Michael; Schweinsberg, Kurhessen; Frische, Elise; Turnau, Baiern; Altrik, Christine; —; —; —

Jakobs; Magdalena; 30-Jul-47; 15-Aug-47; Johann; Weissendorf, Herzogmaura, Baiern; Wunder, Charlotte; Rauschenberg, Neustadt, Baiern; Hoffmann, Magdalena; —; —; —

Januar; Daniel Christian Eduard; 19-Mar-49; 17-May-49; Daniel; Little York, PA; Meyer, Christine Maria; Bretbach, Nekars Ulm, Wurttemberg; Schafer, Christian Jakob; Schafer, Christine Fridrike; Weber, Johann Friedrich; —

Johnson; Wilhelm Heinrich; 9-Mar-43; 2-Jul-43; H.; —; Senft, Magd.; —; —; —; —; illegitimate

Josenhans; Caroline Henrike; 16-Jan-46; 3-May-46; Carl Christoph; Schwieberdingen, Ludwigsburg; Dieterle, Caroline; Enzingen, Faigenheim a.d. Ens, Wurttemberg; Dieterle, Carl Friederich; —; —; —

Josenhans; Emma Olivia; 19-Nov-47; 30-Jan-48; Carl Christoph; Wilperdingen, Ludwigsburg, Wurttemberg; Dieterle, Caroline; Isrigen, Faiingen, Wurttemberg; Dieterle, Carl; Dieterle, Maria; —; —

Jung; Elisabeth; 17-Apr-41; 25-Apr-41; Karl; —; Jung, Eva; —; —; —; —; —

Jungblut; Luise; 1-Jan-49; 11-Feb-49; Carl; Mengringhausen, Waldeck; Marx, Elisabeth; Klein Alpernissen, Hildesheim, Hannover; Troll, Regine; Muller, Juannetta; Schmidt, Luise; —

Kahl; Maria Sophie; 17-Aug-41; 5-Sep-41; Johann; —; Ritter, Maria; —; —; —; —; —

Surname Father; Child's Given Name; Birth Date; Baptismal Date; Father's Given Name; Father's Place of Birth; Mother's Surname and Given Name; Mother's Place of Birth; Witness 1 Surname and Given Name; Witness 2 Surname and Given Name; Witness 3 Surname and Given Name; Comments

Kahle; Johann Heinrich; 1-Nov-47; 13-Nov-47; Gerhard Heinrich; Bissendorf, Osnabruck; Detmers, Catharine Henriette; Essen, Eitlage, Hannover; Bodmann, Johann; parents; —; —

Kahle; Matthaus Friedrich; 21-Jan-50; 27-Jan-50; Johann Christian; Jaxthausen, Neckersulm, Wurttemberg; Heinzmann, Catharine; Jaxthausen, Neckarsulm, Wurttemberg; Kahle, Johannes Mathaus; Heinzmann, Marie; Wust, Johann

Kais; Christian Wilhelm; 4-Apr-47; 18-Apr-47; Johann; Herrnalig, Neuberg, Wurttemberg; Romoser, Elisabeth; Rodensohl, Wurttemberg; Romoser, Georg; Christine; —

Kais; Ernst Georg; 23-Feb-45; 9-Mar-45; Johannes; —; Romoser, Elisabeth; —; Romoser, Georg Friedrich; Romoser, Christine; —

Kais; Jacob Friedrich; 1-May-43; 5-Jun-43; Johann; —; Romoser, Elisab.; —; —; —; —

Kais; Johann Karl; 13-Sep-41; 7-Nov-41; Johann; —; Romoser, Elisab.; —; —; —; —

Kaiss; Caroline Emilie; 12-Jan-49; 18-Feb-49; Jaohnnes; Hermalz; Romoser, Elisabeth; Rodensohl, Neuenbirk, Wurttemberg; Romoser, Charlotta; Romoser, Caroline; —

Kalbfleisch; Elisabetha; 21-Oct-47; 14-Nov-47; Heinrich; Grosseneichen, Grunberg, Hessen; Bär, Maria; Gross eneichen, Grunberg, Hessen; Hoffmann, Elisabetha; —; —

Källing; Heinrich; 14-Nov-45; 3-Aug-47; Heinr. Ludwig; Neustadt am Rubenberge, Hannover; Wiegel, Marie; Lauterbach bei Frankfurth a.M.; Konig, Carl; Konig, Mrs.; —

Kalthof; Maria Magdalena Louise; 26-Dec-65; 31-Dec-65; Friedrich; Wachte, Preussen; Bohn [?], Henriette; Lebben, Preussen; Frese, Christian; Frese, Philippine; —

Kammer; Daniel Wilhelm; 3-Apr-54; 16-Apr-54; Wilhelm; Rodtheim, Hessen; Reiber, Dorothea; —; Schwartz, Daniel; —; —

Kammer; Heinrich; 28-Apr-51; 11-May-51; Wilhelm; Rettheim, Hessen; Reiber, Dorothea; —; Boppler, Heinr.; —; —

Surname Father; Child's Given Name; Birth Date; Baptismal Date; Father's Given Name; Father's Place of Birth; Mother's Surname and Given Name; Mother's Place of Birth; Witness 1 Surname and Given Name; Witness 2 Surname and Given Name; Witness 3 Surname and Given Name; Comments

Kammer; Henriette Karoline; 19-Mar-63; 12-Apr-63; Wilhelm; Rodtheim, Hessen; Reuber, Dorothea; Dohrden, Hannover; Eggers, Heinrich; Schwartz, Elisabeth; —

Kammer; Katharina; 29-Mar-56; 20-Apr-56; Wilhelm; Rothheim, Kurhessen; Rauber, Dorothea; —; Boppler, Katharine; —; —

Kammerzell; Georg Heinrich; 18-Oct-61; 11-May-62; Georg; Sachsen, Gotha; Breithut, Sophie; —; Sieck, Heinrich Adolph; —; —

Kampf; Catharine; 30-Aug-49; 16-Sep-49; Peter; Niederufleiden, Alsfeld, Hessen; Schott, Anna Catharine; Ruppertenroth, Grunberg, Hessen; Schott, Catharine; —; —

Kärcher; Gottfried; 8-Feb-40; 1-Mar-40; Gottfried; —; Manherz, Barbara; —; —; —; —

Karel; Katharine Friedricke; 28-Sep-42; 6-Oct-42; Christoph H.; —; Soekel, Eva; —; —; —; —

Karenroth; Johann Andreas; 31-Mar-53; 17-Apr-53; Johann; Oberdorla, Preussen; Fuller, Maria; —; Karenroth, Joh. Andreas; —; —

Karl; Anna; 25-Jan-57; 8-Feb-57; Karl; Bellmuth, Hessen; Brauer, Elisabeth Maria; —; Ecksturm, Elisabeth; Brauer, Karolina; —

Karl; August; 13-Jan-53; 13-Mar-53; Karl; Belmuth, Hessen; Brauer, Maria; —; Spielmann, Karl; Brauer, Peter; —

Karl; Johanne Elisabeth; 20-Dec-65; 7-Jan-66; Karl; Bellmuth, Hessen; Brauer, Karoline; Lisberg, Hessen; Brauer, Elisabeth; Brauer, Elisabeth; Spilmann, Johann

Karl; Marie Katharina Minna; 3-Oct-63; 11-Oct-63; Karl; Bellmuth, Hessen; Brauer, Karoline; Lisberg, Hessen; Kaufmann, Marie; Broning, Heinrich; Vornkuhl, Minna

Karl; Sophie Karolina Wilhelmine; 20-Dec-65; 7-Jan-66; Karl; Bellmuth, Hessen; Brauer, Karoline; Lisberg, Hessen; Klenke, Sophie; Klenke, Karoline; Schaumlusfel, Wilhelm

Karl; Wilhelm Heinrich Friedrich; 7-Jun-59; 19-Jun-59; Karl; Belmuth, Hessen; Brauer, Maria; —; Schaumloffel, Wilh.; Kaufmann, Eva; Spielmann, Frdch.

Karle; Eva; 18-Oct-44; 15-Dec-44; Heinrich; —; Sunkel, Eva; —; —; —; —

Surname Father; Child's Given Name; Birth Date; Baptismal Date; Father's Given Name; Father's Place of Birth; Mother's Surname and Given Name; Mother's Place of Birth; Witness 1 Surname and Given Name; Witness 2 Surname and Given Name; Witness 3 Surname and Given Name; Comments

Karli; Heinrich Martin; 26-Apr-51; 7-May-51; Konrad; Niederohmen, Hessen; Pfeil, Catharine Margarethe; —; Schneider, Heinr.; Gobel, Martin; father

Karmroth; Elisabeth; 12-Jun-51; 8-Jul-51; Joh.; Ober???; Fuller, Marie; —; mother, ; —; —

Karstens; Christian Friedrich; 6-Apr-64; 17-Apr-64; Johann Heinrich; Engter, Hannover; Kunker, Marie; Husede, Hannover; Weidemeier, Adam; Vordewegsten, Margarethe; Sieck, Adam Frdch.

Karstens; Johann Heinrich Friedrich; 30-Sep-56; 5-Oct-56; Joh. Heinr.; Engeln, Hannover; Kunker, Maria Elsabein; —; Kunker, Heinr.; Radecke, Wilhelmina; Radecke, Dietrich

Karstens; Karl August Heinrich; 27-Jan-67; 10-Feb-67; Johann Heinrich; Engel, Hannover; Kunker, Maria Elsabein; Huseck, Hannover; Schafer, Johann Heinrich; Linckmann, Margaretha; Louis, Karl Friedrich

Karstens; Katherine Marie Elisabeth; 20-Jan-61; 27-Jan-61; Heinrich; Engeln, Hannover; Kunker, Marie; —; Bruns, Rebecca Marie; Radecke, Friedrich; Kunker, Katharine Wilhelmine

Kasmodel; Christiane Katharine Elisabeth; 3-Apr-56; 20-Apr-56; Jakob; Gera, Reuss; Muller, Louise Elisabeth; —; Hoffmann, Katharine; Kowalik, Elisabeth; —

Kassel; Georg Peter; 27-Jun-39; 14-Jul-39; Christoph; —; Oestreicher, Marg.; —; —; —; —; —

Kasten; Wilhelm; 21-Jan-51; 26-Jan-51; Karl; Enkhorst, Preussen; Rosener, Maria Louise; —; father, ; Osterle, Joh.; —; —

Katenkamp; Franz Dietrich; 21-Jan-44; 8-Apr-44; Dietrich; —; Tzschachkenz, Johanne; —; —; —; —; —

Katenkamp; Heinrich Eberhard; 4-Mar-41; 26-Dec-41; Dietrich; —; Tzschapkenz, Juliane; —; —; —; —; —

Katenkamp; Maria Catharina; 4-Oct-49; 11-Nov-49; Dietrich; Hannover; Schitner, Rosine Catharine; Wurttemberg; Fitzberger, Catharine; —; —; —

Katenkamp; Rosine Maria; 20-Aug-48; 17-Sep-48; Dietrich; Ten, Hannover; Schitner, Rosine Catharine; Ten, Wurttemberg; Jung, Jakob; Jung, Anna Maria; —; child died

Kattenkamp; Anna Catharina; 20-Oct-55; 4-Nov-55; Dietrich; Rottner, Hannover; Schickner, Rosina; —; Bruhl, Catharina; —; —; —

Kattenkamp; Juliane Maria; 22-Aug-39; 29-Sep-39; Dietrich; —; Tzschakamz, Julianne; —; —; —; —; —

Kattenkamp; Karoline Rosine; 28-Jul-51; 17-Aug-51; Dietrich; Amt Ehrenburg, Hannover; Schickener, Rosine; —; Meiers, Karoline Katharina; Meiers, Benjamin; —; —

Kattenkamp; Theodor Christian Heinrich; 12-Nov-57; 29-Nov-57; Dietrich; Hannover; Schickner, Rosina; —; Burmann, Elisabeth; Beck, Ernst; Schmidt, Georg; —

Kattenkamp; Wilhelm Thomas; 2-Oct-52; 25-Oct-52; Dietrich; Amt Ehrensburg, Hannover; Schickner, Rosine; —; Wildemuth, Adam; —; —; —

Kaufmann; Barbara Rosine Karoline; 18-Nov-66; 25-Nov-66; Georg Heinrich; Friedegerode, Kurhessen; Eckart, Marie Juliane; Grunberg, Sachsen; Jackel, Barbara Elisabeth; Zink, Rosine; Karl, Karl; —

Kaufmann; Catharine Elisabeth; 5-Apr-47; 10-Aug-47; Heinrich Caspar; Biedenkopf, Hessen; Riemenschneider, Anna Catharine; Robertshaeim, Kurhessen; Wambach, Wilhelm; —; —; —

Kaufmann; Jakob; 12-Apr-46; 13-Apr-46; Heinrich Caspar; Biedenkopf, Hessen; Riemenschneider, Catharine; Ruppersheim, Homberg, Kurhessen; Kaufmann, Luis; —; —; wit is grandfather

Kaufmann; Johann Wilhelm; 15-Mar-55; 25-Mar-55; Georg Heinrich; Friederigerode, Kurhessen; Eckart, Maria Julianne; —; Salzner, Christoph; Bertram, Wilhelm; —; —

Kaufmann; Karl Emil; 7-Jan-53; 16-Jan-53; Georg Heinrich; Friedigerode, Kurhessen; Eckart, Maria Julianne; —; Flemming, Immanuel; Kothe, Kasten; —; —

Surname Father; Child's Given Name; Birth Date; Baptismal Date; Father's Given Name; Father's Place of Birth; Mother's Surname and Given Name; Mother's Place of Birth; Witness 1 Surname and Given Name; Witness 2 Surname and Given Name; Witness 3 Surname and Given Name; Comments

Kaufmann; Katharina Rosina Maria; 14-Jun-57; 28-Jun-57; Georg Heinrich; Friedigerode, Kurhessen; Eckardt, Julianna; —; Schafer, Katharina; Zink, Rosina; —; —

Kaufmann; Louis Johann; 12-Oct-44; 19-Jun-45; Heinrich Caspar; Biedenkopf, Hessen; Riemenschneider, Catharina; Robertshain, Kurhessen; Kaufmann, Ludwig; —; —; wit is grandfather

Kaufmann; Matthaus Wilhelm Heinrich; 17-Oct-61; 27-Oct-61; Georg Heinrich; Fredigerod, Kurhessen; Eckardt, Marie Julianne; —; —; —; —; —

Kaufmann; Rosine Henrietta Elisabeth; 30-Jun-59; 10-Jun-59; Georg Heinrich; Friedigerode, Kkurhessen; Eckardt, Maria Juliane; —; Kattenkamp, Rosina; Schulz, Konrad; Kerl, Elisabeth; —

Kaufmann; Sophia Christine; 12-May-64; 22-May-64; Johann Heinrich; Friedigeroda, Kurhessen; Eckart, Marie Juline; Grunberg, Hessen; Gunther, Sophie; Konig, Christine; —; —

Keil; Georg; 28-Jan-47; 7-Feb-47; Johann; Hegersdorf, Grunberg, Hessen; Traum, Catharine; Hegersdorf, Grunberg, Hessen; Werz, Johann; Werz, Mrs.; —; —

Keil; Heinrich; 3-Sep-48; 15-Oct-48; Johann; Hockersdorf, Grunberg, Hessen; Treum, Catharina; Senroth, Grunberg, Hessen; Ruppel, Heinrich; —; —; —

Keil; Johannes; 14-Jan-45; 13-Apr-45; Johann; Heckersdorf, Hessen; Traum, Catharina; Senerodt, Hessen; Horst, Conrad; —; —; —

Kelling; Maria Christine Greta; 12-Sep-39; 29-Sep-39; Ludwig; —; Wiegel, Maria; —; —; —; —; —

Kepler; Johann August; 9-Mar-43; 24-Sep-43; Johann G.; —; Stoll, Barb.; —; —; —; —; —

Kern; Anna Maria Wilhelmina; 31-Aug-65; 9-Oct-64; Peter; Brucken, Rheinbaiern; Gebhard, Sophia; Markthelbis, Baiern; Kern, Anna Maria; Tormolen, Wilh.; Stetter, Anna Maria; —

Kern; Anna Maria Wilhelmine; —; 9-Oct-64; —; —; —; —; —; —; —; —

Surname Father; Child's Given Name; Birth Date; Baptismal Date; Father's Given Name; Father's Place of Birth; Mother's Surname and Given Name; Mother's Place of Birth; Witness 1 Surname and Given Name; Witness 2 Surname and Given Name; Witness 3 Surname and Given Name; Comments

Kern; Carl August Gottfried; 22-Feb-45; 24-Mar-45; Carl; Marburg; Schuhmacher, Margareth; Marburg; Becker, August; —; —; wit from Marburg

Kern; Elisabeth Kunigunde; 18-Dec-40; 31-Jan-41; Karl; —; Schumacher, Marg.; —; —; —; —; —

Kern; Heinrich Wilhelm Friedrich; 13-Jun-48; 9-Jul-48; Jakob; Ephriegen, Nagold, Wurttemberg; Huis, Anna Christina; Ephriegen, Nagold, Wurttemberg; Raspe, Heinrich Wilhelm Friedrich; —; —; —

Kern; Karl Georg Wilh.; 18-Dec-42; 22-Jan-43; Karl; —; Schumacher, Marg.; —; —; —; —; —

Kern; Mathilde Kunigunde; 12-Jul-49; 10-Aug-49; Carl; Marberg, Kurhessen; Schuhmacher, Margarethe; Marberg, Kurhessen; Schuhmacher, Kunigunde; —; —; —

Kern; Peter Wilhelm; 28-Jul-67; 11-Aug-1867; Peter Wilhelm; Brucken, Baiern; Gebhart, Sophia; Markselbis, Baiern; Stitte, Wilhelm; Kern, Margaretha; —; —

Kern; Reinhard Georg Valentin; 28-Sep-49; 19-Nov-39; Karl; —; Schumacher, Margaretha; —; —; —; —; —

Kerner; Georg Heinrich; 6-Dec-41; 19-Dec-41; Johann; —; Kreuzer, Elisab.; —; —; —; —; —

Kernright; Allis; 31-Jul-35; 24-Nov-40; Nicolas; —; [--?--], Catharine; —; —; —; —; —

Kerth; Emilie Luise; 6-Nov-42; 11-Dec-42; Friedrich; —; Scheppert, Mathilde; —; —; —; —; —

Kettenring; Christian; 14-Nov-38; 6-Jan-39; Peter; —; Weimann, Kathr.; —; —; —; —; —

Kettenring; Georg; 4-Mar-43; 16-Apr-43; Peter; —; Neimann, Kathr.; —; —; —; —; —

Kettenring; Heinrich Andreas; 12-Aug-48; 10-Sep-48; Peter; Hermersberg, Rheinkreis, Baiern; Mezmann, Catharine; Hopstadt, Hessen Homburg; Eggers, Andreas; Eggers, Caroline; —; —

Kettenring; Karl; 6-Jan-41; 17-Feb-41; Peter; —; Weimann, Kathr.; —; —; —; —; —

Surname Father; Child's Given Name; Birth Date; Baptismal Date; Father's Given Name; Father's Place of Birth; Mother's Surname and Given Name; Mother's Place of Birth; Witness 1 Surname and Given Name; Witness 2 Surname and Given Name; Witness 3 Surname and Given Name; Comments

Kettenring; Maria Elisabeth; 3-Aug-45; 28-Sep-45; Peter; Hermersberg, Rheinbaiern; Meimann, Cath.; Sinnhopstate, Homburg; Zulauf, Balthasar; Zulauf, Maria Elisabeth; —; —

Keyl; Agnes Magdalena; 27-Feb-53; 6-Mar-53; Ernst Gerhard Wilhelm; —; Vogel, Sophie Amalie; —; Sommers, Emilie; Sommers, Pastor; Stock, Michael Friedrich; —

Keyl; Bertha Susanne; 18-Dec-61; 29-Dec-61; Ernst Gerhard Wilhelm; Leipzig; Vogel, Sophie Anna; —; Drige, Gesine Marianne; Lettmade, Wilhelm; Rudolph, Adelheid Mathilde; —

Keyl; Caroline Emilie; 20-Feb-51; 27-Feb-51; Ernst Gerhard Wilhelm; —; Vogel, Amalie Sohpie; —; Weidner, Mrs.; Waltjen, Mrs. Georg; Nolting, Bertha; twin

Keyl; Clara Clementine; 3-Sep-64; 17-Sep-64; Rev. Ernst Gerhard Wilhelm; Leipzig; Vogel, Sophie Amalie; Ezbau, Sachsen; Mieth, Karoline; Ruppel, Johann; Lange, Louise; —

Keyl; Daniel Ernst; 14-Aug-57; 23-Aug-57; Ernst Gerhard Wilhelm; —; Vogel, Sophia Amalie; —; Habermehl, Heinr.; Briel, Katharina; Vogel, Emil; —

Keyl; Emma Amalia; 10-Sep-59; 25-Sep-59; Ernst Gerhard Wilhelm; —; Vogel, Sophia Amalia; —; Siegel, Christina; Hampe, Franz; Prufer, Louise; —

Keyl; Hermann Wilhelm; 20-Feb-51; 27-Feb-51; Ernst Gerhard Wilhelm; —; Vogel, Amalie Sophie; —; Beck, Anna Magdalena; Purner, Joh. Andreas; Biehler, Franz; twin

Keyl; Karl August Gerhard; 4-Sep-66; 16-Sep-66; Ernst Gerhard Wilhelm; Leipzig; Vogel, Sophie Amalie; Eibau, Sachsen; Sturken, Rev. Klaus; Ruppel, Emilie Selma; Stellevorbrod, Dora; —

Keyl; Selma Wilhelmine; 28-Oct-55; 4-Nov-55; Ernst Gerhard Wilhelm; Leipzid, Sachsen; Vogel, Sophia Amalia; —; Vogel, Friedrich Wilhelm; Horn, Philippine; Winter, Andreas; child died

Kiefer; Heinrich; 17-Sep-37; 1-Oct-37; Heinrich; —; Wenz, Christine; —; —; —; —; —

Surname Father; Child's Given Name; Birth Date; Baptismal Date; Father's Given Name; Father's Place of Birth; Mother's Surname and Given Name; Mother's Place of Birth; Witness 1 Surname and Given Name; Witness 2 Surname and Given Name; Witness 3 Surname and Given Name; Comments

Kiefer; Kunigunde; 7-Oct-43; 12-Nov-43; Heinrich; —; Schilling, Barb.; —; —; —; —; —

Kimmet; Maria Barbara; 13-Jan-48; 6-Feb-48; Caspar; Diegersheim, Wurzbeurg; Pitzinger, Dorothea; Neustadt, Reuss, Baiern; Pitzinger, Barbara; —; —; —

Kimpel; Anna Margaretha Emilie; 2-Nov-50; 17-Nov-50; Georg; Meiningen, Sachsen Meiningen; Lind, Elisabeth; —; Kimpel, Margaretha; —; —; 2 child

Kirchmeier; Christina Sophia; 15-May-50; 16-May-50; Johann Michael; Deipoldsberg, Nurnberg, Bayern; Thiergartner, Margaretha; Neustadt a.A., Bayern; Neifenbacher, Friedrich; —; —; wit from Leiden, Bayern

Kirchmeyer; Christine Sophia; 17-Jun-49; 21-Jul-49; Johann Michael; Diepholzberg, Markelbach; Thiergert, Margareth; Langenfeld, Markbigardt, Baiern; Reichenbach, Friedrich; Reichenbach, Christine Sophia; —; —

Kister; Christian Wilh.; 13-Apr-38; 14-Oct-38; Ludwig; —; Möller, Friedrieke; —; —; —; —; —

Kister; Ludwig; 11-Aug-45; 12-Nov-45; Ludwig; Breitenbach, Schwarzburg, Sondershausen; Muller, Friderike; Neuhaus, Schwarzburg, Rudolstadt; Ulrich, Wilhelm; —; —; —

Kistner; Margaretha Wilh.; 28-Nov-37; 27-Dec-37; Johann Christoph; —; Gotter, Marg.; —; —; —; —; —

Klärlein; Gustav Adolph; 30-Jun-41; 4-Jul-41; Johann L.; —; Schmidt, Elisab.; —; —; —; —; —

Klärlein; Johann Bernh.; 24-Mar-37; 22-Apr-37; Johann; —; Schmidt, Susanne; —; —; —; —; —

Klein; Elisabeth; 13-Aug-44; 6-Oct-44; Wilhelm; —; Neibert, Kathr.; —; —; —; —; —

Klein; Friedrich Wilhelm; 21-Oct-48; 19-Nov-48; Wilhelm; Bernsburg, Alsfeld, Hessen; Neibert, Catharine; Dittlofsroth, Baiern; Feige, Friedrich; Kramer, Catharine; —; child died

Klein; Georg Jacob; 17-Nov-38; 3-Mar-39; Friedr.; —; Lieblich, Anna R.; —; —; —; —; —

Klein; Margaretha; 8-Oct-46; 15-Nov-46; Eilhwlm; Bernsberg, Hessen; Neubert, Cath.; Detlevsroth bei Wurzburg, Baiern; Geisel, Margarethe; —; —; —

Klein; Sahra Elisab.; 13-Aug-40; 12-Jan-41; Friedrich; —; Wamsley, Elisab.; —; —; —; —; —

Kleinle; Georg Friederich; 23-May-46; 1-Oct-46; Georg Friederich; Wilferdingen, Dollach, Badenr; Siebler, Catharine; Wilferdingen, Dollach, Baden; —; —; —; —

Kleinle; Johann Heinrich; 20-Dec-40; 10-Jan-41; Michael; —; Heinmuller, Kathr.; —; —; —; —; —

Kleinle; Karl; 22-Dec-42; 29-Jan-43; Michael; —; Heinmuller, Katharine; —; —; —; —; —

Kleinle; Luise; 1-Nov-42; 25-Dec-42; Friedrich; —; Siebel, Kathr.; —; —; —; —; —

Kleinle; Maria; 11-Jan-45; 13-Apr-45; Georg Friedrich; Wilferdingen, Baden; Sieble, Cath.; Wilferdingen, Baden; Muller, David; Kramer, Anna Maria; —; —

Klemsen; Eduard Heinrich; 6-Oct-41; 17-Nov-41; Eduard; —; Schmidt, Elisab.; —; —; —; —; —

Klenke; Bertha Karolina; 8-Mar-58; 4-Apr-58; Philipp; Kkurhessen; Brauer, Sophia; —; Schaumloffel, Karoline; Brauer, Karoline; —; —

Klenke; Heinrich Wilhelm Friedrich; 11-Jun-62; 29-Jun-62; Philipp; Altendorf, Kurhessen; Brauer, Sophie; —; Schaumlossel, Wilhelm; Brauer, Heinrich; Spielmann, Frdch.; —

Kleppesch; Anna Maria Martha; 7-Mar-55; 11-Mar-55; Carl Friedrich; Radeberg, Sachsen; Komfortch, Catharine; —; Nolting, Bertha; Purner, Joh. Andreas; Vogel, Catharina; —

Kleppesch; Konstantin Theodor; 15-Sep-57; —; Karl Friedrich; Radeberg, Sachsen; Kamhart, Katharina; —; Hampe, Franz; Imwalde, Katharina; Thiemeyer, Friedrich; —

Kleppisch; Carl Daniel; 28-Sep-50; 10-Oct-50; Friedrich August; Radeberg, Sachsen; Weinhardt, Susanne Margarethe; —; parents, ; —; —; 5 child, 3 son

Kleppisch; Catharina Rosine Elisabeth; 10-Jul-52; 18-Jul-52; Carl Friedrich; Radeberg, Sachsen; Kompfert, Catharina; —;

Imwalde, Catharine; Imwalde, Joh. Hermann; Keyl, Amalie Sophie; —

Kleppisch; Daniel Friedrich; 29-Aug-57; 29-Aug-57; Frdch. Aug.; Radeberg, Sachsen; Weinhardt, Susanna; —; parents, ; —; —; emergency baptism

Kleppisch; Friedrich Theodor; 15-Jan-50; 20-Jan-50; Carl Friedrich; Radeberg bei Dresden, Sachsen; Comfort, Catharine; Baltimore; Kleppisch, August Friedrich; —; —; —

Kleppisch; Georg Andreas; 8-Mar-45; 9-Jun-45; Carl Friederich; Radeberg, Sachsen; Comfort, Catharina; Baltimore; —; —; —; —

Kleppisch; Johann Eduard; 28-Oct-47; 17-Dec-47; Carl Friedrich; Radeberg, Sachsen; Comfort, Catharine; Baltimore; —; —; —; —

Kleppisch; Johann Heinrich; 17-Jun-48; 20-Dec-48; August; Radeberg bei Dresden; Meinhardt, Susanne; Baltimore; —; —; —; —

Kleppisch; Maria Katharina; 8-Jul-53; 19-Jul-53; Friedr. Aug.; Rodeberg, Sachsen; Weinhardt, Susanna; —; Kleppisch, Friedr. Aug.; —; —; father is witness

Kleppisch; Samuel Stephanus; 5-Oct-59; 5-Oct-59; August Friedrich; Radeberg, Sachsen; Weinhardth, Susanna Margaretha; —; —; —; —; emergency baptism

Kleppitsch; Friedrich Ernst; 28-Oct-43; 27-Oct-44; Friedrich Aug.; —; Weinhard, Susanne; —; —; —; —; —

Kleppitsch; Heinrich Michael; 24-Jun-40; 2-Feb-41; Karl Fr.; —; Comfort, Kathr.; —; —; —; —; —

Kleppitsch; Karl Samuel; 11-Dec-38; 16-Jun-39; Karl; —; Comfort, Katharina; —; —; —; —; —

Kleppitsch; Martin Luther; 23-Mar-43; 30-Nov-43; Karl Friedr.; —; Comfort, Kathr.; —; —; —; —; —

Kleppitsch; Susanne Luise; 24-Oct-41; 1-May-42; Friedr.; —; Weinhard, Susanne; —; —; —; —; —

Kleppitsch; Wilhelm August; 14-Dec-38; 7-Jul-39; Friedr. Aug.; —; Weinhard, Susanne M.; —; —; —; —; —

Surname Father; Child's Given Name; Birth Date; Baptismal Date; Father's Given Name; Father's Place of Birth; Mother's Surname and Given Name; Mother's Place of Birth; Witness 1 Surname and Given Name; Witness 2 Surname and Given Name; Witness 3 Surname and Given Name; Comments

Kling; Katharine Elise Mathilde; 21-Aug-60; 2-Sep-60; Philipp; Altendorf, Hessen; Brauer, Sophie; —; Broning, Katharine; Hederich, Marie; —; —

Klingelhofer; Maria Katharine Margarethe; 2-Dec-63; 6-Dec-63; Wilhelm; Rosenthal, Kurhessen; Weiss, Barbara; Beigheim, Baiern; Momberger, Georg; Regener, Anna Katharina; —; emergency baptism

Klingelhofer; Marie Katharine Gertrud; 4-Jan-62; 19-Jan-62; Wilhelm; Rosenthal, Kurhessen; Rossel, Wilhelmine; —; Momberger, Maria; Rossele, Johannes; Regener, Katharine; —

Klingenberg; August; 24-Apr-49; 23-Sep-49; Luis; Stadtoldendorf, Braunscweig; Stamuth, Friederike; Stadtoldendorf, Braunschweig; Peineke, August; —; —; —

Klingler; Johann Jakob Daniel; 12-Mar-55; 18-Mar-55; Jakob; Hohenacker, Wurttemberg; Schwartz, Caroline; —; Schwartz, Daniel; —; —; —

Klinkmeier; [--?--]; 15-Jul-53; —; Aug.; Liebenau, Hannover; , ; —; —; —; —; stillborn

Klinkmeier; Adelheid Katharine Wilhelmine; 20-Aug-65; 10-Sep-65; Wilhelm; Liebenau, Hannover; Thiemeyer, Marie; Engter, Hannover; Meier, Adelheid; Schulz, Gottlieb; Holtgrefe, Katharine; —

Klinkmeier; Anna Henriette Eleonore; 20-Jun-63; 5-Jul-63; Wilhelm; Liebenau, Hannover; Thiemeyer, Maria; Baltimore; Flauaus, Heinrich; Schulz, Eleonore; Hillgartner, Anna; —

Klinkmeier; Christian Heinrich Wilhelm; 2-Nov-58; 14-Nov-58; Heinr. August; Liebenau, Hannover; Fredeking, Friederike; —; Klinkmeier, Wilhelm; Schulz, Gottlieb; Hucksol, Ernst; —

Klinkmeier; Friedrich Wilhelm Heinrich; 30-Jan-55; 4-Feb-55; Heinrich; Liebenau, Hannover; Fredeking, Friederike; —; Schultz, Ferdinand; Heyse, Wilh.; Meier, Christian; —

Klinkmeier; Maria Anna Louise; 12-Nov-59; 27-Nov-59; Wilhelm; Liebenau, Hannover; Thiemeyer, Maria; —; Thiemeyer, Mariea; Thiemeyer, Louis; Schneider, Anna; —

Klinkmeier; Maria Friedericka Charlotta; 3-Nov-57; 15-Nov-57; Wilhelm; Liebenau, Hannover; Thiemeyer, Maria; —;

Surname Father; Child's Given Name; Birth Date; Baptismal Date; Father's Given Name; Father's Place of Birth; Mother's Surname and Given Name; Mother's Place of Birth; Witness 1 Surname and Given Name; Witness 2 Surname and Given Name; Witness 3 Surname and Given Name; Comments

Thiemeyer, Joh. Heinr.; Thiemeyer, Charlotta; Klinkmeier, Friedericka; —

Klinkmeier; Maria Karolina Sophia; 26-Jan-57; 8-Feb-57; Aug.; Liebenau, Hannover; Fredeking, Friedericka; —; Heyse, Maria; Klinkmeier, Maria; Schulz, Sophia; —

Klinkmeier; Marie Henriette Charlotte; 15-Dec-61; 29-Dec-61; Wilhelm; Liebenau,Hannover; Thiemeyer, Maria Elisabeth; —; Thiemeyer, Henriette Charlotte; Morgenstroh, Marie Charlotte; Heyse, Marie; —

Klommann; Paul Cornelius Noabuarn; 22-Nov-52; 12-Dec-52; Louis; Gottingen, Hannover; Thomas, Maria; —; Thomas, Pauline; —; —; —

Klössel; Karl; 16-Oct-44; 15-Dec-44; Johann; —; Hoffmann, Barbara; —; —; —; —; —

Knapp; Georg Ludwig; 4-Jul-41; 8-Aug-41; Johann; —; Horn, Regine; —; —; —; —; —

Knapp; Wihlelm; 3-Dec-44; 15-Dec-44; Wilhelm; —; Ruhl, Elisabeth; —; —; —; —; —

Knauer; Johann Ludwig; 25-Aug-43; 1-Oct-43; Johann G.; —; Friedlein, Barb.; —; —; —; —; —

Knauer; Johann Wilh.; 16-Aug-41; 29-Aug-41; Georg; —; Voglein, Barb.; —; —; —; —; —

Knell; Johann Heinrich; 26-Oct-38; 16-Feb-39; Johann; —; Kräger, Marianne; —; —; —; —; —

Knosp; Johann Anton; 6-Apr-45; 2-Jun-45; Joseph; Orlohen, Baden (?); Schneider, Maria; Kirn, Neupreussen; —; —; —; —

Knosp; Luise Emilie; 27-Sep-44; 2-Jun-45; Joseph; Orlohen, Baden (?); Schneider, Maria; Kirn, Neupreussen; Eggers, Dorothea; —; —; —

Koch; Christian Heinrich; 25-Dec-44; 28-Dec-44; Ludwig; —; Deininger, Dorothea; —; —; —; —; —

Koch; Christiane Elisab.; 4-Dec-39; 25-Dec-39; Ludwig; —; Deiminger, Dorothea; —; —; —; —; —

Koch; Christoph August; 16-Jun-37; 6-Aug-37; Friedrich; —; Gedlach, Elisab.; —; —; —; —; —

Surname Father; Child's Given Name; Birth Date; Baptismal Date; Father's Given Name; Father's Place of Birth; Mother's Surname and Given Name; Mother's Place of Birth; Witness 1 Surname and Given Name; Witness 2 Surname and Given Name; Witness 3 Surname and Given Name; Comments

Koch; Jacob Friedrich; 19-May-42; 12-Jun-42; Ludwig; —; Deininger, Dorothea; —; —; —; —; —

Koch; Johann Philipp Adam; 10-Jul-46; 16-Aug-46; Adam; Wallenhausen, Nidda, Hessen; Runk [Reuk], Viktoria; Nidda; Schmidt, Philipp; Preusch, Adam; —; —

Koch; Luise Kathrine; 8-Dec-37; 4-Feb-38; Ludiwg; —; Feimyer, Dorothea; —; —; —; —; —

Kohl; Anna Charlotte; 26-Oct-66; 25-Nov-66; Philipp; Konig, Hessen; Weckesser, Anna Elisabeth; Baltimore; Funk, Charlotte; —; —; —

Kohl; Johannes; 14-Jul-45; 17-Aug-45; Philipp; Bauerhausen bei Frankfurth a.M.; Germuth, Margaretha; Essig, Baiern; Burger, Joh.; —; —; wit from Lauffen

Kohlus; Andreas; 19-Sep-39; 13-Oct-39; Johann Jacob; —; Reichenbacher, Marg.; —; —; —; —; —

Köhnlein; Dorothea; 13-Oct-39; 20-Oct-39; Georg M.; —; Busch, Rosine; —; —; —; —; —

Kohrs; Heinrich Friederich Wilhelm; 27-Dec-45; 23-Aug-46; Wilhelm; —; Reuter, Sophie Luise; Seelenfeld, Minden, Preussen; Reuter, Friedrich; —; —; illegitimate

Kolb; Jacob Franz; 3-Sep-39; 8-Sep-39; Jacob; —; Stumpf, Luise; —; —; —; —; —

Kolb; Johann Georg; 27-Feb-42; 17-Apr-42; Johann; —; Balz, Anna Elisab.; —; —; —; —; —

Kolb; Karoline; 23-Apr-39; 1-Mar-40; Friedrich; —; Schönthaler, Karoline; —; —; —; —; —

Kolthof; Johann Friedrich Wilhelm; 6-Jul-64; 15-Jul-64; Friedrich Wilhelm; Wechte, Preussen; Bohn, Henriette; Lebern, Preussen; Ruppel, Johann; Bohn, Wilhelmine; —; —

Kommer; [--?--]; 8-May-53; —; Wilhelm; Rottheim, Hessen; , ; —; —; —; —; stillborn

Kommer; Elisabeth; 24-Jan-59; 6-Feb-59; Wilhelm; Rodtheim, Hessen; Reuber, Dorothea; —; Schwarz, Elisabeth; —; —; —

Kommer; Karoline Katharine; 2-Dec-57; 13-Dec-57; Wilhelm; Rotheim, Hessen; Reuber, Dorothea; —; Boppler, Katharina; Eggers, Karoline Katharine; —; —

Surname Father; Child's Given Name; Birth Date; Baptismal Date; Father's Given Name; Father's Place of Birth; Mother's Surname and Given Name; Mother's Place of Birth; Witness 1 Surname and Given Name; Witness 2 Surname and Given Name; Witness 3 Surname and Given Name; Comments

König; Christine Kathr.; 7-Oct-44; 27-Oct-44; Jacob; —; Gais, Elisab.; —; —; —; —; —

König; Elisabeth Regina; 25-Jul-42; 14-Aug-42; Jacob; —; Gais, Elisab.; —; —; —; —; —

König; Johanne Pauline; 6-Mar-47; 5-Apr-47; Jakob Friedrich; Dobel, Wurttemberg; Gais, Elisabeth; Schmalwasser, Baiern; Riehl, Paul; Riehl, Johanne Pauline; —; —

König; Karl Friedr.; 20-Feb-40; 8-Mar-40; Jacob; —; Kayser, Elisab.; —; —; —; —; —

Kopmeyer; Anna Maria Elisab.; 6-Aug-41; 8-Aug-41; Joh. Wilh.; —; Lubben, Anna M.; —; —; —; —; —

Korfhagen; Herrmann Heinrich; 30-Dec-45; 15-Feb-46; Gustav Friedrich; Bennighausen, Minden, Preussen; Doklor, Clara Elisabeth; Kirchspiel, Buur, Melle, Preussen; Donnettel, Herrmann Heinrich; —; —; —

Körner; Herrmann Theodor; 28-Dec-45; 1-Feb-46; Johann; Nürnberg, Baiern; Kreutzer, Elisabeth; Nürnberg, Baiern; Herrmann, Konrad; —; —; —

Korthage; Anna Kathr. Wilh. Charl.; 16-Sep-42; 14-Oct-42; Gustav Fr.; —; Doktars, Clara E.; —; —; —; —; —

Koster; johan Heinrich Ferdinand; 18-Sep-55; 30-Sep-55; Joh. Heinr. Ferdinand; Rehe, Hanover; Schnitker, Louise; —; Burmann, Heinr.; Burmann, Elisabeth; Schnitker, Joh. Friedrich; child died

Kothe; Ferdinand Andreas; 25-May-54; 11-Jun-54; Kasten; Weikershausen, Hannover; Siegmund, Christiane; —; Germuth, Andreas; Siegmund, Ferdinand; —; —

Kraft; Elisabeth; 12-Aug-45; 9-Nov-45; Christian; Bleichenbach, Hessen; Fierdanz, Luise; Bleichenbach, Hessen; List, Elisabeth; —; —

Kraft; Ludwig; 29-Aug-38; 9-Sep-38; Friedrich; —; Samstädt, Elisab.; —; —; —; —

Kramer; Christian; 17-Oct-37; 7-Jan-38; Johann; —; Schleifer, Christiane; —; —; —; —

Kramer; Elisabeth Karoline; 28-Jun-43; 13-Aug-43; Heinr.; —; Loos, Elisab.; —; —; —; —

Surname Father; Child's Given Name; Birth Date; Baptismal Date; Father's Given Name; Father's Place of Birth; Mother's Surname and Given Name; Mother's Place of Birth; Witness 1 Surname and Given Name; Witness 2 Surname and Given Name; Witness 3 Surname and Given Name; Comments

Kramer; Heinrich; 29-Oct-42; 1-Jan-43; Johann; —; Schleicher, Christine; —; —; —; —

Kramer; Wilhelm; 19-Oct-41; 31-Oct-41; Johann; —; Schleicher, Christine; —; —; —; —

Kratzenstein; Johannette Wilhelmine; 7-Mar-47; 24-May-47; Peter; Königstein, Nassau; Fischer, Margaretha; Umstadt, Hessen; French, Wilhelmine; —; —

Kraus; Johann Georg Gottfried; 27-May-57; 1-Jun-57; Christoph; Langensteinach, Baiern; Scheer, Magdalena; —; Schmidt, Christiana; Schimpf, Gottfried; Kraus, Georg

Kraus; Katharina Rosine Augusta; 14-Jun-58; 20-Jun-58; Christoph; Langensteinach, Baiern; Scherr, Magdalena; —; Schimpf, Augusta; Schmidt, Georg; Kraus, Rosina

Krauskopf; Emilie; 13-May-42; 17-Jul-42; Gottfried; —; Schneider, Kathr.; —; —; —; —

Krauskopf; Peter; 8-Jul-40; 9-Aug-40; Gottfried; —; Schneider, Kathr.; —; —; —; —

Kreitmann; Johann Wilhelm; 20-Sep-41; 24-Nov-41; Jacob; —; Herbst, Anna; —; —; —; —

Krell; Georg Konrad; 10-Dec-62; 11-Jan-63; Johann Weigand; Bleichenbach, Hessen; Muller, Anna Friederike; Behrungen, Sachsen Meiningen; Repp, Konrad; Billmann, Georg; —

Krell; Johann Gottlieb Christian; 9-Apr-65; 23-Apr-65; Weiland; Bleichenbach, Hessen; Hartmann, Friedrike; Harzostch, Sacshen; Schmidt, Christian; Kuhnert, Gottlieb; Krell, Elisabeth

Kreutzer; Amalia Barbara; 28-Jul-49; 2-Sep-49; Georg; Leunerstadt, Oberfrancken; Kaiser, Sabina; Dispek, Mittelfrancken; Seitz, Amalia Barbara; —; —

Kreutzer; Friederike; 13-Feb-46; 13-Apr-46; Heinrich; Marburg, Kurhessen; Daubert, Margaretha; Marburg, Kurhessen; Dieterich, Friederike; —; —

Krieger; Maria Elisab.; 18-Jan-39; 11-Aug-39; Georg W.; —; Muller, Magdalene; —; —; —; —; —

Krome; Elisabeth; 22-May-39; 3-Jun-39; Johann; —; Muller, Karoline H.; —; —; —; —; —

Surname Father; Child's Given Name; Birth Date; Baptismal Date; Father's Given Name; Father's Place of Birth; Mother's Surname and Given Name; Mother's Place of Birth; Witness 1 Surname and Given Name; Witness 2 Surname and Given Name; Witness 3 Surname and Given Name; Comments

Krome; Johanne Marg.; 22-May-39; 3-Jun-39; Johann; —; Muller, Karoline H.; —; —; —; —; —

Kroner; Karoline; 20-Jan-42; 20-Feb-42; Georg Fr.; —; Seidler, Karoline; —; —; —; —; —

Kröner; Elisabeth Salome; 3-Jul-37; 9-Jul-37; Georg Fr.; —; Seidel, Karoline; —; —; —; —; —

Kröner; Heinrich; 24-Oct-39; 17-Nov-39; Friedrich; —; Seidler, Barbara; —; —; —; —; —

Kröner; Johann Friedrich; 23-Oct-45; 18-Jan-46; Georg Friedrich; Wilferdingen, Baden; Seidel, Caroline; Hinterweidenthal, Baiern; Dölfeld, Friedrich; Kunkel, Conr.; Schillinger, Heinrich; —

Kröner; Katharina Franziska; 17-Oct-43; 29-Oct-43; Friedr.; —; Seidel, Karoline; —; —; —; —; —

Krose; Sophie Friedrieke; 31-Mar-38; 5-Jun-38; Rodewald; —; Gert, Sophie; —; —; —; —; —

Krotel; Therese Auguste Elisabeth; 5-Mar-60; 18-Mar-60; Valentin; Strebendorf, Hessen; Merkel, Therese; Oberbrachthal, Hessen; Ruppel, Elisabeth; Schimpf, Auguste; —; probably illegitimate

Kugel; Friedrich; 19-Nov-40; 25-Dec-40; Konrad; —; Senbach, Kathr.; —; —; —; —; —

Kuhler; Johann Adam Karl; 27-Sep-44; 3-Nov-44; Jacob; —; Kienzle, Wilhelmine; —; —; —; —; —

Kuhlmann; Anna Maria Charlotte; 2-Feb-51; 21-Apr-51; Joh. Frd. Wilh.; Wedern, Preussen; Koch, Henriette; —; Koch, Anna Marie Charlotte; —; —; —

Kuhlmann; Johann Karl; 9-Jul-64; 24-Jul-64; Wilhelm; Wedern, Preussen; Koch, Henriette; —; Ruppel, Johann; Russel, Karl; —; —

Kuhlmann; Katharine Elisabeth Margarethe; 16-Apr-62; 27-Apr-62; Wilhelm; Weden, Preussen; Koch, Henriette; —; Kunker, Katharine; Schwartz, Donie; Siegel, Margaretha; —

Kuhn; Catharina; 12-Dec-45; 28-Dec-45; Johann; Hersbruck, Baiern; Humadiem, Barbara; Betzenstein, Baiern; Botzner, Cath.; —; —; —

Surname Father; Child's Given Name; Birth Date; Baptismal Date; Father's Given Name; Father's Place of Birth; Mother's Surname and Given Name; Mother's Place of Birth; Witness 1 Surname and Given Name; Witness 2 Surname and Given Name; Witness 3 Surname and Given Name; Comments

Kuhner; Daniel Heinrich Johann; 17-Nov-66; 2-Dec-66; Gottlieb; Oppenweiler, Wuerttemberg; Komm, Karoline; Grabow, Preussen; Schwartz, Daniel; Fuchs, Heinrich; Wachsmann, Johann Gottlieb; —

Kuhnert; Heinrich Gottlieb; 8-Sep-62; 14-Sep-62; Gottfried; Oppenweileg, Wurttemberg; Komen, Karoline; —; Repp, Heinrich; Walther, Heinrich; Krell, Elisabeth; —

Kuhnert; Johann Wilhelm Ludwig; 6-Feb-61; 17-Feb-61; Gottlieb; Oppenweiler, Wurttemberg; Kamen, Karoline; —; Seibel, Joh.; Tormelen, Wilhelm; —; —

Kuhnert; Karoline Marie Christine; 13-Aug-64; 21-Aug-64; Gottlieb; Oppenweiler, Wurttemberg; Löuis, Karoline; Dornow, Pommern; Tormelen, Christine; Schmidt, Karoline; Einwachter, Marie Katharine; —

Kumm; Valentin; 18-Jun-41; 8-Jul-41; Jacob; —; Schwarz, Elisab.; —; —; —; —; —

Kummerer; Johann Heinrich; 2-Aug-43; 2-Sep-43; Johann Bernh.; —; Schiessler, Elisab.; —; —; —; —; —

Kunkel; Johann; 30-Oct-42; 25-Dec-42; Conrad; —; Sebach, Kathr.; —; —; —; —; —

Kunkel; Katharine; 30-Aug-44; 15-Sep-44; Conrad; —; Sebach, Kathr.; —; —; —; —; —

Kunker; [blank]; 14-Jan-57; 19-Jan-57; Joh. Heinr.; Husede, Hannover; Brockmeier, Katharina; —; —; —; —; emergency baptism

Kunker; Anna Maria Louise; 19-Jul-54; 30-Jul-54; Joh. Heinr.; Kespilessen, Hannover; Brockmeier, Catharine; —; Brockmeier, Anna Maria Elise; —; —; —

Kunker; Friedrich Wilhelm; 29-Jun-60; 8-Jul-60; Johann Heinrich; Husede, Hannover; Brockmeier, Katharine; —; Sieck, Adolph Friedrich; Kunker, Johann Heinrich; —; —

Kunker; Heinrich Friedrich; 18-Jan-58; 24-Jan-58; Johann Heinrich; husede Hannover; Brockmeier, Katharine; —; Kastens, Heinrich; Radecka, Wilhelmina; —; —

Surname Father; Child's Given Name; Birth Date; Baptismal Date; Father's Given Name; Father's Place of Birth; Mother's Surname and Given Name; Mother's Place of Birth; Witness 1 Surname and Given Name; Witness 2 Surname and Given Name; Witness 3 Surname and Given Name; Comments

Kunker; Johann Heinrich; 13-Jan-52; 1-Feb-52; Joh. Heinr.; Husite, Hannover; Brockmeyer, Catharine Wilhelmine; —; Sieck, Joh. Heinr.; —; —; —

Kunker; Katharine Wilhelmine; 15-Dec-64; 25-Dec-64; Johann Heinrich; Husede, Hannover; Brockmeier, Katharine; Bargolthausen, Preussen; Kasten, Marie Elsabein; Dankmeier, Wilhelmine; Ortmann, Heinr.; —

Kunker; Marie Wilhelmine Elisabeth; 19-Sep-62; 28-Sep-62; Johann Heinrich; Husede, Hannover; Brockmeier, Katharine; —; Karstens, Marie; Ortmann, Marie Elisabeth; Dankmeier, Wilhelmine; —

Kunker; stillborn child; 15-Mar-67; —; Joh. Heinrich; Huserde, Hannover; Brockmeier, Katharine; Bargolts, Sachsen Preussen; —; —; —; —

Kurtz; Sophia Karolina Louise; 21-Jul-59; 25-Sep-59; Jakob; Heimbuchrathal, Baiern; Diroff, Helena; —; Klenke, Sophia; Brauer, Karoline; —

Kusmaul; Johann; 31-Jan-44; 8-Apr-44; Lorenz; —; Klein, Sophie; —; —; —; —

Kusmaul; Karoline; 3-Apr-41; 19-Sep-41; Lorenz; —; Klein, Sophie; —; —; —; —

Kusmaul; Luise; 28-Dec-36; 14-May-37; Lorenz; —; Klein, Sophia; —; —; —; —

Kusmaul; Wilhelm Friedr.; 9-Jan-39; 4-Aug-39; Lorenz; —; Klein, Sophia.; —; —; —; —

Labahn; Heinrich Ludwig Julius; 20-Oct-66; 17-Nov-66; Heinrich; Liebenau, Hannover; Bothe, Karoline; Engter, Hannover; Kronenberg, Heinrich; Bothe, Ludwig; Bothe, Julius

Labahn; Marie Charlotte Louise; 4-Jan-60; 22-Jan-60; Karl Wilhelm Heinrich; Liebenau, Hannover; Bode, Elise Karoline; —; Thiemeyer, Charlotte; Schulz, Eleonore; Schulz, Louise

Labahn; Marie Louise Regine; 3-Aug-64; 21-Aug-64; Heinrich; Liebenau, Hannover; Bothe, Karoline; Engter, Hannover; Klinkmeier, Marie; Bothe, Louise; Bothe, Anna Marie Regine

Laib; Christina Susanne; 25-Dec-37; 22-Mar-38; Christian; —; Grafe, Sybille; —; —; —; —

Surname Father; Child's Given Name; Birth Date; Baptismal Date; Father's Given Name; Father's Place of Birth; Mother's Surname and Given Name; Mother's Place of Birth; Witness 1 Surname and Given Name; Witness 2 Surname and Given Name; Witness 3 Surname and Given Name; Comments

Laib; Emilie Elisab.; 6-Jul-42; 26-Jul-42; Johann; —; Graf, Sybille; —; —; —; —

Laib; Karl Friedrich; 9-Jun-44; 17-Oct-44; Johann; —; Graf, Sibille; —; —; —; —

Laib; Luise Caroline; 7-Apr-46; 1-Dec-46; Johann Christian; Bergstall, Marbach, Wurttemberg; Graff, Caroline; Rupper bei Carlsruhe, Baden; Laib, Christine; —; —

Laib; Luise Karoline; 11-Oct-39; 1-Dec-39; Christian; —; Graf, Sybille; —; —; —; —

Lais; Maria Katharina; 19-Jan-65; 29-Jan-65; Karl; Lisberg, Hessen; Petri, Margaretha; Niedersema, Hessen; Einwachter, Jr., Alexander; Walther, Marie; Spilmann, Marie

Lais [?]; Karolina Henriette; 15-Jul-67; 28-Jul-67; Karl; Lisberg, Hessen; Petri, Margaretha; Nied..., Hessen; Karl, Karoline; Waltjen, Heinrich; —

Lammer; Georg Heinrich; 16-Apr-61; 5-May-61; Wilhelm; Radtheim, Hessen; Reuber, Dorothea; —; Boppler, Heinrich; —; —

Lang; Elisabeth; 3-Jun-42; 4-Sep-42; Johann; —; Knapp, Anna Kathr.; —; —; —; —; —

Lang; Friedrich Wilhelm; 17-Aug-55; 26-Aug-55; Carl; Gera, Reuss; Muhly, Caroline; —; Muhly, Friedrich; —; —; —

Lang; Johanne Christiane; 15-Mar-45; 10-Oct-45; Johann; Wiesenfeld, Marburg, Hessen Cassel; Töhler, Maria; Kirchspiel, Badbergen, Hannover; —; —; —; —

Lang; Wilhelm; 15-Mar-44; 26-May-44; Sebastian; —; Knapp, Kathr.; —; —; —; —; —

Lange; Anna Henriette Auguste; 19-May-65; 28-May-65; Bernhart; Hosenburen bei Bremen; Lohmuller, Louise Wilhelmine Auguste; Ideweg, Hessen; Lohmuller, Anna Katharina; Lohmuller, Heinrich; Lange, Katharina; —

Lange; Christian Wilhelm; 31-Dec-66; 20-Jan-67; Johann Karl; Gera, Kurhessen; Muhly, Karoline; Elberfeld, Preussen; Muhly, Christian; Bauer, Sarah; —; —

Surname Father; Child's Given Name; Birth Date; Baptismal Date; Father's Given Name; Father's Place of Birth; Mother's Surname and Given Name; Mother's Place of Birth; Witness 1 Surname and Given Name; Witness 2 Surname and Given Name; Witness 3 Surname and Given Name; Comments

Lange; Emilie Louise; 15-Nov-64; 4-Dec-64; Johann Karl; Gera, Furst. Rausch.; Muhly, Karoline Louise; Elberfeld, Preussen; Lange, Emilie; Lange, Gustave; Bauer, Elisabeth; —

Lange; Friedrich Wilhelm; 17-Jul-50; 21-Jul-50; Rudolph; Goslar, Hannover; Reutz, Gottlobine; —; Sorg, Wilhelm; —; —; 1 child

Lange; Georg Eberhard; 19-May-57; 31-May-57; Joh.; Gera, Reuss; Muhly, Karoline; —; Wiessner, Eberhard; Repp, Katharina; Muhly, Eberhard; —

Lange; Gesine Katharine Louise; 27-Nov-59; 11-Dec-59; Borgert; Hasenburrn; Lohmuller, Auguste Wilhelmine Louise; —; Waltjen, Marie; Schulz, Louise; —; —

Lange; Heinrich; 19-Nov-51; 27-Feb-52; Rudolph; Goslar, Hannover; Reutz, Gottliebine; —; Reutz, Helene; —; —; —

Lange; Heinrich Jakob; 9-Sep-58; 26-Sep-58; Johann Karl; Gera, Reuss; Muhly, Karoline; —; Repp, Heinr.; Muhly, Hermann; Rein, Katharine; —

Lange; Johann Eberhard; 5-Aug-62; 17-Aug-62; Karl; Gera, Forsth. Reuss; Muhly, Karoline; —; Muhly, Eberhard; Romester, Johann; —; —

Lange; Johann Wilhelm Heinrich; 4-Jun-60; 24-Jun-60; Johann; Gera, Reuss; Muhly, Karoline; —; Bertram, Wilhelm; Muhly, Louise; Aichele, Johannes; —

Lange; Karl Heinrich Gustav; 15-Jan-65; 29-Jan-65; Gustav; Gera, Furs. Rau.; Trager, Emilie; Baltimore; Lange, Karl; Trager, Heinr.; Hampe, Wilhelmine; —

Lange; Karl Konrad; 29-Jul-53; 7-Aug-53; Karl; Gera, Sachsen Altenburg; Muhly, Maria Karoline; —; Muhly, Konrad; Einwachter, Elisabeth; —; —

Lange; Karoline Louise; 15-Nov-51; 23-Nov-51; Joh. Karl; Gera, Sachsen Altenburg; Muhly, Karoline; —; Muhly, Karoline Louise; —; —; —

Langkam; Friedrich Wilh.; 27-Oct-43; 24-Nov-43; Johann; —; Otto, Barb. Elisab.; —; —; —; —; —

Langschmidt; Adolph August Hermann; 25-Jul-63; 2-Aug-63; Friedrich Wilhelm; Neuenkirchen, Hannover; Schwenker,

Henriette Katharine; —; Gail, Emil Ludwig Adolph; Lettmade, Karl Augst; —; —

Langschmidt; Emma Karoline Louise; 8-Sep-65; 24-Sep-65; Friedrich Wilhelm; Neuenkirchen, Hannover; Schwenker, Henriette Katharine; Neuenkirchen, Hannover; Lettmade, Henriette Louise Wilhelmina; Schroder, Henriette Louise Karoline; —; —

Langschmidt; Friedrich Adolph Wilhelm; 13-Apr-58; 18-Apr-58; Friedrich Wilhelm; Neuenkirchen, Hannover; Schwietker, Henrietta Katharina; —; Lettemade, Georg Wilhelm; Schroder, Frdch. Wilh.; —; —

Langschmidt; Henriette Louise Karoline; 25-Apr-56; 4-May-56; Wilh.; Neuenkirchen, Osnabruck; Schwentker, Henriette; —; Lettmade, Henriette Louise; —; —; —

Langschmidt; Henriette Wilhelmine; 26-Apr-54; 14-May-54; Friedrich Wilh.; Neuenkirchen, Osnabruck; Schwentker, Henriette Caroline; —; Lettmade, Henriette Wilhelmine Louise; —; —; —

Langschmidt; Karl Friedrich Ernst; 31-Jan-60; 12-Feb-60; Friedrich Wilhelm; Neuenkirchen, Hannover; Schwentker, Henriette Katharine; —; Lettmade, Johann Friedrich; Burmann, Ernst Heinr.; —; —

Lapp; Ludwig Andreas; 28-Jul-58; 8-Aug-58; Kaspar; Radtheim, Hessen; Gopein, Katharine; —; Waldschmidt, Ludwig; Brauer, Andreas; Kattenkamp, Rosine; —

Lassig; Anna Catharine Christine; 20-Oct-48; 16-Nov-48; Johann Gottlieb; Untergeisendorf bei Weidam, Sachsen Weimar; Felwinger, Anna; Culmbach, Baiern; Fellwinger, Anna Catharine; Lassig, Christine; —; —

Laufer; Renate Dorothea Louise; 5-Apr-61; 21-Apr-61; Karl; Eisenach, Sachsen Weimar; Hinze, Auguste; —; Ruppel, Elisabeth; Habermehl, Schulleher; Hillgartner, Elisabeth; school teacher

Laumann; Johann Wilh.; 8-Jul-39; 25-Aug-39; Arnold; —; Schepp, Maria; —; —; —; —; —

Surname Father; Child's Given Name; Birth Date; Baptismal Date; Father's Given Name; Father's Place of Birth; Mother's Surname and Given Name; Mother's Place of Birth; Witness 1 Surname and Given Name; Witness 2 Surname and Given Name; Witness 3 Surname and Given Name; Comments

Laumann; Karoline; 2-May-42; 19-Jun-42; Arnold; —; Schepp, Maria; —; —; —; —; —

Lauster; Anna Elisabeth; 2-Aug-46; 13-Sep-46; David; Statten, Ransthal, Wurttemberg; Sellmann, Elisabeth Friederike; Ottenberg, Hessen; Filbert, Anna Dorothea; —; —; —

Lauster; Maria Dorothea; 13-Oct-43; 5-Nov-43; Johann Daniel; —; Rullmann, Elisab. Fr.; —; —; —; —; —

Lechner; Maria Katharine; 15-Sep-41; 7-Nov-41; Peter; —; Emmert, Elisab.; —; —; —; —; —

Lechner; Philip Heinr.; 8-Oct-37; 19-Nov-37; Peter; —; Emmrich, Elisab.; —; —; —; —; —

Ledermann; Joseph; 2-Mar-39; 14-Apr-39; Johann Jost; —; [--?--], Kathr.; —; —; —; —; —

Lehmann; Sophie Margaretha; 21-Sep-40; 26-Dec-40; Friedr.; —; Senger, Rosine M.; —; —; —; —; —

Leipoldt; Barbara; 12-Oct-46; 25-Oct-46; Johann; Kindersbuhl, Lauffen, Baiern; Glausser, Kunigunde; Scholenbach, Erlangen, Baiern; Schickel, Stephan; —; —; —

Leipoldt; Johann Georg; 6-Dec-48; 28-Jan-49; Jakob; Kindersbuhl, Erlangen, Baiern; Klausner, Kunigunde; Schönbach, Erlangen, Baiern; Raab, Johann Georg; —; —; —

Leistner; Johann Christoph; 16-Jun-48; 2-Jul-48; Adam; Dolnitz, Baiern; Bartenhaus, Martha Elisabeth; Baumbach, Rothenburg, Kurhessen; Lassig, Johann Christoph; —; —; —

Lembert; Georg Carl; 9-Jan-46; 22-Apr-46; Christian Carl; Getern; Pracht, Elise; Grunberg, Hessen; Peppler, Georg; Seckel, Dorothea; —; —

Lemmermann; Anna Elisabeth; 20-Dec-63; 10-Jan-64; Johann; Erichshof b. Bremen; Brede, Karoline; Hombrewen, Kurhessen; Hillgartner, Elisabeth; Schwartz, Elisabeth; —; —

Lemmermann; Heinrich Daniel; 6-Mar-66; 1-Apr-66; Johann; Frichshof, hannover; Brede, Karoline; Hofgrismer, Kurhessen; Fuchs, Heinrich; Schwartz, Daniel; —; —

Lemmermann; Marie Katharine; 25-Sep-61; 20-Oct-61; Johann; Erichshof, Hannover; Rode, Karoline; —; Einwachter, Marie Elisabeth; Einwachter, Katharine; —; —

Surname Father; Child's Given Name; Birth Date; Baptismal Date; Father's Given Name; Father's Place of Birth; Mother's Surname and Given Name; Mother's Place of Birth; Witness 1 Surname and Given Name; Witness 2 Surname and Given Name; Witness 3 Surname and Given Name; Comments

Lennert; Johann; 17-Dec-45; 11-Jan-46; George; Munchaurach, Baiern; Ublin, Magdalena; Munchaurach, Baiern; Bauer, Johann; —; —; —

Lentz; Heinrich August; 6-Jul-50; 29-Jul-50; Friedrich August; Breitenbach, Hessen; Rahn, Regina; —; Lentz, Heinrich; —; —; 1 child

Lentz; Johann; 19-Oct-51; 2-Nov-51; Aug.; Bleichenbach, Hessen; Rehn, Rosine; —; Bittroff, Joh.; —; —; —

Lentz; Johann Wilhelm Albert; 29-Mar-62; 6-Apr-62; Heinrich; Bleichenbach, Hessen; Radecke, Anna Adelheid; —; Heyse, Wilhelm; Radecke, Johann Albert; Lenz, Susanne Margarethe; —

Lenz; Andreas; 28-Oct-38; 11-Nov-38; Adam; —; Böhn, Dorothea; —; —; —; —; —

Lenz; Anna Louise; 19-Jul-65; 30-Jul-65; Johannes; Bleichenbach, Hessen; Muller, Margaretha; Dietelsheim, Hessen; Radecke, Anna Adelheid; Burmann, Susanne Margaretha; —; —

Lenz; Georg Friedrich; 15-Jan-67; 3-Feb-67; Johannes; Bleichenbach, Hessen; Traumuller, Margaretha; Dietelsheim, Hessen; Lenz, Heinrich; Stassel, Friedrich; —; —

Lenz; Johann Heinrich Wilhelm; 19-May-60; 27-May-60; Heinrich; Bleichenbach, Hessen; Radecke, Anna Adelheid; —; Radecke, Joh. Frdch.; Heyse, Marie; Burmann, Wilhelm; —

Lenz; Karl Eduard Friedrich; 20-Jan-67; 3-Feb-67; Heinrich; Breitenbach, Hessen; Radeke, Anna Adelheid; Susstedt, Hannover; Shultheiss, Eduard; Stassel, Friedrich; Lindemann, Anna Margaretha; —

Lenz; Karl Friedrich; 6-Mar-65; 19-Mar-65; Heinrich; Bleichenbach, Hessen; Radecke, Anna Adelheid; Susstedt, Hannover; Lenz, Johannes; Radecke, Hermann Frdch.; —; —

Lenz; Ludiwg Heinr.; 6-Dec-40; 26-Dec-40; Johann; —; Oelmann, Elisab.; —; —; —; —; —

Lenz; Maria Sophia; 4-Sep-43; 17-Sep-43; Johann; —; Oelmann, Elisab.; —; —; —; —; —

Lenz; Wilhelm Heinrich Johann; 8-Dec-62; 25-Jan-63; Johannes; Bleichanbach, Hessen; Treumuller, Margarethe; Bittelsheim,

Hessen; Heyse, Wilhelm; Lenz, Susanne Margarethe; Bruns, Johann; —

Leonhard; Christina; 26-Jun-46; 12-Jul-46; Heinrich; Stockheim, Bidingen, Hessen; Ricklefs, Catharine; Fevern, Oldenburg; Bissen, Christine; —; —; —

Leonhard; Elisabeth Kathr; 10-Jul-41; 16-Aug-41; Heinrich; —; Ricklefs, Kathr.; —; —; —; —; —

Leonhard; Johanna; 13-Feb-52; 10-Mar-52; Barthold; Gotha; Kerber, Anna Margaretha Ulrike; —; parents, ; —; —; —

Leonhardt; Johann Heinrich; 16-May-54; 2-Jul-54; Carl; Gotha; Krober, Ulrika; —; Leonhardt, Carl; —; —; Pastor Nordmann

Letenack; Katharine Auguste Maria; 3-Oct-67; 3-Oct-67; Joh. Friedrich; Neuenkirchen, Hannover; Schroede, Henriette Louise; Neuenkirchen, Hannover; Letenack, Katharine Elisabeth; Schimpf ?, Fredericke Auguste; —; Emergency

Lettmade; Friedrich Arnold; 15-Sep-52; 10-Oct-52; Joh. Friedrich; Neuenkirch, Hannover; Schroder, Louise; —; Lettmade, Joh. Friedrich; —; —; father is witness

Lettmade; Friedrich Wilhelm; 26-Oct-66; 18-Nov-66; Heinrich August; Neuenkirchen, Hannover; Stein, Katharine Elisabeth; Burckrota, Sachsen Weimar; Lettmade, Georg Adolph Wilh.; Schrader, Friedrich Wilhelm; Schracke, Karoline Wilheline; —

Lettmade; Friedrich Wilhelm; 30-Jan-54; 12-Feb-54; Wilhelm; Neuenkirch, Osnabruck; Schwentker, Louise; —; Lettmade, Joh. Frdch.; —; —; —

Lettmade; Georg Wilhelm; 29-Dec-54; 7-Jan-55; Johann Friedrich; Neuenkirchen, Osnabruck; Schroder, Henriette Louise; —; Lettmade, Georg Wilhelm; Schroder, Frdch. Wilh.; —; —

Lettmade; Henriette Karoline; 18-Jul-60; 29-Jul-60; Johann Friedrich; Neukirchen, Hannover; Schroder, Louise; —; Langschmidt, Henriette Katharine; Niewohner, Henriette Karoline Louise; —; —

Lettmade; Henriette Louise Wilhelmine; 18-Feb-65; 5-Mar-65; Heinrich August; Neuenkirchen, Hannover; Stein, Katharine Elisabeth; Burckardrotha, Sachsen Weimar; Lettmade,

Henriette Louise Wilhelmine; Lettmade, Henriette Louise; —; —

Lettmade; Henriette Louise Wilhelmine; 5-Feb-58; 14-Feb-58; Johann Friedrich; Neuenkirchen, Hannover; Schroder, Henriette Louise; —; Schroder, Wilhelmine; Lettmade, Henriette Louise Wilhelmine; —; —

Lettmade; infant daughter; 24-Nov-56; —; Goerg Adolph Wilh.; Neuenkirchen, Hannover; Schwatke, Louise; —; —; —; —; stillborn

Lettmade; Julius August Gottfried; 4-Jul-65; 16-Jul-65; Johann Friedrich; Neuenkirchen, Hannover; Schrader, Henriette Louise; Neuenkirchen, Hannover; Lettmade, Heinrich August; Schimpf, Joh. Heinr. Gottfried; —; —

Lettmade; Karl Wilhelm; 15-Nov-62; 23-Nov-62; Johann Friedrich; Neuenkirchen, Hannover; Shroder, Elise; —; Langschmidt, Wilhelm; Lettmade, Karl; —; —

Lettmade; male infant; 25-Dec-58; —; Georg Adolph Wilhelm; Neuenkirchen, Hannover; Schwetker, Louise; —; —; —; —; still born

Leutner; Catharina; 21-Jul-50; 23-Jul-50; Heinrich Christoph; Allendorf, Hessen; Muhly, Christine; —; Leutner, Catharina; Leutner, Friedr.; —; 3 child, 2 dau

Leutner; Catharine; 29-Jan-50; 30-Jan-50; Franz; Allenderof a.d. L., Hessen; Eggers, Dorothea Louise Wilhelmine; Wolbrechtshausen, Moringen, Hannover; Leutner, Anna Catharina; —; —; —

Leutner; Eina Sarah Henriette; 22-Mar-64; 3-Apr-64; Franz; Allendorf a. d. Lumde, Hessen; Egger, Wilhelmine; Wolbreiftshausen, Hannover; Schumacher, Sarah; Mess, Joh.; Beck, Henriette; —

Leutner; Elisabeth Dorothea Louise; 9-Apr-54; 16-Apr-54; Friedrich; Allendorf a.d. Lumda, Hessen; Scherer, Anna Dorothea; —; Immrich, Elisabeth; Leutner, Louise Dorothea; Muhly, Louise; —

Surname Father; Child's Given Name; Birth Date; Baptismal Date; Father's Given Name; Father's Place of Birth; Mother's Surname and Given Name; Mother's Place of Birth; Witness 1 Surname and Given Name; Witness 2 Surname and Given Name; Witness 3 Surname and Given Name; Comments

Leutner; Emil Jakob Eberhard; 8-Jul-60; 8-Jul-60; Friedrich; Allendorf a.d.L, Hessen; Scherer, Anna Katharine; —; Muhly, Eberhard; Boppler, Katharine; Aichele, Jakob; —

Leutner; Friedrich Christoph; 24-Jul-52; 1-Aug-52; Friedrich; Allendorf a.d. Lumda, Hessen; Scherrer, Catharine; —; Schlerf, Philipp; Leutner, Christoph; —; —

Leutner; Heinrich; 20-Jun-48; 21-Jul-48; Friedrich; Allendorf, Hessen; Scherer, Catharine; Wahlen, Alsfeld, Hessen; Leutner, Franz; —; —; —

Leutner; Heinrich Christoph; 8-Jun-52; 13-Jun-52; Franz; Allendorf a.d. Lumda, Hessen; Eggers, Dorothea Louise Wilhelmine; —; Eggers, Georg Heinr.; Leutner, Heinr. Christoph; —; —

Leutner; Katharina; 26-May-50; 26-May-50; Friedrich; Allendorf an d. Lumda, Hessen; Scherer, Anna Katharina; Wahlen, Hessen; Schlerf, Anna Katharina; —; —; wit from Altendorf

Leutner; Louise; 29-Apr-53; 5-May-53; Christoph; Allendorf a.d. Lumda; Muhly, Christine; —; Leutner, Dorothea Wilhelmine; Leutner, Franz; —; —

Leutner; Louise Adelfried Wilhelmine; 16-Apr-67; 5-May-67; Franz; Allenderfad, Hessen; Eggers, Dorothea Louise Wilhelmina; Wolbrechtshausen, Hannover; Wiesner, Eberhard; Eggers, Adelheid Rebecca; Leutner, Wilhelmine; —

Leutner; Maria Florentina Elisabeth; 6-Apr-57; 13-Apr-57; Friedrich; Allendorf, Hessen; Scherer, Catharina; —; Scherer, Maria; Sieck, Heinr. Adolph; Mess, Elisabeth; —

Leutner; Susanna Regina Louise; 22-Jan-58; 31-Jan-58; Franz; Allendorf a.d.L, Hessen; Eggers, Dorothea Louise Wilhelmine; —; Habermehl, Susanna Barbara; Sieck, Heinr. Adolph; Aichele, Regina; —

Leutner; Wilhelm Friedrich Andreas; 31-Jul-55; 5-Aug-55; Franz; Allendorf a.d. Lumda, Hessen; Eggers, Louise Wilhelmine; —; Eggers, Heinrich Andreas; Schlerf, Philipp; Muller, Wilhelmine; —

Lieb; Peter Adam Heinrich; 22-Jan-48; 9-Jul-48; Jakob; Wemlingen, Obernburg, Baiern; Dusenberg, Luise; Munden, Hannover; Brandt, Adam Heinrich; —; —; —

Surname Father; Child's Given Name; Birth Date; Baptismal Date; Father's Given Name; Father's Place of Birth; Mother's Surname and Given Name; Mother's Place of Birth; Witness 1 Surname and Given Name; Witness 2 Surname and Given Name; Witness 3 Surname and Given Name; Comments

Liest; Johann Adam; 22-Jul-50; 9-Sep-50; Johann Jakob; Jugenheim, Hessen; Bing, Elisabeth; —; Liest, Joh. Jakob; —; —; 3 child, 2 son

Lindemann; Anna Maria Elisabeth; 14-Dec-66; 1-Jan-67; Ludolph Gustav; Ottersberg, Hannover; Meier, Anna Margaretha; Susstedt, Hannover; Lenz, Anna Adelheid; Larsten, Joh. Heinrich; Schorrer, Elisabeth Sophie Therese; —

Lindemann; Friedrich; 12-Jan-51; 12-Jan-51; Joh. Gottlob Wilhelm; Gottingen; Hildebrandt, Christine Marie; —; Jung (midwife), Mrs.; Brandes, Mrs.; —; twin

Lindemann; Gustav Ludoph Ernst; 10-May-59; 22-May-59; Ludoph Gustav; Ottersberg, Hannover; Meier, Anna Margaretha; —; Meier, Heinr. Gustav; Lindemann, Otto Ludolph; Schulz, Ernst; —

Lindemann; Johann Heinrich Albert; 18-Mar-63; 29-Mar-63; Ludolph Gustav; Ottersberg, Hannover; Meier, Anna Margarethe; —; Thiemeyer, Joh.; Radecke, Joh.; Meier, Anna Marie; —

Lindemann; Johannes Heinrich Martin; 7-Sep-61; 15-Sep-61; Ludoph Gustav; Liebenau, Hannover; Meiers, Anna Margaretha; —; Eggers, Heinrich; Lindemann, Anna; Radecke, Johann Friedrich; —

Lindemann; Julius; 12-Jan-51; 12-Jan-51; Joh. Gottlob Wilhelm; Gottingen; Hildebrandt, Christine Marie; —; —; —; —; twin

Lindemann; Margaretha Sophie Rebekka; 26-Dec-64; 8-Jan-65; Ludolph Gustav; Otterberg, Hannover; Meier, Anna Margaretha; Susstedt, Hannover; Eggers, Adelheid Rebekka; Radecke, Hermann; Radecke, Sophie; —

Lindner; Christian; 10-May-45; 8-Jun-45; Michael; —; [--?--], Eva; Ansbach, Baiern; —; —; —; —

Lippe; Luise Anna; 8-Jan-38; 4-Mar-38; Georg; —; Kap, Elisab.; —; —; —; —; —

Lischer; Wilhelmina Amalie; 5-Jun-56; 15-Jun-56; Georg; Weiler, Baden; Bargelt, Henriette; —; Bargelt, Wilhelmine; Bargelt, Wilh.; Arnold, Amalie; —

Surname Father; Child's Given Name; Birth Date; Baptismal Date; Father's Given Name; Father's Place of Birth; Mother's Surname and Given Name; Mother's Place of Birth; Witness 1 Surname and Given Name; Witness 2 Surname and Given Name; Witness 3 Surname and Given Name; Comments

List; Abellone; 13-Sep-43; 27-Oct-43; Adam; —; Sommers, Dorothea; —; —; —; —; —

List; Catharine; 1-Sep-48; 17-Sep-48; Johann; Jugenheim, Bernsheim, Hessen; Bing, Catharine; Frischborn, Lauterbach, Hessen; Bing, Catharine; List, Anna Elisabeth; —; —

List; Elisabeth; 1-Feb-41; 28-Feb-41; Adam; —; Sommers, Luise; —; —; —; —; —

List; Elisabeth; 6-Dec-49; 25-Dec-49; Johann; Jugenheim an der Bergstrasse, Hessen; Bing, Catharine; Frischborn, Lautenbach, Hessen; List, Elisabeth; —; —; —

List; Franz; 21-Sep-52; 6-Dec-52; Joh. Jakob; Jugenheim, Hessen; Engelland, Elisabeth; —; Beck, Ernst; —; —; —

List; Jacob; 15-Jan-42; 6-Mar-42; Adam; —; Sommer, Luise; —; —; —; —; —

List; Johann Adam; 7-Oct-44; 22-Dec-44; Adam; —; Sommers, Luise; —; —; —; —; —

List; Johann PHIlipp; 25-Nov-51; 7-Mar-52; Johann; Jugenheim, Hessen Darmstadt; Bing, Catharine; —; List, Joh. Adam; —; —; —

List; Johannes; 19-Feb-48; 1-May-48; Johann Jakob; Jugenheim, Zweigenberg, Hessen; England, Elisabeth; Gemunde, Hessen Kassel; List, Johann; —; —; —

List; Louis; 9-Apr-47; 10-Oct-47; Johann Adam; Jugenheim, Bensheim, Hessen; Sommers, Dorothea; Diepholz, Hannover; Weber, Elisabeth; —; —; child died

List; Luise; 6-Oct-45; 9-Nov-45; Jakob; Jorchinheim, Hessen; Engelland, Elisabeth; Gemund, Kurhessen; Kraft, Luise; —; —; —

List; Maria Luise; 5-Feb-39; 21-Mar-39; Adam; —; Sommer, Luise; —; —; —; —; —

Lobahn; Gottlieb Friedrich Karol; 24-Jul-62; 10-Aug-62; Heinrich; Lisberg, Hannover; Bothe, Elise Karoline; —; Schulz, Gottlieb; Thiemeyer, Friedrich; —; —

Lohmuller; August; 27-Sep-47; 8-Jan-48; Friedrich Wilh.; Edewecht, Zweischenahn, Oldenburg; Behrhorst, Maria

Dorothea; Rhade bei Minden, Preussen; Lohmuller, Aug.; —; —; —

Lohmuller; Dietrich Wilhelm; 18-Aug-46; 12-Sep-46; Friedrich Wilhelm; Edewech, Zwischen Ohn, Oldenburg; Bahrforst, Maria Dorothea; Minden, Preussen; Lohmuller, August; —; —; wit is uncle

Lohmuller; Friedrich Wilhelm; 27-Jun-49; 3-Aug-49; Friedrich Wilhelm; Edewacht, Zwischenahn, Oldenburg; Behrforst, Maria Dorothea; Rhade bei Minden, Preussen; Borcheld, Fried. W.; —; —; —

Lohrfink; Johann; 7-Jul-49; 15-Sep-49; Ludwig; PeterwaideFriedberg, Hessen; Ludmann, Marianne; Eite, Vechte, Oldenburg; Lohrfink, Johann; —; —; —

Lohrmann; Agnes Augustine; 30-Jan-46; 21-May-46; Heinrich; Bergfreisnitz, Waldeck; Kirschner, Maria; Dodtenhausen, Kurhessen; Sanders, Agnes Barbara; —; —; —

Lohrmann; Alexander; 3-Dec-41; 25-Dec-41; Heinrich; —; Kerschner, Maria; —; —; —; —; —

Lohrmann; Christiann Elisabeth; 16-Sep-49; 25-Dec-49; Heinrich; Lergfreiheit, Waldeck; Kirschner, Maria; Totenhausen, Rosenthal, Kurhessen; Eigenbrodt, Christian; Wolff, Elisabeth; —; —

Lohrmann; Heinrich; 7-Jun-38; 19-Aug-38; Heinrich; —; Kirschner, Maria; —; —; —; —; —

Lohrmann; Helene Luise; 5-Mar-44; 14-Apr-44; Heinrich; —; Keschmer, Maria; —; —; —; —; —

Lohrmann; Joahnn Heinrich Louis; 4-Jul-51; 4-Jan-52; Joh. Heinr.; Bregtenscheit, Waldeck; Kirschner, Marie; —; Till, Heinr.; —; —; —

Lohrmann; Maria Emilie Auguste; 25-Oct-47; 25-Dec-47; Johann Heinrich; Bergfreiheit, Waldeck; Kirschner, Maria; Todtenhausen, Waldeck; Litzerich, Elisabeth; —; —; —

Lohrmann; Wilhelm Jacob; 25-Mar-40; 17-May-40; Heinrich; —; Kirschner, Maria; —; —; —; —; —

Long (AKA Lange); Georg Herrmann; 18-Oct-43; 2-Feb-46; Herrmann; —; [--?--], Marie; —; —; —; —; —

Surname Father; Child's Given Name; Birth Date; Baptismal Date; Father's Given Name; Father's Place of Birth; Mother's Surname and Given Name; Mother's Place of Birth; Witness 1 Surname and Given Name; Witness 2 Surname and Given Name; Witness 3 Surname and Given Name; Comments

Long (AKA Lange); Marie Jane; 10-May-41; 2-Feb-46; Herrmann; Nord Deutschland; Bange, Marie; Baltimore; —; —; —; child died

Lotz; Caroline Christine; 24-Apr-47; 24-May-47; Christoph; Rodensohl, Neuenbirk (berg?); Romoser, Jakobine; Rodensohl, Neuenbirk (berg?); —; —; —; —

Louis; Anna Louise; 20-Dec-66; 6-Jan-67; Karl Friedrich; Kalte, Furst. Waldeck; Radecke, Margaretha Adelheid; Susstedt, Hannover; Radecke, Katharine Louise; Radecke, Maria; —; —

Louis; Anna Maria Louise; 14-Nov-53; 27-Nov-53; Karl Friedrich; Kilde, Waldeck; Radecke, Margaretha Adelhied; —; Radeke, Katharine Louise; Dreyer, Anna; —; —

Louis; Carl Herrmann; 27-Oct-45; 23-Nov-45; Carl Friedrich; Bildungen, Waldeck; Radeke, Margaretha Adelheid; Kirchspiel, Vilsen, Hannover; Radeke, Herrmann; —; —; —

Louis; Catharine Margarethe; 10-Jan-51; 9-Feb-51; Karl Friedrich; Altweildungen, Waldeck; Radecke, Margarethe Adelheid; —; Radecke, Catharine Adelheid; parents; —; wit #1 in Hannover

Louis; Heinrich Dietrich; 26-Aug-57; 6-Sep-57; Karl Friedrich; Kalde, Waldeck; Radecka, Adelheid; —; Radecke, Dietrich Eberhard; Radecka, Herm. Heinrich; —; —

Louis; Heinrich Friedrich; 2-Oct-48; 29-Oct-48; Carl Friedrich; Wildungen, Waldeck; Radeker, Margarethe Adelheid; Susstadt, Bruchhausen, Hannover; Dreyer, Friedrich; Radeker, Hermann Heinrich; —; —

Louis; Johann Georg Wilhelm; 9-May-59; 15-May-59; Karl Friedrich; Kalte, Waldeck; Radecke, Margaretha Adelheid; —; Bruns, Joh.; Radecke, Wilhelmina; Kastens, Heinrich; —

Louis; Johann Jakob; 21-Jul-64; 31-Jul-64; Karl Friedrich; Kulte, Waldeck; Radecke, Margaretha; Sustedt, Hannover; Aichele, Jakob; Vonderwegsten, Margarethe; —; —

Louis; Johann Peter Wilhelm; 3-Dec-61; 15-Dec-61; Karl; Lisberg, Hessen; Petri, Margaretha; —; Abel, Johanne; Brauer, Peter; Schaumloffel, Wilhelm; —

Surname Father; Child's Given Name; Birth Date; Baptismal Date; Father's Given Name; Father's Place of Birth; Mother's Surname and Given Name; Mother's Place of Birth; Witness 1 Surname and Given Name; Witness 2 Surname and Given Name; Witness 3 Surname and Given Name; Comments

Louis; Maria Christiana; 26-Apr-57; 3-May-57; Georg Karl; Oberkirchen, Kurhessen; Waltjen, Julianna; —; Waltjen, Maria; Waltjen, Christiana; —; —

Louis; Maria Henriette; 15-Sep-61; 29-Sep-61; Karl Friedrich; Hulte, Waldeck; Radecke, Adelheid Rebecca; —; Bruns, Marie Rebecca; Radecke, Hermann; —; —

Louis; Rebecca Margaretha; 9-May-55; 27-May-55; Carl Friedrich; Altwildungen, Waldeck; Radecka, Margaretha Adelheid; —; Radecke, Rebecca Margare.; Radecke, Rebecca Maria; Radecke, Maria Louise; —

Lubs; Helena Louise; 1-Nov-64; 13-Nov-64; Johann Peter; Morne, Holstein; Droscher, Elisabeth; Hamburg; Lubs, Anna Magdalena; Vogel, Helena; Dors, Maria Elisabeth; —

Ludolph; Caroline; 28-Aug-49; 30-Sep-49; Heinrich; Diepholz, Hannover; Wortmann, Friederike; Diepholz, Hannover; Wortmann, Carl; Wortmann, Caroline; —; —

Ludthardt; Eva; 11-Dec-46; 17-Jan-47; Caspar; Treckenthal, Sachsen Meiningen; Herzog, Kunigunde; Schmelz, Gronach, Baiern; Apler, Thomas; —; —; —

Luft; Carl Ernst; 9-Jun-48; 3-Sep-48; Johannes; Mallernhausen, Nidda, Hessen; Fryh, Helene Elisabeth; Mallernhausen, Nidda, Hessen; Fryh, Conrad; Luft, Weigandt; —; —

Lutz; Carl Gottfried; 3-May-45; 3-Aug-45; Christopfer Dietr.; Rodensohl, Neuenbirk, Wurttemberg; Sirmoher [?], Jakobina; Rodensohl, Neuenbirk, Wurttemberg; Romoser, Johann Philipp; —; —; —

Lutz; Christoph Friedr.; 14-Aug-43; 17-Dec-43; Christoph Friedr.; —; Romoser, Jacobine; —; —; —; —; —

Lutz; Johann; 14-Feb-41; 26-Sep-41; Christoph Fr.; —; Romoser, Jacobine; —; —; —; —; —

Lutz; Margaretha; 12-Feb-50; 6-Jul-50; Christoph; Rothenhol; Romoser, Jacobina; —; —; —; —; —

M---; Christiane Amalie; 18-Oct-43; 21-Jun-44; Heinrich Friedrich; —; Kleinlein, Elisab.; —; —; —; —; —

Magenhard; Erst Fried.; 14-Feb-38; 11-Apr-38; Friedrich; —; Lohbauer, Pauline; —; —; —; —; —

Surname Father; Child's Given Name; Birth Date; Baptismal Date; Father's Given Name; Father's Place of Birth; Mother's Surname and Given Name; Mother's Place of Birth; Witness 1 Surname and Given Name; Witness 2 Surname and Given Name; Witness 3 Surname and Given Name; Comments

Magin; Carl; 17-Oct-49; 21-Oct-49; Johann Peter; Donsiders bei Bermasins, Baiern; Klein, Catharine Barbara; Lemberg, Baiern; Muller, Carl; Muller, Wilhelmine; —; —

Magin; Friedrich; 16-Sep-64; 25-Dec-64; Johann Peter; Biemasrotz, Rheinbaiern; Deiguas, Katharina Barbara; Lemberg, Rheinbaiern; Leutner, Friedrich; Thiemeyer, Frdch.; Tormelen, Marie Elisabeth; —

Magin; Georg; 24-Mar-67; 21-Apr-67; Peter; Dansieder, Baiern; Klein, Anna Barbara; Lemberg, Baiern; Muhly, Georg; Schwab, Wilhelmine; —; —

Magin; Heinrich; 18-Jul-54; 20-Jul-54; Peter; Tonsiders, Baiern; Klein, Catharina Barbara; —; Schwab, Heinrich; Schneider, Anna Maria Louise; —; —

Magin; Katharine; 31-Mar-60; 8-Apr-60; Peter; Donsieder, Rheinbaiern; Klein, Anna Barbara; —; Schwab, Christian; Hoffmann, Magdalena; —; —

Magin; Louise; 27-Sep-62; 14-Nov-62; Peter; Donsiter, Baiern; Klein, Louise; —; Schwab, Louise; Hofmann, August; —; —

Magin; Magdalena; 30-Oct-51; 2-Nov-51; Joh. Peter; Dorfirter, Baiern; Klein, Katharine Barbara; —; Schwab, Karl; —; —; —

Magin; Wilhelmina; 3-Aug-57; 9-Aug-57; Peter; Lemberg, Rheinbaiern; Klein, Katharina Barbara; —; Muller, Karl; Muller, Wilhelmina; —; —

Maienkranz; Wilhelm; 9-Nov-47; 15-Nov-47; Kilian; Waldorf, Sachsen, Meiningen; Lemmer, Anna Elisabeth; Waldorf, Sachsen Meiningen; Maienkranz, Heinrich; —; —; child died

Mans; Wilhelm Jakob; 20-Oct-47; 9-Jan-48; Friedrich; Akmenrodt, Kurhessen; Guntrum, Margaretha; Schlitz, Hessen; Mans, Jakob; Guntrum, Wilhelm; —; —

Mansdorfer; Anna Maria; 14-Mar-41; 2-May-41; Johann G.; —; Fuchs, Kathr.; —; —; —; —; —

Mansdörfer; Friedrich; 11-May-43; 2-Jul-43; Johann; —; Fuchs, Kathr.; —; —; —; —; —

Mansdörfer; Johann Georg; 6-Jan-39; 17-Feb-39; Johann G.; —; Fuchs, Kathr.; —; —; —; —; —

Surname Father; Child's Given Name; Birth Date; Baptismal Date; Father's Given Name; Father's Place of Birth; Mother's Surname and Given Name; Mother's Place of Birth; Witness 1 Surname and Given Name; Witness 2 Surname and Given Name; Witness 3 Surname and Given Name; Comments

Mansdörfer; Johann Georg; 6-Jan-39; 17-Mar-39; Johann G.; —; Fuchs, Kathr.; —; —; —; —; repeated

Mantras; Katharine Juliane; 26-Jan-66; 2-Feb-66; Karl Ferdinand; Preussen; Waldschmidt, Elisabeth; Baltimore; Schwartzenberger, Katharine; Weitz, Juliane; —; illegitimate

Manz; Margaretha; 2-Aug-44; 15-Sep-44; Friedrich; —; Guckrum, Marg.; —; —; —; —; —

Marco; Wilhelmine; 5-Jun-50; 7-Jun-50; Johann; Deuz bei Seen, Preussen; Wehn, Catharina; Wilgersdorf; Leutner, Christine; —; —; wit from Allendorf

Markel; Gerhard; 1-Aug-51; 17-Aug-51; Heinr.; Kreis Salzfeld, Hessen; Heidelbach, Anna Elisabeth; —; Heidelbach, Gerhard; —; —; —

Markel; Heinrich; 12-Sep-49; 30-Sep-49; Heinrich; Strenbedorf, Alsfeld,Hessen; Heidelbach, Anna Elisabeth; Leusel, Alsfeld, Hessen; Schneider, Heinrich; —; —; —

Matthai; Johann Ludwig Herrmann; 26-May-45; 22-Jun-45; Heinrich; Marburg; Kleinlein, Elisabeth; Achsweid, Unter Meinkreis, Baiern; Kleinlein, Johann; —; —; wit is grandfather

Maul; Anna Barbara; 6-Dec-50; 18-May-51; Joh.; Thalreta, Baiern; Muller, Eva; —; Burger, Anna Barbara; —; —; —

Maul; Heinrich; 27-Feb-49; 28-May-49; Johann; Dalherda, Bruckmau, Baiern; Muller, Eva; Dalherda, Bruckmau, Baiern; Menzel, Heinrich; —; —; —

Maul; Johann; 8-Jul-47; 1-Aug-47; Johann; Bruckenau, Baiern; Muller, Eva; Bruckenau, Baiern; Nieboldt, Johann; —; —; —

Maurer; Adolph Heinrich; 18-Jul-40; 2-Aug-40; Heinrich; —; Heldmann, Juliane; —; —; —; —; —

Maus; Friedrich Adam; 29-Nov-38; 30-Dec-38; Friedr.; —; Gunrum, Marg.; —; —; —; —; —

Maus; Karl; 21-Sep-40; 28-Oct-40; Friedrich; —; Guntrum, Marg.; —; —; —; —; —

McMahon; Wilhelm Heinrich; 18-Jul-61; 23-Aug-61; John J.; —; Waltjen, Sophie Dorothea; Baltimore; Waltjen, Wilhelm; Waltjen, Louise; —; illegitimate

Surname Father; Child's Given Name; Birth Date; Baptismal Date; Father's Given Name; Father's Place of Birth; Mother's Surname and Given Name; Mother's Place of Birth; Witness 1 Surname and Given Name; Witness 2 Surname and Given Name; Witness 3 Surname and Given Name; Comments

Medinger; Eduard Gräson; 12-May-38; 7-Oct-38; Christoph; —; Foy, Sophie; —; —; —; —; —

Megenhard; Edmund Friedrich; 28-Jan-37; 20-Feb-37; Friedrich; —; Lohbauer, Pauline; —; —; —; —; —

Megenhard; Edmund Friedrich; 28-Jan-37; 27-Mar-37; Friedrich; —; Lohbauer, Pauline; —; —; —; —; —

Megenhard; Pauline; 10-Jan-43; 28-Mar-43; Friedrich; —; Lohbauer, Pauline; —; —; —; —; —

Megenhardt; Pauline Virginia; 13-Nov-45; 12-Feb-46; Friedrich; Ludwigsburg, Wurttemberg; Leb, Pauline; Stuttgardt, Wurttemberg; —; —; —; —

Mehlgarden; Maria Luise; 16-May-46; 12-Jul-46; August; Erfurt, Preussen; Grein, Elisabeth; Erfurt, Preussen; Trager, Maria Luise; —; —; —

Meier; Adam Christian; 5-Aug-53; 14-Aug-53; Karl Bernhard; Kleinhaibach, Baiern; Morgenroth, Anna Marie; —; Weidemeier, Adam Christian; Schafer, Christine; —; —

Meier; Anna Maria; 15-May-54; 21-May-54; Georg; Baiersdorf, Baiern; Helm, Barbara; —; Friedrich, Anna Maria; —; —; —

Meier; Anna Sophie Wilhelmine; 26-Aug-63; 30-Aug-63; Johann Christian; Mattfeld, Hannover; Dunker, Rebecca Adelheid; Mattfeld, Hannover; Schafer, Anna Marie; Prufer, Katharine; Vornkohl, Wilhelmine; —

Meier; Carol Heinrich; 13-Nov-55; 23-Dec-55; Joh. Gerhard; Gehrde, Hannover; Rosenbaum, Anna Catharina; —; Hoferkamp, Heinr.; —; —; —

Meier; daughter; 30-Nov-61; —; Georg; Baiersdorf, Baiern; Helm, Barbara; —; —; —; —; died before baptism

Meier; Friedrich; 22-Oct-51; 2-Nov-51; Karl; Kleinhaibuch, Baiern; Morgenroth, Maria; —; Leutner, Friedrich; —; —; —

Meier; Friedrich Wilhelm; 18-Dec-47; 30-Jan-48; Friedrich Wilhelm; Emmighausen, Lubbeke, Preussen; Jurgen-Detmars, Maria Engel; Cockhausen, Mitlage, Hannover; Dettmers, Friedrich Wilhelm; —; —; father deceased

Surname Father; Child's Given Name; Birth Date; Baptismal Date; Father's Given Name; Father's Place of Birth; Mother's Surname and Given Name; Mother's Place of Birth; Witness 1 Surname and Given Name; Witness 2 Surname and Given Name; Witness 3 Surname and Given Name; Comments

Meier; Georg Dietrich; 10-Feb-53; 13-Mar-53; Joh. Gerhard; Gehrte, Hannover; Rosengarn, Anna Catharina; —; Rosengarn, Joh. Jurgen; —; —; —

Meier; Heinrich Ludwig; 22-Aug-55; 2-Sep-55; Carl Bernhard; Kleinheibach, Baiern; Margereth, Anna Maria; —; Timmermann, Heinr. Ludwig; —; —; —

Meier; Heinrich Wilhelm August; 9-Oct-50; 27-Oct-50; Johann Friedrich Anton; Eule,Bad Nienburg, Hannover; Vogel, Marie; —; Busching, Heinrich; Waltjen, Wilhelm; Klinkmeier, Aug.; 1 child

Meier; Hermann Dietrich; 29-Sep-50; 26-Jan-51; Joh. Gerhard; Gehrte, Bersenbruch, Hannover; Rosengarn, Anna Catharina; —; Wiedemann, Joh. Gottfried; —; —; child died

Meier; Hermann Heinrich Andreas; 24-Aug-57; 30-Aug-57; Joh. Christian; Mattfelde, Hannover; Dunker, Rebecca Adelheid; —; Purner, Joh. Andreas; Vorderwusten, Margaretha; Dunker, Kasten Heinr.; —

Meier; Johann Hermann Wilhelm; 25-May-66; 3-Jun-66; Christian; Martfeld, Hannover; Dunker, Adelheid; Martfeld, Hannover; Vordwegsten, Johann; Dunker, Karoline; Siemers, Wilhe.; —

Meier; Johann Michael Thomas; 8-May-59; 21-May-59; Georg; Baiersdorf, Baiern; Helm, Barbara; —; Harmes, Thom.; Friedrich, Mich.; Heck, Joh.; in house

Meier; Johann Thomas Michael; 16-Oct-55; 28-Oct-55; Georg; Baiersdorf, Baiern; Helm, Barbara; —; Harmes, Thomas; Friedrich, Anna; Heck, Joh.; —

Meier; Karoline Margaretha Friederike; 1-Sep-59; 4-Sep-59; Christian; Mattfelde, Hannover; Dunker, Adelheid; —; Dunker, Karoline; Vorderwosten, Heinr.; Reitzel, Friederike; —

Meier; Louise Dorothea; 6-Apr-53; 24-Apr-53; Joh. Frdch. Anton; Eule, Hannover; Vogel, Antonette; —; Vogel, Louise; Riemschnucke, Dorothea; —; —

Meier; Martin Heinrich; 4-Mar-51; 11-Mar-51; Heinrich Dietrich; Amt Ehrenburg, Hannover; Dannettel, Wilhelmine; —; Meier, Deitr. Heinr.; Meier, Benjamin Christian; —; —

Surname Father; Child's Given Name; Birth Date; Baptismal Date; Father's Given Name; Father's Place of Birth; Mother's Surname and Given Name; Mother's Place of Birth; Witness 1 Surname and Given Name; Witness 2 Surname and Given Name; Witness 3 Surname and Given Name; Comments

Meier; Peter; 21-Oct-56; 26-Oct-56; Heinrich; Jensbach, Rheinbaiern; Mohring, Anna Maria; —; Mohring, Peter; —; —; —

Meinhard; Friedrich; 15-Jul-40; 2-Aug-40; Peter; —; Beyer, Christine; —; —; —; —; —

Meischke; Karoline Elisabeth; 26-Feb-66; 18-Mar-66; Richard; Stadt Altenburg; Weber, Katharine; Volkartshain, Hessen; Weber, Heinr.; Weber, Elisabeth; Will, Elisabeth; —

Meissner; Amalie Luise; 12-Aug-44; 15-Sep-44; Johann; —; Mechau, Agnes; —; —; —; —; —

Meissner; Wilhelmine; 10-Oct-42; 12-Jan-43; Johann; —; Mecha, Agnes; —; —; —; —; —

Melchior; Carl Friedrich; 2-Oct-48; 24-Dec-48; Nathaniel; Solingen, Preussen; Schachter, Henriette; Solingen, Preussen; Schmidt, Carl; Trell, Friedrich; —; —

Melchior; Daniel Nathaniel; 14-Dec-40; 31-Jan-41; Nathaniel; —; Schlächter, Henriette; —; —; —; —; —

Melchior; Henriette; 11-Dec-45; 19-Jan-46; Nathanael; Solingen, Neupreussen; Schlaihker, Henriette; Solingen, Neupreussen; Ölz, August; Ölz, Henriette Melchior; —; —

Melchior; Herrmann August Abraham; 20-May-46; 20-Dec-46; Nathaniel; Solingen, Preussen; Schlafter, Henriette; Johannelfauth bei Solingen; Oels, August; —; —; —

Melchior; Luise Helene; 16-May-46; 20-Dec-46; Nathaniel; Solingen, Preussen; Fuchs, Bertha; Elberfeld, Preussen; Fuchs, Helene; —; —; wit is grandmother

Menke; Johann Heinr.; 10-Apr-41; 9-May-41; Friedr.; —; Altevogt, Maria; —; —; —; —

Menz; Georg Friedr.; 13-May-37; 2-Jul-37; Georg Fr.; —; Scholl, Johanne; —; —; —; —

Merf; Maria Elisab.; 24-May-43; 12-Nov-43; Friedrich; —; Steinhofer, Emile; —; —; —; —

Mesch; Johann; 6-Oct-46; 22-Nov-46; Caspar; Siefeld, Hochstadt, Baiern; Denner, Dorothea; Ziegenbach, Herrschafts, Rittershausn, Baiern; Mesch, Johann; —; —

Surname Father; Child's Given Name; Birth Date; Baptismal Date; Father's Given Name; Father's Place of Birth; Mother's Surname and Given Name; Mother's Place of Birth; Witness 1 Surname and Given Name; Witness 2 Surname and Given Name; Witness 3 Surname and Given Name; Comments

Mesch; Johannes; 16-Jul-48; 23-Jul-48; Johann Georg; Kinfeld, Hochstadt, Baiern; Beck, Elisabeth; Hannover; Biersack, Johann; —; —

Mess; Friedrich Heinrich Theodor; 20-Mar-58; 28-Mar-58; Johann; Wahlen, Hessen; Schmehl, Elisabeth; —; Leutner, Christoph; Scherrer, Maria; Leutner, Franz

Mess; Johann Jost Friedrich; 16-Nov-55; 25-Nov-55; Johann; Wahlen, Hessen; Schmeer, Elise; —; Leutner, Friedrich; Leutner, Mrs.; Scherer, Joh.

Mess; Karl August; 10-Mar-64; 27-Mar-64; Johann; Wahlen, Hessen; Schmehl, Elisabeth; Wahlen, Hessen; Schlerf, Philipp; Bender, Katharine; —

Mess; Karl Georg Christian; 17-Mar-61; 24-Mar-61; Johann; Wahlen, Hessen; Schmehl, Elisabeth; —; Dunker, Kasten; Meier, Christian; Wagner, Elisabeth

Mess; Stephanus Martin Daniel; 16-Oct-66; 28-Oct-66; Johann; Whalen, Hessen; Schmehl, Elise; Whalen, Hessen; Eggers, Heinrich; Leutner, Mina; Zink, Philipp

Mess; Theodor Wilhelm; 10-Mar-64; 27-Mar-64; Johann; Wahlen, Hessen; Schmehl, Elisabeth; Wahlen, Hessen; Hillgartner, Johann; Rein, Christine; —

Messner; Christoph Daniel; 9-Nov-42; 4-Dec-42; Christoph; —; Hermann, Kathr.; —; —; —; —

Messner; Elisabeth; 18-Nov-40; 21-Feb-41; Johann; —; Romoser, Christine; —; —; —; —

Messner; Johann; 16-Aug-39; 20-Oct-39; Johann; —; Romoser, Christine; —; —; —; —

Metze; Anna Catharine; 12-Feb-46; 22-Feb-46; Adam; Röttenau, Frankenberg, Kurhessen; Dumis, Meta; Warnhoden, Neuenwalde, Hannover; —; —; —

Meyer; Alvina Elise; 17-Dec-42; 16-Apr-43; Joseph; —; Rosengarn, Anna K.; —; —; —; —

Meyer; Anna Josephine; 7-May-46; 14-Jun-46; Heinrich; Heiligenloh, Ehrenburg, Hannover; Dannettel, Margaretha Wilhelmine; Drebber, Diepholz, Hannover; Meyer, Anna Margarethe; —; —

Surname Father; Child's Given Name; Birth Date; Baptismal Date; Father's Given Name; Father's Place of Birth; Mother's Surname and Given Name; Mother's Place of Birth; Witness 1 Surname and Given Name; Witness 2 Surname and Given Name; Witness 3 Surname and Given Name; Comments

Meyer; Anna Maria; 5-May-42; 29-Jan-43; Wilhelm; —; Fetmar, Maria E.; —; —; —; —; —

Meyer; Catharine; 7-Jan-48; 16-Jan-48; Carl; Kleinheubach, Baiern; Morgenroth, Anna Maria; Kleinheubach, Baiern; Weydemeyer, Barbara Elisabeth; —; —; —

Meyer; Catharine Margarethe Adelheid; 11-Apr-49; 17-Jun-49; Johann; Unten, Bruchhausen, Hannover; Bergmann, Maria; Wachendorf, Vieke, Hannover; Bergmann, Margaretha Cathar.; —; —; —

Meyer; Clara Christiane; 8-May-04; 20-Oct-45; Heinrich; Bobenstein, Reuss; Funk, Christiane; Harra bei Loberstein; Hellwig, Clara; —; —; —

Meyer; Georg Heinrich; 3-Mar-41; 28-Mar-41; Johann Gerhard; —; Rosengarn, Adelhaide; —; —; —; —; —

Meyer; Gerhard Wilhelm; 19-Jan-48; 12-Mar-48; Johann Gerhard; Gehrde, Bersenbruck, Hannover; Rosengarm, Anna Cathar; Gehrde, Bersenbruck, Hannover; —; —; —; —

Meyer; Heinrich August; 23-Dec-43; 12-Feb-44; Heinrich W.; —; [--?--], Eleonora; —; —; —; —; twin

Meyer; Jakob; 2-Mar-46; 15-Mar-46; Carl; Klein Heubach, Lowenstein, Baiern; Morgenroth, Anna Maria; Klein Heubach, Lowenstein Baiern; Muller, Jakob; —; —; —

Meyer; Johan nHeinrich; 15-Oct-49; 30-Jun-50; Heinrich; Amt Diepholz, Hannover; Mels, Elisabeth; Baltimore Co.; Fetting, Johann; —; —; wit from Ukermark

Meyer; Johann; 16-Apr-42; 31-Jul-42; Wilhelm; —; Klein, Eva; —; —; —; —; —

Meyer; Johann Heinrich; 29-Apr-46; 19-Jul-46; Wilhelm; Eimighausen, Lubbeke, Preussen; Jurgen-Detmars, Marie Engel; Bockhausen, Wisslage; Strothmann, Johann Heinrich; —; —; —

Meyer; Johann Heinrich Herrmann; 18-Dec-49; 20-Jan-50; August; Dissen bei Osnabruck, hannover; Batzer, Henriette; Dissen bei Osnabruck, Hannover; Rodewald, Johann Heinrich; —; —; —

Meyer; Johann Heinrich Wilhelm; 23-Dec-43; 12-Feb-44; Heinrich W.; —; [--?--], Eleonora; —; —; —; —; twin

Surname Father; Child's Given Name; Birth Date; Baptismal Date; Father's Given Name; Father's Place of Birth; Mother's Surname and Given Name; Mother's Place of Birth; Witness 1 Surname and Given Name; Witness 2 Surname and Given Name; Witness 3 Surname and Given Name; Comments

Meyer; Johannes; 12-Aug-49; 19-Aug-49; Carl; Klein Heubach, Baiern; Morgenroth, Anna Maria; Klein Heubach, Baiern; Bader, Agatha; —; —; —

Meyer; Ludwig Johann Babtist Gottlieb; 9-Jan-43; 30-Oct-43; Wilhelm; —; Bleske, Elise; —; —; —; —; —

Meyer; Magdalena; 14-Jul-39; 18-Aug-39; Wilhelm; —; Klein, Eva; —; —; —; —; —

Meyer; Margarethe Wilh.; 1-Jun-44; 17-Jun-44; Heinrich Dietr.; —; Dannettel, Marg. M.; —; —; —; —; —

Meyer; Maria; 21-Mar-44; 16-Apr-44; Karl; —; Morgenroth, Anna M.; —; —; —; —; —

Meyer; Maria Wilhelmine; 7-Apr-42; 29-May-42; Heinrich Dietrich; —; Dannettel, Marg.; —; —; —; —; —

Meyer; Sophia Caroline; 8-Aug-45; 28-Sep-45; Johann Gerhard; Gehrde, Bersenbruck, Hannover; Rosengarn, Anna Catharine; Gehrde, Bersenbruck, Hannover; Rosengarn, Johann Gerhard; Koch, Henriette; —; —

Meyer; Sophia Caroline; 11-Jul-48; 31-Jul-48; Heinrich Dietrich; Hilgenloh, Ehrenburg, Hannover; Dannettel, Margarethe Wilhelmine; Deka, Diepholz, Hannover; Bruning, Sophia Margarethe; —; —

Meyer; Wilhelm; 23-May-40; 19-Aug-40; Wilhelm; —; Bleske, Elise; —; —; —; —; —

Meyer; Wilhelm Heinrich; 29-Apr-49; 17-Jul-49; Friedrich H.; Heiligenloh, Ehrenburg, Hannover; Jergensen, Mary Rebekka; Lancaster, PA; Meyer, Heinrich Dietr.; Meyer, Benjamin Carl; —; —

Meyer; Wilhelmine Luise; 7-Jun-44; 21-Jul-44; Wilhelm; —; Detmars, Maria; —; —; —; —; —

Michael; Emilie; 14-Dec-47; 9-Jan-48; Luis; Bidenkopf, Hessen; Will, Catharine; Rothheim, Giessen; Will, Andreas; Michael, Emilie; —; —

Michel; Charlotte Clementina Margaretha; 11-Feb-50; 10-Mar-50; Ludwig; Bietenkopf, Hessen; Will, Catharina; —; Will, Margaretha; Will, Andreas; —; —

Surname Father; Child's Given Name; Birth Date; Baptismal Date; Father's Given Name; Father's Place of Birth; Mother's Surname and Given Name; Mother's Place of Birth; Witness 1 Surname and Given Name; Witness 2 Surname and Given Name; Witness 3 Surname and Given Name; Comments

Michel; Georg; 28-Apr-53; 28-May-53; Christian Friedrich Ludwig; Biedekopf, Hessen; Feldner, Margarethe; —; Geldner, Georg; —; —; —

Mieth; Elise; 5-Jan-55; 25-Jan-55; Nikolaus; Volkartshain, Hessen; Weber, Anna Margaretha; —; Weber, Catharina; Will, Elisabeth; —; —

Mieth; Johan Heinrich; 4-Sep-58; 26-Sep-58; Niklaus; Volkertshain, Hessen; Weber, Margaretha; —; Mieth, Joh.; Rahn, Heinrich; Weber, Karoline; —

Mieth; Karl; 29-Mar-62; 30-Mar-62; Johann; Volkertshain, Hessen; Wortmann, Karoline; —; wartmann, Karl; —; —; emergency baptism

Mieth; Karl Heinrich; 18-Dec-64; 8-Jan-65; Niklaus; Volkrothhain, Hessen; Weber, Anna Margaretha; Volkrothhain, Hessen; Frank, Karl; Mieth, Weber; Heinrich; —

Mink; Christine; 13-Feb-43; 26-Mar-43; Anton; —; Somestadt, Sophie; —; —; —; —

Mink; Sohpie; 14-Feb-39; 24-Feb-39; Anton; —; Sonstädt, Sophie; —; —; —; —

Minke; Friedrich Wilh.; 13-Feb-39; 10-Mar-39; Friedrich; —; Altevogt, Maria; —; —; —; —

Minnich; Anna Elisab.; 20-Mar-38; 20-May-39; Johann; —; Eichenbrod, Friedrieke; —; —; —; —

Minnich; Katharine Magd.; 4-Apr-41; 9-May-41; Anton; —; Sonnestädt, Sophie; —; —; —; —

Mohl; Christiane Luise; 18-May-38; 9-Sep-38; Johann; —; Zoeflin, Anna; —; —; —; —

Mohring; Anna Elisabetha; 29-May-62; 8-Jun-62; Philipp; Gedern, Hessen; Ruppel, Marie; —; Ruppel, Heinrich; Mohring, Johann; Trager, Emilie

Mohring; Marie Elisabeth Christiane; 20-Jun-64; 3-Jul-64; Philipp; Gadern, Hessen; Ruppel, Maria Dorothea; Baltimore; Ruppel, Elisabeth; Ruppel, Marie; Ruppel, Marie

Mohring; Marie Louise; 10-Jul-60; 22-Jul-60; Philipp; Gadern, Hessen; Ruppel, Marie; —; Ruppel, Marie; Mohring, Loluise; Ruppel, Heinr.

Mohring; Marie Louise; 19-Nov-61; 1-Dec-61; Johann; Gadern, Hessen; Trager, Louise Karoline; —; Mohring, Marie; Trager, Margarethe Christine; —

Mohring; Marie Sophie; 6-Sep-66; 16-Sep-66; Philipp; Gedern, Sachsen; Ruppel, Maria Dorthea; Baltimore; Mohring, Marie; Ruppel, Marie Elisabeth; —

Mohrmann; Margarethe Kathr. Maria; 8-Sep-41; 26-Sep-41; Joh. R.; —; Henkereness [?], Marg. M.; —; —; —; —

Mohrmann; Maria Elisabeth; 24-Jun-39; 4-Jul-39; Johann R.; —; Hinternesche, Marg. Maria; —; —; —; —

Moins; Johann Michael; 18-Feb-53; 24-Apr-53; Joh.; Hamburg; Menk, Kunigunde; —; Friedrich, Joh. Michael; —; —

Moltz; Christian Heinrich; 19-Feb-32; 18-May-42; August; —; Wolf, Kathr.; —; —; —; —

Moltz; Christoph Jacob; 29-Mar-1829; 18-May-1842; August; —; Wolf, Kathr.; —; —; —; —

Momberg; Johann Friedrich Wilhelm; 16-Aug-61; 1-Sep-61; Georg; Kirschgarten, Hessen; Rossel, Marie; —; Zink, Johann; Friedrich, Michael; Klingmeier, Wilh.; —

Momberger; [--?--]; 22-Jan-53; —; Georg; Kirschgarten, Hessen; Rohl, Maria; —; —; —; —; stillborn twin

Momberger; [--?--]; 22-Jan-53; —; Georg; Kirschgarten, Hessen; Rohl, Maria; —; —; —; —; stillborn twin

Momberger; Johann Adam; 25-Jul-54; 27-Jul-54; Johannes; Merlau, Hessen; [--?--], Magdalena; —; Einwachter, Joh. Adam; —; —; —

Momberger; Johann Georg; 11-Nov-57; 29-Nov-57; Georg; Lieshgarten, Hessen; Rossel, Maria; —; Einwachter, Adam; Regener, Joh.; Momberger, Joh. Georg; —

Momberger; Johannes Wilhelm; 27-Apr-65; 14-May-65; Georg; Kirschgarten, Hessen; Rossel, Marie; Rosenthal, Kurhessen; Ranzbach, Johannes; Klingelhofer, Wilhelm; —; —

Momberger; Karl Johann Friedrich; 13-May-63; 24-May-63; Georg; Kirschgarten, Hessen; Rossel, Marie; Rosenthal, Kurhessen; Rossel, Karl Frdch; Rossel, Maria Barbara; Regener, Johannes; —

Surname Father; Child's Given Name; Birth Date; Baptismal Date; Father's Given Name; Father's Place of Birth; Mother's Surname and Given Name; Mother's Place of Birth; Witness 1 Surname and Given Name; Witness 2 Surname and Given Name; Witness 3 Surname and Given Name; Comments

Momberger; Maria Catharina Elisabeth; 25-Nov-55; 9-Dec-55; Georg; Kirschgarten, Hessen; Rossel, Maria; —; Regener, Maria Catharina; Einwachter, Maria Elisabeth; —; —

Momberger; Maria Katharina; 10-Mar-53; 17-Apr-53; Johannes; Kirschengarten, Hessen; Dehan, Linna; —; Momberger, Maria Katharina; —; —; —

Momberger; Marie Wilhelmine Johanne; 15-Dec-59; 25-Dec-59; Georg; Kirschgarten, Hessen; Rossel, Marie; —; Rossel, Marie; Zink, Joh.; Rossel, Wilhelmine; —

Morschladt; Heinrich; 5-Mar-48; 26-Mar-48; Gerhard Heinrich; Deinhausen,Hannover; [--?--], Sophia Margarethe; Harpstadt, Hannover; Morschladt, Heinrich; —; —; twin

Morschladt; Maria; 5-Mar-48; 26-Mar-48; Gerhard Heinrich; Deinhausen, Hannover; [--?--], Sophia Margarethe; Harpstadt, Hannover; Leimann, Maria; —; —; twin

Morschladt; Maria Margaretha; 17-Apr-48; 14-May-48; Heinrich; Dunhausen, Harpstadt, Hannover; Lindemann, Maria; Gruben, Borgsorn, Hessen; Schafermann, Maria Margarethe; —; —; —

Morschladt; Sophia Elisabeth; 8-Aug-46; 30-Aug-46; Heinrich; Dammhausen, Harpstadt, Hannover; Liedemann, Maria; Gruben, Burgheim, Hessen; Ameyer, Ursula; Koch, Margaretha; —; child died

Mory; Carl Ludwig; 1-Jan-48; 31-Mar-48; Wilhelm; Koppenbruck, Hannover; Oelkers, Elisabeth; Hildesheim; —; —; —; —

Moser; Wilhelmine; 12-Sep-54; 8-Oct-54; Heinrich; Epnith, Baiern; Libbet, Margaretha; —; Winter, Andreas; Winter, Wilhelmine; —; —

Motz; Mari Elisab.; 18-Apr-37; 24-May-38; Johann; —; Wolf, Kathr.; —; —; —; —; —

Muhly; Carl Wilhelm; 12-May-55; 3-Jun-55; Friedrich; Elberfeld, Preussen; Low, Julia; —; Lange, Carol; Lange, Caroline; —; —

Muhly; Catharine; 5-Jul-47; 18-Jul-47; Eberhardt; Allendorf, Hessen; Eitel, Luise; Lemberg, Baiern; Leutner, Catharine; —; —; —

Surname Father; Child's Given Name; Birth Date; Baptismal Date; Father's Given Name; Father's Place of Birth; Mother's Surname and Given Name; Mother's Place of Birth; Witness 1 Surname and Given Name; Witness 2 Surname and Given Name; Witness 3 Surname and Given Name; Comments

Muhly; Cathrina Christina Elisabeth; 26-Feb-55; 4-Mar-55; Eberhard; Allendorf a.d. Lumda, Hessen; Eitel, Louise; —; Schlerf, Anna Catharina; Schmidt, Christine; —; —

Muhly; Christian; 14-Feb-41; 7-Mar-41; Eberhard; —; Eitel, Luise; —; —; —; —; —

Muhly; Emma Louise; 18-Dec-66; 6-Jan-67; Georg Heinrich; Baltimore; Fischer, Barbara Margaretha; Baltimore; Muhly, Christian; Aichele, Regine; —; —

Muhly; Georg Heinr.; 18-Apr-43; 14-May-43; Eberh.; —; Eitel, Luise; —; —; —; —; —

Muhly; Heinrich Anton; 12-Feb-50; 17-Feb-50; Eberhard; Allendorf a. L., Hessen; Eitel, Louise; Lemberg bei Bremesins, Rheinbaiern; Muhly, Heinrich; Wagner, Anton; Wallenfels, Elis.; —

Muhly; Herrmann; 11-Aug-39; 10-Oct-39; Eberhard; —; Klotz, Johanne Karl.; —; —; —; —; —

Muhly; Johannes; 1-Sep-52; 5-Sep-52; Eberhard; Allendorf a.d. Lumda, Hessen; Eitel, Louise; —; Immich, Johannes; —; —; —

Muhly; Luise; 4-Sep-45; 2-Nov-45; Eberhard; Allendorf a.d. Lumda; Eitel, Luise; Kleinberg, Baiern; Leutner, Friederich; Weninghauser, Luise; —; —

Muhly; Maria Elisabeth Wilhelmina; 26-Sep-57; 4-Oct-57; Eberhard; Allendorf, Hessen; Eitel, Louise; —; Hoffmann, Salome; Leutner, Christine; Einwachter, Elisabeth; —

Muhly; Wilhelmine Julianne; 8-Jan-63; 19-Feb-63; Eberhard; Allendorf a.d. Lumda, Hessen; Schneider, Karoline; —; Einwachter, Alexander; Leutner, Frdch.; —; illegitimate

Muhly (deceased); Katharina Elisabetha; 31-May-57; 14-Jun-57; Frdch; Elberfeld, Preussen; Low, Julie; —; Muhly, Louise; Hoffmann, Salome; —; —

Muller; Auguste Friederike; 12-Oct-63; 31-Oct-63; Ernst; Homburg, Preussen; Behrens, Friederike; Glerwink, Preussen; Kowalik, Friedrich; Engel, Auguste Wilhelmine; —; —

Muller; Barbara; 21-May-41; 21-Jun-41; Johann G.; —; Koehlein, Kunigunde; —; —; —; —; —

Surname Father; Child's Given Name; Birth Date; Baptismal Date; Father's Given Name; Father's Place of Birth; Mother's Surname and Given Name; Mother's Place of Birth; Witness 1 Surname and Given Name; Witness 2 Surname and Given Name; Witness 3 Surname and Given Name; Comments

Muller; Barbara Margaretha; 3-Dec-45; 15-Feb-46; David; Wilferdingen, Baden; Brenner, Anna Maria; Essen bei Ashaffenburg, Baiern; Schnellbach, Johann; —; —; —

Muller; Carl; 12-May-49; 13-Nov-49; Andreas; Culmbach; Oedder, Adele; Untersteinach, Baiern; Herold, Carl; —; —; —

Muller; Carl; 12-Dec-48; 12-Aug-49; Christoph; Frickenhofen, Gaildorf, Wurttemberg; Wild, Ursula; Rothenhar, Gaildorf, Wurttemberg; Ruhwin, Heinrich; —; —; —

Muller; Carl Heinrich; 8-May-47; 13-Jun-47; Johann Carl; —; Jungblut, Johannette; —; Heiser, Heinrich; Jungblut, Carl; —; —

Muller; Caroline Henriette; 8-Jul-48; 13-Jul-48; Friedrich Wilhelm; Engan, Rinteln, Kurhessen; Edeler, Dorothea; Obernkirchen, Kurhessen; Edeler, Henriette; —; —; —

Muller; Catharine; 28-Apr-49; 6-May-49; Carl; Obernmoor, Zweibrucken; Klein, Wilhelmine; Lemberg bei Bermehins, Rheinbaiern; Klein, Friedrich; —; —; —

Muller; Christian; 17-Jul-47; 4-Jun-48; Andreas; Culmbach, Baiern; Oele, Ottilie; Untersteinach, Baiern; Rebhuhn, Christine; —; —; —

Muller; Dieterich; 9-Nov-45; 1-Jan-46; Wilhelm; Helsmuhle bei verden, Hannover; Plumer, Anna Margaretha; Barntrupp, Diepholz, Hannover; Dornberg, Dietrich; —; —; —

Muller; Elisabeth; 5-Oct-40; 18-Oct-40; Herrmann; —; Kleinschmidt, Kathr.; —; —; —; —; —

Muller; Georg; 3-Sep-50; 3-Nov-50; Johannes; Durlammen, Hessen; Stein, Elisabeth; —; Steiner, Georg; —; —; 2 child, 2 son

Muller; Georg Heinrich Karl; 28-Aug-66; 16-Sep-66; Ernst; Hornburg, Preussen; Behrends, Friedrike; Osterwink, Preussen; Bauer, Georg; Happel, Heinrich; —; —

Muller; Gertrude; 20-Dec-46; 26-Dec-47; Heinrich; Klein Grove bei Muhlhausen, Preussen; Tochert, Maria Eva; Klein Grave bei Muhlhausen, Preussen; Baur, Gertrud; —; —; —

Muller; Heinrich; 12-Jul-40; 26-Jul-40; Jacob; —; Gaun, Wilhelmine; —; —; —; —; —

Surname Father; Child's Given Name; Birth Date; Baptismal Date; Father's Given Name; Father's Place of Birth; Mother's Surname and Given Name; Mother's Place of Birth; Witness 1 Surname and Given Name; Witness 2 Surname and Given Name; Witness 3 Surname and Given Name; Comments

Muller; Heinrich; 13-Nov-41; 28-Nov-41; Georg; —; Happel, Christiane; —; —; —; —; —

Muller; Heinrich Ludwig; 8-Feb-39; 10-Mar-39; Heinrich; —; Schnathorst, Christine; —; —; —; —; —

Muller; Heinrich Wilhelm; 15-Oct-56; 19-Oct-56; Karl; Obermohr, Rheinbaiern; Klein, Wilhelmina; —; Schwab, Heinr.; Leutner, Elisabeth; —; —

Muller; Hermann Johann; 13-Jan-67; 20-Jan-67; Johann; Lauterbach, Hessen; Huppel, Lina; Carroll County, MD; Gross, Johann; Steiner, Maria

Muller; Jacob Heinr.; 1-Dec-41; 12-Dec-41; Heinrich; —; Eger, Eva; —; —; —

Muller; Johann; 22-Dec-46; 7-Jan-47; Johann David; Wilferdingen, Durlach, Baden; Brenner, Anna Maria; Eschau, Baiern; Bauer, Michael; Bauer, Mrs.

Muller; Johann; 1-Sep-59; 11-Sep-59; Karl; Obermoor, Baiern; Klein, Wilhelmina; —; Schorrer, Johann; Hoffmann, Salome

Muller; Johann; 3-Oct-37; 15-Oct-37; Heinrich; —; Eger, Eva; —; —; —

Muller; Johann; 10-Apr-42; 25-Jun-42; Andreas; —; Oetten, Ottilia; —; —; —

Muller; Johannes; 18-Apr-45; 8-Jun-45; Andreas; Culmbach, Baiern; Ondter, Ottilie; Unter Steinach, Baiern; Nanssen, Johannes; —

Muller; Karl; 12-Mar-51; 26-Mar-51; Karl; Obermohr, Baiern; Klein, Wilhelmine; —; Schwab, Karl; Magin, Anna Barbara

Muller; Katharina; 23-Jan-44; 30-Jan-44; Andreas; —; [--?--], ; —; —; —

Muller; Konrad Karl; 13-Jan-67; 20-Jan-67; Johann; Lauterbach, Hessen; Huppel, Lina; Carroll County, MD; Bockner, Konrad Karl; —

Muller; Ludwig Friedr.; 13-Aug-38; 11-Sep-38; Philip; —; Bets, Elisab.; —; —; —

Muller; Margaretha; 17-Oct-39; 17-Nov-39; Andreas; —; Elter, Ottielie; —; —; —

Surname Father; Child's Given Name; Birth Date; Baptismal Date; Father's Given Name; Father's Place of Birth; Mother's Surname and Given Name; Mother's Place of Birth; Witness 1 Surname and Given Name; Witness 2 Surname and Given Name; Witness 3 Surname and Given Name; Comments

Muller; Maria; 5-Jan-46; 14-Jan-46; Martin; Engelstadt, Hessen; Kuhn, Margaretha; Landwehrshagen, Minden, Hannover; Kuhn, Maria; —

Muller; Minna; 16-Aug-61; 26-Oct-61; Ernst; Halberstadt, Preussen; Trellow, Friederike; —; Spielmann, Johann; Pabst, Andreas

Muller; Rosine Friederike; 3-Nov-46; 15-Nov-46; Nikolaus; Rohr, Culmbach, Baiern; Birner, Gertrud; Gelbsreuth, Holfeld, Baiern; Walther, Auguste; —

Muller; Valentin; 2-May-38; 3-Jun-38; Herrmann; —; Kleinschmidt, Anna; —; —; —

Muller; Valentin; 4-Dec-43; 28-Jan-44; Hermann; —; Kleinschmidt, Kathr.; —; —; —; —; —

Muller; Wilhelmine; 13-Nov-62; 21-Dec-62; Karl; Oberohm, Hessen; Klein, Wilhelmine; —; Leutner, Minna; Schwab, Katharine; —; —

Munk; Heinrich; 2-Aug-37; 13-Aug-37; David; —; Jaus, Barbara; —; —; —; —; —

Nagel; Elisabeth; 6-Feb-49; 8-Apr-49; Peter; Schmalsdorf bei Culmbach, Baiern; Hoffmann, Anna Margarethe; Erlangen, Baiern; Knochel, Christian; Knochel, Elisabeth; —; —

Nagel; Peter; 23-Jan-51; 2-Feb-51; Konrad; Hitzkirchen, Hessen; Hoflin, Marie; —; Baier, Elisabeth Nagel; —; —; —

Nagel; Wilhelmine Catharine; 2-Dec-46; 24-Jan-47; Peter; Schmeistorf, Baiern; Hoffmann, Anna Margaretha; Erlangen, Baiern; —; —; —; —

Nax; Marie Louise; 14-Mar-51; 19-Jun-51; Leonhardt; Budingen, Hessen; Eckardt, Catharine; —; Eckardt, Maria Margar.; —; —; —

Neinweg; Carl Georg; 17-Jan-49; 18-Feb-49; Carl; Borgsteinfurth bei Munster, Preussen; Fritz, Henriette; Hormeln, Hannover; Fritz, Carl; —; —; —

Nessler; Karl Aug.; 8-Jul-38; 26-Jul-38; Karl Im.; —; Kirchhen, Johanne A.; —; —; —; —; —

Neuberger; Christian; 30-Mar-50; 20-May-50; Valentin; Wiesenthal, Bayern; Kappes, Magdalena; Kleinhaubach,

Bayern; Kreig, Christian; —; —; wit from Untereichenbach, Kurhessen

Neuweiler; Elisabeth Katharine; 28-Oct-44; 29-Dec-44; Johann; —; Stocker, Johanne; —; —; —; —; —

Neuweiler; Maria Magd.; 6-Jan-40; 23-Aug-40; Johann; —; Stocher, Johanne; —; —; —; —; —

Niebeling; Georg; 21-Sep-44; 25-Nov-44; Jacob; —; Senger, Katharine; —; —; —; —; —

Niedhammer; Johann Georg; 10-Jul-34; 22-Oct-38; Johann; —; Zeltner, Klara; —; —; —; —; —

Niedhammer; Samuel Ludw.; 23-Feb-39; 28-Apr-39; Johann; —; Zeltmann, Klara; —; —; —; —; —

Niedhammer; Wilhelm; 12-Mar-36; 22-Oct-38; Johann; —; Zeltner, Klara; —; —; —; —; —

Niehaus; Friedrich Heinrich; 25-May-38; 17-Jun-38; Karl; —; Martens, Kathr. Lucia; —; —; —; —; —

Niemeyer; Tobias Friedrich; 8-May-47; 7-Jul-47; Johann Friedr.; —; Kammerzell, [--?--]; —; —; —; —; illegitimate

Nikkolas; Christian Wilh.; 14-Feb-40; 10-Mar-40; Friedrich W.; —; Henkel, Kathr.; —; —; —; —; —

Niklas; Friedrick Wilhelm; 28-Dec-44; 12-Jan-45; Georg; Dorzbach, Wittenberg; Oester, Elisabeth; Ebenth, Baiern; Bauer, Georg; Oster, Margaretha; —; —

Niklas; Georg; 23-Jul-43; 6-Aug-43; Georg; —; Oester, Elisab.; —; —; —; —; —

Niklas; Heinrich Christian; 18-Oct-46; 25-Oct-46; Georg; Dörtsbach, Kinzelsau, Wurttemberg; Oester, Lisette; Ebenett, Weismain, Baiern; Bauer, Neal; Bauer, Georg; —; —

Niklas; Margarethe Barbara; 3-Aug-48; 13-Aug-48; Georg; Dorrbach, Kinzelsau, Wurttemberg; Oester, Elisabeth; Ebenet, Weismain, Baiern; Baur, Marg.; Albrecht, Barbara; —; —

Niklas; Maria Magdalena; 14-Jul-50; 21-Jul-50; Georg Michael; Derzbach, Wurttemberg; Goster, Elisabeth; —; Bauer, Margaretha; —; —; 5 child, 2 dau

Surname Father; Child's Given Name; Birth Date; Baptismal Date; Father's Given Name; Father's Place of Birth; Mother's Surname and Given Name; Mother's Place of Birth; Witness 1 Surname and Given Name; Witness 2 Surname and Given Name; Witness 3 Surname and Given Name; Comments

Niklas; Peter; 8-Jan-47; 2-May-47; Peter; Dresendorf bei Beireuth, Baiern; Nade, Emile; Nordhausen, Preussen; Oechsle, Peter; —; —; —

Niklas; Rosina Anna; 23-Nov-53; 4-Dec-53; Georg; Durzbach, Wurttemberg; Oster, Lisette; —; Krauss, Margaretha; Bauer, Margaretha; —; —

Niklas; Wilhelm Heinrich; 28-Dec-43; 14-Mar-44; Vogt; —; Voz, Elisab.; —; —; —; —; —

Nile; Anna Maria; 15-Aug-50; 25-Aug-50; Conrad; Filzick, Baiern; Hurschmann, Eleonore; —; Hurschmann, Maria; —; —; 1 child

Nith; Joseph Heinrich; 30-Oct-55; 4-Nov-55; Joseph; —; Kuster, Elwira; —; Sunop, Heinr.; Sunop, Maria Elisabeth; —; —

Nobbe; Susanne; 31-Jul-47; 9-Apr-48; Friedrich; Altswede, Lubbeke, Preussen; Kopker, Marie Elisabeth; Engde, Vorden, Hannover; Norris, Richard; Brunnings, Cath. Maria; —; —

Noll; Elisabeth; 5-Nov-41; 26-Dec-41; Adam; —; Valentin, Marg.; —; —; —; —; —

Nonnemacher; Georg Daniel; 18-Jan-47; 2-Jun-47; Jonas; Strassburg, York County, PA; Sommers, Elisabeth; Baltimore; Nonnemacher, Daniel; —; —; child died

Nonnemacher; Henriette Elisabeth; 18-Jan-47; 2-Jun-47; Jonas; Strassburg, York County, PA; Sommers, Elisabeth; Baltimore; Sommers, Henriette; —; —; wit is aunt

Nordt; Christian; 14-May-45; 11-Jun-45; Christian; Eschau, Baiern; Martin, Elisabeth; Eschau, Baiern; —; —; —; —

Nordt; Friedrich; 25-Sep-46; 7-Dec-46; Christian; Eschau, Baiern; Martin, Elisabeth; Eschau, Baiern; Martin, Michael; —; —; —

Nordt; Sophia Magdalene; 18-Sep-48; 29-Sep-48; Christian; Eschau, Baiern; Martin, Elisabeth; Eschau, Baiern; Martin, Magdalena; Berninger, Sophia; —; —

Nothfelter; Christian; 29-Apr-53; 8-May-53; Joseph; Emingen, Wurttemberg; Kampmann, Imrike; Rechenberg, Wurttemberg; Strobel, Christian; —; —; illegitimate

Nutzel; Barbara; 18-Jun-54; 20-Jun-54; Georg; Fruchendorf, Baiern; Meier, Sophie; —; Kieberth, Barbara; —; —; —

Surname Father; Child's Given Name; Birth Date; Baptismal Date; Father's Given Name; Father's Place of Birth; Mother's Surname and Given Name; Mother's Place of Birth; Witness 1 Surname and Given Name; Witness 2 Surname and Given Name; Witness 3 Surname and Given Name; Comments

Nutzel; Elisabeth; 7-Dec-63; 8-Dec-63; Georg; Forchendorf, Baiern; Meier, Margaretha; Hoppurg, Baiern; Happel, Elisabeth; —; —; twin

Nutzel; Johann Georg; 29-Jan-62; 9-Feb-62; Johann; Forchendorf, Baiern; Meier, Sophie; —; Schmidt, Johann; Heck, Georg; —; —

Nutzel; Johann Leonhard; 27-Mar-60; 15-Apr-60; Johann; Volgendorf, Baiern; Meier, Sophie; —; Friedrich, Leonhard; Heck, Johann; —; —

Nutzel; Karoline; 7-Dec-63; 8-Dec-63; Georg; Forchendorf, Baiern; Meier, Margaretha; Hoppung, Baiern; Kasten, Karoline; —; —; twin

Nutzel; Kunigunde Johanne; 12-Feb-66; 18-Feb-66; Johann Georg; Forckendorf, Baiern; Meier, Sophie; Harburg, Baiern; Feurstein, Kunigunde Johanne; —; —; —

Ober; Georg August Friedrich; 17-Jan-49; 25-Apr-49; Jakob; Hanau, Hessen; Waltjen, Sophia; Bossum, Hannover; Waltjen, Georg; —; —; —

Obitz; Christine; 3-Aug-48; 5-Aug-48; Georg Philipp; Hedingen, Ehlingen, Baiern; Strohhacker, Margarethe; Weigesheim a.d. Tauber, Wurttemberg; Muller, Christine; —; —; —

Ochs; Lorenz; 16-Aug-51; 21-Sep-51; Thomas; Lops, Baiern; Eckestine, Eva; —; Ochs, Lorenz; —; —; —

Ochsler; Georg Adam; 30-Mar-47; 29-Apr-47; Thomas; Kups, Krainach, Baiern; Egede, Eva; Kups, Krainach, Baiern; Etzel, Georg Adam; Etzel, Sabine; —; —

Oechsler; Elisabeth; 27-Dec-48; 4-Feb-49; Thomas; Kibs, Kranach, Baiern; Eggede, Eva; Geusnitz, Kranach, Baiern; Ruppel, Johann; Ruppel, Elisabeth; —; —

Oehrl; Johann Georg; 5-Jul-49; 15-Jul-49; Johann; Rieth, Sachsen Meiningen; Renne, Christine; Hosk, Sachsen Coburg; Weydemeyer, Adam; Weydemeyer, Mrs.; Oehrl, Johann Georg; wit #3 is grandfather

Oels; August Ferdinand Friedrich; 8-Jan-48; 5-Mar-48; August; Bargentrug (?), Munden, Preussen; Melchior, Henriette; Solingen, Rheinpreussen; Troll, Friedr.; Melchior, Mrs.; —; —

Surname Father; Child's Given Name; Birth Date; Baptismal Date; Father's Given Name; Father's Place of Birth; Mother's Surname and Given Name; Mother's Place of Birth; Witness 1 Surname and Given Name; Witness 2 Surname and Given Name; Witness 3 Surname and Given Name; Comments

Oels; Carl Heinrich; 27-Feb-46; 10-May-46; August; Burgentreich, Werburg, Preussen; Melchior, Henriette; Solingen, Preussen; Melchior, Daniel; Melchior, Nathaniel; —; wit #1 is grandfather

Oels; Maria Anna Emilie; 25-Aug-49; 15-Sep-49; August; Borgentrug, Minden; Melchior, Henriette; Solingen, Preussen; Troll, Regine Melchior; —; —; —

Oelwein; Friedrich Wilh.; 5-Aug-40; 21-Dec-40; Friedr.; —; Schmidt, Sicilie W.; —; —; —; —; —

Oesterle; Georg Wilh.; 1-May-43; 5-Jun-43; Johannes; —; Gingnagel, Anna M.; —; —; —; —; —

Oesterle; Jakob Adam; 17-Apr-47; 29-Apr-47; Johann; Königsbach, Baden; Gingnagel, Maria; Krumstadt, Hessen; Knipp, Jakob; Knipp, Margarethe; Gingnagel, Sophia; —

Oesterle; Johann Christian; 20-Jan-42; 28-Mar-42; Johann; —; Gingnagel, Anna M.; —; —; —; —; —

Oesterle; Johann Heinrich; 19-Jan-46; 1-Mar-46; Johann; Königsbach, Baden; Gingnagel, Anna Maria; Krumstadt, Hessen; Waltjen, Heinrich; —; —; —

Oesterle; Karl Christoph; 28-May-44; 11-Jul-44; Johann; —; Gingnagel, Anna M.; —; —; —; —; —

Oesterle; Maria Elisabeth; 2-Jun-48; 13-Jun-48; Johann Christoph; Upperspon, Stuttgart, Wurttemberg; Spengler, Margarethe Dorothea; Leitenbach, Waiblingen, Wurttemberg; Oesterle, Maria; —; —; —

Oesterle; Maria Friderike; 8-Oct-49; 21-Oct-49; Johannes; Königsbach, Durbach, Baden; Gingnagel, Anna Maria; Crumstadt, Hessen; Waltjen, Heinrich; Waltjen, Friderike; Gingnagel, Anna Maria; —

Oesterle; Maria Magdlene; 2-Mar-40; 5-Mar-40; Johann; —; Gingnagel, Maria; —; —; —; —; —

Oesterle; Sarah Catharine; 2-May-47; 30-May-47; Christoph; Waiblingen, Wurttemberg; Canley, Elisabeth; Baltimore; Weidner, Franz; —; —; —

Surname Father; Child's Given Name; Birth Date; Baptismal Date; Father's Given Name; Father's Place of Birth; Mother's Surname and Given Name; Mother's Place of Birth; Witness 1 Surname and Given Name; Witness 2 Surname and Given Name; Witness 3 Surname and Given Name; Comments

Ohel; Christine Wilhelmine; 6-Dec-52; 16-Jan-53; Johann; Ried Grosshez. Sachsen Meiningen; Reuer, Barbara Christine; —; Schafer, Christine; —; —; —

Opitz; Eva; 4-Oct-47; 8-Jan-48; Johann Georg; Obernsens bei Baireuth, Baiern; Horde, Anna Barbara; Troppam bei Baireuth; Dill, Michael; Dill, Eva; —; **scan**

Opitz; George Christian; 5-Aug-45; 24-Nov-45; Georg Philipp; Weissenburg, Anspach, Baiern; Strohecker, Margareth; Weigersheim, Wurttemberg; Scharpf, Jaohnn Christian; —; —; —

Opitz; Louise Elisabetha; 1-Jun-50; 16-Jun-50; Georg Philipp; Hottingen, Meissenburg a. S., Bayern; Strohfecker, Margaretha; Meigesheim, Wurttemberg; Muller, Louise Elisabeth; —; —; wit from Baltimore

Ortmack; Friedrich Wilhelm August; 8-Nov-67; 13-Nov-1867; Heinrich Aug.; Neuenkirchen, Hannover; Stein, Katharina Elisabeth; Burkhartrotha, Sachsen; Ortmack, Friedrich; Langschmidt, Wilhelm; —; —

Ortmann; Catharine Wilhelmine Elisabeth; 8-Apr-61; 21-Apr-61; Eberhard Heinrich; Kaspilbalm, Hannover; Kuhlmann, Christine Wilhelmine; —; —; —; —; —

Ortmann; Christine Eleonore; 23-Jun-52; 4-Jul-52; Eberhard Heinr.; Osnabruck; Kuhlmann, Christine; —; Wilker, Joh. Frdch.; Wilker, Christine Eleonore; —; —

Ortmann; Friederike Wilhelmine; 17-Apr-50; 5-May-50; Eberhard Heinrich; Belben bei Osnabruck; Ruhmann, Christina Wilhelmine; Essen, Hannover; Schroder, Friederike Honore; —; —; wit from Diepholz

Ortmann; Johann Heinrich; 21-Nov-63; 6-Dec-63; Eberhard Heinrich; Kalpilbeller, Hannover; Kuhlmann, Christine Wilhelmine; Engter, Hannover; Kunker, Heinrich; Happel, Heinrich; —; —

Ortmann; Johann Heinrich; 10-Apr-48; 23-Apr-48; Eberhart; Osnabruck, Hannover; Kuhlmann, Wilhelmine; Witlage, Hannover; Ortmann, Johann Heinrich; —; —; —

Surname Father; Child's Given Name; Birth Date; Baptismal Date; Father's Given Name; Father's Place of Birth; Mother's Surname and Given Name; Mother's Place of Birth; Witness 1 Surname and Given Name; Witness 2 Surname and Given Name; Witness 3 Surname and Given Name; Comments

Ortmann; Maria Elisabeth; 27-Apr-57; 3-May-57; Eberhard Heinrich; Ossnabruck; Kuhlmann, Christina Wilhelmina; —; Surcop, Sieck; Elisabeth, Sieck; Adam; —

Ortmann; Trihserlein; 26-Nov-59; —; Eberhard Heinrich; Kasbilbelle, Hannover; , ; —; —; —; —; still born

Ortmann; Wilhelm Heinrich; 21-Dec-54; 31-Dec-54; Eberhard Heinrich; Kespilbellen, Hannover; Kullmann, Christine Wilhelmine; —; Succop, Joh. Heinr.; Succop, Maria Kullmann; —; —

Ortwein; Sophia; 28-Oct-37; 10-Dec-37; Hardtmann; —; Burk, Elisab.; —; —; —; —; —

Ostenberg; Gustav Adolph; 21-Mar-61; 31-Mar-61; Karl Wilhelm; Lenneg, Rehinhessen; Lonsberg, Amalie; —; Regener, Johannes; Rossel, Katharine; —; —

Oster; Elisabeth; 6-Jul-47; 22-Aug-47; Johann; Schopp, Bermesins, Baiern; Kaffitz, Barbara; Neuenkirchen, Kaiserslautern, Baiern; Pfad, Elisabeth; —; —; —

Oster; Georg Theodor; 20-May-44; 2-Jun-44; Johann; —; Kafis, Barb.; —; —; —; —; —

Osterle; Emma Francisa; 8-Jun-50; 11-Jul-50; Johann Christoph; Oppelspon, Waiblingen, Wurttenberg; Rauley, Elisabeth; Baltimore; Osterle, Dorothea; —; —; wit is grandmother

Osterle; Johann Friedrich; 4-Dec-50; 22-Dec-50; Friedrich; Stuttgart, Wurttemberg; [--?--], Jane; —; Kreidmann, Magdalena; Kreidmann, Jakob; —; 1 child

Ostermann; Elisabeth; 6-Feb-38; 14-Mar-38; Christian; —; Fischer, Luise; —; —; —; —; —

Otter; Catharine Elisabeth; 5-May-49; 7-Oct-49; Johann; Bobenhausen, Nidda, Hessen; Löffel, Elisabeth; Glashütte, Nidda, Hessen; Hauss, Catharine Elisabeth; —; —; —

Otto; Friedrich August; 30-Jul-43; 14-Aug-43; Friedr.; —; Theiss, Elisab.; —; —; —; —; —

Otto; Karoline Friedricke; 24-Sep-40; 12-Oct-40; Friedrich; —; Deis, Elisab.; —; —; —; —; —

Otto; Sophie Susanne; 9-Aug-38; 27-Aug-38; Friedrich; —; Deis, Elisab.; —; —; —; —; —

Surname Father; Child's Given Name; Birth Date; Baptismal Date; Father's Given Name; Father's Place of Birth; Mother's Surname and Given Name; Mother's Place of Birth; Witness 1 Surname and Given Name; Witness 2 Surname and Given Name; Witness 3 Surname and Given Name; Comments

Oxler; Johann; 4-Nov-44; 15-Dec-44; Thomas; —; Eyeck, Eva; —; —; —; —; —

Pabst; Anna Rosamunde; 5-Mar-66; 18-Mar-66; Andreas; Bobenhausen, Wurttemberg; Horn, Anna Elisabeth; Franklin, Baltimore Co., MD; Mohring, Johann; Horn, Rosa; —; —

Pabst; Elisabeth Frances; 27-Jul-42; 18-Jan-43; Andr.; —; Hey, Maria; —; —; —; —; —

Pabst; Emil Otto; 19-Jul-64; 31-Jul-64; Andreas; Bobenhausen, Hessen; Horn, Anna Elisabeth; Baltimore; Horn, Eulalia; Nolting, Emil Otto; Horn, Valentin; —

Pabst; Heinrich; 19-Feb-45; 30-Mar-45; Adam; Bobenhausen, Hessen; Gro, Catharina; Underseichendrot, Hessen; Sehrt, Heinrich; Emrich, Conrad; —; —

Pabst; Johannes; 17-Feb-50; 1-Apr-50; Adam; Bobenhausen, Hessen; Gro, Catharina; —; Baum, Johannes; —; —; wit from Hirschenhain

Pabst; Ludwig; 25-Feb-43; 23-Apr-43; A.; —; Kern, Kathr.; —; —; —; —; —

Pabst; Marianne; 6-Jun-44; 14-Aug-44; Andr.; —; Hez, Marianne; —; —; —; —; —

Pahmeier; Bertha Friedericke; 17-Oct-54; 18-Feb-56; Gottlieb Dietrich; Herfort, Preussen; Linnenkube, Gertrud; —; Panetti, Eva Friederike; —; —; —

Pahmeier; Maria; 9-Aug-57; 6-Sep-58; Dietrich Gottlieb; Elbersdessen, Westphalen; Linnekugel, Franziska Gertrud; —; Habermehl, School teacher; —; —; —

Panetti; Elisabeth Wilhmina Johanna; 21-Oct-56; 26-Oct-56; Philipp Jakob; Ragelen, Baiern; Wimmer, Friederika; —; Ruppell, Elisabeth; Regener, Joh.; Rossel, Wilhelmina; —

Panetti; Friederike Johanne Dorothea; 19-Dec-59; 1-Jan-60; Philipp Adam Jakob; Ragland, Baiern; Wimmer, Eva Friederike; —; Schimpf, Auguste Friederike; Ruppel, Joh.; Reuter, Dorothea; —

Panetti; Jakobus Paulus David; 2-May-55; 10-May-55; Philipp Adam Jakob; Rugland, Baiern; Wimmer, Eva Friedricke; —; Regener, Johannes; Regener, Anna Catharina; —; child died

Surname Father; Child's Given Name; Birth Date; Baptismal Date; Father's Given Name; Father's Place of Birth; Mother's Surname and Given Name; Mother's Place of Birth; Witness 1 Surname and Given Name; Witness 2 Surname and Given Name; Witness 3 Surname and Given Name; Comments

Panetti; Johannes Elise; 18-Jun-53; 10-Jul-53; Philipp Adam Jakob; Rugland, Baiern; Wimmer, Eva Friedrika; —; Panetti, Jakob Eusebius; Regener, Johannes; Wimmer, Margaretha; child died

Panetti; Johannes Franz Elise; 26-Oct-61; 10-Nov-61; Philipp Adam Jakob; Rugland, Baiern; Wimmer, Eva Friederike; —; Ruppel, Joh.; Ruppel, Elisabeth; Tormelen, Franz; —

Panetti; Lucas Johannes; 18-Oct-63; 23-Nov-63; Philipp Adam Jakob; Rugland, Baiern; Wimmer, Eva Friedrike; Baudenbach, Baiern; Ruppel, Johann; Regener, Anna Katharine; —; —

Papler; Johannes; 15-Sep-46; 22-Oct-46; Heinrich; Helpershain, Grunberg, Hessen; Reuwer, Catharine; Vorden, Wurttemberg; Eisfelder, Joh.; —; —; —

Papst; Alexander Heinrich; 30-Apr-57; 17-May-57; Andreas; Bobenhausen, Hessen; Hay [?], Mariana; —; Einwachter, Alexander; Boppler, Heinr.; —; —

Papst; Andreas; 11-Apr-52; 2-May-52; Adam; Bobenhausen, Hessen; Gro, Catharine; —; Papst, Andreas; —; —; —

Papst; Catharine; 6-Jan-47; 24-Mar-47; Andreas; Bodenhausen, Ulrichstein, Hessen; Hei, Marianna; Baltimore; Bappler, Catharine; —; —; —

Papst; Elisabeth Catharina; 30-Jul-55; 26-Aug-55; Adam; Bobenhausen, Hessen; Groh, Catharina; —; Bach, Elisabeth Catharina; —; —; —

Papst; Elise; 6-Jan-50; 20-Jan-50; Andreas; Bobenhausen, Grunberg, Hessen; Heihaus, Marianne; Baltimore; Einwachter, Elise; —; —; —

Papst; Emma Louise; 11-Nov-54; 26-Nov-54; Andreas; Bobenhausen, Hessen; Hei, Mariane; —; Immich, Elisabeth; —; —; —

Papst; Philipp; 26-Apr-48; 30-Jul-48; Adam; Bobenhausen, Grunberg, Hessen; Gro, Catharine; Unterseibertenort, Grunberg, Hessen; Gro, Philipp; —; —; —

Pechtler; Jakob Friedrich; 23-Sep-51; 5-Oct-51; Michael; Wurzbach, Wuerttemberg; Velde, Johanne; —; Velde, Jakob Frdch.; Bauer, Anna Barbara; —; Pastor Nordmann

Surname Father; Child's Given Name; Birth Date; Baptismal Date; Father's Given Name; Father's Place of Birth; Mother's Surname and Given Name; Mother's Place of Birth; Witness 1 Surname and Given Name; Witness 2 Surname and Given Name; Witness 3 Surname and Given Name; Comments

Peppler; Carl; 10-Nov-45; 13-Apr-46; Georg; Biedenkopf, Hessen; Grossmann, Christiane; Biedenkopf, Hessen; Schneider, Carl; Layr, Christian; —; —

Peppler; Elise Henriette; 19-Aug-44; 3-Oct-44; Georg; —; Peppler, Henriette; —; —; —; —; —

Peppler; Georg Heinrich; 18-Sep-42; 21-Dec-42; Georg; —; Peppler, Henriette; —; —; —; —; —

Peppler; Maria Luise Sophie; 12-Jan-40; 19-Aug-40; Georg; —; Peppler, Henriette; —; —; —; —; —

Peppler; Wilhelmine Kathr. Elise; 28-Sep-38; 17-Mar-39; Georg; —; [--?--], Henriette; —; —; —; —; —

Pertsch; Johann Wilhelm; 5-Oct-49; 19-Nov-49; Jakob; Gronau, Marbach, Wurttemberg; Weber, Dorothea; Heubach, Odenwald, Hessen; —; —; —; child died

Peters; Karoline Christine; 2-May-41; 5-Sep-41; Johann Friedr.; —; Hildebrand, Bertha; —; —; —; —; —

Peters; Margaretha Maria; 3-Sep-39; 12-Sep-39; Karl; —; Kerkhofs, Maria; —; —; —; —; —

Petzer; Carl Heinrich; 14-Apr-46; 10-May-46; Carl; Eikforst, Minden; Luckens, Luise; Eikforst, Minden; Carsten, Carl; —; —; illegitimate

Pfaff; Christian; 19-Sep-48; 8-Oct-48; Jakob; Herleshausen, Eschwege, Kurhessen; Brack, Christine Elisabeth; Herleshausen, Eschwege, Kurhessen; Brack, Christian; —; —; —

Pfaff; Hanna Regina; 4-Sep-39; 23-Sep-39; Jacob; —; Ruppert, Elisab.; —; —; —; —; —

Pfaffenbach; Karl Christian Samuel; 15-May-59; 29-May-59; Arnold Friedrich; Spangenberg, Hessen; Pape, Katharina; —; Roder, Karl; —; —; —

Pfeifer; Elise; 7-Apr-45; 17-Aug-45; Joh. Wilhelm; Gedern, Hessen; Bunding, Maria; Niedergemunde, Hessen; —; —; —; born in New Orleans

Pfeifer; Johanna Catharina Margaretha; 17-Oct-47; 21-Nov-47; Johann Wilhelm; Gedern, Hessen; Binding, Maria; Nieder Gemunden, Hessen; McElvina, Margaretha; —; —; —

Surname Father; Child's Given Name; Birth Date; Baptismal Date; Father's Given Name; Father's Place of Birth; Mother's Surname and Given Name; Mother's Place of Birth; Witness 1 Surname and Given Name; Witness 2 Surname and Given Name; Witness 3 Surname and Given Name; Comments

Pfeiffer; Anna Maria; 12-Jul-39; 5-Aug-39; Heinrich; —; Kampleiter, Anna Marg.; —; —; —; —; —

Pfeiffer; Elisabeth; 10-Apr-38; 29-Apr-38; Johann Ph.; —; Romoser, Kathr.; —; —; —; —; —

Pfeiffer; Jacob Friedr.; 5-Mar-38; 1-Apr-38; Mathaus; —; Kull, Christine; —; —; —; —; —

Pfeiffer; Justus Wilh.; 8-Dec-36; 26-Mar-37; Joh. Friedr.; —; Ruff, Justine; —; —; —; —; —

Pfeiffer; Karoline; 29-Jan-39; 4-Aug-39; Johann G.; —; Bauer, Philipine; —; —; —; —; —

Pfeiffer; Nikolas; 1-Jun-37; 9-Jul-37; Nikolas; —; Furst, Kathr.; —; —; —; —; —

Pfeil; Christine Maria; 26-May-41; 25-Jul-41; Johann; —; Weiss, Karoline; —; —; —; —; —

Pfeil; Johann Adam; 16-Oct-45; 9-Nov-45; Johann Peter; Homberg a.d. Ohm, Hessen; Meyer, Elisabeth; Strasburg, PA; Papst, Adam; —; —; —

Pfeil; Joseph Heinrich; 5-May-44; 27-May-44; Peter; —; Meyers, Elisab.; —; —; —; —; —

Pfeil; Karoline Mathilde; —; 5-May-39; Johann; —; Weiss, Karoline; —; —; —; —; birth date unknown

Pfeil; Maria Karoline; 5-May-37; 11-Jun-37; Johann; —; Weiss, Karoline; —; —; —; —; —

Pfeister; Adam Friedrich; 2-Jan-39; 14-Jan-39; Adam Friedr.; —; Wild, Anna; —; —; —; —; —

Pfeister; Christiane Dorothea; 21-Oct-41; 28-Nov-41; Johann; —; Ruff, Justine; —; —; —; —; —

Pfeister; Christine Martha; 23-Jan-40; 16-Feb-40; Johann Phil.; —; Romoser, Kathr.; —; —; —; —; —

Pfeister; Dorothea Elisab.; 12-Jan-39; 25-Aug-39; Johann Friedr.; —; Ruff, Justine; —; —; —; —; —

Pfeister; Emil; 1-Nov-38; 30-Nov-38; Nikolas; —; Furst, Kathr.; —; —; —; —; —

Pfeister; Heinrich Anastatius; 30-Nov-41; 12-Dec-41; Heinrich; —; Kanzleiter, Anna M.; —; —; —; —; —

Surname Father; Child's Given Name; Birth Date; Baptismal Date; Father's Given Name; Father's Place of Birth; Mother's Surname and Given Name; Mother's Place of Birth; Witness 1 Surname and Given Name; Witness 2 Surname and Given Name; Witness 3 Surname and Given Name; Comments

Pfeister; Jacob Friedrich; 2-Jan-39; 14-Jan-39; Adam Friedr.; —; Wild, Anna; —; —; —; —; —

Pfeister; Katharine; 3-Jul-42; 3-Jul-42; Georg; —; Bauer, Philipine; —; —; —; —; —

Pfeister; Ludwig Jacob Karl; 20-Jun-41; 30-Jun-41; Nikkolas; —; Forster, Kathr.; —; —; —; —; 31 Jun 1841

Pfeister; Maria Elisab.; 24-Dec-41; 6-Feb-42; Mathaus; —; Kull, Christine; —; —; —; —; —

Pfeister; Mathaus; 28-Dec-41; 6-Feb-42; Johann Ph.; —; Romoser, Kathr.; —; —; —; —; —

Pfeister; Matthaus; 17-Nov-39; 15-Dec-39; Matthaus; —; Kull, Christine; —; —; —; —; —

Pfleger; Elise; 2-Mar-34; 6-May-38; Heinrich; —; Albert, Johanne; —; —; —; —; —

Pfleging; Luise Karoline; 2-Feb-37; 30-Jul-37; [--?--]; —; Albert, Johanne; —; —; —; —; —

Philipp; Anna Catharina; 30-Nov-47; 16-Jan-48; Peter; Rossbach, Biedenkopf, Hessen; Straher, Elisabeth; Rossbach, Biedenkopf, Hessen; Schmidt, Catharine; —; —; —

Philipson; Karl Wilh.; 21-Jun-39; 8-Sep-39; Abraham; —; Seich, Renate; —; —; —; —; —

Pieder; Georg; 9-Nov-46; 22-Nov-46; Caspar; Unter Alwa, Dorenbach, Sachsen Weimar; Hoffmann, Elisabeth; Zindelhommer, Baiern; Schumann, Georg; —; —; —

Pimzenbach; Severin Friedrich; 15-May-40; 8-Jun-40; Wilhelm; —; Kirchheim, Johanne; —; —; —; —; —

Pister; Johann Conrad; 10-Sep-39; 13-Oct-39; Conrad; —; Herrmann, Juliane; —; —; —; —; —

Pister; Wilhelimine Elise; 29-Dec-42; 22-Feb-43; Johann Konr.; —; Hermann, Juliane; —; —; —; —; —

Pister; Wilhelm; 28-Jan-41; 15-Mar-41; Conrad; —; Herrmann, Juliane; —; —; —; —; —

Plate; Sophia Rosine Maria; 24-Sep-48; 1-Oct-48; August; Delmenharst, Oldenburg; Weber, Caroline; Nienburg, Hannover; Gottscheck, Rosina; Nordmann, Sophia Margarethe; —; —

Surname Father; Child's Given Name; Birth Date; Baptismal Date; Father's Given Name; Father's Place of Birth; Mother's Surname and Given Name; Mother's Place of Birth; Witness 1 Surname and Given Name; Witness 2 Surname and Given Name; Witness 3 Surname and Given Name; Comments

Plessing; Christiane; 22-Mar-37; 26-Mar-37; Johann; —; Kuhl, Barbara; —; —; —; —; —

Plessing; Ludwig; 6-Sep-38; 13-Sep-38; Johann Fr.; —; Kuhl, Barbara; —; —; —; —; —

Plessing; Luise; 1-Mar-42; 13-Mar-42; Johann; —; Kuhl, Barb.; —; —; —; —; —

Plitt; Catharina Elisabeth; 28-Jun-47; 25-Jul-47; Heinrich; Biedenkopf, Hessen; Heck, Margaretha; Gladenbach, Hessen; Robert, Catharine; —; —; —

Plitt; Friedrich Heinrich; 18-Nov-49; 9-Dec-49; Heinrich; Biedenkopf; Heck, Margarethe; Gladenbach, Biedenkopf, Hessen; Hosbach, Friedrich; Schneider, Friedrich; —; —

Plitt; Johann Leonhardt; 31-Oct-51; 16-Oct-51; Heinrich; Biedekopf, Hessen; Heck, Margarethe; —; Dietrich, Leonhardt; —; —; —

Präbäker; Maria Anna Elisabeth; 22-Nov-44; 16-Mar-45; Georg; Baiern; Brodback, Catharina; PA; Baur, Maria Anna Elis.; —; —; —

Preis; Johann Georg; 16-Jul-44; 18-Aug-44; Michael; —; Hintze, Karoline; —; —; —; —; —

Prior; Philip; 11-Jun-43; 7-Jul-43; Johann; —; Gussmann, Elisab.; —; —; —; —; —

Pripenbrok; Maria Anna; 27-Aug-47; 22-Sep-47; Heinrich; Gutersbach, Preussen; Springmeyer, Cath. Wilhelmine; Dissen, Hannover; Hunemeyer, Wilhelmine; —; —; —

Prufer; Anna Maria; 8-Jun-60; 18-Jun-60; Karl August; Burkersdorf, Sachsen Weimar; Faber, Louise; —; Waltjen, Katharine; Heyse, Wilhelm; Reitzel, Friederike; —

Prufer; Friedrich August; 9-Nov-62; 16-Nov-62; Karl; Burkersdorf, Sachsen Weimar; Faber, Louise; —; Knochele, Christiane; Meier, Christian; Kehl, Marie; —

Prufer; Heinrich Andreas Johann; 13-Jun-55; 24-Jun-55; Carl Aug.; Backersdorf, Sachsen Weimar; Faber, Louise; —; Krauss, Joh. Georg; Keyl, Sophie Amalie; Winter, Joh. Andreas; child died

Prufer; infant daughter; 26-Feb-57; —; Karl Aug.; Burkersdorf, Sachsen Weimar; Faber, Louise; —; —; —; —; stillborn

Surname Father; Child's Given Name; Birth Date; Baptismal Date; Father's Given Name; Father's Place of Birth; Mother's Surname and Given Name; Mother's Place of Birth; Witness 1 Surname and Given Name; Witness 2 Surname and Given Name; Witness 3 Surname and Given Name; Comments

Prufer; Karoline Louise; 1-May-67; 19-May-67; Karl August; Burkersdorf, Sachsen Altenburg; Faber, Louise; Pferdsfeld, Preusen; Hulse, Ferdinand; Dunker, Katharina; —; —

Prufer; Martha Henriette; 17-Mar-65; 26-Mar-65; Karl August; Burckersdorf, Sachsen Weimar; Faber, Louise; —; Keyl, Martha Constantine; Kalthof, Henriette; —; —

Prufer; Wilhelm August; 26-Jun-58; 11-Jul-58; Karl August; Burkersdorf, Sachsen Weimar; Faber, Louise; —; Weidner, Johann; Knochele, Christiane; Keyl, Stephanus; —

Prutz; Christiane Luise; 2-Jan-43; 5-Feb-43; Friedrich; —; Becker, Karoline; —; —; —; —; —

Prutz; Georg Friedr.; 18-Jul-41; 22-Aug-41; Friedrich; —; Becker, Karoline; —; —; —; —; —

Prutz; Karoline Christine; 8-Apr-38; 13-May-38; Christoph Fr.; —; Becker, Karoline; —; —; —; —; —

Prutz; Katharine; 19-Nov-39; 25-Dec-39; Friedr.; —; Becker, Karoline; —; —; —; —; —

Prutz; Margarethe Sophie; 4-Apr-37; 4-Jun-37; Christoph; —; Becker, Caroline; —; —; —; —;

Purner; Johann Immanuel; 21-Oct-55; 4-Nov-55; Franz Carl Joseph; Grafenreuth, Baiern; Blum, Henriette; —; Purner, Joh. Andreas; Kruger, Philipp; Kruger, Catharina; —

Purner; Lydia Margaretha; 7-Nov-55; 11-Nov-55; Joh. Andreas; Schwartzenbach, Baiern; Korf, Sophie; —; Bruhl, Catharina; Kowalick, Friedrich; Korf, Hermina; —

Purner; Wilhelm Heinrich Friedrich; 30-Jun-53; 10-Jul-53; Joh. Andreas; Schwarzenbach, Baiern; Korff, Sophia; —; Stock, Mich. Frdch; Keyl, Amalie Sophie; Waltjen, Heinrich; —

Quehl; Susanne; 26-Feb-43; 11-May-43; Konrad; —; Perths, Maria; —; —; —; —; —

Quick; Karl Heinrich; 29-Apr-43; 16-Aug-43; Johann Heinr.; —; Schmidt, Kathr.; —; —; —; —; —

Quick; Sarah Catharina; 15-Oct-45; 18-Feb-46; Henry James; Baltimore; Schmidt, Catharine Regine; Baltimore; Schmidt, Johann David; Schmidt, Sarah; —; wits are grandparents

Surname Father; Child's Given Name; Birth Date; Baptismal Date; Father's Given Name; Father's Place of Birth; Mother's Surname and Given Name; Mother's Place of Birth; Witness 1 Surname and Given Name; Witness 2 Surname and Given Name; Witness 3 Surname and Given Name; Comments

Quinte; Catharine; 3-Jul-48; 30-Jul-48; Heinrich; Grienberg, Hessen; Papst, Christiane; Bobenhausen, Grunberg, Hessen; Papst, Catharine Gro; Papst, Christine; —; illegitimate

Raab; Georg; 25-May-47; 13-Jun-47; Georg; —; Lederer, Kunigunde; —; Lederer, Waldburg; —; —; Rev. Sands

Raab; Kunigunde; 7-Jan-49; 28-Jan-49; Johann Georg; Heichlingen, Lauf, Baiern; Vogel, Kunigunde; Dorflers, Herzogenaurach, Baiern; Leipoldt, Jakob; —; —; —

Rabe; Andreas; 4-Feb-44; 25-Feb-44; Wilhelm; —; Dehn, Luise; —; —; —; —; —

Rabe; Catharine; 2-Dec-45; 3-Feb-46; Wihelm; Schlagfutze, Wettern, Kurhessen; Dehne, Luise; Brumau, Waldeck; Ress, Cath.; —; —; —

Rabe; Heinrich Wiegand; 20-May-42; 5-Jun-42; Wilhelm; —; Dehn, Luise; —; —; —; —; —

Radecke; Anna Margaretha Wilhelmina; 13-May-58; 23-May-58; Dietrich Eberhard; Susstedt, Hannover; Schwizer, Catharina Louise; —; Radecke, Anna Margaretha; Radecka, Wilhelmina Friederika; —

Radecke; Anna Maria Sophia; 24-Sep-66; 7-Oct-66; Hermann Friedrich; Susstedt, Hannover; Meier, Anna Maria; Leste, Hannover; Lindmann, Anna Marg.; Bruns, Rebecca Maria; Meier, Mar. Adelheid

Radecke; Dietrich Heinrich Wilhelm; 23-Nov-56; 7-Dec-56; Joh. Wilhelm; Susstadt, Hannover; Duvel, Wilhelmina; —; Radecke, Herm. Heinr.; Radecke, Dietrich Eberhard; Louise, Margaretha Adelheid

Radecke; Heinrich Friedrich; 10-May-53; 15-May-53; Dietrich Eberhard; Susstedt, Hannover; Schweitzer, Katharina Louise; —; Radecke, Kasten Friedr.; —; —

Radecke; Karl Heinrich; 26-Dec-64; 8-Jan-65; Dietrich Eberhard; Susstedt, Hannover; Schweitzer, Katharine Louise; —; Louis, Karl Friedrich; Radecke, Sr., Hermann; —

Surname Father; Child's Given Name; Birth Date; Baptismal Date; Father's Given Name; Father's Place of Birth; Mother's Surname and Given Name; Mother's Place of Birth; Witness 1 Surname and Given Name; Witness 2 Surname and Given Name; Witness 3 Surname and Given Name; Comments

Radecke; Katharine Elisabet; 15-Mar-62; 30-Mar-62; Dietrich Eberhard; Susstedt, Hannover; Schweitzer, Katharine Louise; —; Immrich, Elisabeth; Weber, Katharine; —

Radecke; Louise Margaretha; 30-Jun-54; 16-Jul-54; Dietrich Eberhard; Susstedt, Hannover; Schweitzer, Louise Catharine; —; Louise, Margaretha Adelheid Louise; —; —

Radecke; Maria Rosine Rebecca; 8-Oct-56; 19-Oct-56; Dietrich Eberhard; Susstadt, Hannover; Schweitzer, Katharina Louise; —; Brockmeier, Maria; Aruns, Rebecca; —

Radecke (deceased); Katharina Friedericka Margaretha; 8-Feb-57; 15-Feb-57; Kasten Friedrich; Sustadt, Hannover; Brockmeier, Wilhelmina; —; Kunker, Katharina; Louis, Margaretha; Radecka, Margaretha

Radeke; Sophie Albine Charlotte; 23-Feb-67; 10-Mar-67; Friedrich Eberhard; Susstedt, Hannover; Schweitzer, Louise Katharine; Wurttemberg; Feiertag, Sophie Maria; Bruggemann, Albine Charlotte; —

Radeker; Anna Margaretha; 18-Jul-49; 19-Aug-49; Johann Friedrich; Sustadt, Bruchhausen, Hannover; Thielbahr, Rebekka Margareth; Sustadt, Bruchhausen, Hannover; Bachmann, Anna Margareth; —; —

Rahn; Christian Louis; 26-Jan-67; 6-Feb-67; Heinrich; Bobenhausen, Hessen; Selhardt, Elisabeth; Hessen; Rahn, Elisabetha; Strobel, Christian; —

Rahn; Friedrich Heinrich; 14-Apr-61; 28-Apr-61; Heinrich; Bobenhausen, Hessen; Sillhard, Elisabeth; —; Weber, Heinrich; Weber, Marie; Rahn, Elisabeth

Rahn; Heinrich Niklaus; 20-Aug-58; 5-Sep-58; Heinrich; Bobenhausen, Hessen; Silhardt, Elisabeth; —; Papst, Adam; Mieth, Nikolaus; Weber, Heinr.

Rahn; Karl Christian; 17-Jun-65; 30-Jun-65; Heinrich; Bobenhausen, Hessen; Silhardt, Elisabeth; Diebach, Hessen; Strobel, Christian; —; —

Rahn; Karl Johann; 6-Jun-63; 21-Jun-63; Heinrich; Bobenhausen, Hessen; Silhard, Elisabeth; —; Burmann, Johann; Weber, Elisabeth; —

Surname Father; Child's Given Name; Birth Date; Baptismal Date; Father's Given Name; Father's Place of Birth; Mother's Surname and Given Name; Mother's Place of Birth; Witness 1 Surname and Given Name; Witness 2 Surname and Given Name; Witness 3 Surname and Given Name; Comments

Rapp; Richard; 12-Sep-37; 13-Nov-37; Hans; —; Hartmeyer, Christine; —; —; —; —; —

Raquet; Karoline; 15-Aug-37; 10-Apr-38; Adam; —; Muller, Marg.; —; —; —; —; —

Rau; Elisabeth Magd.; 31-Jul-38; 5-Aug-38; Gidz; —; Schwieger, Elisab.; —; —; —; —; —

Rau; Katharine Elisabeth; 14-Nov-1860; 17-Mar-61; Ferdinand; Seldner, Hessen; Bauer, Christine; —; Rahn, Elisabeth; Weber, Katharine; —; —

Raubling; Georg Heinrich; 12-Dec-49; 13-Jan-50; Johann; Eifa, Alsfeld, Hessen; Klingel, Kunigunde; Hofgarten, Alsfeld, Hessen; Raubling, Georg Heinrich; Markel, Georg Heinr.; —;

Raund; Margarethe; 21-Oct-47; 31-Oct-47; Georg; Henfenfeld, Hersbruck, Baiern; Luger, Dorothea; Sadt, Velden, Baiern; Späth, Martin; Späth, Margarethe; —; —

Rausch; Georg; 28-Feb-41; 21-Feb-41; Johann; —; Dehnhart, Marg.; —; —; —; —; —

Rausch; Valentin; 17-Nov-38; 6-Jan-39; Georg; —; Henrich, Marg.; —; —; —; —; —

Reddiger; Anna Hanna; 2-Apr-64; 8-May-64; Johann; —; , ; —; Blum, Katharine; Richerein [?], Anna; —; —

Reddiger; Catharine; 21-Feb-54; 19-Mar-54; Joh.; Baiern; Reikmann, Maria; —; Blum, Catharina; —; —; —

Reddiger; Johann; 29-Jul-55; 12-Aug-55; Johann; Baiern; Rudemann, Barie; —; Immich, Joh.; —; —; —

Rediger; Ernst Johann; 19-Feb-59; 20-Mar-59; Johann; Ulzenheim, Baiern; Rickmann, Maria Elisabeth; —; Beck, Ernst; Bruns, Johann; —; —

Regener; [--?--]; 30-Oct-53; —; Johannes; Rosenthal, Kurhessen; Ronzbach, Katharina; —; —; —; —; stillborn

Regener; Augusta Wilhelmina Katharina; 20-Nov-57; 29-Nov-57; Johann; Rosenthal, Kurhessen; Ransbach, Katharina; —; Rossel, Wilhelmina Katharina; Engel, Augusta Wilhelmina; —; —

Surname Father; Child's Given Name; Birth Date; Baptismal Date; Father's Given Name; Father's Place of Birth; Mother's Surname and Given Name; Mother's Place of Birth; Witness 1 Surname and Given Name; Witness 2 Surname and Given Name; Witness 3 Surname and Given Name; Comments

Regener; Friedrich Wilhelm Georg; 15-Sep-60; 23-Sep-60; Johannes; Rosenthal, Kkurhessen; Ronsbach, Katharine; —; Rossel, Friedrike Wilhelmine; Klingelhofer, Wilhelm; Momberger, Georg; —

Regener; Georg Wilhelm Jakob; 27-Mar-56; 6-Apr-56; Joh.; Rosenthal, Kurhessen; Ronsbach, Katharine; —; Panetti, Philipp Ad. Jak.; Momberger, Georg; Rossel, Wilhelmine; child died

Regener; Maria Katharina; 30-Oct-53; 3-Nov-53; Johannes; Rosenthal, Kurhessen; Ronzbach, Katharina; —; Panetti, Philipp Adam Jakob; Momberger, Maria; Momberber, Georg; —

Rehbein; Adam Theodor; 10-May-45; 2-Feb-46; Georg; Schenkbergsfeld, Hirschfeld, Kurhessen; Orr, Catharine; Lifford, Co. Donegal, Ireland; Rehbein, Heinrich; —; —; —

Rehbein; Georg Samuel; 10-Mar-43; 2-Feb-46; Georg; Schenkbergsfeld, Hirschfeld, Kurhessen; Orr, Catharine; Lifford, Co. Donegal, Ireland; Goetz, Adam; —; —; —

Rehbein; Wilhelm Heinrich Harrison; 21-Oct-40; 2-Feb-46; Georg; Schenkbergsfeld, Hirschfeld, Kurhessen; Orr, Catharine; Lifford, Co. Donegal, Ireland; —; —; —; —

Rehberger; Luise; 7-Sep-44; 10-May-46; Valentin; Kreinfeld, Nidda, Hessen; Kleinschmidt, Gertrud; Bermuthsheim, Nidda, Hessen; Dietmann, Heinrich; —; —; —

Reich; Friederich; 13-May-46; 6-Sep-46; Bernhard; Klein Seelheim, Kurhessen; Ludovici, Maria; Wettern, Kurhessen; Kuhn, Friederich; —; —; —

Reichert; Johann Nikolas; 14-Jan-42; 13-Feb-42; Johann N.; —; Dengel, Karoline; —; —; —; —; —

Reiling; Margarethe; 1-Jun-47; 19-Jul-47; Adam; Kleinstadt, Hessen; Bauerschmidt, Catharine; Stadt Steinach, Baiern; Stertz, Margarethe; —; —; —

Reimann; Katharine Wilhelmine; 16-Oct-37; 14-Nov-37; Ernst Jacob; —; Sande, Kathr. Wilh.; —; —; —; —; —

Surname Father; Child's Given Name; Birth Date; Baptismal Date; Father's Given Name; Father's Place of Birth; Mother's Surname and Given Name; Mother's Place of Birth; Witness 1 Surname and Given Name; Witness 2 Surname and Given Name; Witness 3 Surname and Given Name; Comments

Rein; Elisabeth; 15-Sep-50; 29-Sep-50; Swerin; Allendorf, Hessen; Weiss, Margaretha; —; Reichardt, Elisabeth; —; —; 5 child, 4 dau

Reinhard; Christina Margaretha; 3-Aug-57; 9-Aug-57; Christoph; Allendorf, Hessen; Keil, Wilhelmina; —; Schmidt, Christiana; Weller, Christina; —; —

Reinhard; Maria Wilhelmine Emila; 12-May-59; 22-May-59; Christoph; Allendorf a.d.L., Hessen; Keil, Wilhelmina; —; Bergen, Maria; Leutner, Christoph; Schlerf, Emilia; —

Reinhard; Marie Anna Eleonora; 2-Jun-62; 15-Jun-62; Christoph; Allendorf a.d.L., Hessen; Keil, Wilhelmine; —; Schlerf, Anna Katharine; Bergen, Maria; Fuchs, Eleonora; —

Reinhardt; Georg Niklaus; 1-Jun-49; 25-Jun-49; Johann Christoph; Allendorf a.d. Lumda; Horst, Catharine Elisabeth; Zellen, Alsfeld, Hessen; Hoffmann, Georg Niklaus; —; —; —

Reinhardt; Johann Christoph; 14-May-49; 27-May-49; Christoph; Allendorf a.d. Lumbda, Kurhessen; Schmidt, Elisabeth; Warzenbach, Kurhessen; Reinhardt, Johann Christoph; —; —; —

Reinhardt; Magdalena; 15-Jun-47; 23-Jun-47; Christopfer; Allendorf a.d. Lumbda, Giessen, Hessen; Horst, Catharine; Zell, Alsfeld, Hessen; Eitel, Christine; —; —; —

Reinhardt; Maria; 28-Sep-45; 19-Oct-45; Christoph; Allendorf an d. Lumda, Hessen; Horst, Catharine; Zelle, Alsfeld, Hessen; Horst, Maria; —; —; wit is aunt

Reinke; Johann Heinrich; 28-Nov-49; 1-Dec-49; Johann; Neuenbruchhausen; Schuhmacher, Anna Maria; Monninghausen, Altenbruchhausen, Hannover; Breibe, Heinrich; —; —; child died

Reister; Caroline Elisabeth; 4-Nov-45; 23-Nov-45; Johann Georg; Stein bei Pforzheim, Baden; Hachtel, Anna Margaretha; Stilzisdorf in Schillingsfurst; Preis, Michel; Preis, Caroline; —; —

Reister; Eva Marg.; 30-Sep-42; 6-Nov-42; Johann G.; —; Hachtel, Anna M.; —; —; —; —; —

Reister; Johann Christian; 14-May-44; 16-Jun-44; Johann G.; —; Hachtel, Marg.; —; —; —; —; —

Reitzel; Maria Anna Adelheid; 4-May-58; 9-May-58; Matthaus Joseph; Forchtenberg, Wurttemberg; Fraske, Friederike; —; Strobel, Katharina Maria; Strobel, Nannette Hannette; Meier, Rebecca Adelheid; —

Renhoff; Friedrich Jakob; 9-Jun-48; 6-Aug-48; Friedrich; Todtenhausen, Kurhessen; Stremberger, Maria Elisabeth; Spachbruken bei Darmstadt, Hessen; Renhoff, Jakob; —; —; —

Renkel; Adam; 22-Apr-45; 6-Jul-45; Otto; Steinbach, Erbach, Hessen; Walther, Cath.; Steinbach, Erbach Hessen; Rösrig, Adam; Rösrig, Eva Elisabeth; —; —

Renz; Elisabeth Mathilde; 25-Oct-40; 25-Dec-40; Jacob Friedr.; —; Muller, Kathr.; —; —; —; —; —

Renz; Georg Friedr.; 17-Aug-37; 30-Sep-38; Jacob Fr.; —; Muller, Kathr.; —; —; —; —; —

Renz; Georg Friredrich; 30-Jan-39; 21-Mar-39; Georg Fr.; —; Scholl, Johanne Chr.; —; —; —; —; —

Renz; Karl; 22-Jan-43; 16-Apr-43; Jacob Friedr.; —; Muller, Kathr.; —; —; —; —; —

Repp; Catharine Caroline; 31-Dec-55; 6-Jan-56; Heinr. Conrad; Eichelsdorf, Hessen; Krell, Katharine; —; Imwalde, Catharine; Luck, Caroline; —; —

Repp; Elisabeth; 26-Sep-53; 9-Oct-53; Heinr. Konrad; Eichelsdorf, Hessen; Krell, Katharine; —; Krell, Rosine; Lenz, Susanna; —; —

Repp; Heinrich Christian Wilhelm; 8-Mar-58; 14-Mar-58; Heinrich Konrad; Einfelsdorf, Hessen; Krell, Katharina; —; Schmidt, Christine; Heyse, Wilhelm; Krell, Elisabeth; —

Repp; Johann Heinrich Melchior; 25-Apr-59; 1-May-59; Heinrich Konrad; Eichelsdorf, Hessen; Krell, Katharina; —; Schlerf, Melchior; Lenz, Heinr.; Krell, Joh.; —

Repp; Johann Karl; 31-Aug-61; 8-Sep-61; Heinrich Konrad; Eichelsdorf, Hessen; Krell, Katharine; —; Seibel, Johann; Lange, Karl; —; —

Surname Father; Child's Given Name; Birth Date; Baptismal Date; Father's Given Name; Father's Place of Birth; Mother's Surname and Given Name; Mother's Place of Birth; Witness 1 Surname and Given Name; Witness 2 Surname and Given Name; Witness 3 Surname and Given Name; Comments

Reppert; Maria Elisabeth; 7-Jun-43; 8-Oct-44; Ludwig; —; Johnson, Elisab.; —; —; —; —; —

Resch; Georg Carl; 8-May-55; 13-May-55; Georg; Munchen, Baiern; Bertram, Caroline; —; Bertram, Wilhelm; —; —; —

Retberg; Heinrich Conr. Ludw.; 12-Dec-41; 16-Jan-42; Jacob; —; Koch, Luise; —; —; —; —; —

Rettiger; Maria Elisabeth; 9-Aug-57; 27-Sep-57; Georg; Ulzenhain, Baiern; Rickmann, Elisabeth; —; Blum, Katharina; —; —; —

Reuter; Albert Georg; 1-Jul-54; 16-Jul-54; August; Michelstadt, Hessen; Blum, Dorothea; —; Stiegler, Georg; Waltjen, Maria; Purner, Joseph; —

Reuter; Anna Wilhelmine; 10-Dec-61; 22-Dec-61; August; Michelstadt, Hessen; Blum, Dorothea Auguste; —; Friedrich, Anna; Regener, Anna Katharine; Klingelhofer, Wilhelm; —

Reuter; Eduard; 25-Nov-38; 1-Jan-39; Andreas; —; Hussong, Elisab.; —; —; —; —; —

Reuter; Friedrich Ludw.; 17-Apr-37; 6-Jun-37; Andreas; —; Hussong, Elisabeth; —; —; —; —; —

Reuter; Johann Herrmann Gottlieb; 18-Aug-45; 5-Oct-45; Friedrich; Seelenfeld, Petershagen, Preussen; Witten, Elisabeth; Seelenfeld, Petershagen, Preussen; Hitzmann, Friedrich; Struckmann, Mrs.; —; —

Reuter; Johann Jakob Friedrich; 13-Jan-58; 24-Jan-58; August; Michelstadt, Hessen; Blum, Dorothea; —; Panetti, Philipp Adam Jakob; Panetti, Eva Friederike; Ruppel, Johann; —

Reuter; Johann Maria Wilhelmine; 19-Oct-59; 30-Oct-59; August; Michelstadt, Hessen; Blum, Dorothea; —; Rossel, Maria; Friedrich, Michael; Westermann, Wilhelmine; —

Reuter; Wilhelm Karl; 31-Dec-63; 17-Jan-64; August; Michelstadt, Hessen; Blum, Dorothea; Zellersfeld, Hannover; Klingelhofer, Wilhelm; Regner, Katharine; —; —

Rexe; Johann Gerhard; 16-Mar-51; 21-May-51; Joh. Aug.; Amt Sicken, Hannover; Begmann, Margaretha; —; father, ; —; —; —

Surname Father; Child's Given Name; Birth Date; Baptismal Date; Father's Given Name; Father's Place of Birth; Mother's Surname and Given Name; Mother's Place of Birth; Witness 1 Surname and Given Name; Witness 2 Surname and Given Name; Witness 3 Surname and Given Name; Comments

Riedel; Heinrich Philipp; 6-Aug-57; 20-Aug-57; Konrad; Altenblass, Baiern; Ruppel, Anna Elisabeth; —; Ruppel, Joh. Heinrich; Konig, Philipp; —; —

Riedel; Johann Adam Heinrich; 7-May-59; 19-May-59; Konrad; Altenbloss, Baiern; Ruppel, Elisabeth; —; Ruppel, Joh.; Bach, Adam; Habermehl, School teacher; in house

Riegeler; Johann Christoph; 12-Jan-47; 19-Mar-47; Johann Christoph; Biegarten, Herzog Aurach, Baiern; Gries, Elisabeth; Baiersdorf, Forchheim, Baiern; Billmann, Marg.; —; —; father deceased

Riehn; Hermann Heinrich; 2-Aug-67; 18-Aug-67; Christian Heinrich; Osnabruck, Hannover; Arndt, Auguste; Baltimore; Ellermann, Hermann Heinrich; Arndt, Jakob; —; —

Riemenschneider; Maria Dorothea; 5-Jan-53; 23-Jan-53; Gottlieb; Bad Rethburg, Hannover; Stroh, Dorothea; —; Waltjen, Dorothea; Waltjen, Herm.; Waltjen, Maria; —

Riemenschneider; Sophie Magdalena; 20-Jun-51; 29-Jun-51; Gottlieb; Bad Rohtler, Hannover; Stroh, Magdalena; —; Stroh, Dor. Magdalena; —; —; —

Riethmuller; Catharine; 5-Oct-45; 3-Feb-46; Heinrich; Brumau, Waldeck; Dehne, Elisabeth; Brumau, Waldeck; Rabe, Catharine Ress; —; —; child died

Riethmuller; Wilhelm Ludw. Friedr. Adam; 11-May-41; 29-May-41; Heinr.; —; Dahn, Elisab.; —; —; —; —; —

Rietmuller; Luise; 19-Oct-42; 18-Dec-42; Heinrich; —; Dehn, Elisab.; —; —; —; —; —

Rietzel; Johann Georg Heinrich; 26-Oct-55; 4-Nov-55; Matthaus; Forchtenberg, Wurttemberg; Fraske, Friederike; —; Dunker, Joh. Kasten; Schmidt, Joh. Georg; Strobel, Joh. Georg; —

Rietzel; Karl Andreas; 12-Jul-56; 27-Jul-56; Joh. Georg; Forchendorf, Baiern; Meier, Sophia; —; Kasten, Karl; Kasten, Louise; —; —

Rinkel; Rutilia Marianna; 10-Mar-47; 21-Nov-47; Otto; Steinbach bei Erbach, Hessen; Walther, Catharine; Steinbach bei Erbach, Hessen; Hubner, Maria; —; —; —

Risau; Johann Heinrich; 3-May-43; 7-Jul-43; Johann Heinr.; —; Vansandern, Marg.; —; —; —; —; —

Ritter; Schejo [?] Heinr. Gustav; 5-Feb-41; 9-Apr-41; Heinrich A.; —; Pfluger, Emilie; —; —; —; —; —

Ritz; Anna Maria; 19-Sep-47; 21-Nov-47; David; Little York, PA; Ebele, Maria; Little York, PA; Ritz, Anna Maria; —; —; —

Ritz; David; 21-Jun-47; 27-Jun-47; Daniel; Little York, PA; Schüttrempf, Maria; Friedewald, Kurhessen; Sus, Georg Michael; —; —; —

Ritz; Margaretha Magdalena; 12-Feb-52; 8-Mar-52; Daniel; York, PA; Schietrumpf, Marie; —; Ziegler, Catharine Margarethe; —; —; —

Rixe; Anna Maria; 20-Nov-46; 30-Dec-46; Johann Albert; Godesdorf, Sieke, Hannover; Bergmann, Marg.; Wachendorf, Sieke, Hannover; Meyer, Anna Catharine; —; —; —

Rixe; Anna Sophia; 13-Aug-48; 28-Sep-48; Johann August; Godesdorf, Sieke, Hannover; Bergmann, Gesche Margarethe; Wachendorf, Sieke, Hannover; Meyer, Maria; Vogelsang, Anna Dorothea; —; —

Roese; Katharine Luise; 17-Sep-42; 16-Oct-42; Heinrich; —; Seipel, Magd.; —; —; —; —; —

Rohlfing; Anna Maria; 2-Oct-67; 27-Oct-1867; Ludwig; Friedwalde, Preussen; Funk, Elisabeth; Huchelheim, Preussen; Stetter, Anna Maria; Funk, Maria; Brauer, Margaretha; —

Rolfing; Auguste Lisette Katharine; 7-Dec-62; 21-Dec-62; Ludwig; Friedwald, Preussen; Jung, Elise; —; Schimpf, Auguste Friedrike; Kowalik, Lisette; Jung, Katharine; —

Rolfing; Elisabeth Philippine Susanne; 17-Sep-65; 1-Oct-65; Ludwig; Klinden, Preussen; Junk, Elisabeth; Sochelstein, Preussen; Kunker, Katharine; Bremer, Katharina; Schimpfe, Leuzuste [?]; —

Rolfing; Katharine Marie Margarethe; 5-Feb-64; 28-Feb-64; Ludwig; Friedewald, Kurhessen; Funk, Elise; Hochelsheim, Preussen; Funk, Katharine; Dietel, Konrad; Arras, Margarethe; —

Surname Father; Child's Given Name; Birth Date; Baptismal Date; Father's Given Name; Father's Place of Birth; Mother's Surname and Given Name; Mother's Place of Birth; Witness 1 Surname and Given Name; Witness 2 Surname and Given Name; Witness 3 Surname and Given Name; Comments

Roll; Johann; 26-Nov-45; 28-Jan-46; Johannes; Detweiler, Elsass; Reitz, Charlotte; Hochberger, Glashutte, Litzelstein, Elsass; Oster, Johann; —; —; —

Roll; Ludwig; 19-Jun-42; 28-Jan-46; Johannes; Detweiler, Elsass; Reitz, Charlotte; Hochberger, Glashutte, Litzelstein, Elsass; Reitz, Ludwig; —; —; —

Rollmann; Wigand Johann; 14-Oct-45; 28-Dec-45; Johann; Odenberg, Hessen; Holtz, Friederike; Stadt Oldendorf, Braunschweig; Rollmann, Wigand; —; —; wit is grandfather

Romeser; Johann Jakob; 29-Oct-53; 20-Nov-53; Joh. Gottfried; Rodensohl, Wurttemberg; Ohmenhauser, Louise Regina; —; Romeser, Jakob Frdch.; Ohmenhausen, Susanne; —; —

Romeser; Maria Katharine; 24-Nov-57; 6-Dec-57; Johann Gottfried; Rotensohl, Wurttemberg; Ohmenhauser, Louise Regina; —; Einwachter, Alexander; Einwachter, Katharine; Omenhauser, Susanna; —

Romesser; Emilie Karoline; 9-Oct-51; 9-Nov-51; Georg Friedr.; Rothenzoh, Wurttemberg; Trautmann, Charlotte; —; Trautmann, Albert Friedr.; —; —; —

Romesser; Louise Susanne; 30-Apr-51; 25-May-51; Gottfried; Rothensohl, Wurttemberg; Ohmenhauser, Louise Regine; —; Ohmenhauser, Susanne; —; —; —

Romester; Wilhelm Heinrich; 20-Feb-60; 4-Mar-60; Johann Gottfried; Rothensohl, Wurttemberg; Ohmenhaufer, Louise Regine; —; Mohring, Joh.; Spielmann, Joh. Heinrich; —; —

Romig; Karl Heinrich; 20-May-39; 23-Jun-39; Dr. Johann; —; Mattin, Susanne; —; —; —; —; —

Romoser; Anna Elisab.; 24-Aug-40; 28-Mar-41; Johann Ph.; —; Spengel, Eva; —; —; —; —; —

Romoser; Anna Margarethe; 29-Mar-49; 3-Jun-49; Jakob; Rodensohl, Steinebirk, Wurttemberg; Bötcher, Caroline; Nandershausen, Rothenburg, Kurhessen; Schlessinger, Anna Marg.; —; —; —

Romoser; Anna Maria; 2-Jul-38; 22-Jul-38; Johann Martin; —; Finkbein, Johanne; —; —; —; —; —

Surname Father; Child's Given Name; Birth Date; Baptismal Date; Father's Given Name; Father's Place of Birth; Mother's Surname and Given Name; Mother's Place of Birth; Witness 1 Surname and Given Name; Witness 2 Surname and Given Name; Witness 3 Surname and Given Name; Comments

Romoser; Caroline; 16-Dec-45; 13-Mar-46; Johann Martin; Rodensohl, Neuenbirk, Wurttemberg; Fenkbeiner, Johanne; Götelfingen, Friedenstadt, Wurttemberg; Pfeifer, Johann Philipp; —; —; —

Romoser; David Franklin; 8-May-42; 17-Dec-43; Johann Ph.; —; Spengler, Eva; —; —; —; —; —

Romoser; Eduard Martin; 8-Nov-47; 12-Dec-47; Johann Martin; Rodensohl; Fenkbeiner, Johanne; Guttelfingen, Wurttemberg; Pfeifer, Johann Philipp; —; —; —

Romoser; Karl Philip; 3-Nov-38; 15-Apr-38; Johann; —; Spenger, Eva; —; —; —; —; —

Romoser; Karl Philip; 25-May-43; 17-Dec-43; Johann M.; —; Finkbein, Johanne; —; —; —; —; twin

Romoser; Maria Christine; 26-Jan-47; 21-Mar-47; Jakob Fried; Rodensohl, Wuerttemberg; Bottcher, Anna Sawina; Stentershausen, Rotenburg, Kurhessen; Romeser, Joh. Gottfried; Romeser, Christine; —; —

Romoser; Maria Elisab.; 5-Jan-40; 16-Feb-40; Johann; —; Finkbein, Johanne; —; —; —; —; —

Romoser; Samuel Friedrich; 10-Mar-50; 6-Jul-50; Johann Martin; Rothenhols, Wurttemberg; Fingseiner, Johanna; Gottelfingen, Wurttemberg; —; —; —; —

Romoser; Sophie Christine; 18-Oct-49; 18-Nov-49; George Friedrich; Rodensohl, Neuenbirk, Wurttemberg; Trautmann, Amalie Charlotte; Klagfurth, Sachsen, Preussen; Trautmann, Gustav; Romoser, Caroline; —; —

Romoser; Wilhelm; 25-May-43; 17-Dec-43; Johann M.; —; Finkbein, Johanne; —; —; —; —; twin

Romussen; Karl Friedrich; 5-Dec-63; 20-Dec-63; Johann Gottfried; Rothensohl, Wurttemberg; Ohmens, Louise Regine; Philadelphia; Schlerf, Philipp; Schorrer, Paul; Karle, Katharine; —

Roos; Christoph Adam; 7-Oct-38; 4-Nov-38; Christoph; —; Köhler, Ottilie; —; —; —; —; —

Surname Father; Child's Given Name; Birth Date; Baptismal Date; Father's Given Name; Father's Place of Birth; Mother's Surname and Given Name; Mother's Place of Birth; Witness 1 Surname and Given Name; Witness 2 Surname and Given Name; Witness 3 Surname and Given Name; Comments

Rosch; Anna Maria Elisabeth; 15-Feb-57; 22-Mar-57; Georg; Munchen; Bertram, Anna Maria; —; Bertram, Elisabeth; Balz, Elisabeth; —; —

Rosch; Franz Johann Paul; 16-Jan-59; 13-Mar-59; Georg; Munchen, Baiern; Bertram, Karoline; —; Zink, Georg Frdch.; Schorrer, Paul; —; —

Rosch; Wilhelm; 3-Sep-53; 11-Sep-53; Georg; Munchen, Baiern; Bertram, Karoline; —; Bertram, Wilh.; —; —; —

Rosengarn; Sophie; 4-Jul-51; 3-Aug-51; Karl; Gehrte, Hannover; Henzen, Catharine; —; parents, ; —; —; —

Rosius; Georg; 27-Jan-46; 2-Feb-46; Jakob; Strasburg; Schmidt, Luise; Rixhenau, Lippe; Schmidt, Friederich; —; —; —

Rössler; Anna Luise; 24-Jun-42; 21-Aug-42; Johann Andreas; —; Schmidt, Kathr. B.; —; —; —; —; —

Rossmark; Johann Christian Friedrich; 21-Aug-45; 23-Nov-45; Johann; Seidesheim, Baiern; Cordes, Marie; Rethem, Hannover; Kernhaas [?], Johann; Seifert, Christian Friedrich; Dodenhof, Adelheid; —

Rossmark; Malvine Sophie; 23-Feb-52; 28-Apr-52; Georg; Schweinfurt, Baiern; Cordes, Marie; —; Kordes, Sophie; Sormuller, Malvine; —; —

Rossmarkt; Ferdinand; 22-Oct-47; 15-Dec-47; George; Zeilenheim, Volkach, Baiern; Cordes, Maria; Rethem, Hannover; Fick, Ferdinand; —; —; —

Rost; Maria Barbara; 1-Oct-48; 22-Oct-48; Johann Martin; Igtheim, Mindheim, Baiern; Kopp, Anna Dorothea; Igtheim, Mindheim, Baiern; Pitzinger, Maria Barbara; —; —; —

Roth; Margaretha Magdalene; 20-Feb-46; 13-Apr-46; Conrad; Niedhausen, Hessen; Schwartz, Catharine; Dietelsheim, Hessen; Roth, Margaretha Magdalene; —; —; —

Rubsaame; Johann Georg Martin; 6-Mar-46; 7-Jun-46; Johann Martin; Metzlar; Handwerk, Christiane; Metzlar; Kammerer, Georg; —; —; —

Rubsame; Johann Peter; 5-Jul-39; 4-Aug-39; Heinrich; —; Zecher, Elisab.; —; —; —; —; —

Surname Father; Child's Given Name; Birth Date; Baptismal Date; Father's Given Name; Father's Place of Birth; Mother's Surname and Given Name; Mother's Place of Birth; Witness 1 Surname and Given Name; Witness 2 Surname and Given Name; Witness 3 Surname and Given Name; Comments

Ruckauer; Elisabeth; 23-Dec-59; 15-Aug-50; Sebastian; Herschbruck, Wurttemberg; Kittler, Maria; —; Bracht, Elisabeth; —; —; 1 child

Ruckert; Agnes Medora Constretia; 10-Nov-45; 13-Feb-46; Philipp; Zwingenberg, Hessen; Dietz, Maria; Wolf, Bindingen, Hessen; Horn, Medora Constretia; —; —; —

Ruckert; Georg Friedrich; 20-Jul-64; 31-Jul-64; Philipp Ludwig; Baltimore; Trabant, Anna Katharine; Baltimore; Breil, Georg; Kleppesch, August; Vogel, Selma; —

Ruckert; Johann Philip; 16-Dec-43; 28-Dec-43; Philip; —; Dietz, Maria; —; —; —; —; —

Ruckert; Johannes; 1-Dec-49; 14-Jan-50; Philipp; Zweigenberg, Hessen; Dietz, Maria; Wolf bei Hiessen; Ruppel, Johannes; —; —; child died

Ruckert; Ludwig; 8-Sep-36; 14-May-38; Ludwig; —; Roges, Kathr.; —; —; —; —; —

Ruckert; Maria Dorothea; 20-Oct-38; 5-Nov-38; Philip; —; Dietz, Maria; —; —; —; —; —

Ruckert; Maria Friedricke Elisabeth; 1-Nov-67; 17-Nov-1867; Philipp Ludwig; Baltimore; Trabant, Katharina; Baltimore; Hofmann, Katharina Elisabeth; Kastner, Maria; Kowalik, Friedrich; —

Ruckert; Maria Lisette; 24-Jul-47; 18-Oct-47; Philipp; Zwiegenberg, Hessen; Dietz, Anna Maria; Wolf, Bidingen, Hessen; Ruckert, Lisette; —; —; child died

Rudolph; Anna Adelheid; 28-Mar-59; 10-Apr-59; Ernst Benjamin; Ezbau, Sachsen; Vogel, Adelheid Mathilda; —; Schultheiss, Lisette; Vogel, Emil; Knochele, Christiane; —

Rudolph; Ernst Emil Theodor; 26-Sep-60; 30-Sep-60; Ernst; Ezbau, Sachsen; Vogel, Adelheid Mathilde; —; Vogel, Selma; Habermehl, Frau; Laufer, Karl; —

Rudolph; Ernst Wilhelmn Emmanuel; 17-Aug-62; 29-Aug-62; Ernst Benjamin; Egbar, Sachsen; Vogel, Adelheid Mathilde; —; Keyl, Sophie Amalie; Keyl, Stephanus; Bruggemann, Elise Wilhelmine; —

Surname Father; Child's Given Name; Birth Date; Baptismal Date; Father's Given Name; Father's Place of Birth; Mother's Surname and Given Name; Mother's Place of Birth; Witness 1 Surname and Given Name; Witness 2 Surname and Given Name; Witness 3 Surname and Given Name; Comments

Rudolph; Klara Ottilie; 29-Jan-65; 5-Mar-65; Ernst Benjamin; Egbau, Sachsen; Vogel, Adelheid Mathilde; Egbau, Sachsen; Feiertag, Sophie; Vogel, Emilie Juliane; Briel, Johann; —

Rudolph; Mathilda Hermina; 20-May-57; 2-Jun-57; Ernst Benjamina; Ezbau, Sachsen; Vogel, Adelheid Mathilda; —; Vogel, Wihlelm; Schafer, Katharina; Keyl, Rev.; baptized by Rev. Sommer

Ruff; Catharina; 2-Apr-50; 20-Apr-50; Jakob Friedrich; Dobel, Neuenbirk, Wurttemberg; Steiner, Catharina; Untersiemau, Sachsen Coburg; —; —; —; —

Ruff; Christine; 10-Jan-38; 13-Apr-38; Jacob Fr.; —; König, Jacobine; —; —; —; —; —

Ruff; Elisabeth; 21-Oct-43; 13-Dec-43; Jacob; —; Meiner, Kathr.; —; —; —; —; —

Ruff; Georg Christian; 14-Nov-44; 25-Nov-44; Samuel Fr.; —; Kull, Christine; —; —; —; —; twin

Ruff; Jakob Friederich; 5-Jun-45; 7-Jun-45; Jakob Friederich; Dobel, Neuenberg, Wurttemberg; Steiner, Cath.; Untersied bei Coburg; —; —; —; child died

Ruff; Maria Elisabeth; 14-Nov-44; 25-Nov-44; Samuel Fr.; —; Kull, Christine; —; —; —; —; twin

Ruhwer; Karl; 17-Dec-1850; 21-Apr-51; Heinr.; Stade, Hannover; Wagner, Anna; —; Zenge, Nikolaus; —; —; —

Ruhwin; Carl Ludwig; 29-May-49; 12-Aug-49; Heinrich; Stade, Hannover; Wagner, Anna Catharine; Bremen; Muller, Christoph; —; —

Rupp; Elisabeth; 29-Jul-40; 4-Oct-40; Georg; —; Hirt, Luise; —; —; —; —

Ruppel; Elisabeth Maria Lisetta; 13-Sep-57; 27-Sep-57; Niklas; Hopfgarten, Hessen; Reisinger, Maria Christine; —; Ruppel, Elisabeth; Ruppel, Maria; Kowalik, Lisetta

Ruppel; Emalia Dorothea Elisabeth; 28-Jun-66; 8-Jul-66; Nicholaus; Hopfgarten, Hessen; Reisinger, Maria Christianne; Wembach, Hessen; Stegner, Amalie; Reisinger, Dorothea; Ruppel, Elisabeth

Surname Father; Child's Given Name; Birth Date; Baptismal Date; Father's Given Name; Father's Place of Birth; Mother's Surname and Given Name; Mother's Place of Birth; Witness 1 Surname and Given Name; Witness 2 Surname and Given Name; Witness 3 Surname and Given Name; Comments

Ruppel; Henriette Katharine Elisabeth; 10-Aug-66; 26-Aug-66; Georg Eberhard; Alsfeld, Hessen; Happel, Elisabeth; Josbach, Kurhessen; Happel, Heinrich; Happel, Katharine Elsiabeth; —

Ruppel; Johann Friedrich Georg; 19-Sep-64; 2-Oct-64; Niklaus; Hopfgarten, Hessen; Reisinger, Anna Christiane; Weinbach, Hessen; Reisinger, Joh.; Ruppel, Joh.; Kowalik, Frdch.

Ruppel; Johann Niklas; 28-Sep-61; 6-Oct-61; Niklas; Hopfgarten, Hessen; Reisinger, Marie Christiane; —; Ruppel, Joh. Niklas; —; —

Ruppel; Johanne Elisabeth Mariane; 21-Mar-60; 1-Apr-60; Niklas; hofkirchen, Hessen; Reisinger, Marie Christiane; —; Reisinger, Joh.; Ruppel, Elis.; —

Ruppel; Johannes; 13-Jun-47; 4-Jul-47; Heinrich; Hofgarten, Alsfeld, Hessen; Bühler, Maria; Weida, Sulz, Wurttemberg; Ruppel, Johannes; —; —

Ruppel; Johannes; 15-May-49; 20-May-49; Heinrich; Hopfgarten, Alsfeld, Hessen; Biehler, Maria; Weida, Sulz, Wurttemberg; Ruppel, Johannes; —; —

Ruppel; Wilhelmine Selma Mathilde; 3-Sep-66; 16-Sep-66; Kaspar Karl; Alsfeld,Hessen; Vogel, Emilie Selma; Eibau, Sachsen; Vogel, Wilhelmine; Rudolph, Adelheid Mathilde; Keyl, Maria

Ruppell; Johann Wilhelm; 25-Apr-51; 4-May-51; Heinr.; Hofgarten, Hessen; Biehler, Marie; —; Ruppell, Joh.; Fischer, Heinr.; —

Ruprecht; Peter Conrad; 15-Jan-46; 21-Nov-47; Bernhard; Sidigeshagen, Worms, Preussen; Lauterbach, Maria; Sidgeshagen, Worms, Preussen; Weyrich, Johann Peter; —; —

Rusk; Mariane; 20-Nov-47; 12-Dec-47; Jakob Friedrich; Dobe, Neuenbirk, Wurttemberg; Steiner, Catharine; Untersiemens, Sachsen Coburg; —; —; —

Sachs; Albert; 15-Jul-51; 28-Aug-51; Joh.; Mittelsinne, Kurhessen; Heinz, Magdalena; —; Sachs, Melchior; —; —

Sachs; Anna; 7-Mar-51; 2-Apr-51; Melchior; Mittelsinn, Hessen; Bull, Helene; —; Sachs, Anna; Sachs, Joh.; mother

Sachs; Johann; 31-Aug-48; 22-Oct-48; Johannes; Mittelsins, Orch., Baiern; Heinz, Magdalene; Burkseis, Gemunde, Baiern; Voigt, Johannes; —; —; —

Surname Father; Child's Given Name; Birth Date; Baptismal Date; Father's Given Name; Father's Place of Birth; Mother's Surname and Given Name; Mother's Place of Birth; Witness 1 Surname and Given Name; Witness 2 Surname and Given Name; Witness 3 Surname and Given Name; Comments

Sachs; Margaretha; 4-Jan-46; 20-Apr-46; Johann; Mittelsinn, Baiern; Heintz, Magdalena; Burgsin, Gemunde Baiern; Barth, Margarethe; —; —; —

Sachs; Maria; 10-Jan-50; 3-Feb-50; Johannes; Mittelsin, Baiern; Heinz, Magdalen; Burgsein, Baiern; Schafer, Maria; —; —; —

Sahm; Philipine; 27-Oct-38; 23-Dec-38; Karl; —; Doll, Kathr.; —; —; —; —; —

Sander; Alexander; 5-Nov-39; 14-Nov-39; Peter; —; Hertz, Barbara; —; —; —; —; twin

Sander; Georg Heinrich; 10-Dec-54; 25-Dec-54; Georg; Balitmore; Duncker, Susanna; —; Sander, Barbara; Sander, Alexander; —; —

Sander; Heinrich; 18-Sep-43; 24-Sep-43; Peter; —; Hertz, Barb.; —; —; —; —; —

Sander; Peter; 5-Nov-39; 14-Nov-39; Peter; —; Hertz, Barbara; —; —; —; —; twin

Sarbacher; Georg; 20-Jul-45; 10-Aug-45; Franz; —; Georg, Dorothea; Waismain, Baiern; Dietrich, Georg; Dietrich, Margaretha; —; —

Sartorius; Carl; 30-May-45; 20-Jun-45; Johann Georg; Monsheim, Worms, Hessen; Pfaff, Catharina; Kaiserslautern, Rheinbaiern; Pfaff, Johann; —; —; —

Schaberg; Emma Catharina; 1-Aug-49; 14-Oct-49; Hermann; Bramsche, Forde, Hannover; Ernste, Elisabeth; Bramsche, Forde, Hannover; Wiegel, Catharine; —; —; —

Schade; Johann Heinr. Dan; 27-May-39; 28-Jul-39; Daniel; —; [--?--], Margaretha; —; —; —; —; —

Schaefer; Karl heinr. Wilh.; 24-Jul-39; 26-Sep-39; Johann Jacob; —; Jenter, Anna M.; —; —; —; —; —

Schafer; Anna Kathr.; 7-Aug-40; 6-Jan-42; Augustin; —; Gross, Kathr.; —; —; —; —; —

Schafer; Barbara Christine; 15-Jan-58; 14-Feb-58; Niklaus; Gernheim, Baiern; Riedel, Barbara; —; Riedel, Christine; Rausch, Barbara; —; —

Surname Father; Child's Given Name; Birth Date; Baptismal Date; Father's Given Name; Father's Place of Birth; Mother's Surname and Given Name; Mother's Place of Birth; Witness 1 Surname and Given Name; Witness 2 Surname and Given Name; Witness 3 Surname and Given Name; Comments

Schafer; Christiane; 28-Oct-46; 28-Oct-46; Christian Jakob; Weinberg, Wurttemberg; Meyer, Christiane; Waldbach, Wurttemberg; —; —; —; —

Schafer; Christiane Maria; 5-May-42; 12-Jun-42; Christian Jacob; —; Meyer, Christiane Fr.; —; —; —; —; —

Schafer; Christopher Ludwig; 20-Mar-45; 20-Apr-45; Christian Jakob; Weinsberg, Wurttemberg; Meyer, Christiane; Waldeck, Wurttemberg; Hacker, Christoph; Hacker, Mrs.; —; child died

Schafer; Daniel Wilhelm; 17-Nov-38; 16-Dec-38; Christian Jac.; —; Meyer, Christiane; —; —; —; —; —

Schafer; Dorothea Amalie; 11-Sep-40; 4-Oct-40; Jacob; —; Gunther, Anna M.; —; —; —; —; —

Schafer; Elisabeth; —; 24-Dec-54; Georg; —; Riedel, Barbara; —; Riedel, Elisabeth; —; —; —

Schafer; Eva Luise; 27-Oct-47; 21-Nov-47; Christian Jakob; Weinsberg, Wurttemberg; Meyer, Christiane; Waldbach, Wurttemberg; Hacker, Luise; —; —; —

Schafer; Georg Elik; 17-Nov-37; 3-Jan-39; Jacob; —; Muller, Anna M.; —; —; —; —; —

Schafer; Heinrich Adam Emil; 12-May-56; 25-May-56; Heinrich; Lisberg, Hessen; Hillgartner, Katharine; —; Bach, Adam; Leutner, Christoph; Vogel, Emil; —

Schafer; Hermann; 19-Dec-41; 6-Feb-42; Heinrich; —; Schmidt, Elisab.; —; —; —; —; —

Schafer; Jacob; 25-Dec-41; 6-Jan-42; Augustin; —; Gross, Kathr.; —; —; —; —; —

Schafer; Jacob Christian; 7-Jun-43; 7-Jul-43; Christian Jacob; —; Meyer, Christiane; —; —; —; —; —

Schafer; Johann; 21-Apr-46; 10-May-46; Georg; Dalherda, Bruckenau, Baiern; Wensen, Gertrud; Dalherda, Bruckenau, Baiern; Schafer, Johann; —; —; —

Schafer; Johann Friedrich; 24-Jun-37; 12-Jun-42; Christian Jacob; —; Meyer, Christiane Fr.; —; —; —; —; —

Schafer; Johann Georg; 2-Mar-46; 2-Dec-46; Johann; Baltimore; Dölfel, Maria; Homberg, Neustadt a.d. Reuss, Baiern; Dölfel, J. G.; —; —; illegitimate

Surname Father; Child's Given Name; Birth Date; Baptismal Date; Father's Given Name; Father's Place of Birth; Mother's Surname and Given Name; Mother's Place of Birth; Witness 1 Surname and Given Name; Witness 2 Surname and Given Name; Witness 3 Surname and Given Name; Comments

Schafer; Johann Heinrich Friedrich; 31-Dec-57; 10-Jan-58; Heinrich; Lisberg, Hessen; Hillgartner, Katharina; —; Kaufmann, Heinrich; Hillgartner, Joh.; Spielmann, Joh.; —

Schafer; Johann Jakob; 25-Jun-43; 23-Apr-46; Jakob; Esslingen, Wurttemberg; Genter, Anna Maria; Waldstatten, Balingen, Wurttemberg; —; —; —; —

Schafer; Johann Melchior Wilhelm; 15-Dec-61; 25-Dec-61; Heinrich; Lisberg, Hessen; Hillgartner, Katharine; —; Schaumloffel, Wilhelm; Spielmann, Marie; Schlerf, Melchior

Schafer; Johann Peter; 20-Dec-48; 26-Aug-49; Abraham; Manchester, Baltimore Co., MD; Kufer, Elisabeth Margareth; Canstadt, Wurttemberg; Fetting, Johann; Fetting, Sophie; —

Schafer; Karl August Joseph; 25-Aug-57; 6-Sep-57; Heinrich; Bremen; Mansdorfer, Katharina; —; Schafer, Karolina; Bertram, Wilh.; Siegel, Katharina Margaretha

Schafer; Karl Heinrich Friedrich; 27-Feb-64; 13-Mar-64; Heinrich; Lisberg, Hessen; Hillgartner, Katharine; —; Spilmann, Karl; Walther, Heinr.; Berger, Maria

Schafer; Karl Heinrich Wilhelm; 31-Jan-62; 8-Mar-63; Ernst; Bremen; Berger, Kunigunde; Bambert, Baiern; Wittler, Karl; Schafer, Heinrich; —

Schafer; Karl Wilhelm Martin; 23-Sep-59; 2-Oct-59; Heinrich; Bremen; Mansdorfer, Katharine Margarether; —; Engel, Wilhelmine; Wittler, Karl; Mansdorfer, Maria

Schafer; Katharine Friederike; 5-Oct-61; 13-Oct-61; Heinrich; Bremen; Mansdorf, Katharine Margarethe; —; Siegel, Katharine Margarethe; Schafer, Karoline Friederike; —

Schafer; Lisette Katharine; 4-Mar-66; 18-Mar-66; Heinrich; Lisberg, Hessen; Hillgartner, Katharine; Londorf, Hessen; Hillgartner, Elisabeth; Hillgartner, Heinr.; Sieck, Elisabeth

Schafer; Maria Christine; 20-Aug-49; 23-Sep-49; Christian Jakob; Meiersberg; Meyer, Christiane; Waldbach, Wurttemberg; Januar, Daniel; Januar, Christine; —

Schafer; Maria Elisabeth; 11-Oct-50; 1-Dec-50; David; Wulferdingen, Baden; Seidler, Caroline; —; Konkel, Conrad; Siegel, Catharina Margaretha; —

Surname Father; Child's Given Name; Birth Date; Baptismal Date; Father's Given Name; Father's Place of Birth; Mother's Surname and Given Name; Mother's Place of Birth; Witness 1 Surname and Given Name; Witness 2 Surname and Given Name; Witness 3 Surname and Given Name; Comments

Schafer; Maria Mathilde Christiane; 4-Feb-60; 12-Feb-60; Heinrich; Lisberg, Hessen; Hillgartner, Katharine; —; Kastens, Maria; Walther, Heinrich; Rudolph, Marie

Schafer; Rosine Karoline; 16-Sep-40; 27-Sep-40; Christian Jacob; —; Meyer, Christiane; —; —; —; —

Schafer; Rosine Kathr.; 20-Nov-37; 26-Dec-37; Jacob; —; Junkel, Anna M.; —; —; —; —

Schafermann; Conrad Heinrich Wilhelm; 31-May-49; 22-Jul-49; Heinrich; Bramsche bei Osnabruck, Hannover; Imfange, Catharine Marie; Engter, Osnabruck Hannover; Leimann, Conrad; —; —

Schäfermann; Maria; 23-Apr-47; 9-May-47; Hermann; Engtern, Vorden, Hannover; Imfange, Margareth Maria; —; Moschle, Marg.; —; —

Schäflein; Helena Friederike; 26-Jul-47; 22-Aug-47; Georg; Ebneth, Waisman; Treutser, Dorothea; Ebneth; Heilmann, Helena Friederike Sophia; —; —

Schaible; Amalie Wilh.; 10-Aug-41; 29-Aug-41; Karl Fr.; —; Kienzle, Regina; —; —; —; —; —

Schaible; Anna Elisabeth Catharine; 2-Jan-46; 21-Mar-46; Mathias; Dobel bei Stuttgart, Wurttemberg; List, Anna Elis. Catharine; Jucsenheim, Hessen; List, Grandmother; —; —; —

Schaible; Carl Ferdinand Kienzle; 26-Feb-48; 22-Oct-48; Carl Friedrich; Dobel, Neuenbruk, Wurttemberg; Kienzle, Regina Catharine; Grosstaschbach,Backnang, Wurttemberg; Brandes, Friedrich Ferdinand; Kienzle, Jakob; —; —

Schaible; Elisabeth Kathr.; 3-Oct-39; 17-Nov-39; Karl; —; Kienzle, Regine; —; —; —; —; —

Schaible; Elisabeth Regina; 1-May-40; 21-Jun-40; Mathaus; —; List, Elisab. Kathr.; —; —; —; —; —

Schaible; Johann; 10-Mar-44; 27-May-44; Mathais; —; List, Elisab. K.; —; —; —; —; —

Schaible; Karl Jacob Friedr.; 22-Apr-38; 27-May-38; Karl Fr.; —; Kienzle, Regine; —; —; —; —; —

Schaible; Luise Dorothea; 7-Mar-46; 1-Jul-46; Carl Friedrich; Dobel, Neuenbirk, Wurttemberg; Kienzle, Regine Catharine; Gross Aschbach, Wurttemberg; —; —; —; —

Schaible; Maria Magdalena; 12-May-50; 21-May-50; Carl Heinr.; Dobel, Old. Neunburk, Meirtenberg; Kienzle, Regina Catharina; Gross Aschbach, Wurttemberg; Hotter, Dorothea; —; —; wit from Gross Aschbach

Schaible; Philipp; 13-Jun-47; 23-Oct-47; Mathaus; Dobel, Neuenbirk, Wurttemberg; List, Catharine; Jugenheim, Zwiegenberg, Hessen; List, Anna Elisabeth; —; —; wit is grandmother

Schaible; Regine Karoline; 19-Feb-38; 21-Mar-39; Bernhard; —; König, Elisab.; —; —; —; —; —

Schaible; Samuel; 26-Sep-39; 1-Dec-39; Andreas; —; Wedekind, Elisab.; —; —; —; —; —

Schaible; Sophie Christiane; 3-Nov-43; 31-Dec-43; Karl; —; Kienzle, Regine Kathr.; —; —; —; —; —

Schardel; Ernst Wilhelm Caspar; 7-Jun-55; 17-Jun-55; Paulus; Kriegenbaum, Baiern; Koch, [--?--]; —; Beck, Ernst; Beck, Caspar; —; —

Schärer; Maria Barbara; 8-Nov-44; 15-Dec-44; Johann C. A.; —; Stieglitz, Dorothea; —; —; —; —; —

Scharlitzky; Wilhelm Heinrich; 17-Feb-64; 16-Mar-64; Anton; Baltimore; Mohring, Maria; —; Mohring, Elisabeth; Horr, Maria; —; —

Scharpf; Rosine Barbara; 20-Feb-47; 18-Apr-47; Johann Christian; Rotenberg ad. Tauber, Baiern; Fraas, Rosina; Schmelz, Gronau, Baiern; —; —; —; —

Schauffelberger; Heinrich Karl; 2-Nov-42; 12-Jan-43; Heinrich; —; Weingärtner, Elisab.; —; —; —; —; —

Schauffelberger; Katharine Friedrieke; 27-Feb-39; 14-Apr-39; Heinrich; —; Weingartner, Elisab.; —; —; —; —; —

Schauffelberger; Magdalene; 2-Feb-41; 12-Apr-41; Heinrich; —; Weinkgärtner, Elisab.; —; —; —; —; —

Schaumburg; Franz Friedrich; 20-Sep-64; 16-Oct-64; Lorenz; Fraunau, Waldeck; Schmidt, Elsie; —; Leutner, Friedrich; Leutner, Franz; —; —

Schaumburg; Marie Catharine; 10-Aug-55; 12-Aug-55; Jakob; —; Kramer, Elise; —; Imwalde, Catharine Maria; —; —; —

Schaumloffel; Heinrich Karl Wilhelm; 9-Apr-57; 26-Apr-57; Wilhelm; Oberweschutz, Kurhessen; Brauer, Karoline; —; Broning, Heinr.; Eckstrum, Heinr.; —; —

Schaumloffel; Johanne Louise; 25-Oct-52; 26-Oct-52; Wilhelm; Obervorschutz, Kurhessen; Brauer, Caroline; —; Brauer, Johanne Louise; —; —; child died

Schaumloffel; Maria Sophia Karoline; 3-Sep-58; 19-Sep-58; Wilhelm; Obersvoyschutz, Kurhessen; Brauer, Karoline; —; Klenk, Sophia; Spielmann, Maria; Kunzelmann, Anna Elisabeth; —

Schele; Johann Peter Stuardt; 2-Jul-40; 10-Sep-40; Jacob Fr.; —; Haley, Ellen; —; —; —; —; —

Schellenpfläger; Johann; 18-Aug-44; 13-Oct-44; Matthais; —; Fellmann, Marg.; —; —; —; —; —

Schellenschläger; Mathaus; 24-Jul-42; 21-Aug-42; Mathaus; —; Jellmann, Marg.; —; —; —; —; —

Schellkopf; Johann Friedr.; 15-Jan-39; 10-May-39; Johann Fr.; —; Wacker, Elisab.; —; —; —; —; —

Schellkopf; Luise Maria; 7-Sep-37; 12-Nov-37; Matthias; —; Gauser, Luise; —; —; —; —; —

Schellkopf; Matthaus; 9-Apr-39; 14-Jul-39; Matthaus; —; Hauser, Luise; —; —; —; —; —

Schenk; Christine Henriette; 6-Feb-47; 7-Feb-47; Wolfgang; Ebermaustadt bei Baireuth, Baiern; Kalb, Anna Barbara; Schweinefurth, Baiern; Kalb, Christine; —; —; child died

Schenkel; Jacob Friedrich; 25-May-38; 7-Jun-38; Johann Friedr.; —; Keller, Maria; —; —; —; —;

Scherer; Anna Elise Roseina; 3-Jul-58; 11-Jul-58; Johannes; Gersenbusseck, Hessen; Wagner, Maria; —; Leutner, Anna Katharina; Mess, Johannes; Kattenkamp, Rosina; —

Surname Father; Child's Given Name; Birth Date; Baptismal Date; Father's Given Name; Father's Place of Birth; Mother's Surname and Given Name; Mother's Place of Birth; Witness 1 Surname and Given Name; Witness 2 Surname and Given Name; Witness 3 Surname and Given Name; Comments

Scherers; infant son; 31-Oct-56; —; Joh.; Grosswohlen, Hessen; , ; —; —; —; —; stillborn

Schertel; Anna Katharine; 3-Dec-57; 20-Dec-57; Oaul; Kriegenbrunn, Baiern; Koch, Christine; —; Hoffmann, Katharine; Bach, Katharina; —; —

Schickle; Maria Elisab.; 1-Jul-39; 14-Jul-39; Karl; —; Wacken, Maria; —; —; —; —; —

Schieber; Christian; 10-Mar-38; 25-Mar-38; Christian; —; [--?--], Christiane; —; —; —; —; —

Schieber; Gottlieb; 30-Mar-37; 9-Apr-37; Christian; —; Schneider, Kathr.; —; —; —; —; —

Schiekle; Maria Elisab.; 25-Jan-38; 11-Mar-38; Karl; —; Wacker, Marg.; —; —; —; —; —

Schiess; Elisabeth; 10-Dec-38; 11-Dec-38; Wilhelm; —; Muller, Christine; —; —; —; —; —

Schiess; Luise; 14-Nov-41; 24-Nov-41; Wilhelm; —; Muller, Christiane; —; —; —; —; —

Schiess; Maria Luise; 21-Dec-43; 7-Jan-44; Wilhelm; —; Muller, Christine; —; —; —; —; —

Schiessler; Heinrich; 23-Mar-43; 17-Apr-43; Georg; —; Emmrich, Maria; —; —; —; —; —

Schiessler; Johann Adam; 7-Nov-38; 25-Dec-38; Heinrich; —; Kummerer, Christine; —; —; —; —; —

Schiessler; Johann Heinrich; 20-Jun-41; 18-Jul-41; Heinrich; —; Kummerer, Christine; —; —; —; —; —

Schiessler; Ludwig; 4-Dec-43; 27-Apr-44; Heinrich; —; Kummer, Christine; —; —; —; —; —

Schiessler; Margaretha Elisabeth; 16-Dec-36; 2-Jan-37; Heinrich; —; Kummer, Christine Elise; —; —; —; —; —

Schillinger; Eleonore; 30-Jan-43; 19-Mar-43; Philip; —; Kop, Sophie; —; —; —; —; —

Schillinger; Georg Friedr.; 20-Nov-42; 25-Dec-42; Georg; —; Kop, Friedricke; —; —; —; —; —

Schillinger; Georg Philip; 7-Oct-37; 5-Nov-37; Georg; —; Kopp, Kathr.; —; —; —; —; —

Surname Father; Child's Given Name; Birth Date; Baptismal Date; Father's Given Name; Father's Place of Birth; Mother's Surname and Given Name; Mother's Place of Birth; Witness 1 Surname and Given Name; Witness 2 Surname and Given Name; Witness 3 Surname and Given Name; Comments

Schillinger; Georg Philip; 16-Sep-44; 24-Nov-44; Georg; —; Rupp, Friedricke; —; —; —; —; —

Schillinger; Heinrich Philipp; 12-Apr-44; 28-Apr-44; Philipp; —; Kop, Sophia; —; —; —; —; —

Schillinger; Henriette Mathilde; 14-Jul-46; 19-Aug-46; Georg; Grunberg, Hessen; Kopp, Friederike; Dutweil, Neupreussen; Kopp, Sophia; —; —; wit is grandmother

Schillinger; Johann Heinr.; 23-Mar-39; 14-Apr-39; Georg; —; Kop, Friedrieke; —; —; —; —; —

Schillinger; Luise; 28-Aug-44; 6-Oct-44; Heinrich; —; Pfeister, Johanne; —; —; —; —; illegitimate

Schillinger; Maria Magdalene; 15-Jun-48; 16-Jul-48; Heinrich; Grunberg, Hessen; Grimm, Sophia Magdalene; Weiler, Weissenburg, Elsass; Koster, Maria; —; —; —

Schillinger; Samuel Heinrich; 2-Jun-46; 12-Jul-46; Heinrich; Grunberg, Hessen; Breim, Sophia Magdalena; Weilerin Elsass; —; —; —; —

Schillinger; Sopfia Amalia; 7-Dec-45; 18-Jan-46; Philipp; Grunberg, Hessen; Kopp, Sophia; Dudweilern bei Saarbruck, Preussen; Schillinger, Sophia; —; —; —

Schillinger; Sophie Emilie; 17-Oct-40; 15-Dec-40; Georg; —; Kopp, Friedricke; —; —; —; —; —

Schimmel; Karl Friedr.; 20-Jan-41; 25-Apr-41; Stephan; —; Härter, Maria; —; —; —; —; —

Schimmel; Wilhelm Heinrich; 18-May-48; 13-Jul-48; Stephan; Klein Munster, Hasfort, Baiern; Herder, Maria; Leutershausen, Manheim, Baden; Muller, Friedrich Wilhelm; —; —; —

Schindler; Immanuel Johannes Friedrich; 2-Nov-56; 30-Nov-56; Joh. Friedr.; Schnabelweide, Baiern; Selzner, Agnes; —; Flemming, Immanuel Gottlob; —; —; baptised in house

Schindler; Philipp Adolphus; 22-Nov-60; 1-May-61; —; —; , ; —; —; —; —; —

Schindler; Wilhelm Immanuel Theodor; 1-Feb-58; 11-Apr-58; Johann Friedrich; Schwabelweide, Baiern; Salzner, Agnes Dorothea; —; Vogelmann, Karl Wilhelm; Flemming, Immanuel; —; —

Surname Father; Child's Given Name; Birth Date; Baptismal Date; Father's Given Name; Father's Place of Birth; Mother's Surname and Given Name; Mother's Place of Birth; Witness 1 Surname and Given Name; Witness 2 Surname and Given Name; Witness 3 Surname and Given Name; Comments

Schirmer; Johann Georg; 18-Feb-43; 21-May-43; Kasper; —; Knauer, Maria; —; —; —; —; —

Schlag; Adam; 16-Oct-42; 6-Nov-42; Jacob; —; Weidemeyer, Anna M.; —; —; —; —; —

Schlag; Anna Maria; 16-Jul-40; 9-Aug-40; Jacob; —; Weidemeyer, Anna M.; —; —; —; —; —

Schlag; Katharine; 2-Oct-38; 7-Oct-38; Georg; —; Weidemeyer, Martha; —; —; —; —; —

Schlenbecker; Rosine; 17-Jun-41; 11-Jul-41; Johann; —; Lapp, Elisab.; —; —; —; —; —

Schlerf; Anna Henrietta Louise; 24-May-58; 30-May-58; Philipp; Allendorf a.d.L., Hessen; Leutner, Anna Katharina; —; Leutner, Anna Katharina; Habermehl, Heinr.; Muhly, Louise; —

Schlerf; Auguste Elisabeth; 3-Sep-62; 14-Sep-62; Melchior; Allendorf a. d. L., Hessen; Busch, Katharine; —; Brauer, Elisabeth; Ruppel, Elisabeth; Schimpf, Gottried; twin

Schlerf; Christian Niklaus Melchior; 10-Jan-64; 24-Jan-64; Melchior; Allendorf a. d. Lumda, Hessen; Buschmann, Katharina; Barges, Kurhessen; Ruppel, Niklaus; Strobel, Christian; Schwartz, Katharina; —

Schlerf; Friedrich; 6-Jul-51; 13-Jul-51; Philipp; Allendorf a.d. Lumda, Hessen; Leutner, Catharine; —; Leutner, Friedr.; —; —; —

Schlerf; Friedrich Wilhelm Anton; 25-Aug-55; 2-Sep-55; Philipp; Allendorf a.d. Lumda, Hessen; Leutner, Anna Catharina; —; Leutner, Franz; Schlerf, Margaretha; Merkel, Anton; —

Schlerf; Friedrich Wilhelm Christian; 7-May-61; 19-May-61; Philipp; Allensdorf a.d.L., Hessen; Leutner, Anna Katharine; —; Ruppel, Johann; Bertram, Wilhelm; Reinhard, Christoph; —

Schlerf; Johann Heinrich Christoph; 20-Mar-53; 27-Mar-53; Philipp; Allendorf a.d. Lumde, Hessen; Leutner, Anna Katharina; —; Leutner, Heinr. Christoph; —; —; —

Surname Father; Child's Given Name; Birth Date; Baptismal Date; Father's Given Name; Father's Place of Birth; Mother's Surname and Given Name; Mother's Place of Birth; Witness 1 Surname and Given Name; Witness 2 Surname and Given Name; Witness 3 Surname and Given Name; Comments

Schlerf; Karl Wilhelm Edwuard; 13-Jan-64; 31-Jan-64; Philipp; Allendorf a. d. Lumda, Hessen; Leutner, Anna Katharine; Allendorf a. d. Lumda, Hessen; —; —; —; —

Schlerf; Katharina Elisabeth; 2-Nov-56; 9-Nov-56; Melchior; Allendorf a.d. Lumda, Hessen; Tappmann, Emilie; —; Immich, Elisabeth; Schafer, Katharina; Weber, Katharina; —

Schlerf; Katharina Wilhelmina Henriette; 6-May-67; 19-May-67; Wilhelm; Allendorf a.d. Lunda, Hessen; Busch, Katharina; Kurhessen; Strobel, Katharina; Leutner, Wilhelmine; Weller, Heinrich; —

Schlerf; Katharine Henriette Friedrike; 15-Oct-62; 2-Nov-62; Johann Georg; Allendorf a.d.L., Hessen; Schmidt, Margarethe; —; Beck, Henriette; Schlerf, Katharine; Schlerf, Philipp; —

Schlerf; Marie Katharine; 3-Sep-62; 14-Sep-62; Melchior; Allendorf a. d. L., Hessen; Busch, Katharine; —; Bergen, Marie; Schafer, Heinrich; Shortz, Katharine; twin

Schlerf; Marie Wilhelmine; 21-May-60; 27-May-60; Melchior; Allendorf a.d.L., Hessen; Trappmann, Emilie; —; Reinhard, Christoph; Bergen, Marie; Leutner, Wilhelmine; —

Schlerf; Susanna Margaretha Christina; 21-Oct-54; 29-Oct-54; Melchior; Allendorf a.d. Lumda, Hessen; Troppmann, Emilia; —; Seibel, Susanna; Schlerf, Christina; —; —

Schlerf; Wilhelm Melchior Gottlieb; 5-Jul-65; 16-Jul-65; Melchior; Allendorf a. d. Lunda, Hessen; Busch, Katharina; Barken, Kurhessen; Stetter, Wilhelm; Weller, Melchior; Wachsmann, Heinrike; —

Schlerf; Wilhelmina Katharina; 12-Aug-58; 22-Aug-58; Melchior; Allendorf, Hessen; Trappmann, Emilie; —; Arnold, Katharine; Rieinhard, Wilhelmina; Weller, Katharine; —

Schlitt; Elisabeth Katharine; 8-Jan-64; 24-Jan-64; Eduard; Schabenroth, Hessen; Bohn, Louise; Philadelphia; Bohn, Katharine; Fischer, Elisabeth; Eggers, Ernst Aug.; —

Schlorbecker; Samuel Ludwig; 22-Jun-43; 1-Oct-43; Johann; —; Lappe, Elisab.; —; —; —; —; —

Schlott; Conrad; 7-Dec-41; 21-Jan-42; Conrad; —; Klemper, Kathr.; —; —; —; —; —

Surname Father; Child's Given Name; Birth Date; Baptismal Date; Father's Given Name; Father's Place of Birth; Mother's Surname and Given Name; Mother's Place of Birth; Witness 1 Surname and Given Name; Witness 2 Surname and Given Name; Witness 3 Surname and Given Name; Comments

Schmalz; Friedrich Wilh.; 12-Mar-38; 29-Apr-38; Georg; —; Becker, Christine Magd.; —; —; —; —; —

Schmalz; Georg Dietrich; 14-Sep-39; 11-Feb-40; Georg; —; Becker, Christine; —; —; —; —; —

Schmeener; Ernstine; 17-Jun-45; 1-Aug-45; Daniel; Marburg; Tiedemann, Elisabeth; Kaltern bei Marburg, Kurhessen; —; —; —; —

Schmelz; Caroline; 1-Oct-45; 26-Dec-45; Wilhelm; Neumerschen; Muller, Maria; Marburg, Kurhessen; Muller, Conrad; —; —; —

Schmelz; Georg Wilhelm; 20-Nov-48; 25-Dec-48; Wilhelm; Neuen Merschen, Melzungen, Kurhessen; Muller, Maria; Marburg; Schmidt, Georg; —; —; —

Schmelz; Johann Wilh.; 26-Sep-43; 22-Oct-43; Wilhelm; —; Muller, Maria; —; —; —; —; —

Schmelz; Margarethe; 20-Sep-42; 20-Oct-42; Wilhelm; —; Muller, Maria; —; —; —; —; —

Schmemer; Daniel; 4-Oct-47; 22-Nov-47; Daniel; Marburg, Kurhessen; Tidemann, Elisabeth; Caldem, Kurhessen; —; —; —; —

Schmick; Ursula; 20-May-49; 10-Jun-49; Johann; Bidinger, Hessen; Schmidt, Barbara; Kissingen, Baiern; Ameyer, Ursula; —; —; —

Schmidt; Anna Marie Katharine; 21-Dec-60; 30-Dec-60; Christian; Eichelsdorf, Hessen; Luck, Katharine; —; Thiemeyer, Marie; Engelhaupt, Marie; Kunder, Katharine; —

Schmidt; Catharina Elisabeth; 1-Sep-50; 9-Sep-50; Hartmann; Josbach, Kurhessen; Thomas, Barbara Maria; —; Schmidt, Elisabeth; Schmidt, Catharina; Thomas, Regina Barbara; 3 child, 3 dau

Schmidt; Elise Charlotte; 5-Sep-45; 17-Mar-46; Heinrich; Oldendorf, Kurhessen; Bischoff, Elise; Gerde, Bersenbruck, Hannover; —; —; —; —

Schmidt; Georg Andreas; 17-Oct-45; 14-Dec-45; Georg Peter; Klausterhausen, Baden; Kramer, Maria; Sanger, Baden; Schmidt, Andreas; Schmidt, Catharine; —; —

Surname Father; Child's Given Name; Birth Date; Baptismal Date; Father's Given Name; Father's Place of Birth; Mother's Surname and Given Name; Mother's Place of Birth; Witness 1 Surname and Given Name; Witness 2 Surname and Given Name; Witness 3 Surname and Given Name; Comments

Schmidt; Georg Gottlieb Heinrich; 16-Mar-66; 25-Mar-66; Christian; Eichelsdorf, Hessen; Luck, Karoline; Himmron, Kurhessen; Felder, Georg; Kuhner, Gottlieb; Wittler, Heinrich; —

Schmidt; Georg Heinr.; 23-May-38; 15-Jul-38; Johann Jac.; —; Jordan, Marianne; —; —; —; —; —

Schmidt; Heinrich; 24-Jul-50; 1-Sep-50; Conrad; Oberromern, Grunberg, Hessen; Schmidt, Anna; —; Rausch, Heinr.; —; —; 1 child

Schmidt; Jacob Philip; 12-Nov-41; 13-May-42; Jacob; —; Steuber, Florentine; —; —; —; —; —

Schmidt; Jakob Peter; 7-Mar-48; 30-Apr-48; Mathaus; Oberbruchen, Limburg, Naussau; Gabel, Maria; Haseldorf, Hanau, Kurhessen; Beisswanger, Jakob Peter; Beisswanger, Christine; —; —

Schmidt; Johann Georg; 5-Dec-50; 29-Dec-50; Peter; Berndorf b. Beireuth, Baiern; Fuchs, Elisabeth; —; Buring, Joh. Georg; Link, Georg Christian; —; wit #1 from Wilhelmsdorf

Schmidt; Johann Heinrich; 27-Dec-38; 6-Jan-39; Heinrich; —; Klark, Marianne; —; —; —; —; —

Schmidt; Johann Heinrich Konrad; 2-Feb-57; 8-Feb-57; Christian; Eichelsdorf, Hessen; Luck, Karoline; —; Repp, Heinr. Konrad; Emwalde, Katharina; Schafer, Heinrich; —

Schmidt; Johann Kasten Adam; 13-Nov-59; 21-Nov-58; Christian; Eichelsdorf, Hessen; Lucke, Karoline; —; Dunker, Kasten; Vorderwusten, Margarethe; —; —

Schmidt; Johann Valentin; 30-Oct-60; 11-Nov-60; Joh. Adam; Steinbach, Preussen; Kreuger, Margarethe; —; Ruppel, Joh.; Wolf, Valentin; —; —

Schmidt; Joseph; 23-Dec-44; 2-Feb-45; Matthais; —; Walthers, Wilhelimina; —; —; —; —

Schmidt; Karoline Margarethe Josephine; 8-Sep-63; 13-Sep-63; Christian; Eichelsdorf, Hessen; Luck, Karoline; —; Kuhner, Karoline; Herbst, Josephine Ferdinandine; Schmidt, Heinr.

Schmidt; Katharine; 29-Nov-38; 7-Jan-39; Jacob; —; Schneider, Elisab.; —; —; —; —

Schmidt; Katharine; 26-Aug-39; 29-Sep-39; Heinrich; —; Angersbach, Anna M.; —; —; —; —

Schmidt; Katharine Marg.; 22-Jul-40; 27-Jul-40; Johann; —; Willershauser, Maria K.; —; —; —; —

Schmidt; Luise; 4-Dec-36; 10-Feb-37; Jacob; —; Schneider, Elisabeth; —; —; —; —

Schmidt; Luise; 12-Oct-39; 17-Oct-39; Martin; —; Walter, Wilhelmine; —; —; —; —

Schmidt; Luise; 17-Nov-47; 16-Jan-48; Johann; Bernsburg, Alsfeld, Hessen; Lose, Catharine; Bernsburg, Alsfeld, Hessen; Kreiner, Elisabeth; —; —

Schmidt; Margaretha Louise; 10-Jul-58; 18-Jul-58; Georg; Kairlindoch, Baiern; Damann, Katharina; —; Billmann, Margaretha; Billmann, Georg; Kattenkamp, Rosine

Schmidt; Maria Catharine; 18-Nov-46; 9-Dec-46; Mattias; Oberbrechen, Lenburg, Nassau; Walther, Wilhelmine; Hainichen, Nidda, Hessen; Stroh, Maria Catharine; —; —

Schmidt; Rosina Margaretha; 6-Aug-54; 13-Aug-54; Georg; Kairlinde, Baiern; Damann, Catharina; —; Krauss, Rosina; —; —

Schmidt; Susanne; 12-Apr-41; 9-May-41; Heinrich; —; Angelskach, Anna M.; —; —; —; —

Schmidt; Wilhelm Heinrich; 23-Oct-42; 4-Dec-42; Mathaus; —; Walter, Wilhelmine; —; —; —; —

Schmidt; Wilhelmine; 20-Nov-40; 27-Dec-40; Mathaus; —; Walter, Wilhelmine; —; —; —; —

Schmiermund; Heinrich Ludwig; 8-Apr-50; 28-Apr-50; Johannes; Oberseibertenroth, Grunberg, Hessen; Cramer, Elisabetha; Wahl,Alsfeld, Hessen; Cramer, Heinrich; Schmiermund, Ludwig; —

Schnabel; Christine; 28-Oct-55; 4-Nov-55; Ludwig; Allendorf a.d. Lumda, Hessen; Wagner, Catharina; —; Schmidt, Christine; Schlerf, Georg; Leutner, Christine

Schnabel; Katharine; 14-May-60; 23-Jul-60; Ludwig; Allendorf; Wagner, Katharine; —; —; —; —; emergency baptism

Surname Father; Child's Given Name; Birth Date; Baptismal Date; Father's Given Name; Father's Place of Birth; Mother's Surname and Given Name; Mother's Place of Birth; Witness 1 Surname and Given Name; Witness 2 Surname and Given Name; Witness 3 Surname and Given Name; Comments

Schnabel; Louis; 2-Jan-58; 13-Jan-58; Ludwig; Allendorf, Hessen; Wagner, Katharina; —; Leutner, Christoph; Rein, Widow; —; emergency baptism

Schneemann; Paul Wilhelm; 22-Feb-64; 20-Mar-64; Karl; Rittmarshausen, Hannover; Fladtmann, Anna Margaretha; Buschhausen, Hannover; Schorrer, Paul; Heyse, Wilhelm; —; —

Schneider; Adam; 18-Aug-43; 3-Sep-43; Adam; —; Hornung, Marg.; —; —; —; —; —

Schneider; Agnes Wilhelmine; 15-Aug-43; 3-Sep-43; Peter; —; Klein, Christine; —; —; —; —; —

Schneider; Anna Margaretha; 18-Mar-48; 28-May-48; Heinrich; Leidheim, Nidda, Hessen; Feld, Elisabeth; Bleichenbach, Hessen; Schafer, Margarethe; —; —; —

Schneider; Anna Maria Caroline; 22-Aug-45; 10-Oct-45; Herrmann; Engte, Vorden, Hannover; Lubben, Elisabet; Engte, Vorden, Hannover; Vor der Wusten, Anna Maria Caroline; —; —; —

Schneider; Anna Veronika; 6-Nov-37; 10-Dec-37; Math.; —; Pfeiffer, Jacobine; —; —; —; —; —

Schneider; August; 17-Dec-45; 13-Apr-46; Wilhelm; Merzhausen, Ziegenhain; Werner, Maria; Rosenthal bei Barburg, Kurhessen; Werner, August; —; —; —

Schneider; Caroline; 20-Jan-49; 4-Mar-49; Gottfried; Metzdorf bei Culmbach; Bopp, Anna; Culmbach, Baiern; Hubner, Matthias; Hubner, Charlotte; —; —

Schneider; Catharine Christine; 15-Oct-48; 22-Oct-48; Johann Georg; Gontershausen, Alsfeld, Hessen; Eitel, Christine; Lemberg, Bermesins, Rheinbaiern; Schneider, Catharine; —; —; —

Schneider; Charlotte Sophie; 25-Mar-50; 14-Apr-50; Johannes; Kuhessen, Marburg; Spielmann, Katharina; Nidda, Hessen; Spielmann, Sophie; —; —; wit is grandmother

Schneider; Christian; 10-Dec-51; 25-Dec-51; Friedrich; Birmasenz, Baiern; Viertel, Elisabeth; —; Fulle, Christian; —; —; —

Surname Father; Child's Given Name; Birth Date; Baptismal Date; Father's Given Name; Father's Place of Birth; Mother's Surname and Given Name; Mother's Place of Birth; Witness 1 Surname and Given Name; Witness 2 Surname and Given Name; Witness 3 Surname and Given Name; Comments

Schneider; Dorothea; 17-Apr-55; 21-Apr-55; Johann; Nordeck, Kurhessen; Spielmann, Catharine Maria; —; Brauer, Caroline; Weldermuth, Maria; —; child died

Schneider; Eleonore; 19-Oct-47; 19-Dec-47; Adam; Oberklingen, Creilberg, Hessen; Hornung, Maria; Oberamstadt, Hessen; —; —; —; —

Schneider; Elisabeth; 9-Nov-50; 12-Jan-51; Johann Georg; Guntershausen, Hessen; Eitel, Christine; —; Eitel, Elisabeth; Muhly, Friedrich; —; —

Schneider; Elisabeth; 24-Jan-38; 7-Nov-38; Johann; —; Arnold, Marg.; —; —; —; —

Schneider; Elisabeth; 28-Dec-39; 31-Jan-40; Matthaus; —; Pfeister, Jacobine; —; —; —; —

Schneider; Elisabeth Catharina; 10-May-55; 20-May-55; Heinrich; Feldau, Hessen; Jager, Catharina; —; Bach, Elisabeth Catharina; —; —

Schneider; Elise Friederike; 17-Oct-60; 28-Oct-60; Heinrich; Fulda, Hessen; Jager, Katharine; —; Wolf, Elise; Dietrich, Friedericke; —

Schneider; Friederich; 23-Oct-46; 29-Nov-46; Johann Georg; Gertershausen, Alsfeld, Hessen; Eitel, Christine; Bermasins, Rheinbaiern; Leutner, Georg Friedrich; —; —

Schneider; Friedrich Michael Leonhard; 5-Apr-58; 11-Apr-58; Heinrich; Felda, Hessen; Jager, Katharina; —; Hoffmann, Leonhard; Kowalik, Frdch.; Fritze, Mich.

Schneider; Friedrich Wilhelm; 5-Dec-48; 21-Jan-49; Hermann; Engter bei Osnabruck, Hannover; Lubben, Maria Elisabeth; Engter bei Osnabruck, Hannover; Brunings, Friederike; —; —

Schneider; Georg Heinrich; 2-Jan-53; 16-Jan-53; Heinrich; Felde, Hessen; Jager, Catharine; —; Niklas, Georg Heinrich; —; —

Schneider; Georg Wilhelm; 26-May-41; 13-Jun-41; Adam; —; Hornung, Maria; —; —; —; —

Schneider; Heinrich August; 13-Mar-51; 30-Mar-51; Friedrich; Engter, Hannover; Lange, [--?--]; —; Langermann, Franz Heinr.; —; —

Schneider; Heinrich Wilhelm; 15-Jul-65; 23-Jul-65; Heinrich; Felda, Hessen; Jager, Katharine; Oberohm, Hessen; Harmes, Thomas; Fritzen, Anna; Wolf, Valentine

Schneider; Heinrich Wilhelm; 22-Jul-64; 31-Jul-64; Heinrich; Haubern, Kurhessen; Wagner, Elisabeth; Grosstubussock, Hessen; Wagner, Heinrich; Scherer, Johann; —

Schneider; Herrmann Friedrich; 20-May-48; 7-Aug-48; Johann Friedrich; Engter bei Osnabruck, Hannover; Lange, Maria Engel; Engter bei Osnabruck, Hannover; Thiemeyer, Herrmann Friedrich; —; —

Schneider; Johann; 27-Apr-46; 6-Dec-46; Gottried; Culmbach, Baiern; Bop, Anna Margaretha; Culmbach, Baiern; Hahn, Johann; Hahn, Dorothea; —

Schneider; Johann Christian; 26-Sep-43; 25-Dec-43; Wilhelm; —; Werner, Maria; —; —; —; —

Schneider; Johann Georg; 7-Nov-44; 29-Dec-44; Johnn G.; —; Eitel, Christine; —; —; —; —

Schneider; Johann Gottfried; 16-Jun-52; 26-Jun-52; Gottfried; Metzdorf, Baiern; Popp, Anna Margarethe; —; Schmidt, Joh.; —; —; —

Schneider; Johann Heinrich; 31-Dec-43; 20-Feb-44; Johann; —; Wiegand, Kath.; —; —; —; —; —

Schneider; Johann Heinrich; —; 21-Mar-39; Herm.; —; [--?--], Elisabeth; —; —; —; —; birth date unknown

Schneider; Johann Wilh.; 5-Jan-44; 18-Feb-44; Hermann; —; Enter, Anna M.; —; —; —; —; —

Schneider; Karl Heinrich; 15-Jan-43; 20-Feb-44; Mathaus; —; Pfezker, Jacobine; —; —; —; —; —

Schneider; Karl Philipp Thomas; 9-Jun-63; 21-Jun-63; Heinrich; Felda, Sachsen; Jager, Katharine; Oberohm, Hessen; Konig, Philipp; Seum, Karoline; Harmes, Thomas; —

Schneider; Karoline; 31-Jan-40; 29-Apr-40; Wilhelm; —; Werner, Maria; —; —; —; —; —

Schneider; Katharine; 1-Sep-41; 5-Oct-41; Hermann; —; Lubben, Maria; —; —; —; —; —

Surname Father; Child's Given Name; Birth Date; Baptismal Date; Father's Given Name; Father's Place of Birth; Mother's Surname and Given Name; Mother's Place of Birth; Witness 1 Surname and Given Name; Witness 2 Surname and Given Name; Witness 3 Surname and Given Name; Comments

Schneider; Margaretha; 17-Jan-37; 14-May-37; Heinrich; —; Lutz, Marg.; —; —; —; —; —

Schneider; Maria; 31-Oct-39; 17-Nov-39; Peter; —; Klein, Christina; —; —; —; —; —

Schneider; Maria; 13-Jun-40; 28-Jul-40; Wendel; —; Sauer, Maria; —; —; —; —; —

Schneider; Maria Anna; 14-Apr-41; 13-Jun-41; Heinrich; —; Klark, Marianne; —; —; —; —; —

Schneider; Maria Katharina; 18-Jun-50; 7-Jul-50; Heinrich; Fulda, Hessen; Jager, Katharina; Oberomen, Hessen; Jager, Maria; Schneider, Katharina; —; —

Schneider; Philipp; 18-Dec-49; 30-Dec-49; Caspar; Rohrbach bei Wurzburg, Baiern; Luchsler, Catharine; Bermesins, Rheinbaiern; Wagner, Philipp; Buchsler, Eva; —; —

Schneider; Sophia Christine; 17-Aug-47; 7-Nov-47; Johann; Remsfeld, Homberg, Kurhessen; Wiegand, Catharine; Iba, Rothenburg, Kurhessen; Wigand, Sophia; —; —; —

Schneider; Wilhelm Christian; 19-Aug-45; 18-Oct-46; Johann; Remsfeld, Homburg, Kurhessen; Wigand, Catharine; Iba, Rothenburg, Kurhessen; Wigand, Wilhelm Christian; —; —; wit is grandfather

Schneider; Wilhelm Heinrich; 8-Nov-41; 26-Dec-41; Wilh.; —; Werner, Maria; —; —; —; —

Schnellbach; Johann; 12-Jun-45; 20-Jul-45; Johann; Dorfgrozelden, Baiern; Bremer, Barbara; Wilferdingen, Baden; Bremer, David; —; —

Schnermann; Elise Susanne Katharine; 23-Sep-66; 21-Oct-66; Karl; Retmanshausen, Hanover; Klatmann, Anna; Ochshausen, Hannover; Burmann, Susanne; Lenz, Katharine; —

Schofield; Sarah Anna; 29-Jul-66; 19-Aug-66; Benjamin T.; —; Krell, Elisabeth; —; Lenz, Katharine; Stussel, Friedrich; Krell, Johann

Schönberg; Christian Georg; 16-Dec-40; 7-Feb-41; Christian Fr.; —; Schmidt, Elisab.; —; —; —; —

Surname Father; Child's Given Name; Birth Date; Baptismal Date; Father's Given Name; Father's Place of Birth; Mother's Surname and Given Name; Mother's Place of Birth; Witness 1 Surname and Given Name; Witness 2 Surname and Given Name; Witness 3 Surname and Given Name; Comments

Schorrer; Karl Johann; 10-Dec-59; 25-Dec-59; Georg; Herroldsberg, Baiern; Reichtsheid, Barbara; —; Muller, Karl; Schorrer, Sr., Johann; Muth, Karoline

Schorrer; Paulina Maria Christiana; 8-Sep-57; 20-Sep-57; Johann; Heroldsberg, Baiern; Richtsheid, Barbara; —; Schorrer, Paul; Waltjen, Christian; —

Schorrer; Therese Lisette Karoline; 27-Dec-61; 12-Jan-62; Paul; Heroldsberg, Baiern; Bertram, Sophie Elisabeth; —; Dieffenbach, Conradine; Scharrer, Lisette; Bertram, Thomas

Schorter; Johann Georg Wilh.; 25-Feb-41; 6-Feb-42; Georg L.; —; Vogelmann, Kathr. W.; —; —; —; —

Schott; Karl Christopher; 14-Aug-42; 17-Oct-42; Christian; —; Bauer, Kathr.; —; —; —; —

Schott; Maria Barbara; 4-Dec-39; 15-Dec-39; Georg; —; Winkler, Maria; —; —; —; —

Schrader; Christian Friedrich Wilhelm; 24-Jul-63; 2-Aug-63; Christian Wilhelm; Neuenkirchen, Hannover; Niewafner [?], Louise Henriette Karoline; Neuenkirchen, Hannover; Lettmade, Friedrich; Gail, Christian; Langschmidt, Wilh.

Schrader; Karl Wilhelm Heinrich; 29-Jun-65; 16-Jul-65; Friedrich Wilhelm; Neuenkirchen, Hannover; Nierofner, Karoline Louise; Neuenkirchen, Hannover; Lettmade, Georg Adolph Wilh.; Burmann, Ernst Heinr.; —

Schreiber; Catharina; 17-Jun-45; 3-Jul-45; Jakob; Honstorf, Waldeck; Wolf, Cath.; Wildungen, Waldeck; Schreiber, Philipp; Urschrung, Cath.; —

Schreiber; Joahnn Georg; 25-Feb-41; 7-Mar-41; Georg; —; Wolf, Kathr.; —; —; —; —

Schreiber; Maria Katharine; 23-May-43; 4-Jun-43; Jacob; —; Wolf, Kathr.; —; —; —; —

Schreiber; Maria Luise; 28-May-47; 9-Jul-47; Jakob; Hundsdorf, Waldeck; Wolf, Catharine; Wildungen, Waldeck; Lohrmann, Maria; —; —; —

Schreier; Johann Konrad Wilhelm; 31-Aug-63; 13-Sep-63; Johann; Wuhmels, Baiern; Arnold, Kunigunde; Ebelsheim, Baden;

Kunzelmann, Joh.; Bremer, Wilh.; Dickel, Margaretha Dorothea; —

Schreiner; Susanne Katharine Margarethe; 21-Dec-60; 13-Jan-61; Johann; Rehmelse, Baiern; Arnold, Kunigunde; Heidelberg, Baden; Arras, Katharine Margarethe; Bremer, Susanne Katharine; —; —

Schreiver; Johann Heinrich Louis; 2-Oct-48; 26-Oct-48; Jakob; Hunstorf, Waldeck; Wolf, Catharine; Albildungen, Waldeck; Lohrmann, Johann Heinrich; Eigenbrodt, Maria; —; —

Schrode; Henriette Lisette Emilie; 28-Sep-67; 13-Oct-67; Friedrich Wilhelm; Neuenkirchen, Hannover; Wieckofner, Henriette Karolina; —; Langschmidt, Henriette; Ortmade, August; Nobbe, Lisette; —

Schroder; Franz August; 18-Jun-56; 13-Jul-56; Karl Friedrich; Steinburg, Preussen; Hedom, Christiane Wilhelmine; —; Reuter, Aug.; Purner, Joseph; Purner, Henriette; —

Schroder; Otto Heinrich Eduard; 16-Aug-48; 10-Sep-48; Ludwig Friedrich Wilhelm; Osnabruck, Hannover; Geinersbach, Friederike Elenore; Barnstorf, Diepholz, Hannover; Wiestroh, Johann Heinrich; —; —; —

Schroder; Wilhelmine Louise; 27-May-62; 8-Jun-62; Friedrich Wilhelm; Neuenkirchen, Hannover; Niewohner, Karoline; —; Lettmade, Louise; Schroder, Wilhelmine; —; —

Schröder; Anna Catharine Wilhelmine Henriette; 10-Nov-45; 21-Dec-45; Heinrich Ludwig; Holzhausen, Minden, Preussen; Bussmann, Margaretha Magdalene Henriette; Vilsen, Truchhausen, Hannover; —; —; —; —

Schröder; Johann Heinr. Eduard; 19-Sep-42; 2-Oct-42; Joh. Fr.; —; Fattinger, Martha E.; —; —; —; —; —

Schuchart; Johann Ernst; 6-Mar-42; 26-Jun-42; Heinrich; —; Schafer, Anna E.; —; —; —; —; —

Schuck; Johann Heinr.; 26-Mar-37; 3-Apr-37; Heinrich; —; Mebold, Anna; —; —; —; —; —

Schuhmacher; Georg Konrad; 30-Dec-55; 20-Jan-56; Reinhard; Marburg, Kurhessen; Quaid, Sara; —; Stroh, Konrad; —; —; —

Surname Father; Child's Given Name; Birth Date; Baptismal Date; Father's Given Name; Father's Place of Birth; Mother's Surname and Given Name; Mother's Place of Birth; Witness 1 Surname and Given Name; Witness 2 Surname and Given Name; Witness 3 Surname and Given Name; Comments

Schuhmacher; Wilhelm August; 2-Jul-50; 28-Jul-50; Reinhard; Marburg, Kurhessen; James, Sarah; —; Becker, Aug.; Schreiber, Maria Elisabeth; —; 3 child, 3 son

Schuhmann; Elisabeth Catharina; 7-Feb-44; 11-May-45; Conrad; Rossdorf, Hessen; Drass, Elisabeth Catharina; Sisselsheim, Hessen; Appel, Heinrich; Appel, Mrs.; —; —

Schüler; Wilhelm; 24-Oct-44; 3-Nov-44; Heinrich; —; Satzmann, Elisab.; —; —; —; —; —

Schulte; Adolph Christian; 30-Sep-45; 2-Oct-45; Franz Gerhard; Hördinghausen, Witlage, Hannover; Meyer, Maria Clara; Hördinghausen, Witlage, Hannover; Hetmeyer, Adolph Christian; —; —; twin

Schulte; Ernst August; 30-Sep-45; 2-Oct-45; Franz Gerhard; Hördinghausen, Witlage, Hannover; Meyer, Maria Clara; Hördinghausen, Witlage, Hannover; father, ; —; —; twin, died

Schultheiss; Albertine Margarethe Lisette; 24-Dec-66; 13-Jan-67; Eduard; Baltimore; Radecke, Sophia Margaretha; Baltimore; Radecke, Margarethe; Radecke, Johann Albert; Schultheiss, Lisette; —

Schultheiss; Friedrich Theodor; 19-Oct-51; 10-Nov-51; Joh.; Monberg, Kurhessen; Fischer, Lisette; —; Bruggemann, Friedrich; —; —; —

Schultheiss; Karl; 18-Dec-49; 10-Nov-51; Joh.; Monberg, Kurhessen; Fischer, Lisette; —; Hein, Karl; —; —; emergency baptism

Schultheiss; Karoline Mathilda Christina; 4-May-57; 10-May-57; Joh.; Manberg, Kurhessen; Buscher, Lisette; —; Buscher, Karolina; —; —; —

Schultz; Constantin Emil; 20-Jan-51; 16-Feb-51; Konrad; Biedekopf, Hessen; Funk, Henriette; —; Funk, Amalie Dorothea; —; —; —

Schultz; Friedrich Ludwig; 24-Aug-52; 29-Aug-52; Conrad; Biedenkopf, Hessen; Funk, Henriette; —; Thiemeyer, Friedr. Ludwig; Bruhl, Elisabeth; —; —

Surname Father; Child's Given Name; Birth Date; Baptismal Date; Father's Given Name; Father's Place of Birth; Mother's Surname and Given Name; Mother's Place of Birth; Witness 1 Surname and Given Name; Witness 2 Surname and Given Name; Witness 3 Surname and Given Name; Comments

Schultz; Friedrich Rudolph; 19-May-56; 25-May-56; Konrad; Biedekopf, Hessen; Funk, Henriette; —; Hollebein, Friedr.; Funk, Rudolph; —; —

Schultz; Heinrich August; 25-Apr-55; 6-May-55; Ernst; Liebenau, Hannover; Meier, Sophie; —; Meier, Heinr. Gustav; Klinkmeier, Aug.; —; —

Schultz; Johann Rudolph; 1-Sep-54; 17-Sep-54; Conrad; Biedekopf, Hessen; Funk, Henriette; —; Bruhl, Joh.; Funk, Rudolph; —; —

Schultz; Maria Johanne Elisabeth; 3-Dec-65; 25-Dec-65; Gottlieb; Liebenau, Hannover; Schneider, Louise; Engter, Hannover; Heise, Fr. Maria; Schneider, Georg; Klinkmeier, Marie; —

Schultz; Wilhelm Karl; 13-Feb-67; 17-Mar-67; Karl; Schwedt a. d. Oder, Preussen; Glissmann, Augusta; Petershagen, Preussen; Lahr, Karl; Hofer, Joh. Heinrich; —; —

Schulz; Agnes; 18-Feb-47; 5-Dec-47; Rudolph; Osnabruck; Reidler, Agnes; Sleddehusen, Asnabruck, Hannover; —; —; —; —

Schulz; Friederike Katharine; 8-Jun-63; 5-Jul-63; Karl; Schwedt a. d. Oder, West Holbein; Glekmann, Auguste; Petershagen, Preussen; Bertram, Friederike; Broning, Katharine; —; —

Schulz; Georg Karl Theodor; 20-Jul-59; 31-Jul-59; Konrad; Biedkopf, Hessen; Funk, Henrietta; —; Kaufmann, Georg Heinr.; Weddiger, Theodor; Ernst, Katharine; —

Schulz; Heinrich Ludwig Wilhelm; 23-Sep-61; 13-Oct-61; Ferdinand; Liebenau, Hannover; Falken, Eleonora; —; Heyse, Wilhelm; Lange, Borchart; Schulz, Louise

Schulz; Johann Wilhelm; 20-Nov-66; 2-Dec-66; Konrad; Biedenkopf, Hessen; Funk, Henriette; Wetter, Kurhessen; Spilmann, Johann; Schaumlusel, Wilhelm; Brauning, Katharine

Schulz; Josephina Katharine; 29-Jan-65; 22-Jan-65; Karl; Schweth, Preussen; Gleichmann, August; Petershagen, Preussen; Herbst, Josephine; Webbermann, Katharina; —

Schulz; Julie Amalie; 4-Sep-61; 15-Sep-61; Konrad; Biedkopf, Hessen; Funck, Henriette; —; Brockmann, Dorothea Emilie; Kattenkamp, Julie; Gerlach, Peter

Surname Father; Child's Given Name; Birth Date; Baptismal Date; Father's Given Name; Father's Place of Birth; Mother's Surname and Given Name; Mother's Place of Birth; Witness 1 Surname and Given Name; Witness 2 Surname and Given Name; Witness 3 Surname and Given Name; Comments

Schulz; Karl Wilhelm Franz; 8-Dec-66; 6-Jan-67; Franz Wilhelm Ferdinand; Liebenau, Hannover; Falke, Eleonore; Liebenau, Hannover; Prufer, Karl; Klinkmeier, Wilhelm; Bergen, Maria

Schulz; Karoline Mathilde; 28-Apr-40; 7-Sep-40; Heinrich; —; Andres, Karol.; —; —; —; —

Schulz; Margaretha Maria Friedericka; 1-May-57; 10-May-57; Ernst; Liebenau, Hannover; Meier, Sophia; —; Bachmann, Margaretha; Schulz, Maria Minna; Klinkmeier, Friedericka

Schulz; Maria Louise Eleonora; 1-Mar-05; 23-Apr-65; Franz Wilhelm Konrad; Liebenau, Hannover; Falke, Eleonora; Liebenau, Hannover; Klinkmeier, Maria; Schulz, Louise; Fuchs, Eleonore

Schulz; Sophie Marie; 4-Mar-64; 13-Mar-64; Conrad; Beidekopf, Preussen; Funk, Henriette; Wetten, Kurhessen; Hollebein, Sophie Dorothea; Burmann, Marie Elisabeth; Zink, Georg Frdch.

Schulz; Wilhelm Gustav Heinrich; 2-Apr-60; 8-Apr-60; Ernst; Liebenau, Hannover; Meier, Sophie; —; Lindemann, Gustav; Eggers, Heinrich; Meier, Adelheid Marie

Schulz; Wilhelm Heinrich Gottlieb; 18-Jan-59; 23-Jan-59; Ferdinand; Liebenau, Hannover; Falk, Eleonora Maria; —; Schulz, Gottlieb; Ecksturm, Christian; Laban, Heinr.

Schulze; Elisabeth Marie; 3-May-62; 18-May-62; Gottlieb; Liebenau, Hannover; Schneider, Marie; Engter, Hannover; Happel, Elisabeth; Lobahn, Karoline; —

Schulze; Friederike Karoline Maria; 23-Jul-59; 31-Jul-59; Friedr. Aug. Gottlieb; Liebenau, Hannover; Schneider, Louise; —; Klinkmeier, Friederike; Schulz, Eleonora; Ober, Elise.

Schulze; Louise Maria Eleonora; 12-May-57; 17-May-57; Gottlieb; Liebenau, Hannover; Schneider, Louise; —; Schulze, Ferdinand; Schneider, Anna Louise; Schneider, Maria Engel

Schumacher; Kunigunde Elisabeth; 18-Sep-53; 2-Oct-53; Reinhard; Marburg, Kurhessen; James, Sara; —; Stroh, Kunigunde; Stroh, Konrad; —

Surname Father; Child's Given Name; Birth Date; Baptismal Date; Father's Given Name; Father's Place of Birth; Mother's Surname and Given Name; Mother's Place of Birth; Witness 1 Surname and Given Name; Witness 2 Surname and Given Name; Witness 3 Surname and Given Name; Comments

Schumacher; Louise Maria; 26-Oct-58; 14-Nov-58; Reinhard; Marburg, Kurhessen; Hamer, Sara; —; Leutner, Franz; Leutner, Mrs. Franz; —

Schumann; Anna Margaretha; 18-Jan-38; 29-Apr-38; Friedr.; —; Behrens, Sophie; —; —; —; —; —

Schumann; Caroline; 1-Mar-47; 18-Apr-47; Conrad; Rossdorf, Dieburg; Drass, Elisabeth; Risselsheim, Dornberg, Hessen; Apel, Caroline; —; —; —

Schumann; Helene Marg.; 14-Jan-42; 28-Feb-42; Friedrich; —; Behrens, Dorothea; —; —; —; —; —

Schumann; Johann Augste; 25-Sep-40; 26-Apr-40; Friedr. Heinr.; —; Behrens, Sophie; —; —; —; —; [probably 1839]

Schürer; Karl August; 27-May-42; 3-Jul-42; Johann K. A.; —; Stieglitz, Barbara; —; —; —; —; —

Schurmann; Carl Wilhelm; 17-Jan-48; 29-Oct-48; Carl; Gronach,, Steinach, Baiern; Schneider, Sophie; Baltimore; Pick, Carl; Ashton, William; —; —

Schurz; Anna Maria; 16-May-50; 2-Jun-50; Johann; Watnersbach, Uffenheim, Bayern; Kramer, Katharina; Stothenburg a.d. Tauber, Bayern; Menth, Anna Maria; —; —; wit from Brackenlohr

Schussler; Heinrich; 20-Apr-47; 23-May-47; Heinrich; Dodtenhausen, Kurhessen; Kammerer, Christine; Beckenir, Wurttemberg; Lohrmann, Heinrich; —; —; —

Schutte; Carl Heinrich Ludwigt; 25-Sep-48; 29-Oct-48; Ludwig; Hellenthal, Braunschweig; Seits, Johanne; Hellenthal, Braunschweig; Seits, Sr., Heinrich; Seits, Jr., Heinrich; —; —

Schutz; Johann Heinrich; 2-Jul-39; 21-Jul-39; Johann; —; Hilgen, Kathr.; —; —; —; —; —

Schutze; Johann Wilhelm; 2-Sep-43; 1-Oct-43; Heinrich; —; Späth, Marg.; —; —; —; —; —

Schwab; August; 28-Mar-53; 3-Apr-53; Karl; Obermohr, Rheinbaiern; Klein, Wilhelmine; —; Hoffmann, August; —; —; —

Schwab; Carl; 14-Nov-67; 15-Nov-67; Christian; Gerdbach, Rheinbaiern; , ; —; Schwab, Heinr.; —; —; Schulmeister

Surname Father; Child's Given Name; Birth Date; Baptismal Date; Father's Given Name; Father's Place of Birth; Mother's Surname and Given Name; Mother's Place of Birth; Witness 1 Surname and Given Name; Witness 2 Surname and Given Name; Witness 3 Surname and Given Name; Comments

Schwab; Catharina; 19-Aug-54; 1-Oct-54; Carl; Gonsbach, Pirmessens; Klein, Catharina; —; Schwab, Heinr.; Muller, Wilhelimina; —; —

Schwab; Christian; 25-Jun-58; 1-Jul-58; Christian; Gersbach, Rheinbaiern; Wenz, Louise; —; Schwab, Heinrich; —; —; —

Schwab; Christian Friedrich Melchior; 1-Oct-62; 9-Nov-62; Ludwig; Allendorf a.d.L., Hessen; Wagner, Katharine; —; Schlerf, Melchior; Reinhard, Christoph; Schlerf, Anna Katharine; —

Schwab; Christian Heinrich Karl; 25-May-61; 8-Jun-61; Christian; Gersbach, Rheinbaiern; Wenz, Louise; —; Schwab, Heinrich; Schorer, Maria Karoline; Muller, Karl; —

Schwab; Christine; 19-Jul-52; 25-Jul-52; Carl; Gersbach, Rheinbaiern; Klein, Catharina; —; Muller, Carl; Nonnemacher, Widow; —; —

Schwab; Friedrich Wilhelm; 13-Feb-63; 1-Mar-63; Heinrich; Gersbach, Rheinbaiern; Weckesser, Eva; Baltimore; Leutner, Franz; Scherrer, Marie; Muller, Karl; —

Schwab; Georg Adam Philipp; 11-Sep-67; 29-Sep-67; Heinrich; Gerdebach, Rheinbaiern; Weckesser, Eva; Baltimore; Stubeuruch, Georg; Weckesser, Johann Adam; Leutner, Helena Katharina; —

Schwab; Heinrich Johann Ludwig; 11-Apr-64; 24-Apr-64; Christian; Gersbach, Rheinbaiern; Wenz, Louise; Wolfersheim, Rheinbaiern; Scherer, Johann; Muller, Wilhelmine; —; —

Schwab; Heinrich Karl; 12-Oct-56; 14-Dec-56; Karl; Gersbach, Rheinbaiern; Klein, Katharine; —; Schwab, Heinr.; Muller, Karl; —; out of the country

Schwab; Heinrich Karl Christian; 23-Jun-60; 19-Aug-60; Karl; Gersbach, Rheinbaiern; Klein, Katharine; —; Schwab, Heinr.; Muller, Karl; Schwab, Christian; —

Schwab; Johann Christian Wilhelm; 10-Oct-62; 21-Dec-62; Karl; Gersbach, Rheinbaiern; Klein, Katharine; —; Schwab, Christian; Muller, Wilhelmine; —; —

Surname Father; Child's Given Name; Birth Date; Baptismal Date; Father's Given Name; Father's Place of Birth; Mother's Surname and Given Name; Mother's Place of Birth; Witness 1 Surname and Given Name; Witness 2 Surname and Given Name; Witness 3 Surname and Given Name; Comments

Schwab; Johann Gottfried; 21-Jul-65; 6-Aug-65; Heinrich; Gerdbach, Rheinbaiern; Weckesser, Eva; Baltimore; Leutner, Friedrich; Einwachter, Alex.; Schwab, Louise; —

Schwab; Johann Heinrich Karl; 24-Jan-57; 8-Feb-57; Heinrich; Gersbach, Rheinbaiern; Weckesser, Eva; —; Schwab, Karl; Germuth, Andreas; Leutner, Louise; —

Schwab; Johann Karl; 24-May-61; 9-Jun-61; Heinrich; Gersbach, Rheinbaiern; Weckesser, Eva; —; Weckesser, Johann; Weckesser, Karoline Amalie; —; —

Schwab; Karl Heinrich Wilhelm; 29-Sep-58; 14-Nov-58; Karl; Gersbach, Rheinbaiern; Klein, Karoline; —; Muller, Karl; Schwab, Heinr.; —; —

Schwab; Katharina Elisabeth Wilhelmina; 3-Sep-58; 19-Sep-58; Heinrich; Gersbach, Rheinbaiern; Weckesser, Eva; —; Schwab, Christian; Germuth, Elisabeth; Muller, Wilhelmine; —

Schwab; Louise Katharina; 3-Jul-59; 17-Jul-59; Christian; Gersbach, Rheinbaiern; Wenz, Louise; —; Schwab, Heinrich; Schwab, Eva; —; —

Schwab; Magdalena; 28-Mar-63; 28-Mar-63; Christian; Gersbach, Rheinbaiern; Wenz, Louise; —; Schwab, Heinrich; —; —; emergency baptism

Schwab; Wilhelm Friedrich Theodor; 11-May-66; 27-May-66; Christian; Gersbach, Rheinbaiern; Wenz, Louise; Wolfowshain, Rheinbaiern; Schwab, Eva; Mess, Johann; —; —

Schwab; Wilhelmine; 9-Feb-50; 10-Feb-50; Carl; Gersbach,; Klein, Catharine; Lemberg, Rheinbaiern; Muller, Carl; Muller, Wilhelmine Klein; —

Schwackendirck; Georg August Hermann; 5-Feb-56; 24-Feb-56; Georg; Erzen, Hannover; Lange, Elise; —; Burmann, Heinr.; Lettmade, Wilh.; Bach, Adam

Schwartz; Georg Heinrich; 29-Jul-56; 10-Aug-56; Daniel; Unterschonthal, Wurttemberg; Rauber, Elisabeth; —; Boppler, Heinr.; —; —

Surname Father; Child's Given Name; Birth Date; Baptismal Date; Father's Given Name; Father's Place of Birth; Mother's Surname and Given Name; Mother's Place of Birth; Witness 1 Surname and Given Name; Witness 2 Surname and Given Name; Witness 3 Surname and Given Name; Comments

Schwartz; Georg Heinrich; 4-Nov-54; 12-Nov-54; Daniel; Unterschonthal, Wurttemberg; Reiber, Elisabeth; —; Boppler, Joh. Heinr.; —; —

Schwartz; Johann Alexander Daniel; 8-Jan-66; 21-Jan-66; Daniel; Unterschonthal, Wurttemberg; Reuber, Elisabeth; Sehrder, Hannover; Einwachter, Jr., Bapler; Joh.; —

Schwartz; Johann Daniel; 4-Jul-62; 20-Jul-62; Daniel; Unterschonthal, Wurttemberg; Reuber, Elisabeth; —; Immich, Johann; Hillgartner, Johann; Kammer, Dorothea

Schwartz; Wilhelm Heinrich; 19-Dec-59; 26-Dec-59; Daniel; Unterschonthal, Wurttemberg; Reuber, Elisabeth; —; Kommer, Wilh.; Bopler, Jr., Heinrich; —

Schwarz; Elise Katharina; 5-Jan-58; 18-Jan-58; Daniel; Unterschonthal, Wurttemberg; Reuber, Elisabeth; —; Boppler, Kathar.; Einwacther, Elisabeth; —

Schwarz; Gustav; 25-Nov-35; 23-Jan-37; Gustav; —; Beard, Katharine; —; —; —; —

Schwarzenbach; Conrad; 13-Oct-43; 5-Nov-43; Johann Fr.; —; Löwe, Anna M.; —; —; —; —

Schweigart; Catharine; 3-May-48; 12-May-48; Friedrich Wilhelm; Aich bei Tubingen, Wurttemberg; Riedel, Elisabeth; Nietau bei Hanau, Hessen; Burker, Margareth; —; —

Schweigert; Margarethe; 3-May-44; 27-May-44; Friedrich Wilh.; —; Ritte, Elisab.; —; —; —; —

Schweikert; Friedrich Wilh.; 18-Apr-38; 12-May-38; Friedr. W.; —; Riedel, Elisab.; —; —; —; —

Schweitzer; Jacob Franklin; 22-Oct-42; 7-Mar-43; Georg; —; Stahl, Marg.; —; —; —; —

Schwensen; Johann Christian Marcus; 7-Aug-39; 14-Aug-39; Markus; —; [--?--], [--?--]; —; —; —; —

Seckel; David; 23-Jan-44; 28-Feb-44; Heinrich; —; Erke, Kathr.; —; —; —; —

Seib; Maria Elisab.; 10-Feb-39; 21-Apr-39; Conrad; —; Kerwig, Marg.; —; —; —; —

Surname Father; Child's Given Name; Birth Date; Baptismal Date; Father's Given Name; Father's Place of Birth; Mother's Surname and Given Name; Mother's Place of Birth; Witness 1 Surname and Given Name; Witness 2 Surname and Given Name; Witness 3 Surname and Given Name; Comments

Seibel; Christiane Anna Marie; 15-Jan-61; 20-Jan-61; Johann; Niederotterbach, Baiern; Schlotthauer, Susanne; —; Tormelen, Christine; Winter, Christine; Stetter, Anna Marie

Seibel; Georg Immanuel Melchior; 10-Jul-56; 20-Jul-56; Johann; Niederotterbach, Baiern; Schlotthauer, Susanne; —; Flemming, Immanuel; Reisinger, Georg; Schlerf, Melchior

Seibel; Josephine Susanne Elisabeth; 4-Oct-65; 15-Oct-65; Johann; Niederotterbach, Baiern; Schlotthauer, Susanna; Leimen, Baden; Josephine, Herbst; Felder, Elisabeth; Schmidt, Christian

Seibel; Katharine Karoline Henriette; 23-Aug-63; 6-Sep-63; Johann; Niederotterbach, Baiern; Schlotthauer, Susanne; Grunstadt, Baiern; Walther, Heinrich; Repp, Katharine; —

Seibel; Mariane Selma; 1-Aug-54; 6-Aug-54; Johann; Niederotterbach, Baiern; Schlotthauer, Margaretha; —; Flemming, Selma; Reisinger, Mariane; —

Seibel; Marie Christine; 2-May-51; 1-Jun-51; Joh.; Niederotterbach, Baiern; Schlotthauer, Margar. Susanne; —; Siebel, Marie Christine; Louis, Margaretha Adelheid; —

Seibel; Wilhelmina Henrietta; 21-Sep-58; 3-Oct-58; Johann; Niederottenbach, Baiern; Schlotthauer, Susanna; —; Reinhard, Wilhelmine; Jackel, Henriette; —

Seibold; Alexander; 24-Dec-48; 1-Jul-49; Michael; Remmelshausen, Canstadt, Wurttemberg; Muller, Dorothea; Biedenkopf, Hessen; —; —; —

Seibold; Dorothea Margaretha; 10-Apr-42; 15-Apr-42; Michael; —; Steinmeyer, Dorothea; —; —; —; —

Seibold; Johann Georg; 3-Feb-38; 24-Mar-38; Michael; —; Steinmeyer, Dorothea; —; —; —; —

Seibold; Philip Ludwig; 14-Feb-40; 12-Mar-40; Michael; —; Steinmeyer, Dorothea; —; —; —; —

Seich; Andreas; 23-Jul-48; 20-Aug-48; Paulus; Segnitz bei Wurzburg, Baiern; Hahnemann, Dorothea; Segnitz bei Wurzburg, Baiern; Fleischer, Andreas; —; —

Seifried; Elisabeth; 15-Sep-48; 19-Jul-49; Friedrich; Dortingen, Maulbronn, Wurttemberg; Kussmaul, Rosine; Dortingen,

Maulbronn, Wurttemberg; Roeder, Jakob; Seifried, Friederike; —

Seigel; Rudolph; 19-May-49; 10-Jun-49; Conrad; Eichelsachsen, Nidda, Hessen; Martin, Elisabeth; Romeroth bei Alsfeld, Hessen; Laud, Conrad; Colpus, Heinrich; —

Seip; Maria Elisab. Emmelie; 16-Jan-37; 12-Feb-37; Conrad; —; Kerbin, Amalia; —; —; —; —

Seippel; Emil Melchior; 8-Mar-53; 13-Mar-53; Johann; Niederotterbach, Baiern; Schlotthauer, Margaretha; —; Schlerf, Melchior; Trappmann, Emilie; —; —

Seitz; Catharine Sophie; 27-Jun-45; 5-Jul-46; Georg; Heubach, Hessen; Krupfhauser, Sophie; Wertheim, Baden; Krupfhause, Sophie; —; —; wit is grandmother

Seitz; Georg Heinrich; 16-Mar-66; 3-May-66; Georg Michael; Engelhardshausen, Wurttemberg; Dorsey, Lise; Baltimore; Whitte, Georg Andreas; Schneider, Heinrich; —; —

Seitz; Georg Louis; 9-Jan-46; 15-Feb-46; Daniel; Kusel, Rheinbaiern; Kreutzer, Anna Barbara; Kusel, Rheinbaiern; Kreutzer, Georg Louis; Fruhwald, Kunigunda; —; —

Seitz; George; 27-Oct-43; 5-Jul-46; George; Heubach, Hessen; Krupfhauser, Sophie; Wertheim, Baden; Willner, George; —; —; —

Seitz; Katharine Friedrike; 11-Sep-42; 11-Sep-42; Georg; —; Krophausen, Sophie; —; —; —; —; —

Semmelmann; Louis; 19-Jun-45; 25-Jul-45; Albrecht; Altorf, Holfeld, Baiern; Nebb, Maria; Dollar bei Giessen, Neupreussen; —; —; —; —

Senft; Wilhelmine; 28-Aug-43; 29-Oct-43; Heinrich; —; Steinhofer, Luise; —; —; —; —; —

Sepaller; Margaretha Franziska; 21-May-45; 13-Jul-45; Theodor; Prenzlau, Ukermark; Zimmisch, Charlotte; Minden, Preussen; Zimmisch, Elisabeth; —; —; —

Serbach; Elisabeth; 27-Jan-50; 8-Sep-50; Heinrich; Hinderweitenthal, Rheinbaiern; Keschme, Catharina; —; Cyprian, Joh.; Kunkel, Catharina; Serbach, Elisabeth; 8 child, 4 dau

Surname Father; Child's Given Name; Birth Date; Baptismal Date; Father's Given Name; Father's Place of Birth; Mother's Surname and Given Name; Mother's Place of Birth; Witness 1 Surname and Given Name; Witness 2 Surname and Given Name; Witness 3 Surname and Given Name; Comments

Seybold; Wilhelm Friedrich; 3-Nov-45; 1-Jul-46; Michael; Rummelshausen, Caustadt, Wurttemberg; Muller, Dorothea; Biedenkopf, Hessen; Doberer, Johann; —; —; —

Sickel; Carl Heinrich; 15-Sep-45; 8-Oct-45; Heinrich; Buchenbach, Kinzelsau, Wurttemberg; Erck, Catharine; Nidda, Hessen; —; —; —; —

Sickel; Georg Carl; 16-Apr-47; 21-May-48; Heinrich; Buchenbach, Wurttemberg; Erck, Catharina; Nidda, Hessen; Steinweg, Georg Carl; —; —; —

Sickel; Ludwig Ferdinand; 19-Oct-52; 8-Dec-52; Heinrich; Burgenbach, Wurttemberg; Carrier, Wilhelmine; —; Sickel, Heinrich; —; —; father is witness

Sickel; Sabina Charlotte; 26-Apr-50; 23-May-50; Heinrich; Wurtenberg, Kinzelsua, Buchenbach; Lurrier, Wilhlemina Sabina; Hofgaismar, Hessen Kassel; Lurrier, Sabina Charlotte; —; —; wit is grandmother

Sieck; Adam Friedrich; 17-Sep-53; 25-Sep-53; Adolph Heinrich; Husede, Hannover; Ebeler, Florentine Louise; —; Sieck, Adam Friedrich; Sieck, Joh. Heinr.; —; —

Sieck; Anna Eleonora Charlotte; 10-Feb-58; 21-Feb-58; Adolph Heinrich; Husede, Hannover; Ebeler, Florentine; —; Wilker, Eleonora Christine; Schulz, Konrad; Leutner, Anna Katharina; —

Sieck; Anna Maria Catharina; 30-Dec-55; 6-Jan-56; Heinrich Adolph; Susstedt, Hannover; Ebeler, Maria; —; Sieck, Elisabeth; Kunker, Catharina; Sieck, Maria; —

Sieck; Caroline; 14-Jun-55; 24-Jun-55; Joh. Heinrich Friedrich; Husede, Hannover; Schafer, Anna Maria; —; Schaumloffel, Caroline; —; —; —

Sieck; Christina Wilhelmine Charlotte; 23-Jan-53; 10-Feb-53; Adam Friedrich; Husede, Hannover; Wilke, Maria Elisabeth; —; Ortmann, Christine Wilhelmine Charlotte; —; —; —

Sieck; Christine Margarethe; 25-Jun-60; 4-Jul-60; Adam Friedrich; Husede, Hannover; Wilker, Marie Elisabeth; —; Sieck, Adolph Heinr.; Vorderwusten, Margarehte; Wilder, Christine Eleonore; at house

Surname Father; Child's Given Name; Birth Date; Baptismal Date; Father's Given Name; Father's Place of Birth; Mother's Surname and Given Name; Mother's Place of Birth; Witness 1 Surname and Given Name; Witness 2 Surname and Given Name; Witness 3 Surname and Given Name; Comments

Sieck; Eleonora Elisabeth; 13-Feb-57; 22-Feb-57; Joh. Henir. Friedr.; Husede, Hannover; Schafer, Anna Maria Elisabeth; —; Wilker, Christina Eleonora; Sieck, Maria Elisabeth; Sieck, Adolph Heinr.; —

Sieck; Florentina Louise; 23-Apr-53; 19-Jun-53; Joh. Heinr.; Husede, Hannover; Schafer, Anna Maria; —; Sieck, Florentine Louise; Sieck, Heinr.; —; born at see

Sieck; Florentina Louise; 7-Nov-67; 24-Nov-67; Adolph Heinr.; Susret, Hannover; Ebeler, Florentina; Buwe ?, Hannover; Mohring, Carl; Sommer, Henriette; —; —

Sieck; Florentine Elisabeth; 18-Jul-50; 17-Aug-50; Adam Friedrich; Osnabruck, Hannover; Wilke, Maria Elisabeth; —; Sieck, Florentine; Sieck, Henrich; —; 2 child, 1 dau

Sieck; Florentine Katharine; 19-Mar-60; 25-Mar-60; Jobst Heinrich Friedrich; Husede, Hannover; Schafer, Anna Marie; —; Sieck, Florentine Louise; Sieck, Heinr. Adolph; Wilker, Maria Katharine; —

Sieck; Florentine Louise; 24-Aug-55; 2-Sep-55; Adam Friedrich; Husede, Hannover; Wilker, Maria Elisabeth; —; Sieck, Florentine Louise; Succop, Maria Elise; —; —

Sieck; Jobst Heinrich Friedrich; 17-Jan-58; 21-Jan-58; Adam Friedrich; Husede,Hannover; Wilker, Maria Elisabeth; —; Sieck, Klaus Heinr.; Sieck, Heinr. Friedrich; Wilker, Maria Katharina; —

Sieck; Johann Adam Friedrich; 5-Mar-66; 21-Mar-66; Adam Friedrich; Husede, Hannover; Wilker, Maria Eilsabeth; Boba, Hannover; Lettmade, Johann Friedrich; Sieck, Karoline Louise; Schimpf, Joh. Heinr. Gottfried; —

Sieck; Johann Heinrich; 1-Jan-51; 19-Jan-51; Heinrich; Amt Wittler, Hannover; Ebeler, Florentine Marie; —; Sieck, Klaus Heinrich; —; —; —

Sieck; Karl Heinrich; 8-Jul-65; 12-Jul-65; Adolph Heinrich; Husede, Hannover; Ebeler, Florentine Louise; Bar, Hannover; Sieck, Klamer Heinrich; Leutner, Franz; Ebeler, Joh. Heinrich; —

Surname Father; Child's Given Name; Birth Date; Baptismal Date; Father's Given Name; Father's Place of Birth; Mother's Surname and Given Name; Mother's Place of Birth; Witness 1 Surname and Given Name; Witness 2 Surname and Given Name; Witness 3 Surname and Given Name; Comments

Sieck; Katharine Wilhelmina; 30-Sep-58; 17-Oct-58; Jobst Heinrich Friedrich; Husede, Hannover; Schafer, Anna Maria Elisabeth; —; Kunker, Katharine Wilhelmine; Radecke, Wilhelmine Friederike; Sieck, Adam Friedrich; —

Sieck; Maria Elisabeth; 1-May-66; 10-Jun-66; Jobst Heinrich; Sustade, Hannover; Schafer, Anna Maria Elisabeth; Sustade, Hannover; Burmann, Ernst Heinrich; Burmann, Fr. Elisabeth; —; —

Sieck; Marie Katharine; 25-Jun-63; 4-Jul-63; Adam Friedrich; Husede, Hannover; Wilker, Maria Elisabeth; —; Kunker, Heinrich; Karstens, Heinrich; Karstens, Marie; —

Sieck; Sophie Emma Dorothea; 3-Feb-63; 15-Feb-63; Heinr. Adolph; Fulde, Hannover; Ebeler, Louise Florentine; Bure, Hannover; Burmann, Marie Elisabeth; Treide, Marie Dorothea; Wilker, Maria Katharine; twin

Sieck; Wilhelm Ernst Gustav; 3-Feb-63; 15-Feb-63; Heinr. Adolph; Fulde, Hannover; Ebeler, Louise Florentine; Bure, Hannover; Lettmade, Wilh.; Sieck, Marie Elisabeth; Lindemann, Ludolph Gustav; twin

Sieck; Wilhelmine Louise Johanne; 13-Sep-60; 23-Sep-60; Adolph Heinr.; Husede, Hannover; Ebeler, Florentine; —; Leutner, Dorothea Wilhelmine Louise; Ebeler, Ernst; Treide, Joh. Katharine Louise; —

Siedling; Johann Friedrich Heinrich; 17-Aug-48; 9-Sep-48; Georg Heinrich; Salz der Hulden, Hannover; Pfaff, Juliane Henriette Friederike; Clausthab, Hannover; Weber, Fried. Wilh.; —; —; —

Siegel; Anna Margaretha Magdalena; 15-Aug-65; 24-Aug-65; Ferdinand; Huckelsheim, Baden; Fixes [?], Eva; Strassburg, PA; Siegel, Katharine Margaretha; Schafer, Katharine Margaretha; —; —

Siegel; Johannes Melchior; 20-May-67; 2-Jun-67; Simon; Hugelsheim, Baden; Meusdorf, Maria; Oberohm, Hessen; Ranzbach, Johannes; Ranzbach, Wilhelmina; Schlerf, Melchior; —

Surname Father; Child's Given Name; Birth Date; Baptismal Date; Father's Given Name; Father's Place of Birth; Mother's Surname and Given Name; Mother's Place of Birth; Witness 1 Surname and Given Name; Witness 2 Surname and Given Name; Witness 3 Surname and Given Name; Comments

Siegel; Karl Heinrich Joseph; 19-Sep-64; 25-Oct-64; Simon; Hukelsheim, Baiern; Mansdorf, Maria Margaretha; Homberg a. d. Ohm, Hessen; Wittler, Karl; Siegel, Kath. Marg.; Wittler, Heinr.; —

Siegel; Katharine Margarethe; 22-Nov-60; 2-Dec-60; Simon; Hugelsheim, Baden; Mansdorf, Marie Margarethe; —; Siegel, Katharine Marie; Wittler, Karl; Schafer, Katharine; —

Siegel; Louise Henriette Auguste; 15-Sep-62; 21-Sep-62; Simon; Hugelsheim, Baden; Mensdorf, Marie; —; Wittler, Louise; Schafer, Heinrich, Engel; Wilhelmine; —

Siegle; Johann Wilh.; 21-Aug-37; 31-Aug-37; Cunrad; —; Weiss, Kathr.; —; —; —; —; —

Siegle; Ludwig Eduard; 4-Apr-40; 15-Sep-40; Conrad; —; Weis, Kathr.; —; —; —; —; —

Siegle; Margaretha; 2-Apr-38; 16-Apr-39; Conrad; —; Weiss, Kathr.; —; —; —; —; —

Siegler; Amalie Laura; 30-Jan-43; 10-Feb-43; Conrad; —; Weiss, Kathr.; —; —; —; —; —

Siegmund; Karl Ferdinand; 27-Nov-56; 21-Dec-56; Ferdinand; Sutelfinger, Wurttemberg; Ganshorn, Katharine; —; Kerber, Joh. Xtian Albert; —; —; —

Siegmund; Louise Caroline; 28-Jul-54; 6-Aug-54; Ludwig Ferdinand; Sintelfinger, Wurttemberg; Ganshorn, Catharina; —; Kothe, Sophie; —; —; twin

Siegmund; Ludwig Ferdinand; 28-Jul-54; 6-Aug-54; Ludwig Ferdinand; Sintelfinger, Wurttemberg; Ganshorn, Catharina; —; Kothe, Kasten; —; —; twin died

Siegrist; Karl; 8-Jun-40; 29-Jul-40; Karl; —; Haas, Magdalene; —; —; —; —; adopted child

Siek; Caroline Elise; 22-Mar-48; 7-May-48; Adolph Heinrich; Husede, Wicklaga, Hannover; Eberle, Florentine Maria; Buhr, Molle, Hannover; Brohm, Clara Elisabeth; —; —; —

Siek; Johann Heinrich; 4-Aug-47; 22-Nov-47; Aaron Friederich; Usede, Witlage, Hannover; Wilkes, Maria Elisabeth; Bern bei Osnabruck; Siek, Adolph Heinrich; —; —; —

Surname Father; Child's Given Name; Birth Date; Baptismal Date; Father's Given Name; Father's Place of Birth; Mother's Surname and Given Name; Mother's Place of Birth; Witness 1 Surname and Given Name; Witness 2 Surname and Given Name; Witness 3 Surname and Given Name; Comments

Singewald; Karl; 21-Jun-39; 16-Jul-39; Gottlieb; —; Winter, Friedrieke; —; —; —; —; —

Sivereng; Heinrich Karl; 21-Mar-39; 20-Oct-39; Simon; —; Ziegenfelder, Anna M.; —; —; —; —; —

Sohl; Georg; 16-Jan-39; 17-Mar-39; Adam; —; Appel, Kathr.; —; —; —; —; —

Sohl; Heinrich; 15-Aug-43; 11-Aug-44; Adam; —; Appel, Kathr.; —; —; —; —; —

Sohl; Johann; 21-Apr-41; 23-May-41; Adam; —; Appel, Kathr.; —; —; —; —; —

Soller; Wilhelm Ludwig; 4-Apr-37; 4-Jun-37; Johann; —; Werz, Sara; —; —; —; —; —

Söller; Maria Elisab.; 27-Nov-38; 6-Jan-39; Johann; —; Wirt, Sara; —; —; —; —; —

Sollmann; Johann Georg; 26-Nov-39; 1-Mar-40; Johann; —; Muller, Barbara; —; —; —; —; —

Sollmann; Maria Dorothea; 15-Feb-38; 16-Apr-38; Johann; —; Muller, Barbara; —; —; —; —; —

Sommer; David; 30-Jun-42; 27-Jan-50; Jakob; Kleinfulle, Canton Bern, Schweitz; Steinmeyer, Hanna Sophie Marie; Pyrmont, Waldeck; —; —; —; —

Sommer; Elisabeth; 2-Jul-40; 19-Jul-40; Heinrich; —; Knapp, Jacobine; —; —; —; —; —

Sommer; Hanna Sophie; 14-Feb-46; 27-Jan-50; Jakob; Kleinfulle, Canton Bern, Schweitz; Steinmeyer, Hanna Sophie Marie; Pyrmont, Waldeck; —; —; —

Sommer; Jakob; 12-Jul-1835; 27-Jan-50; Jakob; Kleinfulle, Canton Bern, Schweitz; Steinmeyer, Hanna Sophie Maria; Pyrmont, Waldeck; —; —; —

Sommer; Joseph; 30-Jun-1840; 27-Jan-50; Jakob; Kleinfulle, Canton Bern, Schweitz; Steinmeyer, Hanna Sophie Marie; Pyrmont, Waldeck; —; —; —

Sonnenmeyer; Johann Herm. Theodor; 12-Apr-37; 11-Jul-37; Gerh.; —; Strotmann, Kathr.; —; —; —; —

Spaller; Auguste Charlotte; 3-Aug-37; 20-Aug-37; Theodor; —; Zimmitsch, Charlotte; —; —; —; —

Surname Father; Child's Given Name; Birth Date; Baptismal Date; Father's Given Name; Father's Place of Birth; Mother's Surname and Given Name; Mother's Place of Birth; Witness 1 Surname and Given Name; Witness 2 Surname and Given Name; Witness 3 Surname and Given Name; Comments

Spaller; Friedrich Wilh. Theodor; 6-Mar-39; 7-Apr-39; Theodor; —; Zimmisch, Charlotte; —; —; —; —

Spaller; Johann Theodor; 11-May-43; 6-Aug-43; Theodor; —; Zimmisch, Charlotte; —; —; —; —

Spaller; Maria Luise; 23-Dec-40; 29-Dec-40; Theodor; —; Zimmisch, Sophie Chr.; —; —; —; —

Spamer; Christian August; 25-Sep-43; 29-Oct-43; Ludwig; —; Martin, Julie; —; —; —; —

Spamer; Georg; 16-Oct-39; 17-Nov-39; Conrad; —; Heinzenberger, Johannette; —; —; —; —

Spangenberg; Karoline DorotheaElisabeth; 20-Dec-63; 17-Jan-64; Georg Johannes; Eichelsdorf, Hessen; Euler, Karoline; Daubringen, Hessen; Dorn, Elisabeth; Geblein, Elisabeth Dorothea; —

Spangenberger; Georg Friedrich Peter; 1-Oct-65; 22-Oct-65; Georg Johann; Eichelsdorf, Hessen; Euler, Karolina; Daubringen, Hessen; Waltjen, Wilhelm; Winkel, Friedrich; Treu, Peter

Spangenberger; Georg Jakob Wilhelm; 27-May-61; 16-Jun-61; Georg Johann; Eichelsdorf, Hessen; Euler, Karoline; —; Walther, Wilhelm; Waltjen, Wilhelm; —

Spangenberger; Louise; 12-Dec-59; 24-Dec-59; Georg; Eichelsdorf, Hessen; Eiler, Karoline; —; Spangenberger, Louise; Louise; —

Spielmann; Johann Friedrich; 10-Dec-58; 19-Dec-58; Johann Heinrich; Lisberg, Hessen; Gantenbein, Maria; —; Briel, Joh.; Wildermuth, Joh.; Spielmann, Joh.

Spielmann; Johann Heinrich; 3-Aug-60; 12-Aug-60; Karl Peter Konrad; Lisberg, Hessen; Wildermuth, Marie Elisabeth; —; Spielmann, Joh. Heinr.; Wildermuth, Joh.; Brauer, Heinr.

Spielmann; Karl Johann Heinrich; 21-Nov-56; 30-Nov-56; Johann Heinr.; Lisberg, Hessen; Gantenbein, Margaretha; —; Spielmann, Karl; Brauer, Heinr.; Mohring, Joh.

Spielmann; Katharine Louise Sophie; 26-Nov-60; 2-Dec-60; Johann Heinrich; Lisberg, Hessen; Gandenbein, Marie; —; Bach, Katharine Elisabeth; Broning, Katharine; Romester, Louise

Surname Father; Child's Given Name; Birth Date; Baptismal Date; Father's Given Name; Father's Place of Birth; Mother's Surname and Given Name; Mother's Place of Birth; Witness 1 Surname and Given Name; Witness 2 Surname and Given Name; Witness 3 Surname and Given Name; Comments

Spielmann; Maria Sophia Elisabeth; 22-Aug-59; 4-Sep-59; Karl; Lisberg, Hessen; Wildermuth, Maria; —; Spielmann, Sophia; Wildermuth, Elisab.; —

Spielmann; Rosine Karoline; 12-Apr-62; 27-Apr-62; Karl; Lisberg, Hessen; Wildermuth, Elisabeth; —; Kattenkamp, Rosine; Schaumelossel, Karoline; Spielmann, Friedrich

Spilmann; Friedrich Wilhelm; 3-Aug-67; 18-Aug-67; Karl; Lisberg, Hessen; Wildenmuth, Maria Elisabeth; Baltimore; Thiemeier, Friedrich; Brauer, Heinrich; Schafer, Katharine

Spilmann; Johann Heinrich; 25-Apr-64; 8-May-64; Karl; Lisberg, Hessen; Wildermuth, Marie Elisabeth; Baltimore; Feiertag, Benjamin; Broning, Katharine; Schimpf, Gottfried

Spilmann; Karl Johann; 23-Feb-66; 11-Mar-66; Karl; Lisberg, Hessen; Wildermuth, Maria; Baltimore; Spilmann, Johann Heinrich; Brauer, Karl; Wildermuth, Karoline

Spilmann; Katharine Wilhelmine Marie; 18-Jan-63; 1-Feb-63; Johann Heinrich; Lisberg, Hessen; Gandenbein, Marie Margarethe; Baltimore; Schafer, Katharine; Schaumlossel, Wilhelm; Spilmann, Marie

Stahl; Catharine Pauline; 13-Dec-45; 18-Jan-46; Carl Gottlieb; Oppelsspohn, Wurttemberg; Leins, Luise Sybille; Beutelsbach, Wurttemberg; Leins, Johanne; —; —

Stahl; Christian Magdalene; 25-Aug-42; 18-Dec-42; Karl; —; Leinz, Sibilla; —; —; —; —

Stahl; Karoline Wilhelmine; 28-Oct-39; 10-Nov-39; Karl; —; Leins, Mrs.; —; —; —; —

Stahl; Luise Maria; 16-Jan-38; 4-Feb-38; Karl Gottl.; —; Leinz, Sybille; —; —; —; —

Stahl; Rosine Koncordine; 20-Aug-43; 24-Sep-43; Karl G.; —; Leins, Luise; —; —; —; —

Staib; Johann Michael; 22-May-42; 3-Jul-42; Michael; —; Christmann, Magd.; —; —; —; —

Staib; Karl Wilh.; 21-May-43; 26-Dec-43; Michael; —; Christmann, Magdal.; —; —; —; —

Stang; Anna Susanne; 16-Nov-43; 31-Dec-43; Joseph; —; Hahn, Anna; —; —; —; —

Surname Father; Child's Given Name; Birth Date; Baptismal Date; Father's Given Name; Father's Place of Birth; Mother's Surname and Given Name; Mother's Place of Birth; Witness 1 Surname and Given Name; Witness 2 Surname and Given Name; Witness 3 Surname and Given Name; Comments

Stange; Anna Louise; 27-Apr-51; 25-May-51; Dietrich; Ufelgonne, Oldenburg; Wrede, Anna Maria; —; Wrede, Anna Margar.; Woltmann, Widow Anna Elis.; —; twin

Stange; Louis Valentin; 27-Feb-46; 2-Feb-46; Johann Ludwig; Liebenzell, Neuenbirk, Wurttemberg; Roots, Catharine; Goldheim, Kurhessen; Blum, Valentin; —; —; —

Stanger; Anna Maria; 13-Mar-43; 26-Mar-43; Johann; —; Roth, Kathr.; —; —; —; —; —

Stanger; Elisabeth Kathr.; 10-Sep-41; 19-Sep-41; Johann Ludw.; —; Roth, Kathr.; —; —; —; —; —

Stassfort; Karl Aug.; 18-Dec-43; 14-Apr-44; Ludwig; —; Egers, Elisab.; —; —; —; —; —

Stauch; Jakob Ludwig; 14-Nov-47; 21-May-48; Jakob Georg; Hofstetten, Sachsen Coburg; Mohlmann, Maria; Bohmde, Hannover; Schafer, Jakob Ludwig; —; —; —

Staupitz; Anna Barbara; 17-Jan-37; 22-Jan-37; Wiegand; —; Sonnstädt, Christine; —; —; —; —; —

Staupitz; Christine; 27-Nov-38; 9-Dec-38; Wiegand; —; Somstädt, Christina; —; —; —; —; —

Stecker; Christiane Caroline; 1-Dec-44; 24-Mar-45; Georg; Kaisersbach, Wurttemberg; Klein, Caroline; Mahlheim, Wurttemberg; Blohm, Herrmann; —; —; —

Stecker; Katharine Karline; 19-May-43; 18-Feb-44; Georg; —; Klein, Karoline; —; —; —; —; —

Steckert; Maria Elisabeth; 6-Sep-48; 17-Sep-48; Ambrosius; Bermbach, Sachsen Weimar; Eitel, Maria; Lemberg, Bermisins, Baiern; Hoffmann, Salomine Eitel; —; —; —

Stehl; Justus Valentin; 28-Nov-43; 28-Feb-44; Johann; —; Boucsein, Maria; —; —; —; —; —

Stein; Elisabeth Franziska; 28-Nov-50; 15-Dec-50; Johannes; —; Sander, Anna Maria; —; Sander, Agnes Barbara; —; —; wit is grandmother

Stein; Heinrich Adam Andreas; 16-Feb-66; 11-Mar-66; Caspar; Oberohm, Hessen; Helfenbein, Juliane; Lomdenhausen, Hessen; Bach, Adam; Bach, Katharine; —; —

Surname Father; Child's Given Name; Birth Date; Baptismal Date; Father's Given Name; Father's Place of Birth; Mother's Surname and Given Name; Mother's Place of Birth; Witness 1 Surname and Given Name; Witness 2 Surname and Given Name; Witness 3 Surname and Given Name; Comments

Stein; Heinrich Friedrich Andreas; 29-Aug-67; 22-Sep-67; Kaspar; Oberohm, Hessen; Helfenbein, Julianne; Landenhausen, Hessen; Stein, Katharina Elisabeth; Bach, Friederich; —; —

Stein; Maria Karoline; 6-Mar-64; 27-Mar-64; Jakob; Lingelbach, Kurhessen; Habermehl, Maria Katharine; —; Weber, Maria; Kratz, Wilhelmine; Ruppel, Adam; —

Stein; Philippine Elisabeth; 21-Feb-62; 2-Mar-62; Jakob; Lingelbach, Hessen; Habermehl, Katharine; —; Koch, Philippine; Hillgartner, Elisabeth; —; —

Steiner; Carl Wilhelm; 4-Jan-54; 15-Jan-54; Joh.; Frauenaurach, Baiern; Bausch, Elisabeth; —; Vogelmann, Carl Wilhe.; —; —; —

Steiner; Friedrich; 28-Sep-51; 12-Oct-51; Joh.; Frauenaurach, Baiern; Bausch, Elisabeth; —; Leutner, Friedrich; —; —; —

Steinweg; Catharine Henriette; 17-Jul-50; 28-Jul-50; Carl; Borgsteinfort, Westfalen; Fritz, Henriette; —; Fritz, Catharina Wurz; —; —; 6 child, 3 dau

Steinweg; Johann; 25-Mar-49; 22-Jun-49; Johann Abraham; Bergsteinfurth, Westphalen, Preussen; Pedal, Maria Aurora; Gotha, Sachsen Gotha; Bartzer, Johann; —; —; —

Steinweg; Marianne Helene; 11-Oct-46; 26-Nov-46; Carl Georg; Burg Steinfurth bei Munster, Preussen; Fritz, Henirette; Hameln, Hannover; Fritz, Maria; —; —; —

Steinweg; Susanne; 16-Sep-45; 22-Sep-45; Carl; Steinfurth, Preussen; Fritz, Henriette; —; —; —; —; died 22 Sep 45

Steinweg; Wilhelm Louis; 31-Oct-52; 13-Feb-53; Karl Georg; Steinfurtch, Preussen; Fritz, Henriette; —; Sickel, Heinr.; —; —; emergency baptism

Stengel; Catharina Regina; 5-Nov-47; 28-Nov-47; Jakob; Oberritzeingen, Weisingen, Wurttemberg; Diper, Anna Martha; Spangenberg, Kurhessen; Benker, Catharina; —; —; —

Stephan; Maria Elisabeth; 14-Mar-40; 20-Apr-40; Johann; —; Hussel, Maria; —; —; —; —; —

Sternweiss; Katharine; 26-Jan-44; 3-Mar-44; Johann; —; Adams, Elisab.; —; —; —; —; —

Surname Father; Child's Given Name; Birth Date; Baptismal Date; Father's Given Name; Father's Place of Birth; Mother's Surname and Given Name; Mother's Place of Birth; Witness 1 Surname and Given Name; Witness 2 Surname and Given Name; Witness 3 Surname and Given Name; Comments

Stetten; Emilia Susannna Eva; 20-Jul-59; 7-Aug-59; Wilh.; Buchen, Baden; Kern, Anna Maria; —; Schlerf, Emilia; Seibel, Susanna; Weisbrod, Eva; —

Stetter; Johann Friedrich Wilhelm; 17-Aug-63; 30-Aug-63; Wilhelm; Buchen, Baden; Kern, Anna Marie; —; Klingelhofer, Wilh.; Jackel, Barbara; Seibel, Johann; —

Stetter; Matthaus Heinrich Melchior; 2-Oct-61; 6-Oct-61; Wilhelm; Buchs, Baden; Kern, Marie; —; Reitzel, Friederike; Schneider, Heinrich; Schlerf, Melchior; —

Steub; George Heinrich; 19-Aug-45; 27-Nov-45; Michael; Lairrn bei Pforzheim, Baden; Christmann, Magdelena; Bischweiler bei Hagenau, Elsass; Preiss, Michael; —; —; —

Steub; Lorenz; 3-Jun-37; 4-Jul-37; Michael; —; Christmann, Magdal.; —; —; —; —; —

Steudler; Johann Heinrich; 2-Sep-39; 20-Oct-39; Johann; —; Ruff, Jacobine; —; —; —; —; —

Steudler; Laura Viriginia; 22-Mar-44; 15-Jul-44; Johann; —; Ruff, Jacobine; —; —; —; —; child died

Steuernagel; Johann Heinr.; 18-Aug-40; 22-Aug-40; Joh. Ph.; —; Gerth, Marg. W.; —; —; —; —; —

Stewart; Klara Emilie; 15-Sep-44; 11-Oct-44; David; —; Orckwein, Dorothea; —; —; —; —; —

Stibolt (Dr. Jur.); Erasmus Unkas; 2-Apr-48; 16-May-48; Jens Peter; Hadersluben, Schleswig Holstein; Ehlert, Carolina Wolfhilde Dorothea; Schleswig; Stibolt, Erasmine; Stibolt, Christiane; —; child died

Stief; Auguste Sophie; 9-Oct-39; 14-Feb-40; Karl M.; —; Rösch, Kathr.; —; —; —; —; —

Stief; Gottlob Michael; 12-Jan-37; 6-Aug-37; Karl; —; Rösch, Kathr. Regine; —; —; —; —; —

Stierhofen; Johanna Margaretha; 18-Oct-45; 23-Nov-45; Johann Georg; Hierfeld, Biber, Baiern; Bauer, Barbara; Neustadt a.d. Reuss, Baiern; Bauer, Susanne; —; —; wit is grandmother

Stierhoff; Anna Elisabeth; 13-Jan-48; 12-Mar-48; Johann Georg; Herfeld, Mittelfranken; Baier, Catharine Marg.; Oberhochstadt, Mittelfranken; Baier, Johann; —; —; —

Surname Father; Child's Given Name; Birth Date; Baptismal Date; Father's Given Name; Father's Place of Birth; Mother's Surname and Given Name; Mother's Place of Birth; Witness 1 Surname and Given Name; Witness 2 Surname and Given Name; Witness 3 Surname and Given Name; Comments

Stierhoff; Johann Friedrich; 10-Jul-50; 17-Aug-50; Johann; Suchenheim, Baiern; Baier, Catharina Margaretha; —; Baier, Joh. Friedrich; —; —; 3 child, 1 son

Stock; Andreas Friedrich; 29-Sep-52; 3-Oct-52; Michael Friedrich; Bebenau, Pommern; Muhlbrodt, Wilhelmine; —; Purner, Joh. Andreas; Keyl, Sophie Amalie; Waltjen, Friedrich; child died

Stock; Heinrietta Sophia; 13-May-54; 21-May-54; Michael Friedrich; Revenow, Pommern; Muhlbrodt, Wilhelmina; —; Beck, Anna Maria Magdalena; Winter, Andreas; Panetti, Eva Friedricke; —

Stockert; Philipp August Ambrosius; 29-Mar-46; 26-Apr-46; August Ambrosius; Bernbach, Sachsen Weimar; Eitel, Anna Maria; Lemberg bei Bermesins, Baiern; Eitel, Philipp; Eitel, Maria; —; wits are grandparents

Stolp; Johann Ludwig; 17-Feb-38; 4-Mar-38; Jacob Fr.; —; Scherer, Gottliebin; —; —; —; —; —

Stolz; Karoline Christine; 7-Mar-39; 24-Mar-39; Jacob; —; Scheurer, Gottliebin; —; —; —; —; —

Stolz; Luise Regine; 11-Feb-41; 14-Mar-41; Johann Jac.; —; Scheurer, Gottliebin; —; —; —; —; —

Stoni; Johann Peter; 15-Nov-52; 5-Dec-52; John; —; Sander, Anna Maria; —; Sander, Peter; —; —

Stout; Elisabeth; 26-Mar-38; 27-Mar-38; Samuel; —; Stahl, Elisab.; —; —; —; —

Stout; Katharina Anna; 31-May-39; 15-Jun-39; Samuel; —; Stahl, Elisab.; —; —; —; —

Stover; Anna Margarethe; 10-May-49; 22-Jul-49; Jakob; Milferdingen, Jurlach, Baden; Oelmann, Rebekka; Baltimore; —; —; —

Stover; Jacob; 23-Jun-37; 21-Aug-37; Jacob; —; Oelmann, Rebecca; —; —; —; —

Stover; Johann Wihl.; 10-Mar-40; 1-Nov-40; Jacob; —; Oelmann, Rebecca; —; —; —; —

Strafeiger; Sophie Wilhelmine; 15-Mar-46; 14-Jun-46; Christian; Auerbach, Hessen; Keil, Margaretha; Auerbach, Hessen; Keil, Friedrich; —; —

Surname Father; Child's Given Name; Birth Date; Baptismal Date; Father's Given Name; Father's Place of Birth; Mother's Surname and Given Name; Mother's Place of Birth; Witness 1 Surname and Given Name; Witness 2 Surname and Given Name; Witness 3 Surname and Given Name; Comments

Strafinger; Lisette; 21-Aug-48; 17-Nov-48; Christian; Auerbach, Zweigenberg, Hessen; Keil, Anna Margarethe; Auerbach, Zweigenberg, Hessen; Stiel, Christiane Margarethe; —; —

Strässinger; Johann Jac.; 13-Feb-44; 26-May-44; Christian; —; Keil, Anna M.; —; —; —; —

Straus; George Franklin; 4-Nov-47; 16-Jan-48; Johann; Holzhausen, Windsheim, Baiern; Weiss, Mary Ann; Martin's County, VA; Opitz, Georg; Losser [?], Franklin; —

Strekhart; Johann Henrich August; 8-Sep-49; 25-Nov-40; Carl; Landwehrhagen, Münden, Hannover; Drucke, Elise; Münden, Hannover; Fein, Heinrich; Drucke, Ernst August; —

Strobel; Anna Philippine Heinricke; 29-Sep-64; 16-Oct-64; Johann Georg; Rorchstenberg, Wurttemberg; Muller, Katharine Maria; Wachendorf, Hannover; Strobel, Nanette Frannette; Reitzel, Friederike Philippine Dorothea; Wachsmann, Heinrike

Strobel; Christian Heinrich; 13-Feb-55; 25-Feb-55; Johann Georg; Forchtenberg, Wurttemberg; Muller, Catharina Maria; —; Strobel, Georg Christian; Muller, Joh. Heinrich; —

Strobel; Dorothea Nannette; 1-Jan-54; 4-Jan-54; Joh. Georg; Forchtenberg, Wurttemberg; Muller, Catharina Maria; —; Strobel, Dorothea Nannette; —; —

Strobel; Eduard Jakob Christian; 22-Apr-61; 28-Apr-61; Johann Georg; Forchtenberg, Wurttemberg; Muller, Marie Katharine; —; Kampmann, Heinrike; Strobel, Georg Christian; Stein, Jakob

Strobel; Georg Heinrich Matthaus; 22-Apr-57; 3-May-57; Joh. Georg; Forchtenberg, Wurttemberg; Muller, Katharina Maria; —; Strobel, Georg Christian; Kampmann, Henrietta; Reitzel, Joseph Matthaus

Strobel; Gottlieb; 18-Apr-63; 19-Apr-63; Joh. Georg; Forchtenberg, Wurttemberg; Muller, Maria Katharina; —; —; —; —; emergency baptism

Strobel; Johann Georg; 28-Feb-52; 14-Mar-52; Joh. Georg; Falkenberg, Wurttemberg; Muller, Catharine Marie; —; Muller, Joh. Heinr.; —; —; —

Surname Father; Child's Given Name; Birth Date; Baptismal Date; Father's Given Name; Father's Place of Birth; Mother's Surname and Given Name; Mother's Place of Birth; Witness 1 Surname and Given Name; Witness 2 Surname and Given Name; Witness 3 Surname and Given Name; Comments

Strobel; Johann Heinrich; 22-Jan-50; 3-Feb-50; Johann Georg; Forchtenberg, Oehringen, Wurttemberg; Muller, Catharina Maria; Wachendorf, Sieke, Hannover; Muller, Johann Heinrich; Brendel, Johann Georg; —; —

Strobel; Katharine Christiane Sophie; 8-Nov-66; 2-Dec-66; Johann Georg; Forstenberg, Wuerttemberg; Muller, Katharine Marie; Osterholz, Hannover; Schlerf, Anna Katharine; Strobel, Johann Christian; Schulz, Sophie; —

Strobel; Margaretha Catharine; 2-Jan-48; 23-Jan-48; Johann Georg; Forchtenberg, Ehringen, Wurttemberg; Muller, Maria Catharina; Osterholz, Sieke, Hannover; Muller, Margarethe Adelheid; —; —; —

Strobel; Matthaus Christian Robert; 15-Nov-59; 27-Nov-59; Johann Georg; Forchtenberg, Wurttemberg; Muller, Katharine Maria; —; Reitzel, Matthaus; Strobel, Georg Christian; Kampmann, Heinrich; —

Stroh; Georg Reinhard; 21-Jan-59; 6-Feb-59; Konrad; Lorbach, Hessen; Schumacher, Kunigunde; —; Schumacher, Reinhard; —; —; —

Stroh; Maria Margaretha; 11-Feb-54; 5-Mar-54; Conrad; Lohrbach, Hessen; Schumacher, Kunigunde; —; Kerns, Maria Margaretha; —; —; —

Stroh; Philipp Heinrich; 20-Apr-48; 18-May-48; Wilhelm; Hainchen, Ortenberg, Hessen; Brotmann, Catharine; Mark Oebel, Kurhessen; Henigel, Maria Magdalena; —; —; —

Stroh; Sara Elisabeth; 11-Feb-56; 24-Feb-56; Konrad; Lorbach, Hessen; Schumacher, Kunigunde; —; Schumacher, Sara; —; —; —

Strohmann; Eduard Friedrich; 1-Oct-44; 17-Nov-44; Gerh. Fr.; —; Todt, Amalie; —; —; —; —; —

Strössinger; Sophie; 12-Jul-38; 2-Sep-38; Christian; —; Keil, Anna M.; —; —; —; —; —

Stroth; Georg Caspar; 4-Jan-48; 2-Nov-49; Caspar; Lautenbach, Hessen; Weiss, Catharine; Steinfurth, Siesheim, Baden; Kohnemann, Kunigunde; —; —; —

Surname Father; Child's Given Name; Birth Date; Baptismal Date; Father's Given Name; Father's Place of Birth; Mother's Surname and Given Name; Mother's Place of Birth; Witness 1 Surname and Given Name; Witness 2 Surname and Given Name; Witness 3 Surname and Given Name; Comments

Stührke; Johann Hermann; 17-Dec-43; 10-Mar-44; Johann G.; —; Puarts, Anna M.; —; —; —; —; —

Stumpf; Friedrich Wilhelm; 6-May-52; 11-May-52; Carl; Dresden, Sachsen; Hofer, Friederike; —; Lindemann, Christoph Wilhe.; —; —; born deformed

Stumpf; Heinrich Friedrich; 14-Aug-48; 20-Aug-48; Griedrich Traugott Carl; Dresden, Sachsen; Häfer, Johanne Friederike; Pahrnes bei Lommartsch, Sachsen; Stikeler, Johann Heinrich; Hornung, Dorothea; —; —

Stumpf; Johann Car; 11-Nov-49; 25-Nov-49; Friedrich Carl; Dresden; Hefer, Friederike; Barenz bei Lommatsch, Sachsen; Schlosser, Johann; Ziegler, Michael; —; —

Stumpf; Peade (!); 27-Mar-40; 14-May-40; Peter; —; Stumpf, Elisab.; —; —; —; —; —

Stussel; Johann Wilhelm; 5-Aug-67; 18-Aug-67; Friedrich; Obervorschutz, Kurhessen; Lenz, Katharine Margarethe; Baltimore; Lenz, Johann; Schaumelestel, Wilhelm; Buckmann, Susanna; —

Stutelberg; Johann Heinrich; 28-Jul-45; 7-Sep-45; Ehler; Osterholz, Sieke, Hannover; Meyer, Margarethe; Thedinghausen, Braunschweig; Reinke, Johann; Brunner, Casten Heinr.; —; —

Stutelberg; Margareth Elisabet; 25-Apr-49; 10-Jun-49; Ehlert; Osterholz, Sieke, Hannover; Meyer, Anna Margarethe; Ihedinghausen, Braunschweig; Wernden, Anna Marg.; Lindemann, Elisabeth; —; —

Stutt; Dorothea; 6-Oct-41; 6-Dec-41; Johann; —; Hundtmann, Maria; —; —; —; —; —

Stuttelberger; Friedrich Ernst; 3-Jul-54; 30-Jul-54; Heinrich; Osterhols, Hannover; Dresch, Dorothea; —; Stuttelberger, Elers; Hollebein, Friedrich; —; —

Sudmeier; Carolina Sophia Amalia; 30-Dec-53; 20-Aug-54; Wilhelm; Hartum, Preussen; Helbig, Sophie; —; Helbig, Emilie; Bertram, Sophie; —; —

Sumptner; Christian; 2-Sep-46; 8-Sep-46; Simon; OberAichenbach, Herzog Aurach, Baiern; Hubschmann, Ursula Barbara;

Middelndorf, Herzog Auerach, Baiern; Drummach, Christian; —; —; child died

Sus; Catharine Margarethe; 22-May-47; 30-May-47; Georg Michael; Kalberbach, Gerbronn, Wurttemberg; Bohm, Rosine Margarethe; Schrotsberg, Gerbronn, Wurttemberg; Ziegler, Marg. Cath.; Sus, Cath.; —; —

Sus; Johann Georg; 2-Mar-46; 13-Mar-46; Georg Michael; Kalberbach, Gerabronn; Böhm, Rosine; Schrotsberg, Gerabronn, Wurttemberg; Sus, Johann Georg; —; —; child died

Süss; Augusta Lina; 8-Feb-50; 20-May-50; Friedrich Karl; Langendensbach, Weimar; Jung, Maria; Rosslin, Preussen; Korber, Lina; —; —; wit from Etzleben, Preussen

Suthmeyer; Heinrich Ludwig; 19-Oct-49; 25-Dec-49; Wilhelm; Harting bei Preussitch Minden; Hellwig, Sophie; Lubbeke, Preussen; Hellwig, Ludwig; —; —; —

Suthoff; Maria Kathr.; 9-Oct-39; 20-Oct-39; Friedr.; —; Buscher, Anna K.; —; —; —; —; —

Tarer; Maria Sophia; 19-Nov-44; 14-Jan-45; Jacob; —; Oehlmann, Rebekka; —; Beitz, Elisabetha; —; —; —

Taubert; Heinrich Adam; 11-Nov-64; 4-Dec-64; Gottlieb; Niederniehrohop, Sch. Altenburg; Atzroth, Marie; —; Fuchs, Heinrich; Ruppel, Adam; —; —

Taubert; Wilhelm Heinrich; 27-Mar-67; 21-Apr-67; Gottlieb; Niederwiera, Sachsen Altenberg; Atzrott, Wilhelmine Fredricke Christiana; —; Siemers, Wilhelm; Fuchs, Heinrich; —; —

Tegeler; Heinrich Christian; 19-May-54; 28-May-54; Christian; Sudbruck, Hannover; Langlett, Julianne; —; Kattenkamp, Dietrich; Meier, Heinr. Gustav; —; —

Tegeler; Margaretha Louise; 9-Sep-56; 19-Oct-56; Christian; Sudbruch, Hannover; Langelett, Julianne; —; Bachmann, Margar.; Sieck, Florentina Louise; —; —

Teichmann; August; 26-Jan-39; 19-Feb-39; Johann H.; —; Sippel, Sophie; —; —; —; —; —

Surname Father; Child's Given Name; Birth Date; Baptismal Date; Father's Given Name; Father's Place of Birth; Mother's Surname and Given Name; Mother's Place of Birth; Witness 1 Surname and Given Name; Witness 2 Surname and Given Name; Witness 3 Surname and Given Name; Comments

Teudel; Karl; 15-Sep-41; 3-Oct-41; Johann; —; Ruff, Maria; —; —; —; —; —

Thene; Johann Adam; 13-Feb-40; 3-Dec-40; Adam; —; Buschatt, Maria; —; —; —; —; illegitimate

Thesing; Johann Heinrich; 30-Sep-48; 8-Oct-48; Johann Herman Dietrich; Osnabruck, Hannover; Ruckweg, Christine; Catenhusen, Oberbruck, Hannover; Imwolde, Johann; Weismann, Marie Adelheid; —; —

Thiemeier; Hermann Friedrich; 17-May-67; 2-Jun-67; Friedrich Louis; Baltimore; Ober, Maria Elisabeth; Baltimore; Thiemeier, Hermann Friedrich; Ober, Sophie; —; —

Thiemeyer; Anna Amalie; 21-Feb-54; 5-Mar-54; Hermann; Freidrich; Engter, Osnabruck, Im Sonde; —; Horstmann, Anna Maria Amalie; —; —; —

Thiemeyer; Anna Maria; —; 15-Apr-37; August Herrm.; —; Neumann, Kathr.; —; —; —; —; birth is blank

Thiemeyer; Anna Maria Carolina; 31-Jan-45; 16-Mar-45; Herrmann Friederich; Enchte bei Osnabruck,Hannover; Imsande, Marg. Charl.; Enchte bei Osnabruck Hannover; Vor der Wüsten, Anna Maria Caroline; —; —; —

Thiemeyer; Anna Marianne Julianne; 25-Jul-56; 2-Aug-56; Joh. Heinr.; Engter, Hannover; Vorderingsten, Anna Maria; —; Thiemeyer, Louis; Thiemeyer, Marie Elise; Thiemeyer, Anna Maria Julianna; child died

Thiemeyer; Caroline Juliane; 22-Mar-51; 4-May-51; Heinr. Frdch; Engter, Hannover; Insande, Margaretha Charlotte; —; Theimeyer, Julinne Marie Caroline Vorderwosten; —; —; —

Thiemeyer; Charlotte Sophia; 8-Feb-49; 4-Mar-49; Herrmann Friedrich; Engter bei Osnabruck, Hannover; Imsande, Margareth Charlotte; Engter bei Osnabruck, Hannover; Brumeys, Marie Henrietta; Holthus, Friedrich; Borchelt, Anna Maria; —

Thiemeyer; Elisabeth; 24-Apr-48; 14-May-48; Johann Heinrich; Engter, Vorden, Hannover; Vorder Wosten, Maria Caroline; Engter, Vorden, Hannover; Brunnings, Henriette; —; —; —

Surname Father; Child's Given Name; Birth Date; Baptismal Date; Father's Given Name; Father's Place of Birth; Mother's Surname and Given Name; Mother's Place of Birth; Witness 1 Surname and Given Name; Witness 2 Surname and Given Name; Witness 3 Surname and Given Name; Comments

Thiemeyer; Emilie; 26-Sep-49; 11-Nov-49; Johann Henrich; Engter, Vorden, Hannover; vor der Worsten, Anna Maria Caroline; Engter, Vorden, Hannover; Thiemeyer, Charlotte; —; —; —

Thiemeyer; Emma; 26-Jan-51; 9-Feb-51; Joh. Heinrich; Engter, Hannover; Vonderwusten, Anna Marie Caroline; —; Vonderwusten, Catharine Margarethe; —; —; —

Thiemeyer; Friedrich Wilhelm; 24-Jul-54; 31-Jul-54; Johann; Engter, Hannover; Vorderwosten, Maria Caroline; —; Vorderwosten, Heinrich; —; —; —

Thiemeyer; Heinrich; 27-Jan-56; 27-Jan-56; Friedrich; Engter, Hannover; [--?--], Margaretha Charlotte; —; parents, ; —; —; child died

Thiemeyer; Heinrich Ernst Ludwig; 15-Jul-58; 25-Jul-58; Johann Heinrich; Engter, Hannover; Vordewuster, Anna Maria Karoline; —; Habermehl, Heinr.; Vorderwuster, Margaretha; Waltjen, Heinrich; —

Thiemeyer; Henriette Charlotte; 29-May-43; 23-Aug-43; Hermann Friedr.; —; Sande, Marg. Ch.; —; —; —; —; —

Thiemeyer; Hermann Friedrich Stephanus; 27-Aug-60; 2-Sep-60; Johann Heinrich; Engter, Hannover; Vonderwusten, Anna Marie Karoline; —; Thiemeyer, Frdch.Louis; Klinkmeier, Heinrich Wilhelm; Molkenstroth, Charlotte; —

Thiemeyer; Johann Christian Friedr. Wilh.; 18-Jun-41; 8-Aug-41; Herm. Fr.; —; Imsande, Marg.; —; —; —; —; —

Thiemeyer; Johann Friedrich; 15-Apr-46; 14-Jun-46; Herrmann Friedrich; Engter, Vorden, Hannover; Imsande, Charlotte; Engter, Vorden, Hannover; Thiemeyer, Johann Heinrich; —; —; wit is uncle

Thiemeyer; Johann Heinrich; 19-Sep-46; 22-Nov-46; Johann Heinrich; Engter, Vorden, Hannover; Vorder Wusten, Anna Maria Caroline; Engter, Vorden, Hannover; Thiemeyer, Herrmann Friedrich; —; —; —

Thiemeyer; Josephine; 16-Oct-52; 31-Oct-52; Joh. Heinrich; Engter, Hannover; Vonderwusten, Anna Maria; —; Thiemeyer, Anna Maria; —; —; —

Surname Father; Child's Given Name; Birth Date; Baptismal Date; Father's Given Name; Father's Place of Birth; Mother's Surname and Given Name; Mother's Place of Birth; Witness 1 Surname and Given Name; Witness 2 Surname and Given Name; Witness 3 Surname and Given Name; Comments

Thiemeyer; Maria Elisab.; 9-Oct-39; 15-Dec-39; Hermann Fr.; —; Imsande, Marg. Ch.; —; —; —; —; —

Thierrauch; Albrecht Columbus; 14-Jun-40; 26-Jul-40; Georg M.; —; Cuddy, Rachel; —; —; —; —; —

Thomas; Georg Friedrich; 18-Sep-44; 19-Dec-44; Heinrich; —; Barth, Helene; —; —; —; —; —

Thomas; Johann Andreas; 15-Aug-50; 9-Sep-50; Joh. Andreas; Niedersrodta, Wurttemberg; Weissmann, Rosina; —; Schmidt, Hartmann; —; —; 3 child, 1 son

Thomas; Luise; 17-Apr-46; 23-Apr-46; Abraham; Berungen, Sachsen Meiningen; Herbert, Luise; Berungen, Sachsen Meiningen; Thomas, Elisabeth; —; —; —

Timmermann; Emma Margaretha; 22-May-55; 3-Jun-55; Heinrich Ludwig; Heede, Hannover; Danettel, Margaretha Dorothea; —; Weber, Henriette; Bruning, Margaretha; —; —

Timmermann; Georg Heinrich; 4-Sep-50; 19-Sep-50; Heinrich Ludwig; Amt Diepolts, Hannover; Dannettel, Margarethe Dorothea; —; Dannettel, Heinr. Ludwig; Dannettel, Wilhelmine Margaretha; —; 2 child, 2 son

Timmermann; Heinrich Ludwig; 18-Dec-48; 1-Jan-49; Heinrich Ludwig; Hede bei Diepholz; Dannettel, Dorothea Margarethe; Deka bei Diepholz, Hannover; Bruning, Heinrich Hermann; Bruning, Marg. Sophia; Bruning; —

Timmermann; Sophia Henrietta; 20-Mar-57; 12-Apr-57; Heinr. Ludwig; Gerde, Hannover; Donattel, Dorothea; —; Weber, Margaretha Henrietta; —; —; —

Timmermann; Wilhelm Eberhard; 6-Sep-52; 19-Sep-52; Heinrich Ludwig; Hede, Hannover; Danettel, Margaretha Dorothea; —; Weber, Heinrich Eberhard; —; —; —

Tippel; Johann Wilh.; 9-Oct-41; 31-Oct-41; Johann; —; Naumann, Elisab.; —; —; —; —; —

Toefler [?]; Christine; 16-Sep-45; 27-Sep-45; Carl; —; , ; —; —; —; —; —

Tönges; Anna Margarethe; 8-Nov-41; 26-Dec-41; Conrad; —; Emrich, Kathr.; —; —; —; —; —

Surname Father; Child's Given Name; Birth Date; Baptismal Date; Father's Given Name; Father's Place of Birth; Mother's Surname and Given Name; Mother's Place of Birth; Witness 1 Surname and Given Name; Witness 2 Surname and Given Name; Witness 3 Surname and Given Name; Comments

Tormelen; Eberhard; 19-Nov-58; 19-Nov-58; Wilhelm; Osnabruck, Hannover; Regenwegs, Christine; —; Muhly, Eberhard; —; —; emergency baptism

Tormelen; Elisabeth; 25-Jun-54; 2-Jul-54; Franz Carl; Osnabruck; Aubke, Maria Elise; —; Ruppel, Elisabeth; —; —; —

Tormelen; Franz Karl; 28-Mar-51; 6-Apr-51; Frdch. Wilh.; Osnabruck, Hannover; Reckenwegs, Christine; —; Tormelen, Franz Karl; —; —; —

Tormelen; Georg Karl Christian; 21-May-65; 28-May-65; Friedrich Wilhelm; Atter, Hannover; Reggeweg, Karoline Marie Christine; Goldenhausen, Preussen; Gahm, Georg Karl; Strobel, Christian; —; —

Tormelen; Heinrich Gottfried Wilhelm; 31-May-61; 16-Jun-61; Franz; Osnabruck, Hannover; Jaubke, Marie Elis.; —; Habermehl, Heinr.; Schimpf, Gottfried; Tormelen, Wilh.; —

Tormelen; Johann Heinrich; 4-Jan-58; —; Franz Karl; Hebommeatter [?], Hannover; Aupke, Marie Elise; —; Stuttelberger, Maria; —; —; emergency baptism

Tormelen; Johann Jakob Christian; 2-Jan-59; 16-Jan-59; Franz; Atter, Hannover; Jabke, Elise; —; Ruppel, Johann; Panetti, Jakob; Strobel, Christian; —

Tormelen; Louise Charlotte; 23-Jun-56; 29-Jun-56; Wilhelm; Osnabruck; Regeweg, Christine; —; Thiemeyer, Marg. Charlotte; Muhly, Louise; Thiemeyer, Joh. Heinr.; —

Tormelen; Margaretha Charlotte; 14-Oct-56; 2-Nov-56; Franz; Osnabruck; Aubke, Marie Elise; —; Thiemeyer, Margaretha Charlotte; —; —; child died

Tormelen; Maria Elise; 1-Oct-53; 9-Oct-53; Wilhelm; Osnabruck, Hannover; Reckenwegs, Christine Elisabeth; —; Tormelen, Christine Elise; Tormelen, Franz; —

Tormelen; Wilhelm Niklaus; 12-Nov-63; 29-Nov-63; Franz Karl; Osnabruck, Hannover; Aubke, Mariai Elise; Sleehausen, Hannover; Bertram, Wilhelm; Ruppel, Niklaus; Ruppel, Elisabeth

Tormohlen; Friedrich Wilhelm; 12-Nov-48; 26-Nov-48; Friedrich Wilhelm; Osnabruck, Hannover; Seidweg, Maria Christine;

Katenhofen bei Osnabruck, Hannover; Breis, Martin Heinrich; Schulte, Friedrich Wilhelm; —

Tosing; Maria Elisa Charlotte; 10-Feb-53; 20-Feb-53; Johann; Quackenbruck, Hannover; Beissmann, Maria; —; Thiemeyer, Charlotte; Thiemeyer, Frd.; Borgelt, Mrs.

Trabank; Anna Maria; 26-Dec-42; 18-Feb-43; Georg; —; Urbach, Elisab.; —; —; —; —

Trager; Johann Heinrich; 23-Jun-61; 30-Jun-61; Heinrich; Gottingen; Bauer, Margarethe Christine; —; Bauer, Georg; Hampe, Franz; Mohring, Joh.

Trager; Maria Elisabeth; 19-Jan-64; 31-Jan-64; Heinrich; Gottingen; Bauer, Christiane; Baltimore; Hampe, Wilhelmine; Trager, Henriette Wilhelmine; Bauer, Elisabeth

Traub; Johann; 11-Sep-40; 20-Sep-40; Johann G.; —; Weller, Ann M.; —; —; —; —

Traub; Sophie; 23-Mar-38; 1-Apr-38; Johann G.; —; Wild, Marg.; —; —; —; —

Trautfeder; Dorothea Elisab.; 24-Feb-39; 10-Mar-39; Johann; —; Weber, Eva; —; —; —; —

Trautvetter; Heinrich Wilh.; 16-Feb-41; 14-Mar-41; Johann; —; Weber, Eva; —; —; —; —

Trebel; Anna Kathr.; 1-Nov-37; 3-Dec-37; Georg H.; —; Liebendahl, Anna; —; —; —; —

Treide; Claus Philipp; 6-Dec-65; 7-Dec-65; Gottlieb heinrich; Karlshafen, Kurhessen; Bagel, Dorothea Louise; Felknerhagen, Kurhessen; Sturken, Rev. Claus; Reisinger, Philipp; —

Treide; Gottfried Andreas Johannes; 11-Aug-54; 20-Aug-54; Joh. Heinr. Gottlieb; Carlshafen, Kurhessen; Bagel, Louise; —; Wiedemann, Gottfried; Germuth, Andreas; Thiemeyer, Joh. Heinr.

Treide; Heinrich Karl Georg; 25-Oct-59; 6-Nov-59; Johann Heinrich; Karlhafen, Kurhessen; Pagel, Louise; —; Habermehl, School teacher; Mieth, Karoline; Frank, Georg

Treide; Immanuel Georg Heinrich; 23-Jan-57; 1-Feb-57; Joh. Heinr. Gottlieb; Karlshafen, Kurhessen; Pagel, Louise; —; Flemming, Immanuel; Sieck, Florentina Maria; Frank Georg

Surname Father; Child's Given Name; Birth Date; Baptismal Date; Father's Given Name; Father's Place of Birth; Mother's Surname and Given Name; Mother's Place of Birth; Witness 1 Surname and Given Name; Witness 2 Surname and Given Name; Witness 3 Surname and Given Name; Comments

Treide; Karoline Louise; 1-Jan-63; 19-Jan-63; Heinrich Gottlieb; Karlhofen, Kurhessen; Bagel, Louise; Fockerhagen, Kurhessen; Mieth, Johann; Mieth, Karoline; —; —

Treide; Sophie Wilhelmine Louise; 1-Jul-51; 13-Jul-51; Joh. Heinr. Gottlieb; Carlshofen, Kurhessen; Begel, Louise; —; Corff, Sophie Wilh. Louise; —; —; —

Treude; Daniel Wilhelm; 27-Jun-47; 18-Jul-47; Johann Heinrich Gottlieb; Karlshafen, Kurhessen; Pagel, Luise; Eckershagen, Kurhessen; Fricke, Andreas Daniel; —; —; —

Treutling; Margaretha Elisabet; 21-Aug-48; 3-Sep-48; Joseph; Trappstadt, Baiern; Ziegler, Anna; Heroldsberg, Baiern; Korner, Margerthe Elisabeth; —; —; —

Triebert; Juliane; 6-Jul-47; 6-Jul-47; Heinrich; Grosseneichen, Hessen; Steube, Martha; Homberg, Kurhessen; —; —; —; child died

Troll; Maria Wilhelmine; 25-Jul-48; 24-Sep-48; Friedrich; Snellinghausen, Waldeck; Melchior, Regina; Solingen, Elbersfeld, Preussen; Melchior, Anna Maria Catharina; —; —; child died

Ubert; Johann Philip; 23-Dec-38; 7-Jan-39; Johann; —; Schneider, Marg.; —; —; —; —; —

Uhl; Heinrich; 6-Apr-38; 29-Apr-38; Heinrich; —; Weihert, Maria; —; —; —; —; —

Ulrich; Anna Elisabeth; 2-Feb-48; 24-May-48; Georg; —; Wuber, Elisabeth; Spetzweikel, Kirchheim, Kurhessen; Debus, Elisabeth; —; —; illegitimate

Ulrich; Heinrich; 25-Jan-41; 21-Jan-42; Wilhelm; —; Schmelz, Christine; —; —; —; —; —

Ulrich; Maria; 6-Sep-44; 19-Oct-44; Wilhelm; —; Schmalz, Christine; —; —; —; —; —

Unverzagt; Christina; 12-Aug-39; 22-Sep-39; Christian; —; Tiemann, Kathr.; —; —; —; —; —

Valentin; Wilhelm; 8-Jul-32; 27-May-46; Heinrich; York County, PA; Rupp, Elisabeth; Allen County, PA; —; —; —; —

Vehn; Johanna Margaretha; 9-Aug-46; 6-Sep-46; Johann Stephan; Simmershofen, Affenheim, Baiern; Oehlschlagel, Caroline;

Steben bei Hoff, Baiern; Oehlenschlagel, Johanna Marg.; —; —; wit is aunt

Vehn [Behn]; Rosine Barbara; 19-Dec-47; 27-Feb-48; Stephan; Simmershofen, Uffenheim, Baiern; Ohlenschlagel, Caroline; Staben, Neulau, Baiern; Glaser, Rosine; —; —; —

Vetter; Anna Maria Marg.; 3-Apr-44; 28-Apr-44; Gottlieb; —; Oestricher, Anna K.; —; —; —; —; —

Vetter; Christian Heinrich; 26-Jul-46; 23-Aug-46; Johann Gottlieb; Ottmarshain, Marbach, Wurttemberg; Oestericher, Anna Catharina; Dolgesheim, Oppenheim, Hessen; Götz, Christian; —; —

Viertel; Johann; 21-Dec-45; 4-Jan-46; Johann Fr.; Eirnsbach, Herzogenau, Baiern; Vogel, Elisabeth; Sauerheim, Baiern; Viertel, Joh.; —; —

Viertel; Johann; 15-Oct-48; 18-Oct-48; Johann Friedrich; Eilersbach, Herzogaurach, Baiern; Vogel, Anna Elisabeth; Sauersheim, Herzogaurach, Baiern; Viertel, Johann; —; —

Vogel; Carl Anton; 11-Apr-52; 14-Apr-52; Ludwig; Allendorf a.d. Lumda, Hessen; Martin, Johanne; —; Wagner, Anton; —; —

Vogel; Christine Emilie Albine; 4-Nov-63; 15-Nov-63; Emil; Ezbau, Sachsen; Bruggemann, Christine Elise Wilhelmine; Baltimore; Vogel, Juliane Emilie; Rudolph, Ernst; Bruggemann, Christine Charlotte

Vogel; Christoph Ludwig Friedrich; 6-Jun-56; 29-Jun-56; Heinr. Ludwig; Allendorf a.d.L., Hessen; Martin, Johanne; —; Reinhard, Christoph; —; —

Vogel; Conrad Reinhard; 20-Dec-53; 1-Jan-54; Ludwig; Allendor a.d. Lumda, Hessen; Martin, Johanna; —; Reinhard, Conrad; —; —

Vogel; Emma Mathilde Selma; 15-Nov-65; 21-Nov-65; Wilhelm Emil; Eibau, Sachsen; Bruggemann, Wilhelmine; Lubbecke, Preussen; Ruppel, Kaspar Karl; Vogel, Emilie Selma; —

Vogelmann; Carl Ludwig; 15-Oct-52; 31-Oct-52; Carl Wilhelm; Donnhof, Wurttemberg; Leipoldt, Margarethe; —; Altvater, Catharine; —; —

Surname Father; Child's Given Name; Birth Date; Baptismal Date; Father's Given Name; Father's Place of Birth; Mother's Surname and Given Name; Mother's Place of Birth; Witness 1 Surname and Given Name; Witness 2 Surname and Given Name; Witness 3 Surname and Given Name; Comments

Vogelmann; Catharine Elisabeth Susanna; 10-Mar-55; 25-Mar-55; Carl Wilhelm; Denhof, Wurttemberg; Leippold, Margaretha; —; Erwold, Catharine; —; —

Vogelmann; Georg Heinrich Wilhelm; 11-Apr-58; 2-May-58; Wilhelm; Ammerteweiler, Wurttemberg; Leipold, Margaretha; —; Ermold, Georg; Sander, Heinr.; —

Vogelmann; Karl Heinrich; 2-Dec-56; 14-Dec-56; Karl Wilhelm; Ammertweiler, Wurttemberg; Leipold, Margarehta; —; Schnepter, Heinr.; —; —

Vogelmann; Katharine Margarethe; 13-Jan-60; 29-Jan-60; Karl Wilhelm; Meinhard, Wurttemberg; Leipold, Margaretha; —; Ermold, Katharine; —; —

Vogelmann; Louis Christian Albert; 28-Mar-62; 6-Apr-62; Karl Wilhelm; Trunhof, Wurttemberg; Leipold, Margarethe; —; Winter, Christian; Winter, Christine; Muhly, Louise

Vogelmann; Rothwunde, Baiern; 19-Apr-65; 25-Apr-65; Karl Wilhelm; Amertzweiler, Wurttemberg; , Leipold; Margaretha; Hast, Barbara; Putschke, Margaretha; —

Vogelsang; Georg Philip; 14-Sep-42; 9-Oct-42; Eduard; —; Strube, Johanne; —; —; —; —

Vogelsang; Karl Friedr.; 12-Mar-37; 11-Jul-40; Eduard; —; Strube, Johanne; —; —; —; —; —

Vogelsang; Regina Johanna; 25-Dec-39; 11-Jul-40; Eduard; —; Strube, Johanne; —; —; —; —; —

Volkers; Marianne; 24-Nov-41; 24-Dec-41; Friedr.; —; Harpers, Maria; —; —; —; —; —

Vollbrecht; Johann Georg; 4-Mar-39; 24-Mar-39; Georg; —; Kardel, Maria; —; —; —; —; —

Vollmer; Andreas Karl; 14-Nov-43; 3-Dec-43; Friedrich; —; Halbes, Maria; —; —; —; —; —

Vollmers; Johann Friedrich; 12-Sep-40; 23-Sep-40; Friedrich; —; Herbers, Anna M.; —; —; —; —; —

von der Holden; Georg Friedrich; 9-Feb-50; 14-Apr-50; Peter; Ottendorf, Hannover; Bott, Mathilde; Osnabruck, Hannover; Brandtau, Friedrich; —; —; —

Surname Father; Child's Given Name; Birth Date; Baptismal Date; Father's Given Name; Father's Place of Birth; Mother's Surname and Given Name; Mother's Place of Birth; Witness 1 Surname and Given Name; Witness 2 Surname and Given Name; Witness 3 Surname and Given Name; Comments

von Holden; Johann Heinrich; 3-Oct-45; 16-Nov-45; Johann Peter; Stenau; Buts, Catharine; Schledehausen, Osnabruck, Hannover; —; —; —; —

von Holten; Wihelm Randolph; 25-Feb-48; 16-Apr-48; Johann Peter; Stenau; Buts, Catharine; Schledehausen, Osnabruck, Hannover; Burgheimer, Peter; Buts, Maria; —; child died

von Thurn; Christina; 11-Apr-50; 9-Jun-50; Wolfgang; Langenstadt, Bayreuth; Opsenbrenner, Margaretha; Schwadenfels, Kurhessen; Frisch, Christine; —; —; wit from Hutschdorf, Bayreuth

Vonderwesten; Anna Dorothea Elisabeth; 27-Jan-65; 5-Feb-65; Johann Heinrich; Engter, Hannover; Dunker, Meta Margarethe; Mattfeld, Hannover; Dunker, Kasten; Sieck, Elisabeth; Thiemeyer, Elisabeth; —

Vonhof; Katharine; 30-Oct-42; 9-Dec-42; Philip; —; Seib, Elisab.; —; —; —; —; —

Vorderwosten; Christian Johann; 2-Sep-62; 3-Sep-62; Heinrich; Engter, Hannover; Dunker, Meta Margarethe; —; Meier, Christian; Dunker, Karoline; —; —

Vorderwosten; Johann Hermann Heinrich; 7-Feb-60; 12-Feb-60; Johann Heinrich; Engter, Hannover; Dunker, Martha Margaretha; —; Thiemeyer, Johann; Meier, Adelheid; Kastens, Heinrich; —

Vorderwusten; Johann Kasten Heinrich; 24-Oct-57; 1-Nov-57; Heinrich; Engter, Hannover; Dunker, Margaretha; —; Dunker, Kasten Hermn.; Waltjen, Heinr.; Thiemeyer, Anna Maria; —

Wachsmann; Anna Katharina Elisabeth; 20-Dec-65; 7-Jan-66; Johann Gottlieb; Nimmgsth., Preussen; Kampmann, Henrike; Rechenberg, Wurttemberg; Reitzel, Josph Matthaus; Weber, Elisabeth Katharina; Strobel, Katharine Maria; —

Wachsmann; Friedrich Wilhelm; 17-Feb-67; 3-Mar-67; Johann Gottlieb; Raschkareitz, Schlesien; Kampmann, Heinrike; Rachenberg, Wurttemberg; Strobel, Johann Georg; Reitzel, Friedrike; Kuhner, Gottlieb; —

Wachsmann; Katharine Henriette Friederike; 22-Mar-63; 5-Apr-63; Johann Gottlieb; Roschkowitz, Schlesien; Kampmann,

Friederike; —; Schimpf, Auguste Friederike; Strobel, Joh. Georg; Weber, Katharine Elisabeth; —

Wack; Friedrich; 2-Sep-45; 28-Sep-45; Heinrich Christian; —; , ; —; Zelft, Carl; —; —; —

Wacker; Katharine; 29-Oct-42; 1-Nov-42; Ernst; —; Marquardt, Kathr. M.; —; —; —; —; —

Wacker; Maria Wilhelmina Karolina; 17-Nov-1867; 24-Nov-1867; Heinrich; Liebenau, Hannover; Nulle, Charlotte; Holzhausen, Hannover; Klinkmeier, Wilhelm; Labahn, Karoline; Kronnenberg, Maria; —

Wadermann; Johann Georg Conrad; 5-Aug-50; 15-Sep-50; Heinrich Aug.; Ostendorf, Hessen Schaumberg; [--?--], Susanne Veronike; —; Stengel, Georg Conrad; —; —; —

Wagner; Christoph Melchior Karl; 9-Mar-60; 29-Mar-60; Karl; Hoschbach, Rheinbaiern; Keil, Christine; —; Leutner, Christoph; Schlerf, Melchior; Seibel, Susanna; in house

Wagner; Emilie Wilhelmine Elisabeth; 03-Oct-1856; 29-Jan-60; Karl; Hoschbach, Rheinbaiern; Keil, Christine; —; Reinhard, Wilhelmine; Schlerf, Emilie; —; father in Philadelphia

Wagner; Eva; 2-Oct-44; 13-Oct-44; Johann; —; Betz, Marg.; —; —; —; —; —

Wagner; Ludwig; 16-Sep-39; 29-Sep-39; Georg; —; Giessler, Kathr.; —; —; —; —; —

Wagner; Magdalena; 27-Oct-50; 10-Nov-50; Philipp; Lemberg, Baiern; Schufft, Susanne; —; Feldner, Adam; Klein, Magdalena; —; 1 child

Wagner; Maria; 11-Feb-40; 8-May-40; Philip; —; Lind, Elisab.; —; —; —; —; —

Wagner; Maria; —; 22-Mar-48; Johann; Nagel, Kranach, Baiern; Butz, Margaretha; Schmelz, Kranach, Baiern; Schmidt, Maria; —; —; —

Wagner; Maria Caroline Sophie; 15-Nov-52; 5-Dec-52; Joh. Heinrich; Wolfshagen, Kurhessen; Kuhneweg, Christine; —; Heck, Sophie; Heck, Friedrich; —; —

Wagner; Philipp Jakob; 16-Feb-53; 6-Apr-53; Franz; Dolen, Rudolstadt; Riedel, Friederika; —; Panetti, Philipp Adam Jakob; —; —; —

Wahl; Eleonora Charlotte; 21-Apr-38; 16-Jul-39; John; —; [--?--], Anna; —; —; —; —; —

Wahl; Friedrich; 28-Jan-43; 30-Mar-43; Heinrich; —; Leck, Maria; —; —; —; —; —

Wahl; Heinrich; 26-Jan-40; 22-Mar-40; Heinrich; —; Leik, Maria; —; —; —; —; —

Wahl; Maria; 11-Oct-38; 4-Nov-38; Heinrich; —; Leik, Maria; —; —; —; —; —

Waldschmidt; Elisabeth; 26-Dec-46; 14-Feb-47; Ludwig; Fellingshausen, Giessen, Hessen; Nern, Anna Maria; Waldgerens, Giessen, Hessen; Bremer, Georg Johann; Fuld, Elisabeth; —; —

Waldschmidt; Heinrich Ludwig; 12-May-52; 23-May-52; Ludwig; Fellingshausen, Hessen; Nern, Anna Maria; —; Dietz, Heinrich Ludwig; Bruhl, Elisabeth; —; —

Waldschmidt; Jakob; 28-Jul-49; 22-Jul-49; Ludwig; Jelingshausen, Giessen, Hessen; Nern, Maria; Waldgernes, Giessen, Hessen; Waldschmidt, Jakob; —; —; —

Waldschmidt; Ludwig; 19-Dec-38; 6-Jan-39; Ludwig; —; Nern, Maria; —; —; —; —; —

Waldschmidt; Ludwig Wilh.; 18-Jun-37; 27-Aug-37; Jacob; —; Reider, Christine; —; —; —; —; —

Waldschmidt; Margaretha; 6-Nov-41; 25-Dec-41; Ludw.; —; Nern, Maria; —; —; —; —; —

Walkemeier; Hermann Ludwig; 6-Apr-51; 20-Apr-51; Friedr.; Barkhausen, Hannover; Schurmann, Klara Elisabeth; —; Dippner, Heinr. Ludwig; —; —; —

Walkenmeyer; Maria Elisabeth; 5-Jun-49; 17-Jun-49; Friedrich; Trokhausen, Witlage; Schurmann, Elisabeth; Buhr, Hannover; Brunsmann, Maria Elise; —; —; —

Walker; Elisabeth Luise; 3-Oct-45; 16-Nov-45; Ernst; Itersbach bei Carlsruh, Baden; Marquard, Catharine; Leopoldshafen, Baden; —; —; —; —

Surname Father; Child's Given Name; Birth Date; Baptismal Date; Father's Given Name; Father's Place of Birth; Mother's Surname and Given Name; Mother's Place of Birth; Witness 1 Surname and Given Name; Witness 2 Surname and Given Name; Witness 3 Surname and Given Name; Comments

Walther; Adam; 10-Apr-53; 1-May-53; Aug.; Grunensen, Hannover; Borner, Rosine; —; Bach, Adam; —; —; —

Walther; Anna Charlotte; 7-Jan-47; 26-Mar-47; Ludwig; Grimsen, Erkersburg, Hannover; Muller, Maria; Dietelsheim, Biedeigen, Hessen; Walther, Sophia Charlotte; —; —; wit is grandmother

Walther; Anna Margarethe; 29-Jun-47; 25-Jul-47; August; Grimsen, Hundsruck, Hannover; Berner, Rosine; Gelbsreuth, Landau, Baiern; Muller, Marg.; —; —; —

Walther; Katharine Friedrike; 12-Apr-43; 4-Jun-43; August; —; Werner, Friedrike R.; —; —; —; —; —

Walther; Wilhelmiine; 20-Feb-45; 26-Mar-45; Louis; Krimensen bei Eimbede, Hannover; Muller, Maria; Hessen; Muller, Wilhelmine; —; —; —

Waltjen; Amalie Dorothea; 7-Nov-52; 14-Nov-52; Georg Heinrich Friedrich; Bossum, Hannover; Mohn, Elise Catharine; —; Keyl, Sophia Amalie; Waltjen, Elisabeth; —; —

Waltjen; Anna Elisabeth Eulalia; 11-May-60; 20-May-60; Heinrich; Bossum, Hannover; Horn, Maria Magdalena; —; Horn, Marie Philippine Eulalia; Horn, Anna Elisabeth; —; —

Waltjen; Anna Johanna; 19-Oct-51; 9-Nov-51; Friedrich; Bossum, Hannover; Kirchhof, Maria; —; Waltjen, Joh.; Kirchhof, Widow; —; —

Waltjen; Anna Katharina Henrietta; 13-Jan-58; 24-Jan-58; Andreas; Bossum, Hannover; Hildebrand, Christiane; —; Briel, Katharina; Kruger, Katharine; Waltjen, Joh. Frdch.; —

Waltjen; Anna Maria; 2-Jul-40; 28-Sep-40; Friedrich; —; Kirchhof, Anna M.; —; —; —; —; —

Waltjen; Anna Maria; 30-May-54; 2-Jul-54; Aug. Friedr.; Bossum, Hannover; Luninde, Martha; —; Waltjen, Anna Maria; —; —; —

Waltjen; Auguste Elisabeth Johanne; 29-Oct-60; 4-Nov-60; Georg Heinrich Friedrich; Bossum, Hannover; Muhn, Elisabeth Katharine; —; Einwachter, Elisabeth Katharine; Schimpf, Auguste; Vordewosten, Joh. Heinr.; —

Surname Father; Child's Given Name; Birth Date; Baptismal Date; Father's Given Name; Father's Place of Birth; Mother's Surname and Given Name; Mother's Place of Birth; Witness 1 Surname and Given Name; Witness 2 Surname and Given Name; Witness 3 Surname and Given Name; Comments

Waltjen; Caroline Dorothea; 31-Mar-48; 9-Apr-48; Heinrich; Bossum, Hannover; Stoll, Maria; Statten, Canstadt, Wurttemberg; Waltjen, Dorothea; —; —; wit is grandmother

Waltjen; Catharina Elisa; 1-Oct-50; 6-Oct-50; Heinrich; Amt Bossum, Hannover; Stoll, Friederike; —; Waltjen, Elisa Catharina; Waltjen, Georg; —; 5 child, 4 dau

Waltjen; Catharina Johanna; 27-Nov-50; 22-Dec-50; Andreas; Bossum, Hannover; Hildebrandt, Christiane; —; Waltjen, Catharine; Waltjen, Georg; Waltjen, Johann; 3 child, 2 dau

Waltjen; Christiane Johanna Louise; 31-Oct-58; 14-Nov-58; Georg Heinrich Friedrich; Bossum, Hannover; Muhn, Katharine; —; Thiemeyer, Joh.; Thiemeyer, Mrs. Joh.; Prufer, Louise; —

Waltjen; Christine; 24-Dec-44; 6-Apr-45; Wilhelm; Bassum, Hannover; Kirchhoff, Maria; Ehrenburg, Hannover; Hildebrandt, Christine; —; —; —

Waltjen; Dorothea Maria; 21-May-46; 6-Dec-46; Andreas; Bossum, Hannover; Hildebrandt, Christiane; Bleichenbach, Hessen; Waltjen, Dorothea; Dietrich, Carla Marie; —; wit #1 is grandmother

Waltjen; Elisa Catharina; 8-Oct-54; 12-Oct-54; Georg; Bossum, Hannover; Muhn, Catharina; —; Waltjen, Dorothea; Waltjen, Maria; —; twin

Waltjen; Emilie Rebecca Elisabeth; 18-Apr-55; 29-Apr-55; Friedrich Wilhelm; Bossum, Hannover; Kirchhof, Maria; —; Waltjen, Sophie Marie Elisabeth; Lange, Robert; Waltjen, Sophie Emilie; —

Waltjen; Friderike Auguste; 15-Sep-49; 30-Sep-49; Joh. Friedrich Wilhelm; Bossum, Freidenberg; Kirchhoff, Anna Maria; Blockwinkel, Ehrenburg, Hannover; Dude, Friedrich Wilhelm; Waltjen, August Fr.; —; —

Waltjen; Friederike Sophie; 9-Feb-53; 13-Feb-53; Andreas; Bossum, Hannover; Hildebrandt, Christiane; —; Waltjen, Maria Friedrike; Waltjen, Heinr.; Bruhl, Johann; —

Waltjen; Friedrich Johann Heinrich; 23-Jul-65; 30-Jul-65; Wilhelm Heinrich; Baltimore; Spangenberg, Louise; Eichelsdorf,

Hessen; Waltjen, Friedrich; Waltjen, Heinrich; Spangenberger, Georg Johann; —

Waltjen; Georg Michael Hermann; 25-Feb-54; 19-Mar-54; Joh. Gerhard; Lentol Co. Pa.; Bauer, Elisabeth; —; Waltjen, Hermann Friedrich; —; —; —

Waltjen; Hermann Valentin; 30-Jul-58; 8-Aug-58; Heinrich; Bossum, Hannover; Horn, Maria Magdalena; —; Ober, Sophia; Horn, Joh. Valentin; —; —

Waltjen; Herrmann Heinrich; 18-Jul-45; 31-Aug-45; Heinrich; Bossum, Hannover; Stoll, Maria; Stätten, Canstadt, Wurttemberg; Waltjen, Grandfather; —; —; child died

Waltjen; infant son; 8-Oct-54; 12-Oct-54; Georg; Bossum, Hannover; Muhn, Catharina; —; —; —; —; stillborn twin

Waltjen; Johann; 18-Apr-52; 22-Jun-52; Adam; Spillsteinhoy, Coburg; Hartner, Margarethe; —; Reisenweber, Joh.; Kaiser, Barbara; —; —

Waltjen; Johann Heinrich; 24-Dec-62; 1-Jan-63; Hermann Heinrich; Bossum, Hannover; Horn, Maria Magdalena; Baltimore; Thiemeyer, Johann Heinrich; Thiemeyer, Jr., Heinrich; Thiemeyer, Marie; —

Waltjen; Johann Jakob Hildebrandt; 20-Aug-48; 10-Sep-48; Andreas; Bossum, Hannover; Hildebrandt, Christine; Bleichenbach, Hessen; Hildebrandt, Johann Jakob; —; —; —

Waltjen; Julia Pauline Emilie; 13-Jul-55; 22-Jul-55; Andreas; Bossum, Hannover; Hildebrand, Christiane; —; Heck, Julie; Lenze, Theodor; Waltjen, Sophie Emilie; —

Waltjen; Louise Katharine Christine; 14-Apr-61; 28-Apr-61; Wilhelm Heinrich; Baltimore; Spangenberg, Louise; —; Heck, Juliane; Spangenberg, Georg; Dieterle, Marie Elisabeth; —

Waltjen; Maria Catharine; 15-Apr-47; 27-May-47; Johann Friedrich Wilhelm; Bossum, Hannover; Kirchoff, Anna Maria; Neuenkirchen, Ehrenburg, Hannover; Bauer, Maria Cath.; —; —; —

Waltjen; Maria Elisabeth; 16-May-43; 27-Aug-43; Heinrich; —; Stoll, Maria; —; —; —; —; —

Surname Father; Child's Given Name; Birth Date; Baptismal Date; Father's Given Name; Father's Place of Birth; Mother's Surname and Given Name; Mother's Place of Birth; Witness 1 Surname and Given Name; Witness 2 Surname and Given Name; Witness 3 Surname and Given Name; Comments

Waltjen; Maria Sophia; 29-Jun-45; 23-Jul-45; Andreas; Bassum, Hannover; Hildebrand, Christiane; Bleichenbach, Hessen; Dieterle, Maria; Ober, Sophie; —; —

Waltjen; Marie Sophie; 19-Feb-51; 23-Feb-51; Georg Aug. Frdch.; Amt Bossum, Hannover; Muhn, Caroline; —; Waltjen, Friedrich; Waltjen, Mrs. Heinrich; Ober, Sophie; —

Waltjen; Rebecca Christiana; 12-Sep-52; 19-Sep-52; Heinrich; Bossum, Hannover; Stoll, Friederike; —; —; —; —; —

Waltjen; Sarah; 24-Dec-54; 1-Jan-55; Heinrich; Bossum, Hannover; Stoll, Friederika; —; Korf, Hermine; Heck, Georg; Waltjen, Maria; —

Waltjen; Sophia Amalia; 25-May-41; 29-Aug-41; Heinrich; —; Stoll, Maria; —; —; —; —; —

Waltjen; Sophia Augusta Elisabeth; 29-Dec-56; 4-Jan-57; Georg Heinr. Frch.; Bossum, Hannover; Muhn, Elisabeth Katharina; —; Waltjen, Sophia Emilia; Heck, Georg; Ober, Maria Elisabeth; —

Waltjen; Sophia Dorothea; 20-Sep-42; 27-Aug-43; Friedrich; —; Kirchhof, Anna M.; —; —; —; —; —

Waltjen; Stephanus Andreas; 14-Nov-58; 21-Nov-58; Johann Friedrich Wilhelm; Bossum, Hannover; Kirchhof, Anna Maria; —; Waltjen, Heinr.; —; —; —

Waltjen (deceased); Henriette Auguste; —; 16-Mar-56; Aug.; —; [--?--], [--?--]; —; Waltjen, Maria (wife of Heinr.); Waltjen, Heinr.; Waltjen, Katharina (wife of Georg); —

Walz; Abraham; 16-Feb-38; 6-Dec-38; Johannes; —; Romoser, Regine; —; —; —; —; —

Walz; Christine; 22-Oct-36; 6-Dec-38; Johannes; —; Romoser, Regine; —; —; —; —; —

Wambach; Auguste; 19-Nov-46; 2-Apr-47; August; Biedenkopf, Hessen; Pfeifer, Elisabeth; Biedenkopf, Hessen; —; —; —; —

Wambach; Catharine Christine; 3-Nov-44; 9-Jun-45; Wilhelm; Biedenkopf, Hessen; Kaufmann, Elisabeth; Biedenkopf, Hessen; —; —; —; —

Surname Father; Child's Given Name; Birth Date; Baptismal Date; Father's Given Name; Father's Place of Birth; Mother's Surname and Given Name; Mother's Place of Birth; Witness 1 Surname and Given Name; Witness 2 Surname and Given Name; Witness 3 Surname and Given Name; Comments

Wambach; Emma Louise; 21-Feb-50; 24-Mar-50; Georg; Zwestern, Kurhessen; Steffen, Louise; Binde, Preussen; parents, ; —; —; —

Wambach; Luise; 6-Nov-46; 2-Apr-47; Wilhelm; Biedenkopf, Hessen; Kaufmann, Elisabeth; Biedenkopf, Hessen; —; —; —; —

Warneken; Henriette Karoline; 9-Feb-44; 9-Jun-44; Lühr; —; Koch, Anna; —; —; —; —; —

Warneken; Hermann; 5-Nov-53; 18-Dec-53; Luhr; Meinershausen, Hannover; Koch, Anna; —; Bolden, Klaus Henry; —; —; —

Warneken; Johann Gerhard; 11-Mar-51; 25-May-51; Luhe; Meinershausen, Bremen; Koch, Anna; —; Meyer, Joh. Gerhard; —; —; child died

Warneken; Ludwig; 22-Oct-41; 7-Aug-42; Lühr; —; Koch, Anna; —; —; —; —; —

Warnke; Johann Wilhelm; 29-Jul-46; 11-Oct-46; Lühr; Ottersberg, Hannover; Sachs, Anna; Gerden, Bersenbruck, Hannover; —; —; —; —

Warnken; Heinrich; 14-Jan-49; 17-Jun-49; Luhr; Meinershausen, Ottersberg; Koch, Anna; Gehrde, Bersenbruck, Hannover; Koch, Adelheid; —; —; —

Webber; Karl Friedrich; 18-Nov-50; 21-Apr-51; Frdch.; Wedern, Preussen; Hohn, Anna; —; Muhlenbruck, Karl; —; —; —

Weber; Dorothea Sophia; 19-Sep-47; 24-Sep-47; Heinrich; Ossenbeck, Diepholz, Hannover; Dannettel, Henriette; Deka, Diepholz, Hannover; Dannettel, Doris; Bruning, Sophia; —; —

Weber; Elisabeth Catharine; 15-Feb-46; 22-Feb-46; Johann Heinrich; Bernsburg, Hessen; Umscheid, Genoveva; Dorfprozelten, Unterfranken, Baiern; Weber, Elisabeth Cath.; —; —; —

Weber; Georg Heinr.; 27-May-44; 9-Jun-44; Heinrich; —; Umscheit, Feva [?]; —; —; —; —; —

Weber; Heinrich Thomas; 7-Jan-41; 31-Jan-41; Heinrich; —; Losekanne, Elisab.; —; —; —; —; —

Surname Father; Child's Given Name; Birth Date; Baptismal Date; Father's Given Name; Father's Place of Birth; Mother's Surname and Given Name; Mother's Place of Birth; Witness 1 Surname and Given Name; Witness 2 Surname and Given Name; Witness 3 Surname and Given Name; Comments

Weber; Heinrich Wilhelm; 11-Apr-53; 20-Apr-53; Eberhard Heinr.; Ossenbecck, Hannover; Danettel, Henriette; —; Bruning, Herm. Heinr.; —; —; —

Weber; Johann Friedrich; 27-Mar-50; 4-Apr-50; Eberhard Heinrich; Ossenbeck, Tiepholz, Hannover; Dannettel, Margarethe Fr. Henrietta; Deckau, Tiepholz; Dannettel, Johann Heinrich; Meyers, Margaretha Wilhelmina; —; wit #1 mother's brother

Weber; Johann Heinrich; 24-Sep-50; 13-Oct-50; Johann; Bernsburg, Hessen Darmstadt; Keller, Maria; —; Heinz, Heinrich; —; —; 1 child

Weber; Karl; 6-Jun-53; 19-Jun-53; Heinrich; Volkertshain, Hessen; Herget, Philippine; —; Weber, Christian; Winter, Johannes; —; —

Weber; Lorenz Wilhelm; 23-Mar-44; 12-May-44; Karl; —; Bachmann, Auguste; —; —; —; —; —

Weber; Malvina; 12-Aug-46; 29-Nov-47; Johann Heinrich; Bremen; Garret, Elisabeth; Philadelphia; Medwey [?], Marianne; —; —; —

Weber; Margarethe Emma; 6-May-56; 18-May-56; Eberhard Heinrich; Ossenbeck, Hannover; Donettel, Maria Friederike Henriette; —; Timmermann, Margarethe Dorothea; —; —; —

Weber; Philip Georg; 18-Oct-38; 18-Nov-38; Heinrich; —; Losekamp, Elisab.; —; —; —; —; —

Webersberger; Elisabeth; 30-Jan-51; 23-Feb-51; Joh.; Mitteldorf, Baiern; Bauer, Elisabeth; —; parents, ; —; —; —

Webersperger; Ernst; 26-Mar-48; 2-Apr-48; Johann; Mittelsdorf, Herzogenaurach, Baiern; Bauer, Elisabeth; Angenhof, Herzogenaurach, Baiern; Eckart, Ernst; Eckart, Barbara; —; child died

Webersperger; Michael; 13-Mar-47; 19-Mar-47; Johann; Mitteledorf, Herzogaurach, Baiern; Bauer, Elisabeth; Weissendorf, Herzogaureach, Baiern; Webersperger, Michael; —; —; wit is uncle

Weckesser; Anna Elisab.; 30-Sep-41; 31-Oct-41; Johann; —; Eger, Anna Elisab.; —; —; —; —; —

Surname Father; Child's Given Name; Birth Date; Baptismal Date; Father's Given Name; Father's Place of Birth; Mother's Surname and Given Name; Mother's Place of Birth; Witness 1 Surname and Given Name; Witness 2 Surname and Given Name; Witness 3 Surname and Given Name; Comments

Weckesser; Anna Kathr.; 29-Jan-43; 13-Feb-43; Johann; —; Eger, Anna K.; —; —; —; —; —

Weckesser; Elisabeth; 17-Feb-37; 26-Mar-37; Joh.; —; Eger, Kathr.; —; —; —; —; —

Weckesser; Eva; 6-Dec-38; 23-Dec-38; Johann; —; Eger, Kathr.; —; —; —; —; —

Weckesser; Heinrich; 13-Feb-38; 4-Mar-38; Johanne; —; Eger, Anna El.; —; —; —; —; —

Weckesser; Heinrich Jacob; 14-Apr-40; 17-May-40; Johann; —; Eger, Elisab.; —; —; —; —; —

Weckesser; Johann Adam; 26-Nov-49; 30-Dec-49; Johann; Jusbach, Kirchhain, Kurhessen; Ezer, Anna Catharine; Jusbach, Kirchhain, Kurhessen; Briehl, Johann; —; —; —

Weckesser; Johann Heinrich; 22-Mar-45; 25-May-45; Johann; Josbach, Kurhessen; Eger, Anna Catharina; Josbach, Kurhessen; —; —; —; —

Weckesser; Maria; 14-Dec-40; 14-Dec-40; Johann; —; Eger, Kathr.; —; —; —; —; —

Weckesser; Tobias; 12-Sep-47; 10-Oct-47; Johann; Josbach, Rauschenberg, Kurhessen; Eger, Anna Catharine; Josbach, Rauschenberg, Kurhessen; Eger, Tobias; —; —; —

Weckesser, Jr.; Katharine; 8-Feb-42; 10-Feb-42; Johann; —; Eger, Katharine; —; —; —; —; —

Weddigen; Anna Maria; 26-Nov-51; 14-Dec-51; Theodor Julius Wilhelm; Preuss. Minden; Schwartz, Auguste Wilhelmine; —; Mohlmann, Anna Maria; —; —; —

Weddigen; Auguste Katharine Louise; 23-Feb-66; 11-Mar-66; Theodor Julius Wilhelm; Schusselburg, Preussen; Schwartz, Wilhelmine; Minden, Preussen; Blum, Katharine; Schorrer, Louise; —; —

Weddigen; Mathilde Emilie Sophie; 9-Dec-53; 8-Jan-54; Theodor; Minden, Preussen; Hinz, Auguste; —; Bruggemann, Mathilde; —; —; —

Weddigen; Sophia Wilhelmina Auguste; 14-Apr-56; 20-Apr-56; Theodor Julius Wilh.; Minden, Preussen; Schwartz, Auguste; —; Bach, Adam; Bruhl, Katharine; Flemming, Elisabeth; —

Surname Father; Child's Given Name; Birth Date; Baptismal Date; Father's Given Name; Father's Place of Birth; Mother's Surname and Given Name; Mother's Place of Birth; Witness 1 Surname and Given Name; Witness 2 Surname and Given Name; Witness 3 Surname and Given Name; Comments

Weddigen; Theodor Karl Johann; 15-Apr-58; 25-Apr-58; Theodor; Minden, Preussen; Schwarz, Augusta; —; Briel, Joh.; Schorrer, Joh.; Schulz, Louise; —

Weddiger; Emilie Katharine Margaretha; 27-Jun-61; 14-Jul-61; Theodor Julius Wilhelm; Schlusselburg, Preussen; Schwarz, Auguste; —; Bach, Katharine; Gerlach, Marg.; Spielmann, Joh.; —

Weddiger; male infant; 14-Dec-59; —; Theodor Jul. Wilhelm; Munde, Preussen; Schwarz, Auguste; —; —; —; —; still born

Wedel; Katharine Karoline; 27-Jun-64; 10-Jul-64; Adam; Oberlangenstadt, Baiern; Schaumlussel, Anna Elisabeth; Obervegschutz, Kurhessen; Schaumlussel, Karoline; Broning, Katharine; —; —

Wedig; Karl Wilhelm; 22-Jan-53; 6-Feb-53; Karl; Galen, Regbrg, Minden; Hiese, Anna Rebecca; —; Bertram, Wilhelm; —; —; —

Wehr; Johann Ludwig; 15-May-46; 19-Jul-46; Johann Adam; Oberhochstadt bei Neustadt a.d. Reuss, Baiern; Hahnemann, Elisabeth; Segnitz, Ochsenfurth, Baiern; Glock, Johann Ludwig; —; —; —

Wehr; Maria Rosina; 29-Apr-45; 29-May-45; Johann Adam; Oberhöchstadt, Neustadt an der Reuss, Baiern; Hahnemann, Elisa; Segnitz, Baiern; Hahnemann, Maria Rosina; —; —; —

Weide; Luise Dorothea; 26-Mar-45; 8-Jun-45; Caspar; Weidecken bei Hanau, Kurhessen; Westphal, Cath; Weidecken bei Hanau, Kurhessen; Pick, Luise Schneider; —; —; —

Weidemann; Georg Tobias; 24-Jan-59; 6-Feb-59; Johann; Jagshausen, Wurttemberg; Horrack, Christiane; —; Ermold, Georg; Dietz, Tobias; —; —

Weidemeier; Anna Regine; 9-Jan-62; 26-Jan-62; Adam; Gross Roppershausen, Kurhessen; Richter, Marie Engel; —; Karstens, Heinrich; Briel, Anna Katharine; Rommeser, Louise; —

Weidemeier; Christine Rebecca; 4-Jun-51; 8-Jun-51; Adam; Grossropperhausen, Kurhessen; Schafer, Barbara Elisabeth; —; Schafer, Christine; —; —; —

Surname Father; Child's Given Name; Birth Date; Baptismal Date; Father's Given Name; Father's Place of Birth; Mother's Surname and Given Name; Mother's Place of Birth; Witness 1 Surname and Given Name; Witness 2 Surname and Given Name; Witness 3 Surname and Given Name; Comments

Weidemeier; Karl Friedrich Adam; 6-Sep-59; 4-Sep-59; Adam; Gersropperhausen, Kurhessen; Richter, Maria Engel; —; Kasten, Karl; Leutner, Friedrich; Einwachter, Adam; —

Weidemeier; Maria Catharina; 15-Mar-55; 25-Mar-55; Adam; Grossrupperhausen, Kurhessen; Richter, Maria Engel; —; Lenz, Maria; —; —; —

Weidemeier; Maria Louise; 25-Mar-56; 6-Apr-56; Adam; Grossvoppershausen, Kurhessen; Richter, Maria Engel; —; Kasten, Maria Louise; —; —; —

Weidemeyer; Georg Adam; 4-Jun-43; 18-Jun-43; Adam; —; Schaefer, Barb. Elisab.; —; —; —; —; —

Weider; Maria Elisabeth; 30-Sep-42; 23-Oct-42; Caspar; —; Westphal, Kathr.; —; —; —; —; —

Weider; Regine Magdalene; 11-Oct-38; 21-Oct-38; Kaspar; —; Westphal, Kathr.; —; —; —; —; —

Weidmeier; Ludwig Adam; 17-Sep-64; 25-Sep-64; Adam; Gross Ruppershausen, Kurhessen; Richter, Marie Engel; Bissendorf, Hannover; Sieck, Adam Frdch.; Ermald, Katharine; —; —

Weidner; Caroline Elisabeth; 13-May-45; 1-Jun-45; Franz Michael; Mulfingen, Kinselsbau, Wurttemberg; Oesterle, Christine; Oppelspohm, Wurttemberg; Oesterle, Andreas; —; —; —

Weidner; Christine Elisabeth; 2-Apr-49; 12-Aug-49; Andreas; Mulfingen, Kinzelbau; Oesterle, Caroline; Obelsspohn, Waiblingen, Wurttemberg; Cweidner, Christine; Michael, Franz; —; —

Weidner; Franz Michael; —; 2-Apr-48; Andreas; Mulfingen, Kinzelbau; Oesterle, Caroline; Lauterbach, Waiblingen, Wurttemberg; Weidner, Franz; Weidner, Christiana Oesterle; —; —

Weidner; Friederike Apollonia; 8-Jul-47; 25-Jul-47; Franz Michael; Mulfingen, Wurttemberg; Oesterle, Christina; Opelsschohn, Wurttemberg; Kreidmann, Jakob; —; —; —

Weigel; Elisabetha; 15-Oct-44; 3-Aug-45; Johann; Niederstadt, Wurttemberg; Thomas, Margaretha; Niederstadt, Wurttemberg; —; —; —; —

Surname Father; Child's Given Name; Birth Date; Baptismal Date; Father's Given Name; Father's Place of Birth; Mother's Surname and Given Name; Mother's Place of Birth; Witness 1 Surname and Given Name; Witness 2 Surname and Given Name; Witness 3 Surname and Given Name; Comments

Weigel; Georg Philip; 21-Oct-39; 17-Nov-39; Georg; —; Senger, Magd.; —; —; —; —; —

Weigel; Johann Georg; 21-May-46; 19-Jul-46; Johann; Niederstatten, Wurttemberg; Thomas, Margaretha; Niederstatten, Wurttemberg; Frank, Georg; Senft, Johann; —; —

Weigel; Johann Georg; 27-Feb-42; 27-Mar-42; Georg A.; —; Senger, Magdalene; —; —; —; —; —

Weigel; Lisette Dorothea; 24-Jun-44; 25-Aug-44; Andr.; —; Senger, Magd. M.; —; —; —; —; —

Weigel; Maria Magd. Kathr.; 1-Oct-37; 29-Oct-37; Georg; —; Senger, Magd.; —; —; —; —; —

Weihrauch; Catharine; 16-May-47; 14-May-48; Johann; Elmanshausen, Zwiegenberg, Hessen; Kohler, Margarethe; Zwingenberg; Pollmann, Thomas; Pollmann, Mrs.; —; child died

Weihrauch; Catharine; 11-May-45; 13-Jul-45; Johannes; Senheim, Hessen; Köhler, Margaretha; Zweigenberg, Hessen; Lautenschlager, Cath.; —; —; —

Weihrauch; Elisabeth; 12-Jun-43; 23-Aug-43; Johann; —; Kehler, Marg.; —; —; —; —; —

Weihrauch; Johann; 9-Mar-41; 11-Apr-41; Johann; —; Kehler, Marg.; —; —; —; —; —

Weihrauch; Maria; 25-Jun-49; 29-Jun-49; Johann; Elmenshausen, Zweigenberg, Hessen; Kohler, Margaretha; Zweigenberg; Hanseler, Maria; —; —; child died

Weiker; Johann; 14-Apr-49; 9-Jun-49; Georg; Billertshausen bei Alsfeld, Hessen; Klehn, Auguste; Bremen; Weiker, Johann; —; —; —

Weil; Emilia; 6-Jan-45; 13-Apr-45; Heinrich; Tiefenbach, Elsass; Schmidt, Maria; Baltimore; Brodbeck, Maria; —; —; —

Weil; Heinrich; 25-Nov-42; 25-Dec-42; Ernst Ph.; —; Schütz, Christiane; —; —; —; —; —

Weil; Heinrich; 17-Jul-43; 1-Oct-43; Heinrich; —; Schmidt, Maria; —; —; —; —; —

Surname Father; Child's Given Name; Birth Date; Baptismal Date; Father's Given Name; Father's Place of Birth; Mother's Surname and Given Name; Mother's Place of Birth; Witness 1 Surname and Given Name; Witness 2 Surname and Given Name; Witness 3 Surname and Given Name; Comments

Weil; Johann Christian; 8-Oct-46; 8-Nov-46; Ernst Philipp; Echzel, Nidda, Hessen; Schutz, Christiane; Biedingen, Nidda, Hessen; Schutz, Johann; Hermann, Christian; —; —

Weinhard; Heinrich; 27-Aug-37; 17-Sep-37; Peter; —; Beyer, Christine; —; —; —; —; —

Weinhold; Andreas; 21-Jun-41; 1-Aug-41; Andreas; —; Röhrmann, Kathr. Elise; —; —; —; —; —

Weinrich; Johannes; 9-Dec-56; 25-Dec-56; Joh. Adam; Rouenberg, Baiern; Schedel, Katharine; —; Rogener, Joh.; Rogener, Katharine; —; —

Weis; Elisabeth Kathr.; 1-Oct-40; 26-Dec-40; Jacob; —; Loos, Elisab.; —; —; —; —; -- Oct 1840

Weiss; Anna Amalie; 29-Apr-42; 26-Jun-42; Jacob; —; Loos, Elisab.; —; —; —; —; —

Weiss; Dorothea Margaretha; 30-Dec-65; 22-Feb-66; Karl; Catonsville, Baltimore, MD; Monnich, Johanne Katharine; Wanhers, Baiern; West, Anna Margaretha; —; —; —

Weiss; Elise Caroline; 22-Nov-46; 26-Dec-46; Jakob; Helfenberg, Marbach, Wurttemberg; Lors, Elisabeth; Bernsburg, Alsfeld, Hessen; Weber, Anna Elisabeth; —; —; —

Weiss; Georg; 15-Aug-50; 8-Oct-50; Georg; Simgrechtshausen, Wurttemberg; Steg, Friedericke; —; —; —; —; 1 child

Weiss; Wilhelm; 13-May-44; 28-Jul-44; Jakob; —; Loos, Elisab. M.; —; —; —; —

Weller; Caroline Luise; 2-Jan-46; 20-Jul-46; Christopher; Friedenhofen, Gelldorf, Wurttemberg; Wild, Ursula; Rotenhaar, Gelldorf, Wurttemberg; Heritz, Sophie; Seibold, Luise Dorothea; —

Weller; Elisabeth Christine Maria; 30-Aug-67; 8-Sep-67; Melchior; Altenbusseck, Hessen; Jung, Katharine Elisabeth; Hackelheim, Preussen; Rolfing, Elisabeth; Winter, Christine; Weller, Maria

Weller; Emil Johann Christian; 19-Nov-60; 25-Nov-60; Philipp; Altenbusseck, Hessen; Schlerf, Katharine; —; Winter, Christian; Scherer, Joh.; Schlerf, Emilie

Weller; Georg; 22-Sep-40; 4-Oct-40; Christoph; —; Wild, Ursula; —; —; —; —

Surname Father; Child's Given Name; Birth Date; Baptismal Date; Father's Given Name; Father's Place of Birth; Mother's Surname and Given Name; Mother's Place of Birth; Witness 1 Surname and Given Name; Witness 2 Surname and Given Name; Witness 3 Surname and Given Name; Comments

Weller; Nikolaus Heinrich; 9-Aug-62; 17-Aug-62; Philipp; Alltenbuspeck, Hessen; Schlerf, Katharine; —; Mieth, Nikolaus; Waltjen, Heinrich; Wille, Elisabeth

Weller; Sophie; 21-Nov-42; 12-Jan-43; Christoph; —; Wild, Ursula; —; —; —; —

Weller; Wilhelm Eberhard; 28-Apr-59; 8-May-59; Philipp; Altenbusseck, Hessen; Schlerf, Katharina; —; Stetten, Wilhelm; Bergen, Eberhard; —

Weltner; Catharine Marie; 25-Jun-51; 10-Jul-51; Joh.; Heimershausen, Hessen; Schaumberg, Catharine; —; Weltner, Catharine; —; —

Wendel; Friedrich Adolph; 30-Oct-66; 18-Nov-66; Adam; Oberlangenstadt, Baiern; Schaumlusfel, Anna Elisabeth; Obervorschutz, Kurhessen; Staffel, Friedrich; Kohlmann, Adolph; —

Wendel; Wilhelm Heinrich; 13-Mar-62; 23-Mar-62; Adam; Oberlangenstadt, Baiern; Schaumlossel, Anna Elisabeth; —; Schaumlossel, Ecksturm; Heinrich; —

Wermann (deceased); Agnes Barbara; 18-Jan-54; 22-Jan-54; John Frdch; Sachsen; Schultz, Sophia; —; Salzner, Agnes Barbara; —; —

Werth; Heinrich; 9-Nov-41; 19-Dec-41; Conrad; —; Schwelm, Marg; —; —; —; —

Werth; Jacob; 12-Sep-44; 29-Sep-44; Conrad; —; Schwalb, Magdal.; —; —; —; —

Wesseler; Maria Elise Kathrine; 9-Oct-37; 11-Oct-37; Wilh.; —; Ottings, Kathr.; —; —; —; —

West; Johann Klemens; 21-Jan-65; 6-Apr-65; Konstantin; —; Munsch, Anna Margaretha; Wansers; Weiss, Johanne Margaretha; —; —

Wetter; Ludwig; 26-Aug-50; 9-Sep-50; Georg; Berleburg, Preussen; Rothstein, Wilhelmine; —; Wetter, Ludwig; Gottsched, Rosina; —; 1 child

Wetzler; Johannes; —; 2-Aug-40; Conrad; —; Nev, Barbara; —; —; —; —; not known

Surname Father; Child's Given Name; Birth Date; Baptismal Date; Father's Given Name; Father's Place of Birth; Mother's Surname and Given Name; Mother's Place of Birth; Witness 1 Surname and Given Name; Witness 2 Surname and Given Name; Witness 3 Surname and Given Name; Comments

Weydemeier; Peter Jakob; 8-Oct-48; 15-Oct-48; Adam; Gross Roppenhausen, Ziegenhain, Kurhessen; Schafer, Barbara Elisabeth; Metzebach, Spangenberg, Kurhessen; Weydemeyer, Peter; —; —; —

Weydemeyer, Sr.; Martha Elisabeth; 20-Mar-46; 10-May-46; Adam; Gross Rupperhausen, Ziegenhain, Kurhessen; Schafer, Barbara Elisabeth; Metzebach, Spangenberg, Kurhessen; Schafer, Anna Martha; —; —; wit is grandmother

Wick; Heinrich; 23-Feb-43; 6-Mar-43; Heinrich; —; Scherber, Elisab.; —; —; —; —; twin

Wick; Jacob; 23-Feb-43; 6-Mar-43; Heinrich; —; Scherber, Elisab.; —; —; —; —; twin

Wicklein; Georg Leonhard; 24-Jun-47; 11-Jul-47; Carl; Molmerz, Sonneberg, Sachsen Meiningen; Schem, Anna Maria; Windsheim, Baiern; Schem, Georg Leonhard; —; —; —

Wicklein; Heinrich Leonhard; 3-Aug-49; 12-Aug-49; Carl; Molmertz bei Coburg, Sachsen Meiningen; Schäm, Maria; Windsheim, Mittelfranken, Baiern; Omeyer, Dietrich Heinr.; Schäm, Leonhard; —; —

Wicklein; Johann Georg; 22-Oct-41; 17-Nov-41; Karl; —; [--?--], Maria; —; —; —; —; —

Wicklein; Johannes; 29-Oct-45; 9-Nov-45; Carl; Wollmertz, Sachsen Meiningen; Schem, Anna Maria; Windsheim, Baiern; Schem, Johann; —; —; —

Wideg; Heinrich Philip; 25-Jul-42; 4-Sep-42; Heinrich; —; Bruckenberg, Charlotte; —; —; —; —; —

Wieb; Anna Barb.; 3-Jan-44; 18-Feb-44; Johann; —; Limroth, Elisab.; —; —; —; —; —

Wiebking; Friedrike Wilhelmine; 6-Oct-61; 10-Nov-61; Heinrich; Liebenau, Hannover; Thiemeyer, Amalie; —; Klinkmeier, Wilhelm; Thiemeyer, Johann; —; —

Wiebking; Heinrich Friedrich Wilhelm; 26-Aug-66; 16-Sep-66; Heinrich Konrad; Liebenau, Hannover; Thiemeier, Amalie; Engter, Hannover; Baumann, Georg; Nobbe, Wilhelm; —; —

Wiebking; Hermann Friedrich Ludwig; 18-Sep-59; 2-Oct-59; Heinr. Krdch. Konrad; Liebenau, Hannover; Thiemeyer, Anna Maria

Amalie; —; Thiemeyer, Heinr. Frdch; Schulz, Fred.; Thiemeyer, Anna Maria Emalie; —

Wiebking; Maria Emilie Julianne; 2-Jul-64; 17-Jul-64; Heinrich Friedrich Konrad; Liebenau, Hannover; Horstmann, Anna Maria Amalie; Engter, Hannover; Wiebking, Maria Sophie; Thiemeyer, Anna Marie Julianne; Ober, Heinrich; —

Wiede; Georg; 4-May-45; 3-Aug-45; Heinrich; Wiednitz be Baireuth; Jobst, Elisabeth; Tiefenkleinbe, Baiern; Jobst, Georg; —; —; —

Wiedeker; Elisabeth; 18-Feb-38; 20-Feb-38; Andreas; —; Schneider, Maria; —; —; —; —; —

Wiedemann; Christian Friedrich; 27-Jan-67; 10-Feb-67; Johann Christoph; Forthausen, Wurttemberg; Horack, Christiane; Forthausen, Wurttemberg; Dietz, Tobias; Wiedemann, Christiane; —; —

Wiedemann; Georg Gustav; 17-Jan-58; 24-Jan-58; Johann; Jagsthausen, Wurttemberg; Horak, Christiane; —; Dietz, Johanna; Wiedemann, Gustav; —; —

Wiedemann; Gottfried Heinrich; 29-Aug-63; 13-Sep-63; Johann; Jagsthausen, Wurttemberg; Horock, Christiane; Jagsthausen, Wurttemberg; Wiedemann, Christiane; Dietz, Tobias; —; —

Wiedemann; Johann Georg; 26-Feb-56; 9-Mar-56; Joh.; Forcthausen, Wurttemberg; Horack, Christine; —; Ermold, Georg; Wiedemann, Christiane; Dietz, Tobias; —

Wiedemann; Johanne Christine; 19-Oct-54; 29-Oct-54; Joh.; Jagsthausen, Wurttemberg; Horack, Christiane; —; —; —; —; —

Wiedemann; Wilhelm; 4-Feb-61; 10-Feb-61; Johann; Jagthausen, Wurttemberg; Horack, Christine; —; Dietz, Tobias; Bertram, Friedrike; —; —

Wiedemeier; Anna Emilie Johanna; 29-Oct-57; 1-Nov-57; Adam; Grossroppershausen, Kurhessen; Richter, Maria Engel; —; Briel, Joh.; Briel, Katharina; Schlerf, Emilie; —

Wiedmann; Johanne Albine Karoline; 23-Feb-66; 11-Mar-66; Gustav; Jagsthausen, Wurttemberg; Beck, Wilhelmine;

Langenberg, Hessen; Wiedemann, Johanne; Beck, Albine; —; —

Wiegel; Elisabeth Juliane; 15-Dec-46; 24-Jan-47; Heinrich; Nauses, Ziegenhain, Kurhessen; Hollmann, Catharine Maria; Bramsche bei Osnabruck, Hannover; Schaberg, Herrmann; Ernst, Elisabeth; —; —

Wiegel; Ellen Rosa Anna; 3-Apr-49; 28-May-49; Heinrich; Stein Nauses, Wiegenhain, Kurhessen; Hollmann, Catharine Marie; Bramsche, Hannover; Hollmann, Anna Margarthe; Anna Regina; —; —

Wiegel; Johann Adam; 1-Aug-40; 30-Aug-40; Heinrich; —; Hollmann, Kathr.; —; —; —; —; —

Wiegel; Maria Luise; 27-Jul-41; 8-Sep-43; Heinrich; —; Hollmanns, Katharine M.; —; —; —; —; —

Wiegel; Wilhelm Heinrich; 14-Oct-38; 4-Nov-38; Heinrich; —; Hollmanns, Kathr.; —; —; —; —; —

Wiel; Philipp Henrich; 17-Jan-49; 8-Apr-49; Ernst Philipp; Echzel, Hessen; Schutz, Christine; Budingen, Hessen; Ostheim, Heinrich; —; —; child died

Wieland; Ludwig; 10-Sep-49; 16-Sep-49; Johann Gottfried; Vordermurrharle, Backnang, Wurttemberg; Traub, Christine; Mittelbruding, Backnang, Wurttemberg; Schippert, Ludwig; —; —; —

Wiese; Anna Marg.; 30-Jan-44; 3-Mar-44; Wilhelm; —; Brunner, Kathr.; —; —; —; —; —

Wiese; Christine Wilhelmine; 17-Dec-48; 18-Feb-49; Wilhelm; Hamelwarren, Oldenburg; Bummers, Catharine; Siegstadt, Bednokesa, Hannover; Schmidt, Heinrich; Schmidt, Christine; —; —

Wiesner; Emma Christiane; 29-Dec-65; 28-Jan-66; Eberhard; Allendorf a. d. Lumda; Lessner, Barbara Regina; Igsheim, Baiern; Zink, Christine; Schlerf, Philipp; —; —

Wiesner; Heinrich Hartmann Eduard; 23-Feb-62; 2-Mar-62; Eberhard; Allendorf a.d.L., Hessen; Lessner, Barbara Regina; —; Wiesner, Hartmann; Broning, Heinrich; —; —

Surname Father; Child's Given Name; Birth Date; Baptismal Date; Father's Given Name; Father's Place of Birth; Mother's Surname and Given Name; Mother's Place of Birth; Witness 1 Surname and Given Name; Witness 2 Surname and Given Name; Witness 3 Surname and Given Name; Comments

Wiesner; Katharine Elise; 24-Sep-63; 11-Oct-63; Eberhard; Allendorf a. d. Lunda, Hessen; Lessner, Barbara Regina; Igsheim, Baiern; Leutner, Franz; Bender, Katharine; —; —

Wietler; Caroline Henriette; 27-Sep-46; 4-Oct-46; Johann; Deljehausen, Uslar, Hannover; Freinhagen, Christine; Deljehausen, Uslar, Hannover; Eggers, Caroline; —; —; child died

Wild; Christian; 12-Jun-38; 13-Jun-38; Christian; —; Koch, Karoline; —; —; —; —; —

Wild; Johann Franz; 25-Sep-37; 1-Oct-37; Franz; —; Pfeister, Dorothea; —; —; —; —; —

Wild; Johann Friedr.; 19-Jul-39; 25-Aug-39; Philip Jac.; —; Eckert, Anna M.; —; —; —; —; —

Wild; Johannes; 21-Oct-39; 14-Nov-39; Christian; —; Koch, Kathr.; —; —; —; —; —

Wild; Juliane; 8-Sep-37; 1-Oct-37; Philip Jacob; —; Egert, Marg.; —; —; —; —; —

Wild; Rosine Margaretha; 25-Sep-37; 1-Oct-37; Michael; —; Traub, Kathr.; —; —; —; —; —

Wildemuth; Georg; 21-Dec-53; 15-Jan-54; Adam; Bleitelsheim, Wurttemberg; Funck, Elisabeth; —; Kattenkamp, Dietrich; Kattenkamp, Rosine; —; —

Wildemuth; Johann Adam; 16-Sep-42; 25-Oct-42; Adam; —; Fink, Elisab.; —; —; —; —; —

Wildemuth; Katharine; 19-Aug-38; 30-Sep-38; Wilhelm; —; Frank, Gottliebine; —; —; —; —; —

Wildemuth; Maria Elisab.; 28-Apr-39; 9-Jun-39; Adam; —; Fink, Elisab.; —; —; —; —

Wildermuth; Elisabetha Maria; 21-Feb-50; 28-Apr-50; Adam; Bleidelsheim, Wurttemberg; Finke, Elisabeth; Essen, Oldenburg; Doberer, Johannes; —; —

Wildermuth; George Heinrich; 27-Jun-46; 1-Jul-46; Adam; Bleidelsheim, Marbach, Wurttemberg; Fink, Elisabeth; Essen, Aurkderbruck, Hannover; —; —; —

Surname Father; Child's Given Name; Birth Date; Baptismal Date; Father's Given Name; Father's Place of Birth; Mother's Surname and Given Name; Mother's Place of Birth; Witness 1 Surname and Given Name; Witness 2 Surname and Given Name; Witness 3 Surname and Given Name; Comments

Wildermuth; Karl Heinrich Georg; 1-May-67; 12-Apr-67; Joh. Karl; Baltimore; Frank, Karoline Elisabeth; Baltimore; Spilmann, Karl; Mieth, Karoline; Frank, Georg

Wildermuth; Karoline Marie Lisete; 4-Apr-65; 16-Apr-65; Johann; Baltimore; Frank, Karoline; Baltimore; Frank, Lisette Friederike; Frank, Karl August; Wildermuth, Elisabeth

Wildmuth; Elisabeth; 7-Mar-45; 15-Mar-45; Adam; Bleidelshaim, Wurttemberg; Fenken, Elisabeth; Quackenbruck, Hannover; Doberer, Johannes; Doberer, Mrs.; —

Wilhelm; Herman Wilhelm; 27-Jun-67; 7-Jul-67; Peter; Hornberg a.d. Ohm, Hessen; Feldmann, Rebecca; Altenbruch, Hannover; Wilhelm, Wilhelm; Wilhelm, Katharina; —

Wilhelm; Johanna Justine Katharine; 16-Jan-66; 28-Jan-66; Peter Wilhelm; Homberg a.d. Ohm, Hessen; Feldmann, Wilhelmine Rebecca; Altenbruch, Hannover; Wilhelma, Anna Katharine; Hillgartner, Johann, Wihlelm; Justine

Wilhelms; Georg Luther; 30-Oct-47; 9-Apr-48; Friedrich; Hedemunden, Hannover; Struve, Martha; Weidenrode, Kurhessen; Bauer, Georg; —; —

Wilhelms; Louise; 22-Jan-50; 3-Feb-50; Friedrich; Hedemunde, Hannover; Strube, Anna Martha; Weiterode, Hessen Cassel; Curd, Louise; —; —

Wilhelms; Maria Elisabeth; 22-Nov-52; 20-Feb-53; Friedrich Wilhe.; Hedeminden, Hannover; Strube, Martha Anna; —; Bauer, Georg; —; —

Wilkens; Johann Heinrich; 3-Nov-44; 29-Dec-44; Johann Heinr.; —; Pois, Anna Chr.; —; —; —; —

Wilkens; Margarethe Adelh.; 24-Dec-42; 19-Mar-43; Heinrich; —; Poys [?], Anna; —; —; —; —

Wilker; Adolph Friedrich; 22-Dec-55; 30-Dec-55; Gerhard Friedrich; Kasbilbern, Hannover; Sieck, Christine Eleonore; —; Sieck, Adolph; Sieck, Friedrich; —

Wilker; Heinrich Friedrich; 28-May-61; 9-Jun-61; Gerhard Friedrich; Balle, Hannover; Sieck, Christine Elenore; —; Ortmann, Eberhard Heinrich; Sieck, Jobst Heinrich; Sieck, Florentine Louise

Wilker; Johann Heinrich; 8-Dec-53; 11-Dec-53; Gerhard Friedrich; Bobe, Hannover; Seick, Eloenore Marie; —; Sieck, Kluas Heinrich; —; —

Wilker; Maria Elisabeth; 20-Oct-58; 31-Oct-58; Johann Gerhard Friedr.; Kasbilbelle, Hannover; Sieck, Christine Eleonore; —; Sieck, Maria Elisabeth; Sieck, Maria Elisabeth; Wilker, Maria Katharina; —

Winkelmann; Herrmann Heinrich; 15-Aug-46; 24-Jan-47; Heinrich; Quakenbruck, Hannover; Briegel, Henriette; Feldbach, Canstadt, Wurttemberg; —; —; —; —

Winkelmann; Johann Heinr.; 21-Jun-42; 31-Jul-42; Heinrich; —; Brügel, Henriette; —; —; —; —; —

Winkelmann; Margaretha Henrietta; 29-Jun-44; 22-Sep-44; Heinrich; —; Brügel, Henriette; —; —; —; —; —

Winter; Adam Daniel; 22-Dec-58; 2-Jan-59; Christian; Weidnitz, Baiern; Schlerf, Christine; —; Schlerf, Emilie; Lindemann, Daniel; —; —

Winter; Anna Wilhelmina; 25-Aug-56; 31-Aug-56; Andreas; Volkertshain, Hessen; Weidner, Wilhelmina; —; Weidner, Mrs.; Winter, Johannes; Mohring, Augusta; —

Winter; Christoph Matthaus; 5-Nov-60; 11-Nov-60; Christian; Weidnitz, Baiern; Schlerf, Christine; —; Reinhard, Christoph; Reitzel, Matthaus; —; —

Winter; Ernst Emil; 24-Dec-60; 30-Dec-60; Johann Andreas; Volkeortshain, Hessen; Winter, Wilhelmine; —; Beck, Ernst; Ecksturm, Katharine; Vogel, Emil; —

Winter; Johann Andreas; 6-Aug-58; 15-Aug-58; Johann Andreas; Volkartshain, Hessen; Weidner, Wilhelmine; —; Ecksturm, Joh. Heinr.; Prufer, Louise; Keyl, Stephanus; —

Winter; Johann Andreas; 01-May-1858; 16-May-58; Johannes; Volkartshain, Hessen; Thomas, Louise; —; Winter, Andreas; Weber, Katharina; —; —

Winter; Johann Friedrich; 18-Jul-63; 26-Jul-63; Johann Andreas; Volkartsheim, Hessen; weidner, Wilhelmine; Gadern, Hessen; Weidner, Johann; Eckart, Johann; —; —

Surname Father; Child's Given Name; Birth Date; Baptismal Date; Father's Given Name; Father's Place of Birth; Mother's Surname and Given Name; Mother's Place of Birth; Witness 1 Surname and Given Name; Witness 2 Surname and Given Name; Witness 3 Surname and Given Name; Comments

Winter; Johann Melchior; 30-Jan-57; 8-Feb-57; Christian; Weidnitz, Baieren; Schlerf, Christina; —; Seibel, Joh.; Schlerf, Melchior; —; —

Winter; Johannes; 1-Mar-50; 28-Mar-50; Andreas; Nolkhardsheim, Hessen; Weidner, Wilhelmine; Gaden, Hessen; Weidner, Johann; —; —; wit is grandfather

Winter; Karl Christian Gottlieb; 3-Nov-64; 13-Nov-64; Christian; Weidnitz, Baiern; Schlerf, Christine; Allendorf a. d. L., Hessen; Schmidt, Christian; Schlerf, Kath.; Kuhnert, Gottlieb; —

Winter; Katharine Susanne; 7-Dec-64; 25-Dec-64; Johann Andreas; Volkartshain, Hessen; Winter, Wilhelmine; Gedern, Hessen; Bach, Katharine; Mohring, Joh.; Sommer, Fr. Pastorin; —

Winter; Louise Katharine; 18-Mar-67; 31-Mar-67; Christian; Weudnitz, Baiern; Schlerf, Christine; Allendorf a. d. Lumbda, Hessen; Harmes, Louise; Weller, Katharine; —; —

Winter; Luise; 22-Jun-47; 1-Aug-47; Heinrich; Weidnitz; Jobst, Elisabeth; Tiffenklein,, Weismain, Baiern; Ochslin, Luise; —; —; —

Winter; Martha Magdalena; 18-Aug-53; 28-Aug-53; Andreas; Volkertshain, Hessen; Weidern, Friedrike; —; Keyl, Sophia Amalie; Krauss, Johann Georg; Nolting, Bertha; —

Winter; Martin; 28-Dec-51; 11-Jan-52; Andreas; Volkertshain, Hessen; Weidner, Wilhelmine; —; Mohring, Jakob; —; —; child died

Winter; Philipp Heinrich Eberhard; 31-Oct-62; 9-Nov-62; Christian; Weidnitz, Baiern; Schlerf, Christine; —; Weller, Philipp; Schafer, Heinrich; Bergen, Eberhard; —

Wintler; Maria; 1-Jul-48; 16-Jul-48; Johann; Delgenhausen, Uslar, Hannover; Koch, Christine; Delgenhausen, Uslar, Hannover; Baumann, Christine; —; —; —

Wirth; Andreas; 7-Dec-43; 24-Dec-43; Georg; —; Schmidt, Marg.; —; —; —; —; —

Wirth; Lorenz; 27-Feb-46; 8-Apr-46; Georg; Buchendorf, Tadtsteinhoff, Baiern; Schmidt, Margaretha; Buchendorf, Tadtsteinhoff, Baiern; Schmidt, Johann; —; —; child died

Surname Father; Child's Given Name; Birth Date; Baptismal Date; Father's Given Name; Father's Place of Birth; Mother's Surname and Given Name; Mother's Place of Birth; Witness 1 Surname and Given Name; Witness 2 Surname and Given Name; Witness 3 Surname and Given Name; Comments

Wirth; Magdalene; 23-Oct-41; 31-Oct-41; Georg; —; Schmidt, Marg.; —; —; —; —; —

Witmar; Maria Dorothea; 11-Jun-41; 4-Jul-41; Johann A.; —; Bühler, Anna M.; —; —; —; —; —

Wittekind; Anna Martha; 16-Apr-45; 2-Jun-45; Heinrich; Rauschenberg, Kurhessen; Geiger, Anna Martha; Rauschenberg, Kurhessen; Geiger, Anna Eva; —; —; wit is grandmother

Wittekind; Wilhelm Heinrich; 20-Mar-44; 5-May-44; Heinrich; —; Geyer, Anna M.; —; —; —; —; —

Wittler; Hanna Emilia Virginia; 11-Mar-64; 20-Mar-64; Heinrich Friedrich Wilhelm; Dellinhausen, Hannover; Heyse, Wilhelmine Johanne Louise; Fredeltle, Hannover; Wittler, Frdch Christian; Bader, Katharine Regine; Wittler, Karl Friedrch Aug.; —

Wittler; Heinrich Louis Friedrich; 24-Mar-66; 8-Mar-66; Friedrich Wilhelm; Dellerhausen, Braunschweig; Heise, Wilhelmine Johanna Louise; Ferdelsloh, Wurttemberg; Schafer, Heinrich; Obittler, Louise; Becker, ???; —

Wittler; infang male; 20-May-57; —; Karl; —; Mansdorfer, Louise; —; —; —; —; stillborn

Wittler; Karl Friedrich Heinrich; 24-Jan-59; 30-Jan-59; Friedrich August; Dellinhausen, Braunschweig; Mansdorfer, Louise; —; Wittler, Friedrich; Siegel, Katharina; Schafer, Heinrich; —

Wolf; Elisabeth Amalie; 28-Jan-65; 5-Feb-65; Valentin; Strebendorf, Hessen; Martel, Elisabeth; Strebendorf, Hessen; Ruppel, Elisabeth; Stegner, Amalie; —; —

Wolf; Georg Aug. Andr.; 15-Jul-43; 6-Aug-43; Heinrich; —; Wagner, Anna Doroth.; —; —; —; —; —

Wolf; Jakob; 28-Jun-45; 27-Jul-45; Heinrich; Homburg auf der Höhn; Wagner, Dorothea; Homburg auf der Höhn; Dahl, Jakob; —; —; —

Wolf; Johann Heinrich; 5-Dec-58; 19-Dec-58; Valentin; Strebzendorf, Hessen; Markel, Anna Elisabeth; —; Ruppel, Joh.; Dickel, Konard; Schneider, Heinr.; —

Surname Father; Child's Given Name; Birth Date; Baptismal Date; Father's Given Name; Father's Place of Birth; Mother's Surname and Given Name; Mother's Place of Birth; Witness 1 Surname and Given Name; Witness 2 Surname and Given Name; Witness 3 Surname and Given Name; Comments

Wolf; Johann Ludwig; 8-Jan-42; 27-Feb-42; Heinrich; —; Wagner, Dorothea; —; —; —; —; twin

Wolf; Louise Konrad Nikolaus; 2-May-62; 25-May-62; Valentin; Strebendorf, Hessen; Markel, Anna Elisabeth; —; Ruppel, Elisabeth; Asmann, Konrad; Ruppel, Nikolaus; —

Wolf; Martin Wilhelm; 8-Jan-42; 27-Feb-42; Heinrich; —; Wagner, Dorothea; —; —; —; —; twin

Wolf; Ricfine Barbara; 19-Jul-46; 13-Sep-46; Johann Michael; Haundorf, Feuchtwangen, Baiern; Ellinger, Maria Appollonia; Steinach a. d. Ens bei Rothenburg, Baiern; Ellinger, Anna Barbara; —; —; wit is aunt

Wolfangel; Anna Caroline; 14-Mar-49; 9-Apr-49; August; Minden, Preussen; Romoser, Christine; Rodensohl, Neuenbirk, Wurttemberg; Lutz, Jakobine; —; —; —

Wolfangel; Friedrich Wilhelm; 29-Jan-47; 24-May-47; August; Minden, Preussen; Romeser, Christine; Rodensohl, Wurttemberg; Lotz, Christoph; Lotz, Mrs.; —; —

Wolfangel; Hlene Christine; 25-Oct-42; 25-Dec-42; August; —; Romoser, Christine; —; —; —; —; —

Wolfangel; Johann Christian; 26-Jan-44; 23-Mar-45; Christian August; Minden, Preussen; Romoser, Anna Maria; Neuburg, Wurttemberg; Lutz, Christoph Friedr.; Lutz, Jakobine; —; —

Wolfangel; Karl Heinrich; 25-Dec-50; 9-Jun-51; Christian August; Minden, Preussen; Romesser, Christine; —; Romesser, Regine; —; —; —

Wolfangel; Maria Elisab.; 14-Jul-41; 29-Aug-41; August; —; Romoser, Christine; —; —; —; —; —

Wolff; Georg Louise; —; 14-Oct-47; Heinrich; —; Weckesser, Anna Elisabeth; —; Weckesser, Elisabeth; —; —; illegitimate

Wollenweber; Katharine; 7-Jun-42; 11-Sep-42; Johann; —; Aut, Marg.; —; —; —; —; —

Wolters; Margaretha Anna; 23-Nov-49; 7-Apr-50; Friedrich; Mermner, Hannover; Dobke, Dorothea Louise; Wagenfeld, Hannover; Johnson, Anna Marg.; —; —; wit from Hannover

Wortmann; Anna Doroth. Karol.; 18-Oct-38; 30-Dec-38; Karl; —; Fredelhacken, Magd.; —; —; —; —; —

Surname Father; Child's Given Name; Birth Date; Baptismal Date; Father's Given Name; Father's Place of Birth; Mother's Surname and Given Name; Mother's Place of Birth; Witness 1 Surname and Given Name; Witness 2 Surname and Given Name; Witness 3 Surname and Given Name; Comments

Wovneken; Friedrich Alexander; 19-Mar-56; 20-Apr-56; Luhe; Meinershausen, Hannover; Koch, Anna; —; Einwachter, Alexander; —; —; —

Wrede; Friedrich Wilhelm; 16-Nov-44; 8-Dec-44; Johann G.; —; Niemeyer, Anna M.; —; —; —; —; —

Wrede; Johann Heinrich Friedrich; 10-Apr-48; 18-Jul-48; Johann Heinrich; Freidorf, Bruchhausen, Hannover; Niemeyer, Anna Margaretha; Freidorf, Bruchhausen, Hannover; Stittelberg, Ehlert; Meyer, Heinrich Gustav; —; —

Wunder; Andreas; 2-May-48; 2-Jun-48; Conrad; Streitberg, Ebermannstadt, Baiern; Zimmermann, Elisabeth; Oberfallendorf, Ebermannstadt, Baiern; Flock, Andreas; —; —; —

Wunder; Barbara; 9-May-51; 1-Jun-51; Konrad; Streiberg, Baiern; Zimmermann, Elisabeth; —; Ruppell, Joh.; —; —; —

Wust; Christoph Heinrich; 8-Jul-49; 15-Jul-49; Johann; Jaxthausen, Wurttemberg; Hein, Elise; Schieferbach, Rauschenberg, Kurhessen; Ganer, Christoph; Carle, Christian; —; —

Wust; Friedrich Carl; 19-Oct-50; 17-Nov-50; Johann Gottfried; Jaxthausen, Wurttemberg; Hanel, Elisabeth; —; Carle, Catharina; Hauer, Christoph; —; 3 child, 3 son

Wust; Johann Christian; 14-Apr-48; 16-Apr-48; Johann; Jaxthausen, Neckarsulm, Wurttemberg; Carle, Cathar.; Jagsthausen, Neckarsulm, Wurttemberg; Carle, Christian Heinr.; Heinzmann, Heinrich; —; —

Wyneken; Ernst Friedrich; 10-Feb-47; 14-Feb-47; Friedrich Conr. Dietrich; Verden, Hannover; Buck, Soophia; Windheim, Preussen; Wyneken, Ernst; Ruperti, Ernst; Stoppenhagen, Ernst; child died

Wyneken; Maria Caroline Charlotte; 17-May-48; 21-May-48; Friedrich Conrad Dietrich; Verden, Hannover; Auck, Sophia Maria; Windheim, Preussen; Stuppenhagen, Charlotte; Wyneken, Caroline; —; —

Zeigler; Maria Friederike; 6-Aug-49; 23-Sep-49; Michael; Schrotsberg, Herbronn, Wurttemberg; Marquart, Margaretha;

Heifewindefer, Herbronn, Wurttemberg; Stumpf, Carl; Blattmer, Marie; —; —

Zeihler; [--?--]; 9-Jun-51; 29-Jun-51; Louis; Haunau, Schlesien; Felgler, Julie; —; Nix, Jakob; Steinbach, Robert; Warmuth, Sophie; —

Zeller; David Friedr.; 7-May-43; 30-Jun-43; Christoph; —; Augustin, Kathr.; —; —; —; —; —

Ziegenfelder; Karoline Marg.; 15-Oct-39; 20-Oct-39; Karl Fr.; —; Weisbrod, Anna C.; —; —; —; —; —

Ziegler; Caroline; 3-Apr-46; 3-May-46; Michael; Schrotsberg, Gerbronn; Marquard, Margarethe; Gammersfeld, Gerbronn, Wurttemberg; Wirths, Catharine Schafer; Sieck, Rosine Bohm; Kraft, Margarethe Fischer; —

Ziegler; Georg Leonhard; 18-Apr-48; 7-May-48; Johann Michael; Schrotberg, Gerbronn, Wurttemberg; Marquart, Catharine Margarethe; Hiefewude, Wurttemberg; Sies, Michael; —; —; —

Zimmermann; Eduard Adam; 7-Oct-46; 27-Dec-46; Christoph; Spitzaltheim, Diburg, Hessen; Stablein, Maria; Giesfeld, Gerlshofen, Baiern; Sommer, Eduard; —; —; —

Zimmermann; Maria Luise; 4-Jun-47; 2-Aug-47; Albrecht; Baiereuth, Baiern; Neeb, Maria; Dolla bei Coblenz, Preussen; —; —; —; —

Zink; Anna Katharine Karoline; 8-Jul-60; 22-Jul-60; Johann; Saxen, Baiern; Obelhardt, Maria Barbara; —; Friedrich, Anna; Rossel, Karl; Momberger, Katharine; —

Zink; Anna Maria Barbara; 17-Sep-58; 26-Sep-58; Johann; Sachsen, Baiern; Obelhardt, Maria Barbara; —; Friedrich, Anna Maria; Rossel, Maria Barbara; —; —

Zink; Anna Marie Friedrike; 15-Dec-62; 28-Dec-62; Johann; Saxon, Baiern; Obelhardt, Marie Barbara; —; Momberger, Marie; Friedrich, Linna; Fleischmann, Georg Friedrich; —

Zink; Catharina; 2-Apr-55; 9-Apr-55; Georg Friedrich; Neuhof, Baiern; Büttner, Rosina; —; Hoffmann, Leonhard; —; —; —

Zink; Ernst Heinrich Friedrich; 10-Feb-67; 17-Feb-67; Georg Friedrich; Neuhof, Baiern; Buttner, Eva Rosina; Langrenzren,

Baiern; Burmann, Ernst Heinrich; Engelhaupt, Anna Maria; —; —

Zink; Friedrike Wilhelmine; 16-Sep-53; 15-Oct-53; Heinrich; Flachslandern, Baiern; Renner, Friederike; —; Winter, Friederike Wilhelmine; —; —; born at see

Zink; Georg Heinrich Wilhelm; 2-Nov-56; 9-Nov-56; Goerg Friedrich; Neuhof, Baiern; Büttner, Eva Rosina; —; Bertram, Wilhelm; Kaufmann, Georg Heinrich; —; —

Zink; Georg Karl; 30-May-56; 8-Jun-56; Joh.; Saxhen, Baiern; Oberhardt, Barbara; —; Momberger, Georg; Rossel, Karl; —; —

Zink; Johann; 11-Sep-54; 17-Sep-54; Johann; Saxsen, Baiern; Obenhardt, Maria Barbara; —; Rose, Joh.; —; —; —

Zink; Johann Christian Kasten; 7-Mar-64; 20-Mar-64; Georg Friedrich; Neuhof, Baiern; Buttner, Eva Rosine; Langengrenz, Baiern; Meier, Joh. Christian; Dunker, Kasten; Hollebein, Sophie Dorothea; —

Zink; Johann Heinrich Karl; 10-Feb-67; 17-Feb-67; Georg Friedrich; Neuhof, Baiern; Buttner, Eva Rosina; Langrenzren, Baiern; Spilmann, Johann Heinrich; Brauning, Katharine; —; —

Zink; Konrad Friedrich Wilhelm; 13-Dec-58; 25-Dec-58; Georg Friedrich; Neuhof, Baiern; Büttner, Eva Rosina; —; Schulz, Conrad; Engelhaupt, Frdch. Wilh.; —; —

Zink; male child; 14-Mar-63; —; Georg Friedrich; Neuhof, Baiern; Büttner, Eva Rosine; Langrenzell, Baiern; —; —; —; stillborn child

Zink; Rosine Dorothea Dora; 26-Nov-60; 9-Dec-60; Georg Friedrich; Neuhof, Baiern; Büttner, Rosine; —; Hollebein, Sophie Dorothea Johanne; Schreiner, Sarah Barbara

Zollenhafer; Anna Catharine; 28-Nov-48; 10-Dec-48; Georg; Zollenhofen, Baiern; Schmidt, Catharina; Rossbach, Hessen; Schmidt, Catharine; —

Zwanzger; Barbara; 1-Sep-44; 13-Oct-44; Johann Georg; —; Beck, Marg.; —; —; —

Surname of Deceased; Given Name of Deceased; Date of Death; Date of Burial; Age or Date of Birth; Survivor(I), Surname, Given; Birthplace Deceased or Parent; Survivor (II), Surname, Given; Birthplace of Survivor (II); Comment

Aichele; Caroline; 8-Jun-46; 9-Jun-46; 13 Feb 1846; Aichele, Jakob; Furstenhoff, Backnang, Wuerttemberg [f]; Frank, Rosine; Gross Aschbach, Wuerttemberg [m];

Aichele; Sophia; 23-Nov-47; 24-Nov-47; 20 Jun 1847; Aichele, Jakob; Fürstenhoff, Backnang, Wuerttemberg [f]; Frank, Regina; Gross Aschbach, Wuerttemberg [m];

Albrecht; Christian Friederich; 16-Jun-45; 17-Jun-45; 36y, 11m, 3w; —; Elgehausen bei Göttingen, Hannover; —; —; —

Albrecht; stillborn daughter; 19-Sep-57; 20-Sep-57; —; Albrecht, Karl Jul.; Sangerhausen, Preussen [f]; —; —; —

Alsfels (nee Keils); Widow Elisabeth; —; 1-Nov-48; 75y; —; Hannover in Pennsylvania; —; —; —

Alt; Margarethe; 23-Feb-54; 25-Feb-54; 14y; Alt, Joh.; Windsheim, Baiern [f]; —; —; deaf mute

Amrhein; Ludwig; 4-Apr-48; 5-Apr-48; 23 Aug 1846; Amrhein, Johann; Wahlen, Alsfeld, Hessen [f]; Wahl, Elisabeth; Philadelphia [m];

Amthar; Johann Andreas; 20-Jun-63; 21-Jun-63; 1y, 1m, 3d; Amthar, Joh. Michael Andreas; —; —; —; —

Angelmeyer; Georg; 21-Jan-48; 23-Jan-48; 16 Aug 1843; Angelmeyer, Mathaus; Gundelbach, Maulbron, Wuerttemberg [f]; Lugensland, Catharina; Übtingen, Wuerttemberg [m];

Apel; Johann; 1-Jan-47; 2-Jan-47; 18 Dec 1846; Apel, Caspar; Hain, Weisman, Baiern [f]; Hopf, Margar.; Horp a.m., Zuhtenfels, Baiern [m];

Apt; Luise; 11-Jul-44; 12-Jul-44; 4 May 1842; —; —; —; —; —

Arndt; Catharina; 22-Nov-48; 23-Nov-48; 14 Nov 1848; Arndt, Jakob; Humpfershausen, Sachsen-Meiningen [f]; Betzenberger, Catharina; Tiedorf, Sachsen-Weimar [m];

Arndt; Johann; 1-Feb-47; 3-Feb-47; 27 Jan 47; Arndt, Jakob; Hempfershausen, Sachsen-Meiningen [f]; Betzenberger, Cath.; Dernbach, Sachsen-Weimar [m];

Arnold; Johann Heinrich; 7-Jul-56; 9-Jul-56; 1y, 3w, 5d; Arnold, Richard Hugo; Lommetzsch, Sachsen [f]; —; —; —

Arnold; Sophie Louise; 11-Aug-53; 12-Aug-53; 1y, 1m; Arnold, Richard Hugo; Lommatzsch, Sachsen [f]; —; —; —

Surname of Deceased; Given Name of Deceased; Date of Death; Date of Burial; Age or Date of Birth; Survivor(I), Surname, Given; Birthplace Deceased or Parent; Survivor (II), Surname, Given; Birthplace of Survivor (II); Comment

Arnold; stillborn daughter; 16-Jan-57; 16-Jan-57; —; Arnold, Richard Hugo; Lommatzsch, Sachsen [f]; —; —; —

Auermann; Eleonore Wilhelmine; 11-May-1850; 13-May-50; 9 May 1813 or 1814; Auermann, Jakob; Naumturg a.d. Saale, Sachsen; —; —; spouse

Aul; Georg; 6-May-44; 7-May-44; 14 Apr 1838; —; —; —; —; —

Axler; Elisabeth; 5-Dec-50; 5-Dec-50; 1y, 11m; Axler, Thomas; Kups, Baiern [f]; —; —; —

Bach; Georg Heinrich; 5-Jun-66; 6-Jun-66; 3m, 14d; Bach, Adam; Eckartsborn, Hessen [f]; —; —; —

Bach; Karl Heinrich Theodor; 4-Dec-60; 6-Dec-60; 3y, 6m, 11d; Bach, Adam; Eckartsborn [f]; —; —; —

Bach; premature son; 21-Dec-54; 21-Dec-54; 15min; Bach, Adam; Eckartsborn, Hessen [f]; —; —; —

Bachmann; Margarethe; 8-Apr-61; 10-Apr-61; 5y, 5m, 28d; Bachmann, Wilh. Heinrich; —; —; —; father deceased

Bader; Cyriak; 14-Jul-61; 15-Jul-61; 60y, 6m; —; Gemund, Wurttemberg; —; —; —

Baierlein; Maria Regine; 14-Dec-52; 16-Dec-52; 6y, 6m; Baierlein, Johann; Baireuth, Baiern [f]; —; —; —

Baiswanger; Wilhelm Gottfried; 15-Jun-44; 16-Jun-44; 17 Jun 1843; —; —; —; —; —

Balla; Weinhold; 19-May-38; 20-May-38; 16 Feb 1834; —; —; —; —; —

Baltz; Katharine; 4-Jul-42; 5-Jul-42; 21 Sep 1841; —; —; —; —; —

Balz; Philipine; 1-Aug-40; 2-Aug-40; 24 Aug 1839; —; —; —; —; —

Bäpler; Johannes; 29-Apr-49; 30-Apr-49; 32y; —; Helpersheim, Grünberg, Hessen; —; —; —

Barth; Michael; 24-Nov-37; 25-Nov-37; 25 Apr 1810; —; —; —; —; —

Barthold; Christian Albert; 9-Jun-50; 11-Jun-50; 6 May 1794; —; Schlerz, Sachsen; —; —

Bartholomai; Adolph Friedrich; 6-Jun-52; 6-Jun-52; 9y, 11m; Bartholomai, Christian Gottlieb; Bremen [f]; —; —

Bauer; Georg Friedrich; 11-Jul-44; 12-Jul-44; 18 Jun 1843; —; —; —; —

Surname of Deceased; Given Name of Deceased; Date of Death; Date of Burial; Age or Date of Birth; Survivor(I), Surname, Given; Birthplace Deceased or Parent; Survivor (II), Surname, Given; Birthplace of Survivor (II); Comment

Bauer; Heinrich Ludwig; 13-Aug-61; 15-Aug-61; 8m; Bauer, Georg Ludwig; Dorzbach, Wurttemberg [f]; —; —

Bauer; Henriette Wilhelmine; 18-Mar-64; 19-Mar-64; 1y, 5m; Bauer, Georg Ludwig; Tortzbach, Wurttember [f]; —; —

Bauer; Johann; 10-Aug-39; 11-Aug-39; 26 Feb 1839; —; —; —; —

Bauer; Louise Juliane; 17-Aug-57; 18-Aug-57; 9d; Bauer, Georg Ludwig; Tortzbach, Wurttemberg [f]; —; —

Bauer; Maria; 12-Jul-44; 13-Jul-44; 9 Oct 1843; —; —; —; —

Beck; Anna Elisabeth; 23-Nov-49; 24-Nov-49; 19 Feb 1846; Beck, Ernst; Wixhausen bei Darmstadt [f]; Koch, Anna Magdalena; Oberrad bei Frankfurth a.M. [m]

Beck; Ernst; 16-Aug-65; 18-Aug-65; 59y; —; Darmstadt, Hessen; —; —

Beck; Ferdinand Ludwig; 10-May-50; 12-May-50; 18 Mar 1849; Beck, Ernst; Wixhausen bei Darmstadt [f]; Koch, Anna Magdalena; Oberrad bei Frankfurt a.M. [m]

Beck; Johann Caspar; 23-Sep-55; 24-Sep-55; 14y, 2m; Beck, Joh. E. W. P.; Wirhausen, Darmstadt [f]; —; —

Beck; Karl; 3-Dec-60; 5-Dec-60; 18y, 1w; —; Darmstadt, Hessen; —; —

Beckel; Margaretha Eleonore; 3-Apr-57; 4-Apr-57; 45; —; Lisberg, Hessen; —; —

Beckemeyer; Heinrich Ludwig; 2-Sep-44; 3-Sep-44; 17 Aug 1843; —; —; —; —

Becker; Friedrich Wilh.; 5-Nov-42; 5-Nov-42; 25 Nov 1817; —; —; —; —

Becker; Johannes; 14-Feb-67; 16-Feb-67; 4y; Becker, Johannes; Grossenbusseck [f]; —; —; father deceased

Becker; Maria Sophia; 18-Jul-45; 19-Jul-45; 11m, 7d; Becker, Heinrich Ludwig; Nidda, Hessen [f]; Karnrodt, Eva Elisabeth; Dorner, Neupreussen [m];

Becker; Marie; 10-Jul-53; 11-Jul-53; 6m, 16d; Becker, Konrad; Marburg, Kurhessen [f]; —; —; —

Becker (nee Areularius); Mrs. Barbara Katharine; 1-Jul-63; 3-Jul-63; 58y, 2m, 3w; —; Marburg, Kurhessen; —; —; —

Bedker; Catharine Augustine; 24-Sep-45; 25-Sep-45; 31 Aug 1845; Bedker, Johann Peter; Kaichen, Hessen [f]; Goldeis, Eva Kunigunde; Mainleus, Obermainkens, Baiern [m];

Beitz; Heinrich; 5-Aug-49; 6-Aug-49; about 64y; —; Windhausen, Grunberg, Hessen; —; —; —

Berger; Heinrich Christian; 15-Aug-62; 16-Aug-62; 1y, 3m, 24d; Berger, Eberhard; Allendorf a.d.L, Hessen [f]; —; —; —

Bergmann; Hermann; 7-Jul-52; 8-Jul-52; 22y; —; Dannendorf, Hannover; —; —; —

Berlau; Elisabeth; 15-Jul-54; 16-Jul-54; 14w; Berlau, Johann; Rheinroth, Hessen [f]; —; —; twin

Bernhard; Elisabeth; 5-Jul-47; 6-Jul-47; 26 May 1846; Bernhard, Andreas; Unterlauda, Sachsen-Coburg [f]; Fath, Elisabeth; Klein-Umstadt, Hessen [m];

Bertram; Heinrich Johann Philipp; 9-Jun-64; 10-Jun-64; 4y, 7m, 3d; Bertram, Wilh.; Buren, Preussen [f]; —; —; —

Bertram; Johann Heinrich; 24-Aug-58; 25-Aug-58; 4w; Bertram, Wilhelm; Buren, Presusen [f]; —; —; —

Bertram; Karl Friedrich; 30-Oct-66; 31-Oct-66; 29y, 6m, 12d; —; Buren, Preussen; —; —; —

Bertram; Mrs. Anna Margaretha; 26-May-53; 27-May-53; 26y; Bertram, Wilhelm; Buren, Westphahlen; —; —; spouse

Bertram; Wilhelm; 14-Jun-53; 15-Jun-53; 19w, 2d; Bertram, Wilhelm; Buren, Westfahlen [f]; —; —; —

Bertram (nee Brock); Mrs. Therese; 11-Oct-63; 12-Oct-63; 62y, 8d; —; Buren, Preussen; —; —; —

Billmann; Barbara; 28-Sep-50; 29-Sep-50; 2y, 9m; Billmann, Johann; Egersdorf, Nurnberg [f]; —; —; —

Billmann; Elisabeth; 28-Sep-50; 29-Sep-50; 6m, 8d; Billmann, Johann; Egersdorf, Nurnberg [f]; —; —; —

Billmann; Georg; 3-Dec-46; 4-Dec-46; 26 Nov 1846; Billmann, Johann; Egersdorf, Neustadt, Reuss [f]; Riegler, Margaretha; Bingarten, Aurach, Baiern [m];

Billmann; Johann; 2-Jun-52; 3-Jun-52; 11m; Billmann, Johann; Eggersdorf, Baiern [f]; —; —; —

Billmann; Katharine Elisabeth; 3-Apr-57; 4-Apr-57; 1y, 2m; Billmann, Joh.; Elgersdorf, Baiern [f]; —; —; youngest child

Surname of Deceased; Given Name of Deceased; Date of Death; Date of Burial; Age or Date of Birth; Survivor(I), Surname, Given; Birthplace Deceased or Parent; Survivor (II), Surname, Given; Birthplace of Survivor (II); Comment

Bilmann; Elisabeth Catharina; 14-Jun-54; 15-Jun-54; 8m, 1d; Bilmann, Joh.; Egersdorf, Baiern [f]; —; —; —

Blaich; Johann Georg; 1-Aug-60; 31-Jul-60; 11m; Blaich, Johann Friedrich; —; —; —; school teacher

Blaich; Karl Robert Andreas; 27-Sep-62; 29-Sep-62; 1y, 6m, 11d; Blaich, Johann Gottfried; —; —; —; school teacher

Blittensdörfer; Johann Heinrich; 29-Oct-40; 29-Oct-40; Feb 1816; —; —; —; —; —

Blösing; Johann Friedrich; 28-Nov-63; 29-Nov-63; 66y; —; Hesselworth, Wurttemberg; —; —; —

Blum; Elisa Franzsiska; —; 17-May-53; 7y; Blum, Aug.; Zwickau, Sachsen [f]; —; —; —

Blum; Heinrich; 17-Jul-50; 19-Jul-50; 13y, 7m; Blum, Johann; Dollinghausen, Braunschweig [f]; —; —; drowned in bay

Blum (nee Heysanges); Mrs. Louise; 23-Oct-56; 24-Oct-56; 57y, 7m, 1d; —; —; —; —; —

Bohnhagen; Eva Katharine Charlotte; 7-Jul-61; 8-Jul-61; 7y, 32; Bohnhagen, Charlotte; —; —; —; illegitimate child

Bokelmann; Herrmann Heinrich; 5-Aug-45; 6-Aug-45; 9 Jan 1845; Bokelmann, Johann Heinrich; Asche [f]; Schröder, Sophie; Drebber, Diepholz, Hannover [m];

Bomhorst; Wilhelm Heinrich; 3-Mar-48; 5-Mar-48; 31y; —; Barstorff, Diepholz, Hannover; —; —; —

Boppler; Henriette Karoline Louise; 21-Jul-63; 22-Jul-63; 4m, 3w; Boppler, Heinr.; Helpersheim, Wurttemberg [f]; —; —; —

Borgelt; Hermann Heinrich; 18-Aug-56; 19-Aug-56; 74y, 15d; —; Engter, Hannover; —; —; —

Bothe; Johanne Christine; 4-Oct-62; 5-Oct-62; 16m; Bothe, Hermann Heinrich; Engter, Hannover [f]; —; —; —

Botsch; Joh. Michael Ludwig; 27-Mar-51; 28-Mar-51; 5m, 6d; Botsch, Joh. Adam; Shrotzberg, Wuerttemberg [f]; —; —; —

Botsch; Johann; 1-Jul-47; 2-Jul-47; 27 Sep 1846; Botsch, Johann Adam; Schrotberg, Gerbronn, Wuerttemberg [f]; Gschwinde, Anna Barbara; Schrotberg, Gerbronn, Wuerttemberg [m];

Böttcher; Heinrich Wilhelm; 15-Aug-44; 16-Aug-44; 56y; —; —; —; —; —

Surname of Deceased; Given Name of Deceased; Date of Death; Date of Burial; Age or Date of Birth; Survivor(I), Surname, Given; Birthplace Deceased or Parent; Survivor (II), Surname, Given; Birthplace of Survivor (II); Comment

Brand (nee Haag); Katharine; 15-Aug-42; 17-Aug-42; 10 Feb 1810; —; —; —; —; —

Brauer; Conrad; 7-Jan-54; 8-Jan-54; 4m; Brauer, Johann; Armsfeld, Waldeck [f]; —; —; only son

Brauer; Heinrich; 15-Nov-65; 17-Nov-65; 2y, 7m, 14d; Brauer, Heinrich; Lisberg, Hessen [f]; —; —; —

Brauer; Peter; 21-Mar-65; 23-Mar-65; 66y, 4m, 20d; —; Lisberg, Hessen; —; —; —

Brauer; Sophie Karoline Marie; —; 20-Jun-66; 1y, 6m; Brauer, Karl August; Lisberg, Hessen [f]; —; —; —

Bredemeier; Anna; 28-Jul-54; 29-Jul-54; 8w, 5d; Bredemeier, Frdch.; Moslingen, Preussen [f]; —; —; —

Bredemeier (nee Ameier); Mrs. Maria; 5-Jul-54; 6-Jul-54; 28y; —; Wietze, Hannover; —; —; —

Breiswanger; Johann Jacob; 24-Apr-40; 25-Apr-40; 31 Jan 1840; —; —; —; —; —

Bremer; Joh. Ludwig; 24-Dec-63; 26-Dec-63; 6y, 18d; Bremer, Joh. Andreas; —; —; —; father deceased

Brendel; Johann Heinrich; 10-Aug-48; 11-Aug-48; 16 Dec 1847; Brendel, Johann Georg; Unternichenbach, Hergozauerch, Baiern [fm]; Muller, Dorothea; Osterholz, Siette, Hannover [m];

Brendel; Johann Matthias; 21-Aug-50; 22-Aug-50; 5m; Brendel, Johann Georg; Unterrieichtbach, Baiern [f]; —; —; only child

Briegel; Mrs. Caroline; 17-Aug-50; 19-Aug-50; 21y, 3m, 17d; Briegel, Joseph Friedrich; —; —; —; consumption

Briegel; Philipine Karoline; 10-Aug-38; 11-Aug-38; 6 Jun 1838; —; —; —; —; —

Briegel; Samuel Andreas; 14-Jan-47; 15-Jan-47; 9 Dec 1845; Briegel, Johann Jakob; Feldbach, Canstadt [f]; Burk, Margaretha; Schminden, Canstadt [m];

Briehl; Johannes; 30-Aug-48; 31-Aug-48; 29 Aug 1848; Briehl, Johann; Wollmar, Melber, Kurhessen [f]; Urbach, Catharine; Schluchten, Kurhessen [m];

Briel; Ernst Wilhelm Heinrich; 27-Mar-64; 28-Mar-64; 6m, 25 d; Briel, Joh.; Wollmar, Kurhessen; —; —; twin

Surname of Deceased; Given Name of Deceased; Date of Death; Date of Burial; Age or Date of Birth; Survivor(I), Surname, Given; Birthplace Deceased or Parent; Survivor (II), Surname, Given; Birthplace of Survivor (II); Comment

Briel; Wilhelm; —; 25-Nov-65; 8d; Briel, Johann; Wollmar, Kurhessen [f]; —; —; —

Brock; Katharine Wilhelmine Karoline; —; 12-Apr-64; 1y, 8m, 10d; Brock, Gottlieb; Meiningen [f]; —; —; —

Brockmeyer; Herrmann Heinrich; 23-Dec-49; 24-Dec-49; 24 Jul 1844; Brockmeyer, Wilhelm; Burghobohausen, Hall, Preussen [f]; Brockmeyer, Catharina Marie; Burghobohausen, Hall, Preussen [m];

Broning; Friederike Marie; 13-Jan-60; 14-Jan-60; 8m; Broning, Heinr; Langenbergheim, Hessen; —; —; youngest daughter

Bröning; Heinrich; 7-Feb-66; 9-Feb-66; 39y; —; Langenbergheim, Hessen; —; —; —

Brugel; Wilhelm Jakob; 16-Jul-50; 17-Jul-50; 5m, 2w; Brugel, Joseph Friedrich; Fellbach, Wuerttemberg [f]; —; —; dysentery

Bruggemann; Friedrich; 12-Oct-61; 14-Oct-61; 54y, 10m, 10d; —; Tossen b. Einbeck, Hannover; —; —; —

Bruggemann; Gerhard Eduard; 19-Mar-51; 20-Mar-51; 4y, 2m, 9d; Bruggemann, Christian Friedrich; —; —; —; pox

Bruhl (nee Tinius); Mrs. Elisabeth; 20-Jan-53; 21-Jan-53; 57y; Bruhl, Martin; —; —; —; widow

Bruning; Hermann Heinrich; 27-Jul-53; 28-Jul-53; 45y; —; Dickel, Amt Diepholz, Hannover; —; —; —

Bruns; Johann Dietrich; 3-Sep-55; 4-Sep-55; 3y, 2m; Bruns, Joh.; Dellinghausen, Braunschweig [f]; —; —; —

Bruns; Maria Anna; 12-Aug-55; 13-Aug-55; 2m, 18d; Bruns, Johann; Dellinghause, Braunschweig [f]; —; —; —

Bruns; Mrs. Maria Dorothea; 9-Sep-55; 10-Sep-55; 28y, 11m; —; —; —; —; —

Bucking; stillborn daughter; 25-May-62; 25-May-62; —; Bucking, Franz; Marburg, Kurhessen [f]; —; —; —

Bühler; Franz; 9-Feb-40; 11-Feb-40; 11 Feb 1834; —; —; —; —; —

Bühler; Marianne; 25-Mar-44; 27-Mar-44; 27 Feb 1841; —; —; —; —; —

Burmann; Joh. Heinrich Wilhelm; 23-Dec-63; 24-Dec-63; 2y, 3m, 3w; Burmann, Ernst Heinr.; Euer, Hannover [f]; —; —; —

Surname of Deceased; Given Name of Deceased; Date of Death; Date of Burial; Age or Date of Birth; Survivor(I), Surname, Given; Birthplace Deceased or Parent; Survivor (II), Surname, Given; Birthplace of Survivor (II); Comment

Burmann; Johann Friedrich Wilhelm; 27-Jun-58; 28-Jun-58; 1y, 9m; Burmann, Ernst Heinr.; Bur, Hannover [f]; —; —; —

Burmann; stillborn daughter; 17-Jul-1867; 17-Jul-1867; 0; Burmann, Ernst Heinr.; Bur, Hannover [f]; —; —; —

Burmann; Wilhelm; 20-Jan-63; 22-Jan-63; 31y, 8m; —; Potzwenden, Hannover; —; —; —

Carle; Conrad; 8-Oct-52; 10-Oct-52; 27y; —; Niederohm, Hessen; —; —; —

Carle; Gerhard Heinrich; 28-Aug-47; 30-Aug-47; about 23y; —; Lüstringen, Osnabruck, Hannover; —; —; —

Carrey; Francis; 11-Aug-38; 11-Aug-38; 4 Apr 1837; —; —; —; —; —

Carrey; Jane; 16-Jul-1838; 17-Jul-38; 4 Sep 1837; —; —; —; —; —

Christ; Anna Martha; 19-Aug-50; 19-Aug-50; 2m; Christ, Maria; —; —; —; illegitimate

Christmann; Michael; 6-Jun-44; 8-Jun-44; 56y; —; —; —; —; —

Claridge; Catharine; 30-Jun-46; 1-Jul-46; 80y; —; —; —; —; 35 Jahr Mittwergewesen

Claridge; Henry; 5-Apr-46; 6-Apr-46; 52y, 1d; —; —; —; —; —

Conrad; Jakob; 12-Apr-54; 14-Apr-54; 73y, 7m; —; Grossaschdorf, Wuerttemberg; —; —; —

Crome; Johann Friedr; 18-Jul-38; 19-Jul-38; 29 Jan 1838; —; —; —; —; —

Dankmeier; Heinrich Theodor; 1-Dec-65; 3-Dec-65; 3y, 5m; Dankmeier, Joh. Frdch; Robber, Hannover [f]; —; —; —

Dannettel; Mrs. Isabella; 7-Aug-50; 8-Aug-50; 28y, 5m; Dannettel, Heinrich Ludwig; —; —; —; pox

Dannettel; Mrs. Maria Martharetha; 29-Aug-50; 30-Aug-50; 39y, 7m; Dannettel, Heinrich; —; —; —; spouse

Deckert; Johann Ernst; 16-Jul-66; 17-Jul-66; 6m; Deckert, August; Winkel, Wiemar [f]; —; —; —

Dehfing; Maria Adelheid; 30-Apr-48; 1-May-48; 31 Jul 1847; Dehfing, Johann; Quakenbruck, Hannover [f]; Imwolde, Catharine; Quackenbruck, Hannover [m];

Dehfing (nee Imwolde); Catharine; 14-Aug-47; 15-Aug-47; 31 Dec 1827; Dehfing, Johann; Quackenbruck, Hannover; —; —; —

Deifel; Marianne; 4-Aug-43; 5-Aug-43; 54y; —; —; —; —; —

Surname of Deceased; Given Name of Deceased; Date of Death; Date of Burial; Age or Date of Birth; Survivor(I), Surname, Given; Birthplace Deceased or Parent; Survivor (II), Surname, Given; Birthplace of Survivor (II); Comment

Desaga; Joseph; 25-Aug-50; 26-Aug-50; 61y; —; Bensheim, Hessen; —; —; —

Desaga; Mrs. Philippine; 21-Jul-50; 22-Jul-50; 64y; Desaga, Joseph; —; —; —; liver disease

Dickel; Chrisian; 25-Feb-62; 27-Feb-62; 8y, 1m; Dickel, Konrad; Romeroth, Hessen [f]; —; —; oldest son

Dickel; Elisabeth; 25-Apr-61; 26-Apr-61; 2y, 10m; Dickel, Konrad; Romeroth, Hessen [f]; —; —; youngest child

Diering; Maria Katharine; 24-Jul-63; 26-Jul-63; 7m, 1w, 3d; Diering, Heinr. Ludwig; Baltimore, MD [f]; —; —; —

Dieterle; Christoph; 15-May-48; 16-May-48; 37y; —; Enzingen, Faigenheim, Wuerttemberg; —; —; —

Dieterle; Jakob; 31-Jan-50; 2-Feb-50; 6 Oct 1844; Dieterle, Jakob; Furstenhoff, Backenang, Wuerttemberg [f]; Frank, Regina; Grossenaschbach, Wuerttemberg [m];

Dieterle; Jakob Carl; 9-May-45; 11-May-45; 12 Nov 1783; —; Ensingen, Wuerttemberg; —; —; —

Dieterle; Maria Catharine; 7-Feb-50; 10-Feb-50; 24 Aug 1839; Dieterle, Christoph; Ensingen, Weisingen, Wuerttemberg [f]; Hildebrandt, Maria; Bleichanbach, Hessen [m];

Dieterle (nee Klopp); Rosine Barbara; 5-Oct-43; 6-Oct-43; 4 Mar 1778; —; —; —; —; —

Dietert; Heinrich; 28-Oct-41; 29-Oct-41; 12 Jun 1839; —; —; —; —; —

Dietrich; Elisabeth; 17-Jun-44; 18-Jun-44; 2 Apr 1844; —; —; —; —; —

Dietrich; Elisabeth; 14-Jun-49; 14-Jun-49; 14 Jun 1849; Dietrich, Leonhard; Marburg, Kurhessen [f]; Schneider, Friederike; Bermasins, Rheinbaiern [m]; lived one hour

Dietrich; Heinrich; 6-Aug-54; 7-Aug-54; 1y, 16d; Dietrich, Heinr.; Marburg, Kurhessen [f]; —; —; —

Dietrich; Johann Heinrich; 5-Feb-46; 6-Feb-46; 29 Aug 1845; Dietrich, Leonhard; Marburg, Kurhessen [f]; Schneider, Friederike; Permasens bei Zweibrucken [m];

Dietz; Christian Gottfried; 10-Mar-1867; 11-Mar-1867; 17y, 5w; Dietz, Andreas; Jaxthausen, Wurttemberg [f]; —; —; oldest son

Surname of Deceased; Given Name of Deceased; Date of Death; Date of Burial; Age or Date of Birth; Survivor(I), Surname, Given; Birthplace Deceased or Parent; Survivor (II), Surname, Given; Birthplace of Survivor (II); Comment

Dietz; Christian Karl; 16-Sep-59; 17-Sep-59; 10m, 15d; Dietz, Georg Andreas; Jaxthausen, Wurttemberg [f]; —; —; youngest child

Dietz; Johann Gottfried; 18-Sep-59; 19-Sep-59; 7m, 5d; Dietz, Georg Tobias; Jaxthausen, Wurttemberg [f]; —; —; youngest child

Dietz; Johanne Barbara; 25-Jun-55; 26-Jun-55; 6m, 2w; Dietz, Georg Tobias; Jaxthausen, Wuerttemberg [f]; —; —; —

Dietz; Wilhelm; 19-Jun-65; 21-Jun-65; 29y, 2w, 2d; —; Westerburg, Hessen Nassau; —; —; —

Dirrenberger; Georg; 8-Sep-44; 9-Sep-44; 16 Jan 1813; —; —; —; —; —

Doberer; Johann Christian; 24-Dec-43; 25-Dec-43; 1 Sep 1841; —; —; —; —; —

Doberer; Luise Dorothea; 26-Aug-48; 27-Aug-48; 16 Sep 1839; Doberer, Johann; Lehnenberg, Waiblingen, Wuerttemberg [f]; Ackermann, Anna Maria; Lehnenberg, Waibling, Wuerttemberg [m];

Dobler; Karl Heinrich Dorotheus; 4-Sep-63; 6-Sep-63; 21y, 7m, 8d; —; —; —; —; member St. Peter's English Lutheran

Dobler (nee Ihler); Mrs. Christine; 17-Jun-1867; 18-Jun-1867; 63y, 7d; —; Karnetestheim, Wurttemberg; —; —; —

Doktor; Friedrich Wilhelm; 11-Apr-49; 12-Apr-49; 30y; —; Kirchspiel, Buhren, Gruneberg, Hannover; —; —; —

Dolch; Margaretha; 20-Jan-48; 21-Jan-48; 9 Sep 1847; Dolch, Conrad; Trefurth, Preussen [f]; Freitag, Maria; Trefurth, Preussen [m];

Dölfel; Carl; 17-Feb-46; 18-Feb-46; 14 Feb 1846; Dölfel, Friedrich; Dibbeck bei Neustadt a.d. Reuss [f]; Mathail, Elisabeth; Theldweiler, Bermisen, Baiern [m];

Donges; Elisabeth; 30-Jun-50; 1-Jul-50; 1766 (?); —; Bleichenbach, Nidda, Hessen; —; —; —

Donges; stillborn son; 5-Jun-1867; 5-Jun-1867; 0; Donges, Heinrich; Bleichenbach, Hessen [f]; —; —; —

Dörr; Friedrich; 26-Jul-54; 27-Jul-54; 6y; Dörr, Joh.; Wuerttemberg [f]; —; —; —

Surname of Deceased; Given Name of Deceased; Date of Death; Date of Burial; Age or Date of Birth; Survivor(I), Surname, Given; Birthplace Deceased or Parent; Survivor (II), Surname, Given; Birthplace of Survivor (II); Comment

Dörr (nee Muller); Johanna Christiana Elisabeth; 13-Feb-50; 15-Feb-50; 26 Dec 1807; Dörr, Johann Leonhard; Holzern, Weinsberg, Wuerttemberg; —; —; widow

Dörrenberger; Philipp Georg; 2-Jul-45; 3-Jul-45; 11 Oct 1841; Dörrenberger, Christian; —; Riehl, Saloma; Niedernmodern bei Pforffenhofen, Elsass [m];

Dunker; Johann Heinrich Christian; 5-Aug-57; 6-Aug-57; 7w; Dunker, Kasten Heinr.; Mattfelde, Hannover, [f]; —; —; —

Dunker; Johann Karl Wilhelm; 6-Mar-67; 8-Mar-67; 8m,16d; Dunker, Kasten Heinrich; Martfeld, Hannover; —; —; youngest son

Dürr; Johann; 28-Jun-42; 29-Jun-42; 23 Oct 1816; —; —; —; —;

Eberhard; Ludwig; 14-Aug-45; 15-Aug-45; 26 Nov 1842; Eberhard, Friedrich; —; Reitz, Sophia; Bielsteck bei Saarbruck;

Eberle; Johann Jacob Friedr; 6-Aug-43; 7-Aug-43; 28 Nov 1841; —; —; —; —; —

Eberle; Wilhelm; 30-Mar-51; 1-Apr-51; 2y, 3m; Eberle, Friedrich; Stuttgart [f]; —; —; measles

Ebert; Gottfried; 13-Oct-54; 14-Oct-54; 75; —; Brumath b. Strassburg; —; —; —

Ebert; Mrs. Anna Amalie; 3-Mar-63; 5-Mar-63; 80y, 3m; —; Brumoth, Elsass; —; —; —

Eckardt; Johann August Andreas; 12-Aug-62; 13-Aug-62; 3y, 3w, 3d; Eckardt, Johann; Nidda, Hessen [f]; —; —; —

Eckardt; Johann Wilhelm; 23-May-57; 25-May-57; 2y, 8m, 5d; Eckardt, Joh.; Nidda, Hessen [f]; —; —; —

Eckart; Elisabeth Wilhelmine; 22-Dec-65; 26-Dec-65; 1y, 8m; Eckart, Johann; Nidda, Hessen [f]; —; —; —

Eckart; Friedricke; 6-Aug-50; 7-Aug-50; 1y, 7m; Eckart, Ernst; Herrndorf, Sachsen-Altenburg [f]; —; —; third daughter

Eckhard; Johann; 29-Jul-42; 30-Jul-42; 18 Oct 1818; —; —; —; —; drowned

Egger; Georg Heinrich; 3-Aug-57; 5-Aug-57; 62y; —; Walbrechtshausen, Hannover; —; —; —

Surname of Deceased; Given Name of Deceased; Date of Death; Date of Burial; Age or Date of Birth; Survivor(I), Surname, Given; Birthplace Deceased or Parent; Survivor (II), Surname, Given; Birthplace of Survivor (II); Comment

Egger; Wilhelm; 5-Jul-45; 5-Jul-45; 7 Aug 1844; Egger, Heinrich; Cassel [f]; Butzmer, Catharine; Schweinsberg bei Marburg [m]; between 1-2 o'clock

Einwächter; Anna Maria; 10-Aug-1838; 10-Aug-38; 22 Nov 1837; —; —; —; —; —

Einwächter; Catharina Margaretha; 28-Oct-45; 29-Oct-45; 24 Jul 1838; Einwächter, Georg Alex.; Niederohm, Grunberg, Hessen [f]; Häger, Cath.; Langensteinbach, Baden [m];

Einwächter; Elisabeth; 11-Aug-52; 12-Aug-52; 2y, 2m; Einwächter, Adam; Niederohm, Hessen [f]; —; —; —

Einwächter; Maria; 5-Jan-52; 6-Jan-52; 6y, 11m; Einwächter, Alexander & Catharine; —; —; —; —

Eitel; Philipp; 1-Oct-61; 2-Oct-61; 68y, 5m, 5d; —; Dollwingen, Lothringen; —; —; —

El; Johann Friedrich; 2-Jan-51; 3-Jan-51; 2y, 2m; El, Joseph; Warenbrunn, Baiern [f]; —; —; —

Emmerich; Anna Margarethe; 17-Feb-62; 18-Feb-62; 2y, 1m; Emmerich, Georg; Bleichenbach, Hessen [f]; —; —; father deceased

Emmerich; Elisabeth; 21-May-62; 23-May-62; 9y, 7m, 6d; Emmerich, Georg; Bleichenbach, Hessen; —; —; oldest daughter, father deceased

Emmerich; Heinrich; 31-Jan-50; 2-Feb-50; 11 Feb 1829; —; Bleichenbach, Hessen; —; —; —

Emmerich; Johann; 28-Jan-44; 29-Jan-44; 4 Sep 1843; —; —; —; —; —

Engel; Mathaus; 23-Dec-43; 24-Dec-43; about 80y; —; —; —; —; —

Engelhaupt; stillborn son; 1-Dec-56; 1-Dec-56; —; Engelhaupt, Friedr. Wilh.; Belzig, Preussen [f]; —; —; —

Erbe; Heinrich Georg; 7-Aug-51; 8-Aug-51; 1y, 7m, 17d; Erbe, Heinrich; Sterkelshausen, Kurhessen [f]; —; —; —

Ermold; Georg Michael; 13-Jan-60; 15-Jan-60; 47y, 3w, 2d; —; Jaxthausen, Wurttemberg; —; —; —

Ermold; Maria Elise; 1-Jun-47; 3-Jun-47; 18 Feb 1846; Ermold, Johann Christoph; —; Lux, Maria Christine; —; —

Surname of Deceased; Given Name of Deceased; Date of Death; Date of Burial; Age or Date of Birth; Survivor(I), Surname, Given; Birthplace Deceased or Parent; Survivor (II), Surname, Given; Birthplace of Survivor (II); Comment

Ernst; August; 1-Mar-64; 3-Mar-64; 17y, 5m; Baltimore, MD; —; —; —;

Ernst; Georg Christoph Martin; 3-Mar-49; 5-Mar-49; 26 Aug 1818; —; Steben, Keila, Baiern; —; —; —

Ernst; Marie Katharine; 21-Jan-63; 22-Jan-63; 13y, 6m; —; Baltimore, MD; —; —; —

Eschrich; Johann Andreas; 1-Aug-51; 2-Aug-51; 1y, 3m; Eschrich, Georg; Arnstadt, Schwartzb. Sondershausen; —; —; —

Farenau; Maria; 2-Jan-42; 3-Jan-42; 16y; —; —; —; —; —

Fashler; Catharine Karoline; 10-Jan-46; 11-Jan-46; 8 Aug 1844; Fashler, Heinrich; Zaisersweiler, Maulbronn [f]; Mauthin [?], Cath.; Elbronn, Wuerttemberg [m]; died 1 o'clock

Fassler; Philip Gottlieb; 13-Apr-43; 14-Apr-43; 26 Jun 1842; —; —; —; —; —

Fath; Maria Magdalene; 9-Aug-48; 10-Aug-48; 23 Apr 1847; Fath, Heinrich; Klein-Umstadt, Diburg, Hessen [f]; Oster, Maria Magdalena; Schopp, Waldfischbach, Baiern [m];

Faust (Wittmann); Widow Catharine; 6-Aug-48; 7-Aug-48; Jan 1763; —; Lancaster, PA; —; —; —

Feger; Friedrich Wilhelm; 14-Nov-51; 16-Nov-51; 1y; Feger, Joseph; Wuerttemberg [f]; —; —; —

Feger; Josephine; 26-Aug-50; 27-Aug-50; 2y; Feger, Joseph; Ulm, Wuerttemberg [f]; —; —; youngest daughter

Feger; Wilhelm; 25-Aug-50; 27-Aug-50; 11y; Feger, Joseph; —; —; —; drowned

Fetesturm; Elisabeth; 17-Jun-63; 18-Jun-63; 24y; —; Useborn, Hessen; —; —; —

Fetting; Anna Sophia; 18-Feb-50; 20-Feb-50; 3 Dec 1843; Fetting, Johann Friedrich; Schwedt in der Ukermark [f]; Meyers, Sophia; Bossum, Diepholz, Hannover [m];

Fetting; Johann Heinrich; 5-Feb-50; 7-Feb-50; 24 Apr 1846; Fetting, Johann Friedrich; Schwert, Ukermarkt, Preussen [f]; Meyers, Sophia; Bossum, Diepholz, Hannover [m];

Fick; Jakob; 22-Sep-51; 23-Sep-51; 8y, 9m; Fick, Georg Adam; Memmelsdorf, Baiern [f]; —; —; from exposure [?]

Filbert; Sophia Elisabeth; 21-Mar-48; 22-Mar-48; 2 April 1848; Filbert, Georg; Eschau, Baiern [f]; Medinger, Dorothea; Reinsthal, Wuerttemberg [m];

Filbert (nee Medinger); Anna Dorothea; 19-May-49; 20-May-49; 20 Feb 1818; Filbert, Georg; Staten in Remsthal, Wurttemberg; —; —; —

Filpert; Gertrud; 4-May-53; 5-May-53; 66y; Filpert, Andreas; —; —; —; bur: Baltimore Cem.

Filpert; Johannes; 6-Jul-53; 7-Jul-53; 16m; Filpert, Georg; Eschau, Baiern; —; —; twin, bur: Baltimore Cem.

Finkbohner; Jakob; 4-Sep-46; 5-Sep-46; 1808; —; Silz am Neckar, Wurttemberg; —; —; —

Finke; Margarethe Wilhelmine; 11-Sep-48; 12-Sep-48; 27 Feb 1848; Finke, Friederich; Diepholz, Hannover [f]; Winkelmann, Margarethe; Kirischpiel, Essen, Oldenberg [m];

Fischer; Catharina Elisabeth; 21-Sep-45; 23-Sep-45; 23 Oct 1844; Fischer, Ernst; Sickingen, Baden [f]; Schröder, Helena; Wachendorf, Sieke, Hannover [m];

Fischer; Georg; 27-Oct-45; 28-Oct-45; 49y, 1d; —; Riberg, Baden; —; —; —

Fischer; Heinriette Agnes; 2-Sep-40; 2-Sep-40; 25 Jul 1840; Rev. J. H. Fischer [f]; —; —; —; —

Fischer; Johann; 6-Aug-38; 7-Aug-38; —; —; —; —; —; —

Fischer; Martin; 23-Jun-49; 24-Jun-49; 18 May 1805; —; Pommersfelden, Hochstadt, Baiern; —; —; —

Fischer; Mrs. Elisabeth; 10-Feb-54; 12-Feb-54; 45y; —; Oberndorf, Hochstadt a.d. Esch; —; —; —

Fischhaupt (nee Koch); Catharina; 18-Feb-48; 20-Feb-48; 13 Dec 1816; Fischhaupt, Eberhard; Borken, Homberg; —; —; —

Flauaus; Heinrich; 13-Sep-63; 14-Sep-63; 33y, 3w; —; Hergersdorf, Hessen; —; —; —

Flauaus; Wilh. Gottlieb Heinrich; 5-Mar-64; 6-Mar-64; 4d; Flauaus, Heinr.; —; —; —; father deceased

Flemming; Immanuel Gottlieb; 6-Oct-66; 8-Oct-66; 57y, 5m, 2d; —; Grunberg, Hessen; —; —; —

Fluhardt; Rosine; 22-Jun-58; 23-Jun-58; 3m; Fluhardt, Andreas; —; —; —; Konrad Repp foster father

Surname of Deceased; Given Name of Deceased; Date of Death; Date of Burial; Age or Date of Birth; Survivor(I), Surname, Given; Birthplace Deceased or Parent; Survivor (II), Surname, Given; Birthplace of Survivor (II); Comment

Folks; Heinrich; 7-Mar-45; 9-Mar-45; 14m, 7d; Folkes, Nicholaus; —; [--?--], Elisabeth; —; —

Förster; Rosina Magdalena; 21-Aug-50; 22-Aug-50; 2y; Förster, Johann Leonhard; Kunzendorf, Baiern [f]; —; —; —

Förtsch; Anna Elise Johanna; 14-Aug-46; 15-Aug-46; 5 Aug 1846; Förtsch, Joh. Georg; Rothof, Baiern [f]; Hoffmann, Henrieke Wilhelmine; Coburg [m];

Fossberger; Augustins Dorothe Julianne; 3-Aug-61; 4-Aug-61; 4m, 4w, 2d; Fossberger, Aug. Frdch.; —; —; —; illegitimate child

Foy (nee Büschel); Katharina; 25-Mar-39; 26-Mar-39; Feb 1768; —; —; —; —; —

Frank; Gottfried; 16-May-40; 17-May-40; 8 July 1803; —; —; —; —

Franke; Jakob; 23-Feb-51; 24-Feb-51; 8d; Franke, Christian Ludwig; Grossaschbach, Wuerttemberg [f]; —; —

Franke; Johann Wilhelm; 18-Jul-51; 20-Jul-51; 1y, 2m, 12d; Franke, Herm. Wilhelm; Diessen b. Osnabruck [f]; —; —

Freinhagen; Christoph; 18-Nov-49; 20-Nov-49; about 68y; —; Deljehausen [?], Uslar, Hannover; —; —

Freudenberg; Maria; 20-Jun-41; 21-Jun-41; 3 Nov 1839; —; —; —; —

Freudenberg; Martin; 15-May-1850; 16-May-50; 1815; —; Eschau bei Aschaffenburg, Bayern; —; —

Freudenberger; Eva; 13-Feb-46; 14-Feb-46; 14 Nov 1842; Freudenberger, Martin; Eschau bei Aschaffenburg, Baiern [f]; Ruhl, Maria; Steinberg bei Giessen [m]

Friedrich; Hanna; 9-Jun-39; 10-Jun-39; 85y; —; —; —; —

Fritz; Johann; 15-Jan-54; 16-Jan-54; 2y, 4m, 16d; Fritz, Joh.; Eberbach, Wuerttemberg [f]; —; —

Fritz; Johann Adam Thomas; 25-Jul-56; 26-Jul-56; 11m, 3w, 5d; Fritz, Michael; Ebersbach, Wuerttemberg [f]; —; —

Fritz; Katharina; 8-Jun-50; 9-Jun-50; 21 Dec 1849; Fritz, Johann; Eberbach, Kinzelsau, Wuerttemberg [f]; Vogel, Magdalena; Aufdemthal, Grafenberg, Bayern [m]

Fritz; stillborn daughter; 11-May-56; 12-May-56; —; Fritz, Joh.; Ebersbach, Wuerttemberg [f]; —; —

Fritze; stillborn son; 30-Mar-54; 30-Mar-54; —; Fritze, Michael; Eberbach, Wuerttemberg [f]; —; —

Fuchs; Eleonore Marie Christiane; 1-Jun-64; 2-Jun-64; 5m; Fuchs, Heinr.; Frankenberg, Kurhessen [f]; —; —

Fuchs; Marie; 24-Nov-60; 25-Nov-60; 6m; Fuchs,Heinrich; Frandenberg, Kurhessen [f]; —; —

Funk; Marie Wilhelmine; 27-Jun-66; 28-Jun-66; 1y, 10m; Funk, Rudolph; Wetter, Kurhessen [f]; —; —

Funk; Rudolph; 20-Feb-59; 21-Feb-59; 1y, 10m, 3w; Funk, Rudolph; Wetter, Kurhessen [f]; —; —; —

Gahm; Friedrich Wilhelm; 1-Mar-61; 3-Mar-61; 3m, 2d; Gahm, Georg; Trifftshausen, Wurttemberg [f]; —; —; youngest son

Gam; Catharine; 1-May-52; 2-May-52; 12w; Gam, Leonhardt; Wuerttemberg [f]; —; —; only child

Gantinbein; Johann Michael; 21-Aug-39; 22-Aug-39; not given; —; —; —; —; —; —

Gantinbein; Sophie Kathr.; 12-Jul-38; 13-Jul-38; 2 Apr 1837; —; —; —; —; —

Gantner; Joh. Conrad; 25-Dec-45; 26-Dec-45; 31 Dec 1842; Gantner, Johann; Lauffen, Wuerttemberg [f]; Loos, Elisabeth Cath.; Bernsburg, Hessen [m];

Garde; Heinrich; 8-Oct-53; 10-Oct-53; 1y, 3m, 4d; Garde, Johann; Kurhessen [f]; —; —; father deceased, bur: Baltimore Cem

Garthe; Johannes; 21-Jul-52; 22-Jul-52; 24y, 5m, 3d; —; Heismar, Kurhessen; —; —; —

Gärtner; Regina; 24-May-39; 24-May-39; 6 Aug 1834; —; —; —; —; —

Gärtner; Wilhelm; 22-May-39; 24-May-39; 12 Dec 1835; —; —; —; —; —

Gauss; Carl; 14-May-48; 16-May-48; 11 Feb 1844; Gauss, Emanuel Friedrich; Hildritzhausen, Herrenberg, Wuerttemberg [f]; Kiehl, Elisabeth; Babenhausen, Hessen [m];

Gauss; Marie; 8-Aug-47; 9-Aug-47; 30 Jul 1847; Gauss, Friedrich Emanuel; Hildritzhausen, Herrenberg, Wuerttemberg [f]; Kuhl, Elisabeth; Bebenhausen, Hessen [m];

Surname of Deceased; Given Name of Deceased; Date of Death; Date of Burial; Age or Date of Birth; Survivor(I), Surname, Given; Birthplace Deceased or Parent; Survivor (II), Surname, Given; Birthplace of Survivor (II); Comment

Geiger; Anna Eva; 4-Feb-49; 5-Feb-49; 17 Apr 1798; Geiger, Wilhelm; Rauschenberg, Kirchheim, Kurhessen; —; —; died at 4:30

Geiger; Helene; 22-Mar-47; 24-Mar-47; 5 Dec 1828; Geiger, Wilhelm; Rauschenberg, Kurhessen [f]; Heckert, Anna Eva; Rauschenberg, Kurhessen [m];

Geigle; Luise; 1-Jan-46; 2-Jan-46; 1 Nov 1844; Geigle, Johann; Affringen, Wuerttemberg [f]; Luginsland, Carline; Ebdingen, Wuerttemberg [m]; Maria Catharine in bapt record

Gent; Luise; 17-Jun-43; 20-Jun-43; 1 Jan 1843; —; —; —; —;

Gerlach; Johann Konrad; 22-Feb-51; 23-Feb-51; 11y; Gerlach, Peter; Dietelsheim, Hessen [f]; —; —; killed by train

Gerlach; Maria Catharine; 27-Jul-49; 28-Jul-49; 6 Jun 1849; Gerlach, Peter; Dittelsheim bei Hanau, Hessen [f]; Schüsel, Margareth; Dittelsheim bei Hanau, Hessen [m];

Gerlach; Mrs. Margarethe; 18-Aug-62; 20-Aug-62; 51y, 6m; —; Dittelsheim, Hessen; —; —; —

Germuth; Andreas; 13-May-62; 15-May-62; 37y; —; Eschau, Baiern; —; —; —

Gingnagel; Johann Ludwig; 18-Mar-47; 17-Mar-47; Aug 1783; —; Crumstadt, Darmstadt; —; —; —

Ginnagel (nee Ehrenfels); Mrs. Anna Marie; 27-May-61; 28-May-61; 75y, 1m; —; Grumbach, Hessen; —; —; —

Glassner; Catharine; 25-Oct-50; 25-Oct-50; 2y, 3m; Glassner, Ernst Friedrich; Dreichtlingen, Mittelfranken [f]; —; —; pox

Glassner; Johann Georg; 24-Oct-50; 24-Oct-50; 2m; Glassner, Ernst Friedrich; Dreichtlingen, Mittelfranken [f]; —; —; pox

Göbel; Katharine; 27-May-53; 28-May-53; 9m, 18d; Göbel, Martin; Felda, Hessen [f]; —; —; —

Goener; Herm. Heinrich; 19-Nov-48; 21-Nov-48; 4 Dec 1801; —; Kirchspiel, Rehme bei Bilefeld, Preussen; —; —; —

Göflich; Barbara; 11-Mar-43; 12-Apr-43; 29 May 1763; —; —; —; —; Mar is probably an error

Gontrom; Christian; 8-Oct-45; 10-Oct-45; 6 Feb 1792; —; Oberofleiden, Homberg, Hessen; —; —; Jerusalem Lutheran Cemetery

Surname of Deceased; Given Name of Deceased; Date of Death; Date of Burial; Age or Date of Birth; Survivor(I), Surname, Given; Birthplace Deceased or Parent; Survivor (II), Surname, Given; Birthplace of Survivor (II); Comment

Götz; Margaretha; 14-May-44; 15-May-44; —; —; —; —; —; —

Gräf (nee Riemenschneider); Widow Engel; —; 30-Dec-1847; 96y, 10m, 1d; —; Aldensen, Braunschweig; —; —; —

Gross; Johann Emanuel; 7-Aug-49; 8-Aug-49; 14 Jan 1849; Gross, Jakob Wilhelm; Baltimore, MD [f]; Hender, Friederike; Eselshaltershoff bei Schönbach, Wuerttemberg [m];

Gruner; Catharina; 5-Apr-50; 6-Apr-50; 17 Oct 1845; Gruner, Georg Friedrich; Wilferdingen bei Carlsruh, Baden [f]; Seidel, Carolina; Hinterweidenthal bei Birmasens [m];

Grüner; Friederich; 23-Jun-49; 24-Jun-49; 18 May 1806; —; Wilferdingen, Baden; —; —; —

Guehl; Konrad; 30-May-43; 31-May-43; 33y; —; —; —; —; —

Gunther; Marie Margarethe; 27-May-64; 28-May-64; 23y, 2w; —; Weidenschlagel, Baiern; —; —; —

Guth (nee Knödberin); Christine Friederike; 10-Apr-46; 12-Apr-46; 17 Dec 1779; Guth, Georg; Backnang, Wuerrtemberg; —; —; —

Hammann; Elisabeth; 24-Aug-45; 25-Aug-45; 15 Dec 1825; —; Bobenhausen, Grunberg, Hessen; —; —; —

Hammann; Johannes; 16-Jul-45; 17-Jul-45; 24 Feb 1807; —; —; —; —; sudden death

Hammann; Peter; 12-Aug-45; 13-Aug-45; 6 Aug 1845; Hamman, Johannes; —; Bauerle, Anna Barbara; —; —

Hammann (nee Kauter); Elisabeth Dorothea; 16-Oct-40; 17-Oct-40; 20 Jan 1775; —; —; —; —; —

Hammel; Margaretha; 21-Mar-42; 23-Mar-42; 27 Jun 1838; —; —; —; —; —

Hammer; Johann David Friedr.; 20-Dec-41; 21-Dec-41; 11 Oct 1841; —; —; —; —; —

Harris; Heinrich; 29-Jul-42; 30-Jul-42; between 30-40y; —; —; —; —; —

Hartmann; Charlotte Magd.; 25-Sep-40; 26-Sep-40; 19 Mar 1840; —; —; —; —; —

Hauber; Franziska; 27-Jan-48; 28-Jan-48; 23 Oct 1847; Hauber, Philipp; Schriesheim, Baden [f]; Kuhl, Anna Margaretha; Weidehausen bei Metzlar, Preussen [m];

Surname of Deceased; Given Name of Deceased; Date of Death; Date of Burial; Age or Date of Birth; Survivor(I), Surname, Given; Birthplace Deceased or Parent; Survivor (II), Surname, Given; Birthplace of Survivor (II); Comment

Hauff; Christoph Friedrich; 27-May-48; 28-May-48; 12 Dec 1847; Hauff, Christoph Friedrich; —; Welte, Rosine; Aschenbach,, Calw, Wuerttemberg [m];

Hausler; Martha; 10-Dec-49; 11-Dec-49; 17 Apr 1847; Hausler, Johann; Kleinmünster, Hasfurth, Baiern [f]; Sachs, Margaretha; Melzungen, Kurhessen [m];

Hayerl; Eduard Adolph; 5-Aug-45; 6-Aug-45; 1 May 1844; Hayerl, Ferdinand Adolph; Donbra, Sachsen [f]; Bansmer, Maria Amalia; Danzig [m];

Haynel [?]; Carl Heinrich; 30-Aug-46; 2-Sep-46; 11w; Haynel [?], Dr. Ferd. Adolph; Donbra, Sachsen [f]; Bausemer, Marie Amalia; Domzig [m];

Heberle; Johann; 22-May-47; 29-May-47; 43y; —; Rosenthal, Frankenberg, Kurhessen; —; —; drowned

Hebler; Adam; 24-Sep-48; 25-Sep-48; 22 Feb 1808; —; Rosenthal bei Marburg, Kurhessen; —; —; —

Heck; Catharina; 20-Apr-48; 21-Apr-48; 14 Feb 1848; Heck, Andreas; Egloffstein, Grafenburg, Baiern [f]; Keilholz, Barbara; Bieberbach, Bodenstein [m];

Heck; Christine Sophie; 17-Jul-59; 18-Jul-59; 3w, 1d; Heck, Georg Karl Louis; Oberkirchen, Kurhessen [f]; —; —; youngest daughter

Heck; Friedrich Heinrich Andreas; 12-Dec-58; 14-Dec-58; 3y, 10m, 14d; Heck, Georg; Neuenkirchen, Hannover [f]; —; —; —

Heck; Sophie Louise; 19-Jul-65; 20-Jul-65; 5w, 4d; Heck, Karl Louis; Obernkirchen, Kurhessen [f]; —; —; —

Heck; stillborn daughter; 18-Sep-50; 18-Sep-50; —; Heck, Wilhelm; Oberkirchen, Kurhessen [f]; —; —; —

Heck; Thomas; 19-Aug-56; 20-Aug-56; 6y, 3m; Heck, Joh.; Kuhnreut, Baiern [f]; —; —; —

Hecker; Mrs. Katharine Elisabeth; 21-Jun-58; 22-Jun-58; 89y; —; Lehrelbach, Kurhessen; —; —; —

Heinlein; Marie Katharine; 14-Aug-57; 15-Aug-57; 1y, 10d; Heinlein, Joh.; Margrudof, Baiern [f]; —; —; only daughter

Heinlein; Mrs. Katharine; 26-Dec-56; 27-Dec-56; 54y; Heinlein, Michael; Burkersdorf, Baiern; —; —; spouse

Surname of Deceased; Given Name of Deceased; Date of Death; Date of Burial; Age or Date of Birth; Survivor(I), Surname, Given; Birthplace Deceased or Parent; Survivor (II), Surname, Given; Birthplace of Survivor (II); Comment

Heins; Johann Heinrich; 22-Sep-48; 23-Sep-48; 15 Sep 48; Heins, Heinrich; Schornsheim, Hessen [f]; Weber, Elisabeth; Bernsburg, Hessen [m];

Heintz; Johannes; 22-Apr-51; 24-Apr-51; 37y; —; Burgsinn, Baiern; —; —; car accident

Heistermann (nee Konmond); Mrs. Sophie; 30-Oct-52; 1-Nov-52; 42y; —; Amt Bossum, Hannover; —; —; —

Heldmann; Elisabeth; 17-Sep-40; 18-Sep-40; 63y; —; —; —; —; —

Hellbig; Sophia; 25-May-54; 26-May-54; 1y, 11m, 4d; Hellbig, Louis; Lubbeke, Preussen [f]; —; —; —

Hellenthal; Mrs. Katharine; 14-Feb-62; 16-Feb-62; unknown; —; unknown; —; —; —

Hellwig; Florentine Henriette Wilhelmine; 15-Jun-49; 16-Jun-49; 18 Jan 1849; Hellwig, Heinrich Ludwig; Lübbeke, Minden, Preussen [f]; Thüner, Luise; Osnabruck, Hannover [m];

Hellwig; Heinrich Conrad Wilhelm; 25-Dec-45; 26-Dec-45; 24 Nov 1844; Hellwig, Ludwig; —; Thüner, Luise; —; —

Hellwig; Ursine Maria; 16-Nov-47; 17-Nov-47; 6 Jan 1846; Hellwig, August; Lübbeke, Preussen [f]; Gruner, Clara; Lobenstein, Reuss [m];

Helwig; Heinrich Dietrich; 15-Feb-49; 16-Feb-49; 2 May 1848; Helwig, August; Lübbeke, Preussen [f]; Grunner, Clara; Lobenstein, Reuss [m];

Henkel; Johann Peter; 16-Aug-45; 18-Aug-45; 3 Dec 1844; Henkel, Johann Peter; Schuffelbach, Naufhenberg, Kurhessen [f]; Ahlrs, Anna Maria; Aschbach, Wuerttemberg [m];

Henkel; Maria Elisab.; 18-Jul-40; 19-Jul-40; 7 May 1840; —; —; —; —; —

Herbig; Johanne Karoline; 28-Jun-53; 29-Jun-53; 16w; Herbig, Heinr.; Staben, Baiern [f]; —; —; —

Hermann; Christian; 18-Mar-49; 19-Mar-49; 6 Oct 1825; —; Einthinghausen, Thedinghausen, Braunschweig; —; —; —

Herold; Johanne Marie Pauline; 26-Oct-48; 27-Oct-47; 6 Sep 1838; Herold, Friedrich; Eisleben [f]; Ther, Johanne Maria; Lutzendorf bei Eisleben [m];

Herwig; Mrs. Marie; 2-Aug-58; 3-Aug-58; 90y, 4m; —; Marburg, Kurhessen; —; —; Greenmount Cemetery

Surname of Deceased; Given Name of Deceased; Date of Death; Date of Burial; Age or Date of Birth; Survivor(I), Surname, Given; Birthplace Deceased or Parent; Survivor (II), Surname, Given; Birthplace of Survivor (II); Comment

Hessenauer; Friedrich; 10-Nov-52; 11-Nov-52; 1y, 3m; Hessenauer, Johann; Wuerttemberg [f]; —; —; —

Heyser; Elisabeth; 13-Aug-38; 13-Aug-38; 16 Feb 1838; —; —; —; —; —

Heyser (nee Wahl); Elisabeth; 22-Feb-38; 23-Feb-38; 2 Feb 1817; —; —; —; —; —

Hickmann; Georg Samuel; 3-Jan-48; 4-Jan-48; 16 Jan 1840; Hickmann, Georg; Schlitz, Hessen [f]; Hafkemeyer, Catharina; Osnabruck, Hannover [m];

Hickmann; Jakob Eduard; 11-Jan-48; 13-Jan-48; 15 Aug 1843; Hickmann, Georg; Schiltz, Hessen [f]; Hafkemeyer, Catharina; Osnabruck, Hannover [m];

Hickmann; Juliane; 1-Jan-51; 2-Jan-51; 5y, 5m; Hickmann, Georg; —; —; —; oldest daughter

Hiedemuller; Sophie Henriette Elisbeth; 25-Jun-55; 27-Jun-55; 2y, 8m, 24d; Hiedemuller, Wilhelm; Liebenau, Hannover [f]; —; —; —

Hillgartner; Anna Katharine Margarethe; 11-Jul-65; 13-Jul-65; 9m, 9d; Hillgartner, Joh.; Lomdorf, Hessen [f]; —; —; —

Hillgartner; Johann Alexander; 31-Oct-63; 1-Nov-63; 1d; Hillgartner, Joh.; Londorf, Hessen [f]; —; —; —

Hillgartner; unbaptised son; 31-Jul-66; 1-Aug-66; —; Hillgartner, Joh.; Landorf, Hessen; —; —; —

Hinkel; Friederich; 15-Apr-46; 16-Apr-46; 29 Jul 1845; Hinkel, Johann; Sechbach bei Hanau, Kurhessen [f]; Rehberger, Catharine; Kleinfeld, Nidda, Hessen [m];

Hinkel; Heinrich Ferdinand; 19-Feb-65; 21-Feb-65; 7y, 18d; Hinkel, Adam; Mossenheim, Kurhessen [f]; —; —; —

Hinkel; Karoline Emilie Katharine; 26-Feb-65; 27-Feb-65; 6m, 7d; Hinkel, Adam; —; —; —; foster father

Hittmeyer (nee Pagen); Henriette; 25-May-45; 26-May-45; 3 Apr 1816; —; Bemen in Osnabruck, Hannover; —; —; —

Hittmeyer (nee Schulte); Maria Clara; 11-Nov-49; 14-Nov-49; 18 Apr 1826; Hittmeyer, Adolph Christian; —; —; —; —

Hoffmann; Catharine Elisabeth; 12-Sep-55; 13-Sep-55; 8m; —; —; —; —; —

Surname of Deceased; Given Name of Deceased; Date of Death; Date of Burial; Age or Date of Birth; Survivor(I), Surname, Given; Birthplace Deceased or Parent; Survivor (II), Surname, Given; Birthplace of Survivor (II); Comment

Hoffmann; Daniel; 23-Jan-47; 25-Jan-47; 16 Oct 1799; —; Rosenthal, Frankenberg, Kurhessen; —; —; —

Hoffmann; Johannes Adam; 12-May-57; 13-May-57; 1y, 2m, 16d; Hoffmann, Valentin; Nerweiler, Elssass [f]; —; —; —

Hoffmann; Maria Katharine; 24-Jul-59; 24-Jul-59; 10m, 1w; Hoffmann, Aug. Heinr.; —; —; —; youngest daughter

Hoffmannn (nee Bachin); Maria Margaretha; 17-Jul-45; 18-Jul-45; 30 Aug 1795; —; Dauernheim, Nidda, Hessen; —; —; —

Hofmann; Amalie; 6-Mar-50; 7-Mar-50; 20 Feb 1848; Hofmann, Valentin; Elsass [f]; Eitel, Salome; —; second child

Hofmann; Christine; 8-Jun-65; 9-Jun-65; —; Hofmann, Valentin; Elsass; —; —; triplet

Hofmann; Friedrich; 9-Mar-50; 10-Mar-50; 15 Feb 1850; Hofmann, Valentin; Elsass [f]; Eitel, Salome; —; —

Hofmann; Georg; 8-Jun-65; 9-Jun-65; —; Hofmann, Valentin; Elsass; —; —; triplet

Hofmann; Heinrich; 8-Jun-65; 9-Jun-65; —; Hofmann, Valentin; Elsass; —; —; triplet

Hofmann; Karl; 29-Aug-66; 31-Aug-66; 13y; Hofmann, August; Biedekopf, Hessen [f]; —; —; —

Hofmann; Magdalen; 26-Jun-50; 24-Jun-50; 25 Nov 1849; Hofmann, Ernst; Ferkershausen, Möllerstadt, Sachsen-Meiningen [f]; Bachmann, Henriette; —; —

Hofmann; Mrs. Maria; 16-Jul-52; 18-Jul-52; about 60y; Hofmann, Daniel; —; —; —; spouse

Hohmann; Caspar; 5-Nov-45; 6-Nov-45; 21 Jul 1845; Hohmann, Caspar; Statten, Sachsen-Weimar [f]; Bäteln, Elisabeth; Unter-Au vor Röhn, Sachsen-Weimar [m];

Hol; Anna Kathr.; 13-May-38; 14-May-38; 3 May 1778; —; —; —; —; —

Holdgrefe; Anna Katharine Elisabeth; 27-Jul-66; 29-Jul-66; 1y, 2m, 22d; Holdgrefe, Friedrcih Ludwig; Engter, Hannover [f]; —; —; —

Hollebein; Georg Friedrich Leonhard; 11-Oct-61; 12-Oct-61; 8m, 1d; Hollebein, Georg; Hosselbrunn, Hessen [f]; —; —; —

Hollebein; Konrad; 2-Jul-58; 2-Jul-58; 3y; Hollebein, Friedrich; Hasselbrunn, Hessen [f]; —; —; —

Surname of Deceased; Given Name of Deceased; Date of Death; Date of Burial; Age or Date of Birth; Survivor(I), Surname, Given; Birthplace Deceased or Parent; Survivor (II), Surname, Given; Birthplace of Survivor (II); Comment

Holtgrove; Johann Friedrich Louise; 29-Aug-61; 30-Aug-61; 3w; Holtgrove, Louis; Engter, Hannover [f]; —; —; —

Hoppel; Christian; 22-May-58; 23-May-58; 8y, 8m; Hoppel, Johann; Jossbach, Kurhessen [f]; —; —; —

Hormes; Anna Barbara Rosine; 26-Jul-56; 27-Jul-56; 1y, 4w; Hormes, Thomas; Baiersdorf, Baiern [f]; —; —; —

Hormes; Georg Michael; 24-May-61; 26-May-61; 3y, 11m, 3w, 3d; Hormes, Thomas; Baiersdorf, Baiern [f]; —; —; second son

Horn; Leonhardt Friedrich; 4-Nov-51; 5-Nov-51; 3y, 9m; Horn, Joh. Mich.; Grossbernweiler, Wuerttemberg [f]; —; —; —

Horst; Heinrich Martin; 4-Apr-50; 6-Apr-50; 16 Jan 1849; Horst, Conrad; Bobenhausen, Gruneberg, Hessen [f]; Schuster, Catharina; Birdenkorf, Hessen [m];

Horstmann; Jurgen Heinrich; 18-Jul-57; 19-Jul-57; 27y, 10m; —; Holte, Hanover; —; —; —

Horstmann; Marie Elise; 12-Sep-57; 13-Sep-57; 2y; Horstmann, Jurgen, Heinr.; Holte, Hannover [f]; —; —; father deceased

Hossbach; Margarethe; 3-Aug-51; 4-Aug-51; 6m, 16d; Hossbach, Adam; Grossbuschla, Preussen [f]; —; —; —

Huck; Johann; 10-Aug-49; 11-Aug-49; 5 Nov 1844; Huck, Jakob; Diedorf, Eisenach, Sachsen-Weimar [f]; Engelhardt, Catharina; Diedorf, Eisenach, Sachsen-Weimar [m];

Huhn; Christian Wilhelm; 26-Dec-45; 28-Dec-45; 5 Jul 1805; —; Dörrdingen, Maulbronn, Wuerttemberg; —; —; —

Ihde (nee Tewes); Mrs. Marie Dorothea; 4-Sep-61; 5-Sep-61; 67y, 4m; —; Vonlossen, Hannover; —; —; —

Imwalde; Elisabeth; 29-Jan-58; 30-Jan-58; 79y, 10 m; —; Quackenbruck, Hannover; —; —; —

Imwalde; Heinrich Samuel; 23-Jul-54; 24-Jul-54; 1y, 2m, 4d; Imwalde, Joh. Heinr.; Quackenbruck, Hannover [f]; —; —; —

Isermann; Jacob; 4-Oct-43; 5-Oct-45; 22 Aug 1814; —; —; —; —; —

Jaekel; Karl; 21-Nov-53; 22-Nov-53; 1y, 6m; Jaekel, Christoph; Lisberg, Hessen [f]; —; —; —

Jakob; Charlotte Johanne; 24-Sep-46; 25-Sep-46; 1 Sep 1846; Jakob, Lorenz; Wiessendorf, Baiern [f]; Frische, Ursula Margaretha; Wiessendorf, Baiern [m];

Jakob; Lorenz; 12-Apr-46; 13-Apr-46; 3 Apr 1846; Jakob, Johann; Weissendorf bei Nurnberg [f]; Wunder, Charlotte; Rauschenburg bei Neustadt a.d. Reuss [m];

Jakob (nee Frisch); Anna Catharine; 11-Dec-46; 13-Dec-46; 10 Jul 1820; Jakob, Michael; Hammermühl, Kulmbach, Baiern; —; —; —

Jakob (nee Frische); Ursula Margaretha; 9-Sep-46; 9-Sep-46; 1800; Jakob, Lorenz; Weissendorf, Baiern; —; —; —

January; Daniel; 4-Jan-43; 5-Jan-43; 3 Feb 1821; —; —; —; —; —

Jung; Anna Christine; 29-Jun-62; 30-Jun-62; 29y, 8m, 4w; —; Ochelheim, Preussen; —; —; —

Junghause; Philipp Frdch. Julius; 2-Jun-45; 3-Jun-45; 35y; —; Blankenberg, Schwarzburg; —; —; sudden death, 6 days in USA

Kahle (nee Jürgen-Detmers); Henriette; 12-Nov-47; 13-Nov-47; 25y; Kahle, Gerhard Heinrich; —; Essen, Mittlage, Hannover; —; —

Kaiser; Christian; 29-Feb-52; 1-Mar-52; 2y; Kaiser, Heinrich; Maaslingen, Preussen [f]; —; —; daughter

Kampmann; Christian; 20-Aug-53; 21-Aug-53; 3m, 3w; Kampmann, Friederike; Rechenberg, Wuerttemberg; —; —; illegitimate

Kärcher; Jacob; 13-Jun-39; 14-Jun-39; 2 Apr 1837; —; —; —; —; —

Karl; Wilhelm Heinrich Friedrich; 28-Jun-60; 29-Jun-60; 1y, 3w; Karl, Karl; Bellmuth, Hessen [f]; —; —; —

Karl (nee Brauer); Mrs. Elisabeth Marie; 22-Oct-60; 24-Oct-60; 30y, 7m, 1w, 5d; —; —; —; —; —

Karle; Katharina Margaretha; 29-Mar-50; 31-Mar-50; 10 Mar 1850; Carle, Conrad; Hessen [f]; Pfeil, Catharina Margaretha; —; —

Karmroth; Elisabeth; 11-Jul-51; 12-Jul-51; 1m; Karmroth, Joh.; —; —; —; —

Kaster; Joh. Heinrich Ferdinand; 28-Sep-56; 29-Sep-56; 1y, 9d; Kaster, Joh. Heinr.; Rehe, Hannover [f]; —; —; —

Katenkamp; Rosine Maria; 1-Aug-49; 2-Aug-49; 20 Aug 1848; Katenkamp, Dietrich; Hannover [f]; Schitner, Rosine Catharine; Wuerttemberg [m];

Surname of Deceased; Given Name of Deceased; Date of Death; Date of Burial; Age or Date of Birth; Survivor(I), Surname, Given; Birthplace Deceased or Parent; Survivor (II), Surname, Given; Birthplace of Survivor (II); Comment

Katenkamp (nee Tschackony); Juliane Sabine; —; 13-Dec-46; 21 Feb 1822; Katenkamp, Dietrich; Haunesheim, Baiern; —; —; —

Kattenkamp; Heinrich Eberhard; 6-Sep-57; 8-Sep-57; 16y, 6m, 4d; Kattenkamp, Dietrich; Rotterode, Hannover [f]; —; —; —

Kaufmann; Katharine Rosine Marie; 2-Sep-60; 3-Sep-60; 3y, 2m, 2w, 2d; Kaufmann, Georg Heinrich; Friedegerode, Kurhessen [f]; —; —; —

Kaufmann (nee Eckardt); Marie Juliane; 23-Jan-67; 25-Jan-67; 39y; —; Hennberg, Hessen; —; —; —

Keiling (nee Gondd); Dorothea; 15-Mar-46; 16-Mar-46; 2 Nov 1806; —; Langendebach bei Hanau, Kurhessen; —; —; —

Kern; Margarethe; 28-Apr-64; 30-Apr-64; 7y, 3m, 4d; Kern, Conrad; Brugge, Baiern; —; —; father deceased

Kern; Peter; 18-Aug-66; 19-Aug-66; 15y, 7m, 1w; —; Baltimore, MD; —; —; —

Kerschling; Heinrich; 27-Sep-63; 28-Sep-63; 56y; —; Wettesingen, Kurhessen; —; —; —

Keyl; Bertha Susanne; 2-Dec-66; 4-Dec-66; 4y, 11m, 16d; Key, Rev. Gerhard Wilhelm; —; —; —; minister of church

Keyl; Helene Wilhelmine; 12-Jul-56; 13-Jul-56; 8m, 2w; Keyl, Rev. Ernst Gerhard Wilhe.; —; —; —; minister of church

Kiepert (neeMeyer); Mrs. Barbara; 12-Jan-60; 13-Jan-60; 43y, 2m, 1w; —; Hoppurg, Baiern; —; —; —

Kieser; Dorothea; 27-Apr-38; 28-Apr-38; 15 dec 1796; —; —; —; —; —

Kieser; Heinrich; 4-Jan-38; 5-Jan-38; 10 Dec 1802; —; —; —; —; —

Kirchmeier; Christina Sophia; 17-May-50; 18-May-50; 16 May 1850; Kirchmeier, Johann Michael; Dippoldberg, Bayern [f]; Thiergartner, Margaretha; Neustadt, Bayern [m];

Kirchmeier; Johann; 15-Oct-51; 17-Oct-51; 33y; —; —; —; —; —

Kirchmeyer; Christine Sophia; 30-Jun-49; 1-Jul-49; 17 Jun 1849; Kirchmeyer, Johann Michael; Diepholzberg, Markelbach [f]; Thiergart, Margareth; Langenfeld, Markbigart, Baiern [m];

Kister; Ludwig; 7-Jan-46; 9-Jan-46; 2 Feb 1808; —; Breitenbach, Schwarzburg, Sondershausen; —; —; died 9 AM

Surname of Deceased; Given Name of Deceased; Date of Death; Date of Burial; Age or Date of Birth; Survivor(I), Surname, Given; Birthplace Deceased or Parent; Survivor (II), Surname, Given; Birthplace of Survivor (II); Comment

Klein; Friederich Wilhelm; 28-Apr-49; 29-Apr-49; 21 Oct 1848; Klein, Wilhelm; Bernsburg, Alsfeld, Hessen [f]; Seibert, Catharine; Dittlofsroth, Baiern [m];

Klein; Gottfried; 31-Aug-63; 2-Sep-63; 72; —; Lemberg, Rheinbaiern; —; —; —

Klein; Magdalene Arins; 24-Oct-37; 25-Oct-37; 24 Oct 1811; —; —; —; —; —

Kleinlein; Peter; 3-Sep-42; 4-Sep-42; 6 May 1817; —; —; —; —; —

Klenke; Katharine Elise Mathilde; 14-May-62; 15-May-62; 1y, 8m; Klenke, Philipp; Allendorf, Hessen [f]; —; —; —

Kleppisch; Daniel Friedrich; 29-Aug-57; 30-Aug-58; 5h; Kleppisch, Friedr. Aug.; Lommatzsch, Sachsen [f]; —; —; —

Kleppisch; Friedrich Theodor; 7-Jun-53; 8-Jun-53; 3y, 7m; Kleppisch, Karl Frdch.; Radeberg, Sachsen [f]; —; —; —

Kleppisch; Georg Andreas; 16-Dec-47; 17-Dec-47; 8 Mar 1845; Kleppisch, Carl Friedrich; Radeberg, Sachsen [f]; Canfort, Cath.; Baltimore, MD [m];

Kleppisch; Johann Eduard; 22-May-53; 23-May-53; 5y, 5m, 3w, 4d; Kleppisch, Karl Frdch.; Radeberg, Sachsen [f]; —; —; —

Kleppisch; Johannes Heinrich; 11-Mar-49; 12-Mar-49; 17 Jun 1848; Kleppisch, August; Radeberg bei Dresden [f]; Weinhardt, Susanne; Baltimore, MD [m];

Kleppisch; Karl Daniel; 7-Aug-53; 8-Aug-53; 2y, 10m; Kleppisch, Frdch. Aug.; Radeberg, Sachsen [f]; —; —; —

Kleppisch; Katharine Rosine Elisabeth; 24-May-56; 26-May-56; 3y, 10m, 2w; Kleppisch, Karl Frdch.; Radeberg, Sachsen [f]; —; —; —

Kleppisch; Maria Katharina; 14-Aug-53; 16-Aug-53; 1m, 6d; Kleppisch, Frdch. Aug.; Radeberg, Sachsen [f]; —; —; —

Kleppisch; Mrs. Anna Rosine; 9-Mar-61; 11-Mar-61; 80y, 3m, 12d; —; Langenbruck, Sachsen; —; —; —

Kleppisch; Samuel Stephanus; 8-May-61; 9-May-61; 1y, 7m, 2d; Kleppisch, August Friedrich; —; —; —; youngest son

Kleppisch (nee Weinhardt); Mrs. Susanne Anna; 8-Sep-60; 10-Sep-60; 40y, 7m, 8d; —; —; —; —; —

Klingelhofer; Marie Katharine Gertrud; 12-Jul-62; 13-Jul-62; 6 m, 8d; Klingelhofer, Wilhelm; Rosenthal, Kurhessen [f]; —; —; only child

Klingelhofer; Marie Katharine Margarethe; 22-Dec-63; 23-Dec-63; 20d; Klinghofer, Wilhelm; Rosenthal, Kurhessen [f]; —; —; —

Klingelhofer (nee Rossel); Mrs. Katharine Marie Wilhelmine; 1-Feb-62; 2-Feb-62; 24y; —; Rosenthal, Kurhessen; —; —; —

Klinkmeier; Christian Heinrich Wilhelm; 13-Oct-59; 14-Oct-59; 11m, 2w; Klinkmeier, Aug. Heinrich; —; —; —; father deceased

Klinkmeier; Heinrich August; —; 16-Aug-59; 30y, 4m, 1w, 6d; —; Liebenau, Hannover; —; —; —

Klinkmeier; Marie Charlotte Henriette; 10-Jul-62; 12-Jul-62; 7m; Klinkmeier, Wilhelm; Liebenau, Hannover [f]; —; —; —

Klinkmeier; stillborn daughter; 16-Jul-53; 16-Jul-53; —; Klinkmeier, August; Liebenau, Hannover [f]; —; —; —

Klinkmeier (nee Fredking); Mrs. Friedrike; 12-Aug-59; 13-Aug-59; 32y; —; Deckau, Hannover; —; —; —

Knapp (nee Bohn); Eva; 23-Aug-42; 24-Aug-42; 23y; —; —; —; —; —

Knipp; Wilhelm; 19-Oct-54; 21-Oct-54; 2y, 3w; Knipp, Joh.; Lisberg, Hessen [f]; —; —; —

Koch; Charlotte; 29-Sep-63; 30-Sep-63; 60y, 11d; —; Holten, Hannover; —; —; —

Koch; Johann Heinrich; 26-Dec-45; 27-Dec-45; 19 Aug 1756; Koch, Adam; Niederhorn, Eshwege [f]; —; —; —

Koch; Luise Kathr.; 9-Aug-39; 10-Aug-39; 8 Dec 1837; —; —; —; —; —

Koch; Margareth Adelheid; 21-Apr-46; 22-Apr-46; 18y, 7m, less 5d; Koch, Johann; —; Rohdens, Rebeka Margar.; Neuenbruchhausen, Altenbruchhausen, Hannover [m];

Koch (nee Wolbert); Anna; 25-May-40; 26-May-40; 21 Feb 1766; —; —; —; —; —

Kocher; Jacob Ulrich; 26-Nov-37; 27-Nov-37; 24 Aug 1836; —; —; —; —; —

Surname of Deceased; Given Name of Deceased; Date of Death; Date of Burial; Age or Date of Birth; Survivor(I), Surname, Given; Birthplace Deceased or Parent; Survivor (II), Surname, Given; Birthplace of Survivor (II); Comment

Köhler; Thomas; 2-Mar-48; 2-Mar-48; 13 Jun 1845; Köhler, Johann; Butzeldorf bei Beireuth [f]; Richter, Kunigunde; Unterzaunsbach, Grafenberg, Baiern [m];

Kohnlein; Johann Georg; 13-Jul-52; 15-Jul-52; 49y; Baiern; —; —; —; —

Koing (nee Gettier); Elisabeth; 27-Jun-37; 28-Jun-39; 14 May 1785; —; —; —; —; probably Konig

Kolb; Karoline; 22-Mar-40; 23-Mar-40; 23 Apr 1839; —; —; —; —; —

Kommer; Katharine; 5-Jun-57; 7-Jun-57; 14m, 6d; Kommer, Wilh.; Rodtheim, Hessen [f]; —; —; —

Kommer; son; 8-May-53; 9-May-53; 1d; Kommer, Wilhelm; Rottheim, Hessen [f]; —; —; unbaptized son

König; Philipp; 16-Jul-65; 18-Jul-65; 39y, 6m; —; Grosswellensbach, Baden; —; —; —

Koos; Christoph; 28-Mar-43; 29-Mar-43; 1 Feb 1817; —; —; —; —; —

Koppmeyer; Maria; 15-Aug-41; 16-Aug-41; 24y; —; —; —; —; —

Köster; Anna Marg. Charl. Christine; 17-May-42; 18-May-42; 7 Mar 1840; —; —; —; —; —

Kraft; Anna Maria; —; 15-Aug-46; 19y; Kraft, Georg; —; [--?--], Anna Maria; Baltimore, MD [m];

Kraft; Margarethe; 29-May-38; 30-May-38; 26 Dec 1834; —; —; —; —; —

Kramer; Christine; 24-Jan-48; 25-Jan-48; 12 Jun 1830; Kramer, Johann; Sengen, Durlach, Baden [f]; Scheicher, Christine; Sengen, Durlach, Baden [m];

Kramer; Heinrich; 1-Oct-52; 3-Oct-52; 52y, 9m; —; Walen, Hessen; —; —; —

Kramer; Louise; 22-Sep-49; 23-Sep-49; 26 Jun 1843; Kramer, Heinrich; Wahl, Alsfeld, Hessen [f]; —; —; —

Kraus; Johann Georg Gottfried; 2-Dec-57; 3-Dec-57; 27w; Kraus, Christoph; Langensteinach, Baiern [f]; —; —; —

Krell; Georg Heinrich; 23-Jan-66; 25-Jan-66; 3y, 1m, 14d; Krell, Weigand; Bleichenbach, Hessen [f]; —; —; —

Krell; Weigand; 23-Apr-65; 24-Apr-65; 30y; —; Bleichenbach, Hessen; —; —; —

Krome; Elisabeth; 26-Jul-39; 27-Jul-39; 22 May 1839; —; —; —; —; —

Krome; Johanne Marg.; 30-Jul-39; 31-Jul-39; 22 May 1839; —; —; —; —; —

Kröner; Elisabeth; 24-Jul-38; 25-Jul-38; 3 Jul 1837; —; —; —; —; —

Kuhl; Elise; 20-Jan-38; 21-Jan-38; 8 Oct 1809; —; —; —; —; —

Kuhn; Augustus; 30-Jul-51; 1-Aug-51; circa 75y; —; Leipzig, Sachsen; —; —; —

Kuhn (nee Meyer); Marie; 24-Mar-50; 27-Mar-50; 1780 ?; Kuhn, Aug. Chr.; Hannover; —; —; —

Kummer; Georg Heinrich; 24-Sep-62; 25-Sep-62; 1y, 7m, 9d; Kummer, Wilhelm; Rodtheim, Hessen; —; —; after a fall

Kunker; Marie Wilhelmine Elisabeth; 23-Jul-63; 24-Jul-63; 10m, 4d; Kunker, J. Heinr.; Husede, Hannover [f]; —; —; —

Kunker; stillborn son; 24-Mar-1867; 24-Mar-1867; 0; Kunker, Joh. Heinr.; Susede, Hannover [f]; —; —; —

Kunker; un-named child; 19-Jan-57; 20-Jan-57; 6d; Kunker, Heinr.; Husede, Hannover [f]; —; —; —

Kurtz; Friedrich; 21-Dec-57; 22-Dec-57; 14y, 11m, 3w; —; Schinnerhausen, Schwartzburg, Rudolstadt; —; —; —

Labahn; Julius; 20-Oct-61; 21-Oct-61; 9m, 6d; Labahn, Heinrich; Liebenau [f]; —; —; youngest child

Lachner; Georg; 18-Sep-43; 20-Sep-43; 7 Apr 1802; —; —; —; —;

Laib; Louise Karoline; 18-Aug-40; 19-Aug-40; 11 Oct 1839; —; —; —; —; —

Lais; Johann Peter Wilhelm; 21-Feb-62; 23-Feb-62; 3m; Lais, Karl; Lisberg, Hessen [f]; —; —; first child

Lais; Karl; 8-Jun-61; 10-Jun-61; 2y, 4d; Lais, Karl; Lisberg, Hessen [f]; —; —; only son

Lais; Marie; 27-Jul-65; 29-Jul-65; 6m; Lais, Karl; Lisberg, Hessen [f]; —; —; —

Lais (nee Emmerich); Marie Sybille; 16-Jun-46; 17-Jun-46; 4 Dec 1786; Lais, Johann Georg; Lissberg, Hessen; —; —; —

Surname of Deceased; Given Name of Deceased; Date of Death; Date of Burial; Age or Date of Birth; Survivor(I), Surname, Given; Birthplace Deceased or Parent; Survivor (II), Surname, Given; Birthplace of Survivor (II); Comment

Lamann; Eberhard Jakob; 28-Mar-46; 30-Mar-46; 23 Sep 1837; Lamann, Arnold Rudolph; Lienen, Preussen [f]; Schipp, Maria; Homburg, Hessen [m];

Lange; Georg Eberhard; 31-Jul-57; 1-Aug-57; 9w, 4d; Lange, Joh.; Gera, Reuss [f]; —; —; youngest son

Lange; Gustav; 29-Dec-65; 31-Dec-65; 39y, 8m, 18d; —; Gera, Kurhessen Reuss; —; —; —

Lange; Jakob Heinrich; 30-Jul-59; 31-Jul-59; 10m, 3w; Lange, Johann; Gera [f]; —; —; —

Langler; Friedrich Wilhelm; 9-Jan-45; —; 1y, 2m; Langler, Johannes; —; Otto, Barbara Elisabeth; —; —

Langschmidt; Henriette Karoline Louise; 14-Jan-58; 15-Jan-58; 1y, 8m; Langschmidt, Wilh.; Neuenkirchen, Hannover [f]; —; —; sister of next entry

Langschmidt; Henriette Louse Wilhelmine; 26-Jan-58; 28-Jan-58; 3y, 9m; Langschmidt, Wilh.; Neuenkirchen, Hannover [f]; —; —; sister of prior entry

Lapp; Joahn Jakob; 10-Mar-64; 13-Mar-64; 23y, 9m; —; Roitheim, Hessen; —; —; —

Lapp; Kaspar; 7-Apr-59; 8-Apr-59; 21y, 11m, 9d; —; Rodtheim, Hessen; —; —; —

Lapp; Konrad; 24-Jan-43; 25-Jan-43; 12 Feb 1816; —; —; —; —; —

Lapp; Ludwig; 11-Jul-50; 12-Jul-50; 12 Mar 1847; Lapp, Ludwig; Rottheim, Giessen, Hessen [f]; Montler, Katharina Margaretha; Knizenbach, Preussen [m];

Lapp; Mrs. Maria Catharina; 12-Oct-50; 13-Oct-50; 69y; Lapp, Georg; Giessen, Hessen; —; —; spouse

Lassig; Johann Gottlob; 14-Dec-44; 16-Dec-44; 17 Dec 1820; —; —; —; —; —

Lassig (nee Chruschwitzins); Johanna Sophia; 5-Jan-45; —; 53y, 6m, 25d; Lassig, Joh. Christoph; Unterheinsdorf, Sachsen; —; —; —

Laumann; Karoline; 15-Jul-43; 17-Jul-43; 2 May 1842; —; —; —; —; —

Surname of Deceased; Given Name of Deceased; Date of Death; Date of Burial; Age or Date of Birth; Survivor(I), Surname, Given; Birthplace Deceased or Parent; Survivor (II), Surname, Given; Birthplace of Survivor (II); Comment

Ledder; August; 1-Jan-46; 3-Jan-46; 16w; Ledder, Johann; Herzsprunde, Baiern [f]; Ohlenschlager, Margaretha; Stiefen bei Beireuth, Baiern [m]; 10 o'clock

Leipoldt; Barbara; 26-Apr-49; 27-Apr-49; 12 Oct 1846; Leipoldt, Jakob; Kindersbühl, Lauf [f]; Klausner, Kunigunde; Unterschirmbach, Erlangen, Baiern [m];

Leistner; Adam; 2-Jul-49; 4-Jul-49; 16 Oct 1802; —; Döllnitz bei Turnau, Baiern; —; —; —

Leistner (nee Dressel); Elisabeth; 10-Nov-46; 12-Nov-46; 21 Sep 1794; Leistner, Adam; Herrschafts, Thurnau, Baiern; —; —; —

Lenz; Helena; 26-Oct-38; 28-Oct-38; 9 Feb 1834; —; —; —; —; —

Lenz; Karl Friedrich; —; 22-Apr-65; 7w; Lenz, Heinr.; Bleichenbach, Hessen [f]; —; —; —

Lenz (nee Emmerich); Mrs. Susanne Margarethe; 15-Apr-65; 17-Apr-65; 59y; —; Bleichenbach, Hessen; —; —; —

Letmade; Friedrich Wilhelm; —; 26-Jan-67; 12w; Letmade, Heinrich August; Neuenkirchen, Hannover [f]; —; —; —

Letmade; Friedrich Wilhelm August; 13-Nov-67; 14-Nov-67; 5 d; Letmade, Heinr. Aug.; Neuenkirchen, Hannover [f]; —; —;

Lettemade; Friedrich Wilhelm; 3-Jan-58; 5-Jan-58; 3y, 11m, 3w, 3d; Lettemade, Adolph Wilh.; Neuenkirchen, Hannover [f]; —; —; —

Lettmade; Henriette Wilhelmine Louise; 26-May-65; 27-May-65; 2m, 8d; Lettmade, Heinr. August; Neuenkirchen, Hannover; —; —; —

Lettmade; Julius August Gottfried; 30-Oct-66; 31-Oct-66; 1y, 4m; Lettmade, Friedrich; Neuenkirchen, Hannover [f]; —; —; —

Lettmade; Mrs. Katharine Marie; 9-Feb-60; 11-Feb-60; 69y; —; Melle, Hannover; —; —; —

Lettmade; stillborn daughter; 24-Nov-56; 24-Nov-56; —; Lettmade, Wilhelm; Neuenkirchen, Osnabruck [f]; —; —; —

Lettmade; stillborn son; 26-Dec-58; 26-Dec-58; —; Lettmade, Georg Adolph Wilh.; Neuenkirchen, Hannover [f]; —; —; —

Leutner; Christoph; 3-Oct-63; 4-Oct-63; 52y, 2m; —; Allendorf a.d.L., Hessen; —; —; fell out of train

Surname of Deceased; Given Name of Deceased; Date of Death; Date of Burial; Age or Date of Birth; Survivor(I), Surname, Given; Birthplace Deceased or Parent; Survivor (II), Surname, Given; Birthplace of Survivor (II); Comment

Leutner; Elisabeth Dorothea Louise; 18-Apr-56; 19-Apr-56; 2y, 8d; Leutner, Freidr.; Allendorf a.d.L., Hessen; —; —; youngest daughter

Lindemann; Caroline Elisabethe; 6-Aug-50; 7-Aug-50; 4h, 4m, 2w, 3d; Lindemann, Joh. G. Wilh.; —; —; —; school teacher

Lindermann; Anna Maria Elisabeth; 3-Feb-67; 4-Feb-67; 7w, 2d; Lindemann, Ludolph Gutav; Ottersberg [f]; —; —; —

List; Johann Adam; 7-Mar-46; 8-Mar-46; 7 Oct 1844; List, Johann; Ingenheim, Hessen [f]; Sommer, Luise; Diepholz, Hannover [m];

List; Luise; 29-Apr-49; 30-Apr-49; 9 Apr 1847; List, Adam; Jugenheim, Bensheim, Hessen [f]; Sommers, Dorothea; Diepholz, Hannover [m];

List; Maria Elise; 30-Jul-39; 31-Jul-39; 5 Feb 1839; —; —; —; —; —

List; Philip; 28-Jun-39; 30-Jun-39; 17 Mar 1777; —; —; —; —; —

Lohrmann; Alexander; 9-Jun-48; 11-Jun-48; 5 Dec 1841; Lohrmann, Johann Heinrich; Fuopfreiheit [?], Waldeck [f]; Kirschner, Maria; Todtenhausen, Waldeck [m];

Lohrmann; Auguste Agnes; 23-Dec-1847; 25-Dec-47; 30 Jan 1846; Lohrmann, Johann Heinrich; Bergfreiheit, Waldeck [f]; Kirschner, Maria; Todtenhausen, Waldeck [m];

Lohrmann; Luise; 11-May-48; 12-May-48; 5 Mar 1844; Lohrmann, Johann Heinrich; Bergfreiheit, Waldeck [f]; Kirschner, Marie; Todtenhausen, Waldeck [m];

Louis; Anna Maria Louise; 31-May-54; 1-Jun-54; 6m, 2w, 3d; Louis, Carl Frdch.; Altwildungen, Waldeck [f]; —; —; —

Ludolf; Karoline; 11-Nov-51; 12-Nov-51; 2y, 3m, 1d; Ludolf, Heinrich; Nordheim, Hannover [f]; —; —; —

Lutz; Carl Gottfried; 29-Jan-48; 30-Jan-48; 3 May 1845; Lutz, Christoph Friedrich; Rodensohl, Neuenbirk, Wuerttemberg [f]; Romoser, Jacobine; Rodensohl, Neuenbirk, Wuerttemberg [m];

Lutz; Johann; 6-Sep-44; 7-Sep-44; 15 Jul 1841; —; —; —; —; —

Maeser; Georg Adolph; 3-Sep-63; 4-Sep-63; 2y, 1m; Maeser, Karl Wilhelm; Mittel-Ebersbach, Sachsen [f]; —; —; —

Magenhard; Pauline; 16-Mar-44; 17-Mar-44; 10 Jan 1843; —; —; —; —; —

Surname of Deceased; Given Name of Deceased; Date of Death; Date of Burial; Age or Date of Birth; Survivor(I), Surname, Given; Birthplace Deceased or Parent; Survivor (II), Surname, Given; Birthplace of Survivor (II); Comment

Magin; Jakob; 25-Aug-48; 26-Aug-48; 14 Mar 1846; Magin, Peter; Lemberg bei Bermesins, Rheinbaiern [f]; Klein, Anna Barbara; Lemberg bei Bermesins, Rheinbaiern [m];

Maienkranz; Wilhelm; 16-Nov-47; 17-Nov-47; 9 Nov 1847; Maienkranz, Kilian; —; [--?--], Anna Elisabeth; Waldorf, Sachsen-Meiningen [m];

Maier; stillborn daughter; 30-Nov-61; 2-Dec-61; —; Maier, Georg; Baiersdorf, Baiern; —; —; —

Man; Friedrich; 1-Mar-50; 3-Mar-50; 28 Aug 1802; —; Erdmanroth bei Herschfeld; —; —; —

Mansdorf; Heinrich; 7-Feb-66; 9-Feb-66; 68y, 2m, 3w; —; Homberg a.d. Ohm, Hessen; —; —; —

Maul; Johann; 10-Nov-42; 13-Nov-42; 26 Sep 1810; —; —; —; —;

May; Friedrich; —; 18-May-40; age unknown; —; —; —; —; drowned

Megenhard; Eduard Friedrich; 12-Feb-38; 13-Feb-38; 28 Jan 1837; —; —; —; —; —

Megenhard; Wilhelm Heinrich; 27-Mar-43; 28-Mar-43; 24 Dec 1841; —; —; —; —; —

Megenhard (nee Lohbauer); Pauline; 25-Dec-48; 27-Dec-48; 19 Sep 1803; Megenhard, Friedrich; Stuttgart; —; —; —

Meier; Adam Christian; 12-Jun-56; 13-Jun-56; 2y, 10m, 1d; Meier, Karl Bernhard; Kleinhaibach, Baiern [f]; —; —; —

Meier; Anna Maria; 3-Feb-56; 4-Feb-56; 1y, 18d; Meier, Georg; Baiersdorf, Baiern [f]; —; —; only daughter

Meier; Heinrich; 28-Apr-58; 30-Apr-58; 25y; —; Kaiserslautern, Rheinbaiern; —; —; —

Meier; Johann Thomas Michael; 14-Jul-56; 15-Jul-56; 9m; Meier, Georg; Baiersdorf, Baiern [f]; —; —; —

Meier; Johann Thomas Michael; 29-Jun-59; 30-Jun-59; 1m, 2w; Meier, Georg; Baiersdorf, Baiern [f]; —; —; —

Meier; Karoline Margarethe Friederike; 1-Aug-61; 2-Aug-61; 7y, 11m; Meier, Christian; Mattfelds, Hannover [f]; —; —; only daughter

Meier (nee Landwehr); Mrs. Anna Adelheid; 2-Feb-64; 3-Feb-64; 73y, 6m; Neuenkirchen, Hannover; —; —; —; —

Surname of Deceased; Given Name of Deceased; Date of Death; Date of Burial; Age or Date of Birth; Survivor(I), Surname, Given; Birthplace Deceased or Parent; Survivor (II), Surname, Given; Birthplace of Survivor (II); Comment

Melchor; Karl; 17-Jan-44; 18-Jan-44; 14 Jan 1814; —; —; —; —; —

Mengel; Heinrich; 16-Feb-41; 18-Feb-41; 28 Aug 1812; —; —; —; —; —

Menken; Dietrich; 8-Sep-48; 9-Sep-48; between 44-48y; —; Vegesack bei Bremen; —; —; carpenter aboard Ship Albert from Bremen

Merk; Emilie; 11-Aug-42; 12-Aug-42; 24 Jan 1842; —; —; —; —; —

Merk; Maria Elisabeth; 27-Jul-44; 28-Jul-44; 12 May 1843; —; —; —; —; —

Merkel; Therese Auguste Elisabeth; 25-Sep-60; 26-Sep-60; 6m, 2w, 6d; Merkel, Therese; Oberbrechtal, Hessen [m]; —; —; illegitimate

Mess; Karl Georg Christian; 23-Apr-63; 25-Apr-63; 2y, 1m, 6d; Mess, Joh; Wahlen, Hessen [f]; —; —; —

Mess; Theodor Wilhelm; 19-Oct-65; 20-Oct-65; 1y, 7m, 9d; Mess, Johann; Wahlen, Hessen [f]; —; —; —

Messer; Johann; 15-Aug-40; 16-Aug-40; 15 Aug 1839; —; —; —; —; —

Meuert; Carl; 21-Jan-45; —; 47y; —; Stuttgart, Wuerttemberg; —; —; —

Meyer; Karl; 11-Jun-1850; 12-Jun-50; 7 Sep 1848; Meyer, Karl; Hamburg [f]; Weber, Katharina; Frankisch grumbach, Darmstadt [m]; m: Kathr. Weber

Meyer; Ludeke; 29-Mar-49; 1-Apr-49; 1 May 1825; —; Eintinghausen, Thedinghausen, Braunschweig; —; —; —

Meyer; Wilhelm; 14-Sep-47; 15-Sep-47; 14 Mar 1814; —; Emighausen, Lübbeke, Preussen; —; —; —

Meyer; Wilhelm Heinrich; 24-Apr-44; 29-Apr-44; —; —; —; —; —; —

Meyer (nee Rosengarm); Katharine Adelheide; 10-Mar-41; 13-Mar-41; 19 Apr 1817; —; —; —; —; —

Mienich; Heinrich Albert; 28-Jun-46; 29-Jun-46; 15y, 3m, 4d; Mienich, Johann; Baltimore, MD [f]; Eigenbrodt, Friederike; Göttingen, Hannover [m];

Surname of Deceased; Given Name of Deceased; Date of Death; Date of Burial; Age or Date of Birth; Survivor(I), Surname, Given; Birthplace Deceased or Parent; Survivor (II), Surname, Given; Birthplace of Survivor (II); Comment

Mieth; Johannes; 4-Sep-58; 5-Sep-58; 6y, 4m; Mieth, Niklaus; Voldortshain, Hessen [f]; —; —; —

Mieth; Karl; 30-Mar-62; 30-Mar-62; 9h; Mieth, Johann; Volkertshain, Hessen [f]; —; —; —

Mink; Margaretha; 1-Apr-49; 2-Apr-49; 24 May 1847; Mink, Anton; Hamsdorf, Ober-Elsass [f]; Sonstadt, Sophie; Eiwiller, Elsass [m];

Mohrhardt (nee Meerwein); Christine Maria; 26-Aug-49; 27-Aug-49; 62y; —; Mohrhardt, Jakob Friedrich; Pforzheim, Baden; —; —

Mohring; Gertrud Karoline; 1-Dec-60; 3-Dec-60; 17y, 3m, 2w, 5d; —; —; —; —; —

Mohring; Marie Louise; 7-Dec-61; 8-Dec-61; 2w, 6d; Mohring, Mrs. Louise Karoline; —; —; —; mother died same day

Mohring (nee Trager); Mrs. Louise Karoline; 7-Dec-61; 8-Dec-61; 20y, 6m, 4h; —; —; —; —; —

Mohrmann; Ann Marg; 06-Dec-1840; 07-Dec-1840; 65y; —; —; —; —; —

Momberger; Johann Frirednich Wilhelm; 6-Jul-62; 7-Jul-62; 10m, 19d; Momberger, Georg; Kirschgarten, Hessen [f]; —; —; youngest son

Momberger; Maria Katharine; 3-Jul-62; 5-Jul-62; 2y, 7m; Momberger, Georg; Kirschgarten, Hessen [f]; —; —; second daughter

Momberger; stillborn twin boys; 22-Feb-53; 22-Feb-53; —; Momberger, Georg; Kirschengarten, Hessen [f]; —; —; twins

Morhardt; Johann; 9-May-60; 10-May-60; 70y; —; Pforzheim, Baden; —; —; —

Morschladt; Sophia Elisabeth; 11-Sep-46; 12-Sep-46; 8 Aug 1846; Morschladt, Heinrich; Dammhausen, Harpstadt, Hannover [f]; Lindemann, Maria; Gruben, Bergheim, Kurhessen [m];

Muhly; Anton; 12-Apr-54; 13-Apr-54; 71y, 8m; —; Allendorf a.d. Lumda, Hessen; —; —; —

Muhly; Friedrich; 16-Apr-57; 17-Apr-57; 24y, 11m; —; Elberfeld, Preussen; —; —; —

Surname of Deceased; Given Name of Deceased; Date of Death; Date of Burial; Age or Date of Birth; Survivor(I), Surname, Given; Birthplace Deceased or Parent; Survivor (II), Surname, Given; Birthplace of Survivor (II); Comment

Muhly; Katharina; 30-Mar-50; 31-Mar-50; 5 Jul 1847; Muhly, Eberhard; Allendorf, Hessen [f]; Eitel, Louise; —; died at 3 AM

Muhly (nee Eitel); Mrs. Louise; 2-Jul-61; 3-Jul-61; 46y, 3m, 28d; —; —; —; —; —

Muhly (nee Low); Mrs. Juliane; 8-Jun-63; 9-Jun-63; 28y, 11m; —; —; —; —; —

Muller; Andreas; 13-Jul-44; 14-Jul-44; 28 Feb 1796; —; —; —; —; —

Muller; Georg; 26-Aug-43; 27-Aug-43; 10 Feb 1824; —; —; —; —; —

Muller; Georg; 12-Feb-51; 13-Feb-51; 5m, 9d; Muller, Joh.; Hessen [f]; —; —; —

Muller; Joh. Heinrich; 12-Mar-57; 14-Mar-57; 60y, 10m, 3w, 4d; —; Osterholz, Hannover; —; —; —

Muller; Karl Friedr.; 3-Jul-39; 3-Jul-39; 13 May 1837; —; —; —; —; —

Muller; Maria; 20-Jan-46; 21-Jan-46; 5 Jan 1846; Muller, Martin; Engelstadt, Hessen [f]; Kuhne, Margaretha; Landwehrshagen, Hannover [m];

Muller; Rebecka Adelheid; 1-Sep-45; 2-Sep-45; 27 Oct 1828; Muller, Johann Heinrich; Osterholz, Sieke [f]; Wilken, Marg. Adelheid; —; —

Muller; stillborn son; 31-May-1867; 31-May-1867; 0; Muller, Karl Wilhelm; —; —; —; school teacher

Muller; Valentin; 4-Sep-42; 5-Sep-42; 2 May 1838; —; —; —; —; —

Muller (nee Klotte); Mrs. Margarethe; —; 31-May-1867; 39y, 5m, 2w, 4d; —; Arsten b. Bremen; —; —; —

Muller (nee Wilkens); Mrs. Margarethe Adelheid; 16-Oct-63; 18-Oct-63; 68y, 11w, 2d; —; Hannoverston; —; —; —

Neuweiler; Maria Magd.; 27-Jan-42; 28-Jan-42; 6 Oct 1840; —; —; —; —; —

Niklas; Friedrich Wilhelm; 3-Jul-46; 3-Jul-46; 28 Dec 1844; Niklas, Georg; Dörzbach, Kinzelsau, Wuerttemberg [f]; Oester, Elisabeth; Ebneth, Baiern [m];

Surname of Deceased; Given Name of Deceased; Date of Death; Date of Burial; Age or Date of Birth; Survivor(I), Surname, Given; Birthplace Deceased or Parent; Survivor (II), Surname, Given; Birthplace of Survivor (II); Comment

Niklas; Heinrich Christian; 25-Jul-54; 26-Jul-54; 7y, 9m; Niklas, Georg; Tietzbach, Wuerttemberg [f]; —; —; —

Nikolas; Wilhelm; 9-Mar-41; 10-Mar-41; 63y; —; —; —; —; —

Nonnemacher; Georg Daniel; 2-Jun-47; 3-Jun-47; 18 Jan 1847; Nonnemacher, Joanas; Strasburg, York Co., PA [f]; Sommer, Elisabeth; Baltimore, MD [m];

Nordheck; Friedrich Wilhe.; 14-May-38; 15-May-38; 30 May 1807; —; —; —; —; —

Nutzel; Elisabeth; 23-Dec-63; 24-Dec-62; 16d; Nutzel, Georg; Forchendorf, Baiern [f]; —; —; —

Nutzel; Kunigunde Johanne; 25-May-66; 26-May-66; 4m; Nutzel, Joh. Georg; Forchendorf, Baiern [f]; —; —; —

Ochs; Lorenz; 18-Oct-53; 20-Oct-53; 2y, 2m; Ochs, Thomas; Kips, Baiern [f]; —; —; —

Oehlwein; Wilhelm; 22-Apr-42; 23-Apr-42; 5 Aug 1841; —; —; —; —; —

Oels; August Ferdinand Friedrich; 4-May-49; 5-May-49; 8 Jan 1848; Oels, August; Borgentrup, Minden [f]; Melchior, Henriette; Solingen, Preussen [m];

Oesterle; Georg Wilhelm; 26-Jul-43; 27-Jul-43; 1 May 1843; —; —; —; —; —

Oesterle; Johann; 28-Apr-51; 29-Apr-51; 39y; —; —; —; —; —

Oesterle; Johann Christian; 26-Mar-42; 10-Apr-42; 20 Jan 1842; —; —; —; —; —

Oesterle; Johann Heinrich; 9-Apr-46; 10-Apr-46; 19 Jan 1846; Oesterle, Johann; Königsbach, Baiern [f]; Gingnagel, Anna Maria; Krumstadt, Hessen [m];

Ohmenhauser; Gottlieb Friedrich; 15-Jun-53; 16-Jun-53; 68y; —; Backnan, Wuerttemberg; —; —; bur: Western Cem.

Opitz; Georg Christian; 16-Aug-47; 17-Aug-47; 5 Oct 1845; Opitz, Georg Philipp; Weisssenburg, Anspach, Baiern [f]; Stroheck, Margaretha; Weigersheim, Wuerttemberg [m];

Ortmann; stillborn daughter; 27-Nov-59; 27-Nov-59; —; Ortmann, Eberhard Heinr.; —; —; —; —

Ortwein; Sophia; 14-May-38; 15-May-38; 28 Nov 1837; —; —; —; —; —

Surname of Deceased; Given Name of Deceased; Date of Death; Date of Burial; Age or Date of Birth; Survivor(I), Surname, Given; Birthplace Deceased or Parent; Survivor (II), Surname, Given; Birthplace of Survivor (II); Comment

Osenberg; Gustav Adolph; 16-Sep-63; 17-Sep-63; 2y, 5m, 25d; Osenberg, Karl Wilhelm; Lennep, Preussen [f]; —; —; —

Pabst; Ludwig; 1-Feb-45; —; 1y, 11m, 6d; Pabst, Ludwig; —; Gra, Catharina; —; —

Palmer; Marie; 7-Apr-64; 8-Apr-64; 6m; Palmer, Charles; Massachusetts; —; —; father deceased

Panetti; Friederike Johanne Dorothea; 18-Oct-61; 19-Oct-61; 1y, 10m; Panetti, Philipp Adam Jakob; Rugland [f]; —; —; —

Panetti; Jakob Paulus David; 15-May-55; 16-May-55; 13d; Panetti, Adam Jakob; Rugland, Baiern [f]; —; —; —

Panetti; Johannes Elisa; 14-May-55; 15-May-55; 1y, 10m, 3w; Panetti, Adam Jakob; Rugland, Baiern [f]; —; —; son named Elisa ?

Papst; Alexander Heinrich; 23-Jul-58; 25-Jul-58; 1y, 3m; Papst, Andreas; Bobenhausen, Hesen [f]; —; —; —

Papst; Anna Elisa; 14-Mar-53; 16-Mar-53; 3y, 2m, 1w; Papst, Joh. Andreas; Bobenhausen, Hessen [f]; —; —; —

Papst; Elisabeth; 16-Feb-52; 18-Feb-52; 9y, 6m, 3w; Papst, Andreas; Bobenhausen, Hessen [f]; —; —; oldest daughter

Papst; Johannes; 22-Aug-50; 23-Aug-50; 6m; Papst, Adam; Grunburg, Hessen [f]; —; —; —

Peppler; Wilhelmine Kathr. Elise; 11-Nov-39; 12-Nov-49; 28 Sep 1838; —; —; —; —; —

Peppler (nee Peppler); Henriette; 31-Oct-44; 2-Nov-44; 7 May 1811; —; —; —; —; —

Peusch (nee Waltz); Hannah; 31-Dec-45; 1-Jan-46; 29y; Peush, George; Lancaster, PA; —; —; Valentin & Sarah Weltz

Pfeffer; Maria Elisabeth; 23-Aug-44; 24-Aug-44; 24 Dec 1841; —; —; —; —

Pfeifer; Johann Friedrich; 7-Nov-46; 9-Nov-46; 1 Jan 1844; Pfeifer, Heinrich; Blasbach, Metzlar, Preussen [f]; Beutler, Maria; Nagold, Oberland, Wuerttemberg [m]

Pfeifer; un-named daughter; 6-Mar-47; 7-Mar-47; 1839; Pfeifer, Heinrich; Blasbach, Metzlar, Preussen [f]; Beutler, Maria; Nagold, Wuerttemberg [f]

Pfeiffer; Jacob Friedrich; 5-May-40; 6-May-40; 25 Mar 1838; —; —; —; —

Surname of Deceased; Given Name of Deceased; Date of Death; Date of Burial; Age or Date of Birth; Survivor(I), Surname, Given; Birthplace Deceased or Parent; Survivor (II), Surname, Given; Birthplace of Survivor (II); Comment

Pfeiffer; Nikolas; 27-Mar-39; 28-Mar-39; 1 Jun 1837; —; —; —; —
Pfeiffer (nee Kull); Christine; 9-Apr-44; 11-Apr-44; 1806; —; —; —; —
Pfeil; Karoline Maria; 5-Apr-39; 7-Apr-39; 5 May 1837; —; —; —; —
Pfeil; Ludwig David; 29-Aug-41; 30-Aug-41; —; —; —; —; —
Pfeil (nee Meinhard); Eva Margarethe; 9-Mar-43; 11-Mar-43; 3 Jan 1796; —; —; —; —
Pister; Conrad; 26-Feb-44; 27-Feb-44; 37y; —; —; —; —
Plessing; Luise; 5-Jun-42; 6-Jun-42; 1 Mar 1842; —; —; —; —
Potsch; Margaretha; 9-May-45; 10-May-45; 20 Nov 1844; Potsch, Adam; —; Geschwind, Anna Barbara; Gerbronn, Wuerttemberg [m]
Pracht; Johann; 6-Jul-46; 8-Jul-46; 11 Dec 1796; —; Grunberg, Hessen; —; —
Prufer; Anna Marie; 7-Nov-62; 9-Nov-62; 2y, 5m; Prufer, Karl; Burkersdorf, Sachsen-Weimar [f]; —; —
Prufer; Friedrich August; 1-May-64; 3-May-64; 1y, 6m; Prufer, Karl; Burkensdorf, Sachsen-Weimar [f]; —; —
Prufer; Heinrich Andreas Johann; 25-Aug-55; 27-Aug-55; 10w, 4d; Prufer, Carl Aug.; Bakersdorf, Sachsen-Weimar [f]; —; —
Prufer; stillborn daughter; 20-Feb-57; 20-Feb-57; —; Prufer, Karl Aug.; Burkensdorf, Sachsen-Weimar [f]; —; —; —
Prufer; Wilhelm August; 26-Jul-58; 27-Jul-58; 1m; Prufer, Karl; Burkersdorf, Sachsen-Weimar [f]; —; —; —
Prutz; Chritiane Luise; 9-Feb-43; 10-Feb-43; 2 Jan 1843; —; —; —; —; —
Prutz; Karoline Christine; 5-Apr-40; 6-Apr-40; 8 Apr 1838; —; —; —; —; —
Prutz (nee Becker); Caroline; 20-Feb-48; 22-Feb-48; —; Prutz, Christoph Friedrich; Katzenbach, Rheinbaiern; —; —; —
Raba; Heinrich Wiegand; 6-May-44; 8-May-44; 20 May 1842; —; —; —; —; —
Rabe; Andreas; 5-Jun-45; 6-Jun-45; 4 Feb 1844; Rabe, Wilhelm; Schlagwitz, Kurhessen [f]; Dehn, Luise; Brunnau, Waldecken [m];

Radecke; Heinrich Friedrich; 4-Jul-53; 6-Jul-53; 7w; Radecke, Dietrich Eberhard; Sussede, Hannover [f]; —; —; —

Radecke; Kasten Friedrich; 18-Sep-56; 19-Sep-56; 26y, 19d; —; Husstedt, Hannover; —; —; —

Radecke; Mrs. Catharina Adelheid; 30-Jul-54; 31-Jul-54; 60y; Radecke, Hermann Heinr.; Susstedt, Hannover; —; —; spouse

Radecke; Regine Marie Rebecca; 1-Sep-57; 2-Sep-57; 10m, 3w, 2d; Radecke, Dietrich Eberhard; Susstedt, Hannover [f]; —; —; —

Radeker; Casten Dietrich; 22-Aug-49; 23-Aug-49; 13 May 1844; Radeker, Johann Friedrich; Süstedt, Bruchhausen, Hannover [f]; Thielbahr, Rebecka Margarethe; Süstedt, Bruchhausen, Hannover [m];

Rahn; Andreas Louis; 17-Jun-60; 19-Jun-60; 3y, 7m, 11d; Rahn, Louis; Bobenhausen, Hessen [f]; —; —; —

Rahn; Friedrich; 5-Oct-63; 7-Oct-63; 64y; —; Bobenhausen, Hessen; —; —; —

Rahn; Heinrich Friedrich; 23-Apr-64; 24-Apr-64; 3y, 9d; Rahn, Heinr.; Bobenhausen, Hessen [f]; —; —; —

Rahn; Heinrich Ludwig; 20-Apr-64; 22-Apr-64; 10m; Rahn, Heinr.; Bobenhausen, Hessen [f]; —; —; —

Rahn; Karl Christian; —; 12-Jul-65; 3w; Rahn, Heinr.; Bobenhausen, Hessen [f]; —; —; —

Rahn; Louis Christian; 24-Apr-1867; 26-Apr-1867; 3m; Rahn, Heinrich; Bobenhausen, Wurttemberg; —; —; —

Rapp; Christina; 16-May-1838; 17-May-38; 1805; —; —; —; —; —

Rausch; Conrad; 11-Apr-42; 12-Apr-42; 22y; —; —; —; —; —

Rausch; Georg; 29-Aug-41; 30-Aug-41; 28 Jan 1841; —; —; —; —; —

Rausch (nee Baierlein); Mrs. Margarethe Brigitte; 10-Jan-57; 12-Jan-57; 65y, 9m; —; Plankenfeld, Baiern; —; —; —

Regener; Auguste Wilhelmnine; 1-Jul-58; 2-Jul-58; 7m, 10d; Regener, Johann; Rosenthal, Kurhessen [f]; —; —; —

Regener; Friedrich Wilh. Georg; 4-May-64; 7-May-64; 3y, 7m, 19d; Regener, Georg; Rosenthal, Kurhessen [f]; —; —; —

Regener; Georg Wilhelm Jakob; 6-Jul-56; 7-Jul-56; 3m, 8d; Regener, Johannes; Rosenthal, Kurhessen [f]; —; —; —

Surname of Deceased; Given Name of Deceased; Date of Death; Date of Burial; Age or Date of Birth; Survivor(I), Surname, Given; Birthplace Deceased or Parent; Survivor (II), Surname, Given; Birthplace of Survivor (II); Comment

Regener; Maria Catharine; 31-Dec-53; 1-Jan-54; 9w; Regener, Johannes; Rosenthal, Kurhessen [f]; —; —; —

Regener; stillborn daughter; 1-Nov-53; 1-Nov-53; —; Regener, Johannes; Rosenthal, Kurhessen [f]; —; —; twin

Rein; Christoph; 28-Jul-50; 29-Jul-50; 8y, 3m, 6d; Rein, Severin; Allendorf an d. Lumde, Hessen; —; —; dysentery

Rein; Elisabeth; 6-Apr-55; 7-Apr-55; 4y, 6m,; Rein, Severin; —; —; —; father deceased

Rein; Severin; 23-May-51; 24-May-51; between 40 & 50; —; Allendorf a.d. Lumda, Hessen; —; —; pox

Reinhard; Christine Margarethe; 10-Jan-58; 11-Jan-58; 5m, 6d; Reinhard, Christoph; Allendorf, Hessen [f]; —; —; —

Reinhard; Georg Nicolaus; 22-Apr-1850; 29-Apr-1850; 1 Jun 1849; Reinhard, Johann Christoph; Allendorf a.d. Lumbda [f]; Horst, Katharina Elisabeth; Zell, Hessen [m];

Reinhard; Ludwig; 14-Aug-56; 15-Aug-56; 1y, 2m, 5d; Reinhard, Christoph; Allendorf a.d.L., Hessen [f]; —; —; —

Reinhard; Wilhelmine Marie Emilie; 27-Jan-61; 28-Jan-61; 1y, 9m; Reinhard, Christoph; Allendorf a.d. L, Hessen [f]; —; —; youngest child

Reinhardt; Maria; 10-Oct-47; 11-Oct-47; 28 Sep 1845; Reinhardt, Christopher; Allendorf a.d. Lumda, Hessen [f]; Horst, Catharine; Zell, Alsfeld, Hessen [m];

Reister; Caroline Elisabeth; 14-Jun-46; 15-Jun-46; 7m, 10d; Reister, Johann Georg; Stein bei Pforzheim, Baden [f]; Hachtel, Margaretha; Schillingsfurst, Baiern [m];

Reitz; Margarethe; 5-Jan-42; 7-Jan-42; 21 May 1777; —; —; —; —; —

Repp; Heinrich Christian Wilhelm; 30-Mar-58; 31-Mar-58; 22d; Repp, Heinr. Konrad; Eichelsdorf, Hessen [f]; —; —; pox

Repp; Konrad; 2-Apr-65; 4-Apr-65; 38y, 15d; —; Eichelsdorf, Hessen; —; —; —

Reuter; Anna Wilhelmine; 20-Aug-63; 21-Aug-62; 1y, 8m, 12d; Reuter, Aug.; Michelstadt, Hessen [f]; —; —; —

Riedel; Heinrich Philipp; 13-Jan-58; 14-Jan-58; 5m, 18d; Riedel, Konrad; Altenblass, Baiern [f]; —; —; —

Surname of Deceased; Given Name of Deceased; Date of Death; Date of Burial; Age or Date of Birth; Survivor(I), Surname, Given; Birthplace Deceased or Parent; Survivor (II), Surname, Given; Birthplace of Survivor (II); Comment

Riedel (nee Ruppel); Mrs Anna Elisabeth; 8-Jan-66; 10-Jan-66; 42y; —; Hopfgarten, Hessen; —; —; —

Riel; Elisabeth; 12-Feb-51; 13-Feb-51; 9m; Riel, Caspar; Altenhauslar, Hessen [f]; —; —; —

Riemenschneider; Sophie Magdalena; 1-Apr-52; 2-Apr-52; 9m; Riemenschneider, Gottlieb; Bad Reburg, Hannover [f]; —; —; —

Ries; Anna Elisabeth; 21-Mar-44; 22-Mar-44; 17 May 1842; —; —; —; —; —

Riethmuller; Catharine; 16-Sep-46; 17-Sep-46; 5 Oct 1845; Riethmuller, Heinrich; Braunau, Waldeck [f]; Dehnn, Elisabeth; Braunau, Waldeck [m];

Riethmuller (nee Dehn); Elisabeth; 24-Dec-45; 26-Dec-45; Oct 1811; —; Brockau, Waldeck; —; —; —

Ritter; August Ludwig; 8-Apr-41; 9-Apr-41; 16 May 1835; —; —; —; —; —

Rolfing; Auguste Lisette Katharine; 24-Sep-63; 25-Sep-63; 9m, 2w, 3d; Rolfing, Ludwig; Friedewald, Preussen [f]; —; —; —

Romescher; Heinrich; 9-Dec-59; 11-Dec-59; 44y, 6m, 3d; —; Blankenfels, Baiern; —; —; —

Romig; Maria Mathilde; 12-Dec-38; 3-Dec-39; 15 Jan 1838; —; —; —; —; probably bur. 13 Dec

Rommel; Christian Ferdinand; 2-Sep-50; 3-Sep-50; 3y, 1m, 3w; Rommel, Heinrich; Schmalcalden, Kurhessen; —; —; father deceased

Romoser; Carl Philipp; 20-Dec-1847; 21-Dec-47; 25 Nov 1843; Romoser, Johann Martin; Rodensohl [f]; Fenkbeiner, Johanne; Gettelfingen, Wurttemberg [m];

Romoser; Caroline; 21-Mar-46; 22-Mar-46; 16 Dec 1845; Romoser, Johann Martin; Rodensohl, Neuenbirk [f]; Fenkbeiner, Johanne; Götelfingen, Frendenstadt, Wuerttemberg [m];

Romoser; Christine; 10-Mar-48; 12-Mar-48; 15 Nov 1826; Romoser, Jakob Friedrich; Rothensohl, Neienburg, Wuerttemberg [f]; —; —; —

Romoser; Johann Friedr.; 23-Jan-39; 24-Jan-39; 10 Aug 1835; —; —; —; —; —

Surname of Deceased; Given Name of Deceased; Date of Death; Date of Burial; Age or Date of Birth; Survivor(I), Surname, Given; Birthplace Deceased or Parent; Survivor (II), Surname, Given; Birthplace of Survivor (II); Comment

Romoser; Johann Heinrich; 2-Jan-48; 3-Jan-48; 12 Mar 1842; Romoser, Johann Martin; Rodensohl [f]; Fenkbeiner, Johanne; Gettelfingen, Wuerttemberg [m];

Romoser; Johann Martin; 26-Oct-37; 27-Oct-37; 5 Nov 1831; —; —; —; —; —

Romoser; Wilhelm; 6-Jun-45; 7-Jun-45; 25 Nov 1843; Romoser, Johann; Rothensohl, Wuerttemberg [f]; Fenkbeiner, Johanna; Gettelfingen, Wuerttemberg [m];

Romoser (nee Ohmenhauser); Mrs. Louise Regine; 12-Dec-65; 14-Dec-65; 35y, 7m, 5d; —; Rothensohl, Wurttemberg; —; —; —

Romoser (nee Schaber); Christine; 6-Jun-48; 8-Jun-48; 9 Apr 1787; Romoser, Jakob Friedrich; Rodensohl, Wuerttemberg; —; —; —

Romusser; Samuel Friedrich; 18-Apr-52; 19-Apr-52; 2y, 1m; Romusser, Joh. Martin; Wuerttemberg [f]; —; —; —

Rosa; Johann; 3-Oct-54; 3-Oct-54; 40y; —; Burglein, Baiern; —; —; —

Rosengarn; Mrs. Marie; 14-Nov-51; 16-Nov-51; 68y; —; Gehrter, Hannover; —; —; —

Roter (nee Metzler); Catharine; 14-May-49; 15-May-49; 11 Oct 1817; Roter, Johann; Judenbach, Sachsen-Meiningen; —; —; —

Ruckauer; Elisabeth; 27-Aug-50; 28-Aug-50; 8m; Ruckauer, Sebastian; Herschbruck, Wuerttemberg [f]; —; —; —

Ruckert; Johannes; 25-Jan-50; 26-Jan-50; 1 Dec 1849; Ruckert, Philipp; Zwingenberg [f]; Dietz, Marie; Wolf bei Giessen, Hessen [m];

Ruckert; Maria Lisette; 18-Sep-48; 20-Sep-48; 24 Jul 1847; Ruckert, Philipp; Zwingenberg, Hessen [f]; Dietz, Anna Maria; Wolf, Bidingen, Hessen [m];

Rudolph; Johann Hermann; 17-Jun-44; 19-Jun-44; 25 Apr 1760; —; —; —; —; —

Rudolph; Mathilde Hermine; 11-Aug-58; 13-Aug-58; 1y, 2m, 3w; Rudolph, Benjamin; Ezbau, Sachsen [f]; —; —; —

Ruff; Jakob Friederich; 18-Sep-46; 19-Sep-46; 4 Jun 1845; Ruff, Jakob Friedr.; Dobel, Neuenberg, Wuerttemberg [f]; Steiner, Catharine; Unter Simau bei Coburg [m];

Rullmann; Mrs.; 5-Feb-52; 7-Feb-52; —; —; —; —; —; husband refuses to give info

Ruppel; Heinrich; 25-Nov-62; 27-Nov-62; 48y, 8m; —; Hopfgarter, Hessen; —; —; —

Ruppel; Heinrich Johann; 5-Jul-47; 6-Jul-47; 12 Feb 1846; Ruppel, Johann; Hofgarten, Alsfeld, Hessen [f]; Weitzel, Elisabeth; Strebendorf, Alsfeld, Hessen [m];

Ruppel; Johann Frdch. Georg; 30-Jun-65; 1-Jul-65; 9m; Ruppel, Nilaus; Hopfgarten, Hessen [f]; —; —; —

Ruppel; Johanne Elisabeth Mariane; 23-Dec-60; 25-Dec-60; 9m; Ruppel, Nikolaus; Hopfgarten [f]; —; —; —

Ruppel; Johannes; 21-Apr-48; 23-Apr-48; 4 Jul 1847; Ruppel, Heinrich; Hofgarten, Alsfeld, Hessen [f]; Bühler, Maria; Weida, Sulz, Wuerttemberg [m];

Ruppert; Mrs. Elisabeth; 25-Jun-59; 26-Jun-59; 86y, 9m, 3w; —; Rodtheim, Hessen; —; —; —

Ruppert; Wilhelm; 11-May-52; 13-May-52; 61y; —; Dellingshausen, Hessen; —; —; —

Rusk; Marianne; —; 15-Aug-48; 20 Nov 1847; Rusk, Jakob Friedrich; Dobel, Neuenbirk, Wuerttemberg [f]; Steiner, Catharina; Unter Siemens, Sachsen-Coburg;

Sachs; Albert; 27-Sep-51; 29-Sep-51; 2m, 12d; Sachs, Johann; Mittelsinn, Kurhessen [f]; —; —; —

Sartorius; Carl; 24-Jun-45; 25-Jun-45; 30 May 1845; Sartorius, Georg; Monsheim, Hessen [f]; Pfaff, Cath.; Kaiserslautern [m];

Sauft; August; 10-Aug-42; 11-Aug-42; 2 Mar 1805; —; —; —; —; —

Schaberg; Catharina Emma; 31-Aug-50; 2-Sep-50; 1y, 1m; Schaberg, Hermann Heinrich; Bramsch b. Osnabruck [f]; —; —; —

Schafer; Christiane; —; 19-Jan-47; 28 Oct 1846; Schafer, Christian Jakob; Weinsberg, Wurttemberg [f]; Meyer, Christiane; Waldbach, Wuerttemberg [m];

Schafer; Christiane Maria; 13-Feb-44; 14-Feb-44; 5 May 1842; —; —; —; —; —

Surname of Deceased; Given Name of Deceased; Date of Death; Date of Burial; Age or Date of Birth; Survivor(I), Surname, Given; Birthplace Deceased or Parent; Survivor (II), Surname, Given; Birthplace of Survivor (II); Comment

Schafer; Christopher Ludwig; 10-Apr-48; 11-Apr-48; 20 Mar 1845; Schafer, Christian Jakob; Weinsberg, Wuerttemberg [f]; Mayer, Christiane; Waldbach, Wuerttemberg [m];

Schafer; Emilie; 5-Oct-40; 06-Oct-1840; Jan 1829; —; —; —; —; —

Schafer; Jakob; 14-Feb-46; 15-Feb-46; 21 Aug 1801; —; Esslingen, Wuerttemberg; —; —; —

Schafer; Johann Heinrich Friedrich; 23-Feb-60; 24-Feb-60; 2y, 7w, 5d; Schafer, Heinr.; Lisberg, Hessen [f]; —; —; youngest son

Schaible; Bernhard; 21-Oct-42; 22-Oct-42; 10 Aug 1840; —; —; —; —; —

Schaible; Karl Jacob Fr.; 5-Oct-38; 5-Oct-38; 22 April 1838; —; —; —; —; —

Schaible; Maria Magdalene; 28-Jun-52; 29-Jun-52; 2y, 1m; Schaible, Friedrich; Wuerttemberg [f]; —; —; —

Schaumburg; Franz Friedrich; 6-Aug-65; 7-Aug-65; 10m, 2w, 4d; Schaumburg, Lorenz; Braunau, Waldeck [f]; —; —; —

Schaumburg; Marie Katharine; 28-Jun-56; 29-Jun-56; 10m, 2w, 4d; Schaumburg, Jakob; —; —; —; only daughter

Schaumloffel; Johanne Louise; 28-Oct-52; 29-Oct-52; 3d; Schaumloffel, Wilh.; Oberschutz, Kurhessen [f]; —; —; only daughter

Schaumloffel; Marie Sophie Karoline; 13-Aug-59; 14-Aug-59; 1y, 11m, 10d; Schaumloffel, Wilhelm; Obervaschutz, Kurhessen [f]; —; —; youngest child

Scherer; stillborn son; 31-Oct-56; 31-Oct-56; —; Scherer, Joh.; Wahlen, Hessen [f]; —; —; —

Scheuermann; Wilhelm; 6-Mar-45; 9-Mar-45; 18m; Scheuermann, Dr. Franz; —; —; —; —

Scheufle; Samuel; 9-Jul-40; 10-Jul-40; 26 Sep 1839; —; —; —; —; —

Schickle; Maria Elisab; 22-Aug-38; 23-Aug-38; 25 Jan 1838; —; —; —; —; —

Schieber; Christian; 21-Dec-37; 22-Dec-37; 28y; —; —; —; —; —

Schiess; Luise; 4-Mar-43; 5-Mar-43; 13 Nov 1841; —; —; —; —; —

Schiess; Wilhelm; 15-Aug-45; 17-Aug-45; 33y, 6m; —; Bergzabern, Rheinkreis, Baiern; —; —; —

Schillinger; Georg Friederich; 13-Aug-46; 14-Aug-46; 20 Nov 1842; Schillinger, Georg; Grunberg, Hessen [f]; Kopp, Friederike; Dottweil, Neupreussen [m];

Schillinger; Georg Philip; 24-Jan-39; 25-Jan-39; 7 Oct 1837; —; —; —; —; —

Schillinger; Georg Philipp; 4-Sep-45; 5-Sep-45; 15 Sep 1844; Schillinger, Georg Adam; Grunberg, Hessen [f]; Kopp, Friederike; Duttweil, Neupreussen [m];

Schillinger; Heinrich Philipp; 19-Feb-46; 21-Feb-46; 12 Apr 1844; Schillinger, Philipp; Grunberg, Hessen [f]; Kopp, Sophie; Dudweiler, Preussen [m];

Schlaffer; Karl; 10-Sep-43; 11-Sep-43; 22 Nov 1807; —; —; —; —; —

Schlag; Mariane; 5-Sep-42; 7-Sep-42; 16 Jun 1840; —; —; —; —; —

Schlentz; Friederike; 20-Oct-58; 22-Oct-58; 1y, 9m; Schlentz, Ludwig; Flegesen, Hannover [f]; —; —; only daughter

Schlerf; Friedrich Wilhelm Anton; 7-Aug-57; 8-Aug-57; 1y, 11m, 1w, 6d; Schlerf, Philipp; Allendorf, Hessen [f]; —; —; —

Schlerf; Friedrich Wilhelm Christian; 8-Jul-62; 10-Jul-62; 1y, 2m; Schlerf, Philipp; Allendorf a.d.L, Hessen [f]; —; —; —

Schlerf; Katharine Elisabeth; 15-Aug-58; 16-Aug-58; 1y, 9m; Schlerf, Melchior; Allendorf, Hessen [f]; —; —; —

Schlerf; Katharine Henriette Friedrike; 31-Mar-63; 1-Apr-63; 5m, 2w, 3d; Schlerf, Joh. Georg; Allendorf a.d.L, Hessen [f]; —; —; —

Schlerf; Marie Katharine; 8-Jul-63; 9-Jul-63; 10m, 4d; Schlerf, Melchior; Allendorf a.d.L, Hessen [f]; —; —; —

Schlerf; Marie Wilhelmine; 7-Jul-61; 8-Jul-61; 1y, 5w, 6d; Schlerf, Melchior; Allendorf, Hessen [f]; —; —; youngest daughter

Schlerf; Mrs. Emilie; 2-Aug-61; 3-Aug-61; 35y, 2m, 21d; —; Grunstadt, Rheinbaiern; —; —; —

Schlerf; Wilhelm Melchior Gottlieb; 9-Aug-66; 10-Aug-66; 1y, 1m, 3d; Schlerf, Melchior; Allendorf a.d. Lumde, Hessen [f]; —; —; —

Surname of Deceased; Given Name of Deceased; Date of Death; Date of Burial; Age or Date of Birth; Survivor(I), Surname, Given; Birthplace Deceased or Parent; Survivor (II), Surname, Given; Birthplace of Survivor (II); Comment

Schlerf; Wilhlmine Katharine; 26-Jul-59; 27-Jul-59; 1m, 2w; Schlerf, Melchior; Allendorf a.d.L, Hessen [f]; —; —; —
Schmalz; Georg; 9-Feb-40; 11-Feb-40; 8 Feb 1804; —; —; —; —; —

Schmenner; Marianne; 21-Dec-45; 23-Dec-45; 22 Feb 1842; Schmenner, Daniel; Marburg [f]; Thielemann, Elisabeth; Caldern, Kurhessen [m];
Schmidt; Anna; 7-Dec-65; 8-Dec-65; 1y, 2w; Schmidt, Joh.; Breitenbach, Hessen [f]; —; —; —
Schmidt; Heinrich; 6-Jul-51; 8-Jul-51; 11m, 6d; Schmidt, Konrad; Oberohm, Hessen, [f]; —; —; bur: Baltimore Cem.
Schmidt; Johann Georg; 11-May-57; 12-May-57; 5y, 5m; Schmidt, Georg; Kairlindach, Baiern [f]; —; —; —
Schmidt; Johanne; 8-Jun-40; 9-Jun-40; 17 Scp 1834; —; —; —; —; —

Schmidt; Johannes; 28-Nov-66; 30-Nov-66; 25y, 6m, 2w, 4d; —; Langendorf, Kurhessen; —; —; —
Schmidt; Karoline Josephine Susanne; 21-Dec-65; 22-Dec-65; 2y; Schmidt, Christian; Eichelsdorf, Kurhessen [f]; —; —; —
Schmidt; Wilhelm; 21-Jan-44; 22-Jan-44; 23 Nov 1840; —; —; —; —; —
Schmidt (nee Koch); Elisabeth; 3-Dec-46; 4-Dec-46; 62y; Schmidt, Johann; Beutelsbach, Wuerttemberg; —; —;

Schmidt (nee Oesterle); Maria Dorothea; 19-Jul-47; 20-Jul-47; 16 May 1824; Schmidt, Friedrich; Obelspohn, Wuerttemberg; —; —; —
Schmidt (nee Reif); Anna Margaretha; 12-Oct-49; 13-Oct-49; 16 Nov 1780; Schmidt, Johann; Hain, Baiern; —; —; —
Schmidt (nee Walther); Wilhelmina; 21-Nov-46; 22-Nov-46; 3 May 1807; Schmidt, Math.; Hainichen, Nidda, Hesen; —; —; —
Schmiermund; Ludwig Heinrich; 22-Jan-51; 23-Jan-51; 9m, 2w; Schmiermund, Joh.; —; —; —; —
Schnabel; Christine; 19-Aug-56; 20-Aug-56; 9m, 21d; Schnabel, Ludwig; Allendorf a.d.L, Hessen [f]; —; —; —
Schnabel; Katharine; 15-Aug-60; 16-Aug-60; 3m; Schnabel, Ludwig; —; —; —; youngest daughter

Surname of Deceased; Given Name of Deceased; Date of Death; Date of Burial; Age or Date of Birth; Survivor(I), Surname, Given; Birthplace Deceased or Parent; Survivor (II), Surname, Given; Birthplace of Survivor (II); Comment

Schnabel; Ludwig; 3-Mar-66; 5-Mar-66; 8y, 2m; Schnabel, Ludwig; Allendorf a.d. Lumde, Hessen [f]; —; —; —

Schneider; August Heinrich; 3-Aug-56; 5-Aug-56; 5y, 5m, 3w; Schneider, Friedr.; Engter, Hannover [f]; —; —; —

Schneider; Dorothea; 23-Aug-55; 24-Aug-55; 4m, 5d; Schneider, Joh.; Nordeck, Kurhessen [f]; —; —; —

Schneider; Friedrich; 15-Dec-47; 17-Dec-47; 23 Oct 1846; Schneider, Johann Georg; Gondershausen, Alsfeld, Hessen [f]; Eitel, Christine; Lemberg bei Bermesins, Baiern [m];

Schneider; Hermann Friedrich; 14-Mar-54; 16-Mar-54; 6y, 9m, 3w; Schneider, Joh. Frdch.; Engter, Osnabruck [f]; —; —; —

Schneider; Johann Friedrich Wilhelm; —; 15-Apr-62; 26y, 2m, 15d; —; Engter, Hannover [f]; —; —; —

Schneider; Johann Wilh. Martin; 13-Jul-44; 13-Jul-44; 22 Jan 1844; —; —; —; —; —

Schneider; Karl Philipp Thomas; 19-May-64; 21-May-64; 11m, 10d; Schneider, Heinrich; Fulda, Hessen [f]; —; —; —

Schneider; Maria Elisa; 4-Oct-54; 5-Oct-54; 2y, 5m; Schneider, Joh.; Nordeck, Kurhessen [f]; —; —; —

Schneider; Mrs. Catharina; 24-Apr-55; 26-Apr-55; 31y, 10m, 17d; Schneider, Johann; Nordeck, Kurhessen; —; —; spouse

Schneider; Wilhelm Heinrich; 28-Dec-45; 28-Dec-45; 8 Nov 1841; Schneider, Wilhelm; Mertzhaisen [f]; Werner, Maria; Rosenthal, Kirchenheim [m];

Schneider (nee Engel); Mrs. Marie; 24-Jun-66; 26-Jun-66; 58y, 4d; —; Engter, Hannover; —; —; —

Schneider (nee Hagemeyer); Mrs. Marie Adelheid; 2-May-60; 3-May-60; 81y, 6m,; —; Engter, Hannover; —; —; —

Schnezt; Margarethe Wilhelmine; 26-Mar-39; 27-Mar-39; 21 Jan 1839; —; —; —; —; —

Schoenberg; Johann Heinrich; 30-Mar-66; 31-Mar-66; 68y; —; Engter, Hannover; —; —; —

Schog; Johann Christian; 8-Aug-49; 9-Aug-49; 50-60y; Greberg, Ehringen, Wuerttemberg; —; —; —; —

Schortz; Johann; 7-Sep-50; 9-Sep-50; 30y, 6m; —; Wurzburg; —; —; left a widow

Schramm (nee Gunther); Wilhelmine; 16-Mar-49; 18-Mar-49; 5 Mar 1817; —; Diepholz, Hannover; —; —; —

Schreier; Mrs. Marie; 17-Sep-51; 18-Sep-51; 78y, 6m, 7d; —; —; —; —; —

Schroder; Wilhelmine Louise; 14-Aug-62; 15-Aug-62; 11w; Schroder, Wilhelm; Neuenkirchen, Hannover [f]; —; —; —

Schröder; Heinrich Ludwig; 16-Jan-46; 18-Jan-46; 7 Apr 1840; Schröder, Heinr. Friedr. Ludwig; Holzhausen, Hausberge, Minden [f]; Fallinger, Martha Elise; Salzwerth, Sehme, Hannover [m];

Schröder; Johann Eduard Heinrich; 14-Dec-45; 15-Dec-45; 19 Sep 1845; Schröder, Heinrich Friedrich; —; Fattinger, Martha Elise; —; —

Schuhmacher (nee Rodehäuser); Kunigunde; 29-Jun-49; 1-Jul-49; 54y; Schuhmacher, Christoph; Marburg, Kurhessen; —; —; —

Schulte; Adolph Christian; 17-Jul-46; 19-Jul-46; 30 Sep 1845; Schulte, Franz Gerhard; Hördinghausen, Mittlage, Hannover [f]; Meyer, Maria Clara; Hördinghausen, Mittlage, Hannover [m];

Schulte; Ernst August; 11-Oct-45; 12-Oct-45; 30 Sep 1845; Schulte, Gerhardt; Hordinghausen, Mitlage, Hannover [f]; Meyer, Maria Clara; —; —

Schulz; Friedrich Rudolph; 8-Nov-56; 10-Nov-56; 5m, 3w; Schulz, Konrad; Biedekopf,Hessen [f]; —; —; —

Schulz; Karl Wilhelm Franz; 16-Jul-1867; 17-Jul-1867; 7m, 8d; Schulz, Franz Wilhelm Konrad; Liebenau [f]; —; —; —

Schulz; Marie Helene Rosine; 10-May-58; 12-May-58; 7m, 2w, 3d; Schulz, Konrad; Biedekopf, Hessen [f]; —; —; pox

Schulze; Marie Louise Eleonore; 2-Aug-58; 3-Aug-58; 1y, 3m; Schulze, Gottlieb; Liebenau [f]; —; —; —

Schumacher; Kunigunde Elisabeth; 3-Sep-54; 4-Sep-54; 11m, 2w; Schumacher, Reinhard; Marburg, Kurhessen [f]; —; —; —

Schurter; J. Ludwig; 14-Sep-49; 15-Sep-49; 6 Jun 1815; —; Auenheim, Baden; —; —; —

Schurz; Anna Maria; 4-Jul-50; 5-Jul-50; 16 May 1850; Schurz, Johann; Wahnersbach, Bayern [f]; Kramer, Katharina; Rothenburg a.d. Tauber [m];

Surname of Deceased; Given Name of Deceased; Date of Death; Date of Burial; Age or Date of Birth; Survivor(I), Surname, Given; Birthplace Deceased or Parent; Survivor (II), Surname, Given; Birthplace of Survivor (II); Comment

Schwab; Christian; 3-Jul-58; 4-Jul-58; 9d; Schwab, Christian; Gersbach, Rheinbaiern [f]; —; —; —

Schwab; Christian Heinrich Karl; 17-Jul-62; 19-Jul-62; 1y, 1m, 17d; Schwab, Christian; Gersbach, Rheinbaiern [f]; —; —; —

Schwab; Elisabeth Katharine Wilhelmine; 23-Jan-60; 24-Jan-60; 1y, 4m, 20d; Schwab, Heinr.; Gersbach, Rheinbaiern [f]; —; —; only daughter

Schwab; Johann Friedrich; 13-Aug-1867; 15-Aug-1867; 2y, 24 d; Schwab, Heinr.; Gersbach, Rheinbaiern; —; —; —

Schwab; Karl; 19-Nov-1867; 20-Nov-1867; 5 d; Schwab, Christian; Gersbach, Rheinbaiern [f]; —; —; youngest son

Schwab; Karl Heinrich; 13-May-58; 15-May-58; 1y, 7m; Schwab, Karl; Gersbach, Rheinbaiern [f]; —; —; drowned in Muhlbach [?]

Schwab; Magdalene; 13-Apr-63; 14-Apr-63; 16d; Schwab, Christian; Gerbach, Rheinbaiern; —; —; —

Schwab; Philipp; 8-Dec-60; 10-Dec-60; 74y; —; Windsberg, Rheinbaiern; —; —; —

Schwartz; Johann Alexander Daniel; 8-Dec-66; 10-Dec-66; 11m; Schwartz, Daniel; Unterschonthal, Wurttemberg [f]; —; —; —

Schwarz (nee Schulz); Juliane Chatarine Elisabeth; 6-Jun-49; 7-Jun-49; 7 Jan 1776; Schwarz, [--?--]; Magenfeld, Hannover [d]; —; —; husband from Bremen

Schwarzenberger; Friedrich; 4-Feb-61; 6-Feb-61; 1y, 11m; Schwarzenberger, Friedrich; Truterteufstetter Wurttemberg [f]; —; —; —

Schweckendiek; Georg August Hermann; 27-Mar-58; 29-Mar-58; 2y, 1m, 3w; Schweckendiek, Georg; Braunschweig [f]; —; —; —

Schweigerdt (nee Lücke); Barbara; 13-Jan-50; 15-Jan-50; 12 Feb 1777; —; Aich, Nöttingen, Wuerttemberg; —; —; —

Schweigert; Michael; —; 2-Jun-46; 76y; —; Aich, Wuerttemberg; —; —; —

Seckel; David; 3-Mar-50; 5-Mar-50; 10 Jan 1790; —; Kurhessen; —; —; —

Seib; Mrs. Katharine; 17-May-66; 18-May-66; 69y, 3m, 18d; —; Wollmer, Kurhessen; —; —; —

Surname of Deceased; Given Name of Deceased; Date of Death; Date of Burial; Age or Date of Birth; Survivor(I), Surname, Given; Birthplace Deceased or Parent; Survivor (II), Surname, Given; Birthplace of Survivor (II); Comment

Seibel; Maria Magdalena; 2-Sep-55; 3-Sep-55; 1y, 1m; Seibel, Joh.; Niederotterbach, Baiern [f]; —; —; —

Seibold; Dorothea Karoline; 21-Apr-44; 22-Apr-44; 13 Dec 1843; —; —; —; —; —

Seibold; Phlip Franz; 12-Jul-38; 13-Jul-38; 25 May 1836; —; —; —; —; —

Seip; Jakob; 11-Jan-48; 13-Jan-48; 14 Dec 1822; Seip, Johann; —; Dofft, Catharina; Wollmaar, Marburg, Kurhessen [m];

Seippel; Emil Melchior; 31-Jul-53; 1-Aug-53; 4m, 3w; Seippel, Johann; Niederotterbach, Baiern [f]; —; —; —

Seyfried; Carl Friedrich; 17-Dec-47; 18-Dec-47; 1816; —; —; —; —; —

Sickel (nee Erck); Catharina; 20-Nov-48; 21-Nov-48; 31y, 2m; Sickel, Heinrich; Nidda, Hessen; —; —; —

Sieck; Anna Katharine Margaretha; 20-Jun-66; 22-Jun-66; 1y, 11m; Sieck, Jobst Heinrich Friedrich; Susede, Hannover [f]; —; —; —

Sieck; Christoph Heinr.; 7-Nov-54; 8-Nov-54; 37y, 10m; —; Husede, Hannover; —; —; leaves widow & 4 children

Sieck; Eleonore Elisabeth; 10-Apr-58; 12-Apr-58; 1y, 8w; Sieck, Jobst Heinr. Frdch; Husede, Hannover [f]; —; —; —

Sieck; Elise; 5-Oct-52; 6-Oct-52; 7y; Sieck, Claus; Husede, Amt Wittler, Hannover [f]; —; —; —

Sieck; Florentine Elisabeth; 20-Feb-53; 21-Feb-53; 2y, 7m, 2d; Sieck, Adam Friedrich; Husede, Hannover [f]; —; —; oldest daughter

Sieck; Florentine Katharine; 31-Aug-60; 2-Sep-60; 5m, 1w, 6d; Sieck, Heinr. Frdch.; Husede, Hannover [f]; —; —; youngest daughter

Sieck; Florentine Louise; 4-Jun-62; 6-Jun-62; 6y, 9m, 1w, 4d; Sieck, Adam Friedrich; Husede, Hannover [f]; —; —; —

Sieck; Johann Heinrich; 16-Feb-53; 18-Feb-53; 5y, 6m; Sieck, Adam Frdch.; Husede, Hannover [f]; —; —; only son

Sieck; Karoline; 2-Nov-56; 3-Nov-56; 1y, 4m, 3w; Sieck, Joh.; Husede, Hannover [f]; —; —; —

Sieck; Katharine Wilhelmine; 8-Jul-59; 9-Jul-59; 9m, 8d; Sieck, Jobst Heinr. Friedch.; Husede, Hannover [f]; —; —; youngest daughter

Sieck; Klaus Heinrich; 11-Jul-62; 12-Jul-62; 66y, 11m, 3w; —; Husede, Hannover; —; —; —

Siegel; Anna Margaretha Magdalene; 27-Aug-65; 28-Aug-65; 12d; Siegel, Ferd.; Eichelsheim, Baden [f]; —; —; —

Sieghart; Gottlieb; 12-Aug-65; 14-Aug-65; 40y; —; Neustadt a.d. Hayde, Sachsen Coburg; —; —; —

Siegle; Amalie Laura; 23-Feb-43; 28-Feb-43; 31 Jan 1843; —; —; —; —; —

Siegmund; Ludwig Ferdinand; 23-Jan-55; 25-Jan-55; 6m; Siegmund, Ludwig Ferdinand; Sintelfinger, Wuerttemberg [f]; —; —; twin

Sonnstadt; Ludwig; 26-May-38; 27-May-38; 24 Dec 1781; —; —; —; —; —

Spainer; Johann; 5-Jul-38; 6-Jul-38; 5 Jun 1838; —; —; —; —; —

Spalt; Anna Elisabeth; 22-Mar-44; 24-Mar-44; 58y; —; —; —; —; —

Spangenberg; Charlotte; —; 11-Apr-56; 23y; —; Herruden bei Nordhausen, Presussen; —; —; shot [?]

Spangenberger; Georg Jakob Wilhelm; 26-Jun-61; 27-Jun-61; 1m; Spangenberger, Georg; —; —; —; youngest child

Spangenberger; Karoline Dorhothea Elisabeth; 10-May-64; 11-May-64; 5m; Spangenberger, Johannes; Eichelsdorf, Hessen [f]; —; —; —

Spangenberger (nee Muth); Mrs. Katharine Marie; 28-May-64; 29-May-64; 76y; —; Eichelsdorf, Hessen; —; —; —

Späth; Maria Magdalena; —; 19-Oct-46; 8 Feb 1826; Späth, Johann Georg; —; Schneider, Regina Barbara; —; fifth dau of boardmaker

Spielmann; Marie Virginia; 11-Mar-58; 12-Mar-58; 2y, 7m, 5d; Spielmann, Joh. Heinrich; Lisberg, Hessen [f]; —; —; —

Spilmann; Johann Heinrich; 31-Dec-63; 2-Jan-64; 3y, 4m, 4w; Spilmann, Peter Karl; Lisberg, Hessen [f]; —; —; —

Stahl; Jakob; 26-Feb-55; 28-Feb-55; 80y, 2m; Hohenossloch, Wurttemberg; —; —; —; —

Surname of Deceased; Given Name of Deceased; Date of Death; Date of Burial; Age or Date of Birth; Survivor(I), Surname, Given; Birthplace Deceased or Parent; Survivor (II), Surname, Given; Birthplace of Survivor (II); Comment

Stahl; Mrs. Barbara; 27-Feb-57; 1-Mar-57; 78y, 7m; —; —; —; —; —

Stang; Elisabeth; 2-Jun-66; 4-Jun-66; 17m, 6d; Stang, Nikolaus; Frauenaurach, Baiern [f]; —; —; —

Stanger (nee Wolkemuth); Elisabeth Katharina; 29-Feb-44; 1-Mar-44; 7 Sep 1794; —; —; —; —; —

Staupitz; Christine; 27-Sep-39; 28-Sep-39; 27 Nov 1838; —; —; —; —; —

Stecker; Katharine; 7-Sep-44; 9-Sep-44; 19 Nov 1843; —; —; —; —; —

Stegmeyer (nee Herrin); Rosine; 13-Dec-40; 13-Dec-40; 43y; —; —; —; —; —

Steiner; Johann Georg; 21-May-55; 23-May-55; 5y, 9m, 5d; Steiner, Joh.; Frauenaurach, Baiern [f]; —; —; —

Steinweg; Johann; 17-Dec-47; 18-Dec-47; 3 Jan 1844; Steinweg, Carl; Bergsteinhurth bei Münster, Preussen [f]; Fritz, Henriette; Hamele, Hannover [m];

Steinweg; Marie Helene; 13-Dec-47; 14-Dec-47; 11 Oct 1846; Steinweg, Carl; Bergsteinfurth bei Münster, Preussen [f]; Fritz, Henriette; Hamele, Hannover [m];

Steinweg; Susanne; 22-Sep-45; 23-Sep-45; 16 Sep 1845; Steinweg, Carl; Burg Steinfurth, Preussen [f]; Fritz, Henriette; —; —

Stetter; Emilie Susanne Eva; 18-Jun-62; 19-Jun-62; 12y, 10m, 2w, rd; Stetter, Wilhelm; Buche, Baden [f]; —; —; —

Stetter; Heinrich Matthaus Melchior; 15-Aug-62; 16-Aug-62; 10m, 2w; Stetter, Wilhelm; Buche, Baden [f]; —; —; —

Steudler; Karl; 13-Jul-44; 14-Jul-44; 15 Sep 1841; —; —; —; —; —

Steudler; Laura Virginia; 8-Jul-45; 9-Jul-45; 22 Mar 1845; Steudler, Joh.; Dimbach, Bergzabern, Rheinbaiern [f]; Ruf, Jacobine; Dobel, Wuerttemberg [m];

Stierle; Johann Georg; 20-Dec-45; 22-Dec-45; 14 May 1816; —; Oberaichen, Mussberg, Wuerttemberg; —; —; —

Stober; Jakob; 30-Aug-51; 31-Aug-51; 14y; Stober, Jakob; —; —; —; oldest son

Stober; Jakob; 28-Aug-1867; 29-Aug-1867; 64 y, 6 m; —; Wilferdingen, Baden; —; —; —

Stober; Mrs. Rebecca; 22-Aug-50; 23-Aug-50; 41y,; Stober, Jakob; Wolfentingen, Baden; —; —; leaves 6 children

Stock; Andreas Friedrich; 9-Dec-52; 11-Dec-52; 6w; Stock, Michael Friedrich; —; —; —; school teacher

Strobel; Dorothea Nannette; 5-Jan-54; 6-Jan-54; 5d; Strobel, Joh. Georg; Forchtenberg, Wuerttemberg [f]; —; —; —

Strobel; Georg Christian Matthaus; 9-Oct-58; 11-Oct-58; 18m; Strobel, Joh. Georg; Forchtenberg, Wurttemberg [f]; —; —; —

Strobel; Gottlieb; —; 19-Apr-63; —; Strobel, Joh. Georg; —; —; —; miscarriage

Strobel; Johann Georg; 11-Apr-63; 13-Apr-63; 11y; Strobel, Joh. Georg; Forcstenberg, Wurttemberg [f]; —; —; —

Strobel; Johann Heinrich; 28-Jul-53; 29-Jul-53; 3y, 6m, 6d; Strobel, Joh. Georg; Forchten, Wuerttemberg [f]; —; —; —

Strobel; Margaretha Catharina; 12-Apr-1850; 14-Apr-1850; 2 Jan 1848; Strobel, Johann Georg; Forchtenberg, Wuerttemberg [f]; Muller, Katharina Maria; Hannover bei Bremen [m];

Strobel; Matthaus Christain Robert; 8-Feb-60; 9-Feb-60; 2m, 3w, 3d; Strobel, Joh. Georg; Frochtenberg, Wurttemberg [f]; —; —; youngest child

Stroh; Maria Margaretha; 11-Feb-58; 13-Feb-58; 4y; Stroh, Conrad; Lohrbach, Hessen [f]; —; —; —

Strohmann; Heinrich; 27-Jun-60; 29-Jun-60; 20y; Uchte, Hannover; —; —; —; —

Stuckenbrock; Ludwig; 24-Dec-45; —; —; —; Osnabruck, Hannover; —; —; school teacher

Stumptner; Christian; 8-Sep-46; 9-Sep-46; 2 Sep 1846; Stumptner, Simon; Oberaichenbach, Aurach, Baiern [f]; Hubschmann, Ursula Barbara; Middeldorf [m];

Sturken; Marie Christine Elisabeth; 28-Apr-66; 30-Apr-66; 9y, 6m, 3d; Sturken, Rev. Klaus; Pastor of Immanuel Church; —; —; —

Stuterberger; Johann Heinrich; 8-Sep-48; 11-Sep-48; 27 Jul 1845; Stuterberger, Ehlert; Osterholz, Sinke, Hannover [f]; Meyer, Anna Margaretha; Thedinghausen, Braunschweig [m];

Sus; Catharine Margarethe; 06-Aug-1848; 14-Aug-1848; 22 May 1847; Sus, Georg Michael; Kalberbach, Gerbronn,

Wuerttemberg [f]; Böhm, Rosine Margarethe; Schrotsberg, Wuerttemberg [m];

Sus; Johann Georg; 20-Mar-46; 21-Mar-46; 2 Mar 1846; Sus, Georg Michael; Kalberbach, Gerabronn, Wuerttemberg [f]; Böhm, Rosine; Schrotsberg, Wuerttemberg [m];

Taubert; Heinrich Adam; 12-Apr-65; 13-Apr-65; 5m, 1d; Taubert, Gottlieb; Niederwiera, ,Sachsen-Altenburg [f]; —; —; —

Taubert; Ida; 15-Nov-66; 16-Nov-66; 5y, 28d; Tauber, Gottlieb; Sachsen Altenburg; —; —; only child

Thiemeyer; Anna Amelie; 20-Apr-63; 22-Apr-63; 9y, 1m, 29d; Thiemeyer, Friedrich; Engter, Hannover [f]; —; —; —

Thiemeyer; Anna Maria Carolina; 15-Jun-45; 16-Jun-45; 31 Jan 1845; Thiemeyer, Herrmann Friedr.; Engter, Wörden, Hannover [f]; Im Sande, Margaretha Charlotte; Engter, Wörden, Hannover [m];

Thiemeyer; Anna Maria Luise; 8-Feb-42; 9-Feb-42; 12 Mar 1838; —; —; —; —; —

Thiemeyer; Anna Marie Juliane; 13-Aug-56; 13-Aug-56; 2w, 4d; Thiemeyer, Joh. Heinr.; Engter, Hannover [f]; —; —; —

Thiemeyer; Heinrich; 17-Apr-56; 18-Apr-56; 11w, 4d; Thiemeyer, Herm. Frdch.; Engter, Hannover [f]; —; —; —

Thiemeyer; Johann Friedrich; 10-Mar-55; 12-Mar-55; 8y, 10m, 12d; Thiemeyer, Hermann Friedrich; Engter, Hannover [f]; —; —; —

Thiemeyer (nee Klusmann); Anna Maria; 7-Oct-38; 8-Oct-38; 65y; —; —; —; —; —

Thiemeyer (nee Vor der Wusten); Mrs. Anna Marie Karoline; 13-Mar-65; 15-Mar-65; 44y, 4m, 9d; —; Engter, Hannover; —; —; —

Thomas (nee Schneider); Elisabeth; 9-Dec-49; 10-Dec-49; 67y; Thomas, Heinrich; Jusbach, Rauschenberg, Kurhessen; —; —; spouse

Thompson; Johann Jacob; 28-Oct-41; 29-Oct-41; about 60; —; —; —; —; —

Thüner (nee Harhausen); Widow Henriette Amalia; 17-May-48; 19-May-48; 56y; Thüner, Johann Heinrich; Lübbeke, Preussen; —; —; —

Surname of Deceased; Given Name of Deceased; Date of Death; Date of Burial; Age or Date of Birth; Survivor(I), Surname, Given; Birthplace Deceased or Parent; Survivor (II), Surname, Given; Birthplace of Survivor (II); Comment

Timmermann; Eberhard Wilhelm; 24-Nov-53; 25-Nov-53; 1y, 2m; Timmermann, Ludwig; Haide, Hannover [f]; —; —; —

Timmermann; Georg Heinrich; 13-Nov-53; 15-Nov-53; 3y, 2m, 9d; Timmermann, Ludwig; Haide, Hannover [f]; —; —; —

Titus; Rosine; 19-Feb-42; 20-Feb-42; 8 Sep 1841; —; —; —; —; —

Tormelen; Eberhard; 24-Nov-58; 25-Nov-58; 5d, 19h; Tormelen, Wilh.; Osnabruck [f]; —; —; —

Tormelen; Johann Heinrich; 4-Jan-58; 5-Jan-58; 10h; Tormelen, Franz; Atter, Hannover [f]; —; —; —

Tormelen; Louise Johanne Charlotte; 2-Aug-58; 3-Aug-58; 2y, 1m, 9d; Tormelen, Wilhelm; Osnabruck [f]; —; —; —

Tormelen; Margarethe Charlotte; 21-Nov-56; 22-Nov-56; 5w, 4d; Tormelen, Franz; —; —; —; —

Tormolen; Georg Christian; 8-Jun-1867; 9-Jun-1867; 2y, 3w; Tormolen, Frdch. Wilh.; Engter, Hannover [f]; —; —; —

Tormolen (nee Regeweg); Mrs. Christine; 27-Feb-1867; 1-Mar-1867; 38y,27d; —; —; —; —; —

Trabant; Maria; 1-May-45; 2-May-45; 30 Jun 1842; Trabant, Georg; —; Urbach, Elisasbeth; —; —

Traule; Johann Georg; 7-Apr-45; 9-Apr-45; 1 May 1801; —; Backnang, Wuerttemberg [f]; —; —; —

Treide; Karoline Louise; 1-Aug-63; 2-Aug-63; 7m; Treide, Joh. Heinr. Gottlieb; Karlofen, Kurhessen [f]; —; —; —

Treide; Sophie Wilhelmine Louise; 26-Feb-54; 27-Feb-54; 2y, 8m; Treide, Joh. Heinr. Gottlieb; Carlshafen, Kurhessen [f]; —; —; —

Triebert; Juliane; —; 7-Jul-47; unknown; Triebert, Heinrich; Grosseneichen, Grunberg, Hessen [f]; Strube, Martha; Homberg, Hessen [m];

Troll; Maria Wilhelmina; 7-Aug-49; 8-Aug-49; 24 Jul 1848; Troll, Friedrich; Smillinghausen, Waldeck [f]; Melchior, Regina; Solingen, Elberfeld, Preussen [m];

Tschagkeni; Maria; 21-Dec-45; 22-Dec-45; 27 Jun 1823; Tschagkeny, Eberhard; Hauersheim, Baiern [f]; Pfitzer, Juliane; Maulbronn [m]; father is schoolteacher

Tshchagkeny; Eduard; 21-Dec-41; 22-Dec-41; 26y; —; —; —; —; —

Surname of Deceased; Given Name of Deceased; Date of Death; Date of Burial; Age or Date of Birth; Survivor(I), Surname, Given; Birthplace Deceased or Parent; Survivor (II), Surname, Given; Birthplace of Survivor (II); Comment

Turing; Marie Margarethe Barbara; 12-Nov-63; 13-Nov-63; 2y, 6m; Turing, Georg; Schnelldorf, Baiern [f]; —; —; —

Utz; August; 7-Jun-44; 8-Jun-44; 28y; —; —; —; —; —

Viehmeyer; Adam; 18-Aug-40; 19-Aug-40; 6 Feb 1785; —; —; —; —; —

Viertel; Johann Friedrich; 6-Jun-48; 7-Jun-48; 21 Jun 1845; Viertel, Johann Friedrich; Eilersbach, Nurnberg, Baiern [f]; Vogel, Elisabeth; Sauerheim, Baiern [m];

Vogel; Johann; 6-Sep-54; 7-Sep-54; 46y; —; Afalderthel, Baiern; —; —; —

Vogel; Margaretha; 30-Jul-48; 1-Aug-48; 6 Feb 1847; Vogel, Magdalena; Asterthal, Grafenberg, Baiern [m]; —; —; illegtimate

Vogelmann; Karl Heinrich; 16-Dec-56; 17-Dec-56; 2w; Vogelmann, Karl Wilh.; —; —; —; —

Vogelmann (nee Cripold); Mrs. Margarethe; 26-Aug-65; 27-Apr-65; 33y; —; Rothwind, Baiern; —; —; Aug is a mistake

Vogelmann (nee Muller); Mrs. Susanne; 12-Sep-51; 13-Sep-51; 64y, 9m, 8d; —; Neudeck, Wuerttemberg; —; —; —

Volkmar; Andreas Karl.; 11-Sep-44; 12-Sep-44; 14 Mar 1843; —; —; —; —; —

Vollers; Anna Sophie; 15-Aug-61; 17-Aug-61; 24y, 5m; Amt Bewerstedt, Hannover; —; —; —; —

von Holten; Wilhelm Randolph; 10-Apr-49; 11-Apr-49; 24 Feb1848; von Holten, Johann Peter; Stenau [f]; Buts, Catharine; Schledehausen, Osnabruck, Hannover [m];

Vonderwesten; Johann Heinrich; 6-Feb-67; 8-Feb-67; 37y, 11m, 6d; —; Engter, Hannover; —; —; —

Vonhof; Georg Ludwig; 5-Aug-52; 7-Aug-52; 39y; —; Ortruffhez, Sachsen-Gotha; —; —; —

Vorderwusten; Johann Kasten Heinrich; 6-Aug-59; 7-Aug-59; 1y, 9m, 2w; Vorderwusten, Joh. Heinr.; —; —; —; only child

Vorderwuster; Johann Hermann Heinrich; 13-Apr-62; 14-Apr-62; 2y, 9w; Vorderwusten, Joh. Heinrich; Engter, Hannover [f]; —; —; —

Vorderwuster (nee Strubbe); Mrs. Katharine Marie; 30-Jul-63; 31-Jul-63; 75y, 11m; —; Engter, Hannover; —; —; —

Surname of Deceased; Given Name of Deceased; Date of Death; Date of Burial; Age or Date of Birth; Survivor(I), Surname, Given; Birthplace Deceased or Parent; Survivor (II), Surname, Given; Birthplace of Survivor (II); Comment

Vornkahl; Friedrich Theodor; 18-Jun-63; 19-Jun-63; 28y; —; Gross Himstadt, Hannover; —; —; —

Wachsmann; Anna Katharine Auguste; 5-Mar-65; 6-Mar-65; 1y, 11m; Wachsmann, Joh. Gottlieb; —; —; —; —

Wagner; Eva; 11-Apr-49; 12-Apr-49; 1 Oct 1844; Wagner, Johann; Nagel, Kranach, Baiern [f]; Batz, Margaretha; Schmelz, Baiern [m];

Wagner; Johann; 12-May-63; 13-May-63; 53y, 10m, 2w, 3d; —; Nagel, Baiern; —; —; —

Wagner (nee Keil); Mrs. Christine; 6-Feb-60; 7-Feb-60; 38y; —; Allendorf a.d.L, Hessen; —; —; —

Wagner (nee Muller); Mrs. Eleonora; 8-Jun-65; 9-Jun-65; 56y, 6w; —; Giessa; —; —; —

Wahl; Maria; 18-Mar-50; 19-Mar-40; 11 Oct 1839; —; —; —; —; —

Wahl; Mrs. Marie; 10-Jul-52; 11-Jul-52; about 66y; Wahl, Melchior; Kerndorf, Hessen; —; —; spouse

Waldschmidt; Jacob; 6-Mar-50; 7-Mar-50; 14 Jul 1849; Waldschmidt, Ludwig; Hessen bei Giessen [f]; Naern, Anna Maria; —; —

Waldschmidt; Ludwig; 22-Dec-65; 24-Dec-65; 63y, 4m, 11d; —; Rothheim, Hessen; —; —; —

Waldschmidt; Wilhelm; 15-Jan-67; 17-Jan-67; 22y, 11m, 4w, 6d; —; Baltimore, MD; —; —; struck by fellow worker

Walther; Adam; 19-Jan-54; 21-Jan-54; 9m; Walther, Adam; Geimmende, Hannover [f]; —; —; —

Walther; Christine Katharine; 20-Jan-44; 21-Jan-44; 12 Apr 1843; —; —; —; —; —

Walther; Elisabeth; —; 22-Dec-47; —; Walther, Ludwig; —; —; —; —

Walther; Katharine; 27-Nov-60; 29-Nov-60; 16y, 2m, 2w; Walther, Heinrich; Lissberg, Hessen [f]; —; —; oldest daughter

Walther; Martin; 4-May-49; 5-May-49; 18 Aug 1807 or 1808; —; Massnerberg, Thuringen, Sachsen-Coburg; —; —; —

Walther (nee Börner); Mrs. Rosine; 17-Nov-60; 18-Nov-60; 43y, 4m, 23d; —; —; —; —; —

Walther (nee Klein); Mrs. Katharine; 5-Jun-62; 7-Jun-62; 46y, 5m, 1w; Walther, Heinrich; Harten, Hessen; —; —; —

Waltjen; Andreas Stephanus; 7-Feb-62; 10-Feb-62; 3y, 3m, 3w; Waltjen, Johann Friedrich Wilhelm; Bossum, Hannover [f]; —; —; youngest son

Waltjen; Catharina Elisabeth; 15-Jan-55; 16-Jan-55; 4y, 2m, 5d; Waltjen, Heinrich; Bossum, Hannover [f]; —; —; —

Waltjen; Christiane Johanne Louise; 15-Jul-60; 16-Jul-60; 1y, 8m, 2w; Waltjen, Georg Heinr. Friedr.; Bossum, Hannover [f]; —; —; youngest daughter

Waltjen; Georg; 7-Sep-62; 9-Sep-62; 36y; —; Bossum, Hannover; —; —; killed at Sharpsburg

Waltjen; Georg Michael Hermann; 25-Dec-54; 26-Dec-54; 9m; Waltjen, Johann Gerhard; Centre Co., PA. [f]; —; —; —

Waltjen; Heinrich; 26-Jul-65; 28-Jul-65; 46y, 6m, 3w, 3d; —; Bossum, Hannover; —; —; —

Waltjen; Hermann Friedrich; 30-Jul-58; 1-Aug-58; 71y, 10m, 12d; —; Bossum, Hannover; —; —; —

Waltjen; Herrmann Heinrich; 7-Feb-47; 9-Feb-47; 26 Aug 1845; Waltjen, Heinrich; Bossum, Hannover [f]; Stoll, Maria; Stätten, Canstadt, Wuerttemberg [m];

Waltjen; Karl Eduard; 2-Feb-62; 4-Feb-62; 6m, 2w, 3d; Waltjen, Christiane; —; —; —; illegitimate child

Waltjen; Maria Elisabeth; 25-Jun-45; 26-Jun-45; 2y, 1m, 8d; Waltjen, Heinrich; Bossum, Hannover [f]; Stoll, Maria; Sater, Wuerttemberg [m];

Waltjen; Maria Sophia; 19-Dec-45; 21-Dec-45; 29 Jun 1845; Waltjen, Andreas; Bossum, Hannover [f]; Hildebrandt, Christiane; Bleichenbach, Hannover [m];

Waltjen; Mrs. Friederike; 18-Sep-56; 19-Sep-56; 17y, 4m, 11d; Waltjen, Heinrich; Bossum, Hannover; —; —; spouse

Waltjen; Mrs. Marie Dorothea; 25-Feb-56; 26-Feb-56; 65y, 8m, 32; Waltjen, Hermann Heinrich; —; —; —; first funeral in church

Waltjen; Rebecca Christiana; 21-Jan-55; 23-Jan-55; 2y, 4m, 9d; Waltjen, Heinrich; Bossum, Hannover [f]; —; —; —

Waltjen; Sarah; 6-Jun-56; 8-Jun-56; 1y, 5m, 1w, 6d; Waltjen, Heinr.; Bossum, Hannover; —; —; youngest daughter

Surname of Deceased; Given Name of Deceased; Date of Death; Date of Burial; Age or Date of Birth; Survivor(I), Surname, Given; Birthplace Deceased or Parent; Survivor (II), Surname, Given; Birthplace of Survivor (II); Comment

Waltjen; stillborn son; 8-Oct-54; 8-Oct-54; —; Waltjen, Georg; Bossum, Hannover [f]; —; —; —

Warnecken; Johann Gerhard; 20-Apr-54; 21-Apr-54; 3y, 1m, 9d; Warnecken, Biren; Meiershausen, Hannover [f]; —; —; —

Warneken; Henriette Karoline; 4-Jul-62; 6-Jul-62; 18y, 4m, 3w, rd; —; Baltimore, MD; —; —; —

Warneken; Hermann; 5-Aug-62; 6-Aug-62; 8y, 9m, 1d; Warneken, Luhr; Ottersberg, Hannover [f]; —; —; —

Warnken; Cunrad; 27-Jun-65; 28-Jun-65; 57y; —; Meininghausen, Hannover; —; —; —

Weber; Carl; 15-Jul-54; 17-Jul-54; 1y, 6w; Weber, Heinr.; Volkartshain, Hessen [f]; —; —; —

Weber; Heinrich; 24-Mar-47; 26-Mar-47; 3 Nov 1801; —; Langenstein, Kirchheim, Kurhessen; —; —; son of Ludwg & Cath. Weber

Weber; Johann Friedrich; 13-Oct-53; 14-Oct-53; 3y, 6m, 16d; Weber, Eberhard Heinr.; Ossenbeck, Hannover [f]; —; —; —

Weber; Johann Heinrich; 27-Nov-47; 28-Nov-47; 27y; —; Bremen; —; —; —

Weber; Konrad; 25-Apr-51; 26-Apr-51; 68y; —; Bernsburg, Hessen; —; —; dead in bed

Weber; Mrs. Eva Katharine; 25-Jul-51; 27-Jul-51; 65y, 3d; —; —; —; —; —

Weber (nee [--?--]); Anna; 3-Nov-46; 4-Nov-46; 78y; —; Homberg, Wuerttemberg; —; —; —

Webersperger; Ersnt; 17-Jun-50; 18-Jun-50; 26 Mar 1848; Webersperger, Johann; Mitteldorf, Baiern [f]; Bauer, Elisabeth; Angenhof, , Baiern [m];

Webersperger; Michael; —; 22-Mar-47; 8d; Webersperger, Johann; Mittelendorf, Aurach [f]; Bauer, Elisabeth; Weissendorf, Baiern [m];

Weckesser; Heinrich Georg; 23-Jul-40; 24-Jul-40; 14 Apr 1840; —; —; —; —; —

Weckesser; Johann; 3-Aug-1867; 4-Aug-1867; 57y, 7m, 3d; —; Josbach, Kurhessen; —; —; —

Weckesser; Johannes; 7-Mar-41; 8-Mar-41; —; —; —; —; —; —

Surname of Deceased; Given Name of Deceased; Date of Death; Date of Burial; Age or Date of Birth; Survivor(I), Surname, Given; Birthplace Deceased or Parent; Survivor (II), Surname, Given; Birthplace of Survivor (II); Comment

Weckesser; Maria; 1-Mar-41; 3-Mar-41; 14 Dec 1840; —; —; —; —; —

Weckesser; Mrs.; 28-Oct-54; 30-Oct-54; 41y, 7m, 11d; —; Josbach, Kurhessen; —; —; —

Weddigen; Aug. Wilhelm Karl; 20-Aug-59; 22-Aug-59; 24y, 4m, 2w, 2d; —; Schlusselburg, Preussen; —; —; —

Weddigen; stillborn son; 14-Dec-59; 14-Dec-59; —; —; Schlisselburg, Preussen; —; —; —

Weidemeier; Mrs. Barbara Elisabeth; 8-Jul-53; 9-Jul-53; 28y, 7m, 20d; Weidemeier, Adam; —; —; —; spouse

Weigandt; Elisabeth; 27-Jul-48; 28-Jul-48; 7 Nov 1847; Weigandt, August; Fem, Sachsen-Weimar [f]; [--?--], Catharina; Preussen [m];

Weihrauch; Catharine; 27-May-46; 28-May-46; 11 May 1845; Weihrauch, Johannes; Seheim, Hessen [f]; Kohler, Margarethe; Zwingenberg, Hessen [m];

Weihrauch; Catharine Margarethe; 1-Jun-49; 2-Jun-49; 16 May 1847; Weihrauch, Johann; Elmanshausen, Zwingenberg, Hessen [f]; Köhler, Margarethe; Zwingenberg [m];

Weihrauch; Maria; 29-Jun-49; 30-Jun-49; 25 Jun 1849; Weihrauch, Johann; Elmanshausen, Zwingenberg [f]; Köhler, Margarethe; Zwingenberg [m];

Weil; Philipp Heinrich; 15-Sep-49; 17-Sep-49; 17 Jan 1849; Weil, Philipp; Echzell, Hessen [f]; Schütz, Christiane; Büdingen, Hessen [m];

Weinhard; Georg Friedrich; —; 11-Jul-46; 27 Jul 1766; —; Schwabach bei Nurnberg; —; —; —

Weinhardt; Mrs. Anna Elisabeth; 14-Mar-57; 15-Mar-57; 76y, 5m, 1w; —; —; —; —; —

Weisbrod; Anna; 18-Jul-40; 19-Jul-40; 59y; —; —; —; —; —

Weiss; Jacob; 15-Mar-50; 17-Mar-50; Jun 1817; —; Wuerttemberg; —; —; —

Weitemeyer; Georg Adam; 4-Jan-44; 6-Jan-44; 4 Jun 1843; —; —; —; —; —

Welle (nee Messinger); Sophie; 3-Jul-47; 4-Jul-47; 18 Mar 1768; —; Oberbriede, Backknang, Wuerttemberg; —; —; died 1 AM

Surname of Deceased; Given Name of Deceased; Date of Death; Date of Burial; Age or Date of Birth; Survivor(I), Surname, Given; Birthplace Deceased or Parent; Survivor (II), Surname, Given; Birthplace of Survivor (II); Comment

Weller; Christine; 22-Oct-57; 23-Oct-57; 6y, 10m, 22d; Weller, Philipp; Alteenbosseck, Hessen [f]; —; —; —

Weller; Johann Christian; 6-Sep-62; 7-Sep-62; 1y, 9m, 2w, 3d; Weller, Philipp; Altenbosseck, Hessen [f]; —; —; —

Weller; Sophia; 1-Feb-42; 2-Feb-42; about 60y; —; —; —; —; —

Weller (nee Schlerf); Katharine; 30-Mar-66; 1-Apr-66; 44y; —; Allendorf a.d. Lumde; —; —; —

Welte; Georg Friedrich; 17-Jun-48; 17-Jun-48; 9 Mar 1792; —; Meisenbach, Kalw, Wuerttemberg; —; —; —

Widmar; Johann Adam; 5-Nov-42; 6-Nov-42; 12 Jun 1812; —; —; —; —; —

Wiedemann; Georg Gustav; 19-Mar-58; 20-Mar-58; 8w, 6d; Wiedemann, Joh.; Jaxthausen, Wurttemberg [f]; —; —; pox

Wiedemann; Johann Christian; 14-May-62; 15-May-62; 7y, 3m; Wiedemann, Johann; Jaxthausen, Wurttemberg [f]; —; —; —

Wiedemier; Anna Emilie Johanne; 1-Mar-58; 2-Mar-58; 4m; Wiedemier, Adam; Grossrepperhausen, Kurhessen [f]; —; —; —

Wiegandt; Margarethe; 4-May-49; 5-May-49; 15 Apr 1849; Wiegandt, August; Willmanns, Sachsen-Weimar [f]; Fledemeyer, Catharine; Finen [?], Teklenburg, Preussen [m];

Wiegel; Johann Adam; 14-Feb-44; 16-Feb-44; 1 Aug 1840; —; —; —; —; —

Wiese; Heinrich; 30-Aug-47; 31-Aug-47; 23 Apr 1846; Wiese, Wilhelm; Oldenburg [f]; Bremmer, Catharina; Ringstadt, Hannover [m];

Wiesner (nee Schneider); Mrs. Katharine; 17-Mar-66; 19-Mar-66; 56y; —; Rossberg, Kurhessen; —; —; —

Wietler; Caroline Henriette; 4-Oct-46; 5-Oct-46; 27 Sep 1846; Wietler, Johann; Deljehausen, Uslar, Hannover [f]; Freinhagen, Christine; Deljehausen, Uslar, Hannover [m];

Wild; Adam Friedrich; 23-Jan-39; 24-Jan-39; 11 Jan 1839; —; —; —; —; —

Wild; Christian; 18-Jun-38; 19-Jun-38; 12 Jun 1838; —; —; —; —; —

Wild; Jacob Friedrich; 23-Jan-39; 24-Jan-39; 11 Jan 1839; —; —; —; —; —

Surname of Deceased; Given Name of Deceased; Date of Death; Date of Burial; Age or Date of Birth; Survivor(I), Surname, Given; Birthplace Deceased or Parent; Survivor (II), Surname, Given; Birthplace of Survivor (II); Comment

Wildermuth; Adam; 21-Feb-62; 23-Feb-62; 59y, 6m, 1w, 3d; —; Bleidelsheim, Wurttemberg; —; —; —

Wildermuth; George Heinrich; 7-Nov-48; 8-Nov-48; 27 Jun 1846; Wildermuth, Adam; Blleidelsheim, Marbach, Wuerttemberg [f]; Fink, Elisabeth; Essen, Quakenbruck, Hannover [m];

Wildermuth; Mrs. Elisabeth; 8-Mar-61; 10-Mar-61; 47y, 10m; —; —; —; —; —

Wimmer; Eva Margaretha; 31-Aug-53; 1-Sep-53; 26y; —; Marktbauterbach, Baiern; —; —; —

Winter; Adam Daniel; 2-Dec-59; 3-Dec-59; 11m, 11d; Winter, Christian; Weidnitz, Baiern [f]; —; —; youngest son

Winter; Johann Andreas; 6-Jul-66; 8-Jul-66; 7y, 11m; Winter, Joh. Andreas; Volkartshain, Hessen [f]; —; —; —

Winter; Johann Friedrich; 4-Jan-64; 5-Jan-64; 6m; Winter, Andreas; Volkartshain, Hessen [f]; —; —; —

Winter; Johannes; 21-Aug-53; 22-Aug-53; 3y, 2w; Winter, Andreas; Volkartshain, Hessen [f]; —; —; —

Winter; Martin; 29-Aug-52; 1-Sep-52; 8m, 2d; Winter, Andreas; Volkartshain, Hessen [f]; —; —; second son

Winter; Mrs. Elisabeth; 5-Aug-55; 6-Aug-55; 67y; —; Volkartshain, Hessen; —; —; —

Winter; Rosabella; 19-Aug-48; 20-Aug-48; 16 Jul 1847; Winter, Jonas; Glauberg, Nidda, Hessen [f]; Beineweber, Emilie; Manchester, Carrol Co., MD [m];

Wirth; Lorenz; 20-Jun-46; 21-Jun-46; 27 Feb 1846; Wirth, Georg; Buchendorf, Stadt Neinhoff, Baiern [f]; Schmidt, Margaretha; Buchendorf, Stadt Neinhoff, Baiern [m];

Wisser; Elisabeth; 22-Dec-43; 23-Dec-43; Jan 1843; —; —; —; —; —

Wittler; Karl Friedrich Heinrich; 30-Aug-59; 31-Aug-59; 7m, 6d; Wittler, Karl Frdch. Aug.; Dellinghausen, Braunschweig [f]; —; —; —

Wittler; stillborn son; 20-May-57; 20-May-57; —; Wittler, Karl; —; —; —; —

Wittler (nee Prohmann); Mrs. Anna Sophie; 10-Apr-63; 12-Apr-63; 56y, 8m, 2w, 5d; —; Dellinhausen, Hannover; —; —; —

Wohlbfahrt; Catharine; 18-Oct-46; 19-Oct-46; 17m, 14d; Wohlbfahrt, Johann; Biwerer, Sachsen-Meiningen [f]; Exel, Wilhelmine; Biwerer, Sachsen-Meiningen [m];

Wolf; Martin Wilh.; 8-Jul-42; 10-Jul-42; 8 Jan 1842; —; —; —; —; —

Wüst (nee Carle); Catharine; 14-Apr-48; 15-Apr-48; 16 Jun 1827; Carle, Johann; Jaxthausen, Neckarsulm, Wuerttemberg; —; —; —

Wyneken; Ernst Friedrich; 17-Jul-47; 18-Jul-47; 10 Feb 1847; Wyneken, Friedrich Conrad Dietrich; Werden, Hannover [f]; Buck, Sophia; Windheim, Preussen [m]

Zink; Anna Katharine; 28-Jul-62; 29-Jul-62; 7y, 4m, 26d; Zink, Georg Friedrich; Neuhof, Baiern [f]; —; —

Zink; Anna Maria; 5-Aug-59; 6-Aug-59; 11m; Zink, Johann; Sarxa, Baiern [f]; —; —

Zink; Johann; 7-Jul-55; 8-Jul-55; 10m; Zink, Joh.; Saxen, Baiern [f]; —; —

Zink; Rosine Dorothea Susanne; 10-Aug-62; 11-Aug-62; 8m, 2w; Zink, Georg Friedrich; Neuhof, Baiern [f]; —; —

Zink; stillborn daughter; 15-Mar-63; 15-Mar-63; —; Zink, Georg Friedr.; —; —; —

Surname of Deceased; Given Name of Deceased; Date of Death; Date of Burial; Age or Date of Birth; Survivor(I), Surname, Given; Birthplace Deceased or Parent; Survivor (II), Surname, Given; Birthplace of Survivor (II); Comment

Surname; Given Name; Year Confirmed

Ahlers, Magdalene; 1840
Ahles, Friedrich; 1839
Aichele, Joh.; 1856
Aichele, Joh.; 1855
Aisle, Johann; 1839
Albach, Georg; 1840
Albach, Johann; 1843
Albach, Katharine; 1843
Anschütz, Johannette; 1837
Arndt, Jacob; 1867
Arnold, Kunigunde; 1857
Arros, Joh. Wilhelm; 1865
Bachmann, Anna M.; 1862
Bachmann, Rosine; 1864
Bachmann, Sophia; 1866
Bader, Joh. Ferd.; 1855
Bagel, Selma; 1858
Balla, Henriette; 1843
Balz, Anna Kath.; 1855
Balz, Conrad; 1837
Balz, Elisabeth; 1853
Balz, Eva Kath.; 1857
Balz, Ludwig; 1859
Balz, Marie; 1861
Balz, Wilh.; 1855
Bär, Wilhelmine; 1866
Bauer, Elis. Barbara; 1858
Bauer, Georg Ludwig Christian; 1856
Bauer, Joh. Benjamin; 1864
Bauer, Marg. Christiane; 1854
Bauer, Sarah; 1861
Beck, Bernhard Jakob; 1851
Beck, Friedrich; 1844
Beck, Friedrich; 1839
Beck, G. Hermann; 1853
Beck, Henriette; 1858
Beck, Joh. Kaspar; 1854
Beckel, Anna Philippine; 1866
Beckelmeier, Karoline; 1855
Becker, Elis.; 1861
Becker, Elisab.; 1838
Becker, Katharine; 1841
Becker, Maria; 1867
Beier, Joh. Tobias; 1853
Beissweiger, Gottlieb; 1845
Beiswanger, Elise; 1853
Beiswanger, Marie Rebecca; 1851
Benhard, Johann; 1838
Berg, L.A. L.; 1862
Bertram, Elisabeth; 1854
Bertram, Friedrich; 1853
Bertram, Karl; 1851
Bichler, Charlotte; 1853
Biersack, M.; 1862
Blome, Lina; 1852
Blum, Karl; 1841
Blumen, Dorothea; 1841
Bockel, Heinr.; 1857
Bode, Elisabeth; 1838
Bohn, Fr. Wilh.; 1862
Bohn, Henriette; 1854
Bohn, Louis; 1861
Bopler, Andreas; 1863
Bopler, Elisabeth; 1866
Bopler, Heinr.; 1858
Bopler, M.; 1862
Boppler, Johannes; 1860
Borchelt, Ludwig; 1852
Brandes (Schmalz), Frch. Wilh.; 1851
Brauer, Christiane; 1853
Brauer, Heinrich; 1853

Surname; Given Name; Year Confirmed

Brechemacher, Friedrich; 1837
Breden, Johann; 1845
Bremer, A. Maria E.; 1867
Bremer, Agathe; 1864
Bremer, Joh. Wilhelm; 1860
Bremer, Marg.; 1862
Briegel, Wilhelm; 1845
Briel, Elisabeth; 1866
Briel, F. A. Emanuel; 1867
Briel, Georg Martin; 1860
Briel, Joh. Heinrich; 1863
Brockmeier, Heinr. Aug.; 1852
Brockmeier, Maria Frdk.; 1853
Brocks, Moritz; 1865
Brösiun, Heinrich; 1843
Bruens, Marg. A.; 1867
Brügel, Johann Jac.; 1841
Brügel, Joseph; 1839
Brügel, Karl Ferd.; 1841
Brügel, Wilhelmine; 1837
Bruggemann, Karl Aug.; 1856
Bruggemann, Ludwig; 1866
Bruggemann, Mathilde; 1852
Bruggemann, Wilh.; 1858
Bruggemann, Wilh.; 1854
Bruks, K.; 1862
Bruning, Jakob; 1858
Bruning, Marg. Wilh.; 1851
Bruning, Maria Eilh.; 1853
Burk, Sophie; 1843
Burman, A. Maria; 1867
Burmann, Anna Marg.; 1865
Burmann, C. W.; 1862
Burmann, Heinr.; 1859
Burmann, Jobst Heinr.; 1861
Burmann, L. Charlotte; 1863
Busch, Amalie; 1860
Busch, Johanne Wilhelmine; 1864
Buscher, Auguste; 1840
Buscher, Luise; 1841
Butscher, A. M.; 1862
Carlosson, Maria Agnes; 1861
Christ, Christiane; 1840
Christ, Christine; 1837
Christ, Jacob; 1837
Christmann, Elisabeth; 1842
Dannettel, Henriette; 1838
Dannettel, Margaretha; 1843
Deckmann, Elisabeth; 1867
Dickel, Anna Elisabeth; 1865
Diester, Katharine; 1841
Dieter, Elisabeth; 1838
Dieterle, Christoph; 1852
Dieterle, Maria; 1841
Dietrich, Friedricke Hnr.; 1860
Dietrich, Georg; 1866
Dietrich, Juliane; 1863
Dietz, Anna Maria; 1865
Dietz, Gottfried; 1863
Dillmann, Maria; 1838
Dirrenberger, Karoline; 1843
Dirrenberger, Salome; 1842
Dobeler, Gustav Adolph; 1853
Doberer, Marie Kath.; 1851
Dominick, Charl. Fried. Christine; 1851
Drechsel, Barbara; 1842
Dreyer, Heinr. Dietrich; 1866
Ebert, Margaretha; 1839
Eckardt, Louis Karl; 1863
Eckardt, Wilh.; 1853
Eggers, Dorothea; 1844
Eifert, Elisabeth; 1858
Einwachter, Alex.; 1856

Einwachter, Frdch. Ferdinand; 1865
Einwachter, Georg Alexander; 1866
Einwachter, Joh. Adam; 1860
Einwachter, Maria Kath.; 1863
Einwacther, Alex.; 1855
Eisfoller [?], J. Georg Heinr.; 1853
Eitel, Maria; 1845
Eitel, Salome; 1841
Emmerling, Elisabeth; 1841
Emrich, Georg; 1864
Endebroek, Katharine; 1842
Epple, Rosine; 1860
Epple, Wilhelmine; 1857
Erdmann, Wilhelm; 1837
Erick, Caspar; 1840
Erick, Daniel; 1842
Erick, Johann; 1838
Erick, Wilhelm; 1838
Ermold, Christine; 1864
Ermold, Frdch.; 1866
Ernst, August; 1860
Ernst, Heinr. Karl Benj.; 1853
Ernst, Kath.; 1855
Ernst, L. M.; 1862
Ernst, Marie Kath.; 1856
Faber, Johann; 1839
Faber, Johann; 1837
Fanau, Maria; 1841
Fangmeyer, Dorothea; 1863
Farenau, Margaretha; 1844
Feger, Joseph; 1855
Fellen, Mathilde; 1866
Fick, Catharine; 1845
Fischbeck, Katharine; 1840
Fischer, Elise Kath.; 1858
Fischer, Katharine; 1837
Fischer, Kathr.; 1838
Flemming, Maria Magd.; 1856
Frank, Elisabeth F.; 1867
Frank, Johannes; 1851
Frank, Karl Johann; 1861
Frank, Karoline Elis.; 1858
Frank, Magdalene; 1839
Frank, Marie Wilhelmine; 1863
Frank, Regine; 1838
Freudenberg, Joh.; 1855
Freudenberger, Johannes; 1845
Friedrich, August; 1863
Friedrich, Louise; 1865
Fritze, Magdalene; 1866
Fritze, Philipp M.; 1867
Fuchs, Bertha; 1837
Fuerking, Friederike; 1859
Gahm, Wilhelm; 1866
Gebhard, Christian; 1843
Gebhard, Juliane; 1843
Geiger, Engelhard; 1838
Geiger, Jacob; 1843
Geiger, Katharine; 1840
Geiger, Konrad; 1851
Geiglein, Marie; 1851
Gemp, Maria Elisab.; 1842
Gerber, Magdalene; 1839
Gerwig, Christiane; 1841
Gerwig, Jacob; 1838
Gerwig, Mathaus; 1837
Geyer, Helene; 1845
Gieglein, Franz Theodor; 1852
Gingnagel, Sophie; 1842
Grauling, Gottfried; 1842
Grimm, Gustav Franz; 1863
Groner, Karoline; 1855
Gross, Elisabeth; 1839

Surname; Given Name; Year Confirmed

Grosser, Andreas; 1837
Groth, Louise Frdh. Bertha; 1851
Gruner, Jakob Heinr.; 1853
Gruner, Joh. Frdch.; 1859
Gruner, M. K.; 1862
Hacker, Magdalene; 1840
Hammer, Johann; 1837
Hammer, Michael; 1837
Hampe, Franz. Wilh.; 1859
Happel, Elisabeth; 1861
Harken, Emma; 1858
Harken, Marie; 1857
Harmes, Barbara; 1864
Harmes, Joh.; 1866
Hauscher, Rosine; 1837
Hebebrand, Peter; 1843
Heck, August; 1851
Heck, Georg; 1860
Heck, Joh.; 1858
Heibeck, Frdch.; 1866
Heilmann, Georg; 1861
Heimuller, Katharine; 1841
Heimuller, Paul; 1838
Heinlein, Katharine; 1856
Heinlein, Katharine; 1855
Heistermann, Anna; 1852
Helber, Friedrieke; 1837
Hellweg, Emilie; 1854
Herbst, Georg N.; 1867
Herbst, Louise Marg.; 1866
Hermensdörfer, Johann; 1845
Herringel, Gottfr.; 1842
Herringel, Konrad Fr.; 1843
Hersch, Katharine; 1844
Hesse, Henriette Christiane; 1851
Heyse, Wilhelmine; 1854
Hof, Katharine; 1837
Hoffmann, Johanne; 1867
Hofler, Kunigunde; 1865
Hofmann, Friedrich; 1864
Hofmann, Maria Elis.; 1866
Hofmann, Marie Elis.; 1859
Hofmeister, Jacobine; 1844
Holdgrafe, Heinr. Christian; 1866
Horlebein, Georg Ludwig; 1866
Horn, Anna; 1851
Horn, Emma Sophie Amalie; 1866
Horn, Ernst; 1860
Horn, Joh. Frdch. Val.; 1855
Horn, Joh. Frdch. Valentin; 1856
Horn, Rosamunde Albertine; 1863
Horn, Susanne Katharine; 1854
Horn, Wilh.; 1858
Hornung, Katharine; 1842
Horr, Maria; 1851
Horstmann, Anna Elisab.; 1841
Hostmann, Heinrich; 1867
Houslob, Adolph; 1866
Huckel, Georg; 1843
Ihle, Katharine; 1841
Imwalde, Johann; 1861
Imwalde, Karl Frdch.; 1866
Imwalde, M. A.; 1862
Imwolde, Joh. Heinr.; 1859
Isermann, Johann; 1839
Jackel, Henriette; 1856
Jackel, Henriette; 1855
Jackel, Kath.; 1859

Jung (Wiedemann), Georg; 1860
Jung, Barbara; 1842
Jung, Friedrich; 1863
Jurger, Wilhelmine; 1845
Kaleb, Katharine; 1839
Kamer, D. Wilh.; 1867
Kardel, Eva; 1839
Kardel, Nikolas; 1837
Karl, Karl August; 1866
Karle, Heinrich; 1839
Karle, Heinrich Martin; 1864
Karmrodt, Johann Martin; 1840
Karmrodt, Maria; 1844
Karmrodt, Martha; 1839
Kartterweler, Franz; 1864
Kasten, Friedrich; 1858
Kasten, Heinrich; 1853
Kasten, Louise Marie; 1851
Kasten, Marie; 1861
Kasten, Wilh. Karl; 1864
Katenkamp, Wilh. Thomas; 1866
Katharine, Juliane; 1865
Kattenkamp, Franz Deitr.; 1857
Kattenkamp, Franz Dietrich; 1856
Kattenkamp, Heinr. Eberhard; 1854
Kattenkamp, Juline Marie; 1853
Kattenkamp, Karoline Rosine; 1864
Kattenkamp, Marie Katharine; 1863
Kaubatz, Christoph; 1838
Kaufmann, Friedrich; 1842
Kaufmann, Karl Emil; 1866
Keil, Heinne; 1861
Kenper, Johann; 1843
Kern, Aug. Anna Elis. Marg.; 1852
Kern, Heinrich; 1867
Kern, Henriette; 1843
Kern, Peter; 1866
Kern, Peter; 1865
Kettenring, Katharina; 1844
Keyl, Agnes Magdalene; 1866
Keyl, Anna Dorothea; 1857
Keyl, Emilie Karoline; 1864
Keyl, Marie; 1860
Keyl, Martha Constantia; 1862
Kiebeler, Christiane; 1838
Kienzle, Dorothea; 1842
Kienzle, Karoline; 1838
Kienzle, Wilhelmine; 1840
Kieseker, Adam; 1842
Kisher, Barbara; 1859
Kleffmann, Friedrieke; 1838
Klein, Karoline Louise; 1852
Kleppisch, A. M. Martha; 1867
Kleppisch, Frdch. David; 1859

Kleppisch, Heinr. Mich.; 1853
Kleppisch, Karl Sam.; 1852
Kleppisch, Martin Luther; 1856
Kleppisch, Susanne Louise; 1855
Kleppisch, Wilh. Aug.; 1852
Klettmann, Karl; 1838
Klinke, Lina Marie; 1865
Knapp, Sophie; 1854
Knirr, Kathr.; 1838
Knobloch, Johann; 1840
Knobloch, Kathr.; 1838
Knoch, Anna Kath.; 1841

Knoch, Ferdicka [?]; 1841
Koch, Albert; 1845
Koch, Heinrich; 1845
Koch, Henriette; 1841
Koch, Karoline; 1843
Koch, Luise; 1839
Kohlmann, Auguste; 1843
König, Luise; 1838
Kopp, Elis. Susanne; 1866
Korff, Hermine; 1853
Kraft, Juliane; 1837
Kraft, Maria; 1839
Kramer, Elisabeth; 1845
Kramer, Katharine; 1844
Kramer, Magdalena; 1841
Kratz, Karoline; 1860
Krauling, Catharina; 1845
Kreitmann, Jacob; 1837
Kreitmann, Salome; 1841
Krell, Elisabeth; 1854
Krell, Joh.; 1856
Kreter, Eberhard; 1843
Kring, Eduard; 1838
Kromer, Johannes; 1852
Kronenberg, Frdch. Wilh.; 1866
Kruger, Katharine; 1838
Kruger, Marg. Barbara; 1856
Kruger, Marg. Barbara; 1855
Kugelmann, Johannes; 1859
Kuhlmann, Anna Maria Charlotte; 1864
Kuhlmann, Joh. Christoph Frdch.; 1866
Kuhlmann, Joh. Frdch. Wilh.; 1863
Kuhnemund, [blank]; 1853
Künker, Ana M. L.; 1867
Kunker, Joh. Heinr.; 1865
Kunstendorf, Karl; 1842
Kurz, Frdch.; 1857
Kuster, Johanne Elvire; 1851
Kuster, Louis; 1860
Laib, Friedrich; 1840
Lammer, Heinrich; 1865
Lang, Wilhelmine; 1867
Lange, Carl K.; 1867
Lange, Karoline Louise; 1865
Langemann, Joh. Heinr.; 1861
Langemann, Wilh.; 1864
Lapp, Jakob; 1854
Lapp, Kaspar; 1852
Lars, Marie; 1864
Lehmann, Elis. Magdal.; 1852
Leins, Maria; 1839
Leist, August; 1838
Leistner, Jobst; 1845
Lemle, Elisabeth; 1840
Lemle, Georg; 1841
Lemle, Henriette; 1841
Lemle, Johann; 1840
Lenz, Katharine; 1857
Lenz, Susanne Marg.; 1854
Lessig, Heinrich; 1841
Lessig, Johanne; 1844
Letmade, Heinrich; 1861
Letmate, Joh. Frdch.; 1866
Letmate, Karl Dietr. Wilh.; 1866
Letmate, Louise Auguste; 1863
Lettmade (I), Karl Friedrich; 1860
Lettmade (II), Heinr. Frdch; 1860
Lettmade, Henr. Wilhe. Dorothea; 1865

Surname; Given Name; Year Confirmed

Leutner (I), Katharine; 1863
Leutner (II), Katharine; 1863
Leutner (III), Katharine; 1863
Leutner, Frdch. Melchior Franz; 1861
Leutner, Friedrich Christoph; 1866
Leutner, Heinr.; 1861
Leutner, Heinr. Chr.; 1865
Leutner, Louise; 1866
Leutner, Wilhelmine; 1859
Lohmuller, Helene; 1863
Louis, Heinr. Frdch.; 1862
Louis, Karl Herm.; 1859
Louise, Katharine Margarethe; 1864
Magin, Heinrich; 1867
Magin, Karl; 1863
Magin, Magdalene; 1865
Mandler, Johann; 1841
Mandler, Maria; 1841
Manns, Marie; 1865
Mansdorf, Marie Marg.; 1853
Mansdörfer, Elisabeth; 1844
Mansdörfer, Katharina; 1842
Martin, Julianne; 1839
Mebold, Jacob; 1838
Medinger, Friedrich; 1842
Medinger, Johann; 1837
Meier, Anna Helene Marie; 1851
Meier, Anna Marie; 1855
Meier, Elis.; 1855
Meier, Heinr.; 1856
Meier, Heinr. Wilh. Aug.; 1864
Meier, Karl; 1853
Meier, Rebecca Adelh.; 1853
Meis, Maria; 1838
Melchior, Regina; 1845
Melgior, Ferdinand; 1841
Melgior, Otto; 1842
Melgior, Regine; 1838
Merz, Philip; 1839
Messerschmidt, Louise; 1851
Messner, Philip; 1839
Messner, Philip; 1837
Meyer, Alwine Elisa; 1856
Meyer, F. Luise; 1867
Meyer, Friedrich; 1840
Meyer, Margarethe; 1840
Meyer, Sophia; 1838
Mieth, Karoline; 1861
Mohrhard, Karoline; 1839
Mohring, Karoline; 1857
Mohring, Katharine; 1851
Mohring, Marie; 1853
Moltz, Marie; 1851
Muhly, Anton Heinrich; 1863
Muhly, Caroline; 1845
Muhly, Christian; 1854
Muhly, Georg Her.; 1856
Muhly, Herm.; 1854
Muhly, Johann; 1866
Muhly, Karl Wilh. Eberhard; 1851
Muhly, Louise; 1859
Muller, August; 1866
Muller, Christoph; 1844
Muller, Johann; 1837
Muller, Karl; 1864
Muller, Katharine; 1862
Muller, Maria; 1845
Muller, Ursula; 1852
Muller, Wilhelm; 1842
Muth, Elisabeth; 1867
Niebergall, Philipine; 1839

Niklas, Joh.; 1855
Nikolas, Anna; 1841
Ober, Georg; 1862
Ober, Heinrich; 1857
Ober, Marie Elis.; 1855
Ober, Marie Elise; 1856
Ochs, Lorenz; 1862
Oesterle, Christiane; 1842
Oesterle, Friedrich; 1838
Oesterle, Johann; 1837
Oesterle, Karoline; 1843
Oesterle, Maria; 1839
Oesterle, Maria Frdke.; 1863
Oestreicher, Barbara; 1843
Oestreicher, Katharine; 1837
Ommenhauser, Luise; 1844
Orth, Conrad; 1845
Ortmann, Eleonore Christine; 1865
Ortmann, Friederike Wilh.; 1863
Ortmann, Joh. Heinr.; 1861
Ortwein, Dorothea; 1838
Osterle, Adam; 1860
Otto, Georg; 1854
Pabst, Kathrine; 1861
Pabst, Marie; 1858
Pfeifer, Maria; 1845
Pfeil, Katharina; 1844
Pfeister, Georg Fr.; 1841
Pfeister, Johann; 1841
Plessing, Daniel; 1844
Plessing, Friedrich; 1838
Pohl, Charlotte; 1843
Polens [?], Oskar; 1856
Pollack, Frdch.; 1859
Pollack, Georg; 1865
Pollack, Karoline; 1857
Pollack, Katharine; 1862
Priegel, Martin; 1843
Priester, Valentin; 1851
Radecke, Anna Adelheid; 1853
Radecke, Anna Marg.; 1863
Radecke, Herm. Frdch.; 1855
Radecke, Joh. Albert; 1855
Radecke, Marg. Sophie; 1860
Ratzi, Justus; 1838
Regner, Karl Frdch.; 1864
Rehberger, Valentin; 1843
Reibet, Maria; 1842
Rein, Christine; 1858
Rein, Friederike; 1853
Rein, Margarethe; 1861
Reisinger, Friedrich; 1862
Reisinger, Jakob; 1860
Reitzel, Friedrich; 1864
Reppert, Hanna; 1839
Reting, Katharine; 1851
Reuter, Elisabeth; 1865
Reuter, Louise Susanne; 1863
Riddel, Anna Elisabeth; 1845
Ritschmann, Magdalena; 1839
Ritschmann, Magdalene; 1837
Romoser, Christine; 1840
Romoser, Christine; 1838
Romoser, Karoline; 1842
Romoser, Louise Susanne; 1864
Rother, Anna; 1864
Rother, H. Hugo R.; 1867
Rother, Heinrich; 1867
Rother, Maria Elisabeth; 1865
Ruckert, J. Frdch.; 1854
Ruckert, Marie Dorothea; 1853
Ruckert, Philipp Ludwig; 1852
Rullmann, Johann; 1837

Rullmann, Maria; 1843
Rumoser, Joh. J.; 1867
Ruppel (II), Heinr.; 1858
Ruppel (II), Nik.; 1858
Ruppel, Johannes; 1863
Ruppel, Karoline; 1862
Ruppel, Marie; 1854
Ruppel, Wilh. Joh.; 1864
Sahm, Jakob; 1845
Sahm, Karl; 1843
Sahm, Katharine; 1841
Sander, Alexander; 1853
Sander, Anna Maria; 1841
Sander, Heinr.; 1857
Sander, Katharine; 1842
Sander, Peter; 1854
Schaefer, Mathilde; 1842
Schafer, Elisabeth; 1839
Schafer, Maria; 1845
Schaible, Elis. Kath.; 1852
Schaible, Elisabeth; 1837
Scharckl, Marg.; 1855
Scharrer, J. Heinr.; 1858
Schenkel, Rosine; 1843
Scherer, Johann; 1837
Scherer, Wilhelm; 1862
Schertz, Elisabeth; 1845
Scheufler, Luise; 1842
Schindler, [--?--]; 1857
Schitt, Magdalene; 1838
Schlerf, Joh. Heinr. Christoph; 1866
Schmidt, Christine Barb.; 1841
Schmidt, Elisabeth; 1838
Schmidt, Eva; 1854
Schmidt, Johann; 1844
Schmidt, Johann; 1840
Schmidt, Johann; 1838
Schmidt, Joseph; 1857
Schmidt, Katharina; 1839
Schmidt, Katharine; 1840
Schmidt, Mathilde; 1844
Schmidt, Regina; 1843
Schmidt, Sahra Anna; 1844
Schmidt, Susanne; 1842
Schmidt, Wilhelmine; 1838
Schnabel, Konrad; 1862
Schneider, Frdch.; 1854
Schneider, Georg Heinr.; 1866
Schneider, Gerhard Frdch. Wilh.; 1852
Schneider, Joh. Heinr. Frdch.; 1852
Schneider, Katharine; 1854
Schneider, Louise; 1864
Schneider, Maria Kath.; 1863
Schott, Dorothea; 1860
Schrieber, Katharine Elis.; 1851
Schropfer, Hanne Marie; 1851
Schropfer, Magdlene Fried.; 1851
Schuhmacher, Conrad; 1844
Schultheiss, Louise Christine; 1858
Schultheiss, Marie; 1861
Schultz, Ludwig; 1866
Schulz, Dorothea; 1843
Schulz, Eduard; 1865
Schulz, Elisabeth; 1863
Schulz, Emil; 1864
Schulz, Johanne; 1866
Schulze, K. H. Fried.; 1867
Schumacher, Johes.; 1854
Schumacher, Karl; 1858
Schwab, Christina; 1867

Schwab, Wilhelmine; 1863
Schwartzenberger, Maria; 1866
Schwarz, Elisabeth K.; 1867
Schweickert, Elis.; 1856
Schweickert, Elise; 1855
Schweickert, Frdch.; 1853
Seib, Elisabeth; 1838
Seibel, Maria; 1864
Seitz, Joh. Mich.; 1856
Seitz, Joh. Mich.; 1855
Seitz, Leonhard; 1861
Senger, Katharine; 1837
Sickel, Wilh. Heinr.; 1852
Sieck (I), Karoline Louise; 1861
Sieck (II), Apollonia Marie; 1861
Sieck, A. Magdal.; 1867
Sieck, Adolph Friedrich; 1866
Sieck, Ch. Wilhelmine Ch.; 1867
Sieck, Clomer Heinr.; 1851
Sieck, Ernestine Katharine Eleonore; 1866
Sieck, F. Louise; 1867
Sieck, Jobst Heinr.; 1855
Sieck, Joh. Heinrich; 1863
Sieck, Johann Heinrich; 1864
Siemers, Kath. Marie; 1851
Siemers, Marie Elis.; 1852
Sommers, Elisabeth; 1843
Sorei [?], Heinrich; 1841
Spamer, Christian; 1837
Spamer, Kathrine; 1838
Spawer, Heinrich; 1842
Spielmann, Heinr. K. Frdch.; 1856
Spielmann, Heinr. K. Frdch.; 1855
Stanger, Johanne; 1838
Stein, Wilhelm Fr.; 1843
Steiner, Andreas; 1851
Steinhofer, Christian; 1843
Stiefel, Johann Jac.; 1842
Stieler, Sophie; 1838
Stober, Joh.; 1854
Stober, Margar.; 1863
Stock, Maria; 1838
Stoll, Maria; 1837
Stracke, Jacob; 1843
Strobel, Georg; 1843
Stroh, Wilhelm; 1842
Stübner, Agatha; 1844
Stumpf, Catharine (Marie?); 1845
Stutelberg, Albert; 1854
Sucop, Herm. H.; 1858
Tagler, Justine; 1839
Tegler, Geg; 1842
Th…er, Johann; 1838
Thiemeyer, Elisa; 1861
Thiemeyer, Emilie; 1863
Thiemeyer, Emma; 1864
Thiemeyer, Frdch. Ludwig; 1851
Thiemeyer, Henr.; 1857
Thiemeyer, Joh. Heinr.; 1860
Thiemeyer, Josephine; 1866
Thiemeyer, Karoline Julianne; 1864
Thiemeyer, L. S.; 1862
Thiemeyer, Marie Elis.; 1853
Thiemier, F. Wilh.; 1867
Titus, Wilhelmine; 1845
Tormelen, Wilhelm; 1862

Surname; Given Name; Year Confirmed

Tormölem, M. Elisabeth; 1867
Trager, Emilie; 1856
Trager, Emilie; 1855
Trager, Louise Kath.; 1854
Trautmann, Joh. Karl; 1855
Treide, Daniel Wilh.; 1860
Treide, Elis.; 1857
Treide, Marie Elis.; 1856
Treide, Marie Elis.; 1855
Trost, Karoline; 1843
Trost, Wilhelm; 1842
Uhl, Christine; 1837
Urbach, Kathr.; 1838
Uttmann, Katharine; 1838
Vogelmann, Karl Ludwig; 1866
Vogelmann, Karoline; 1841
Vogelsang, Wilhelmine; 1845
Volland, Christian; 1839
Wachler, Joh C. H.; 1867
Wagner (Weidemeier), Friedrike; 1852
Wagner, Frdch. Gotthelf; 1854
Wagner, Marie; 1860
Waldhauer, Karl; 1865
Waldschmidt (Ruppert), Ludwig; 1851
Waldschmidt, Elisabeth; 1860
Waldschmidt, Friedrich; 1865
Waldschmidt, Ludwig; 1852
Waldschmidt, Marg.; 1855
Waldschmidt, Wilh.; 1857
Walther (II), Marie; 1861
Walther, Anna; 1861
Walther, Frdch. Wilh.; 1859
Walther, Kath.; 1858
Walther, Louise; 1863
Waltjen (I), Marie Dorothea; 1861
Waltjen (II), Karoline Dorothe; 1861
Waltjen, Amalie Doroth.; 1866
Waltjen, Anna Johanne; 1865
Waltjen, Anna Marie; 1854
Waltjen, August; 1844
Waltjen, Christine; 1858
Waltjen, Friederike Aug.; 1863
Waltjen, Heinr.; 1852
Waltjen, Kath.; 1860
Waltjen, Marie Sophie; 1864
Waltjen, Sophie Christine; 1856
Waltjen, Sophie Emilie; 1854
Warneken, Georg; 1853
Warneken, Karoline; 1858
Warneken, Louis; 1855
Warneken, Wilh.; 1860
Warnken, Heinrich; 1865
Weber, Elisabeth; 1861
Weber, Friedrich; 1839
Weber, Heinr. Ernst; 1859
Weber, Katharina; 1844
Weber, Maria Magdalena; 1845
Weber, Marie; 1857
Weber, Michael; 1842
Webersberger, Georg; 1852
Weckesser, Anna Cath.; 1845
Weckesser, Anna Elisab.; 1856
Weckesser, Elisabeth; 1851
Weckesser, Elisabeth; 1845
Weckesser, Eva; 1852
Weckesser, J. Heinr.; 1858
Weckesser, Johann Adam; 1863

Weckesser, Tobias; 1861
Weddigen, Anna Marie; 1865
Weddigen, Mathil L. E.; 1867
Wedekind, Dorothea; 1837
Weidemeier, Christine Rebekka; 1864
Weidemeier, Martha Elis.; 1859
Weidemeier, Peter Jakob; 1863
Weihrich, H. D.; 1867
Weihrich, Otto F.; 1867
Weinhard, Sybille; 1838
Weinhold, Thomas; 1845
Weirich, Anna Marg. Elis.; 1855
Weiss, Elis.; 1854
Weiss, Emilie; 1855
Weller, Heinrich; 1863
Weller, Jacob; 1844
Weller, Justine; 1861
Weller, M.; 1862
Weller, Maria Kath.; 1866
Weller, Melchior; 1860
Weller, Sophia Lora; 1843
Welten, Georg; 1839
Wick, Christoph; 1842
Wick, Wilhelm; 1845
Wiegel, Kath. Marg.; 1851
Wiegel, Wilh. Heinr.; 1852
Wieland, Joh. Michael; 1865
Wieland, Ludwig; 1864
Wiesner, Hartm.; 1855
Wiesner, Joh.; 1856
Wiesner, Joh.; 1855
Wildermuth, Anna Elisabeth; 1863
Wildermuth, Georg; 1867
Wildermuth, Joh. Heinr. G.; 1855
Wildermuth, Joh. Hnr.; 1856
Wildermuth, Marie Elisab.; 1852
Will, Katharine; 1842
Wilmann, Theodor; 1841
Winter, Martha Magd.; 1866
Winter, Wilhelmine; 1845
Wittler, Frdch.; 1856
Wittler, Frdch.; 1855
Wittler, Karl August; 1852
Wolf, A. E.; 1862
Wolf, Anna Marie; 1858
Wolf, Ernst; 1843
Wolf, Konrad; 1866
Wolf, Maria; 1844
Wolfram, Elisabeth Samantha; 1863
Wortmann, Karoline; 1852
Wortmann, Lisette; 1838
Wurmstich, Friederike Marg.; 1865
Wust, Katharine; 1840
Zinsky, Johanne; 1841
Zinsky, Katharine; 1841
Zulauf, Catharine; 1845

Name Index

This index includes all names except for the main person who is listed alphabetically.

Place Name Index

www.ingramcontent.com/pod-product-compliance
Lightning Source LLC
LaVergne TN
LVHW020519100826
845148LV00010B/1288

9780788433702